ASCENT®
CENTER FOR TECHNICAL KNOWLEDGE

3DEXPERIENCE CATIA 2022x Introduction to Modeling Part 1

Learning Guide

1st Edition

ASCENT - Center for Technical Knowledge®
3DEXPERIENCE CATIA 2022x
Introduction to Modeling - Part 1

1st Edition

Prepared and produced by:

ASCENT Center for Technical Knowledge
630 Peter Jefferson Parkway, Suite 175
Charlottesville, VA 22911

866-527-2368
www.ASCENTed.com

ASCENT - Center for Technical Knowledge (a division of Rand Worldwide Inc.) is a leading developer of professional learning materials and knowledge products for engineering software applications. ASCENT specializes in designing targeted content that facilitates application-based learning with hands-on software experience. For over 25 years, ASCENT has helped users become more productive through tailored custom learning solutions.

We welcome any comments you may have regarding this guide, or any of our products. To contact us please email: feedback@ASCENTed.com.

AS-3DE22-ICM1-SG1 // RS-3DE22-ICM1-SG1

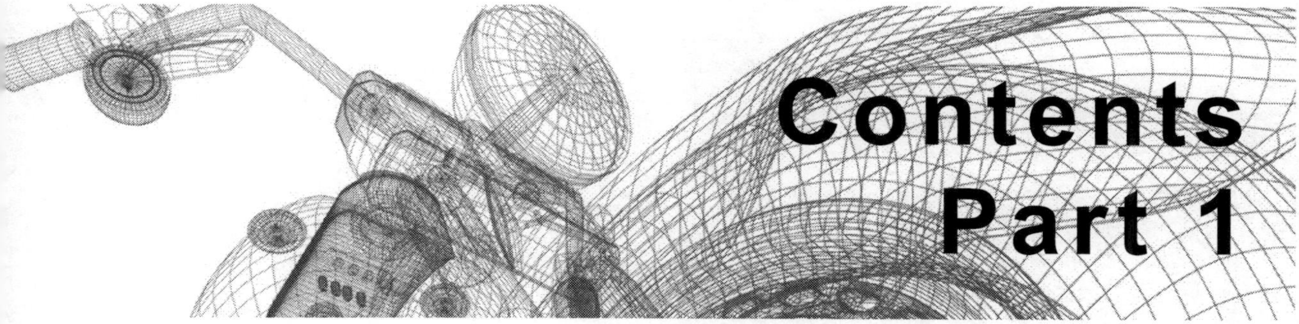

Contents Part 1

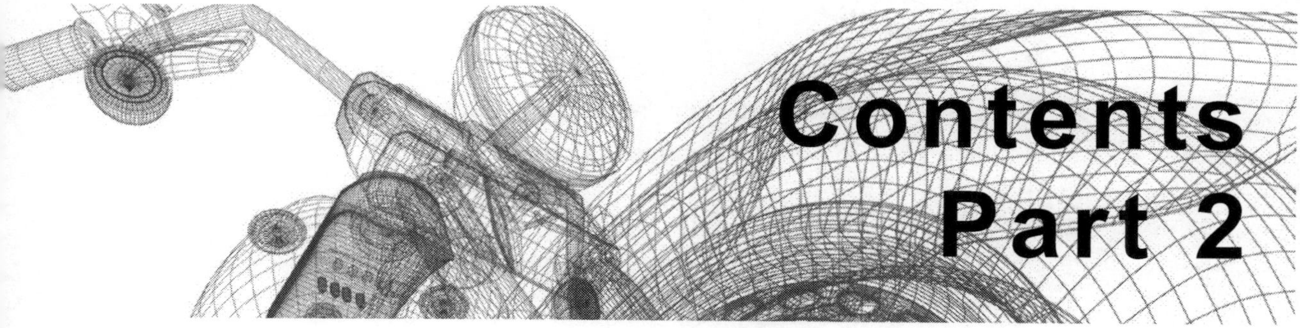

Contents Part 2

Preface

The *3DEXPERIENCE CATIA 2022x: Introduction to Modeling* guide can help you with learning the process of designing models using the 3DEXPERIENCE platform - from conceptual sketching to solid modeling, assembly design, and drawing production. Upon completion of this guide, you will have acquired the skills to confidently work in the 3DEXPERIENCE platform and gained an understanding of the parametric design philosophy of the CATIA apps.

Topics Covered

- 3DEXPERIENCE Platform Overview
- 3DEXPERIENCE Platform PLM Objects
- Launching the 3DEXPERIENCE Platform
- 3DEXPERIENCE Platform User Interface
- Customizing the 3DEXPERIENCE Platform
- Creating and Constraining Sketch Geometry
- Sketched Feature Techniques and Formulas
- Adding Material with Pad and Shaft Features
- Removing Material with Pocket and Groove Features
- Creating Reference Elements for construction and measurement
- Fillet, Chamfer, Hole, Draft, and Shell Dress-Up Features
- Pattern, Copy, and Mirror Duplication Features
- Thin Features, Stiffeners
- Rib and Slot Features
- Multi-sections Solid Features
- Feature Management Using the Hide/Show, Activate/Deactivate Functions
- Parent/Child Relationships and Feature Failure Resolution
- Obtaining Part Information
- Managing Object Lifecycles

- Assembly Design using Engineering Connections and Constraints
- Constraint Creation and Assembly Management
- Obtaining Assembly Information (Measure, Clash, and Bill of Materials)
- Working with Drawings in the 3DEXPERIENCE Platform
- Working with Multi-Body Models
- Effective Modeling Tips and Techniques

Prerequisites

- Access to the 3DEXPERIENCE CATIA 2022x platform, including access to the CATIA Part Design, CATIA Assembly Design, CATIA Drafting, ENOVIA Collaborative Lifecycle, ENOVIA Product Finder, and ENOVIA Design IP Classification apps.
- Permission to import 3DXML files.

Note on Software Setup

This guide assumes a standard installation of the 3DEXPERIENCE platform.

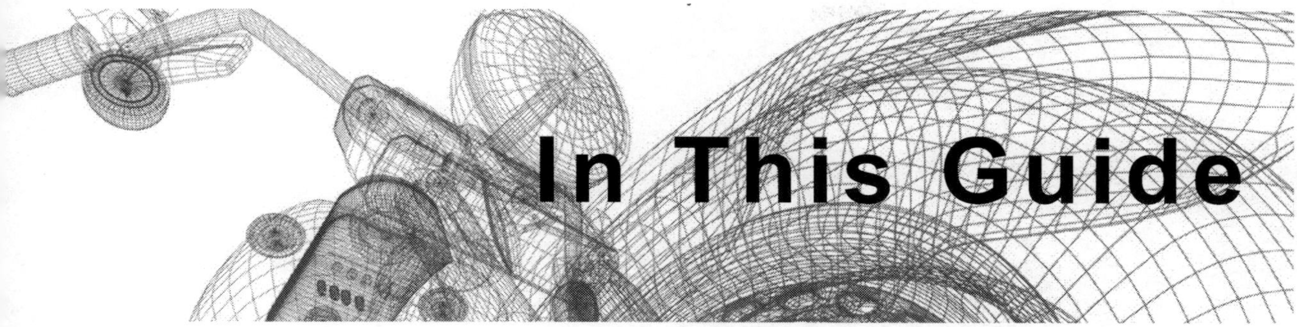

In This Guide

The following highlights the key features of this guide.

Feature	Description
Practice Files	The Practice Files page includes a link to the practice files and instructions on how to download and install them. The practice files are required to complete the practices in this guide.
Chapters	A chapter consists of the following - Learning Objectives, Instructional Content, Practices, Chapter Review Questions, and Command Summary. • **Learning Objectives** define the skills you can acquire by learning the content provided in the chapter. • **Instructional Content**, which begins right after Learning Objectives, refers to the descriptive and procedural information related to various topics. Each main topic introduces a product feature, discusses various aspects of that feature, and provides step-by-step procedures on how to use that feature. Where relevant, examples, figures, helpful hints, and notes are provided. • **Practice** for a topic follows the instructional content. Practices enable you to use the software to perform a hands-on review of a topic. It is required that you download the practice files (using the link found on the Practice Files page) prior to starting the first practice. • **Chapter Review Questions**, located close to the end of a chapter, enable you to test your knowledge of the key concepts discussed in the chapter.

Practice Files

To download the practice files for this guide, use the following steps:

1. Type the URL ***exactly as shown below*** into the address bar of your Internet browser to access the Course File Download page.

   Note: If you are using the ebook, you do not have to type the URL. Instead, you can access the page simply by clicking the URL below.

   https://www.ascented.com/getfile/id/dactylorhizaPF

2. On the Course File Download page, click the **DOWNLOAD NOW** button, as shown below, to download the .ZIP file that contains the practice files.

3. Once the download is complete, unzip the file and extract its contents.

   The recommended practice files folder location is:
   C:\3DEXPERIENCE Introduction to CATIA Modeling Practice Files

   Note: It is recommended that you do not change the location of the practice files folder. Doing so may cause errors when completing the practices.

Stay Informed!

To receive information about upcoming events, promotional offers, and complimentary webcasts, visit:

www.ASCENTed.com/updates

Chapter 1

3DEXPERIENCE Platform Overview

This chapter provides an overview of the 3DEXPERIENCE platform. You learn about the various components comprising the platform, and how working with 3DEXPERIENCE differs from CATIA V5.

Learning Objectives in This Chapter

- Understand the 3DEXPERIENCE platform.
- Understand the various components of the platform, including the 3DDashboard, various apps, and the database.
- Understand the compatibility between CATIA V5 and 3DEXPERIENCE objects.
- Understand the licensing and platform deployment schemes.
- Become familiar with 3DEXPERIENCE platform PLM objects and the 3DEXPERIENCE product structure.
- Learn the general process for accessing the system and search for objects.
- Learn how to import, export, and open objects.

1.1 3DEXPERIENCE Platform Overview

3DEXPERIENCE platform is a unified database and interface from Dassault Systèmes that provides a platform in which business software and application can run, particularly programs related to the design, development, and manufacturing industries, as shown in Figure 1–1.

Figure 1–1

3DDASHBOARD

The 3DDashboard, shown in Figure 1–2, is a front home page for your projects. In here, you can gather information from a variety of sources - reports, 3D models, files, group communications - to gain a holistic view of the project.

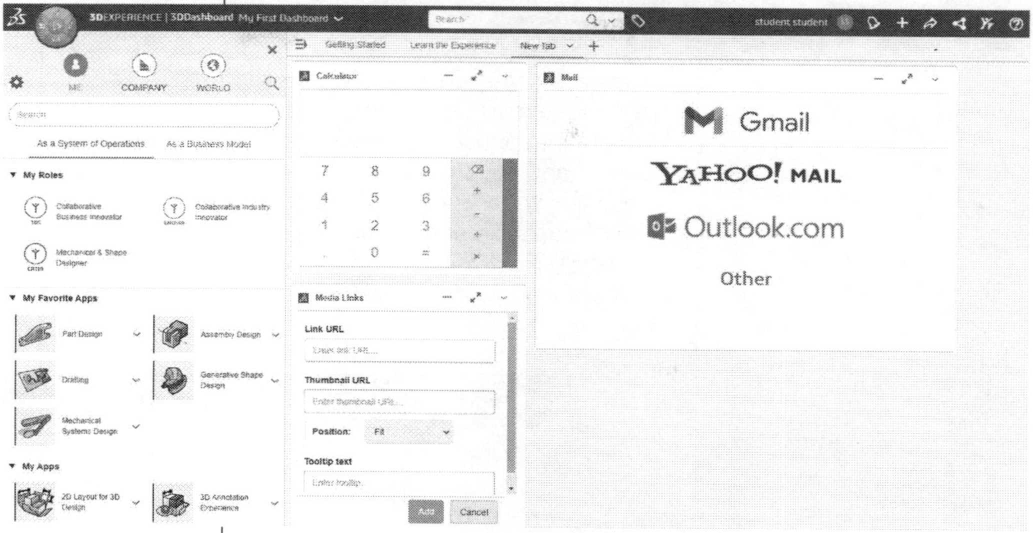

Figure 1–2

Apps

Applications (apps) are the various programs which run in the 3DEXPERIENCE platform. These are equivalent to workbenches in V5. Several apps are shown in Figure 1–3. Each application is made of several commands related to a common task. For example, the CATIA Part Design application contains commands used to build 3D solid models.

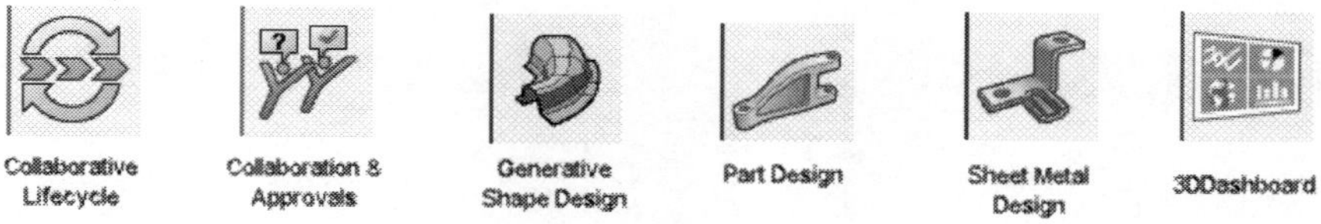

Figure 1–3

Compass

Apps are accessible through the Compass. The Compass is a re-imagined version of the Start menu from V5. The Compass is broken into two selectable regions - the **Play** button (inner circle), and the **Roles, Apps & Solution Portfolio** (outer ring). Selecting the **Play** button in certain applicable apps will start interactions like simulations and animations. The **Roles, Apps & Solution Portfolio** button lists all the available roles and apps that are accessible on the 3D experience platform, as shown in Figure 1–4.

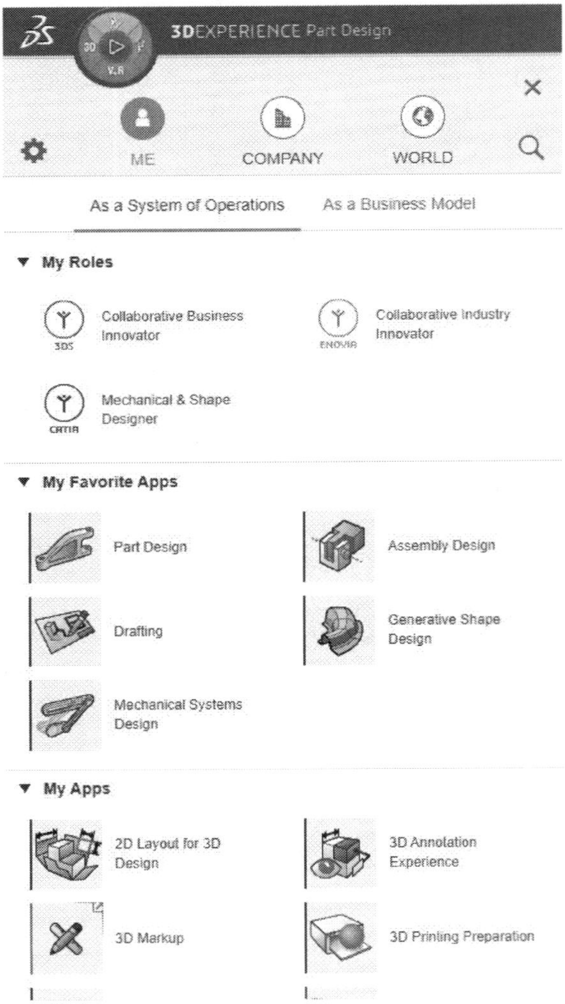

Figure 1–4

While the **Roles, Apps & Solution Portfolio** works as a single button to access apps, there are general categories that a number of these apps fall under. Following is a list of some of the modules capable of being implemented within the 3D Experience.

Social and Collaborative Apps

- **Enovia** - Collaborative Innovation, Document Revisions, Database Management
- **3DEXCITE** - Marketing in the Age of Relationships

3D Modeling Apps

- **CATIA** - Product development and shape creation
- **Solidworks** - Inspiring Innovation
- **Geovia** - Virtual Planet
- **Biovia** - Virtual Biosphere and Materials

Content and Simulation Apps

- **Simulia** - Simulation for product, Nature and Life
- **DELMIA** - Digital Manufacturing and Global Industrial Operations
- **3DVIA** - The consumer experience brand

Information Intelligence Apps

NETVIBES - Dashboard Intelligence

EXALEAD - Data in Business

Database

The goal of the 3DEXPERIENCE platform is to integrate the various disconnected 3D processes. By tying different aspects of product creation, development, and manufacturing, the platform becomes a single source of truth to define the product. As such, all file information is stored in a shared database.

As opposed to simply storing files in folders, a database creates relations between files so that they may be searched, filtered, and connected in meaningful ways that create value and usefulness, making it easier to work with large sets of data and provide individual users with the knowledge that they need.

This database can be accessed through a variety of methods:

1. Webclient
2. Windows integration
3. Tablet
4. Mobile

Since the 3DEXPERIENCE platform is based on a relational database, instead of saving individual files into folders on a network or local drive, all files are stored in the database. This alleviates issues with version control and data backup.

In the database, files can be locked or unlocked to prevent accident over-writing (check-in and check-out). Version control can be applied to models. Different revisions and variations can easily be made. Non-CAD data and information can be stored, broadening the files' scope and depth-of-use.

Compatibility

CATIA V5 and 3DEXPERIENCE use the same geometry modeling engines.

Models from the same release can be transferred back and forth while maintaining feature history, as shown in Figure 1–5.

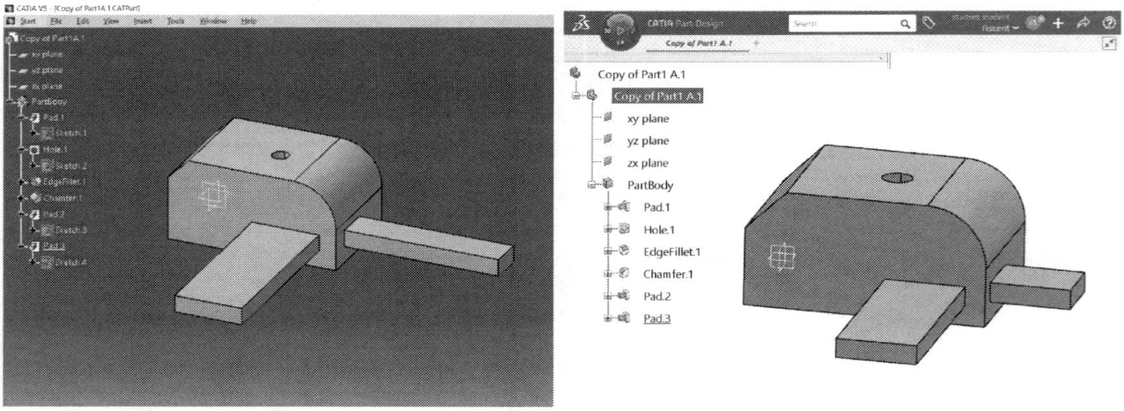

CATIA V5 ***3DEXPERIENCE***

Figure 1–5

1.2 Deployment and Licensing

The 3DEXPERIENCE platform can be integrated to an existing business model using the solution that best serves that business – using the Software-as-a-Service (SaaS), Platform-as-a-Service (PaaS), or Infrastructure-as-a-Service (IaaS) options.

On-Premise Platform Deployment

Basic requirement for on-premise installation:

- License Server
- Database Software
- Webserver

It will take VAR help to setup your on-premise 3DEXPERIENCE installation.

All services are run from and data is stored on your hardware.

On-Cloud Platform Deployment

On-Cloud Advantages:

- Fast deployment
- Only a license server is required for On-Cloud
- Simplicity
- Collaboration and connected
- Security and reliability
- Scalability

Licensing

Both 3DEXPERIENCE platform and V5 use Trigrams to denote licenses. In V5, each trigram represents a product or a package of products. For example, the MCE (Mechanical Product Creation) Package contains PDG (Part Design 2), ASD (Assembly Design 2), GS1 (Generative Shape Design 1), and FM1 (Functional Molded Part).

V5 Licensing

In V5, configurations of licenses are purchases. For example, purchasing a CAC+FPE+HDX+MCE configuration would include these elements:

- CAC – Base V5 PLMExpress
- FPE – Fabricated Product Creation Package
- HDX – Mechanical Shape Design Package
- MCE – Mechanical Product Creation Package

Additional licenses are also available as add-ons and shareable products.

3DEXPERIENCE Platform Licensing

In the 3DEXPERIENCE platform, roles are purchased instead of configurations. The role includes a set of specific licenses that are typically used together for a specific job task. Several roles are shown in Figure 1–6.

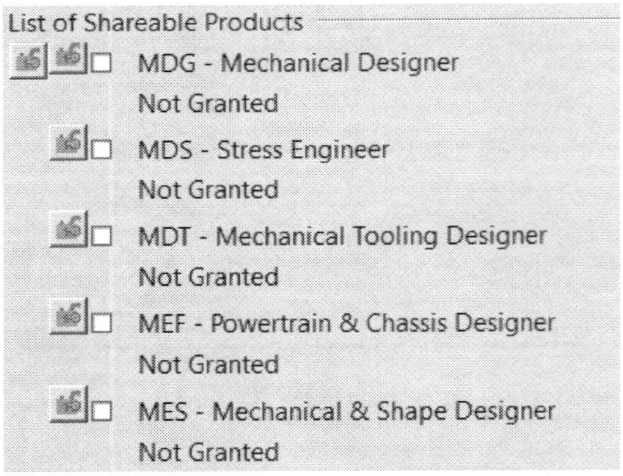

Figure 1–6

For example, the MDG (Mechanical Designer Role) includes 25 different apps. These individual apps are still identified by their trigram.

Roles are available for:

- System Architects
- Mechanical Designers
- Creative Designers
- Surface Designers
- Decision Makers

In the 3DEXPERIENCE platform, all licenses are Named User licenses, which means that administrators must assign these licenses to a specific person.

A license may only be moved to another user after 30 days of inactivity.

1.3 3DEXPERIENCE Platform PLM Objects

Individual files are now referred to as objects and may contain other information than strictly file data. In general, these can be thought of as their V5 counterparts. There are equivalents for parts, products, and drawings. Many object types are available, as shown in Figure 1–7.

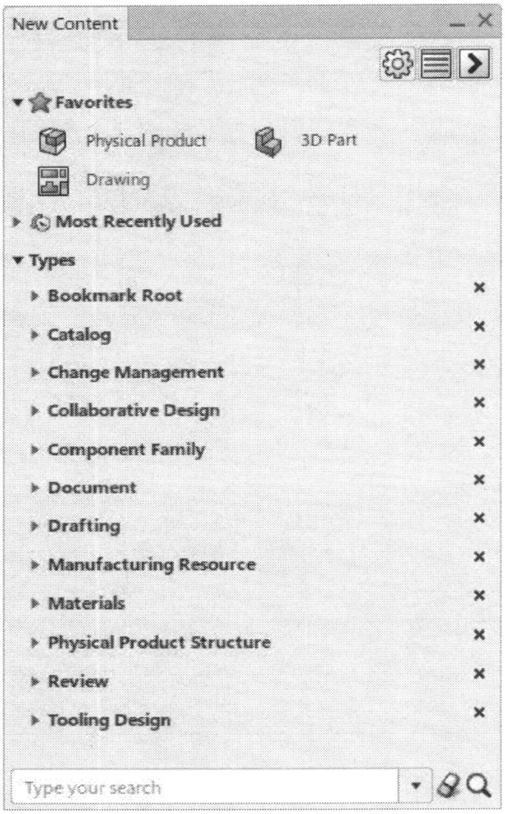

Figure 1–7

Products can be grouped into types. A product file is an assembly that contains representations. A representation is the 3D visualization of a model. It can be a 3D Shape, which would be a V5 Part or CGR (lightweight file). It can also be a drawing or other object that represents the model.

Product Structure

The following table illustrates how V5 objects have been simplified. The entities are now organized into basic categories of Product and Representation.

V5	3DEXPERIENCE	Category
Product	Physical Product	**Product**
Component		
Part Instance	3D Part Instance	**Representation**
Part Representation	3D Shape Representation	

The image shown in Figure 1–8 provides a comparison of the V5 and the 3DEXPERIENCE platform product structures.

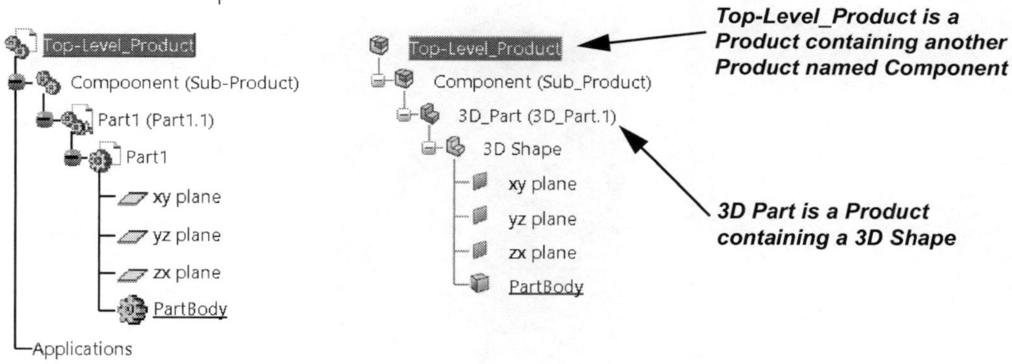

Figure 1–8

1.4 Launching the 3DEXPERIENCE Platform

The 3DEXPERIENCE platform infrastructure is organized around a centralized engineering database. This permits concurrent communication of the latest design data. As a result, the chance of using obsolete data is minimized for all participants with access to the system.

Connecting to the System

The centralized database structure requires that you log into the system with the appropriate credentials to use the software.

When you launch the 3DEXPERIENCE platform, the 3DEXPERIENCE - Login webpage opens as shown in Figure 1–9, in which you must enter your user name and password.

Your administrator must provide this information before you can use the 3DEXPERIENCE platform.

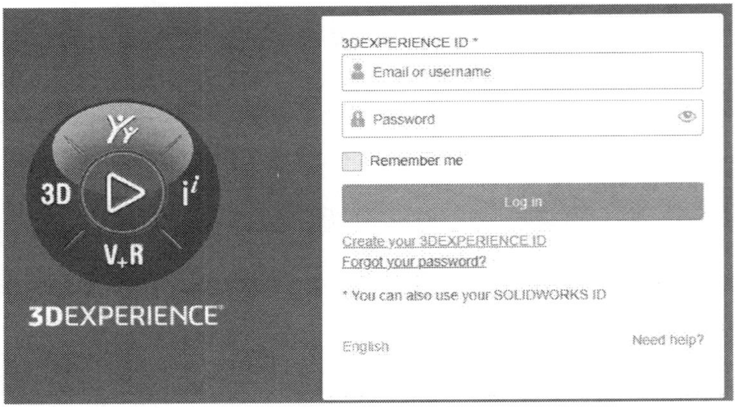

Figure 1–9

Platform Credentials

The 3DEXPERIENCE Platform dialog box, shown in Figure 1–10, determines the specific location and type of data that you can pull from or push to the database by setting your credentials.

Note that if you are not using this content in the Rand 3D environment, use the credentials, Collaborative Space, and Role provided by your System Administrator.

For this training, the Collaborative Space is set to **RAND 3D Models**, and the Access Role is set to **Owner**. Generally, the roles available in the 3DEXPERIENCE platform include:

- **Public Reader**
- **Reader**
- **Contributor**
- **Author**
- **Leader**
- **Owner**
- **Administrator**

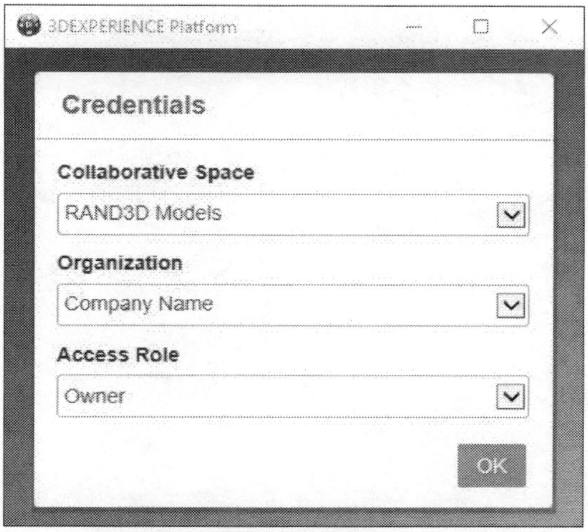

Figure 1–10

If you are using a Native App, these credentials can also be customized by expanding the arrow next to your current Collaborative Space in the upper right corner of the screen, as shown in Figure 1–11.

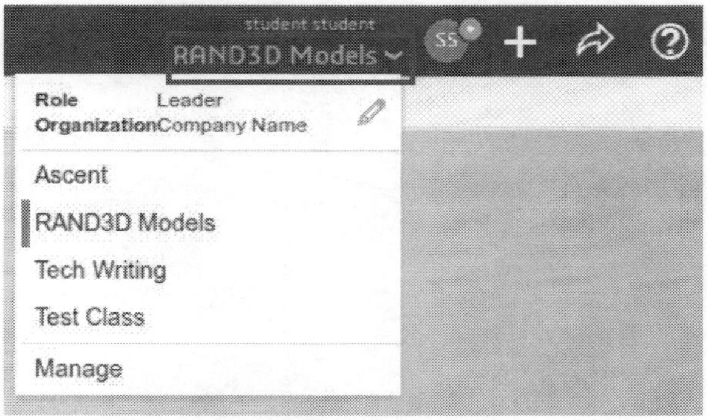

Figure 1–11

1.5 Working with Models

Locating a Model

Models are located in the engineering database using the **Search** tool, as shown in Figure 1–12.

To use the **Search** tool:

1. Enter the filename or a portion of the filename in the *Search* field. Using wildcards (*) is permitted.

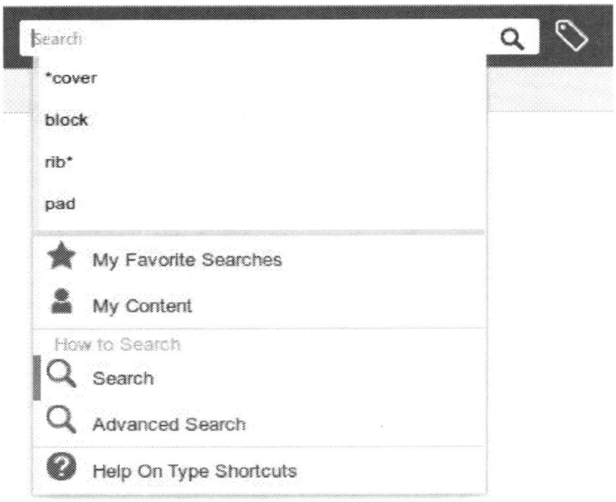

Figure 1–12

2. Searches may be prefaced with the following to further filter the results:

Preface	Description
folder:	Root folder
prd:	Products
fav:	Favorite
prt:	Parts
rvw:	Review

3. Searches can be filtered using the **6W Tags**, as shown in Figure 1–13.

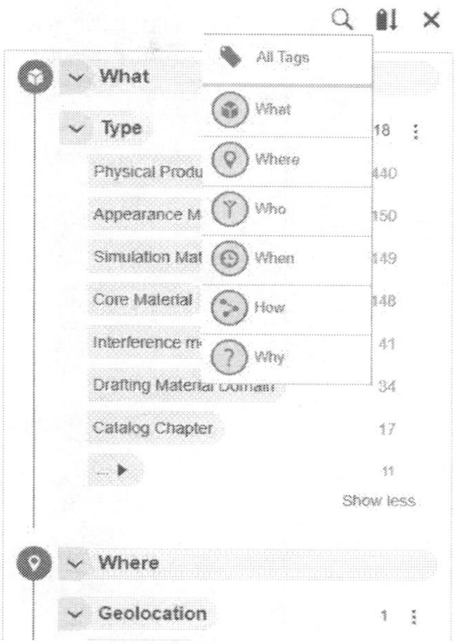

Figure 1–13

4. Open the file by double-clicking it in the list. You can also right-click to access additional options such as **Explore** or **Properties**, as shown in Figure 1–14.

Figure 1–14

Importing a CATIA Model

Standard CATIA files can be imported from your local file system using the following steps:

1. In the Top Bar, click (Add).
2. Click next to Import and select **CATIA File**.
3. Select the file(s) to import and click **Open**.
4. Select the import options, shown in Figure 1–15.
5. Click **OK**.

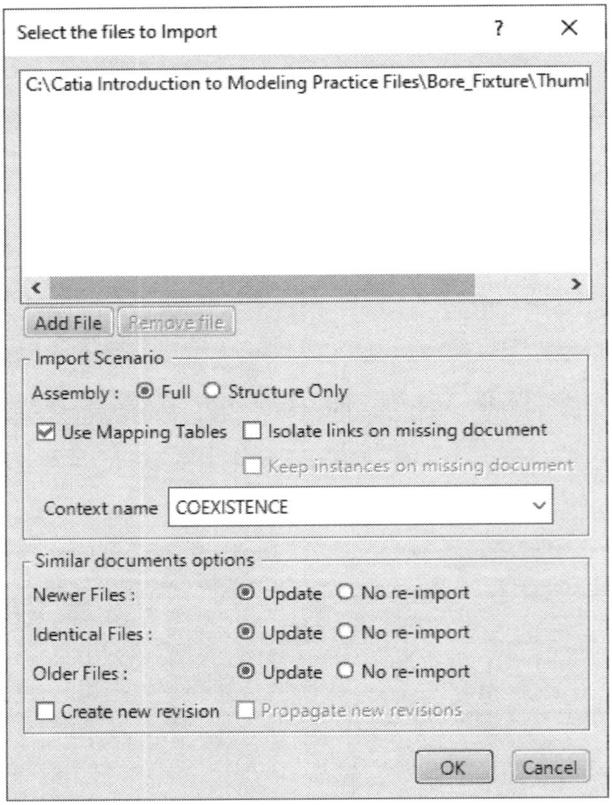

Figure 1–15

Importing a 3DXML File

3DXML is a proprietary format that facilitates transfer of CATIA files in a lightweight proprietary XML format. 3DXML can be in two formats: **With Authoring** (editable format) and **For Review** (non-editable).

3DXML files can be imported from you local file system using the following steps:

1. In the Top Bar, click  (Add).
2. Click **Import**.
3. Select the file to import.
4. Select the import options, shown in Figure 1–16.
5. Click **OK**.

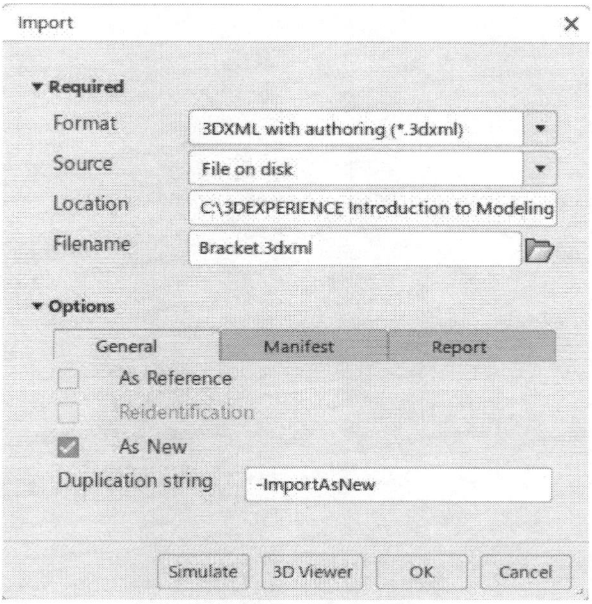

Figure 1–16

Imported objects will open in the Explore mode, and will have to be opened to edit them.

Explore

Assemblies, folders, and other "container" type documents can be explored. This is similar to opening a folder in Windows. All the contents of the parent item will be listed. From there, selected sub elements can be viewed or opened.

To explore:

1. Search and find an assembly or folder.
2. Right-click and select **Explore**.

Turntable

Particularly with large assemblies or folders, it may be useful to engage the turntable view. The turntable will show a 3D representation of the assembly, as shown in Figure 1–17.

Parts are visible based on tree expansion:

- If the tree is expanded and open, the part will be displayed in the turntable.
- If a particular branch of the tree is collapsed and not visible, then that part will not be displayed in the *3D* area.

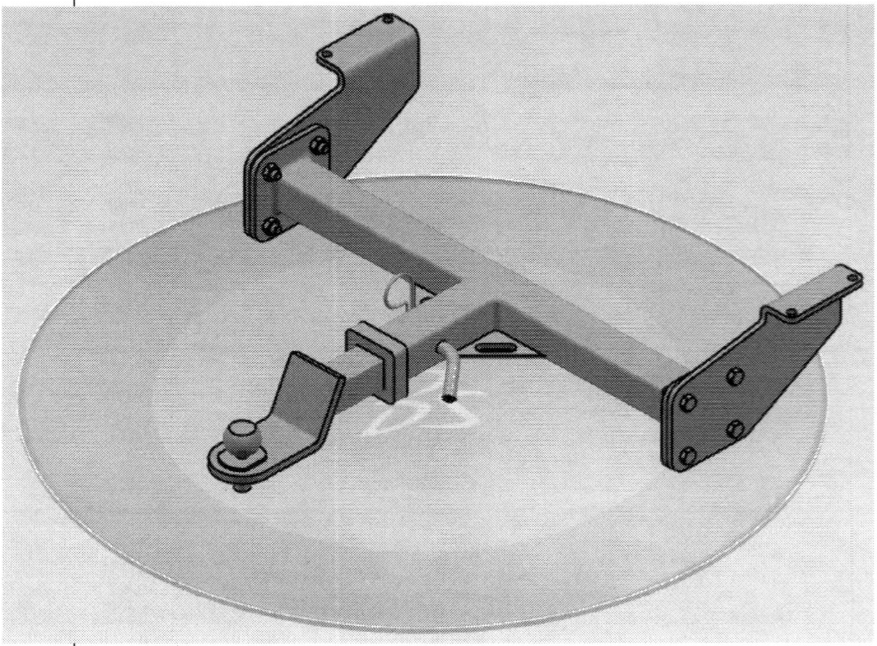

Figure 1–17

Essentially, the turntable is a large preview. To modify and analyze the parts, they will need to be opened.

To use the turntable:

1. Find an assembly or folder and **Explore** it.
2. In the *View* tab of the Action Bar, click  (Swap Turntable/In-place) or press F9 to enable/disable the exploded turntable view.

3. Click  (Text View) to display labels on parts, as shown in Figure 1–18.

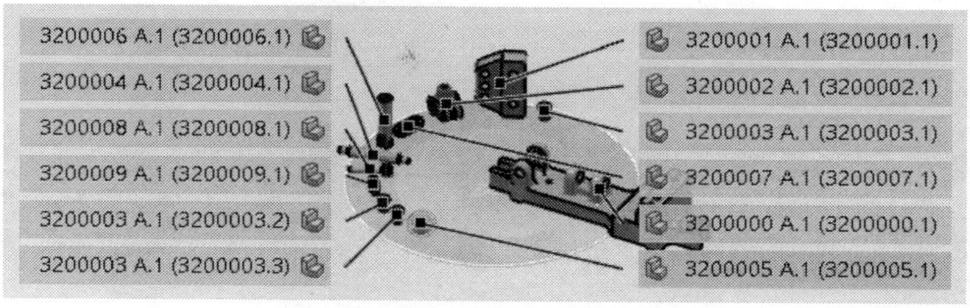

Figure 1–18

4. Click  (Ghost View) and select to hide or show parts from the top of the screen. Select any parts you wish to hide/show.
5. Drag the turntable to rotate parts.

Open

Typically, to open a file, right click it from either a Search Results or an Explorer window, then select **Open**, as shown in Figure 1–19. If opening an assembly, by default all child parts of that assembly will be loaded.

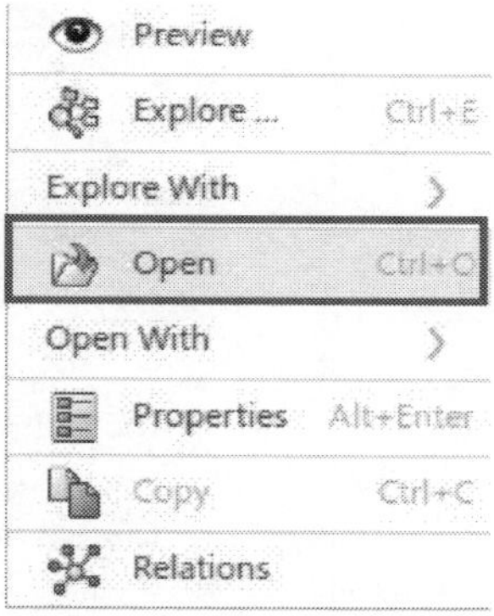

Figure 1–19

Open Advanced

Extra options are available when using **Open With**, as shown in Figure 1–20.

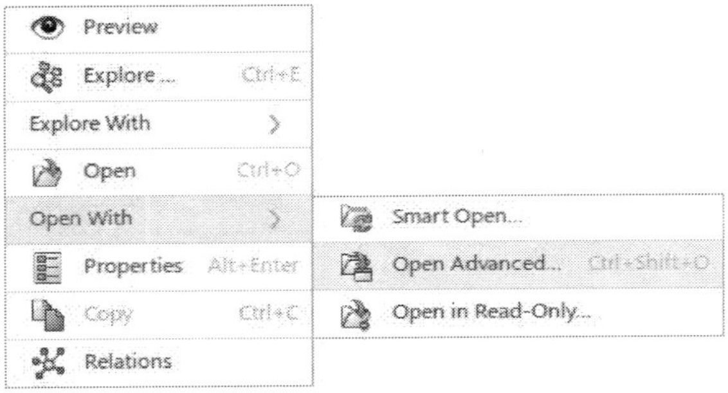

Figure 1–20

Open Advanced displays the Open Advanced dialog box, as shown in Figure 1–21.

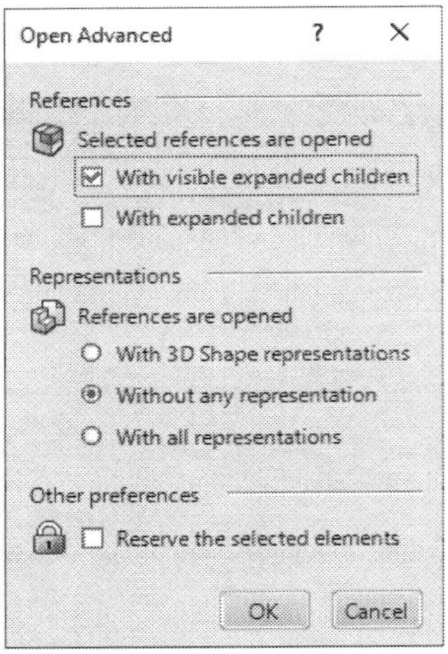

Figure 1–21

The advanced options are described as follows:

Section	Description
References	**With visible expanded children** opens only the parts that are expanded in the tree. **With expanded children** opens all subparts of an assembly, regardless of the tree being expanded.
Representations	Select what type of references will be loaded.
Other Preferences	Select to automatically lock (check out) the selected elements for modification.

Save

Due to the integration of CATIA V6 with a centralized file database, local file storage does not typically occur.

Instead, files are stored in the engineering database for access by other team members or departments. File access is controlled by the database administrator or someone with the appropriate security access.

- Click (Share) and **Save**. The files will be saved to the database using the default settings.
- Click (Share) > **Save with Options** to further control the saving operation.

Save with Options

When using save with Options, the current status of the parts can be checked by viewing the circles on the left, as shown in Figure 1–22. Filters can be used to pick what types of parts are displayed, such as only showing modified items. If a part has been accidentally changed, it can be excluded from being saved. To make a copy of a part, there is Save As New as well as revision options.

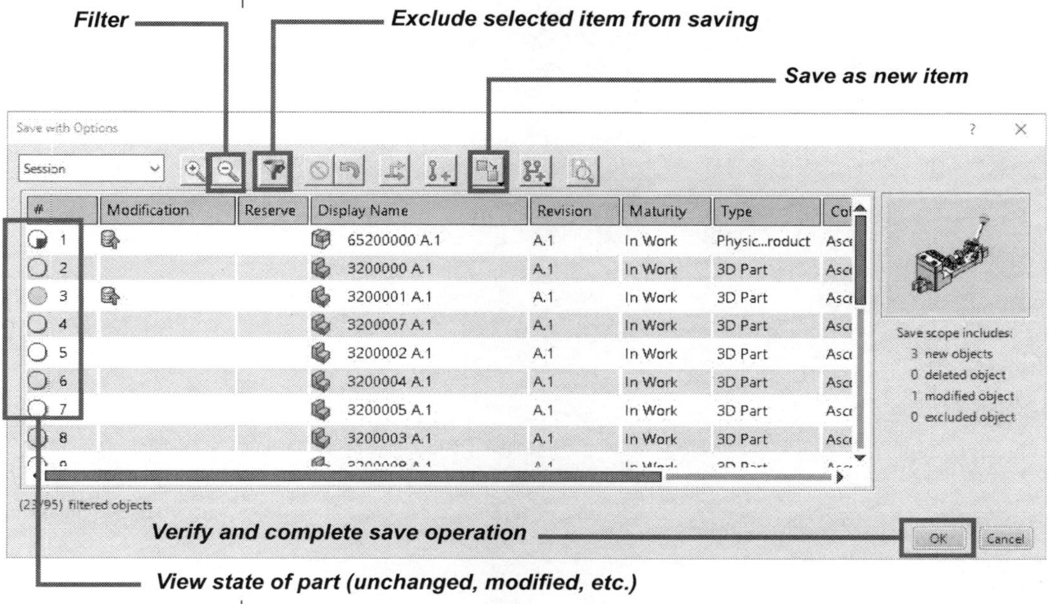

Figure 1–22

The current states of each item is shown by the color of the circle on the right, as shown in Figure 1–23. **Not modified** is white, **New** is blue, **Modified** is yellow, **Excluded** is orange, and **Cannot be saved** is red.

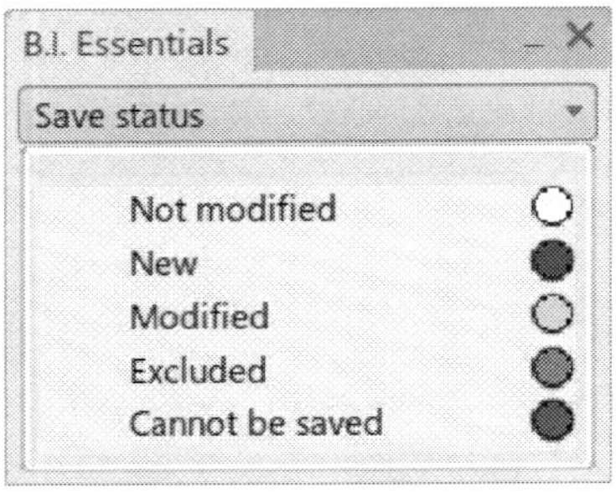

Figure 1–23

Export

Exporting will allow a file to be stored outside of the 3DEXPERIENCE platform vault in order to be shared with users of other systems.

To export a file:

1. Click (Share) > **Export**, and the Export dialog box opens as shown in Figure 1–24.

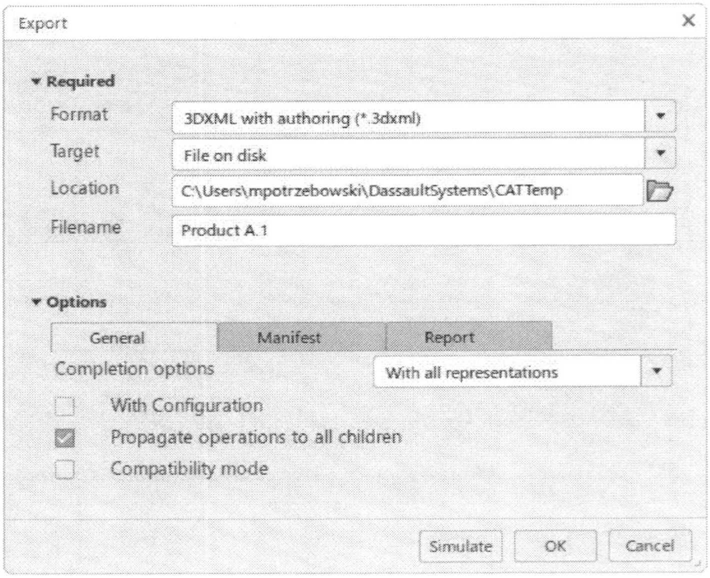

Figure 1–24

2. Select the **Format** drop-down list to change the file type of the exported file, as listed in the following table:

Option	Description
3DXML with authoring	Creates a 3DXML file that contains part feature data. This part can be modified by other users.
3DXML with Review	Creates a 3DXML file that contains a review. Other users will be able to see the file and add notes and markup data.
CATIA file	Creates a file that will be compatible with CATIA V5.
IGES3D	Exports as a neutral .IGS file. Commonly used to transfer surface data between CAD programs.
STEP	Exports as .STP file. Commonly used to transfer solid data between CAD programs.
STL	Exports a Stereo Lithography file; typically used for 3D printing and rapid prototyping.

3. Select the location to save the file.
4. Set exclusion options (Optional).
5. Press **OK**.

While saving, the B.I. Essentials window opens and color codes each part, as shown in Figure 1–25. **To be exported** is green, **To be excluded** is white, **To be delegated** is blue, and **To be waived** is cyan.

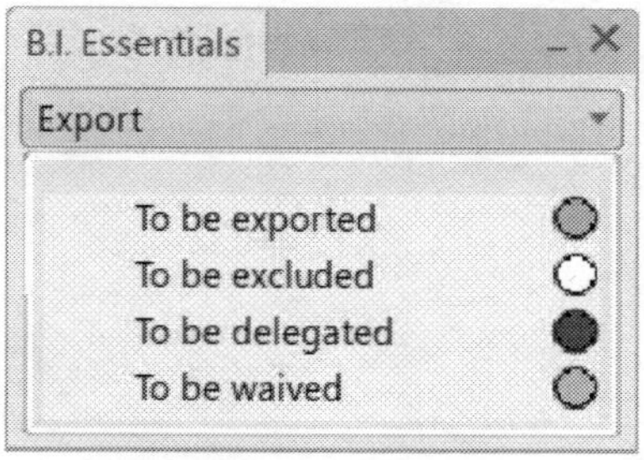

Figure 1–25

To exclude a part from being exported:

1. Select the part while the Export window is open.
2. Click **Exclude** in the floating dialog menu, as shown in Figure 1–26.

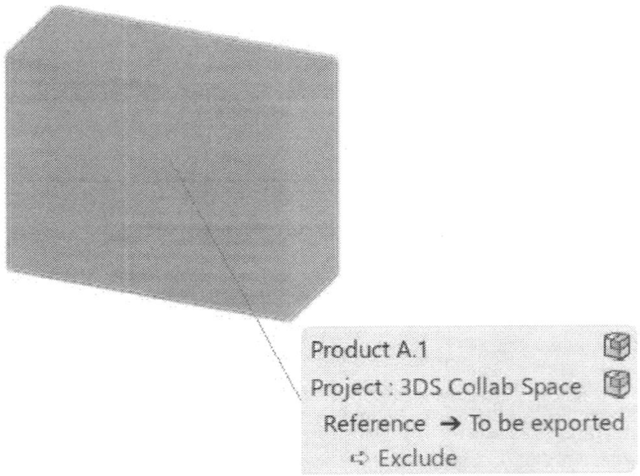

Figure 1–26

Practice 1a Access the 3DEXPERIENCE Platform

Practice Objectives

- Log into the 3DEXPERIENCE platform.
- Import a model.
- Make an edit to the model and save it.
- Open the revised model via search.

In this practice, you will log into the 3DEXPERIENCE platform and import a model. You will change the geometry of a model and save it to the database, then reopen it using search.

Task 1 - Launch the 3DEXPERIENCE platform.

Icon may very depending on implementation.

1. Double-click the **3DEXPERIENCE 2022x** icon on the desktop, as shown in Figure 1–27.

Figure 1–27

2. In the 3DPassport - Login web page, enter the *Username* and *Password* assigned by your administrator, as shown in Figure 1–28.

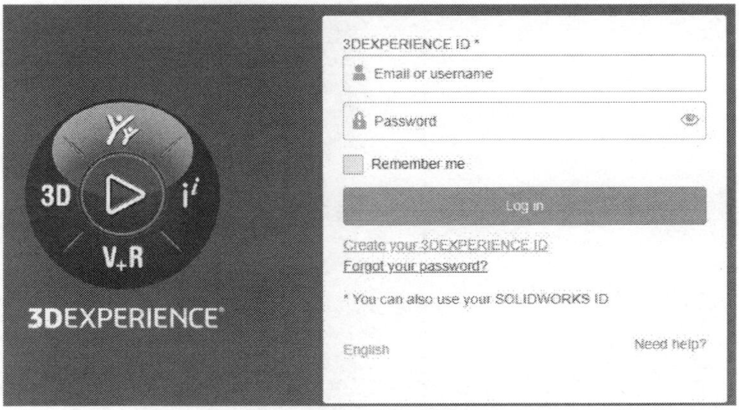

Figure 1–28

3. Click **Log in**.

Note that if you are not using this content in the Rand 3D environment, use the credentials, Collaborative Space, and Role provided by your System Administrator.

4. Once logged in, you will see the **My First Dashboard** within the web browser. This is the web page gives the user access to both the Web and Native apps within the 3DEXPERENCE.

   If presented with the Welcome screen (shown in Figure 1–29), navigate through it with the arrows on the sides or small circles at the bottom, then close it using the **X** in the upper-right corner.

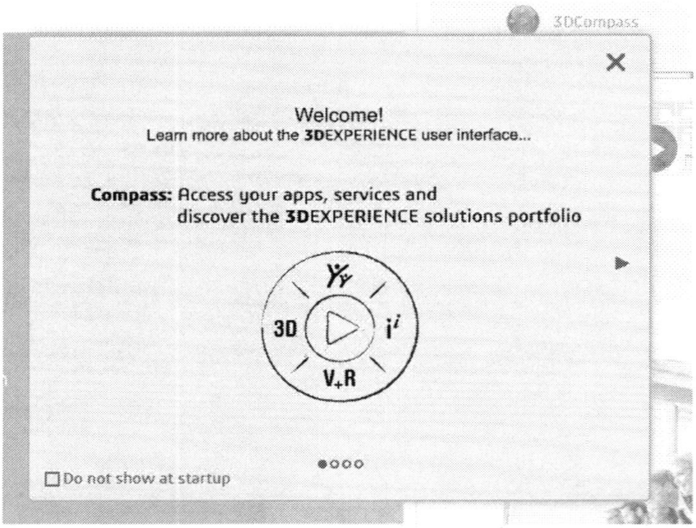

Figure 1–29

5. In the upper left corner Select the outer ring of the compass called the **Roles, Apps & Solutions portfolio** as shown in Figure 1–30. This will expand the list of apps available to you.

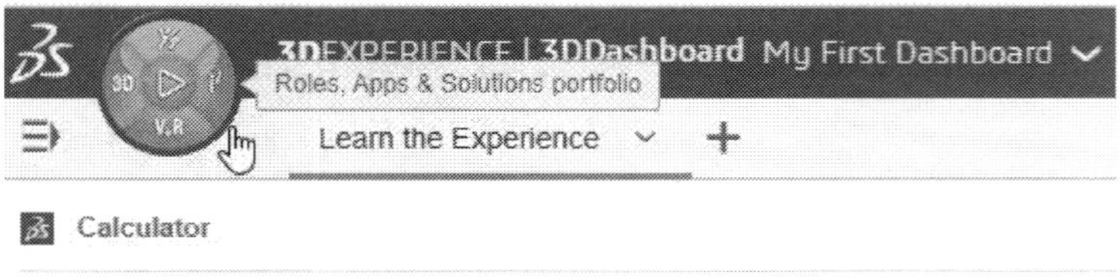

Figure 1–30

6. Next, launch the native app **Part Design** by expanding **My Apps** and selecting  **Part Design** from the list. This might take a moment to load. **Cancel** any 3D Part files that might automatically try to open.

7. If presented with the Welcome screen (shown in Figure 1–31), navigate through it with the arrows on the sides or small circles at the bottom, then close it using the **X** in the upper-right corner.

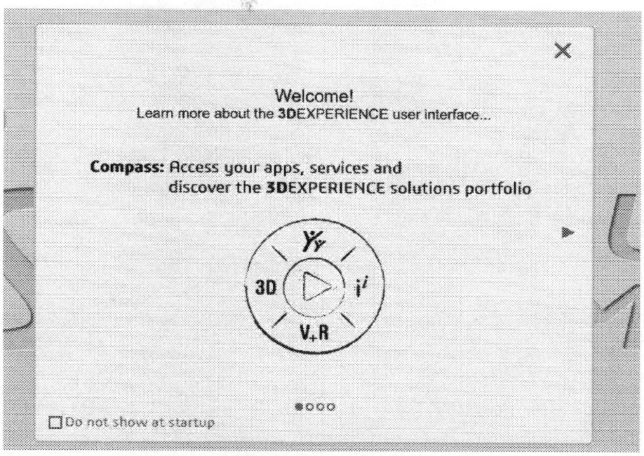

Figure 1–31

Task 2 - Set the 3DEXPERIENCE platform to add your initials to new and imported objects.

1. In the Top Bar, click **ME** (your user icon).
2. Select **Preferences**, as shown in Figure 1–32.

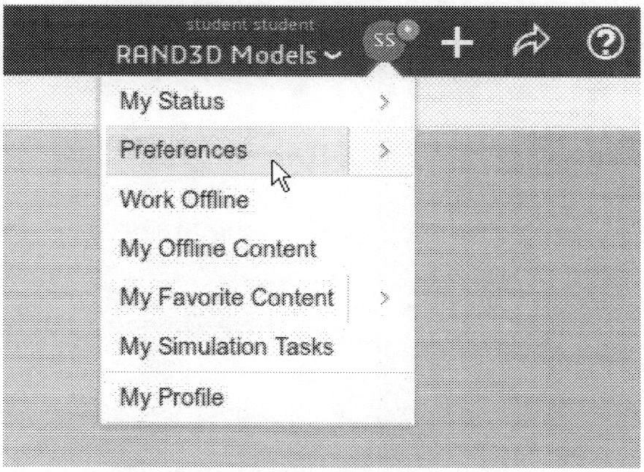

Figure 1–32

3. In the Preferences dialog box, click **App Preferences Tab**, as shown in Figure 1–33.

4. Expand **Social and Collaborative**, and then expand **Global Design Management** and select **Collaborative Lifecycle**, as shown in Figure 1–33.

5. In the *Identification* section, add your initials followed by an underscore, as shown in Figure 1–33.

Note that the images in this guide will not have initials preceding the names.

*Alternatively, you can type **Identification String** into the search settings under the Preferences tab and let it find it for you.*

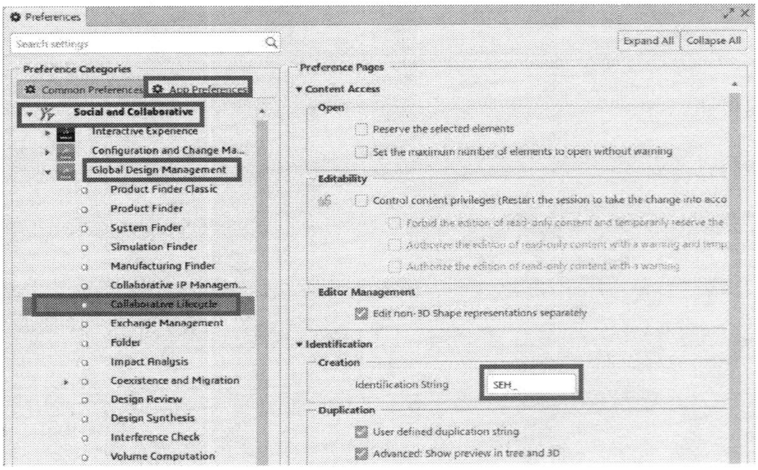

Figure 1–33

6. Click **OK**.

Task 3 - Import a CATIA part.

1. In the Top Bar, click (Add)**>Import**.

2. In the Import dialog box, click (Open).

3. Browse to the Bore_Fixture folder and select **Bore-Device-Assembled.3DXML** and click **Open**.

Note that the Duplication string field shows your initials based on the preference setting you made in Task 2.

4. Ensure that the settings in the Import dialog box match those shown in Figure 1–34.

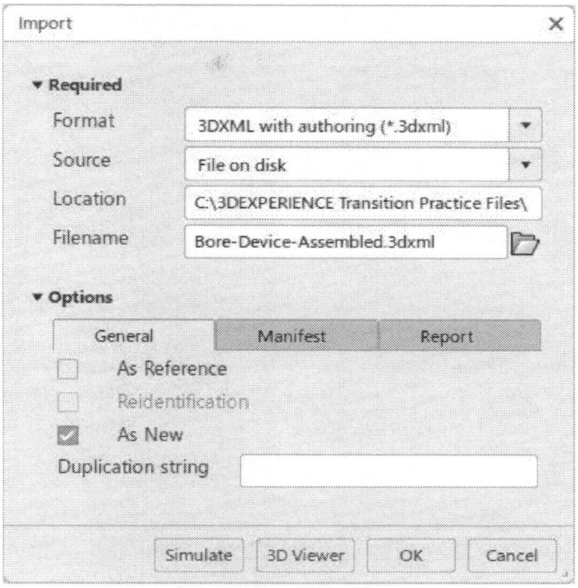

Figure 1–34

5. Click **OK**.

6. Click **OK** in the Operation report dialog box.

Task 4 - Investigate the Explorer.

The initial display in the Explore view is a representation of the model, rather than the geometry.

1. The model displays as shown in Figure 1–35.

Figure 1–35

Note that you may need to click the arrow on the left side of the screen to see the specification tree, the first time you open an object.

Your objects will have your initials as a prefix.

2. Expand the listing in the specification tree as shown in Figure 1–36.

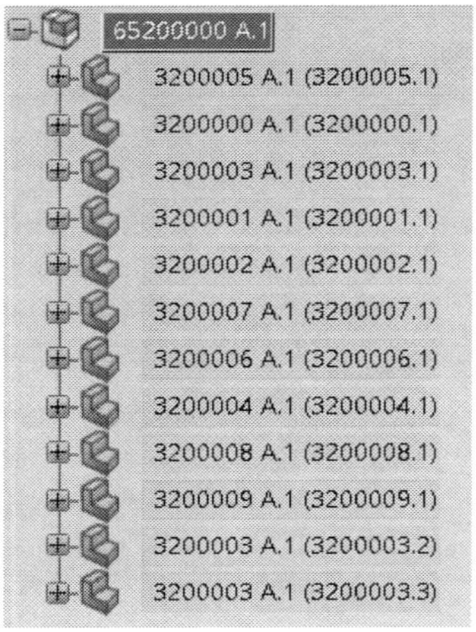

Figure 1–36

3. In the *View* tab of the Action Bar, click (Swap Turntable/In-place) until the assembly displays fully assembled, as shown in Figure 1–37.

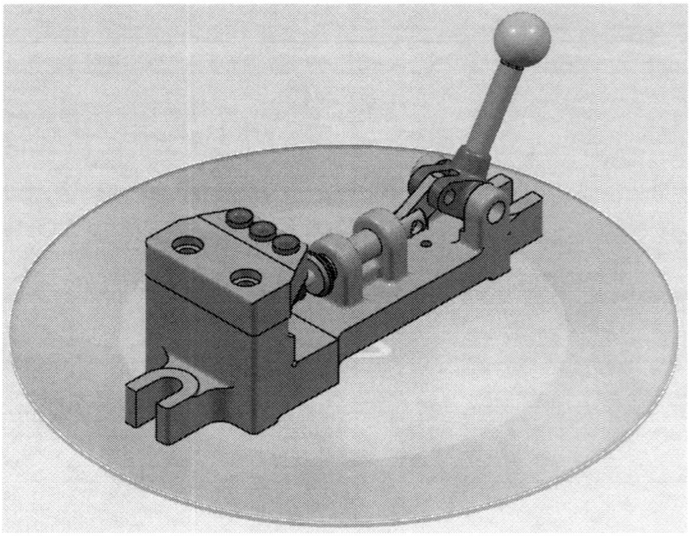

Figure 1–37

4. Click and drag the turntable to rotate the assembly, until it displays approximately as shown in Figure 1–38.

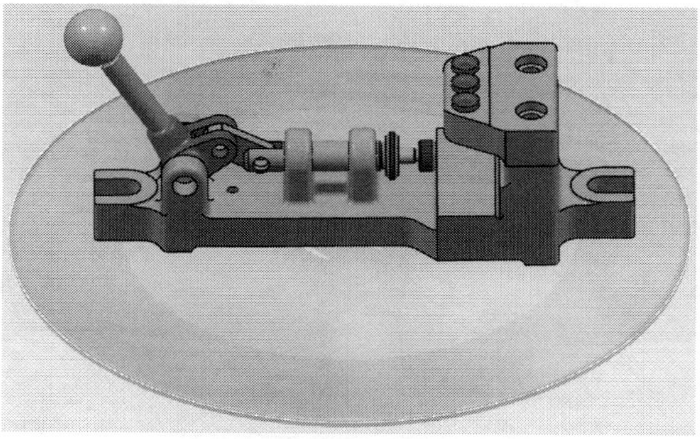

Figure 1–38

5. Click  (Swap Turntable/In-place) to view the components as shown in Figure 1–39.

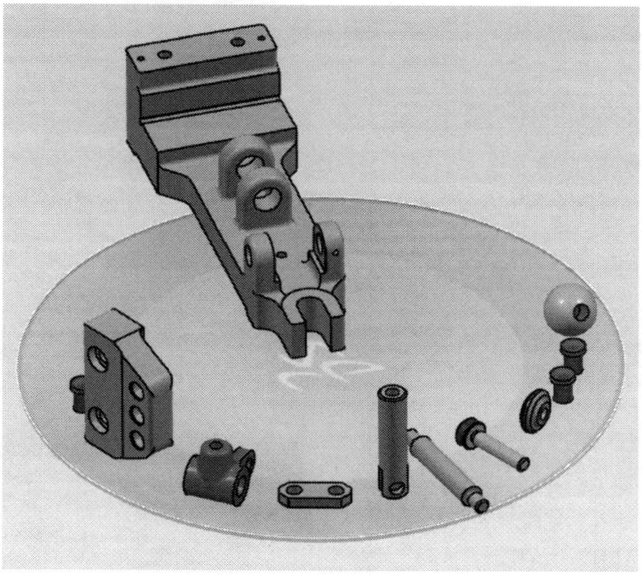

Figure 1–39

6. In the *View* tab, click  (Text View) to view callouts of each component found in the assembly, as shown in Figure 1–40.

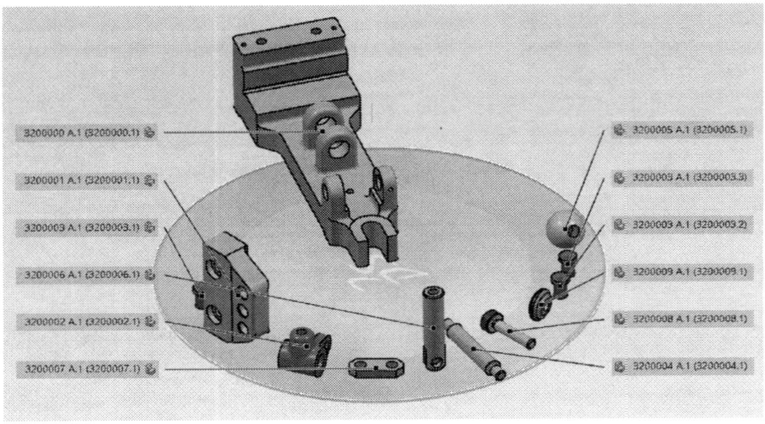

Figure 1–40

7. Select several text labels and note that as they are selected, the applicable model highlights both on-screen and in the specification tree.
8. Click  (Text View) to turn off the callouts.
9. Select the **3200001** component and in the *View* tab of the Action Bar, click  (Ghost View). Note that the object is displayed transparently, as shown in Figure 1–41.

Your objects will have your initials preceding their name. In the text and images in this content, we will show the names without any prefixes.

Note that objects set to Ghost View will have  *next to them in the specification tree.*

Edges have been turned off in the  *View Mode, otherwise the outline will still show.*

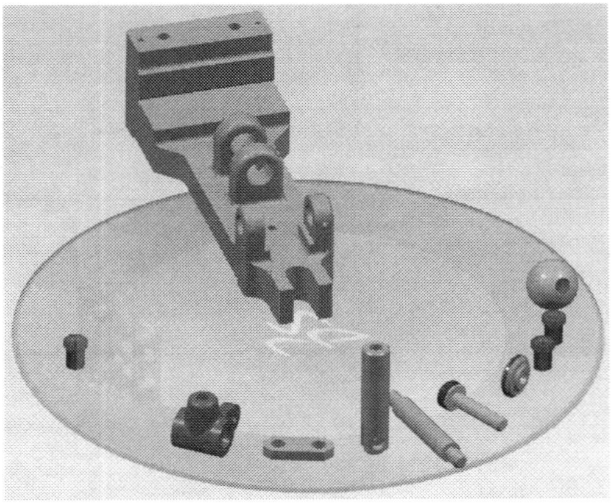

Figure 1–41

10. Select the **3200001** component again and click (Ghost View) to reset it to shaded.

11. Click (Swap Turntable/In-place) to view the assembled model.

Task 5 - Open the assembly for editing.

1. In the specification tree, right-click **65200000** and select **Open**.
2. Select the *Product Edition* tab in the Action Bar. This tab allows you to complete assembly related tasks such as assembling new components.
3. In the specification tree, right-click 3200001, and select **3200001.1 object** > **Open in New App**.
4. The part opens in its own tab, as shown in Figure 1–42.

If you do not see the specification tree, click the arrow on the left side of the screen.

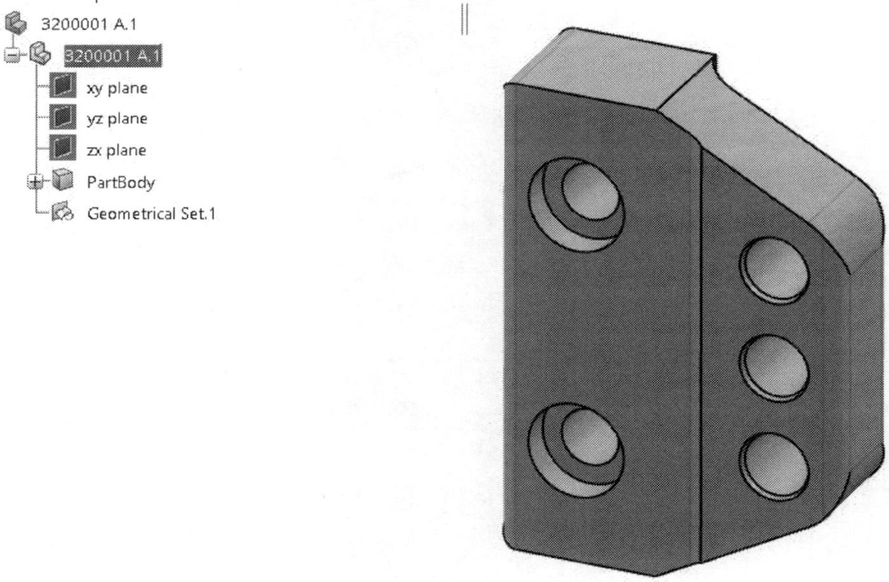

Figure 1–42

5. Double-click the hole shown in Figure 1–43 and edit the Main diameter to **10**.

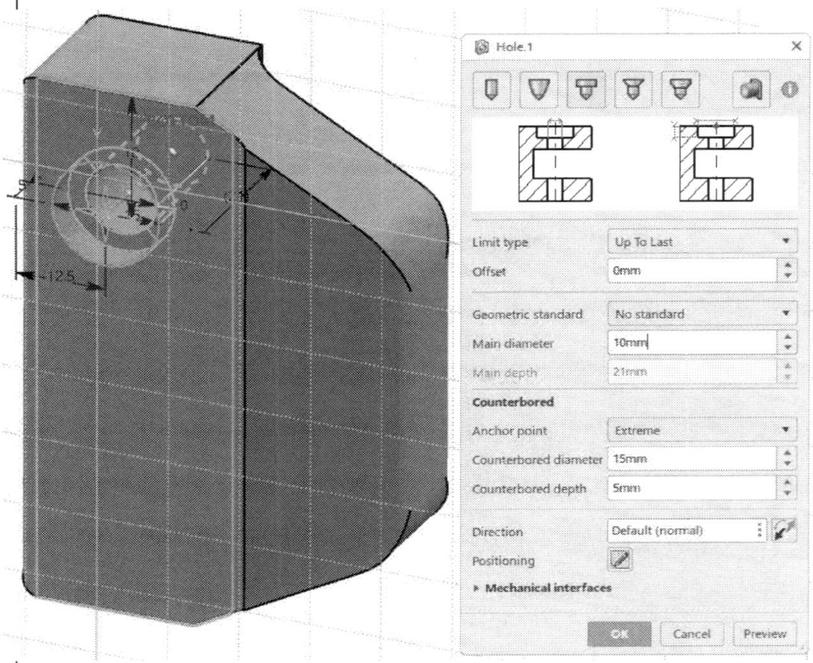

Figure 1–43

6. Click **OK**.

7. Close the 3200001 part tab.

8. In the Action Bar, click (Update) to update the assembly.

Task 6 - Save the assembly, then use Search to reopen it from the database.

1. In the Top Bar, click (Share)>**Save**.

2. Close the open tabs.

3. In the Search Bar at the top of the 3DEXPERIENCE window, type ***Your_Initials*_652*** and press <Enter>.

4. Find the most recent version of the assembly, right-click and select **Open**.

5. In the specification tree, expand **3200001** fully, and double-click on **Hole.1** to activate the part. Then double-click **Hole.1**. Note that the diameter is the original 9mm, as shown in Figure 1–44.

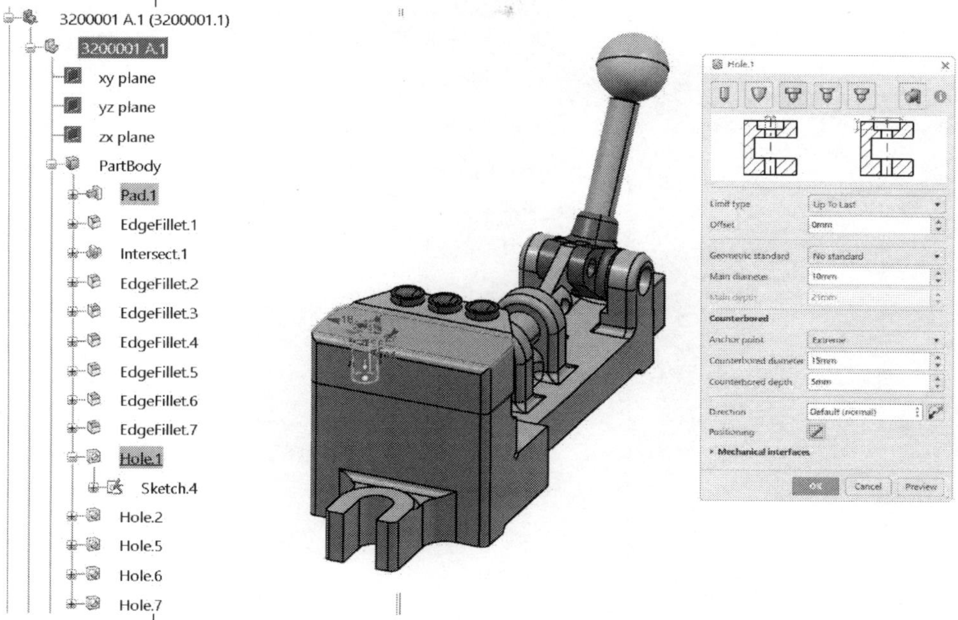

Figure 1–44

6. Click **Cancel** in the Hole Definition dialog box.

7. Close the tab.

Chapter Review Questions

1. 3DEXPERIENCE is a unified database and interface from Dassault Systèmes that provides a platform in which business software and application can run.
   a. True
   b. False
2. The tool used to navigate between various apps is referred to as the:
   a. Start Menu
   b. Compass
   c. Preferences
   d. Me (your user icon)
3. If you have models, even if from the same release of CATIA V5 and 3DEXPERIENCE, they cannot be transferred back and forth.
   a. True
   b. False
4. To find objects, you can use the Search tool in 3DEXPERIENCE by entering text and wildcards.
   a. True
   b. False
5. Among other formats, you can import existing CATIA V5 files as well as 3DXML files.
   a. True
   a. False

Answers: 1a, 2b, 3b, 4a, 5b, 6a

Solid Modeling Overview

This chapter provides an overview of solid modeling, where you use features and parameters to build a model. The relationships created with these features and parameters can be used to establish the design intent on the model. You learn how CATIA maintains associativity between the model, assemblies, and drawings. You gain familiarity with the CATIA user interface and learn how to customize it, making it more efficient to work with.

Learning Objectives in This Chapter

- Understand the basics of solid modeling.
- Understand feature-based modeling.
- Understand the parametric and associative nature of CATIA.
- Understand how and why you capture a model's design intent during modeling.
- Become familiar with the CATIA user interface.
- Learn how to work with a model by opening it, customizing the display settings, and selecting entities.
- Learn how to access the online help system.

2.1 Fundamentals

Solid Modeling

CATIA is used to create three-dimensional (3D) solid models. The software *understands* that the model is *filled* with material. With a solid model, you can perform the following:

- Obtain the mass properties of a part.
- Determine if components in an assembly interfere with one another.
- Create cross-sections of an assembly or display part cross-sections in a drawing. Instead of manually *drawing* the views on the drawing, you can reference the part model to generate views and show the dimensions from the 3D geometry, as shown in Figure 2–1.

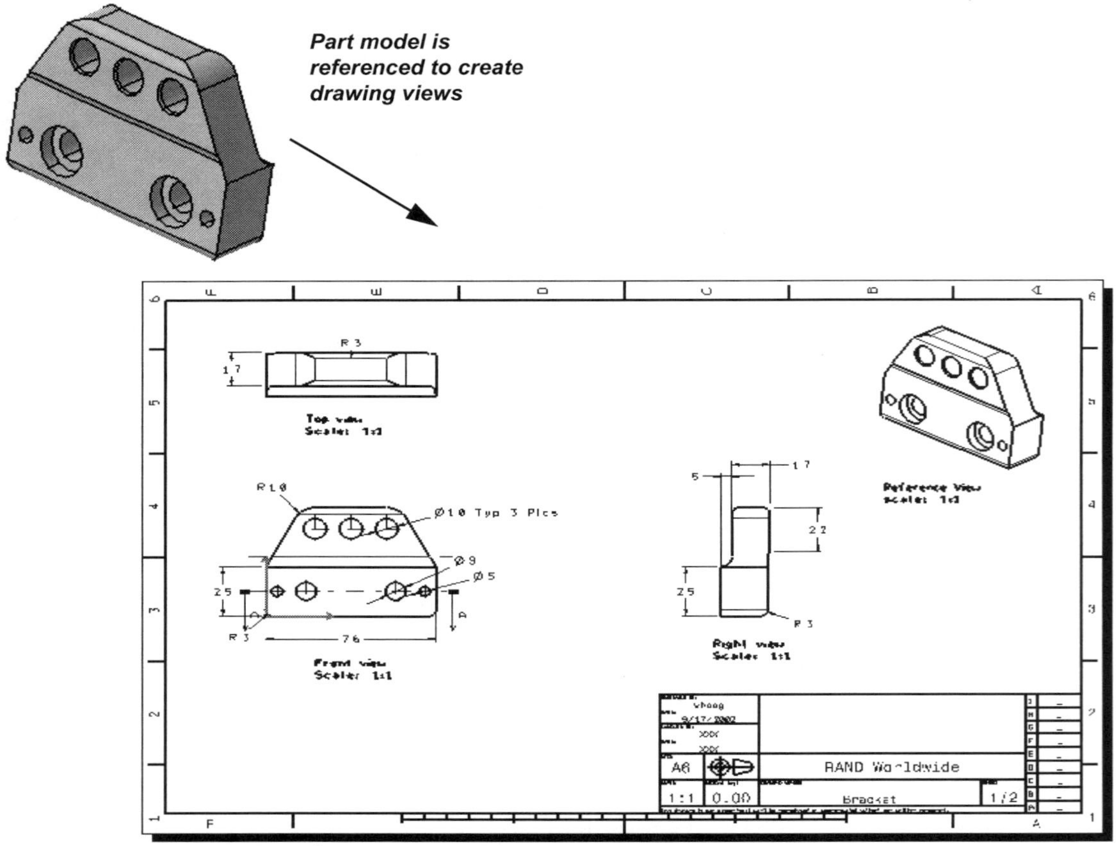

Figure 2–1

This process also applies to assemblies, as shown in Figure 2–2. You can locate existing part and assembly models relative to one another.

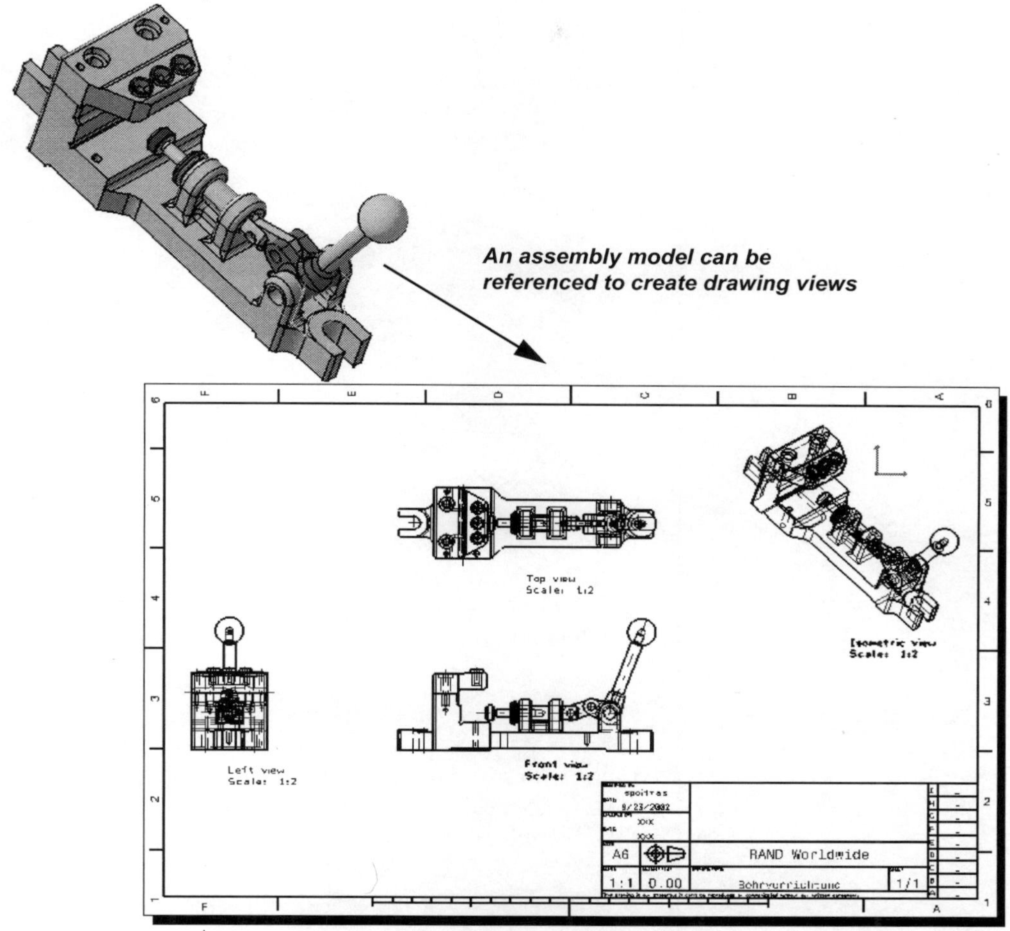

Figure 2–2

Feature-Based

The solid model evolves as features are created, one by one, until the geometry is complete. The part model (shown in Figure 2–3) is constructed by consecutively creating the following features:

1. Create a sketch.
2. Create a Pad feature.
3. Draft several walls of the part using a Draft feature.
4. Remove sharp edges of the geometry by creating a Fillet feature.
5. Create a Shell feature to hollow out the part.

6. Create another Pad feature to act as a cylindrical boss.
7. Center a Hole feature on the cylindrical Pad.
8. Duplicate the boss and hole to create the second boss, as shown in Figure 2–3.

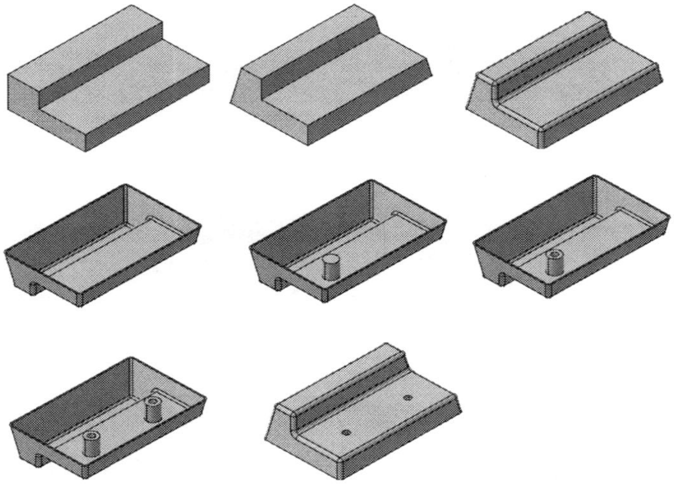

Figure 2–3

You can organize features based on the design intent by initially defining the overall size, major geometric shapes, and then later the finishing details.

Parametric

Features created in CATIA are parametric. All of the dimensional constraints used to define a feature's shape are considered *parameters* and are accessible at any time. Double-click on a feature to display its dimensional constraints and change any of those values to alter the geometry. The dimensional value that positions the Pocket feature (shown in Figure 2–4) has changed. The position of the feature updates to reflect the design change.

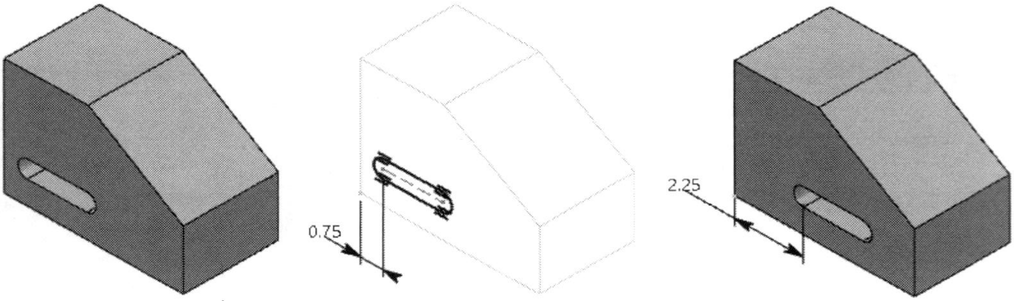

Figure 2–4

Associative

Drawings are created by referencing a model. When the model is changed, any drawings of that model are automatically updated the next time they are opened. Similarly, changing a part model is automatically reflected in the assembly. Also, changes made in the assembly update in all other modes in CATIA, as shown in Figure 2–5.

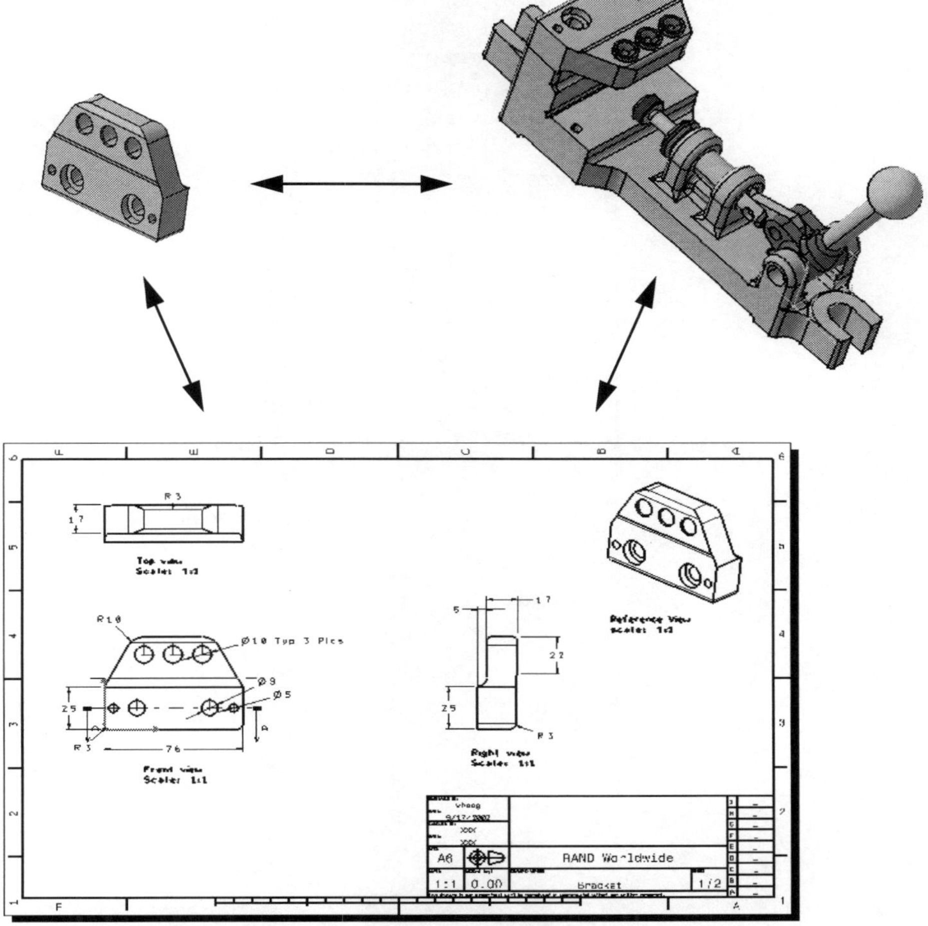

Figure 2–5

Associativity creates a dependency between models. The part models referenced by an assembly and/or drawing must be retrievable to work with the assembly and/or drawing.

2.2 Design Intent

The key to building parametric, feature-based, solid models is to ensure that they have a flexible and predictable behavior. This process is known as capturing *design intent*.

Method 1

One method of capturing design intent is to determine the feature's dimensioning scheme. Figure 2–6 shows an example of a part with a hole. When the Pad feature increases in length, the design intent of the hole determines how it behaves. If the hole is dimensioned to the end of the Pad, the hole moves to remain a distance of 3.00 from that end. If the hole is dimensioned to the face, it remains a distance of 6.00 from that face.

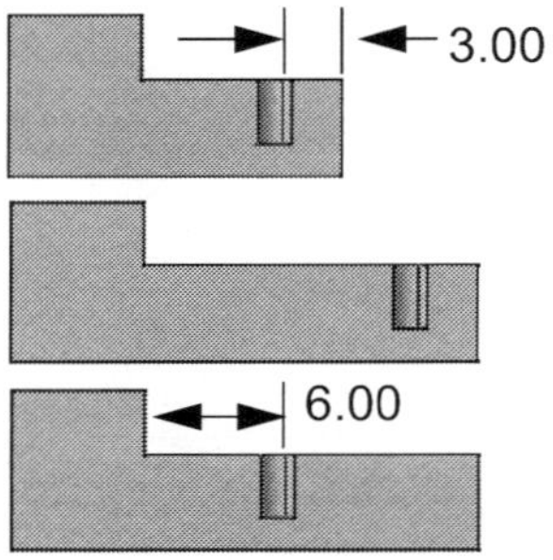

Figure 2–6

Method 2

A second method of capturing design intent is to select an option to limit your feature. A part with a hole is shown in Figure 2–7.

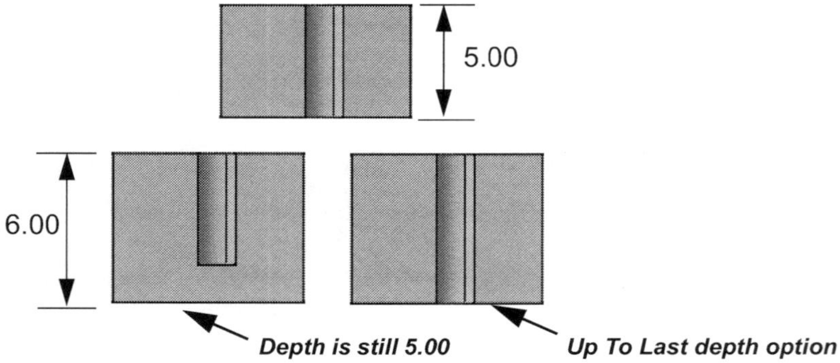

Figure 2–7

The design intent is for the hole to pass through the entire model. When the Pad changes from 5.00 to 6.00, the resulting geometry displays differently depending on how the hole is limited. If the hole was created with a depth of 5.00, it no longer passes though the entire part. It must be changed to maintain the design intent. A better solution is to set the limit of the hole using **Up To Last** option and ensure that it always passes through the part, regardless of the height of the Pad feature.

Method 3

A third method of capturing design intent is to create symmetrical geometry. The design intent for the part (shown in Figure 2–8) is to have the Pocket remain at the center of the part.

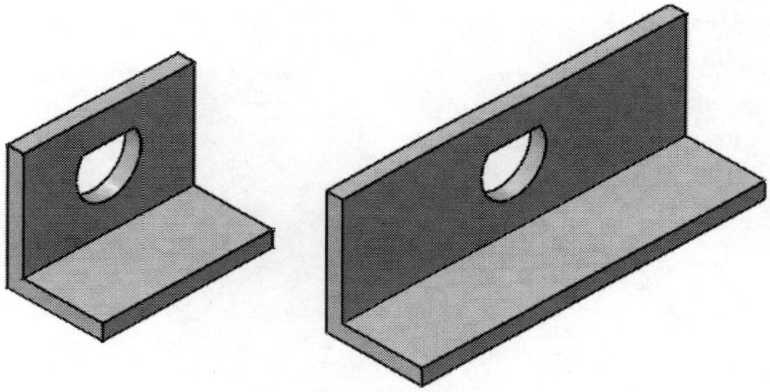

Figure 2–8

Constraining the Pocket from either end of the Pad feature does not capture the design intent. Constructing the Pad and Pocket relative to a center datum reference is preferable.

2.3 User Interface

Screen Layout, Quick Start

When you launch 3DEXPERIENCE, you are presented with a welcome screen, as shown in Figure 2–9.

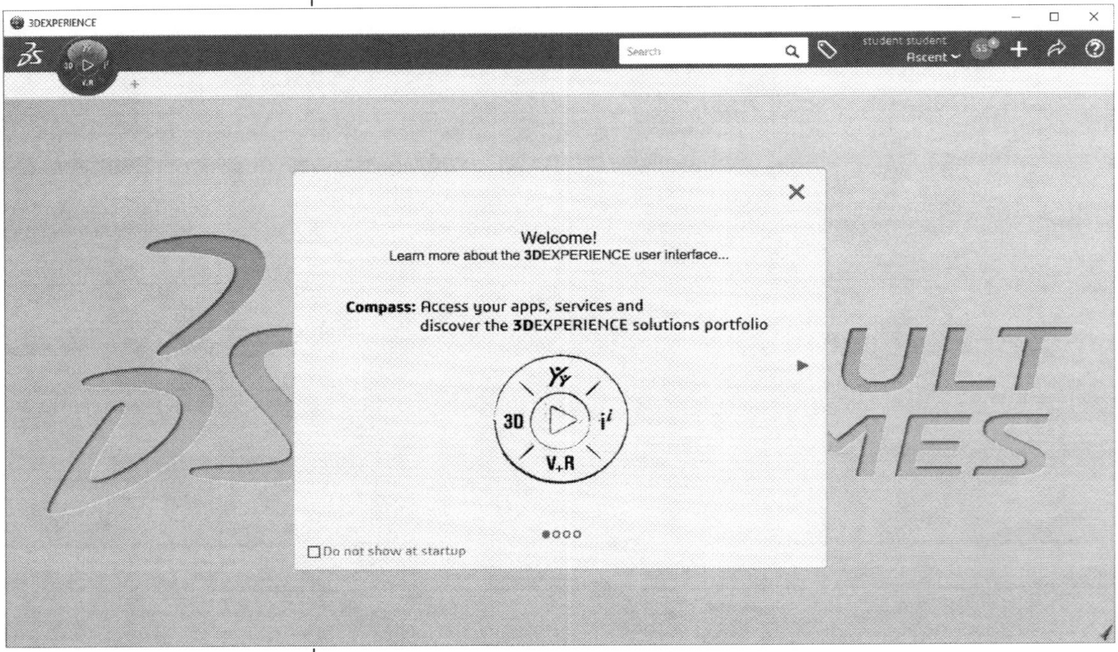

Figure 2–9

This welcome screen has multiple pages, accessed by the arrows on the side or the circular buttons at the bottom, as shown in Figure 2–10. The circular buttons allow you to move to a specific page.

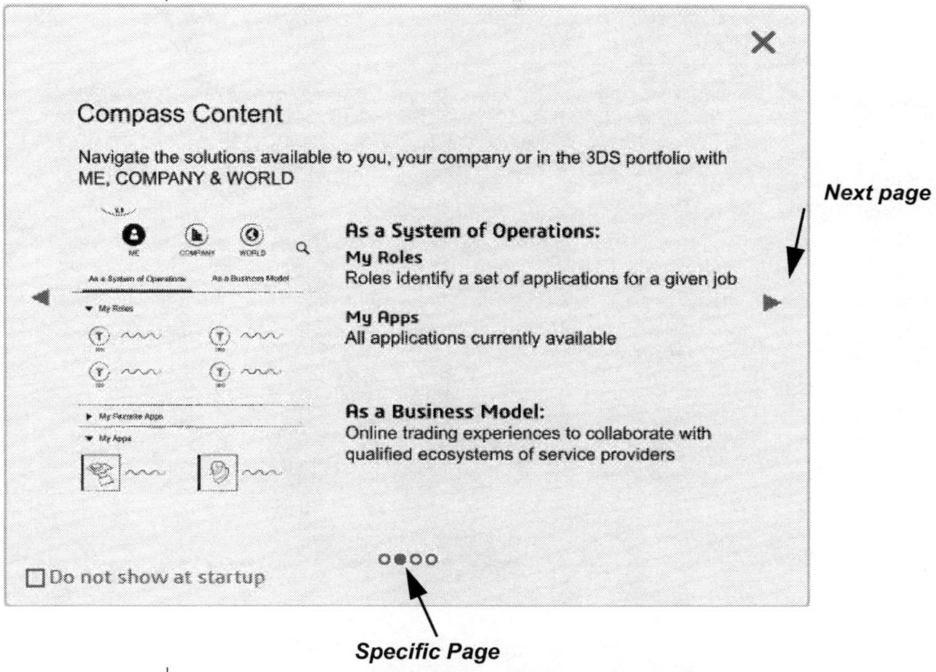

Figure 2–10

You can click through this welcome screen to discover the basics of the 3DEXPERIENCE user interface. If you do not want to see this screen when 3DEXPERIENCE launches, select **Do not show at startup**.

Screen Layout

When you open a model in 3DEXPERIENCE CATIA Part Design, the screen displays as shown in Figure 2–11. The major areas of the interface that are labeled are discussed in the following topics.

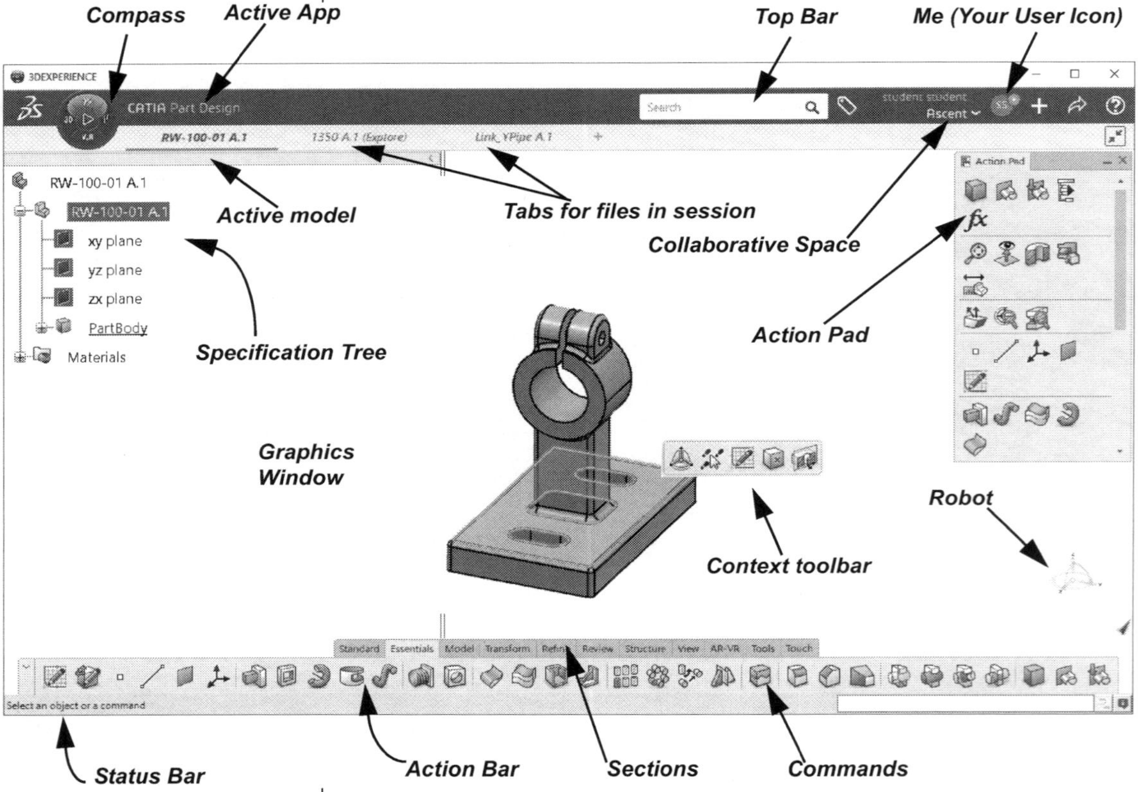

Figure 2–11

Commands

The primary way of interacting with the software is to select icons in the Action Bar, Action Pad or Context toolbar. You can customize the interface by arranging the location of the toolbars and selecting the icons to display.

Compass

The Compass enables you to access various apps. The Compass is broken into two functional areas. The inner circle named the (Play) button and the outer ring named (Roles, Apps and Solution Profile).The outer ring allows you to switch between Rolls and Apps freely, while the play button allows you to interact only with the applicable apps. Some of the major categories in the 3DEXPERIENCE platform system are shown in Figure 2–12.

Social and Collaborative Apps

3D Modeling Apps

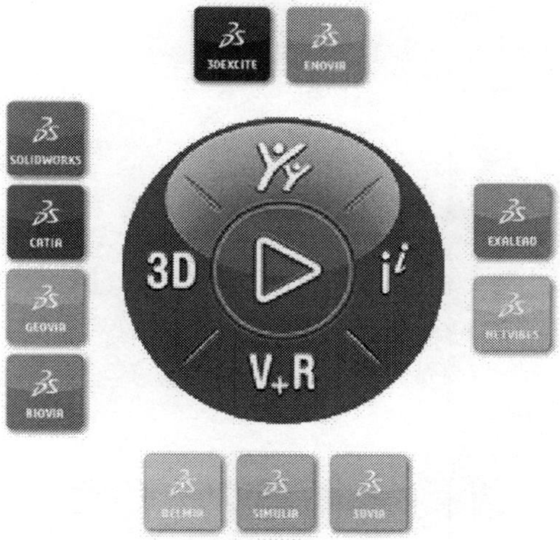

Information Intelligence Apps

Simulation Apps

Figure 2–12

Search Bar

The Search Bar enables you to look up CATIA files within the engineering database. Searches can include wildcard (*) use (as shown in Figure 2–13) and can be refined in various ways. The wildcard (*) is not needed at the beginning or the end of the text because it is implied.

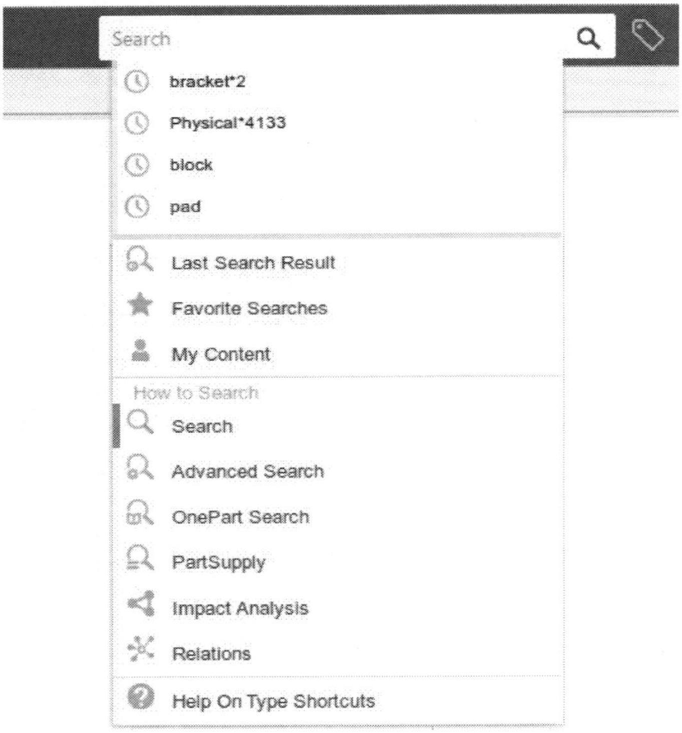

Figure 2–13

Specification Tree

The specification tree can be quickly toggled on and off by pressing <F3>.

The specification tree is available when working with parts, assemblies, and drawings. It displays a variety of information about the model and displays the features of the part in the order in which they were created, as shown in Figure 2–14. This provides quick access to parameters, functions, materials, and commonly used measurements.

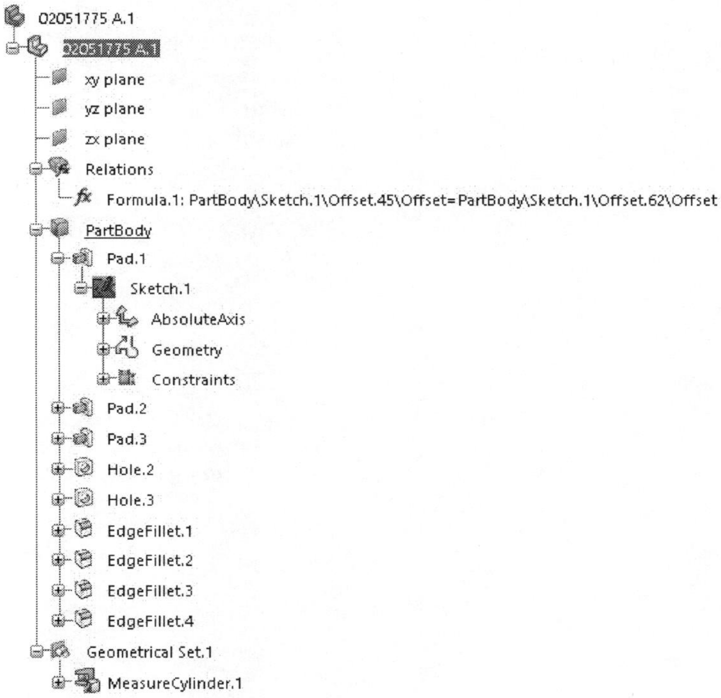

Figure 2–14

Robot

The Robot is available for part and assembly models. It displays in the upper right corner of the model window and can perform various functions, as shown in Figure 2–15Figure 2–17. The Robot is used to:

- Freely rotate the model in all three directions.
- Rotate the model in a plane.
- Pan along one direction.
- Pan in a plane.
- View down an axis direction by selecting the X, Y, or Z letter. Selecting again flips the view in the opposite direction.

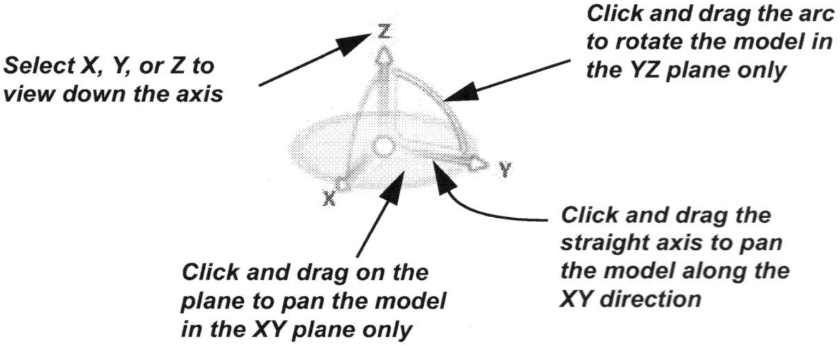

Figure 2–15

Tabs

Multiple objects can be open at the same time. Each object is presented in its own tab, and you can switch back and forth between objects simply by selecting the tab name.

Tabs can also be subdivided into smaller windows called widgets, as shown in Figure 2–16.

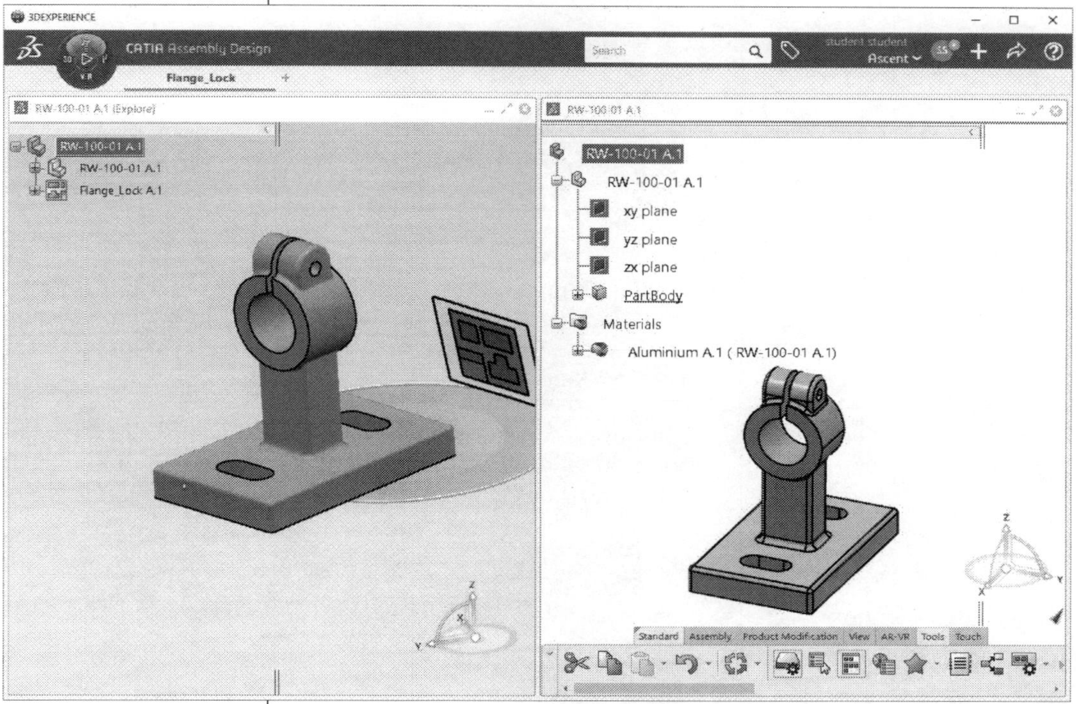

Figure 2–16

You can access options for controlling the display of widgets by right-clicking on the tab where they are stored, as shown in Figure 2–17.

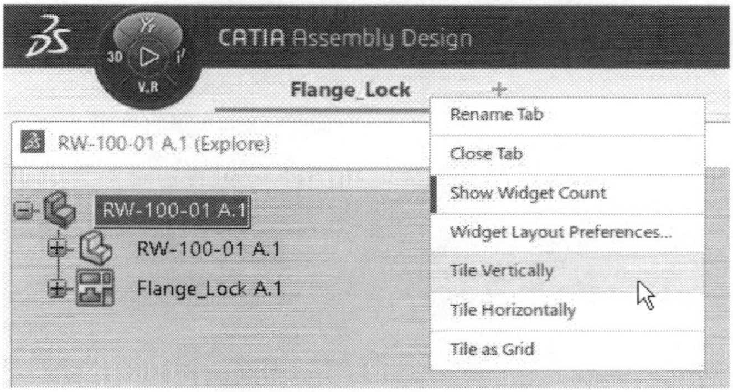

Figure 2–17

Apps

An app is a set of tools used to complete certain tasks. The apps used in this course are described as follows:

Icon	Application Name
	Part Design
	Drafting
	Assembly Design

Additional apps are accessed from within other apps. For example, when in the Part Design app, you will create sketches for features. To create those sketches, the system places you into the Sketch app.

Other apps can be used for Analysis, Manufacturing, Digital Mock Up, and other advanced tasks. The name of the active app is displayed next to the compass, as shown in Figure 2–18.

Part Design app is active

Figure 2–18

2.4 Working with Models

ViewModes

Although you are working with a solid model, you can change how the geometry displays. These options can be accessed using  (View Modes) found in the *View* section of the Action Bar, as shown in Figure 2–19.

Figure 2–19

Selecting  (View Modes) will display the View Modes window, where the user can change the look of the model with standard predefined rendering styles. By selecting one of the many named cylinder shaped icons at the top of the window, the models look will quickly change as shown in Figure 2–20. By expanding the arrow next to **Shading** simple customizations can be made.

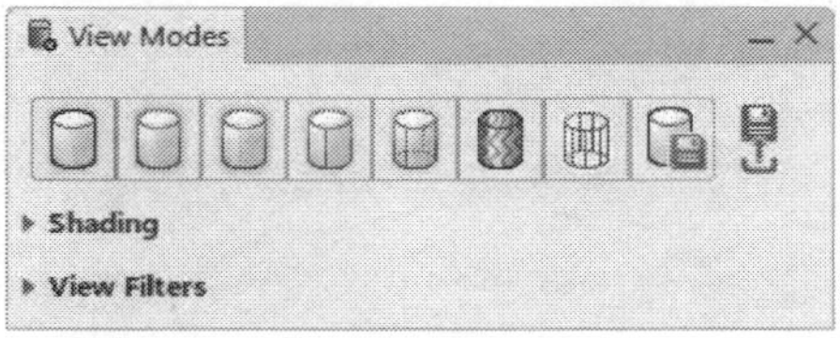

Figure 2–20

Figure 2–21 shows an example of each icon listed in the View Mode window. The **Customized View Mode** option enables you to configure the display with all options to suit your preferences, such as with hidden edges shown, with the material shown, or with faceted faces.

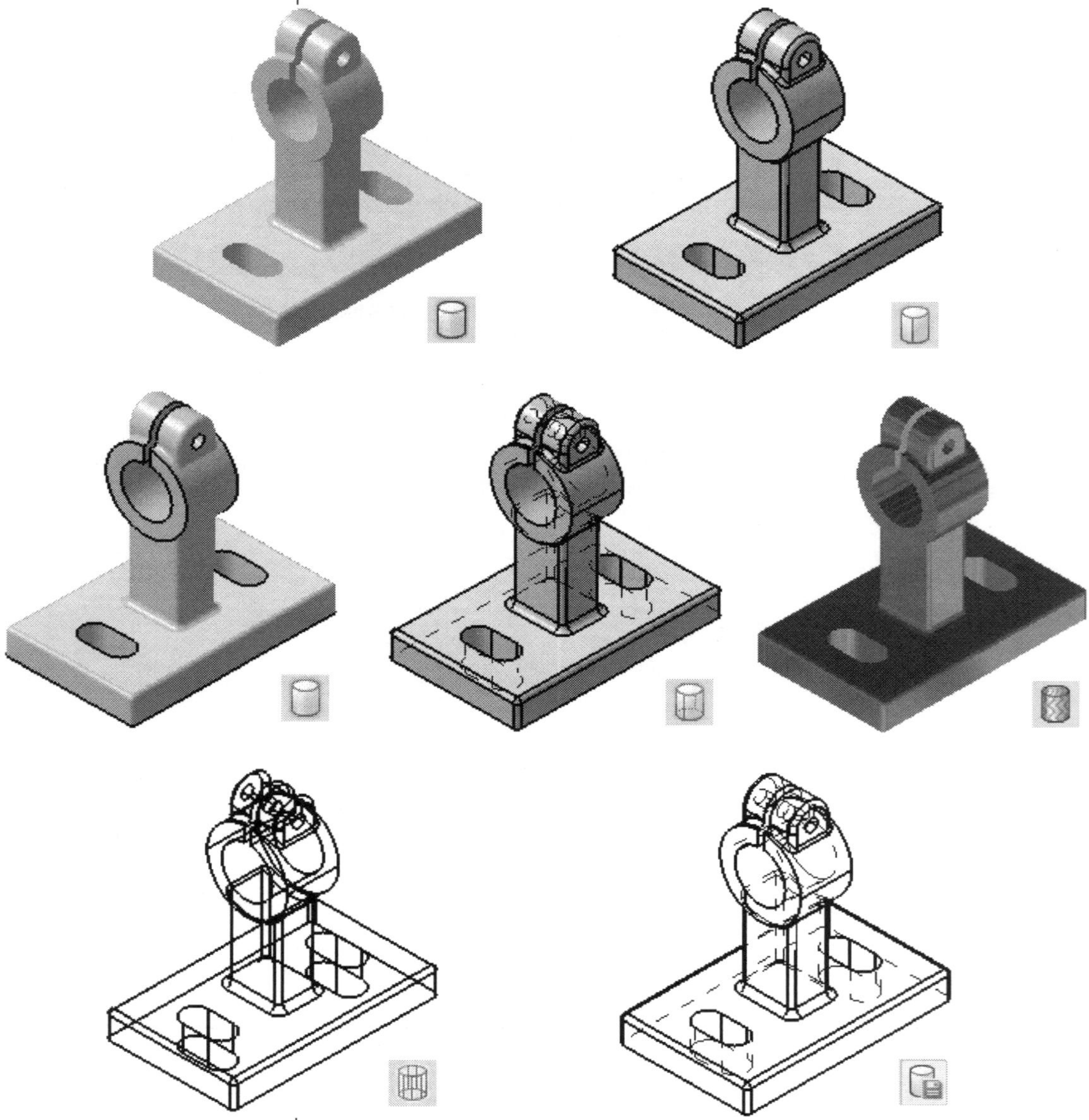

Figure 2–21

Model Navigation

To thoroughly inspect your models, you must learn how to reorient the model, zoom in and out, and pan. There are several methods to navigate a model.

- The Quick Views options in the *View* section of the Action Bar contain predefined model orientations enabling you to view the model from commonly used orientations. Figure 2–22 shows the available Quick Views.

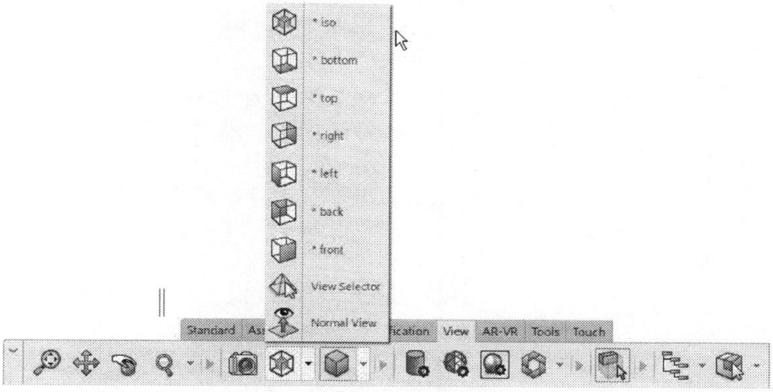

Figure 2–22

To dynamically navigate the model, you can use specific toolbar icons, menu commands, or mouse shortcuts. The navigation functions are listed as follows:

Icon	Function	Mouse
	**Pan**	Hold Middle
	**Rotate**	Hold Middle + Hold Right or Hold Middle + Hold Left
	**Zoom In/Out**	Hold Middle + Click Right or Hold Middle + Click Left
	**Zoom Area**	N/A
	**Fit All In**	N/A
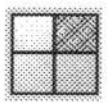	**Create Multi-view**	N/A

	**Re-center on Geometry**	Click Middle on required geometry

Use the **Re-center on Geometry** function to rotate the model around a specific location on the model or geometry. Click the middle mouse button on the required geometry or model location to re-center the model. Then, use the **Rotate** function to spin the model around the centered geometry.

Preselect Navigator

The **Preselect Navigator** tool enables you to select geometric entities that are hidden or difficult to select on a model. The software lists all entities that exist beneath the current cursor position and enables you to scroll through this list to select the required entity.

How To: Use the Preselect Navigator

1. Position the cursor over the geometry that you want to select.
2. Press the <Up Arrow> or <Down Arrow>. The software lists all entities that are beneath the current cursor position, as shown in Figure 2–23. A display window opens, indicating the currently highlighted entity.

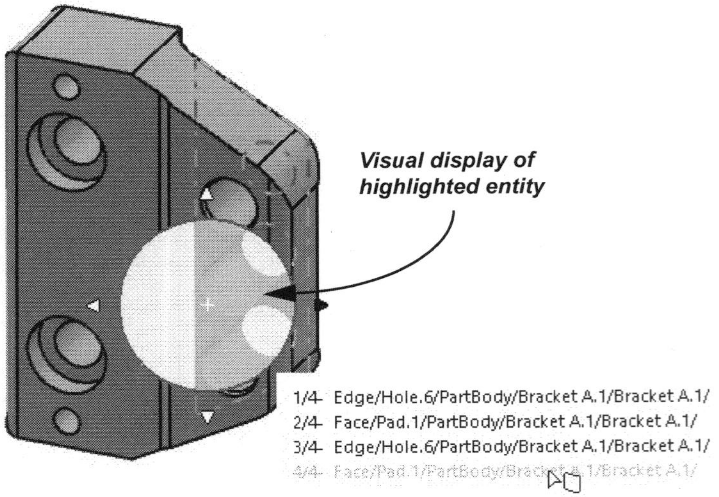

Figure 2–23

3. To scroll through the list, continue pressing the <Up Arrow> or <Down Arrow>. Press the <Left Arrow> and <Right Arrow> to navigate the possible selections for the active component only. You can also navigate the list using the cursor.
4. To select an entity for further operation, select it from the list using the cursor or press <Enter>.

An alternative method is as follows:

1. Position the cursor over the geometry that you want to select.
2. Press and hold <Alt> and then select the model. The software lists all of the entities that are beneath the selection point.
3. Move the cursor to make the appropriate selection. This option is controlled through the **Preselect in Geometry View** option, located in **Me>Preferences>Common Preferences>2D 3D View Display>Selection>Selection**, where Me is your user icon in the Top Bar of the 3DEXPERIENCE window.

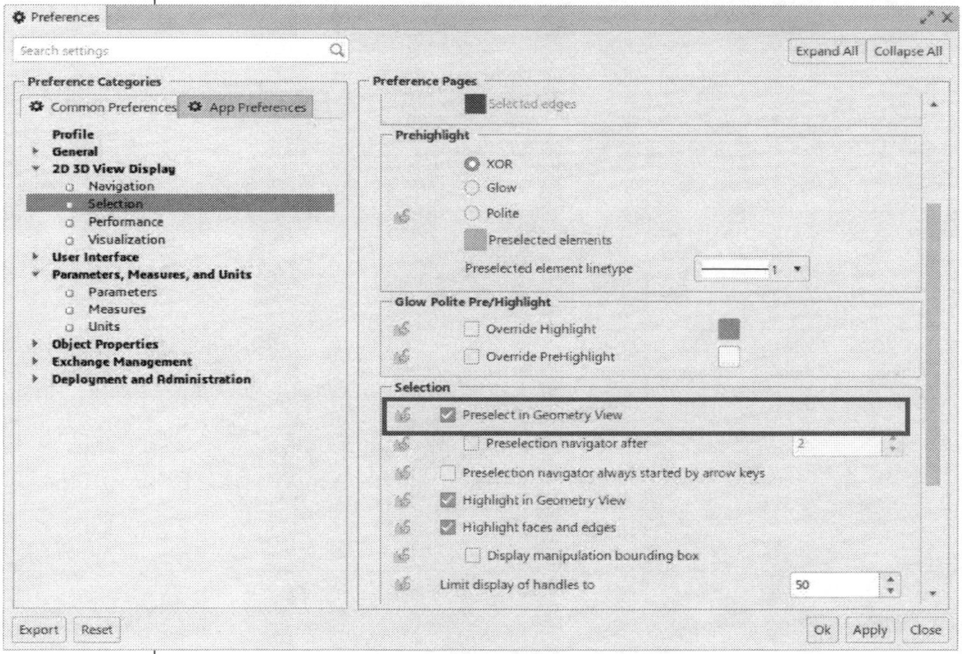

Figure 2–24

2.5 Online Documentation

Online documentation is very useful and easily accessible. To learn about any function, press <F1> when working with that function. This will open the User Assistance window that provides some basic information about that function. For additional information, click on **More help on this topic** at the bottom of the window, and the entire help topic displays on an Internet browser, as shown in Figure 2–25.

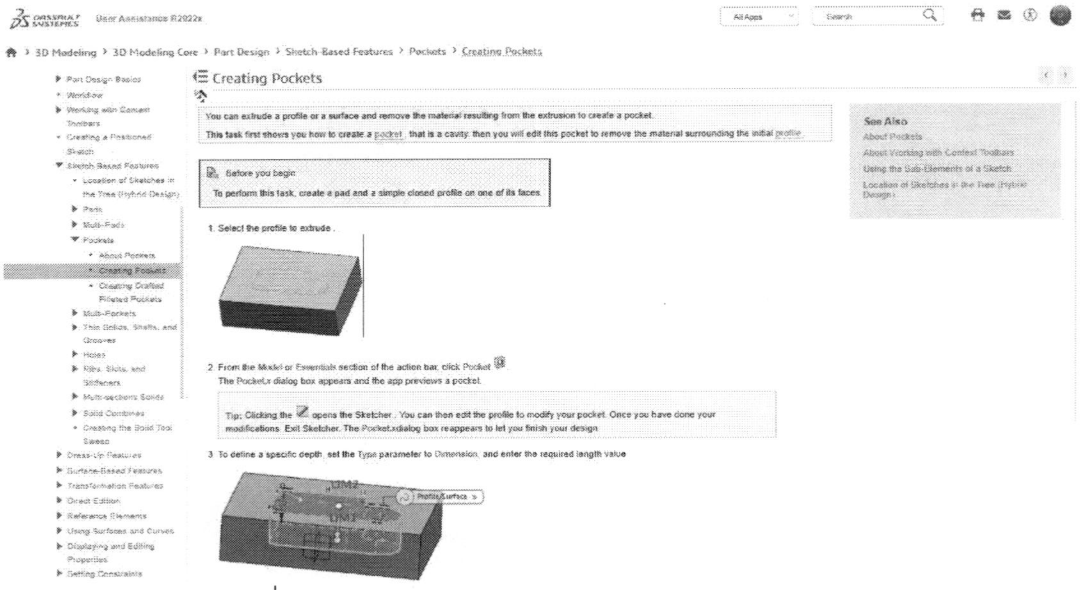

Figure 2–25

Online documentation usually includes structured practices that you can follow to gain hands-on experience with a particular function. At the top of the practice, the name of the component used in the practice displays as a blue hyperlink.

Practice 2a

Viewing a Part

Practice Objectives

- Open a part model and view it from different orientations.
- Change the display settings for the model.
- Investigate associativity between parts, drawings and assemblies.

In this practice, you will open an existing model and work with various visualization tools. You will also change the geometry of a model by editing parameters and deleting features, and note how these changes update in drawings and assemblies.

Task 1 - Import a CATIA part.

1. In the Top Bar, click (Add)>**Import**.
2. In the Import dialog box, click **(Open).**
3. Browse to and select **Flange_Lock_Drawing.3dxml** and click **Open**.
4. Ensure the settings in the Import dialog box match those shown in Figure 2–26.

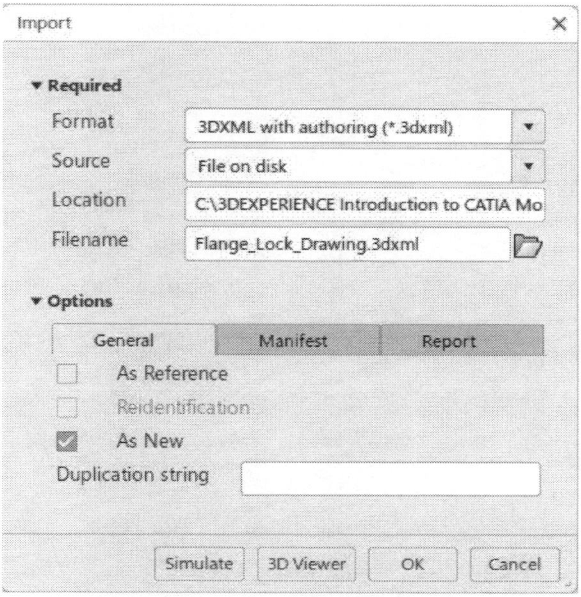

Figure 2–26

5. Click **OK**.
6. The Import Progression dialog box opens momentarily, as shown in Figure 2–27.

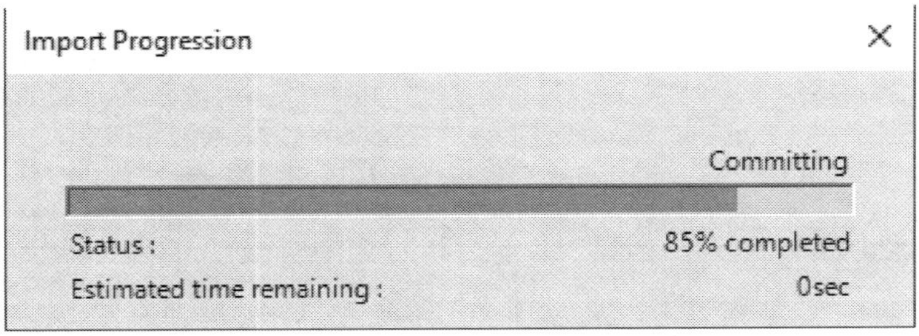

Figure 2–27

7. Then the Operation Report window appears showing the import was successful as shown in Figure 2–28.

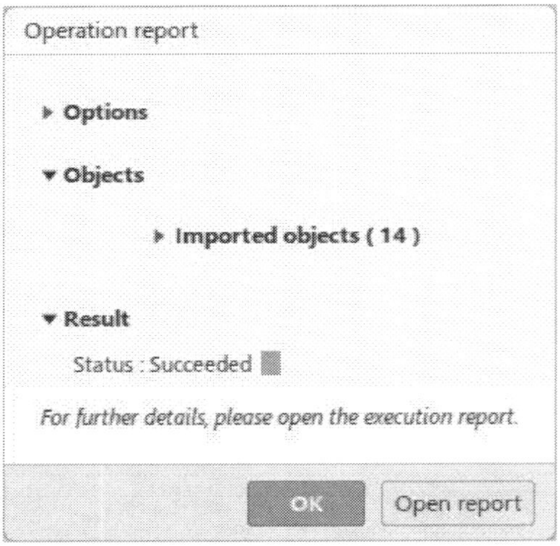

Figure 2–28

8. Click **OK** in the OperationReport dialog box.
9. In the specification tree, right-click **RW-100-01** and select **Open**.

10. The part displays as shown in Figure 2–29.

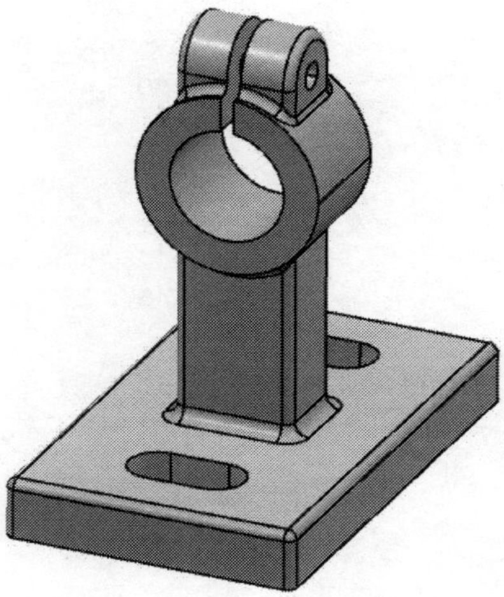

Figure 2–29

Task 2 - Change the display of the model.

1. In the *View* section of the Action Bar, select  (View Modes). This will open a View Modes window, as shown in Figure 2–30, and select  (Shading).

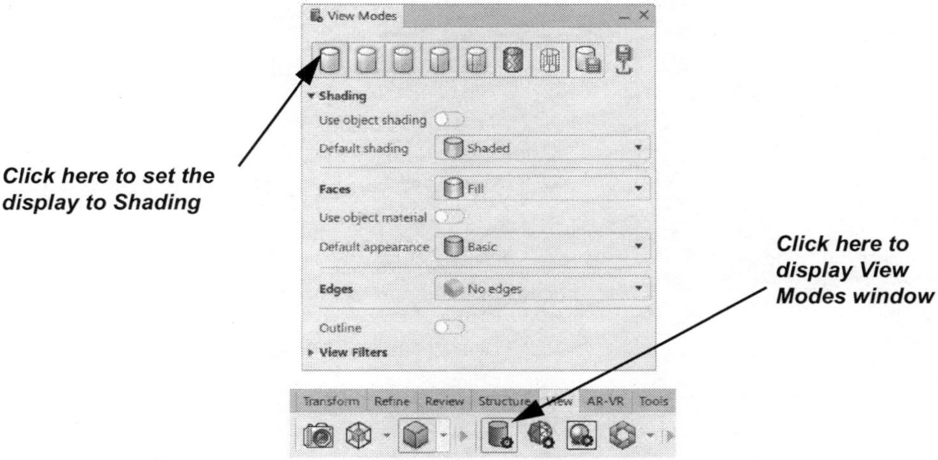

Figure 2–30

2. Repeat Step 1 to set the display to  (Shading With Sharp and Smooth Edges),  (Shading With Material), and  (Shading With Edges and Hidden Edges).

3. Set the display to  (Customize View Mode).

4. Set the options, as shown in Figure 2–31. The model displays as shown in Figure 2–32.

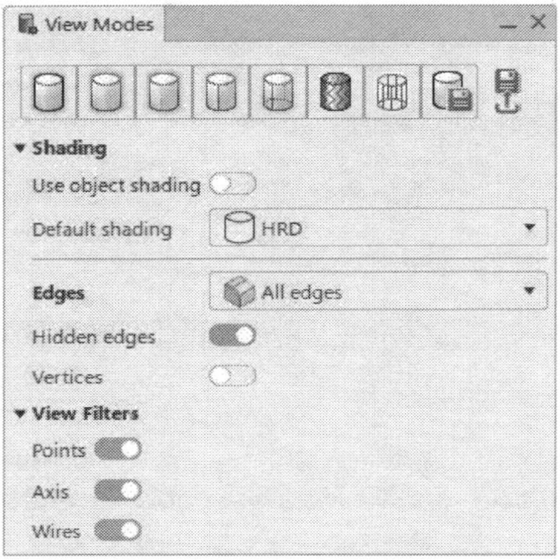

Figure 2–31

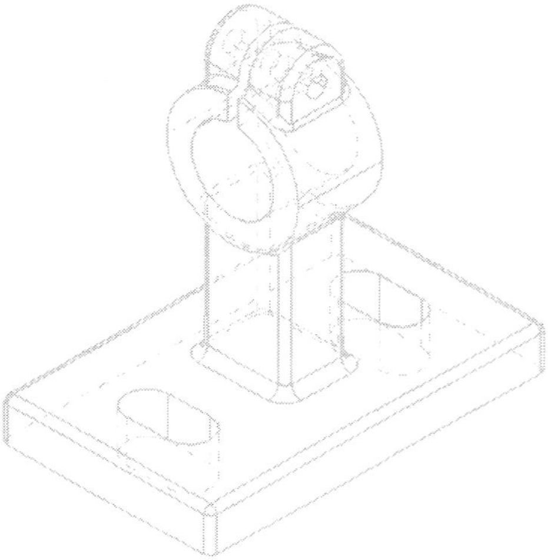

Figure 2–32

Task 3 - Use the Quick Views toolbar to change the model orientation.

1. Click  (Shading With Sharp and Smooth Edges) to set the display to **Shading With Sharp and Smooth Edges**.

2. Close the View Modes window by selecting  (close) in the right-hand corner.

3. Change the display to **Front** by clicking (* front) in the flyout menu, as shown in Figure 2–33.

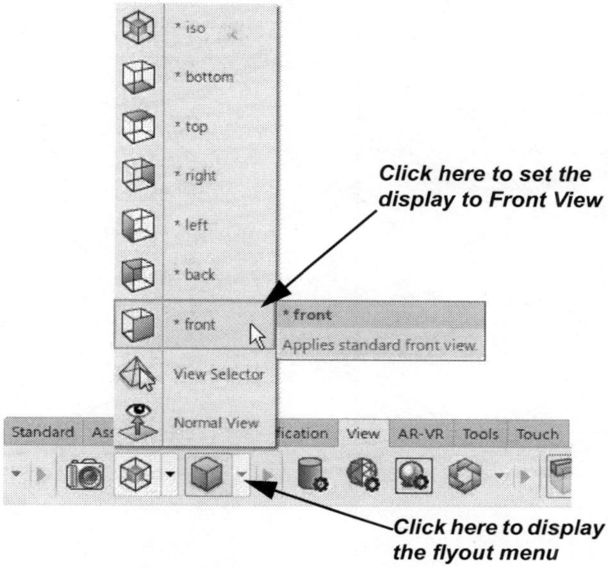

Figure 2–33

4. Repeat Step 2 for the (* back), (* right), (*left), (* top), and (* bottom) quick views.

5. Return to the (* iso) view.

Task 4 - Use the toolbar icons and menus to zoom, pan, and spin the model.

1. Click (Zoom In Out), select on the screen (keep the mouse button in) and drag upward to zoom into the model.

2. Click (Fit All In) to fit the model in the window.

3. Click (Zoom In Out), select on the screen (keep the mouse button in) and drag downward to zoom away from the model to zoom out.

4. Click the small arrow next to (Zoom In Out) and select (Zoom Area).

5. Use the left mouse button to draw a box around the area you want to zoom in to, as shown in Figure 2–34.

In some cases, the zoom area box does not display on the screen, although the functionality works correctly.

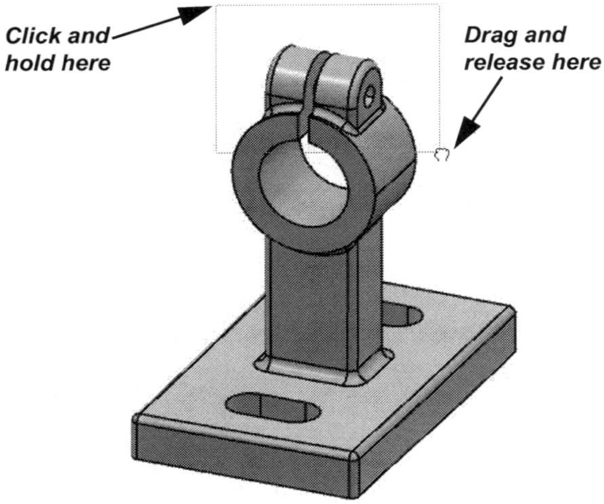

Figure 2–34

6. Click (Pan) to pan the model.

7. Click and drag the cursor around the screen, and the model follows your movements. Note that you must click the icon each time you want to pan.

You learn additional ways of panning and zooming later in the practice.

8. Click (Fit All In) to fit the model in the window.

9. Click (Rotate) to rotate the model. Hold the left mouse button and move the cursor to rotate the model. The **Rotate** tool behaves in the same manner as the **Pan** tool in that you must click the icon each time you want to rotate the model.

Task 5 - Use the robot to dynamically rotate and pan the model.

1. Click (* iso) to return to the Isometric view.

2. Click and drag the curved edge of the XY plane to rotate the model about the Z-axis only, as shown in Figure 2–35.

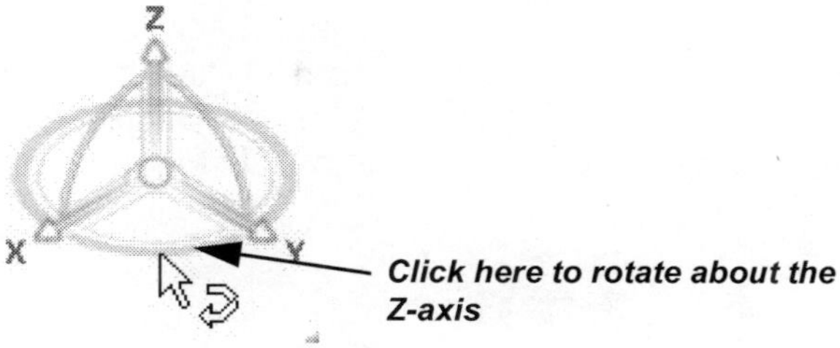

Figure 2–35

3. Repeat Step 4 for the other two curved edges.
4. Return to the Isometric quick view.
5. Click and drag the X-, Y-, and Z-axes of the compass to translate the model along that direction, as shown in Figure 2–36.

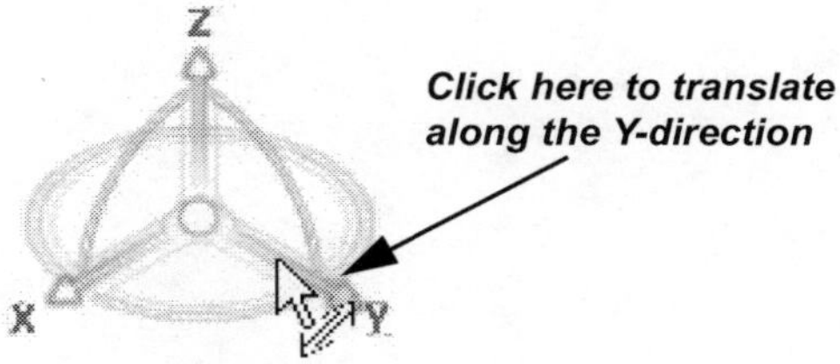

Figure 2–36

Task 6 - Use the mouse to dynamically rotate, pan, and zoom the model.

Click  (Fit All In) to center your model in the graphics window.

Try repeating these mouse shortcuts when possible.

1. Return to the Isometric quick view and fit the entire model in the window.
2. Hold the middle mouse button and move the cursor to pan the model.
3. Hold the middle mouse button and then left-click (or right-click) once. Move the cursor up and down to zoom in and out.
4. Press and hold the middle mouse button and then press and hold the left mouse button (or right mouse button) simultaneously, and move the cursor to rotate the model.

Task 7 - Use the specification tree to review the model geometry.

1. In the specification tree, select **Multipad.1** (you might need to expand PartBody by clicking the **+** symbol). The feature highlights in green in the tree and blue on the model, as shown in Figure 2–37.

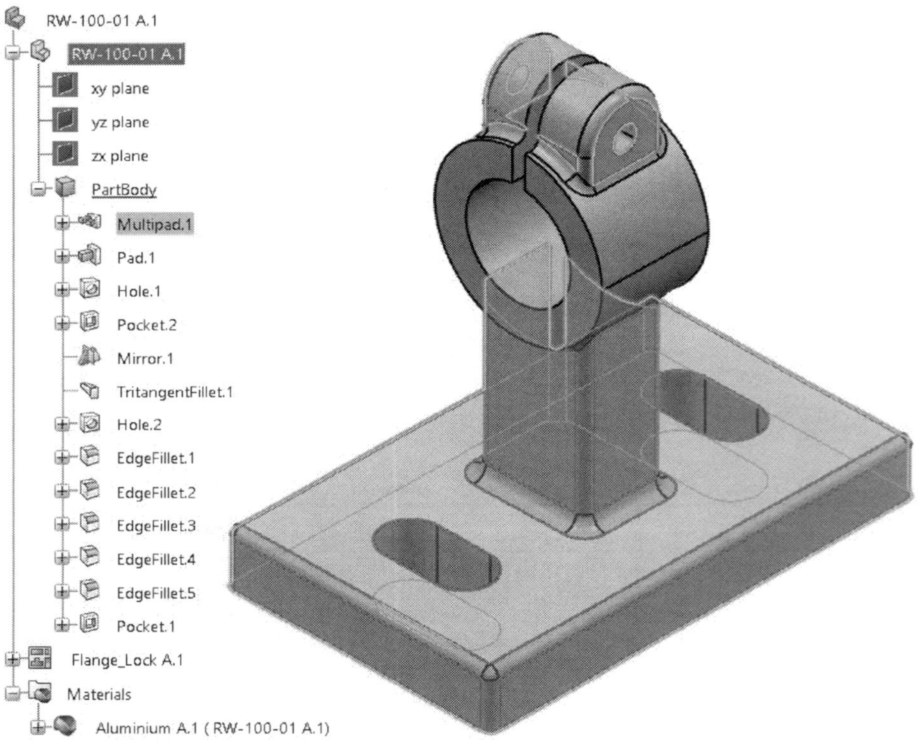

Figure 2–37

2. Repeat Step 1 for each feature under the PartBody branch (i.e., Pad.1, Hole.1, Pocket.2, Mirror.1, etc.). The selected feature is highlighted on the model and in the specification tree.

If you accidentally change the focus to the specification tree, you must understand how to activate the model.

3. Press <F3> several times to hide and show the specification tree.

4. Another method to hide and show (referred to as Pinning and Unpinning) the specification tree, is to select the arrow shown in Figure 2–38.

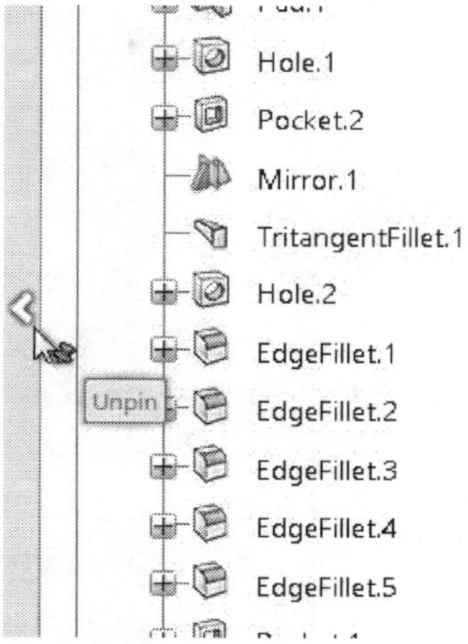

Figure 2–38

Task 8 - Change the size of several features.

1. Place the cursor over the large fillet at the base of the neck to highlight it, as shown in Figure 2–39. Double-click on it to display the radius dimension.

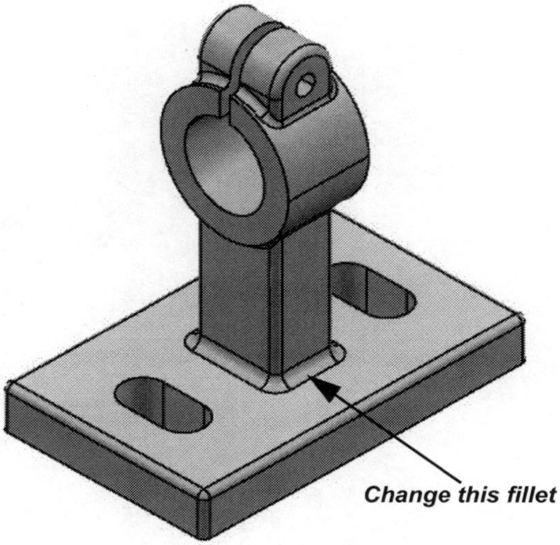

Figure 2–39

2. In the Edge Fillet Definition dialog box, change *Radius* to **6.00 mm (0.236 in),** as shown in Figure 2–40. Click **OK**.

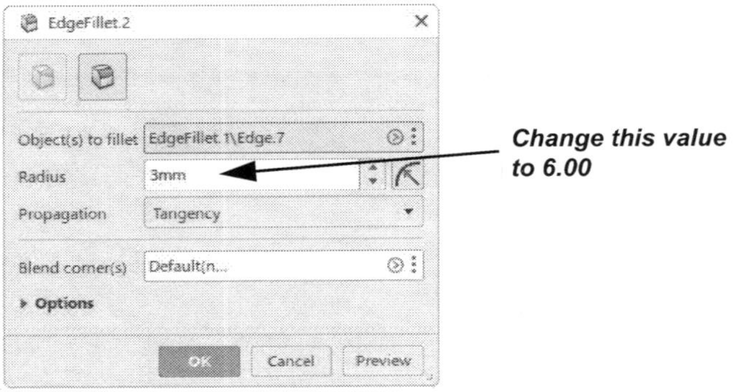

Figure 2–40

3. In the specification tree, double-click on **Hole.1**.

4. In the Hole Definition dialog box, change the *Diameter* to **13.00 mm (0.512 in),** and click **OK**. The updated model is shown in Figure 2–41.

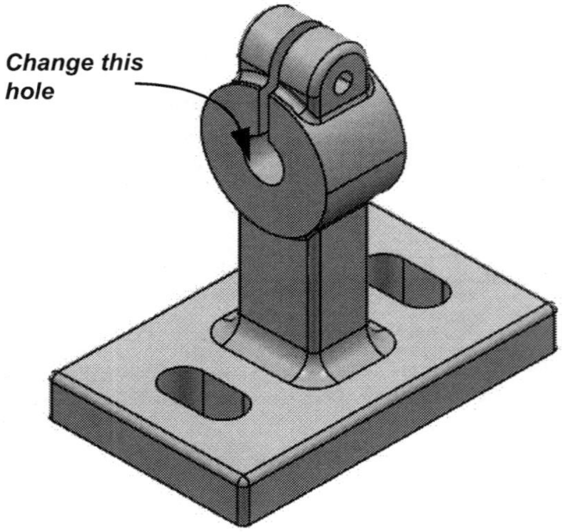

Figure 2–41

Task 9 - Delete features.

1. Select the edge fillet shown in Figure 2–42.

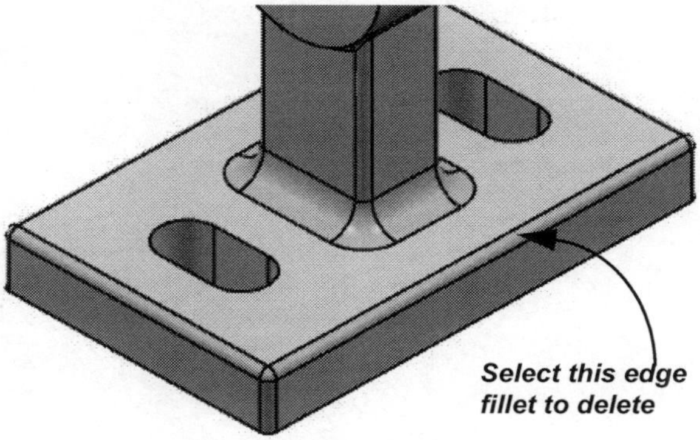

Figure 2–42

2. Right-click and select **Delete**.

3. Delete **Sketch.6** from the specification tree, as shown in Figure 2–43.

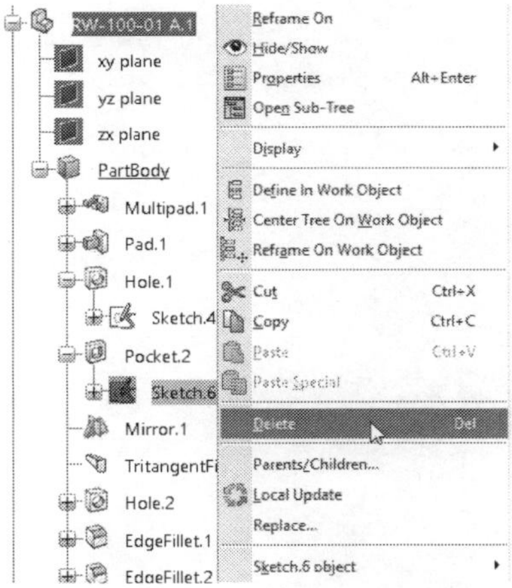

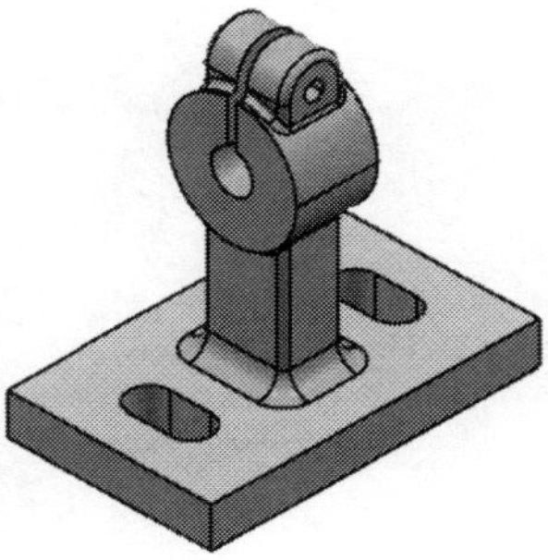

Figure 2–43

4. The Delete dialog box opens, as shown in Figure 2–44. It prompts you that the sketch is a parent feature and when deleted, its children are also deleted.

Figure 2–44

5. Click **OK**. The model displays as shown in Figure 2–45.

6. Click  (Undo) to undo the deleting operations. The model displays as shown in Figure 2–46.

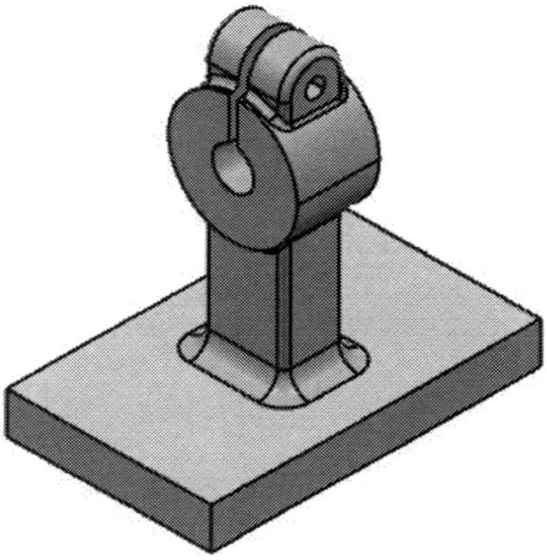

Figure 2–45

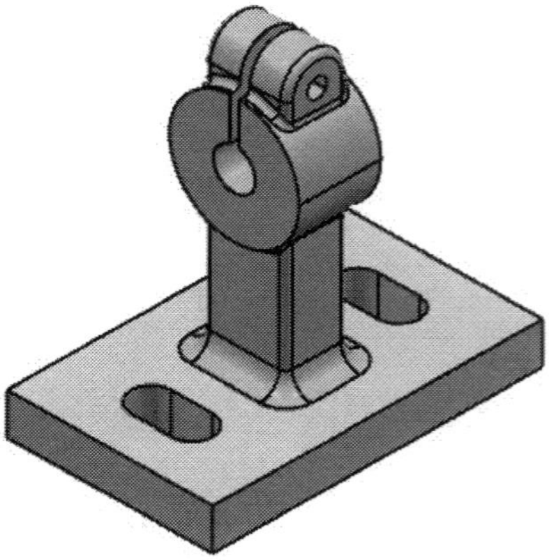

Figure 2–46

Task 10 - Cause a feature to fail.

1. In the specification tree, double-click on **EdgeFillet.2**.
2. Modify the radius of the fillet to **30.00 mm (1.181 in)** and click **OK**.

   The radius of the fillet is too large and causes the **EdgeFillet.2** feature to fail. An Update Diagnosis dialog box opens, as shown in Figure 2–47.

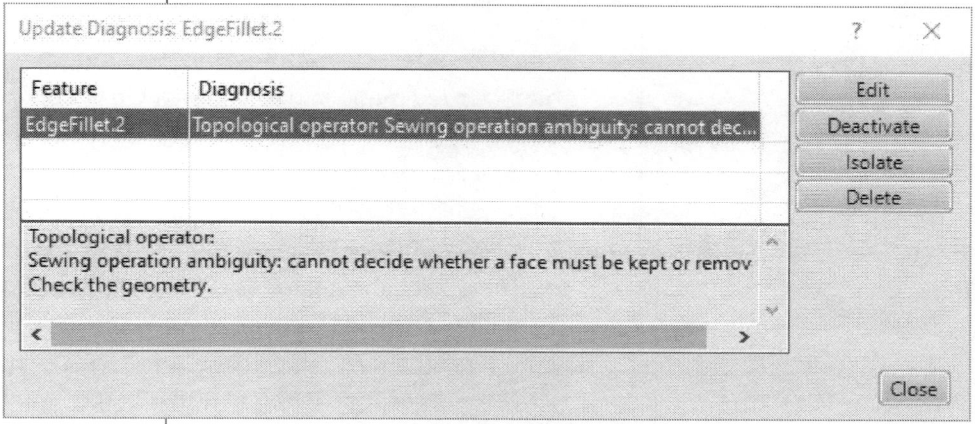

Figure 2–47

3. Select **Close**, and undo the changes made to the Fillet feature and resolve the failure by clicking (Undo).
4. Click (Share)>**Save** to save the model.
5. Close the part tab.

Chapter Review Questions

1. "Solid modeling evolves as features are created one by one until geometry is complete," best describes which attribute?
   a. Parametric
   b. Associative
   c. Feature Based
   d. None of the above
2. Parametric can best be described as:
   a. Changes made in one mode of CATIA update throughout the other modes of CATIA.
   b. Solid models evolve by creating features, one by one, until the geometry is complete.
   c. Three-dimensional solid models.
   d. Dimensional constraints define a feature‘s shape, are considered *parameters*, and are accessible at any time.
3. After editing the dimensions of a part model, you must open all drawings referencing that part and make the same dimensional changes.
   a. True
   b. False
4. The specification tree is useful because:
   a. It provides quick access to parameters, functions, materials, and commonly used measurements.
   b. It is available when working with parts, assemblies, and drawings.
   c. It displays the features of the part in the order in which they were created.
   d. All of the above.
5. CATIA part files have a ______ filename extension.
   a. .PRT
   b. .Part
   c. .CATPart
   d. .CATProduct

6.  enables you to view the Isometric view of the model.
   a. True
   b. False

7. To pan the model using the mouse, you press and hold which mouse button?
   a. Left
   b. Right
   c. Middle

8. To zoom the model using the mouse, press and hold the middle mouse button and click either the left or right mouse button.
   a. True
   b. False

9. Which tool can be used to zoom in or out on the shown geometry so that it fills all the available space?
   a. 
   b. 
   c. 
   d. 

10. You can open multiple windows in a CATIA session.
    a. True
    b. False

Answers: 1c, 2d, 3b, 4d, 5c, 6b, 7c, 8a, 9a, 10a

Customizing 3DEXPERIENCE

In this chapter, you learn how to effectively customize the Preferences dialog box, Action Bar, and apps to suit your preferences and requirements, and to help you work more efficiently.

Learning Objectives in This Chapter

- Understand where settings used to customize 3DEXPERIENCE are stored.
- Review the settings in the Preferences dialog box.
- Review the recommended settings for completing this training.
- Learn how to manipulate the Action Bar to customize the interface and streamline your working environment.
- Customize 3DEXPERIENCE to display your preferred apps.

3.1 Preferences Dialog Box

When first started, the 3DEXPERIENCE platform uses a default set of configurations. These configurations include interface color scheme, model units, sketcher grid, spaceball configuration, and so on.

The Preferences dialog box opens by clicking your user icon (Me) in the top right of the 3DEXPERIENCE window and clicking **Preferences**. The Preferences dialog box is used to customize the 3DEXPERIENCE platform options, shown in Figure 3–1.

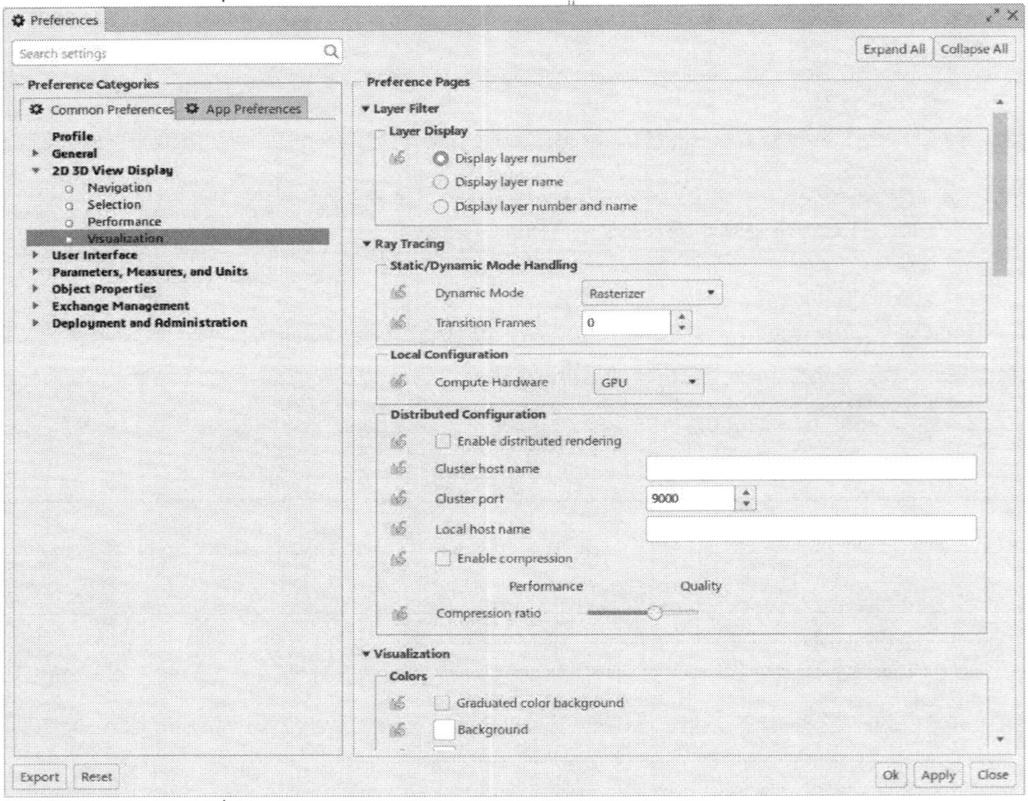

Figure 3–1

When setting the required options, the changes made are written to the files in the *CATSettings* folder.

Recommended Options

You should become familiar with the option menus to maximize efficiency within the CATIA environment. These options impact the results obtained when completing the practices available in this guide. The option menus are described as follows:

Path	Option	Value
Common Preferences> General> Cache and Performance> PCS	**Undo**	The **Stack Size** option controls the number of undo operations that can be performed. Increasing this value also decreases CATIA performance, as the software must store more operation information. The maximum value is 99. It is recommended that you set this option to 15-20.
Common Preferences> User Interface> Tree> Tree Manipulation	**Zoom on Tree**	Disabling the **Tree zoom after clicking on any branch** option helps in working in the CATIA interface. Users often become confused when selecting a branch in the tree, which takes their focus off the model. With this option disabled, the tree can be zoomed by selecting the axis in the lower right corner of the window.
Common Preferences> 2D 3D View Display> Performance> Performance	**3D Accuracy**	These options control the quality of the model display in CATIA. A higher accuracy might result in an increase in system resource requirements. Proportional accuracy varies display quality relative to model size, while fixed accuracy does not. It is recommended that you set a *Proportional value* of **0.04**.
Common Preferences> Parameters, Measures, and Units> Parameters> Parameters & Relations	**Parameter Tree View**	These options control the display of parameter values and formulas in the tree. It is recommended that you select **Display value**.
Common Preferences> Parameters, Measures, and Units> Measures> Measure Tools	**Associativity**	These options control the automatic update of measurements in a part and product model. It is recommended that you enable **Automatic update in product**.

Common Preferences> Object Properties> 3D Shape> Display> Display	**Display In specification tree**	These options control the display of model information in the tree. They include: • External References • Constraints • Parameters • Relations • Bodies under operations • Expand sketch-based feature nodes at creation It is recommended that you enable all of the options in this area.
Common Preferences> Object Properties> 3D Shape> Infrastructure>3D Shape	**Hybrid Design**	Unless your company has standardized on the use of Hybrid Design, clear the **Enable hybrid design inside part bodies and bodies** option. Hybrid Design changes the way wireframe and surface elements are stored in a part model and should not be enabled unless instructed by your CAD Administrator.
App Preferences> 3D Modeling> 3D Modeling Core> Sketcher> Sketcher	**Sketch Plane**	**Minimize viewpoint transformation** orients the sketch along the closest X, Y, and Z directions. It is recommended that you disable this option so that the sketch orients correctly during creation.
App Preferences> 3D Modeling> 3D Modeling Core> Sketcher> Sketcher	**Update**	**Generate update errors when the sketch is under-constrained** enables the software to open an Update Diagnosis dialog box when exiting Sketcher with an under-constrained profile. It is recommended that you enable this option.
App Preferences> Social and Collaborative> Global Design Management/ Collaborative Lifecycle> Identification	**Creation Preferences**	**Identification String** adds a declared prefix to the beginning of new and imported objects. It is recommended that you set the **Identification String** to your initials, followed by an underscore (for example, SEH_) so any new or imported objects are named with your initials as a prefix.

3.2 Action Bar Customization

Once an app is launched, or a model or drawing is opened, the Action Bar displays at the bottom of the 3DEXPERIENCE platform window, as shown in Figure 3–2. The Action Bar is organized into sections, and each section has multiple commands.

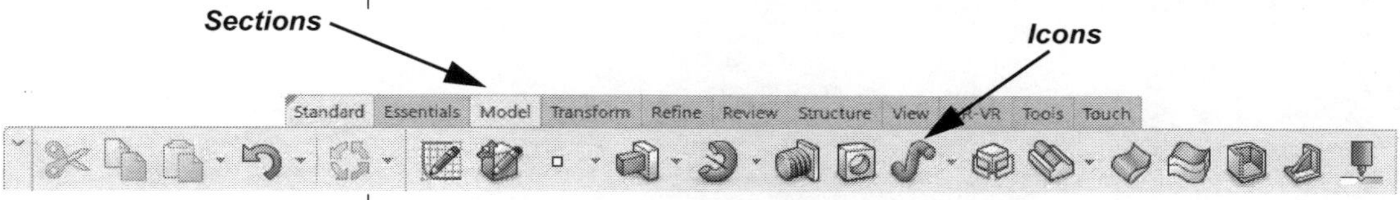

Figure 3–2

The default setting for the Action Bar is to display all the section names in dark gray, but with the name of the selected section displayed with a white background. Additionally, the icons display with their image, but no names. This display mode takes up the minimum amount of screen space, and if you hover your cursor over any of the sections or icons, a tool-tip displays with the applicable name. However, until you are familiar with the modeling environment, you may want more information displayed.

You can right-click on the Action Bar and select **Display Icons and Text**. The Action Bar updates as shown in Figure 3–3. Note that the Action Bar now takes up considerably more space to account for the command names.

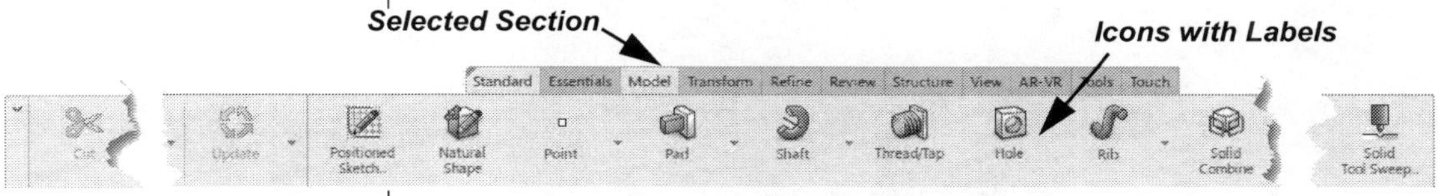

Figure 3–3

Add Commands

This list of options will vary depending on the location on the Action Bar where you right-clicked.

You can rearrange icons in the Action Bar by right-clicking on the Action Bar and selecting **Customize Mode**. When you do, if you right click again anywhere on the Action Bar, you will see an expanded list of options, as shown in Figure 3–4.

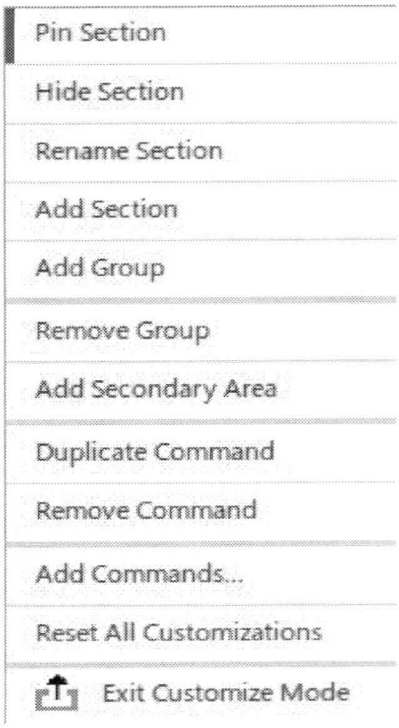

Figure 3–4

The list of options can include:

Command	Result
Pin Section	Pins a section so it continues to display that section's commands even when it is not the active section
Hide Section	Hides the currently active section.
Rename Section	Renames the currently active section.
Add Section	Adds a new empty section to the Action Bar that can be renamed and completely customized.
Add Group	Adds a group to the active section where new commands can be placed.
Remove Group	Removes the group that was right-clicked on.

Add Secondary Area	Adds a "hidden group" to the right of the group that was right-clicked on. Commands can be moved or added to this secondary area. The blue arrow indicating this secondary area can be clicked on to expand or collapse these commands from the display. 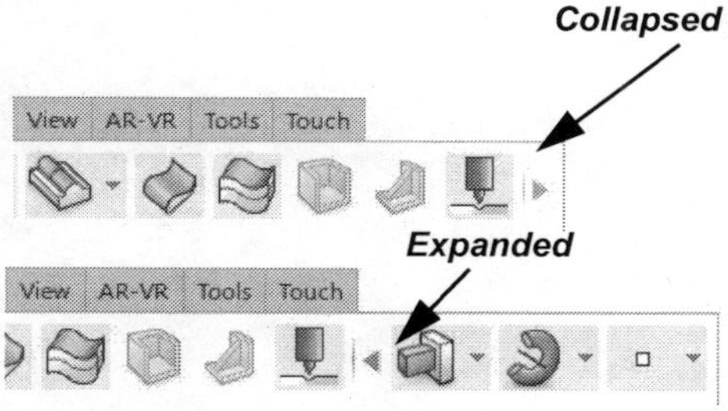
Duplicate Command	Creates a second command that can be moved to new location without moving original.
Add Commands	Opens Customize window that lists all commands that can be added to the Action Bar.
Reset All Customizations	Returns Action Bar back to its default settings.

You can note a change in the way the Action Bar looks when you go into "Customize Mode" as well. When customizing, the Action Bar background will turn white, and the commands will be outlined with a square around them, as shown in Figure 3–5.

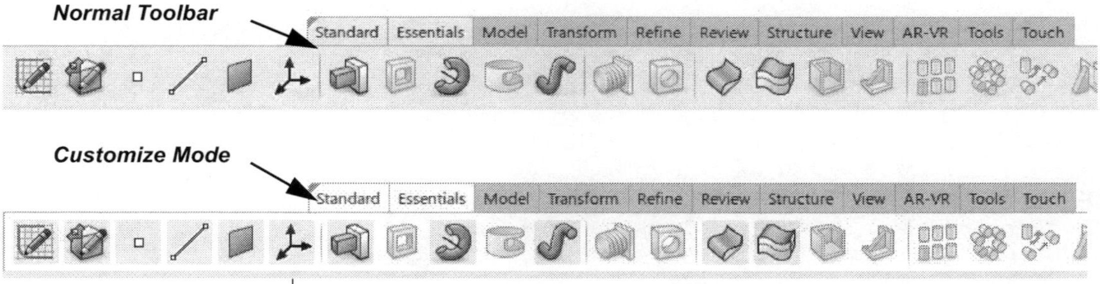

Figure 3–5

To rearrange icons, simply drag them to the new location. When you release the mouse button, the icon will be moved to the location. In the example shown in Figure 3–6, the icon is moved from one location to another.

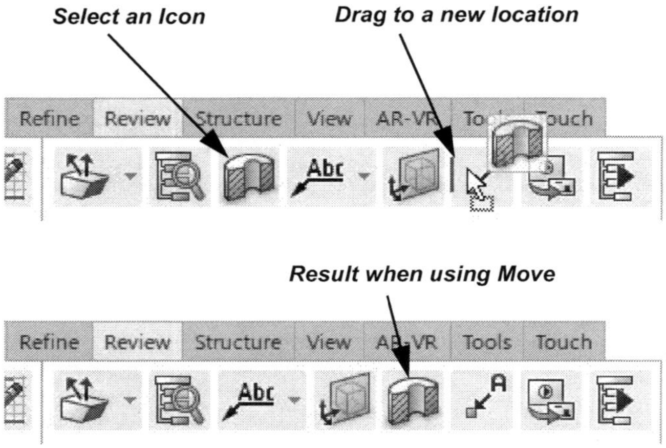

Figure 3–6

Expanding Flyouts

Some Action Bar icons contain flyouts, which display additional icons when selected. For example, the **Pad** feature icon in the *Model* section of the Action Bar contains a flyout, as shown in Figure 3–7.

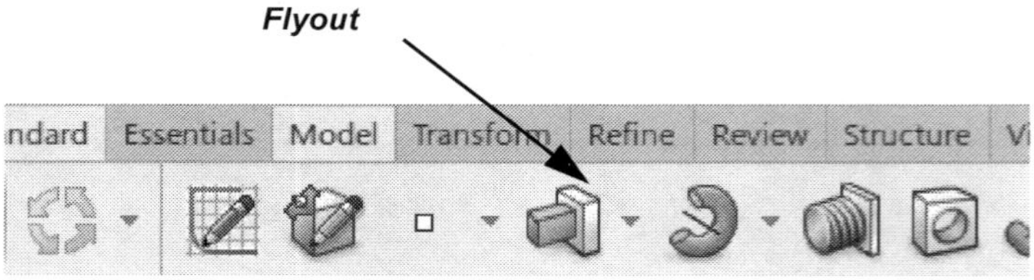

Figure 3–7

Flyout options are grouped by type.

Clicking the flyout (the down arrow) displays the additional icons, as shown in Figure 3–8.

Flyout options are grouped by type.

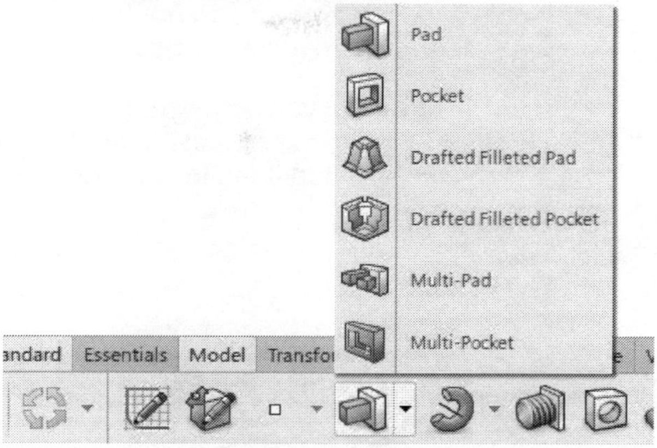

Figure 3–8

When rearranging icons in the Action Bar, you have to move or duplicate all options from the flyout. You cannot select individual options.

Another method for customizing the Action Bar is to select in the Top Bar, right-click, select **Display**>**Customize**, and select the *Sections* tab in the Customize dialog box, as shown in Figure 3–9.

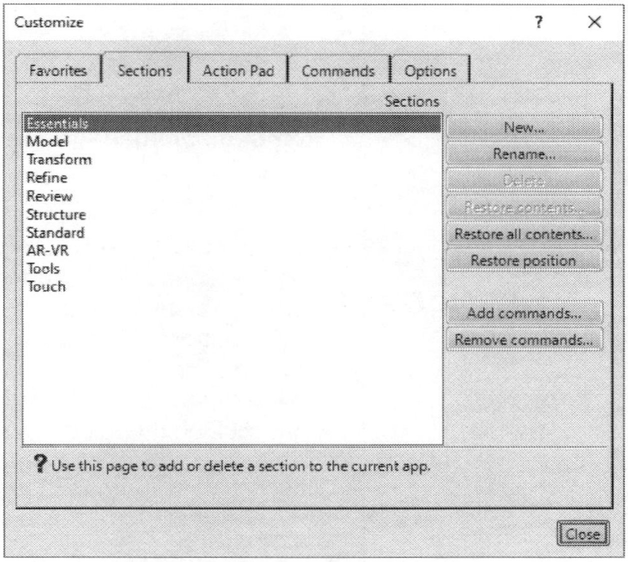

Figure 3–9

Here, you can create **New** Action Bar sections, **Rename** existing sections, or **Delete** custom sections you have added.

If you have added or removed commands, you can use the **Restore all contents** option to reset them. **Restore position** will reset the position of any sections you may have moved.

If you click **Add commands**, the command list dialog box opens, as shown in Figure 3–10. Here, you can select commands and add them to sections.

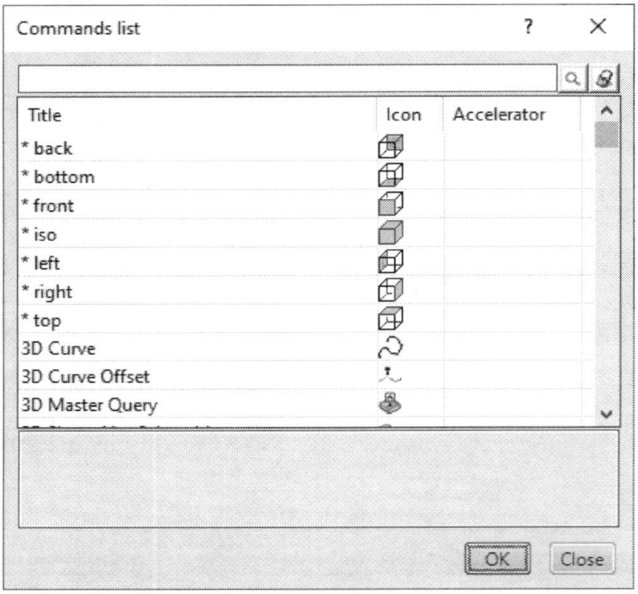

Figure 3–10

Remove commands allows you to remove commands from sections.

Pin/Unpin Sections

By default, when you navigate between sections of the Action Bar, the icons found in each section are displayed and the *Standard* section is pinned. You can set one or more sections to be permanently displayed by right-clicking the Action Bar and selecting **Pin Section**. The selected section will now be pinned and permanently displayed. To turn off a pinned section, right-click on the section's name and select **Pin Section** again.

Pinning a section has the following results:

- The Pinned section title highlights in white with a blue triangle corner.
- If you select another section, the icons in the pinned section continue to display.

- The section displays in the sequence in which it originally exists. For example, if you pin the *Review* section, then select the *Model* section, the *Review* icons display as if added to the end of the *Model* section, as shown in Figure 3–11. Conversely, if you select the *Touch* section, the *Review* icons display as if added to the beginning of the Touch section.

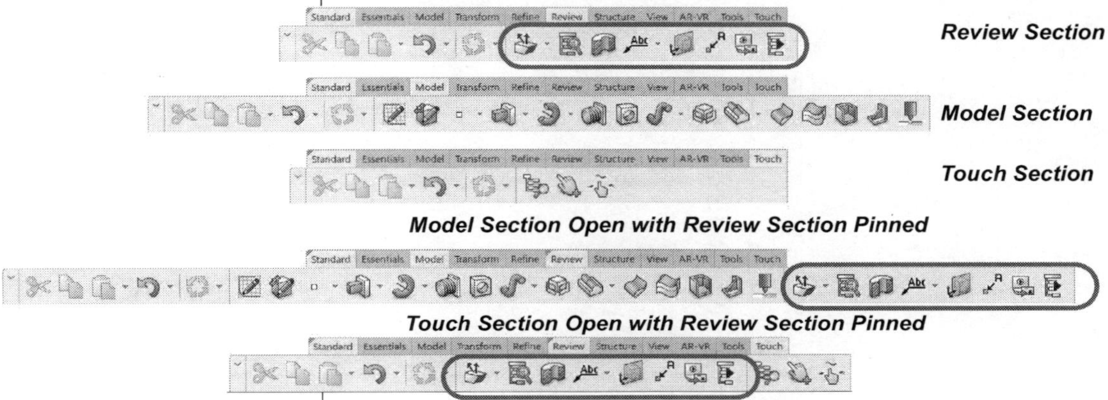

Figure 3–11

Action Pad

The Action Pad enables you to have quick access to your favorite commands in a completely customizable window. The Action Pad, shown in Figure 3–12, is opened by right-clicking in the modeling area and selecting **Display>Action Pad**.

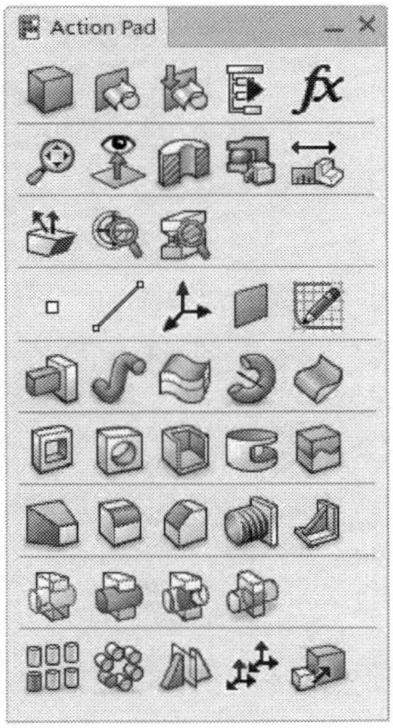

Figure 3–12

To customize the Action Pad, in the Top Bar, right-click, select **Display**>**Customize**, and select the *Action Pad* tab in the Customize dialog box, as shown in Figure 3–13.

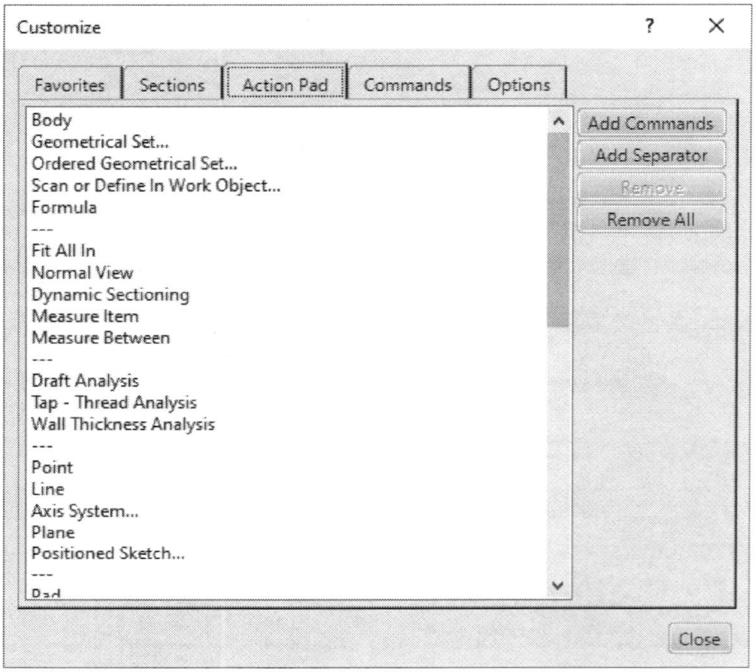

Figure 3–13

Here you can add or remove commands, and can create separators between groups of commands. You can also rearrange commands by dragging and dropping them in different locations in the list.

App Options

The App Options panel provides quick access for managing objects using selection and filter variants. To activate the App Options panel, right-click anywhere on the Top Bar and select **Display>App Options**. You can also find  (App Options) under the *Tools* section in a variety of applications. Once activated, the Actions Panel will display as shown in Figure 3–14.

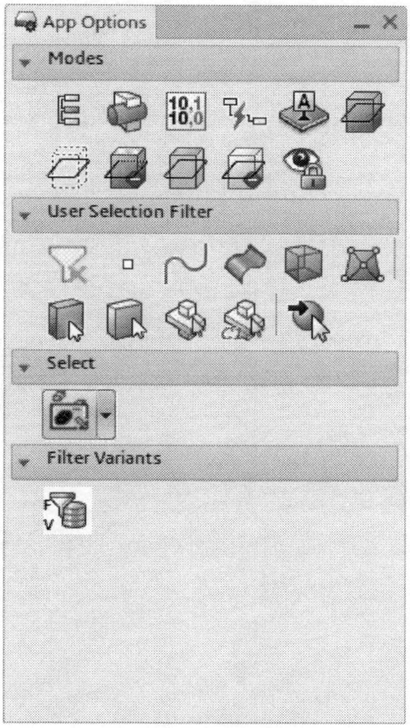

Figure 3–14

3.3 Favorite Apps

By default, when the 3DEXPERIENCE platform is started, you are in the basic 3DEXPERIENCE window, with no apps visible. To access the modeling apps, click the outer ring in the Compass, as shown in Figure 3–15.

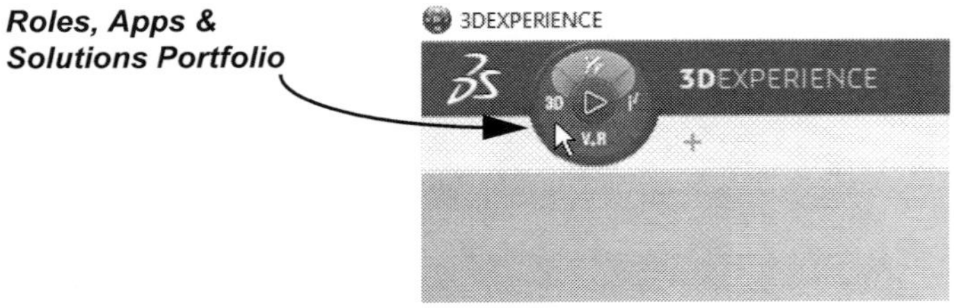

Figure 3–15

The apps available under *My favorite apps* display, as shown in Figure 3–16. The *My favorite apps* section can be customized.

The available apps on your system may differ from those shown, depending on how your system was set up and what licenses you have.

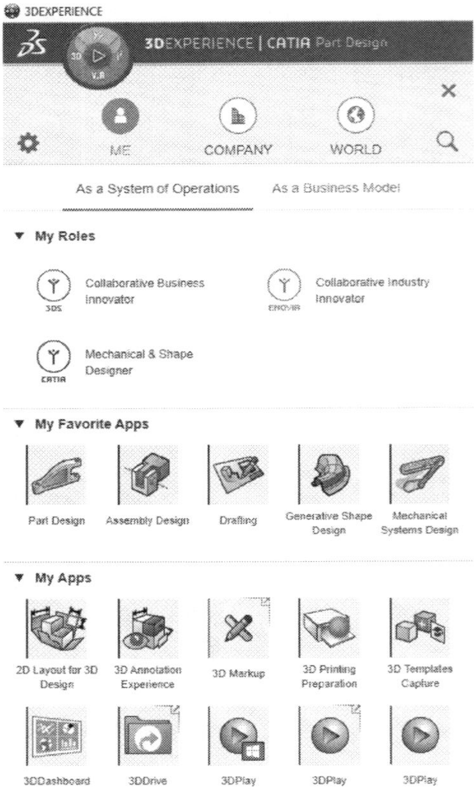

Figure 3–16

Method 1

One way to customize your favorite apps is to move your cursor to the Top Bar, right-click and select **Display>Customize**.

In the Customize dialog box, select the *Favorites* tab, as shown in Figure 3–17.

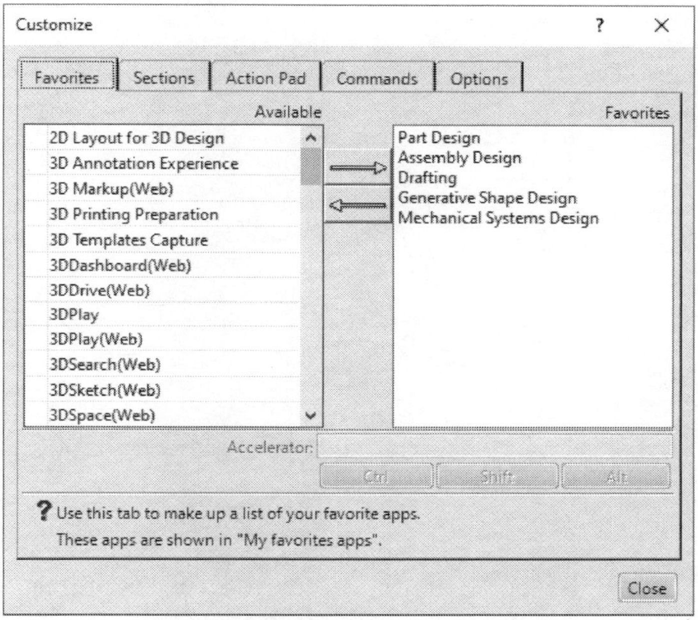

Figure 3–17

You can add or remove apps here by moving them between the *Available* and *Favorites* lists. To add an app to the favorites list, select it in the Available list and click . The app moves to the bottom of the favorites list. Conversely, select an app in the *Favorites* column and click 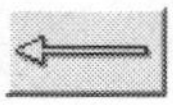 to move it to the Available list.

You can also rearrange the order in which your favorite apps are displayed by dragging and dropping them in the Favorites list.

Method 2

A second method is to click the outer ring of the Compass, then, drag apps from the *My Apps* section and drop them into the *My Favorite Apps area*, as shown in Figure 3–18.

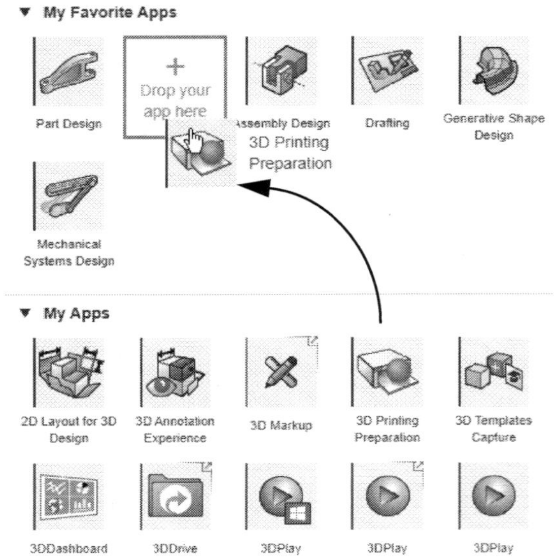

Figure 3–18

To remove an app from your favorites, drag and drop it to the location shown in Figure 3–19.

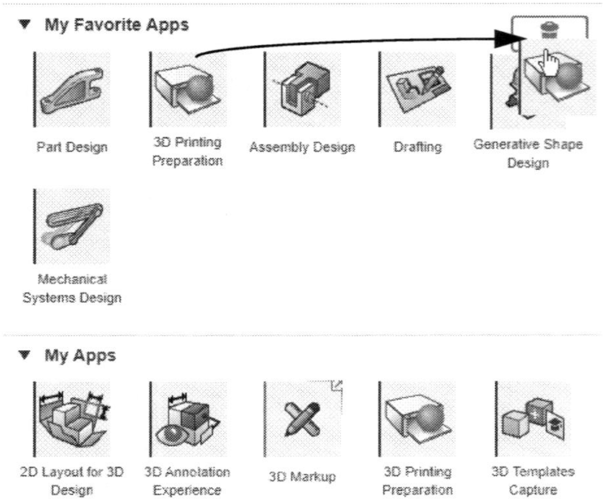

Figure 3–19

Practice 3a Customization

Practice Objectives

- Set up favorite workbenches.
- Customize the on-screen toolbar display.
- Customize the CATIA configuration.

Task 1 - Import a model.

1. In the Top Bar, click (Add)>**Import**.
2. In the Import dialog box, click (Open).
3. Browse and select **Flange_Lock_2.3DXML** and click **Open**.
4. Ensure that the settings in the Import dialog box match those shown in Figure 3–20.

Note how the Duplication string field displays your initials based on the preference setting made in the first practice. The images provided in this guide do not show the duplication string.

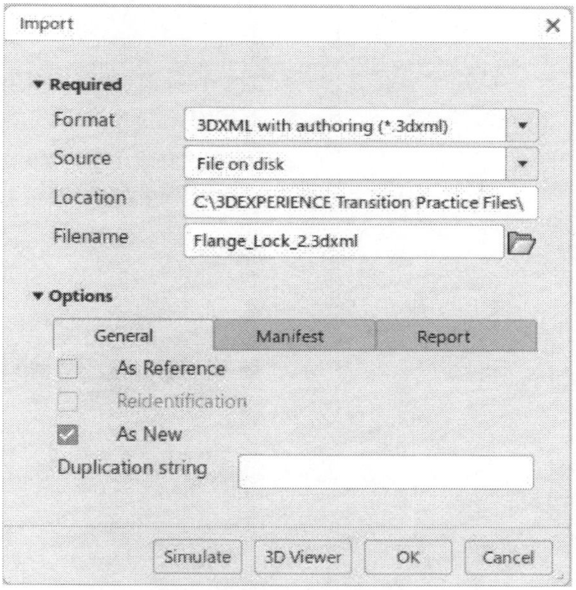

Figure 3–20

5. Click **OK**.
6. Click **OK** in the Operation report dialog box.

7. The model opens in Explore mode as shown in Figure 3–21.

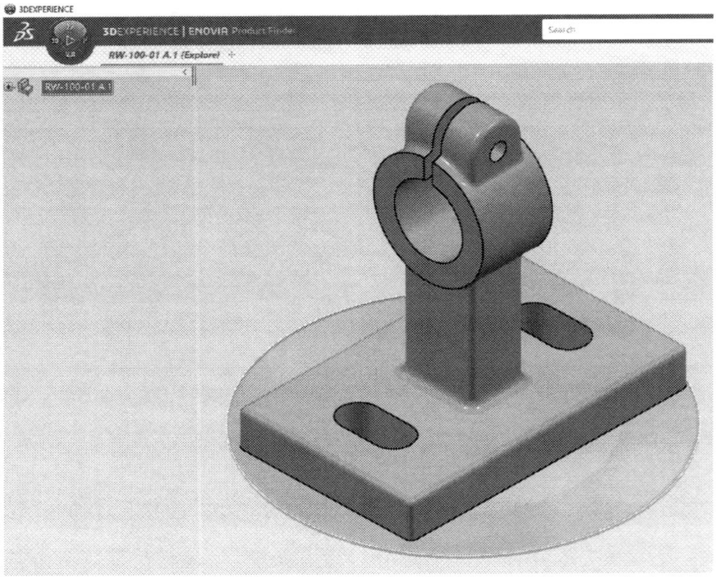

Figure 3–21

8. Right-click on **RW-100-01** in the specification tree and select **Open**.

9. The part opens for editing in a new tab. If the model opens in a widget panel instead of its own tab, in the upper-right of the widget window, click (Maximize), as shown in Figure 3–22.

Figure 3–22

10. Close the *RW-100-01 (Explore)* tab.

Task 2 - Ensure you are prompted for file attributes when creating new files.

1. In the Top Bar, click (Add), and then click **New Content**.
2. In the New Content dialog box, click (Tools).
3. Enable **Set attributes at creation for all types**.
4. Close the New Content dialog box.

Task 3 - View favorite apps.

1. In the Compass, click **Roles, Apps and Solution Portfolio**, as shown in Figure 3–23.

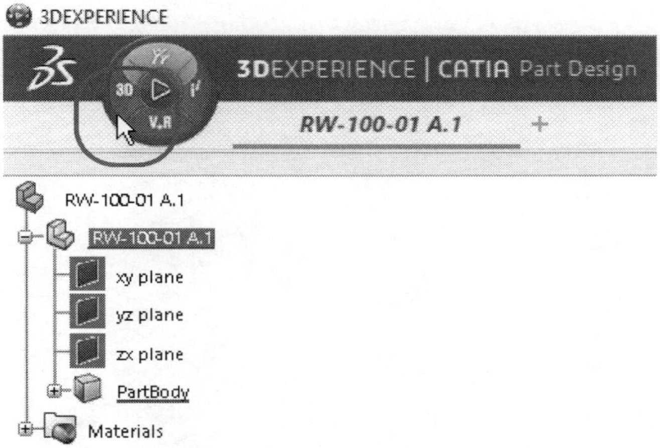

Figure 3–23

The available apps on your system may differ from those shown, depending on how your system was setup and what licenses you have.

2. Note the apps available under *My Favorite Apps*, as shown in Figure 3–24. My Favorite Apps maybe empty if customization has not been done up to this point.

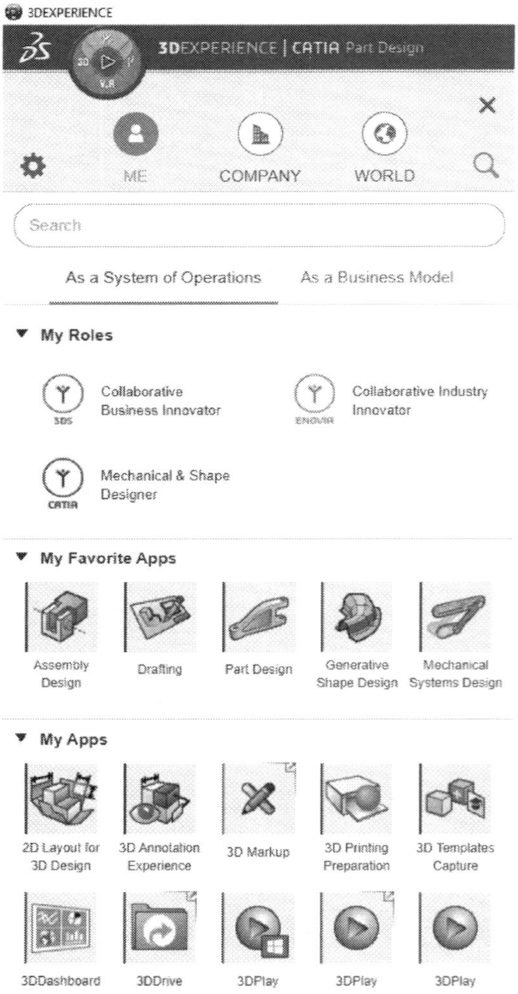

Figure 3–24

3. To customize your favorite apps, move your cursor to the Top Bar, right-click and select **Display>Customize**.

4. In the Customize dialog box, select the *Favorites* tab, as shown in Figure 3–25.

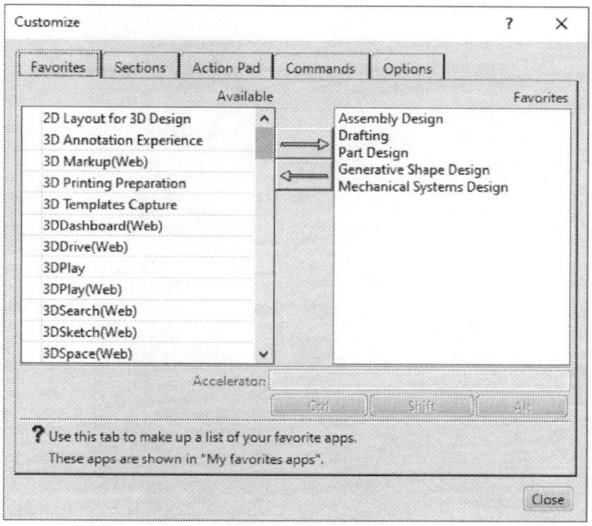

Figure 3–25

5. In the *Favorites* column on the right, remove  (Part Design) by selecting **Part Design** and clicking .

6. Part Design moves to the *Available* column, as shown in Figure 3–26.

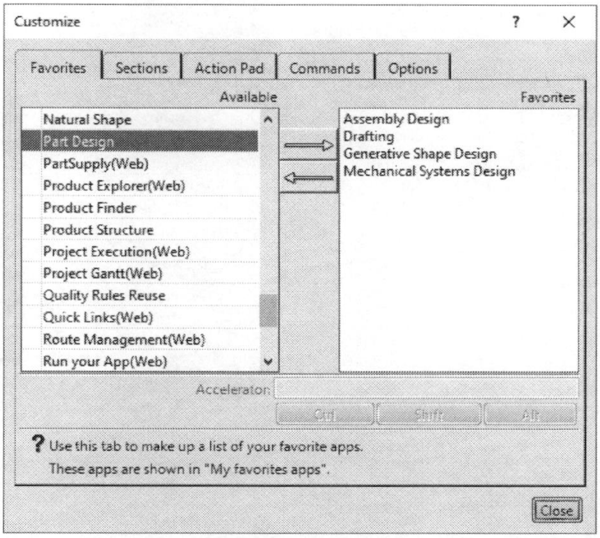

Figure 3–26

7. Close the Customize dialog box.

8. In the *3D Apps* area, expand *My Favorite Apps* if necessary, and note that  (Part Design) has been removed, as shown in Figure 3–27.

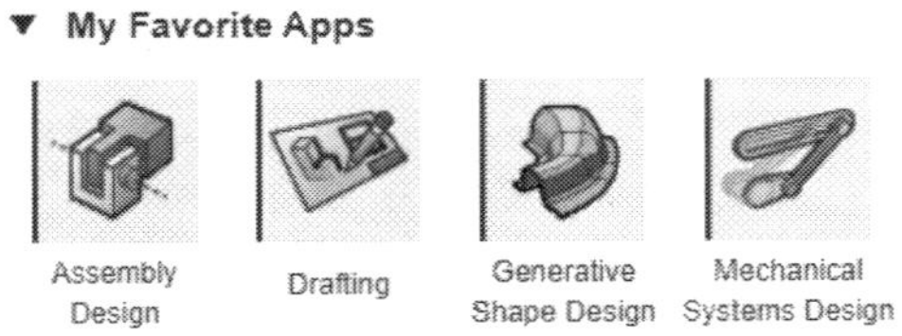

Figure 3–27

9. Add  (Part Design) back into the *My Favorite Apps* section by repeating steps 3-7 but this time, select **Part Design** in the Available list and click .

10. In the *Favorites* area of the Customize dialog box, click and drag **Part Design** to the top of the list (as shown in Figure 3–28), so it appears first in your list of apps.

You can rearrange the order in which any apps appear by dragging them to the correct location.

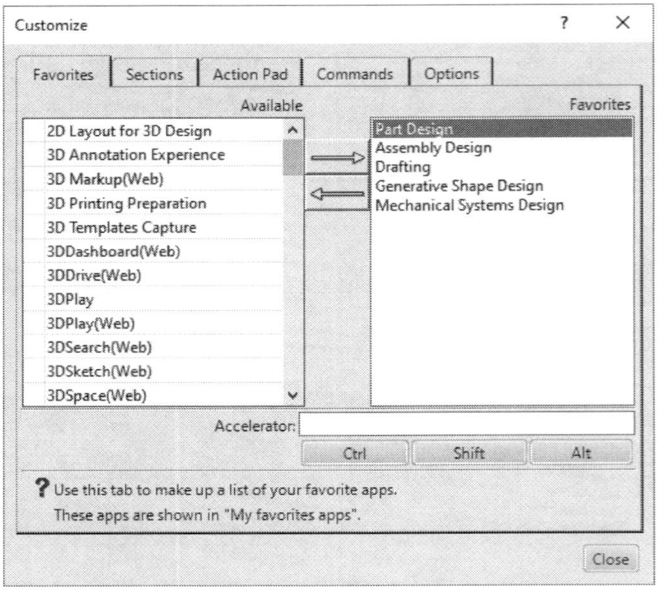

Figure 3–28

11. Close the Customize dialog box.

12. In the *3D Apps* area, expand *My Favorite Apps* (if necessary) and click (Drafting) to activate the Drafting app.

13. Click **OK** to accept the default Drawing Title. All of the Action Bar sections and icons update to drafting functions.

14. Select the *RW-100-01* tab to switch windows back to the **Flange_Lock** part. Note that all of the toolbar icons update to part design functions.

15. Click (Close) in the *Drawing Title* tab.

16. Double-click the **RW-100-01** product at the top of the specification tree.

17. Note that the Drawing is still referenced in the specification tree. This is because it is still in session. Right-click the drawing and select **Unload**, as shown in Figure 3–29.

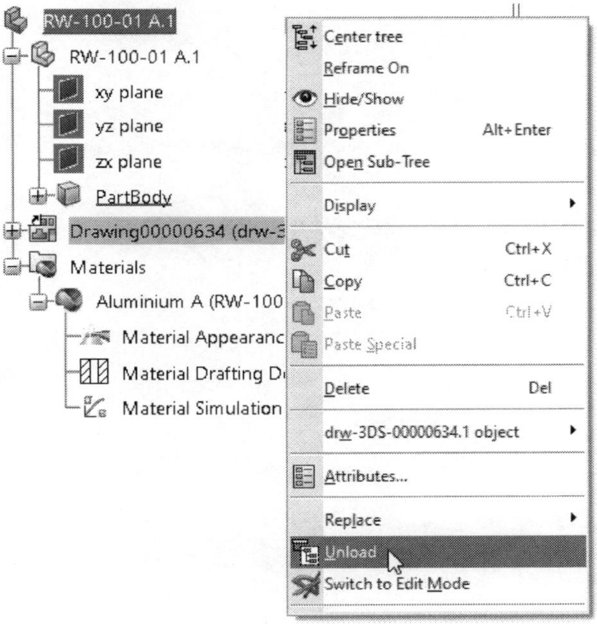

Figure 3–29

18. Click **OK** when prompted.

Task 4 - Change the Action Bar display.

1. Note that, by default, the Action Bar displays with icons only for the selected section, and with no labels for those icons. The *Assembly* section is shown in Figure 3–30.

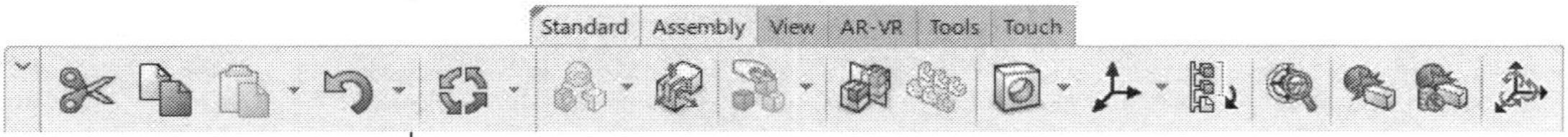

Figure 3–30

2. Right-click on the Action Bar and select **Display Icons and Text**, as shown in Figure 3–31.

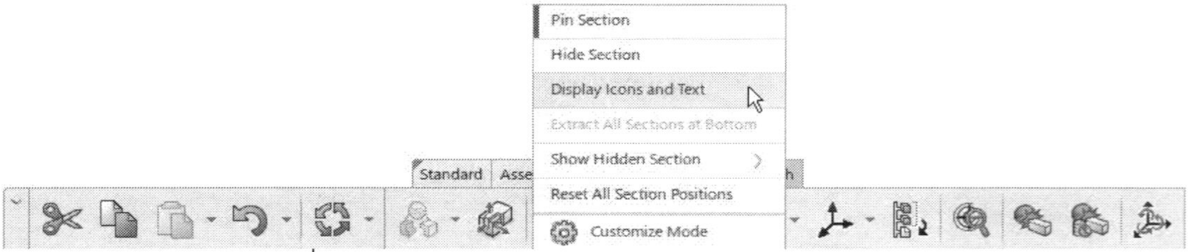

Figure 3–31

The names for the icons display as shown in Figure 3–32.

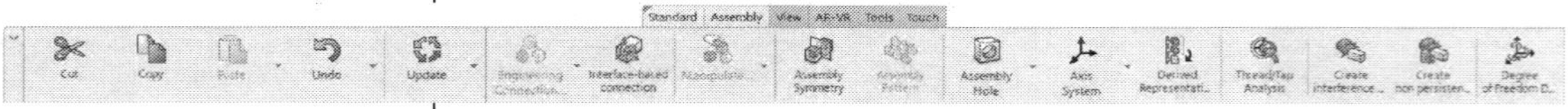

Figure 3–32

3. Right-click on the Action Bar and select **Display Icons Only** again to turn off the labels.

Task 5 - Customize Action Bar icon positioning.

1. Double-click the **RW-100-01** at the part level (2nd level) of the specification tree to switch back to the Part Design app. The tree will display as shown in Figure 3–33.

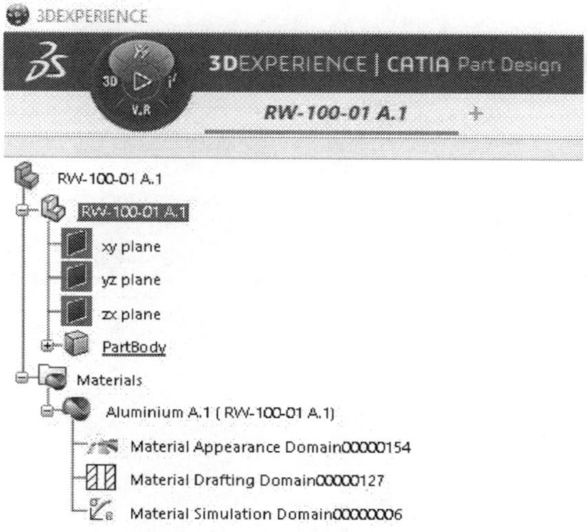

Figure 3–33

2. In the Action Bar, select the *Essentials* section if not already selected.

3. Right-click on the Action Bar and select **Customize Mode**.

4. Right-click on  (Draft) and select **Add Secondary Area** as shown in Figure 3–34.

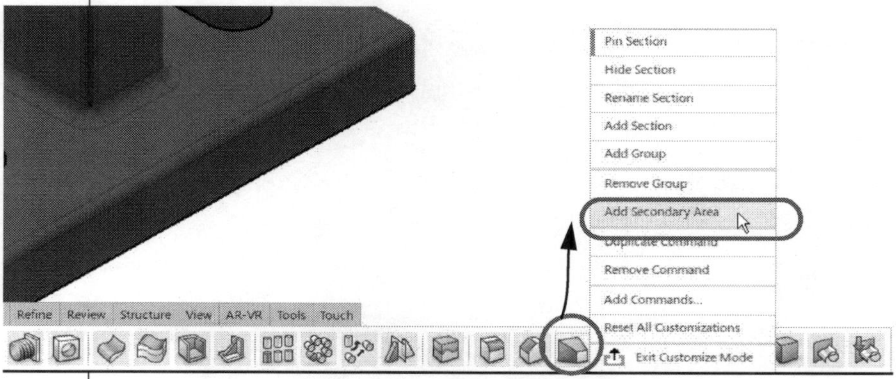

Figure 3–34

This will create a new expandable/collapsible area to the right of **Draft** as shown in Figure 3–35.

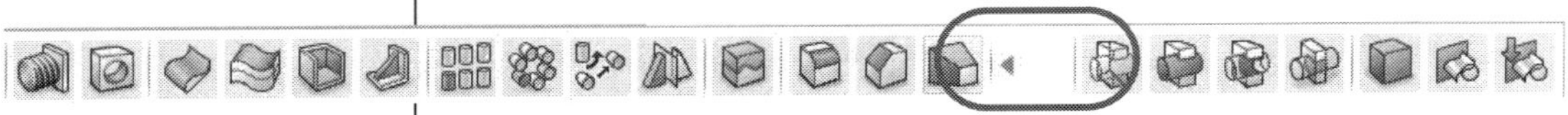

Figure 3–35

5. Select the  (Edge Fillet) and drag it to the secondary area you just created. When a blue vertical bar appears (as shown in Figure 3–36) indicating the location where the icon will be placed, you can let go of the cursor.

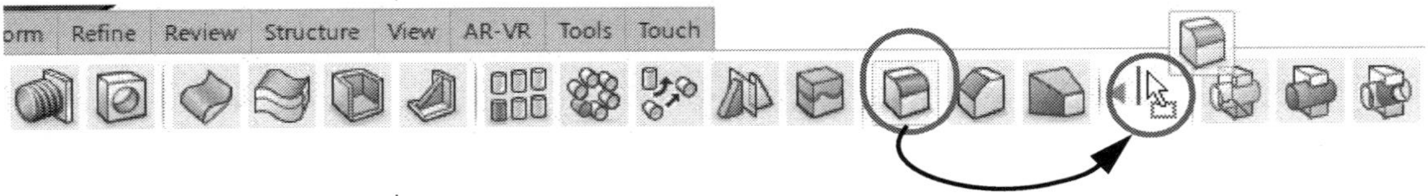

Figure 3–36

The Edge Fillet is relocated to the secondary area as shown in Figure 3–37.

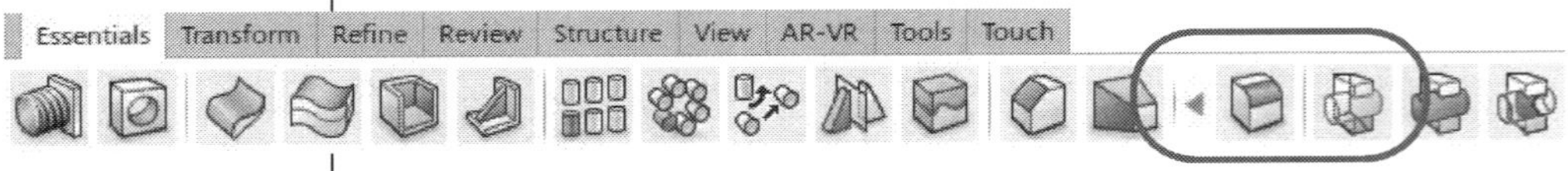

Figure 3–37

6. Repeat the previous step to move the  (Split) icon. The Action Bar updates as shown in Figure 3–38.

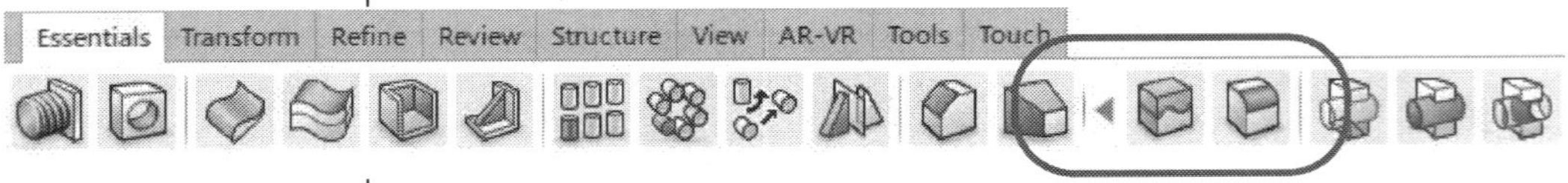

Figure 3–38

7. Right-click on the Action Bar and select  (Exit Customize Mode).

8. Note that the two icons can now be hidden in the Action Bar.

   Click (collapse) to collapse the group, as shown in Figure 3–39.

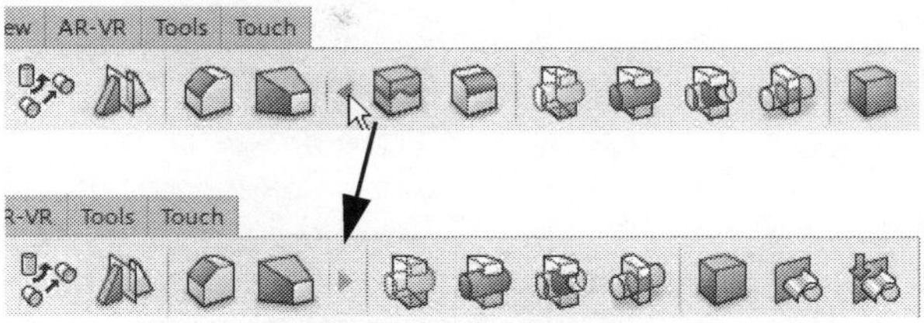

Figure 3–39

9. Click (Expand) to show the two icons again.

Task 6 - Set the Model section of the Action Bar to always be visible.

1. In the Action Bar, select the *Model* section.
2. Right-click on the Action Bar and select **PinSection**, as shown in Figure 3–40.

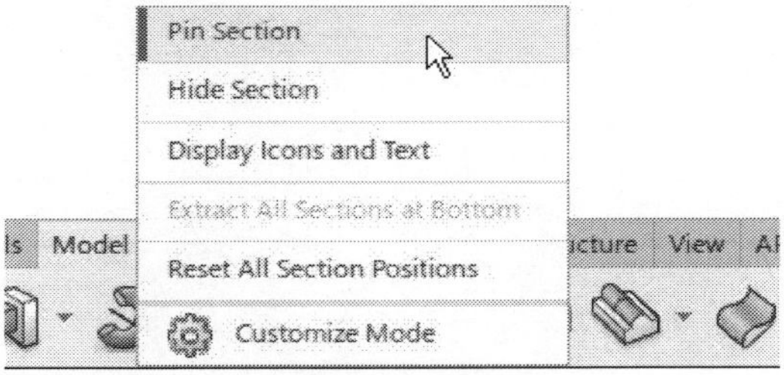

Figure 3–40

- Note that there is a blue triangle in the upper left corner of the *Model* section (as shown in Figure 3–41), indicating that it is pinned.

3. Select the *Refine* section. Note that the icons in the *Model* section are still visible, as shown in Figure 3–41.

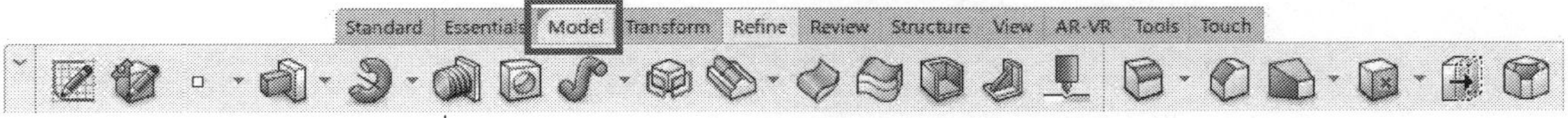

Figure 3–41

4. Select several other sections and note that the Model icons are always visible.

5. Right-click on the Action Bar, and select **Customize Mode**.

6. Right-click on the Action Bar again, and select **Reset All Customizations**. The Action Bar returns to the default setup.

7. Select **OK** to accept the reset.

   IMPORTANT: The images going forward in this content will have the section labels on and the icon labels turned off to save space. You may want to leave the labels displayed until you begin to recognize the icons.

Task 7 - Display the Action Bar.

1. Right-click in the graphic area and select **Display**>**Action Pad**.

2. The Action Pad displays as shown in Figure 3–42.

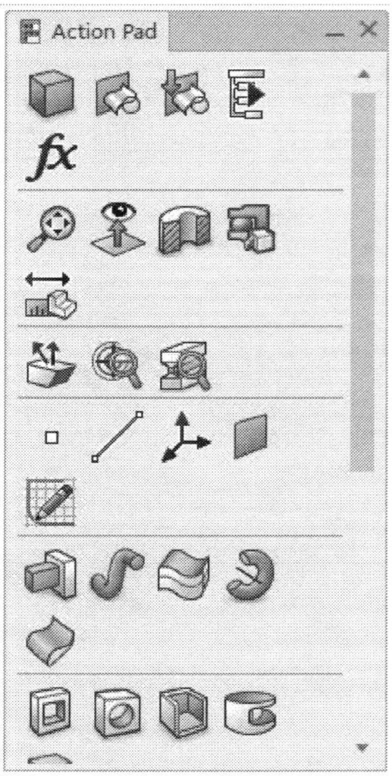

Figure 3–42

3. The Action Pad will allow you to quickly access common commands quickly.

Task 8 - Modifying your CATIA settings.

In this task, you will begin modifying the options in CATIA to the recommended settings for your training session.

1. Modify the display performance of CATIA. Select **Your User Icon>Preferences**.

2. Select **Common Preferences>2D3D View Display> Performance** from the left side of the Preferences window. Set the *3D Accuracy* to **Proportional**, with a value of **0.04**, as shown in Figure 3–43.

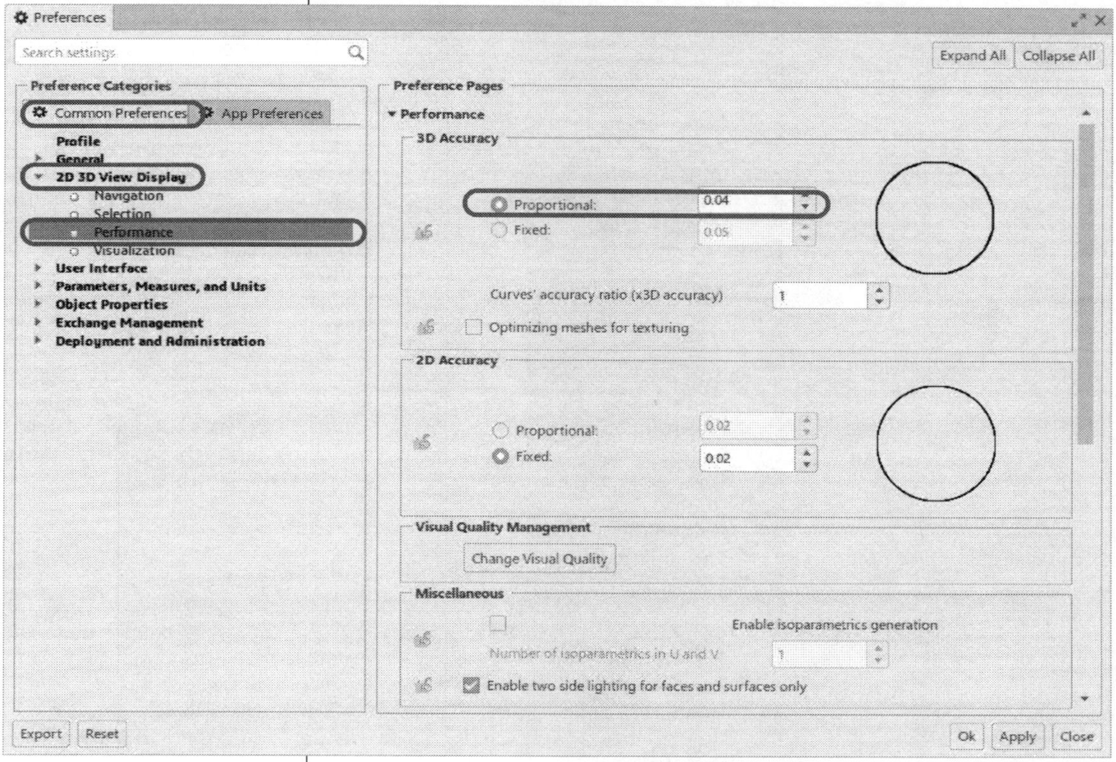

Figure 3–43

Task 9 - Complete the CATIA settings modification.

1. Use the following information as a guide to complete the remaining configurations. All of the configurations are done under **Your User Icon>Preferences**.

Path	Option	Value
Common Preferences> General> Cache and Performance> PCS	**Undo Command**	The **Stack Size** option controls the number of undo operations that can be performed. Increasing this value also decreases CATIA performance, as the software must store more operation information. The maximum value is **99**. It is recommended that you set this option to **15-20**.
Common Preferences> User Interface> Tree> Tree Manipulation	**Zoom on Tree**	Disabling the **Tree zoom after clicking on any branch** option helps in working in the CATIA interface. Users often become confused when selecting a branch in the tree, which takes their focus off the model. With this option disabled, the tree can be zoomed by selecting the axis in the lower right corner of the window.
Common Preferences> Parameters, Measures, and Units> Parameters> Parameters & Relations	**Parameters Tree View**	These options control the display of parameter values and formulae in the tree. It is recommended that you select **Display values**.
Common Preferences> Parameters, Measures, and Units> Measures> Measure Tools	**Associativity**	These options control the automatic update of measurements in a part and product model. It is recommended that you enable **Automatic update in product.**

Common Preferences> Object Properties> 3D Shape> Display> Display	**Display In Tree**	These options control the display of model information in the tree. They include: • External References • Constraints • Parameters • Relations • Bodies under operations • Expand sketch-based feature nodes at creation It is recommended that you enable all of the options in this area.
Common Preferences> Object Properties> 3D Shape> Infrastructure>3D Shape	**Hybrid Design**	Unless your company has standardized the use of Hybrid Design, clear the **Enable hybrid design inside part bodies and bodies** option. Hybrid Design changes the way wireframe and surface elements are stored in a part model and should not be enabled unless instructed by your CAD Administrator.
App Preferences> 3D Modeling> 3D Modeling Core> Sketcher> Sketcher	**Sketch Plane**	Disable the **Minimize viewpoint transformation** option so that the sketch orients correctly during creation.

Chapter Review Questions

1. Changes made to the default configuration for CATIA are saved in the _________ folder.
   a. Settings
   b. CATSettings
   c. Config
   d. Properties
2. To open the Preferences dialog box:
   a. Select **Me>Options**.
   b. Select **>Preferences**.
   c. Select **Me>Preferences**.
   d. Click the .
3. The _______ option keeps the selected section of the Action Bar open at all times.
   a. Pin/Unpin
   b. Fixed
   c. Lock
   d. Position
4. To access your favorite modeling apps, click_____?
   a. The **App** icon
   b. **3D** from the Compass
   c. **Me**>**Favorites**
   d. All of the above

5. What does the small black arrow on an icon (shown in Figure 3–44) indicate?

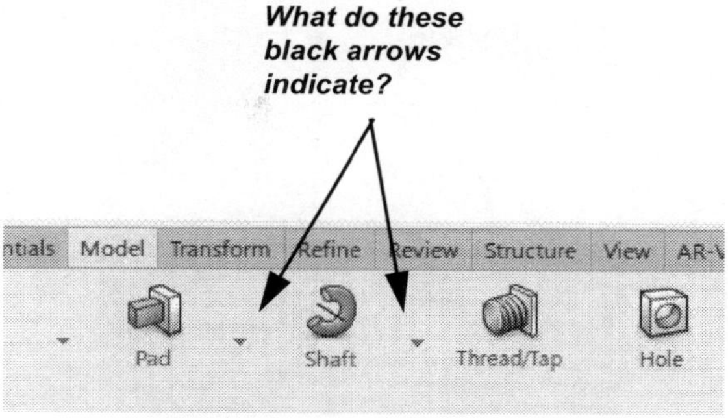

Figure 3–44

   a. The icon is not part of the default icons for this app.
   b. The icon has been locked.
   c. The icon contains a flyout.
   d. The black arrow is used to move the icon.

6. When CATIA is closed and re-opened, it opens using the same options that were set the last time it was customized.
   a. True
   b. False

Answers: 1b, 2c, 3a, 4b, 5c, 6a

Creating Sketches

In this chapter, you learn how sketches are used to create features. You also learn some of the basic capabilities of the Sketch app, which enables you to create sketch-based features. Then, you use reference planes and surfaces to orient and sketch the profile of your first feature.

Learning Objectives in This Chapter

- Understand the basics of sketched features.
- Review the general steps for creating a new part.
- Understand the use of default and reference planes for sketching.
- Review the basic tools that you can use to create entities in sketches.
- Create a sketch for the model profile.
- Understand several operations for editing sketches.
- Learn various tips and techniques for working with sketches.
- Understand how features and sketches display in the specification tree.

4.1 Getting Started on Sketching Features

2D sketches are used to create 3D features. A sketch plane is selected and used to create a sketched feature, as shown in Figure 4–1.

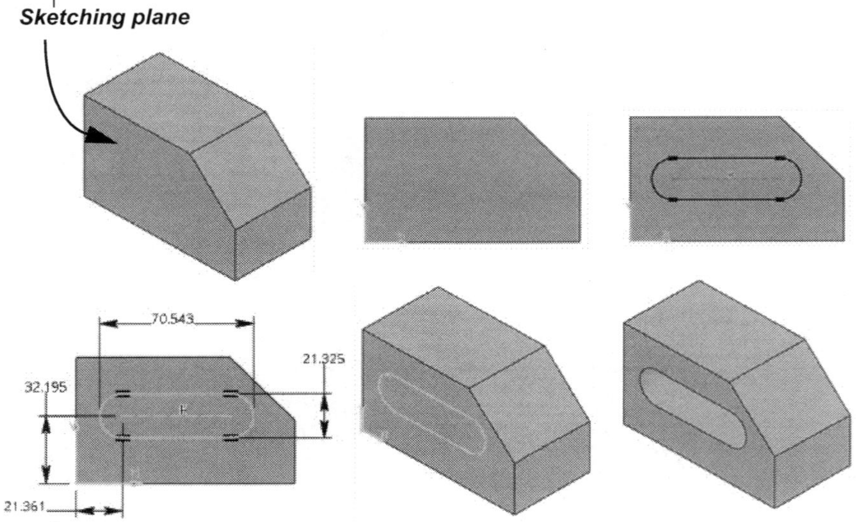

Figure 4–1

How To: Create a Sketched Feature

1. Select a sketch plane and enter the Sketch app. The plane you select is initially oriented parallel to the screen. The Y-axis faces the top of the screen and the X-axis faces the right side of the screen.
2. Sketch the required profile or cross-section.
3. Create constraints/dimensions to define the size and location of the sketch.
4. Exit the Sketch app.
5. Use the sketch to create a solid feature, such as a Pad or Pocket.

4.2 Creating a New 3D Part

The 3DEXPERIENCE Part Design modeling engine is the same as CATIA V5, which ensures file compatibility so V5 data will be able to transfer to 3DEXPERIENCE without any issue. Because of this, most of the modeling commands are very similar and the overall approach to modeling is quite familiar, with a few differences.

Creating a New Part

There are three main ways to create a new 3D part:

1. Use the Compass.
2. Click Add from the Top Bar.
3. Add to an assembly (design in context).

Using the Compass to Create a New Part

The compass is used to access the various apps available in the 3DEXPERIENCE platform. Use the following steps to create a new model.

1. Click the outer ring of the compass, as shown in Figure 4–2.

Figure 4–2

2. Select the app that you would like to use, such as Part Design or Assembly Design, as shown in Figure 4–3.

Figure 4–3

3. A part file is created when entering the app, as shown in Figure 4–4.

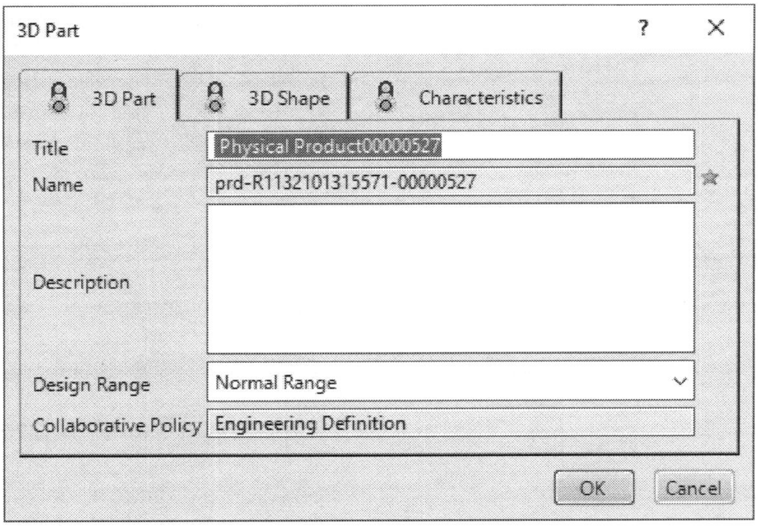

Figure 4–4

Using the Add Command

By clicking the (Add) drop-down, you can select to create Physical Products, Parts, and Drawings directly, as shown in Figure 4–5.

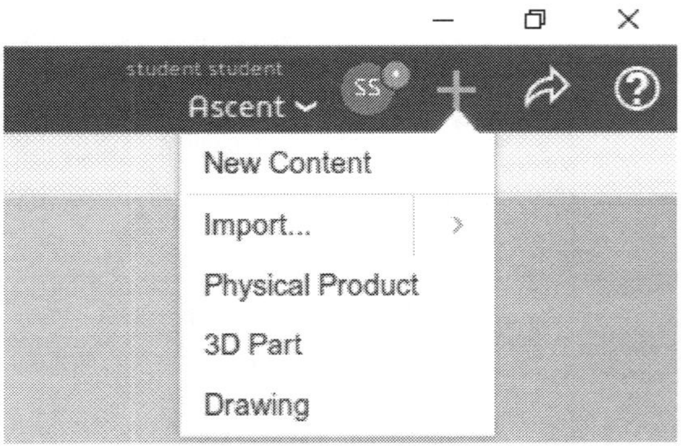

Figure 4–5

Or, by clicking Content, all other 3DEXPERIENCE platform objects can be created, as shown in Figure 4–6.

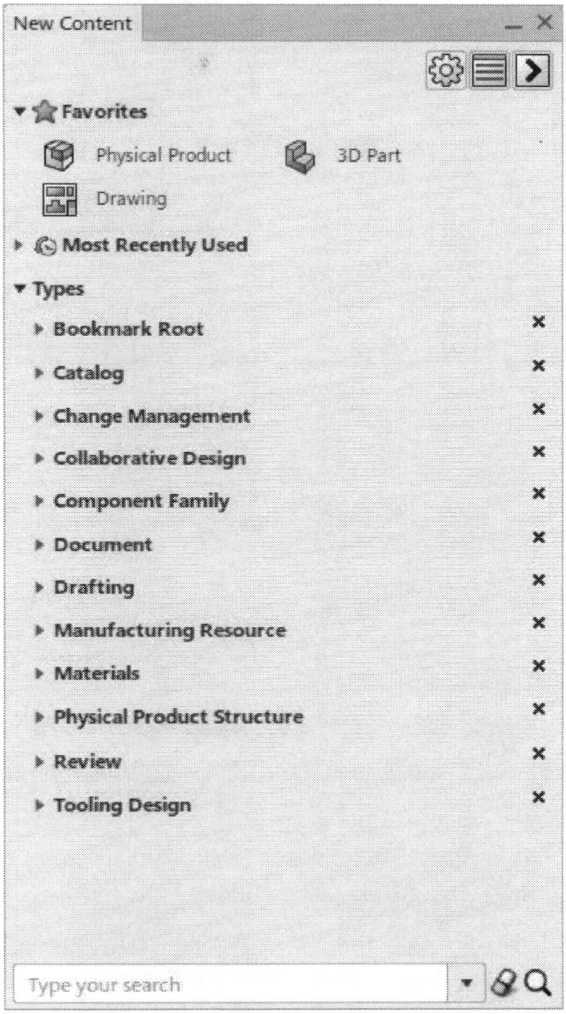

Figure 4–6

Build a New Part in an Assembly (Design in Context)

To create a part in an assembly, right-click the Product and select **Insert** > **3D Part**, as shown in Figure 4–7. Keep in mind that a 3D Part is specifically a 3D shape that contains a product that will only hold a shape file.

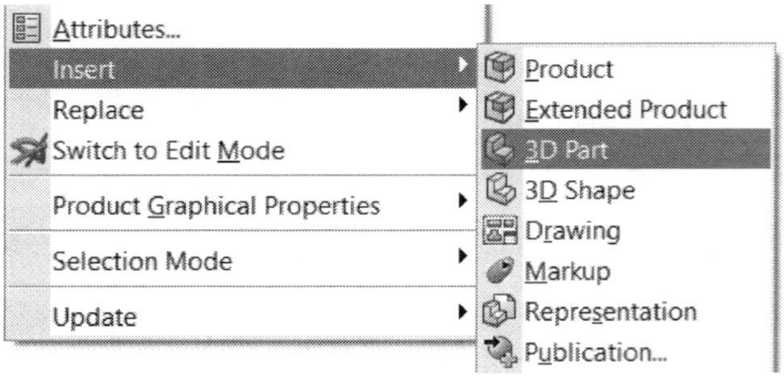

Figure 4–7

Note this is covered in detail in a later section.

4.3 New Part Dialog

The 3D Part dialog box has three tabs. There are two titles, one for the 3D Part and one for the 3D Shape, as shown in Figure 4–8.

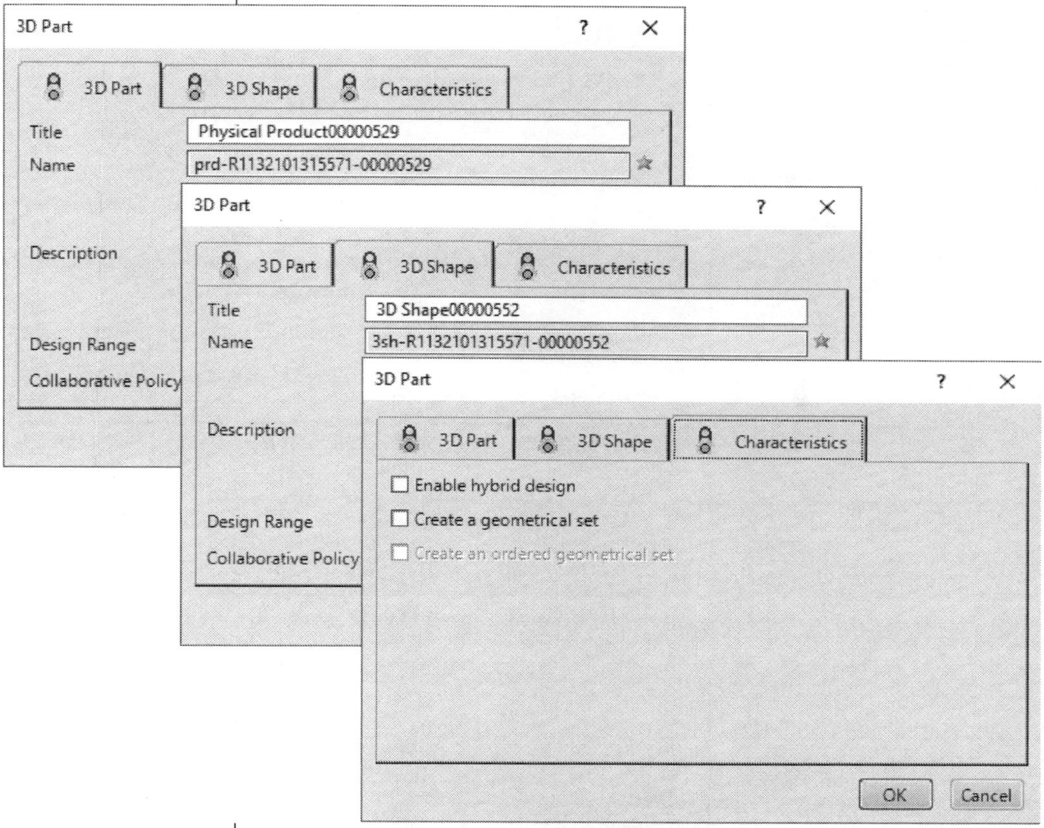

Figure 4–8

There is also a Characteristics tab, allowing you to select additional options for creating the part.

The titles for a part are shown in Figure 4–9. The 3D Part is a container that will contain reference information (such as position in an assembly, reviews, or drawing) for that part. The 3D shape will be the 3D model and contain 3D features, such as Pads, Pockets, Extrudes, Joins, etc.

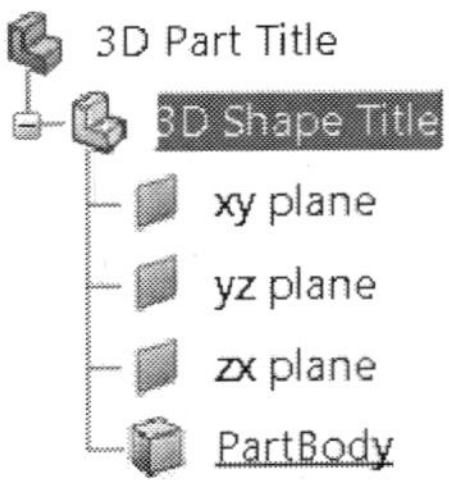

Figure 4–9

The following options can be configured for the new part:

Parameter	**Description**
Enter part Title field	Enter a name for the part model. This name is automatically assigned to the Part Number of the new file.
Enter part *Description* field	Optional description of the model.
Enable hybrid design option	Hybrid design uses a special type of body, called a hybrid body. It can contain both wireframe/surface and solid features. This enables direct integration of the surface and part design environments into a single body. For current purposes, the hybrid design environment is disabled.
Create a geometrical set option	When the hybrid design environment is disabled, a geometrical set is used to store wireframe and surface elements, as well as sketched elements. A geometrical set is automatically added to the new part file when this option is selected.
Create an ordered geometrical set option	When the hybrid design environment is enabled, an ordered geometrical set can be used to group together wireframe or surface geometry with order preserved.

Click **OK** when the part parameters have been specified. The model is created with three default reference planes that can be used as sketching planes, as shown in Figure 4–10.

If the New Part Dialog box is not appearing when you create a new part, it can be turned on by selecting the (Add)> New Content> (Tools) and enabling **Set attributes at creation for all types.**

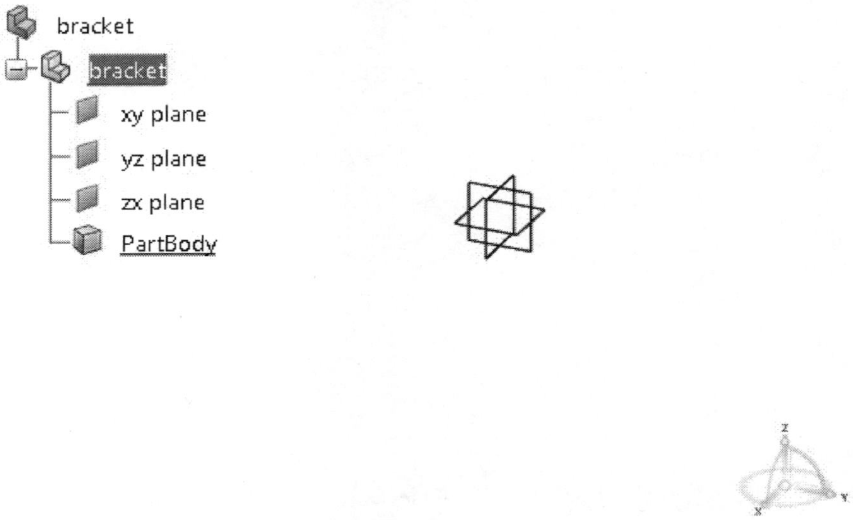

Figure 4–10

4.4 Sketch Planes

A new part always starts with three default reference planes. The model and specification tree display is shown in Figure 4–11. The planes are automatically named to match the directions of the coordinate system that they are parallel to, such as the XY plane.

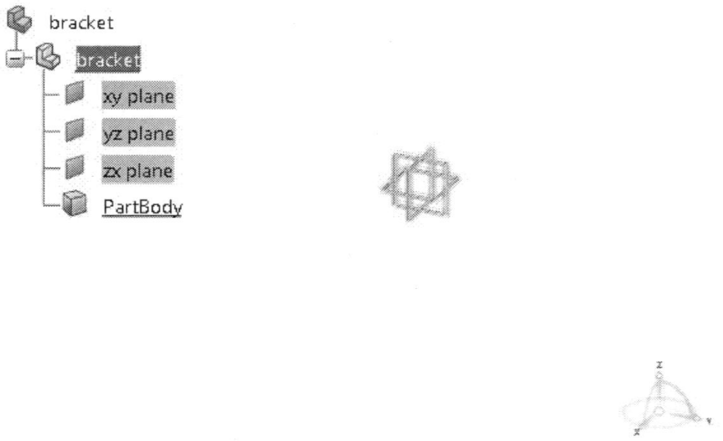

Figure 4–11

Reference Planes

For better visualization, highlight each plane by placing the cursor over a reference plane in the specification tree or on the screen.

All CATIA parts contain default reference planes as the first three features. The default reference planes remain the same size relative to screen, regardless of model size or zoom level, as shown in Figure 4–12.

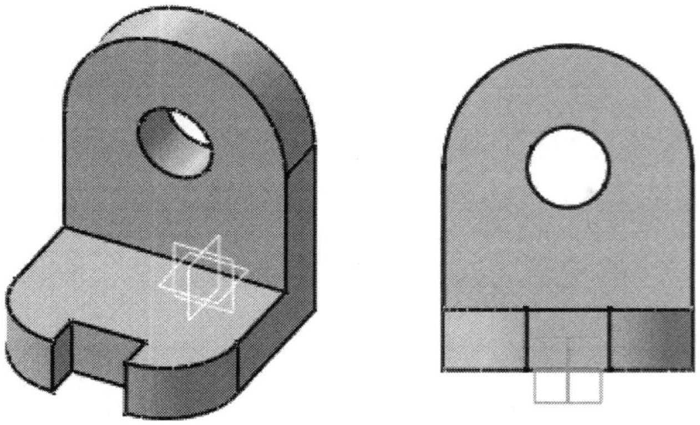

Figure 4–12

Default reference planes are useful for creating a new model because they provide a planar reference to place the first sketch. Figure 4–13 shows three shaded rectangular surfaces to help visualize the reference planes orientation.

Planes cannot be displayed as shaded. This is for illustration only.

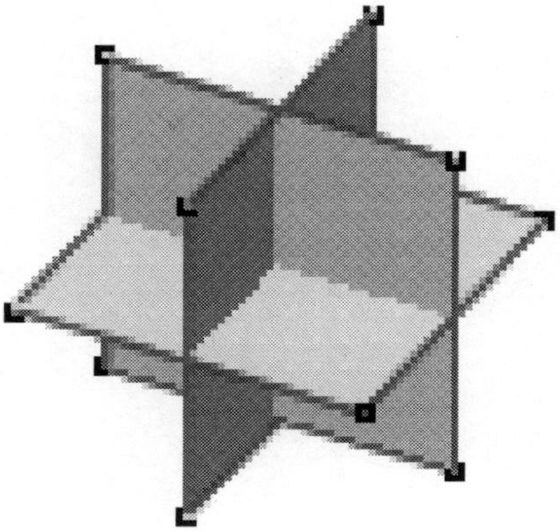

Figure 4–13

Selecting a Plane for Sketching

Selecting one plane over another impacts the Quick Views and the default orientation of the model. The YZ plane is considered the front of the part, as shown in Figure 4–14. However, this does not mean that you always sketch on the YZ plane.

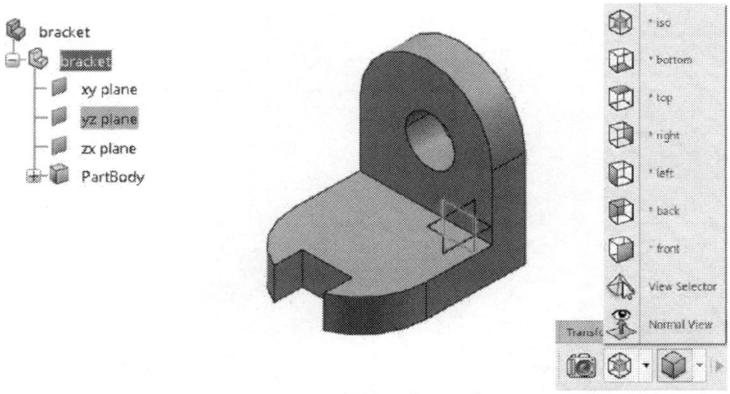

Figure 4–14

The sketch of the bracket part is two lines at right angles, sketched on the ZX plane.

Sketch a front profile on the YZ plane, a side profile on the ZX plane, and a top profile on the XY plane.

Consider the following example. The possible default orientations of a cylinder when one of the default planes is selected, as shown in Figure 4–15.

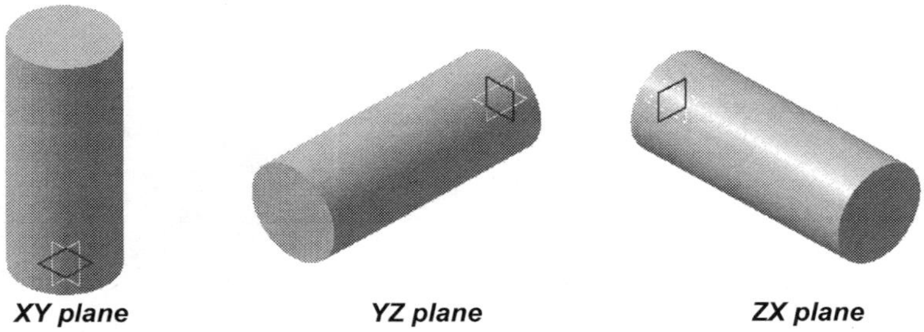

Figure 4–15

4.5 Sketch Application

How To: Create a Sketch

1. Select an appropriate sketching plane and click (Sketch) from the context toolbar.
2. Create your sketch.
3. Click (Exit App) to complete the sketch.

Sketcher Grid

When you first enter the Sketch app, the following objects display, as shown in Figure 4–16:

- Sketcher grid over your sketch plane
- Three default reference planes
- Horizontal and Vertical axes
- Robot
- Specification tree

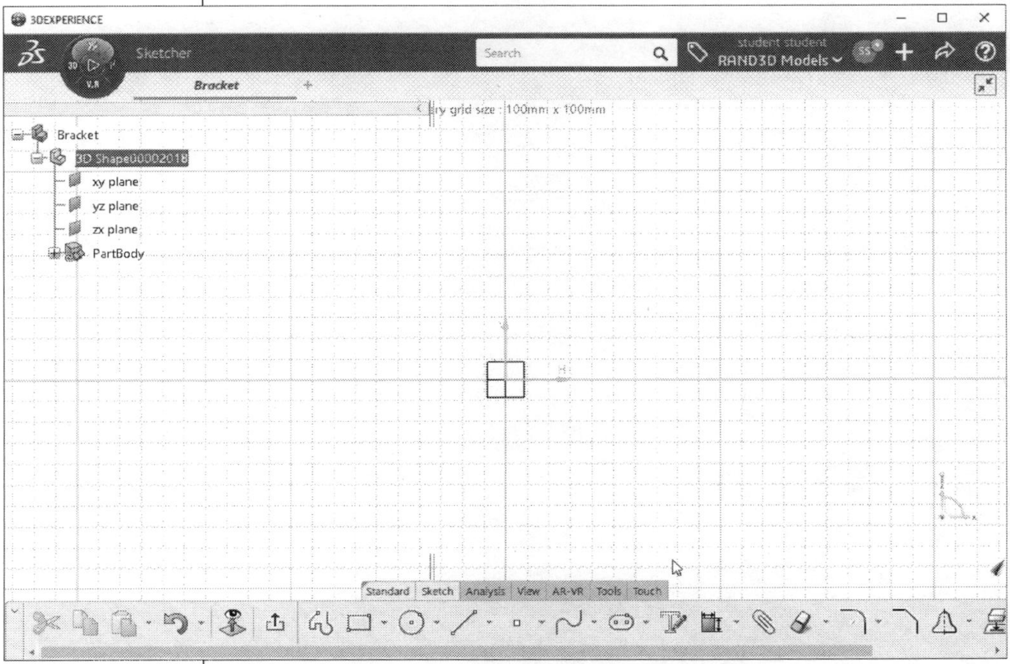

Figure 4–16

(Grid) is also available in the View section of the Action Bar. (Snap to Point) is available in the Sketch section.

To use the sketcher grid, right-click and select **Display>Action Pad** to display the Action Pad, shown in Figure 4–17. You can set the following options:

- Enable/disable the grid: (Grid)
- Enable/disable the snap function: (Snap to Point)

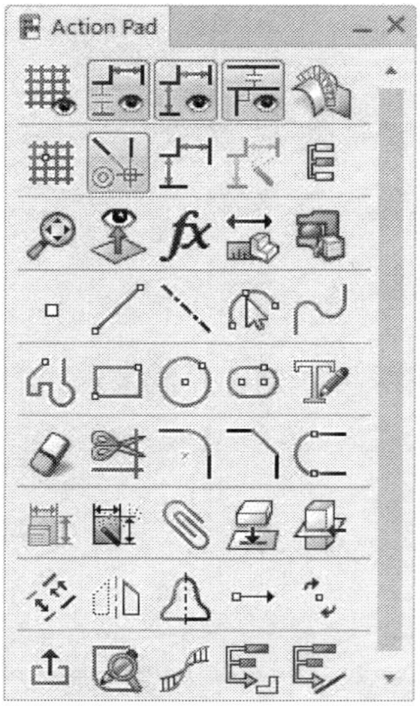

Figure 4–17

4.6 Basic Shapes

Other sketch tools are available. These are covered in a different chapter.

Once inside the Sketch app, the feature's profile (or cross-section) must be sketched. The most commonly used tools for sketching are described as follows.

Icon	Sequence	Description
 (Line)		Select the start and end points of the line.
 (Bi-Tangent Line)	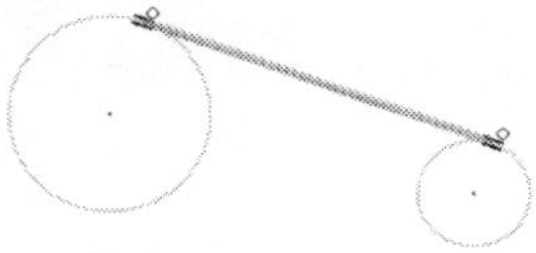	Select two arcs or circles for the line to be tangent to.
 (Line Normal To Curve)	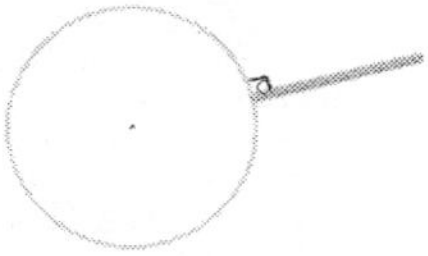	Select a location on a curve, or a point on a curve. Then select the end point of the line.
 (Rectangle)		Select the location for two diagonal corners of the rectangle.
 (Arc)		Select the start point of the arc, end point of the arc, and then another point for the arc to pass through.
 (Circle)	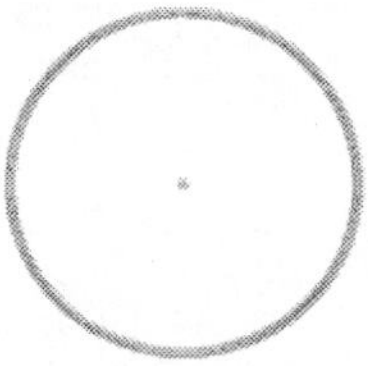	Select the center of the circle and a point on its perimeter to define the diameter.
 (Elongated Hole)		Select the center of each arc, and then select a location on the profile to define the diameter.

 (Corner)	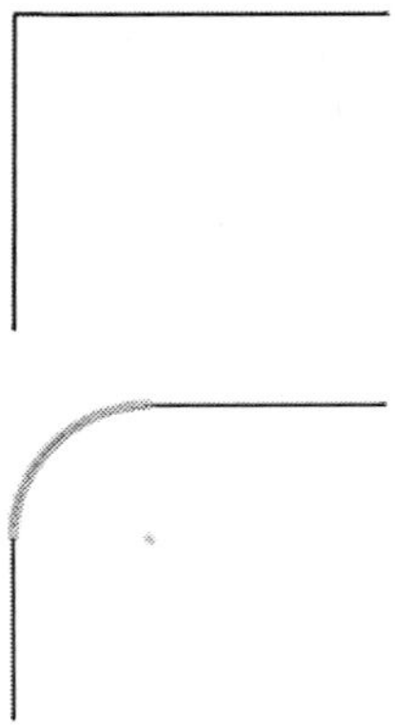	Select the two lines the corner is tangent to, and then drag the corner out to the required size.
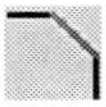 (Chamfer)	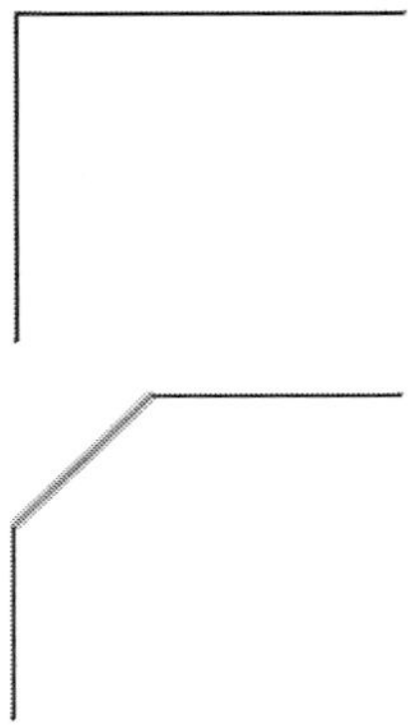	Select the two lines the chamfer contacts, and then drag the chamfer out to the required size.
 (Axis)	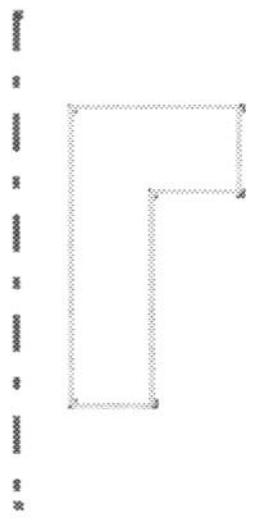	Select the start and end points of the axis.

Manual Definition

With many sketch tools, you can use another toolbar called the Tools Palette that contains additional functions for that specific type of geometry. Some of these options are described as follows:

Option	Description
Lines	Manually enter the coordinates of the start point, end point, line length, and angle into the Sketch Tools toolbar.
Rectangle	Manually enter the coordinates of the first point, the coordinates of the second point, and the height and width of the rectangle.
Circle	Manually enter the coordinates for the circle's center and specify its radius.
Corner	Specify how to trim the existing lines when the corner is completed.

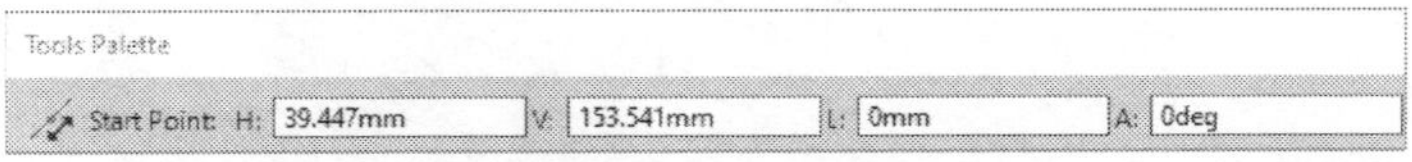

4.7 Profile Sketching

To create a connected series of lines and arcs, use  (Profile). Sketch a series of connected lines, then when you have formed a closed loop, the profile automatically terminates, as shown in Figure 4–18. You can also terminate the profile with an open loop by double-clicking the left mouse button at the end of the last line, as shown in Figure 4–19.

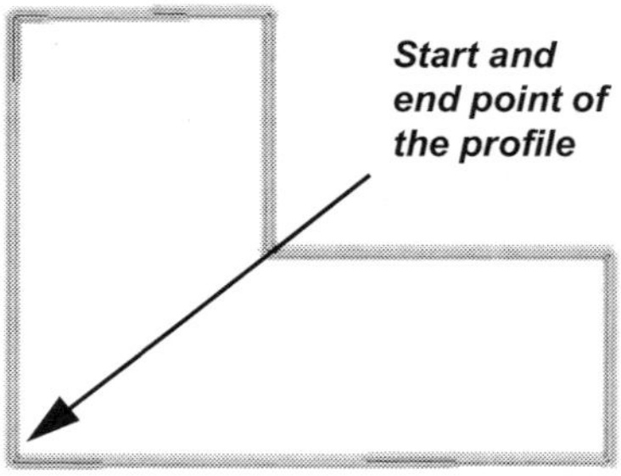

Figure 4–18

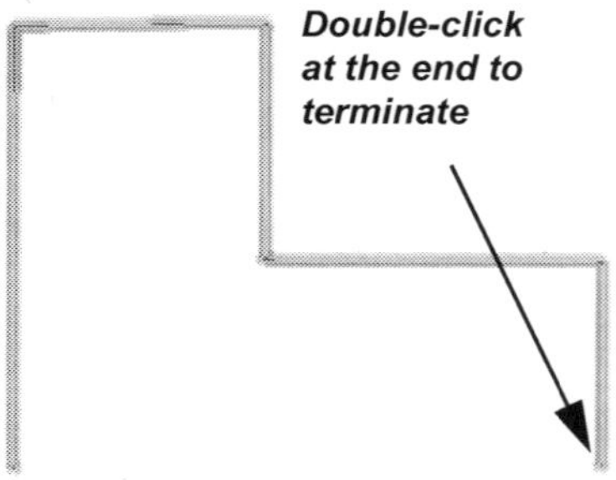

Figure 4–19

You can toggle from sketching a line to sketching a tangent arc (as shown in Figure 4–20) or three-point arc (as shown in Figure 4–21), by using the temporary icons in the Sketch tools toolbar. You return to sketching a line after you finish the arc.

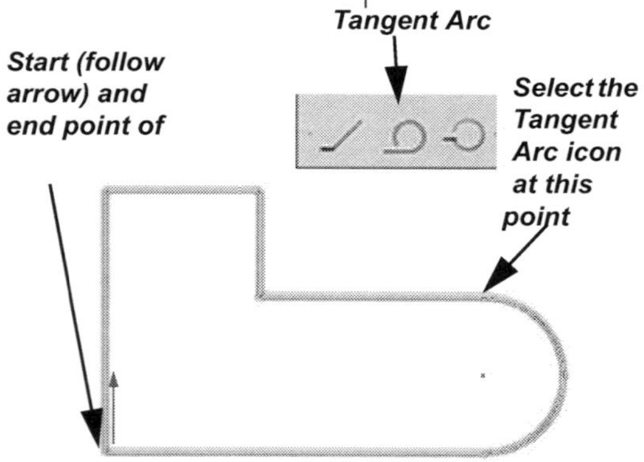

Figure 4–20

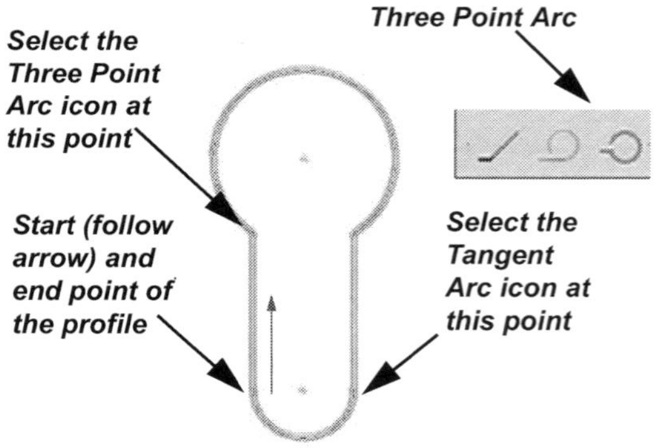

Figure 4–21

4.8 Sketcher Editing Operations

Quick Trim

(Quick Trim) deletes the selected portion of a feature. The software automatically breaks the element at its intersections with other sketched elements.

- The **Quick Trim** method is used to remove the arc segment between two vertical lines, as shown in Figure 4–22.

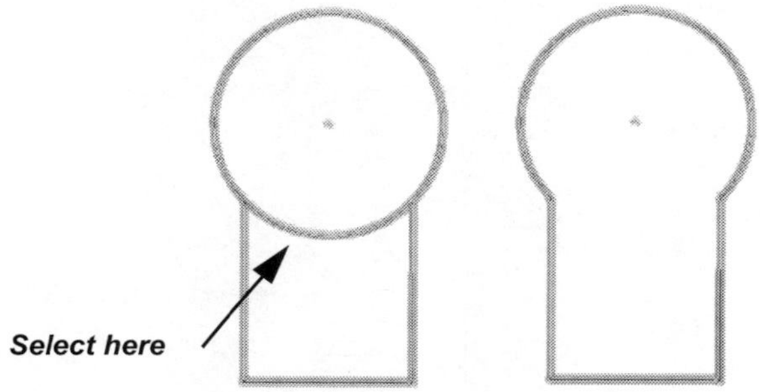

Figure 4–22

Trimming

(Trim) extends or trims sketched entities to form a closed corner. Select each entity on the side of the intersection that you want to keep. Figure 4–23 shows three examples of trimming and extending line segments.

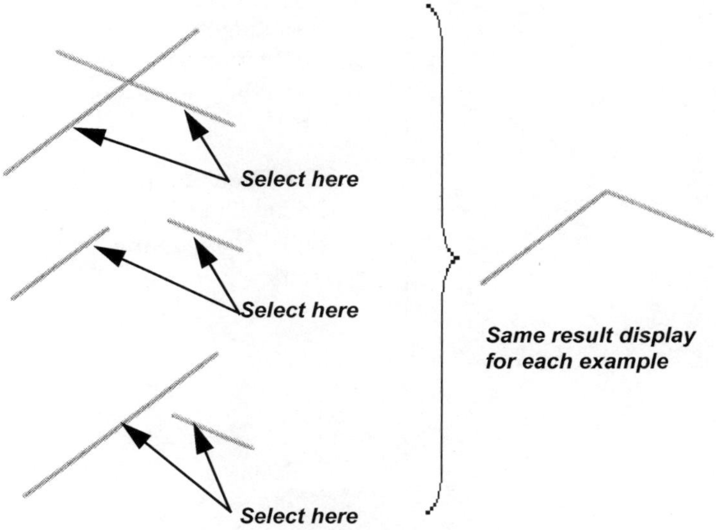

Figure 4–23

You can also choose to trim only the first selected entity by clicking  (Trim First Element) in the Tools Palette toolbar that opens after you click  (Trim), and selecting the entity to which the first element should be trimmed, as shown in Figure 4–24.

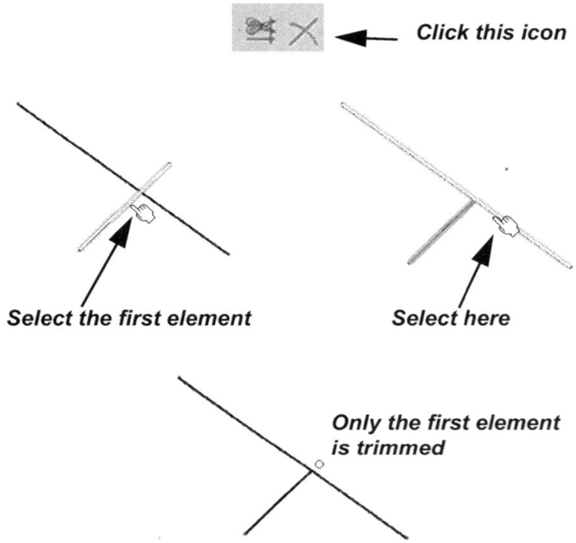

Figure 4–24

Break

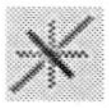 (Break) divides a sketched entity at its intersection with another sketched entity. To use the **Break** tool, select the feature you want to divide and select the intersecting feature. The intersection point is projected if the feature does not intersect the first entity.

- The **Break** tool is used to break circles into arcs using an intersecting line, as shown in Figure 4–25. Note that a closed entity, such as the circle, is also divided by an implicit 360° mark.

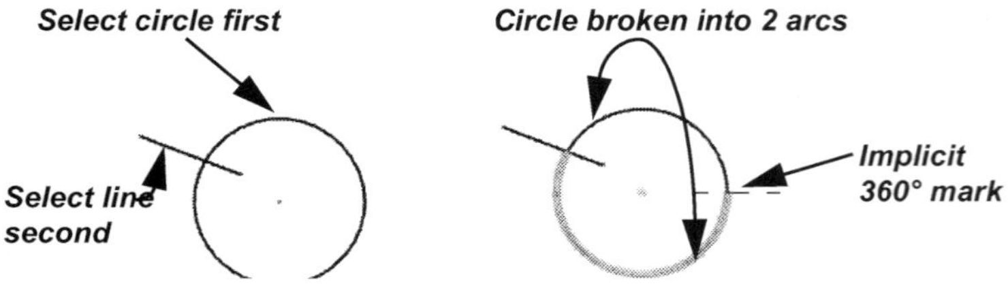

Figure 4–25

Delete and Undo

Pressing <Delete> enables you to remove portions (one or more lines) of a model or the entire sketch (rectangle).

- To completely eliminate a feature you just sketched, you can press <Ctrl>+<Z> or click  (Undo). The keyboard shortcut executes the **Undo** command. CATIA records your previous actions, enabling you to undo multiple times.

  If **Undo** doesn't seem to be working, ensure that you have finished the previous command or hit the **Esc** key to exit the command you are currently using. This should allow **Undo** to be preformed.

4.9 Tips and Techniques

Repeating a Command

When you use any of the geometry creation icons, the command is automatically deactivated once you perform the action. However, by double-clicking on the icon, you can perform that command multiple times.

- Select the icon again to deactivate it. This technique is more efficient than repeatedly selecting the same icon.

Sketching in 3D

Sketching in a 3D orientation can be useful when solid geometry exists and you are sketching on the face of a previously defined feature.

- To return to the planar sketch view, click  (Normal View).

Construction Geometry

You can use construction geometry to help create lines, shapes, and points for your standard geometry. Construction geometry is useful when working with more complex sketches, as shown in Figure 4–26.

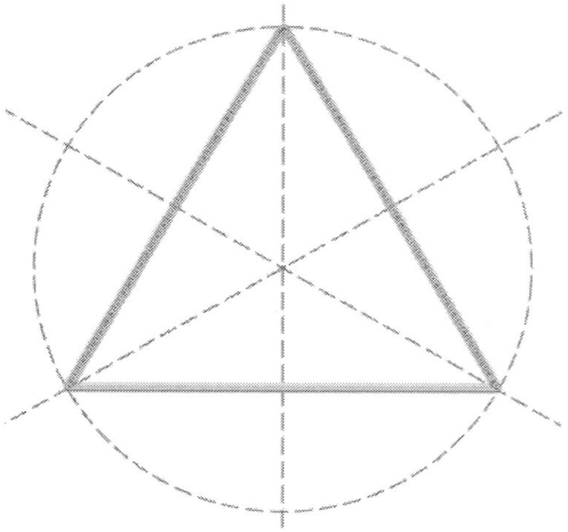

Figure 4–26

You can create construction geometry using one of the following methods:

Do not forget to return to Standard elements when you are done.

- Click (Construction/Standard Element) in the *Sketch* section of the Action Bar, as shown in Figure 4–27. Any geometry you sketch displays as construction geometry.

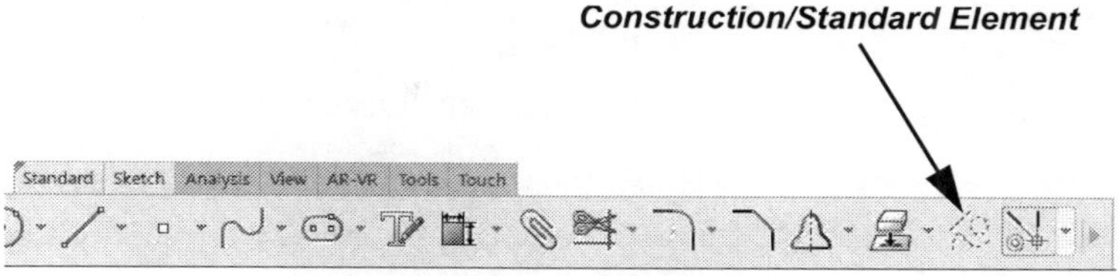

Figure 4–27

- Select the existing standard geometry and click (Construction/Standard Element) to convert it to construction geometry.

Auto Search

Use the **Auto Search** tool to automatically select all entities that are connected to the selected entity.

- To use the **Auto Search** tool, select a sketched entity that belongs to the profile you want to select and click (Auto Search), as shown in Figure 4–28. The continuous chain of entities is highlighted for the next operation.

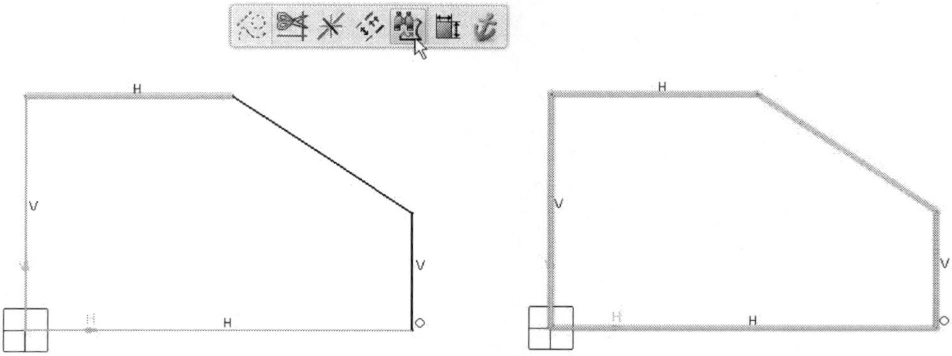

Figure 4–28

- Alternatively, you can select the entity, right-click and select * **object>Auto Search**.

Sketching at Origin

If you select the origin of the sketch during the creation of a profile, CATIA automatically creates an implicit constraint between the vertex of the sketch and the origin. This constraint restricts the vertex of the profile from being moved at a later time, but can be broken by selecting the profile, selecting (Cut) and (Paste) from the Action Bar. This pastes the profile on its original position without the constraint, so you can move it. This only works if the sketched entity has not been referenced by any other features. Any features that reference the entity being cut and pasted fail because the pasted item is considered a new sketched entity and does not maintain the references.

- This type of constraint can be used for a base feature since it is unlikely to move later. However, for other features that should be constrained to the origin, it is recommended to sketch offset from the origin and manually constrain the sketch to it. Figure 4–29 shows a circle that can be manually constrained to the origin using a **Coincident** constraint.

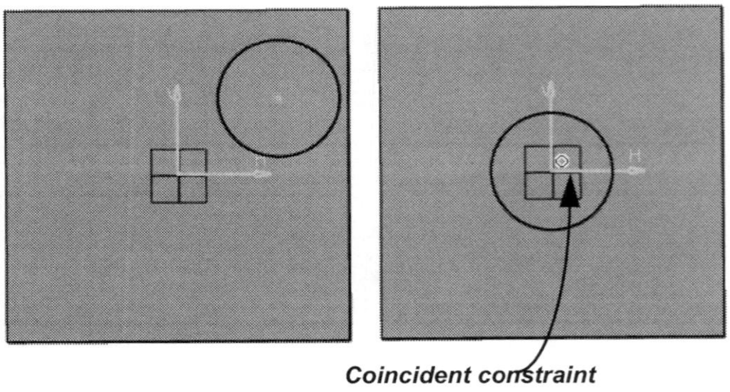

Figure 4–29

4.10 Specification Tree

Sketches are automatically listed under the feature branch that uses them.

The features you create are listed in the specification tree in the order in which you create them. Solid geometry features are listed under PartBody, as shown in Figure 4–30.

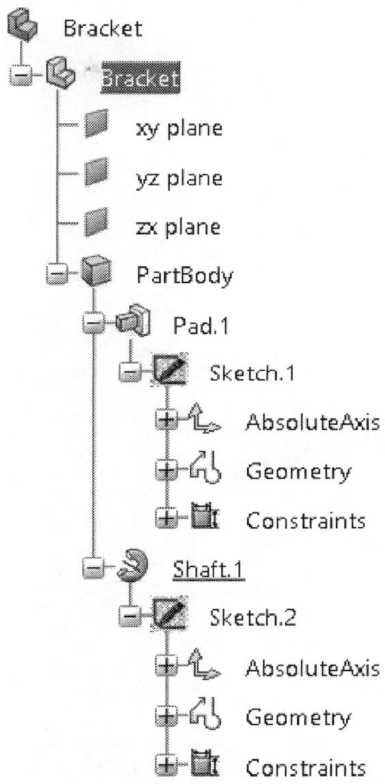

Figure 4–30

- A sketch is automatically hidden once referenced by a solid feature. Right-click on the sketch and select **Hide/Show** to toggle on its display.

Practice 4a Sketching Basic Shapes

Practice Objectives

- Sketch a line, arc, rectangle, circle, and elongated hole.
- Trim overlapping shapes.

In this practice, you will create a sketch as shown in Figure 4–31. You will use various constraints to help constrain the sketch.

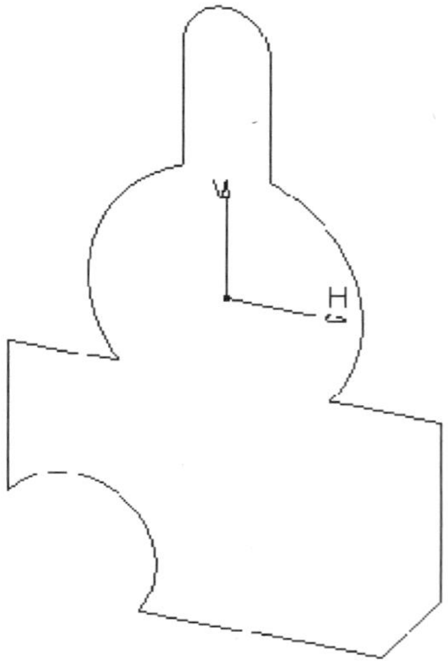

Figure 4–31

Task 1 - Create a new part and set the length units to millimeter.

1. In the Top Bar, click (Add)>**3D Part**.
2. In the 3D Part dialog box, enter ***Your_Initials*_Sketch_1** as the *Title*.
3. Select the *3D Shape* tab and enter **Sketch_1** for the *Title*.
4. Select the *Characteristics* tab and ensure **Enable hybrid modeling** is disabled.
5. Click **OK**.

Task 2 - Select the sketching plane and enter the Sketch app.

1. Select the YZ plane as shown in Figure 4–32.

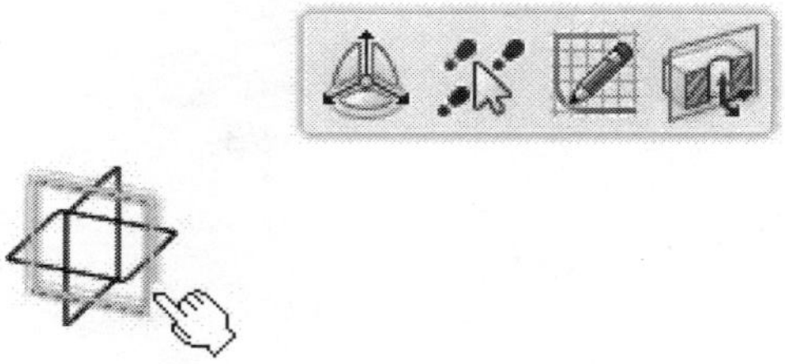

Figure 4–32

2. In the Context toolbar, click (Sketch).
3. The selected reference plane displays parallel to the screen, as shown in Figure 4–33.

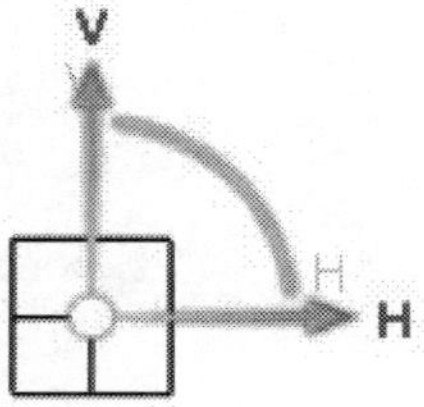

Figure 4–33

Task 3 - Sketch a circle.

Automatic Dimensional Constraints are discussed in more detail in a later chapter.

1. Right-click and select **Display**>**Action Pad** if the Action Pad is not already displayed.
2. Ensure that (Automatic Dimensional Constraints) is toggled off.
3. If necessary, in the Action Pad, click (Grid) to turn off the grid display.
4. If necessary, in the Action Pad, click (Snap to Point) so you can sketch freely.
5. Click (Circle) to sketch a circle.

6. Place the cursor over the intersection of the horizontal and vertical axes. Select the **0.0**, **0.0** location of the XY axis to define the circle's center point.

7. Move the cursor and select a location to define the radius of the circle. The sketch displays as shown in Figure 4–34.

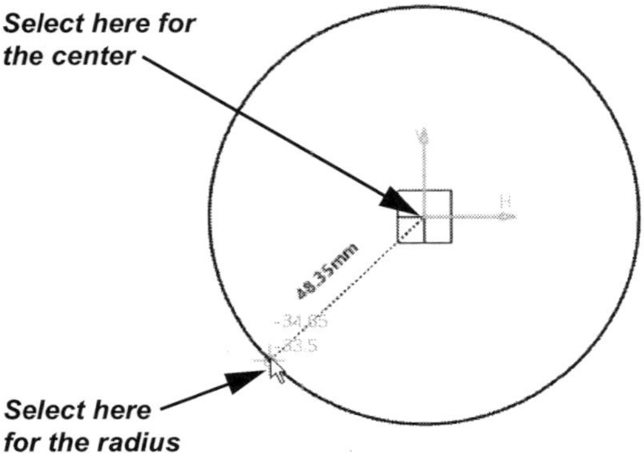

Figure 4–34

Task 4 - Sketch a rectangle that overlaps the circle.

1. Click (Rectangle) to sketch a rectangle.

2. Select the first point of the rectangle and the second point of the rectangle, as shown in Figure 4–35.

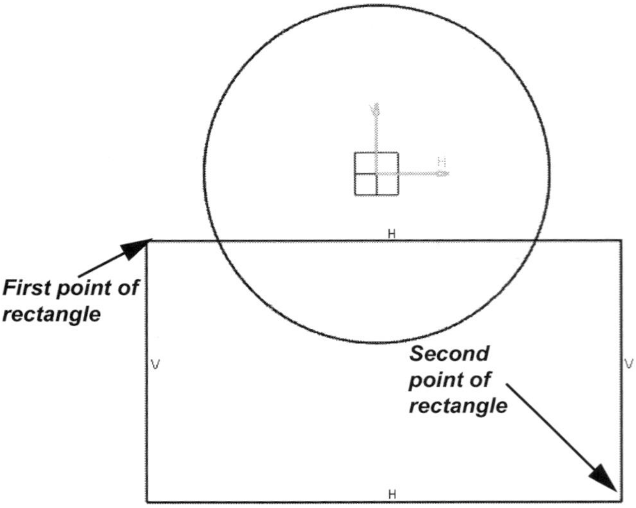

Figure 4–35

Task 5 - Sketch a line.

1. Click  (Line) to sketch a line.
2. Select the locations for the start and end points of the line, as shown in Figure 4–36.

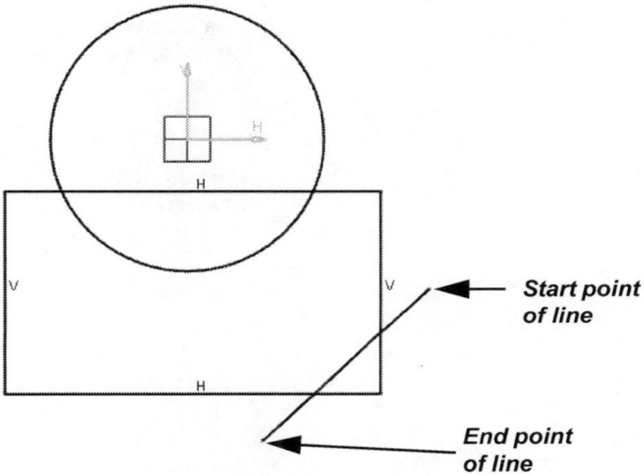

Figure 4–36

Task 6 - Sketch an arc.

1. In the Action Bar, expand the  (Circle) flyout and click  (Three Point Arc) to sketch an arc.

Select the start point of the arc. Note that the lines of the rectangle highlight in blue when the cursor is over them. This color change indicates that the ends of the arc are aligned with that feature.

2. Select the second point that the arc passes through and select the end point of the arc, as shown in Figure 4–37.

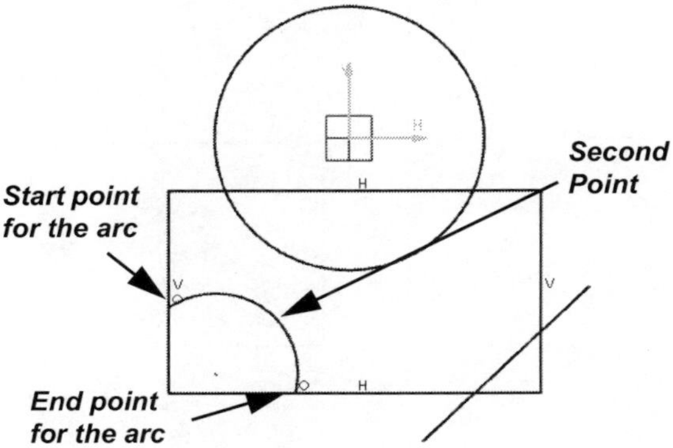

Figure 4–37

Task 7 - Sketch an elongated hole.

1. Click  (Elongated Hole) to sketch an elongated hole.
2. Select the locations for the two arc centers, and a location to define the width of the elongated hole, as shown in Figure 4–38.

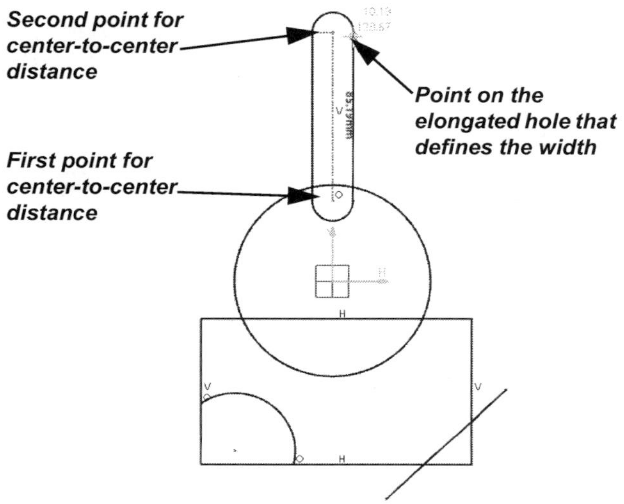

Figure 4–38

Task 8 - Trim the rectangle to the line and the circle.

1. In the Action Bar, expand  (Quick Trim) and click  (Trim) to trim the rectangle.
2. Select the line and the bottom of the rectangle, as shown in Figure 4–39.

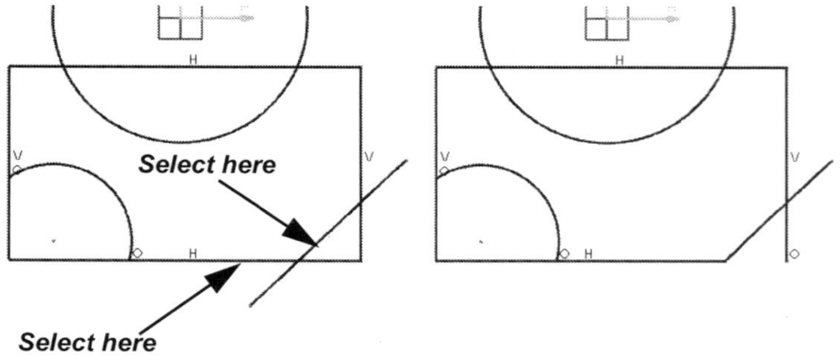

Figure 4–39

3. Note that  (Trim) is no longer highlighted. This means you have to click the icon again to perform another trim.

4. Double-click  (Trim) so it remains active.

5. Trim the other side of the rectangle and the line by clicking the elements labeled **Trim #2** in Figure 4–40.

6. Trim two more times to trim the arc to the box. The elements to select are labeled **Trim #3** and **Trim #4** in Figure 4–40.

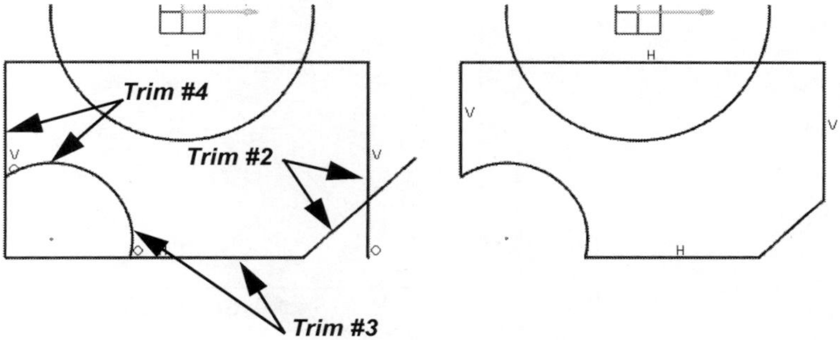

Figure 4–40

Task 9 - Trim the rectangle to the circle and the circle to the elongated hole using the Quick Trim method.

1. In the Action Bar, expand  (Trim), and click  (Quick Trim) to perform a **Quick Trim**.

2. Select the bottom of the circle to delete that segment, as shown in Figure 4–41.

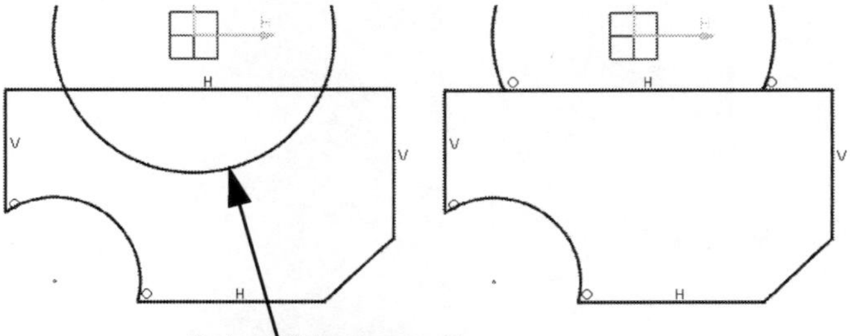

Figure 4–41

3. Double-click (Quick Trim) and trim multiple segments to clean up the sketch, as shown in Figure 4–42.

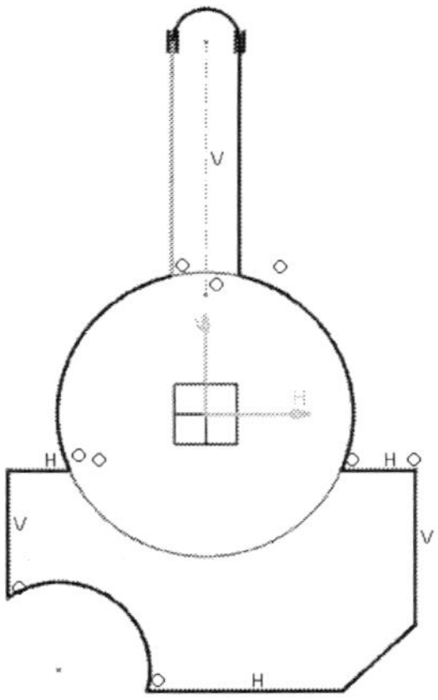

Figure 4–42

Task 10 - Exit the Sketch app and save the part.

1. Click (Exit App) to exit the Sketch app. The sketch displays as shown in Figure 4–43.

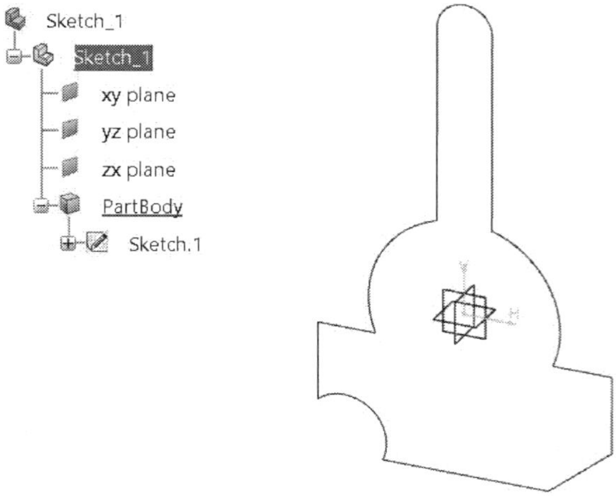

Figure 4–43

2. In the Top Bar,click (Share)>**Save** to save the part.
3. Close the *Sketch_1* tab.

Practice 4b

Profile Sketching

Practice Objective

- Use Profile Sketching to create lines and arcs.

In this practice, you will use the profile sketcher to create the sketch shown in Figure 4–44.

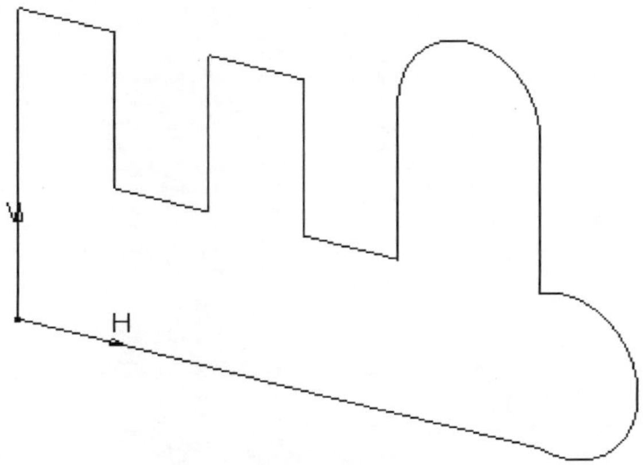

Figure 4–44

Task 1 - Create a new part and begin creating a sketch.

1. In the Top Bar, click (Add)>**3D Part**.
2. In the 3D Part dialog box, enter ***Your Initials*_Sketch_2** as the *Title*.
3. Select the 3D Shape tab and enter **Sketch_2** for the *Title*.
4. Select the *Characteristics* tab and ensure **Enable hybrid modeling** is disabled.
5. Click **OK**.

6. Select the YZ plane as shown in Figure 4–45.

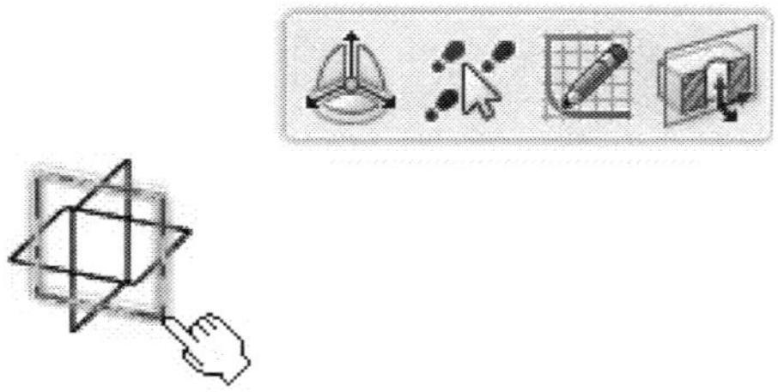

Figure 4–45

7. In the Context toolbar, click (Sketch).

Task 2 - Begin sketching a profile.

1. In the *Sketch* section of the Action Bar, click (Profile).
2. Place the cursor at the intersection of the horizontal and vertical axes, as shown in Figure 4–46. Press the left mouse button to begin sketching.

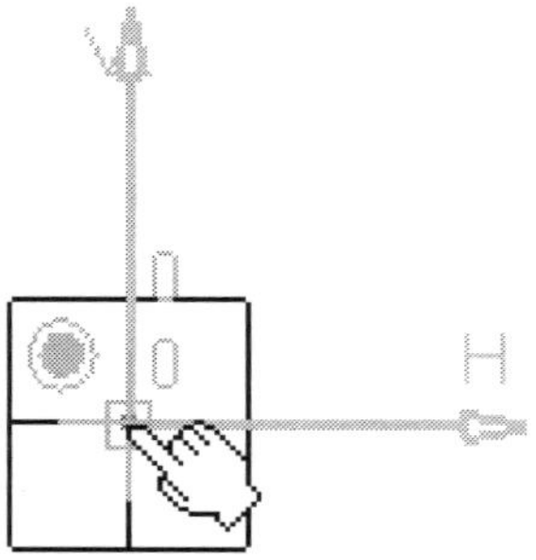

Figure 4–46

3. Sketch the series of connected vertical and horizontal lines, as shown in Figure 4–47. Note that the line turns blue when it is vertical or horizontal. Also note that the software displays a line to indicate when the cursor is coincident with other sketched elements.

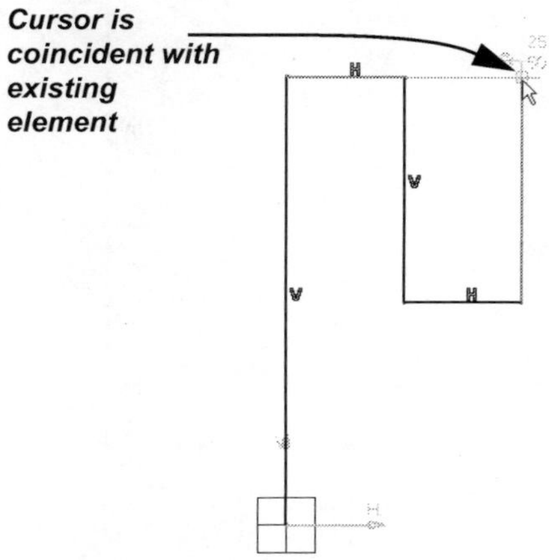

Figure 4–47

4. Continue sketching the profile until the section displays as shown in Figure 4–48. DO NOT end the profile yet.

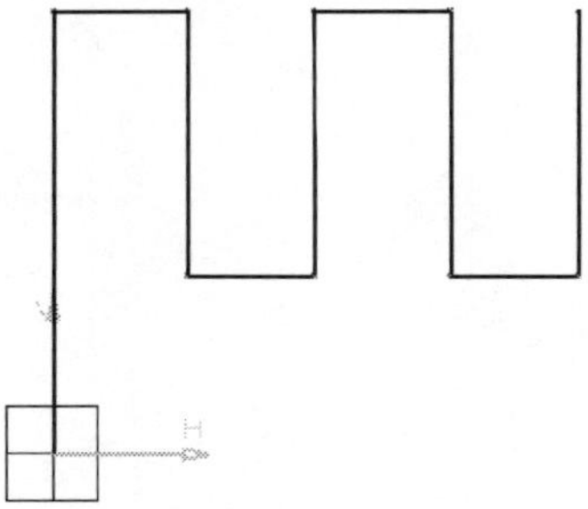

Figure 4–48

5. After selecting the end point of the last vertical line segment, click  (Tangent Arc) in the Tools Palette toolbar, as shown in Figure 4–49.

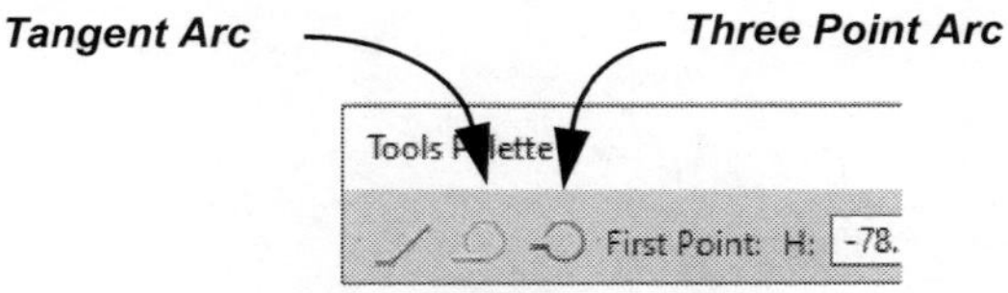

Figure 4–49

*The **Profile** tool needs to be active to display the **Tangent Arc** icon in the Tools Palette toolbar.*

The dimensions at the end of the arc on your sketch will be different. You are currently only concerned about the shape.

6. Drag the arc to **180°**, as shown in Figure 4–50. The arc highlights in blue once you reach 180°.

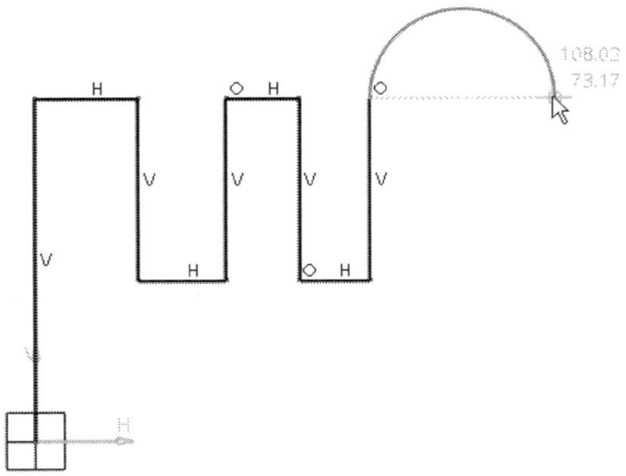

Figure 4–50

7. Draw a vertical line that is coincident with the intermediate horizontal lines, as shown in Figure 4–51.

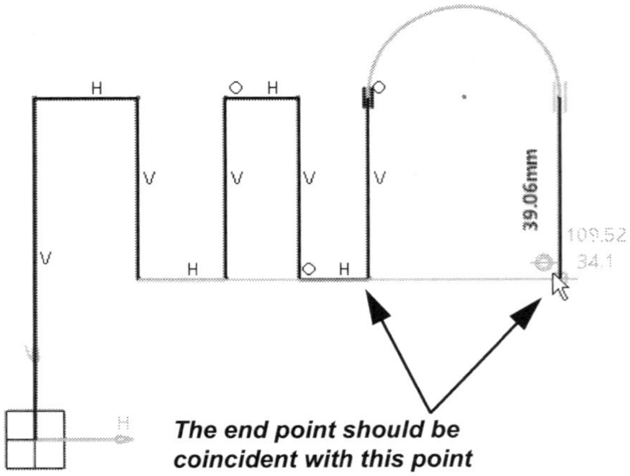

Figure 4–51

8. In the Tools toolbar, click 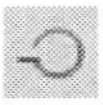 (Three Point Arc).

9. Sketch the three point arc shown in Figure 4–52. Try to make the end of the arc coincident with the horizontal axis and your last vertical line.

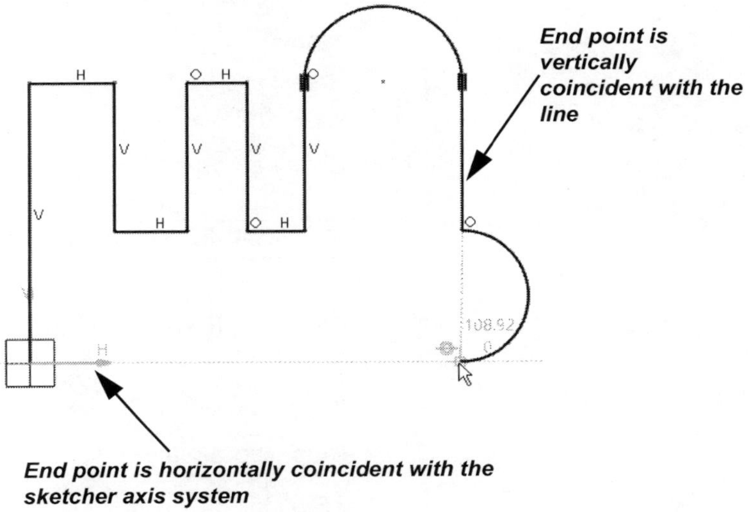

Figure 4–52

10. Drag the last horizontal line and connect it to the start point to close the sketch as shown in Figure 4–53.

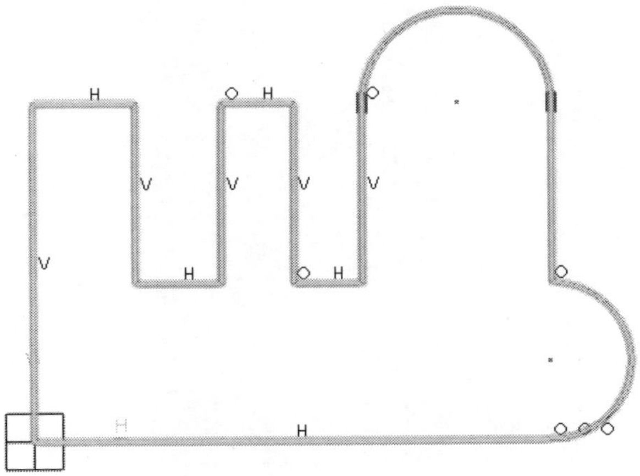

Figure 4–53

Task 3 - Select the profile.

In this task, you will demonstrate the use of the **Auto Search** option by selecting the 13 entities of the sketch.

1. Select any entity in the sketch and click (Auto Search) in the context toolbar. The software highlights the entire profile.
2. Select anywhere on the background to clear the profile.

Task 4 - Exit the Sketch app and save the part.

1. Click (Exit App) to exit the Sketch app.
2. In the Top Bar, click (Share)>**Save** to save the part.
3. Close the *Sketch_2 A.1* tab.

NOTE: Additional sketching practices are found in Practice B1 and Practice B2 at the end of this guide.

Chapter Review Questions

1. What is the process of accessing the Sketch app? (Select all that apply.)
    a. Select an appropriate sketch support and click .
    b. Click  and select an appropriate sketch support.
    c. When a CATIA part is created, the Sketch app is immediately opened.
    d. Select an appropriate sketch support and click .
2. All new parts start with what features?
    a. Pads
    b. Pockets
    c. Surfaces
    d. Default Reference Planes and the Part Body.
3. Which of the following statements best describes the default reference planes?
    a. They are the first solid feature.
    b. They have mass.
    c. They are the foundation of a part.
    d. They are not required and should be deleted.
4. If Figure 4–54 is shown in the Isometric view orientation, what is the sketching plane for the feature?

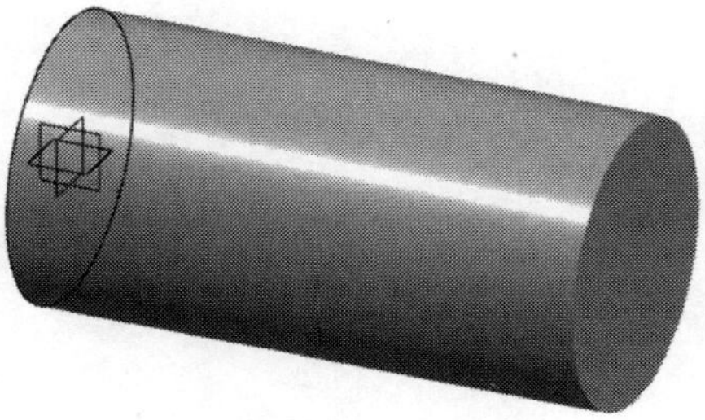

Figure 4–54

    a. XY plane
    b. ZX plane
    c. YZ plane

5. Which of the following icons enables you to sketch construction geometry?

    a. 

    b. 

    c. 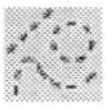

    d. 

6. Sketches are automatically hidden once they are referenced by a solid feature.

    a. True

    b. False

7. Which tool is the most efficient method of creating a series of connected lines and arcs?

    a. 

    b. 

    c. 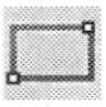

    d. 

8. When is a profile terminated? (Select all that apply.)

    a. When you form a closed loop.

    b. When you click  again.

    c. When you double-click.

    d. When you right-click and select **End Profile**.

Answers: 1ab, 2d, 3c, 4b, 5c, 6a, 7b, 8abc

Constraining Sketches

Constraints can be either geometric or dimensional. Geometric Constraints assess a relationship between geometric elements that forces a limitation, whereas dimensional constraints define the size and location of an element. In addition, the Auto Constraint feature creates the missing constraints to make the profile fully constrained.

Learning Objectives in This Chapter

- Understand the difference between Geometric, Dimensional, and Automatic Dimensional Constraints.
- Understand the advantages of using constraints to control sketches.
- Understand the various geometric constraints.
- Work with constraints and learn how to automatically constrain a sketch.
- Use the Edit Multi-Constraint dialog box to edit multiple dimensions before the section updates.
- Understand the system-defined constraint colors for the sketch status.
- Understand the Sketch Analysis dialog box and how to use its various tabs to analyze a sketch.

5.1 Constraints

Constraints define the size and location of a sketch. You can use dimensional and geometrical constraints, as shown in Figure 5–1.

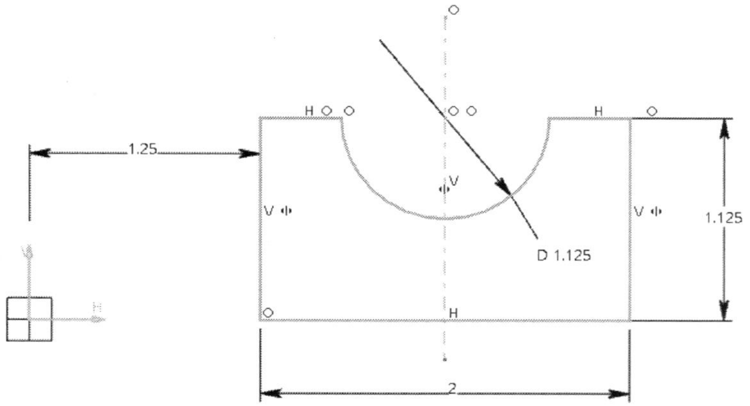

Figure 5–1

The constraints available, along with their icons in the Action Pad, are used to control their display. They are described as follows:

Icon	Constraint	Description
	**Geometrical Constraints**	Relationships between geometric elements that describe how they are oriented.
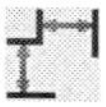	**Dimensional Constraints**	Values used to define the size, distance, or angle of an element.
	**Automatic Dimensional Constraints**	Automatically apply the values used to define the size or angle of elements as you sketch.

You can develop sketches that are completely unconstrained or partially unconstrained. Thus, you do not need to place any unnecessary dimensions on a sketch. However, it is recommended that you fully constrain your sketches.

Figure 5–2 shows an example of a partially constrained sketch. Initially, the box is 50 wide. When this dimensional constraint is changed to 100, the software updates one side of the box and leaves the other side in its original state. If the design intent of this sketch is to create a rectangle, the current design of this part requires additional constraints to maintain the geometry over time.

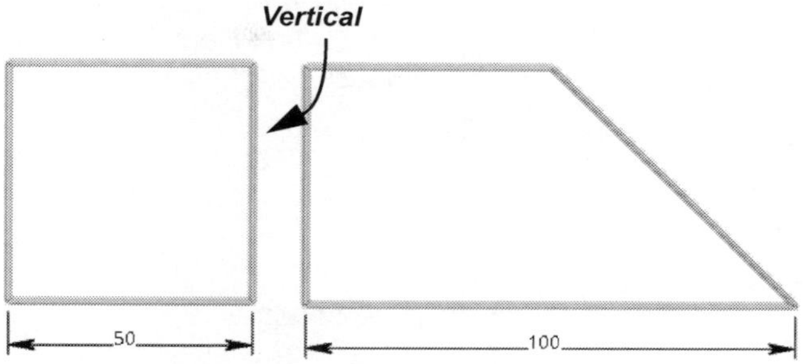

Figure 5–2

Constructing 3D solid models from unconstrained sketches can lead to unpredictable results. Figure 5–3 shows an example of an unconstrained Pocket. If the block is made wider or taller, what happens to the Pocket? Should it remain centered on the block or should it remain the same distance from the right or left side? This unpredictable nature can lead to undesirable shapes and update outcomes.

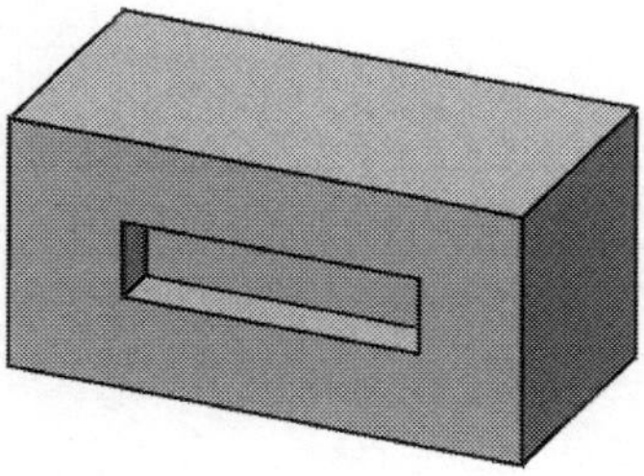

Figure 5–3

Advantages of Using Constraints

Using constraints has the following advantages:

- Dimensional constraints enable you to precisely define the size of your sketch and to quickly and accurately change its size.
- Geometric constraints enable you to incorporate design intent into your sketches, which automates the geometry update process.

5.2 Geometric Constraints

Geometric constraints can be created by selecting entities while 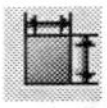 (Constraint) is enabled. As you select entities, the context toolbar displays with constraints applicable to the selected entities. For example, if two lines are selected, the context toolbar provides access to the Dimension, Parallelism Constraint, Perpendicular Constraint and so on, as shown in Figure 5–4.

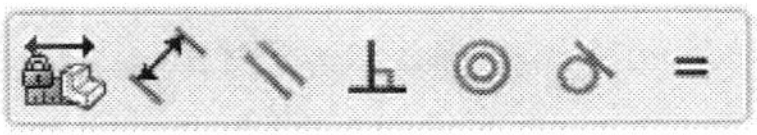

Figure 5–4

The constraints in the context toolbar will vary depending on the type of entity selected.

Geometric constraints consist of a relationship between geometric elements that forces a limitation of some type. For example, you can constrain a line in a sketch to be vertical. With the vertical constraint in place, the line is limited and cannot be at an angle.

The most commonly-used geometric constraints are described as follows:

Constraint	Example	Description
Horizontal 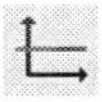	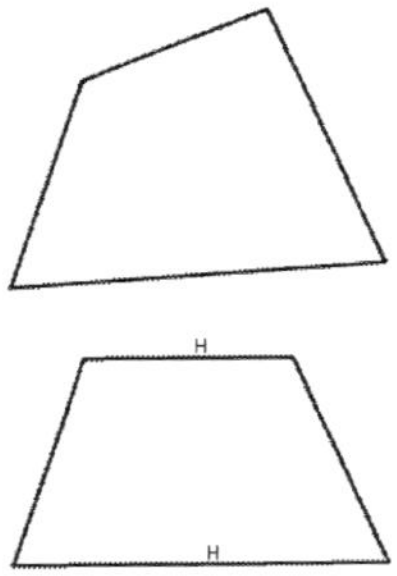	Use <Ctrl> to preselect the lines that are to be horizontal.

Vertical 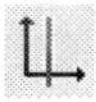	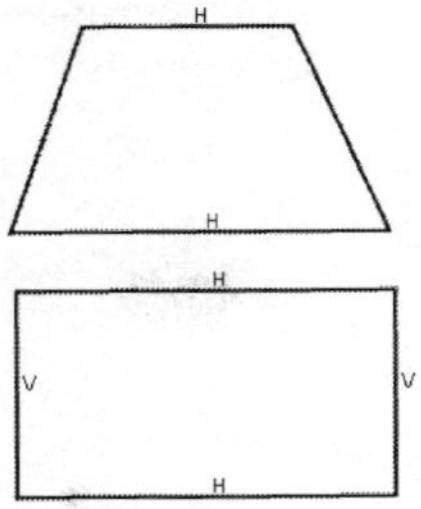	Use <Ctrl> to preselect the lines that are to be vertical.
Parallelism 	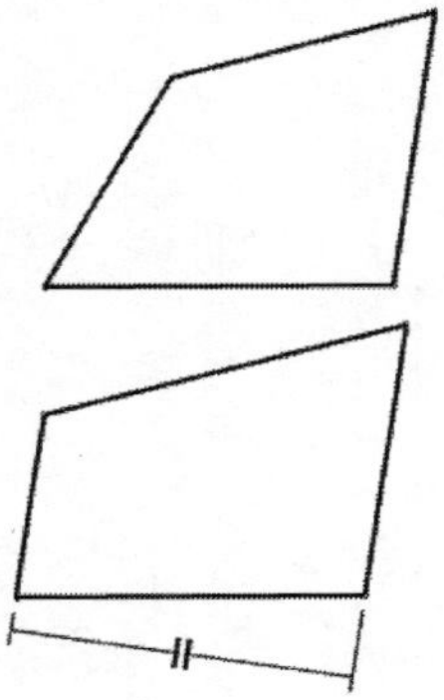	Select the first line to remain fixed, and select the second line to make parallel to the first.
Perpendicular 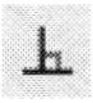	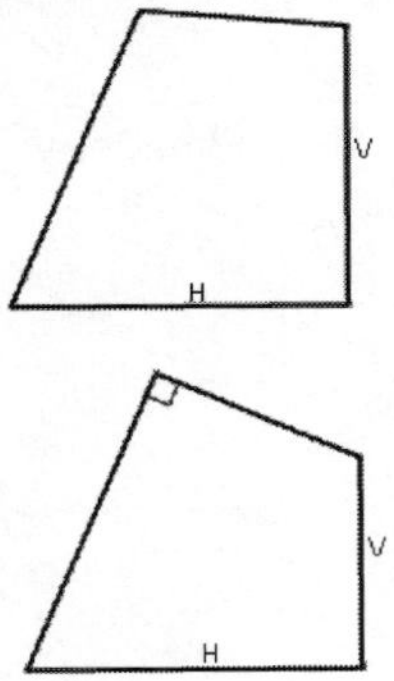	Use <Ctrl> to preselect lines to be perpendicular.

Concentricity or Concentric 	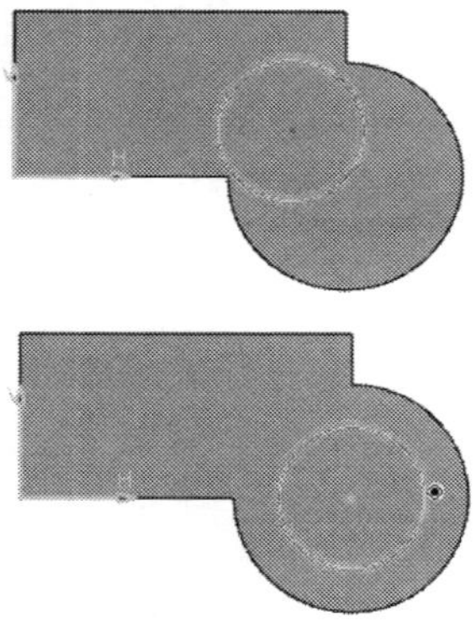	Select a curved edge of a Pad feature and the sketched circle. Concentricity only works with existing geometry.
Tangency 		Use <Ctrl> to preselect the entities to be tangent.
Symmetry 	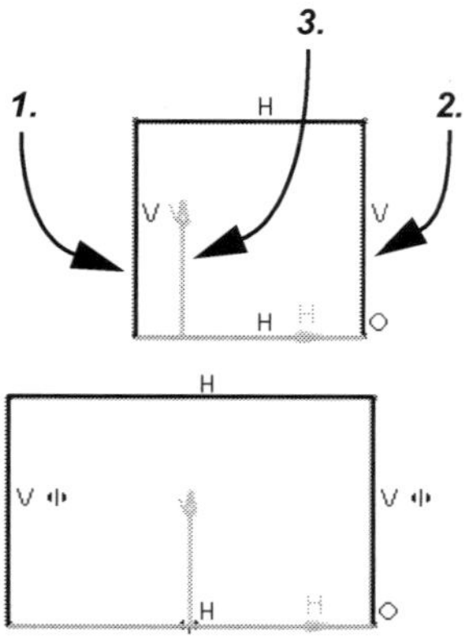	Press and hold <Ctrl> while selecting references in the following order: first symmetric element, second symmetric element, and symmetry reference.

Coincidence 	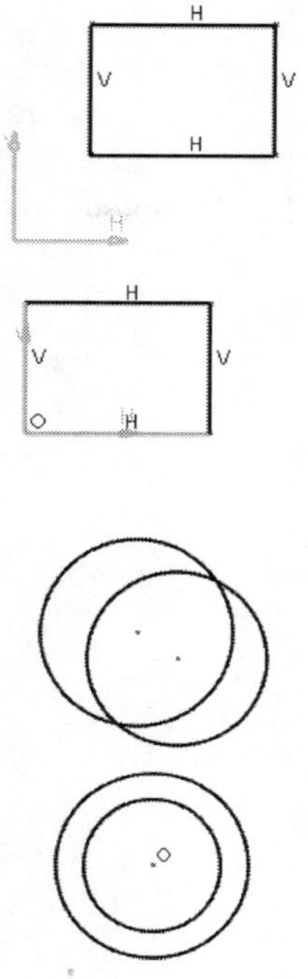	Select end points of entities to be coincident with one another and/or to another point. For circles, you must select the circle centers.
Equal 	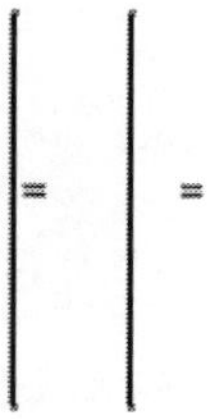	Select two entities to make their length, diameter or radii equal.

Shortcut Menu

The shortcut menu is another method to apply constraints. It provides access to frequently used geometric constraints and operations such as **Horizontal** or **Vertical** constraints for linear elements and **Close** or **Complement** operations for arcs. For example, a slanted line can be vertically constrained by right-clicking and selecting **Line.# object> Vertical**, as shown in Figure 5–5.

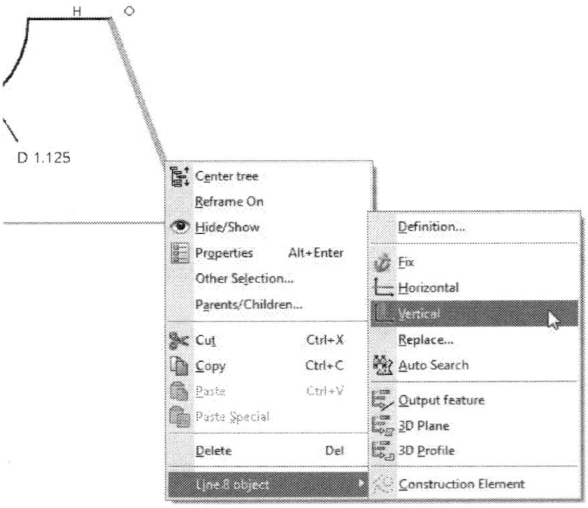

Figure 5–5

Geometric Constraints can also be generated using 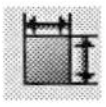 (Constraint) in conjunction with the shortcut menu.

How To: Place Geometric Constraints Using the Shortcut Menu

1. Select one or more geometric entities in your sketch.
2. Select 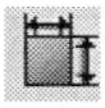 (Constraint) from the context toolbar or the *Sketch* section of the Action Bar.
3. Instead of clicking to place the dimension that displays, right-click to display the shortcut menu shown in Figure 5–6.

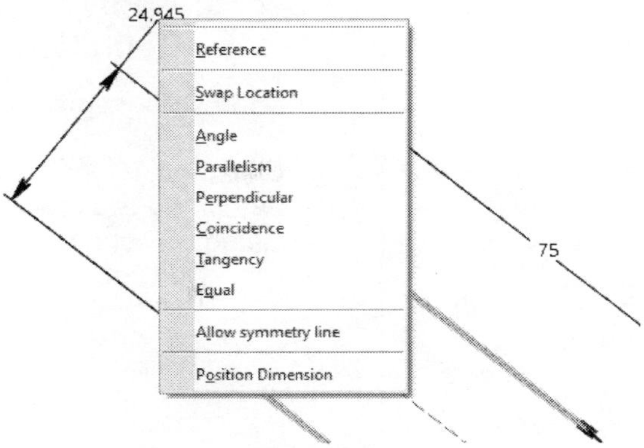

Figure 5–6

4. Select the geometric constraint you want to apply to the selected geometry from the shortcut menu. The geometric constraint is now applied as shown in Figure 5–7.

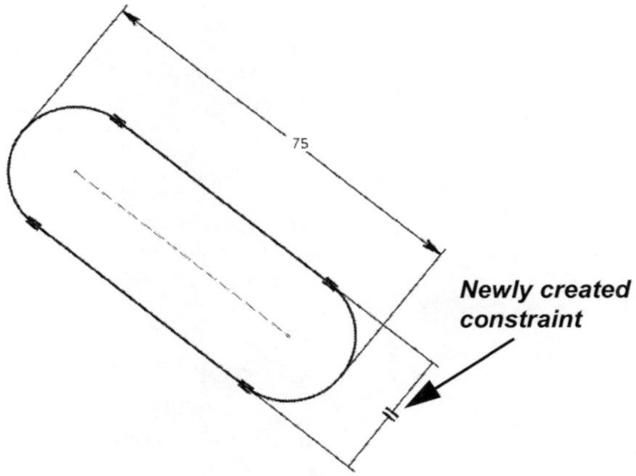

Figure 5–7

Repeat Steps 2 to 4 to place more geometric constraints.

Constraints Defined in Dialog Box

Another method for applying constraints is to use the (Constraints Defined in Dialog Box) option. This option displays a dialog box that shows the available constraints for the selected entities. Here you can select the constraints you want to enable.

How To: Apply a Constraint with the Constraint Definition Dialog Box

1. Use <Ctrl> to preselect the elements in the correct sequence.
2. Click  (Constraints Defined in Dialog Box).
3. Select the required constraint in the Constraint Definition dialog box shown in Figure 5–8.

Only the constraints that are valid for the elements you selected are available.

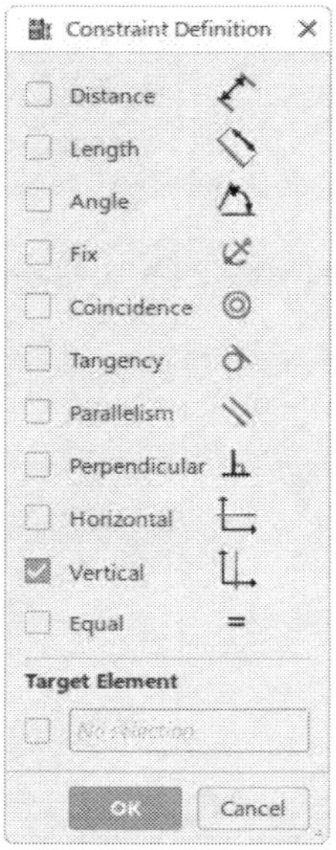

Figure 5–8

4. Click **OK**.

Note that you can apply constraints between entities using the **Target Element** option. Enable **Target Element**, click in the *Target Element* field and select an element from the sketch. The selected element will drive the resulting constraints.

Three lines were selected in Figure 5–9, and the top line, **Line.3**, is used as the Target Element. When the **Distance** constraint is selected, the dimensions for the distance between the lines, are added, using **Line.3** as the baseline.

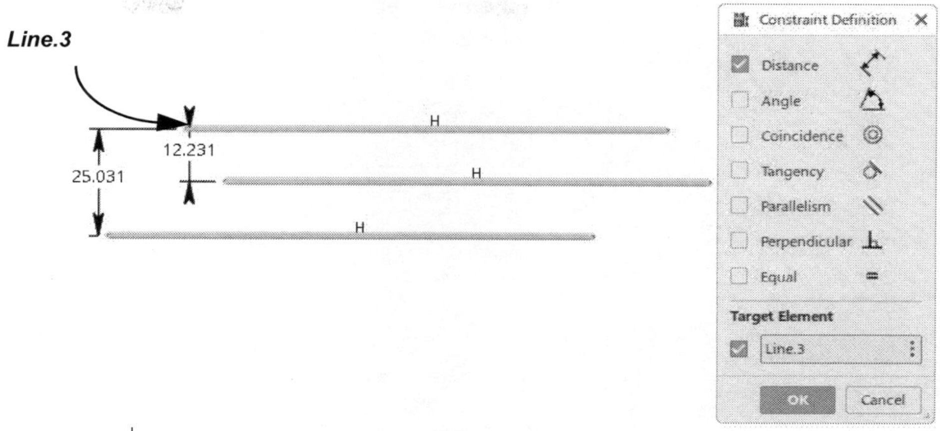

Figure 5–9

Deleting Constraints

Use one of the following methods to remove a constraint:

- Select the constraint symbol on the screen to highlight it, and press <Delete>.
- Select the constraint in the specification tree and press <Delete>.

Centering a Sketch

To center a sketch on a part, sketch an axis and use the **Symmetry** constraint to constrain the axis to the middle of the part. Use <Ctrl> to multi-select the two edges of the part, and then an axis. In the context toolbar, click (Fast Symmetry), and the selected entities are set to be centered around the vertical axis, as shown in Figure 5–10.

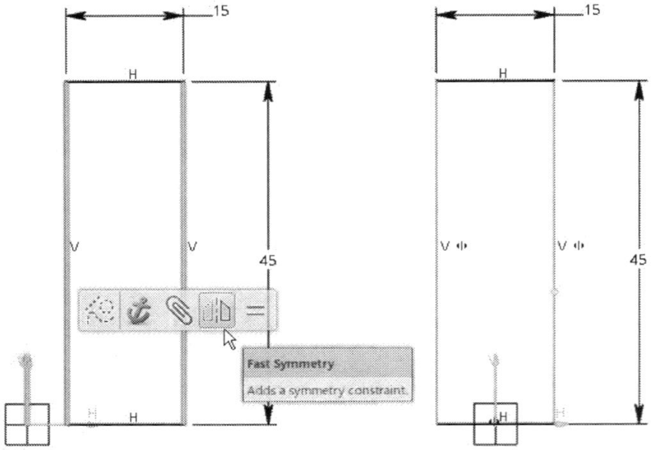

Figure 5–10

Group Constraint

The **Group** constraint constrains selected sketched elements together so that they can be moved as one entity.

How To: Group Elements Together

1. Select the entities to add by drawing a selection box around them, or by multi-selecting with <Ctrl>.
2. Click  (Group). The Group Definition dialog box opens as shown in Figure 5–11.
3. Click **OK**. The sketch elements can be dynamically moved using the cursor, as shown in Figure 5–12.

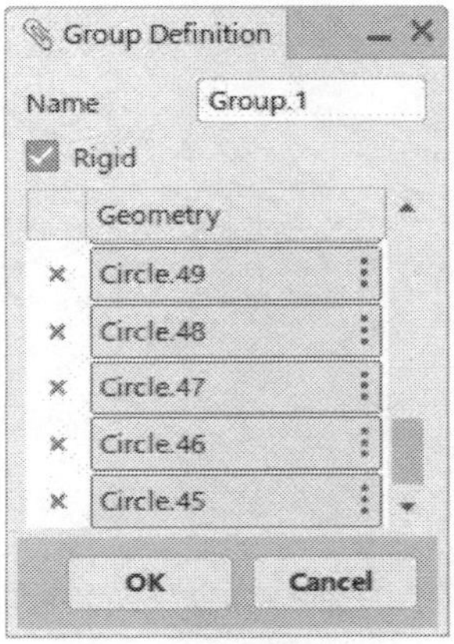

Figure 5–11

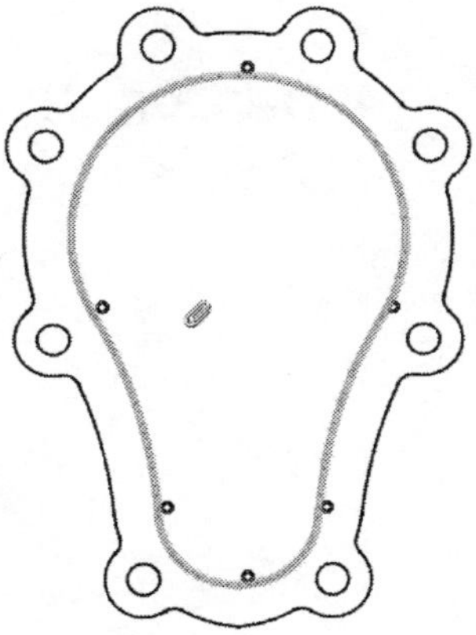

Figure 5–12

5.3 Dimensional Constraints

Dimensional constraints define an element's size and location. In most cases, you need to create several dimensions. Double-click on 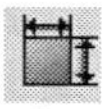 (Constraint) to create as many dimensions as you require without having to click the icon every time.

The following topics describe how to create various dimension types.

Line Length Dimension

To dimension a line, select the line to be dimensioned and drag the dimension to the required location, as shown in Figure 5–13.

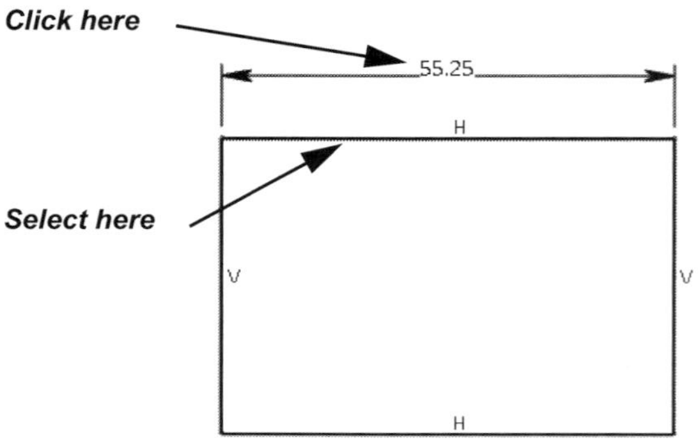

Figure 5–13

Distance between Parallel Lines

To dimension the distance between parallel lines, select the first line. A length dimension displays. Select the second line. The distance between the two lines displays. Click to place the dimension. An example is shown in Figure 5–14.

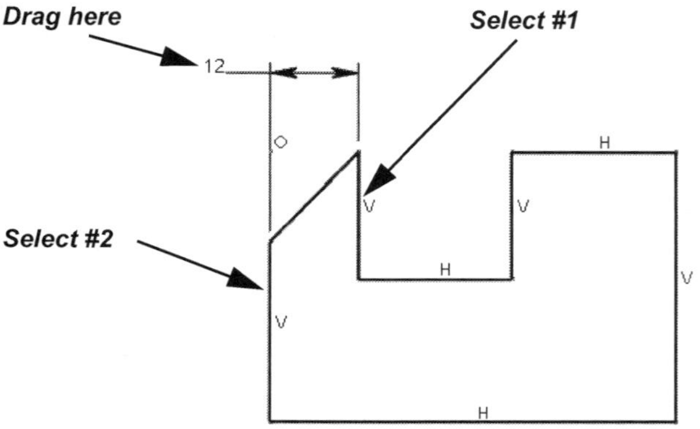

Figure 5–14

Arc Radius

To create an arc radius dimension, sketch a corner and the dimension is automatically created. To manually create an arc radius dimension, select the arc and click a location on the screen to place the dimension, as shown in Figure 5–15.

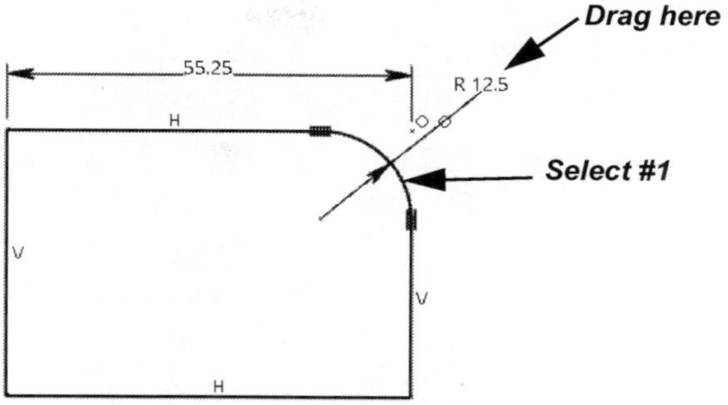

Figure 5–15

Arc Diameter

To dimension an arc as a diameter, you can use one of the following methods:

- A radius dimension displays by default when you select the arc. Before placing the dimension, click  (Diameter Constraint) in the context toolbar, or right-click and select **Diameter**, as shown in Figure 5–16.

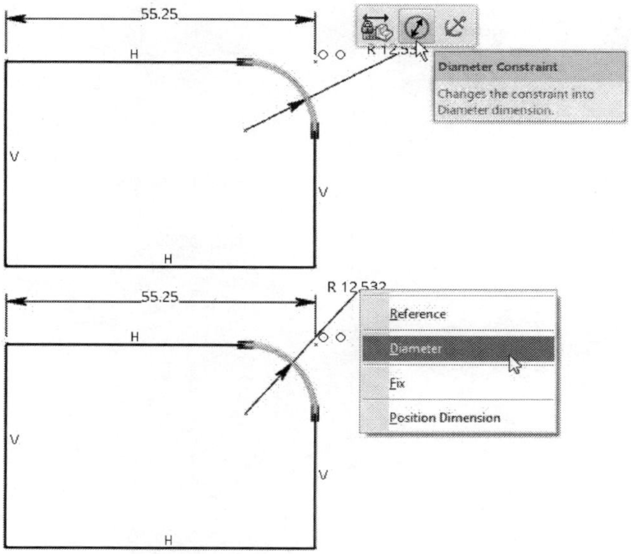

Figure 5–16

- Convert an existing arc radius dimension into a diameter dimension by double-clicking on the radius dimension. The Radius dialog box opens. Select **Diameter** in the dimension drop-down list and click **OK** to complete the change, as shown in Figure 5–17.

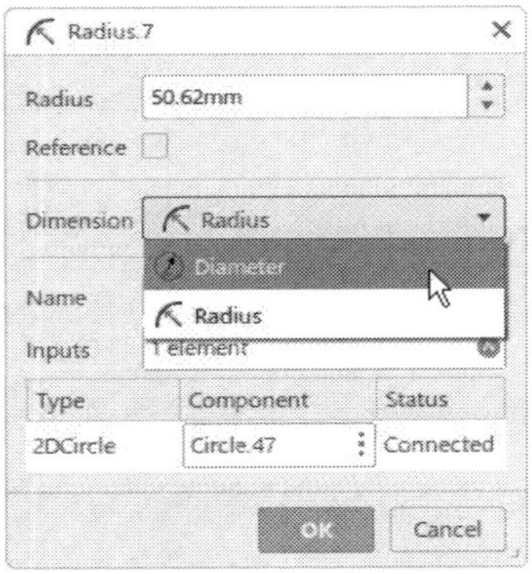

Figure 5–17

Revolved Diameter

The revolved diameter can only be created using an axis and not a construction line.

When creating sketches for revolved features, only half of the profile is sketched. It is then revolved about the centerline. To create this dimension, select a line element and an axis. By default, a dimension representing the distance between the two parallel elements displays. Before placing the dimension, right-click and select **Diameter**, as shown in Figure 5–18.

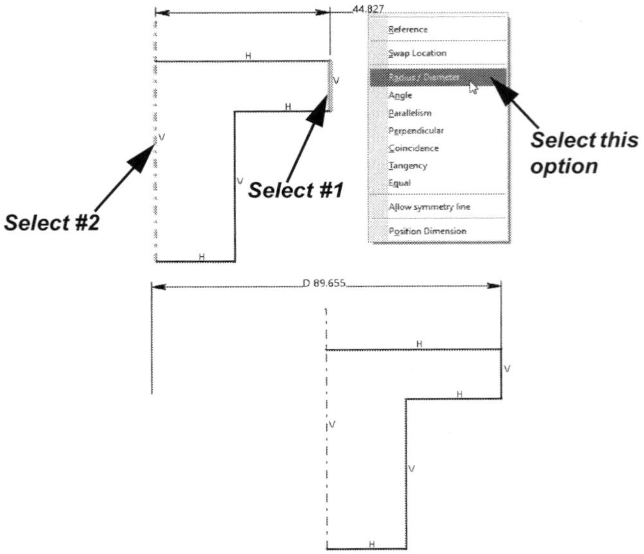

Figure 5–18

Angle Dimension

To create an angle dimension, select two non-parallel lines and an angle dimension displays. The dimension location determines how the angle dimension displays. The result of placing an angle dimension in four different locations is shown in Figure 5–19.

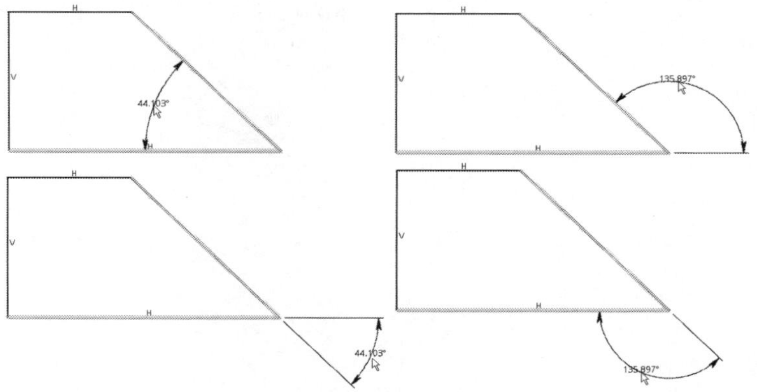

Figure 5–19

Point-to-Point Dimension

Point-to-point dimensions can be created between any two of the following elements:

- Center of an arc or circle
- End of a straight line
- Construction point

By default, the dimension displays as the absolute distance between the points. Before placing the dimension, use the shortcut menu to display the dimension as the horizontal or vertical distance between the points. These dimension options are shown in Figure 5–20.

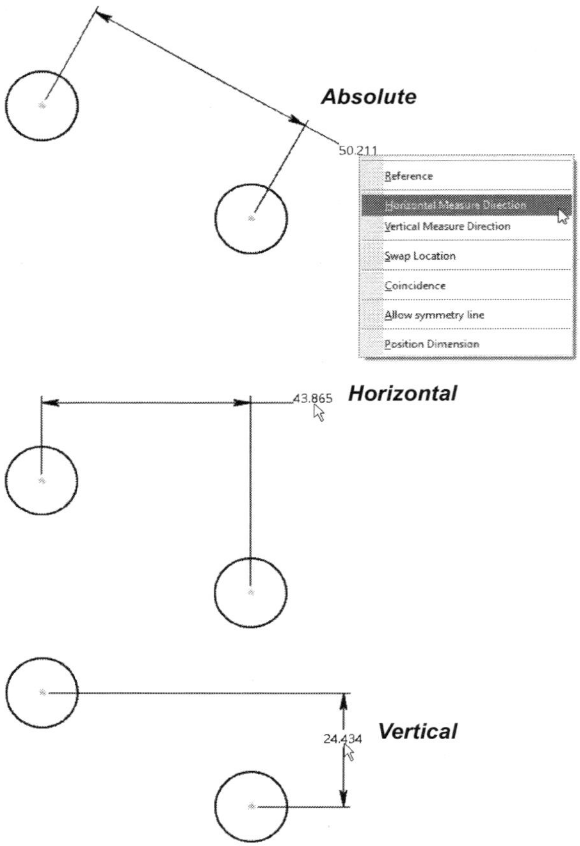

Figure 5–20

Line-to-Arc Tangent

You can also dimension to the arc center by selecting on the point.

To create a line-to-arc tangent dimension, select the line as the first element to dimension from. The line length dimension displays. Ignore this dimension and select the arc. The arc tangent dimension displays as shown in Figure 5–21.

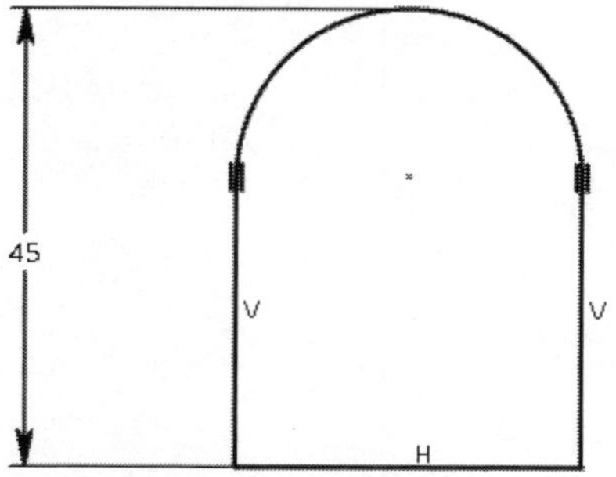

Figure 5–21

Arc Tangent-to-Arc Tangent

Select each of the arcs and drag the dimension to the required location. By default, the dimension displays as the absolute distance between the arc tangents, as shown in Figure 5–22.

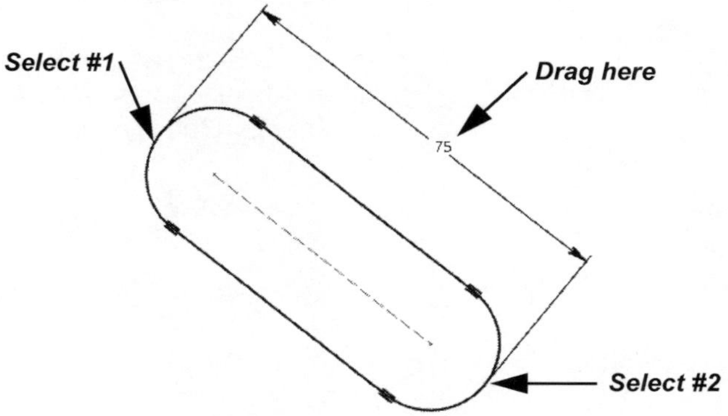

Figure 5–22

Before placing the dimension, you can use the shortcut menu to display the dimension as the horizontal or vertical distance between the arcs.

5.4 Automatic Dimensional Constraints

By default, in the *Sketch* section of the Action Bar, the 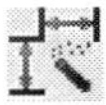 (Automatic Dimensional Constraints) is enabled, as shown in Figure 5–23.

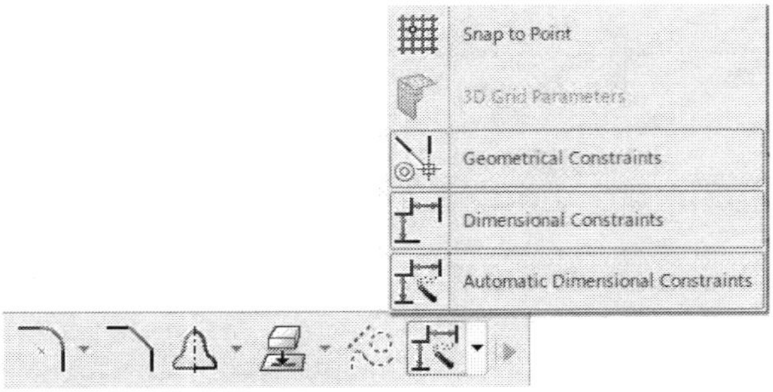

Figure 5–23

With this option enabled, the system automatically adds dimensional constraints as you sketch geometry.

In Figure 5–24, as soon as the rectangle is sketched, the system automatically determined the required dimensions to constrain it and applied them accordingly.

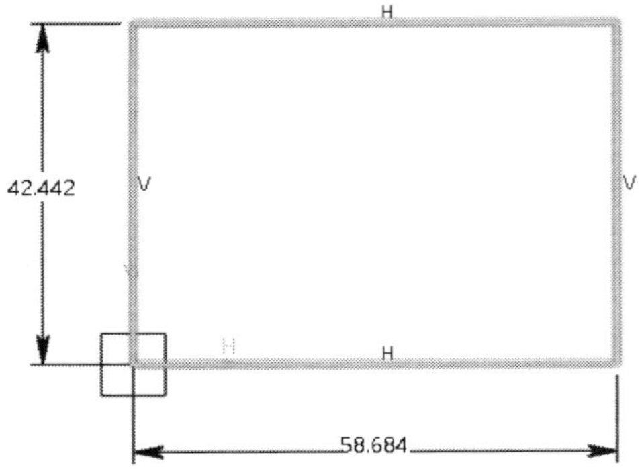

Figure 5–24

You can edit the dimensions to finalize them, as required. Automatic dimensional constraints are only applied to rectangles, circles, arcs and ellipses, and will only be added to define the size of an element, not its location relative to other elements.

5.5 Edit Multi-Constraint Dialog Box

The Edit Multi-Constraint dialog box enables you to modify the value of more than one dimension before updating the section. This is useful when modifying all dimensions of an oversized section. Typically, you would have to select the order of modification carefully to ensure that the modified dimension does not cause the section to fail. Using the **Edit Multi-Constraint** tool, you can modify all dimension values, and then preview and accept the changes.

The **Multi-Constraint** tool is found in the Constraint toolbar shown in Figure 5–25.

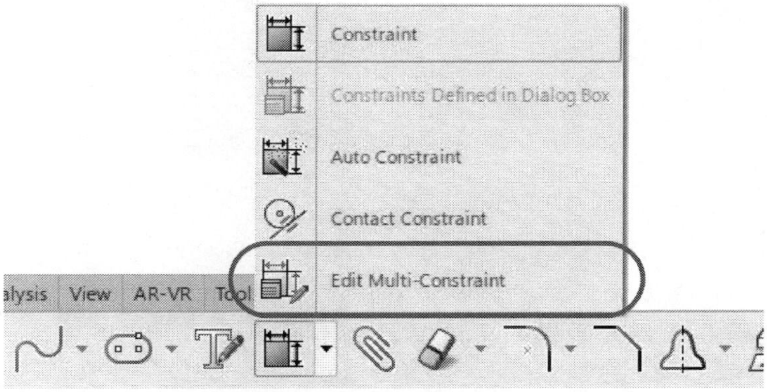

Figure 5–25

How To: Modify Dimensions Using the Edit Multi-Constraint tool

1. Click (Edit Multi Constraint) in the Action Bar.
2. The Edit Multi-Constraint dialog box opens. The software displays the constraint name, initial value, current value, and the maximum and minimum tolerances for each dimension in the section as shown in Figure 5–26.

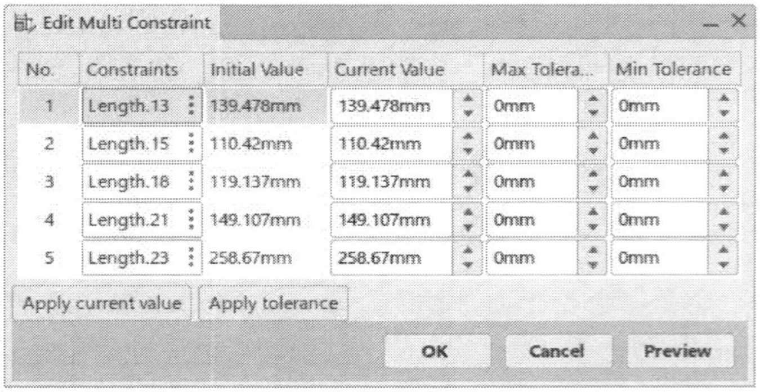

Figure 5–26

3. Select the dimension from the list or directly from the model. The corresponding dimension highlights in light blue on the section.
4. In the *Current value* field, enter a new value. The dimension highlights in cyan to indicate that the initial value has been modified.
5. Once all dimensions have been modified, click **Preview** to preview the changes to the section.
6. Click **OK** to complete the changes. If an error occurs, click **Restore Initial Value** to undo the modification to the selected dimension.

Tips and techniques

- You can modify or restore multiple dimensions by using <Ctrl> to select them.
- Maximum and minimum tolerances can be added to any dimension by selecting it and entering the tolerance in the appropriate field.
- You can right-click in the *Current value* field in the Edit Multi-Constraint dialog box to access standard constraint editing options, as shown in Figure 5–27.

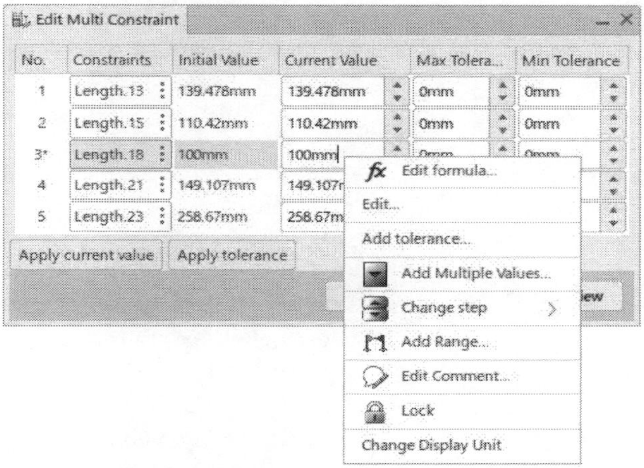

Figure 5–27

- For large, complex sections, click **Preview** frequently to update and test the section. If an error occurs, it is likely a dimension that was modified after the last preview.
- Selecting dimensions before clicking 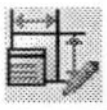 (Edit Multi Constraint) only adds those dimensions to the Edit Multi-Constraint dialog box.

5.6 Constraint Colors

To fully constrain your sketches, you must define the size and location of the sketch. For the first sketch on a new part, you must constrain the sketch to the horizontal and vertical axes, as shown in Figure 5–28.

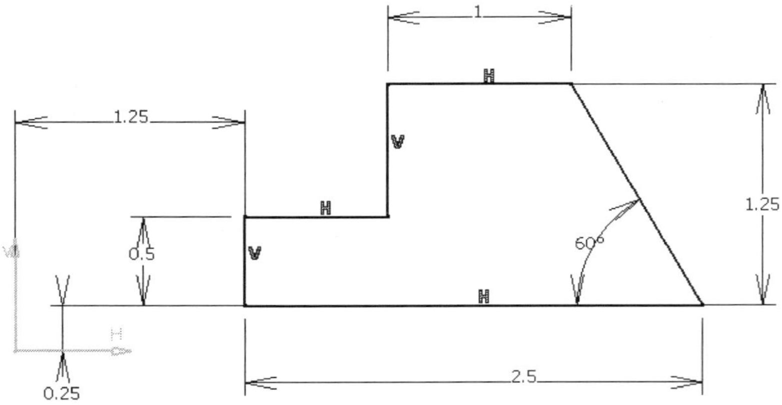

Figure 5–28

The software uses colors on the elements of your sketch to visually indicate the constraint status. These colors are described as follows:

Color	Definition	Description
Black	Under constrained	Some degrees of freedom still remain for the element.
Green	Constrained	The geometry is completely fixed and cannot be moved without altering a dimensional value.
Purple	Over constrained	Too many dimensions or geometric constraints are on the element.
Red	Inconsistent	The sketch cannot be solved with the current combination of constraints and values.
Brown	Not changed	Geometry that is dependent on over-defined or inconsistent elements and is not up to date.

5.7 Sketch Analysis

Once the sketch is created and constrained, you can analyze the sketch by clicking  (Sketch Analysis) in the *Analysis* section of the Action Bar. The Sketch Analysis dialog box opens as shown in Figure 5–29.

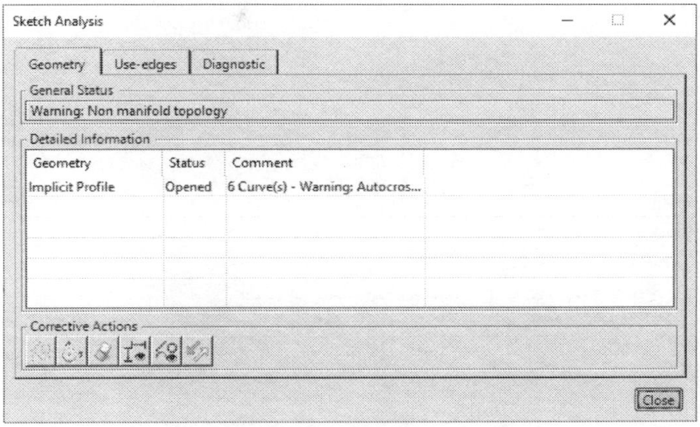

Figure 5–29

The following are examples of the types of analyses that can be performed:

- Ensure that the section meets the design intent.
- Ensure that the section is fully constrained.
- Check the status of projections and intersections.
- Perform corrective actions, as required.

Geometry Tab

The *Geometry* tab is used to analyze individual elements of the sketch. It displays the general status of the elements being analyzed. It is used to analyze the sketched elements and determine the status of each element in the model.

The different values available in the *Status* column are described as follows:

Status	Description
Opened	A collection of sketched entities that form an open loop. Open loops can occur when the start and end points of a loop appear to be touching, but actually have a gap between them.

Closed	A collection of sketched entities that form a closed loop.
Isolated	A single sketched entity that is not touching or connected to any other geometry in the section. This could indicate a line which should be converted to a construction line, or a line which should belong to a loop of entities, but has gaps at either end.
Wrong Point	A sketched point is connected to existing geometry. This indicates that the point should be converted to a construction point to be a valid section to create 3D geometry.

The *Geometry* tab also displays detailed information about each selected element type and general comments, as shown in Figure 5–30.

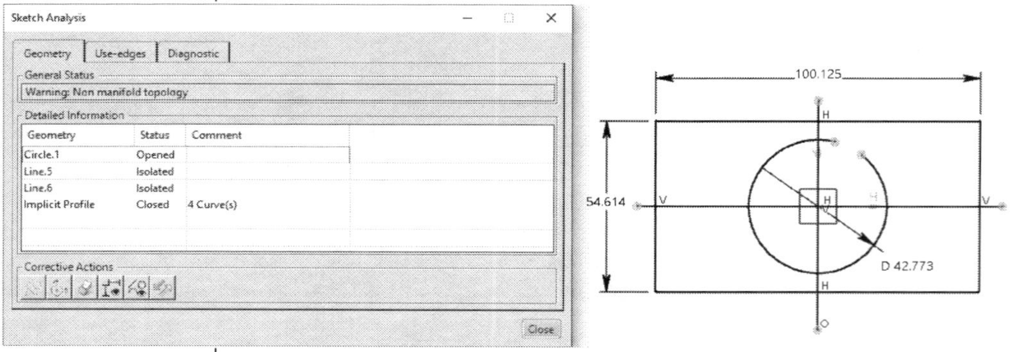

Figure 5–30

If you select an item in the Detailed Information area, the entity highlights on the screen, making it easier to find.

The sketch shown in Figure 5–30 has several problems. The detailed information displays that the circle is not closed (which is not the design intent) and that two line entities in the profile should be construction lines. The icons in the *Corrective Actions* area of the dialog box enable you to correct the problems in your sketch.

These icons are described as follows:

Icon	Description
	Changes the selected entity to a construction entity.
	Closes the open profile.
	Deletes the selected entity from the sketch.
	Toggles the display of constraints on and off in the sketch.
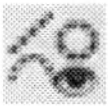	Toggles the display of construction geometry on and off in the sketch.
	Reverses the orientation of the sketched entity.

The icons in the *Corrective Actions* area correct the problem, as shown in Figure 5–31. **Line.5** and **Line.6** were converted to construction entities using . **Circle.1** was closed using .

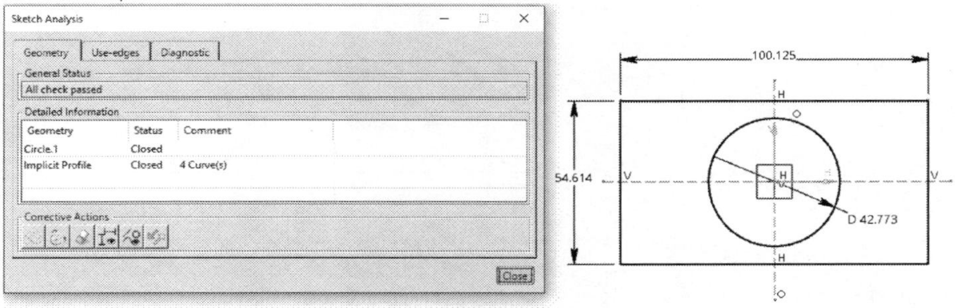

Figure 5–31

Use-edges

The *Use-edges* tab displays the status of all entities that are projected from existing geometry. The contents of this tab are discussed in detail once the concept of projecting 3D geometry has been introduced.

Diagnostic Tab

The *Diagnostic* tab provides a detailed summary of each sketched entity and the solving status of the sketch. A sketched entity can have one of the following three status values:

- **Under-Constrained:** Additional dimensions or constraints must be applied to the sketched entity.
- **Over-Constrained:** Too many dimensions or constraints have been applied to the element.
- **Iso-Constrained:** The entity is fully constrained.

The *Detailed Information* area lists all sketched entities, their current constraint status, and the type of entity (i.e., geometry, constraint, construction geometry, etc.), as shown in Figure 5–32.

You cannot edit the sketch while the tab is open. You must first exit the Sketch Analysis dialog box, solve any constraint issues, and re-open the dialog box to verify.

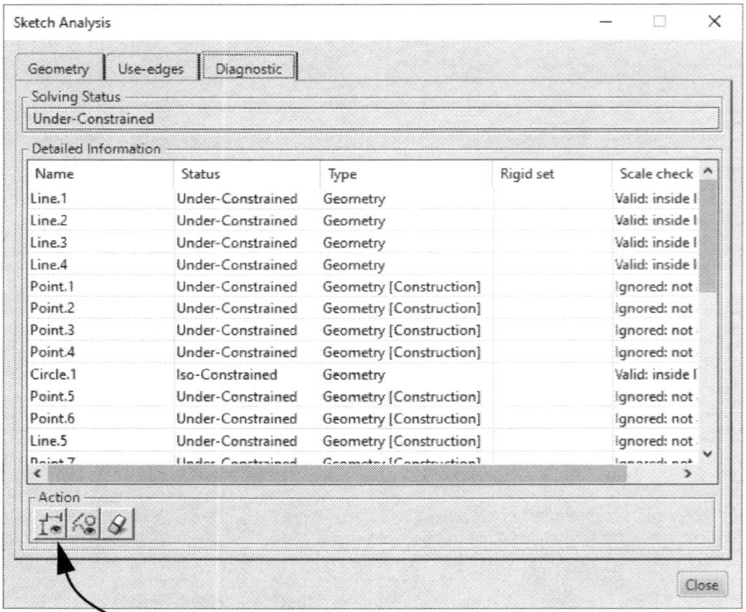

Hide/Show icons

Figure 5–32

The **Hide/Show** icons in the *Action* area can be used to simplify the screen. Select an entity in the *Detailed Information* area and select the appropriate icon to hide or show the entity.

Sketch Solving Status

The Sketch Solving Status dialog box is used to determine the constraint status of the sketch. A sketch can either be under-constrained, over-constrained, or fully constrained (Iso-constrained). If the section is over-constrained or under-constrained, the software highlights the affected entities on the sketch.

Click  (Sketch Solving Status) in the *Analysis* section of the Action Bar to open the Sketch Solving Status dialog box, as shown in Figure 5–33.

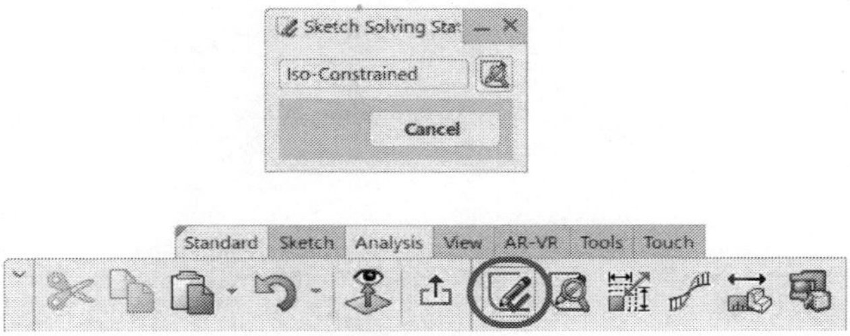

Figure 5–33

You can open the **Sketch Analysis** tool from this dialog box by clicking  (Sketch Analysis).

5.8 Auto Constraint

If you are having trouble eliminating all degrees of freedom, you can use  (Auto Constraint) to fully constrain your sketch. The **Auto Constraint** tool is found in the *Sketch* section of the Action Bar, as shown in Figure 5–34.

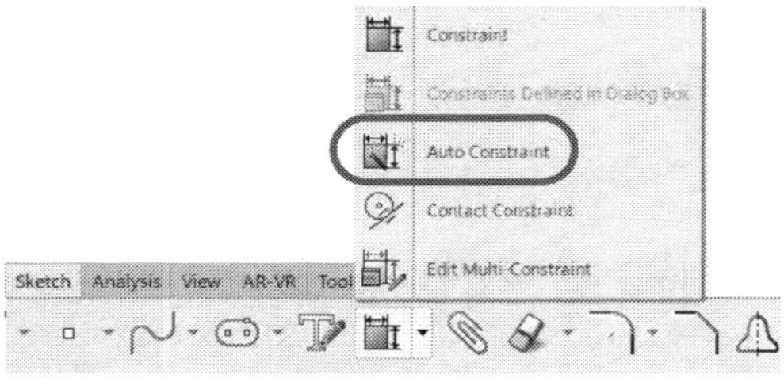

Figure 5–34

The Auto Constraint dialog box requires up to three sets of information. These are described as follows:

Information	Description
Elements to be constrained	These elements of your sketch display in black. When in doubt, select your entire sketch.
Reference elements	These elements are what your sketch is located to. For new sketches, select the horizontal and vertical axes.
Symmetry lines	If you want your sketch to be symmetrical, select the horizontal axis, the vertical axis, or a sketched axis.

The Auto Constraint dialog box opens as shown in Figure 5–35.

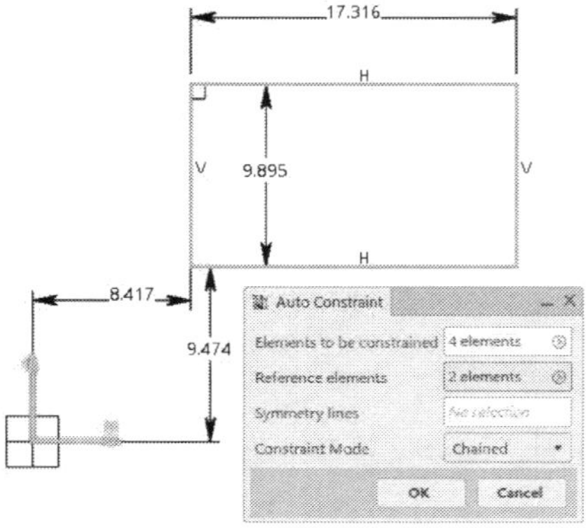

Figure 5–35

Practice 5a Dimensions

Practice Objectives

- Create a sketched profile.
- Create the dimensions required to fully define a sketch.
- Recognize when a sketch is under-constrained or constrained.

In this practice, you will create the sketch shown in Figure 5–36. You will constrain the sketch using geometrical and dimensional constraints. You will also be able recognize whether a sketch is under-constrained or over-constrained.

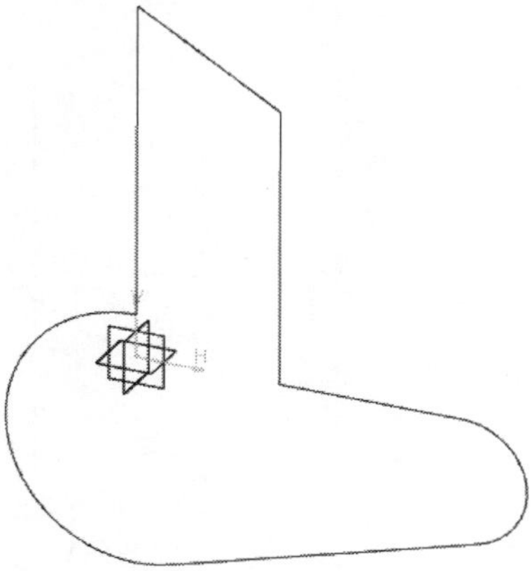

Figure 5–36

Task 1 - Create a new part and begin creating a sketch.

1. In the Top Bar, click  (Add)>**3D Part**.
2. In the 3D Part dialog box, enter **Constraints_1** as the *Title*.
3. Select the *3D Shape* tab and enter **Constraints_1** for the *Title*.
4. Select the *Characteristics* tab and ensure **Enable hybrid modeling** is disabled.
5. Click **OK**.
6. In the specification tree, select the YZ plane.
7. In the Action Bar, click  (Sketch).

Task 2 - Begin sketching the profile.

1. If necessary, right-click and select **Display>Action Pad**.

An activated icon displays with a blue highlight.

2. Verify  (Geometrical Constraints) is selected to enable automatic geometric constraints.

3. Ensure  (Automatic Dimensional Constraints) is disabled.

4. Sketch the part profile shown in Figure 5–37 using  (Profile). Verify that the arcs are tangent in the locations shown.

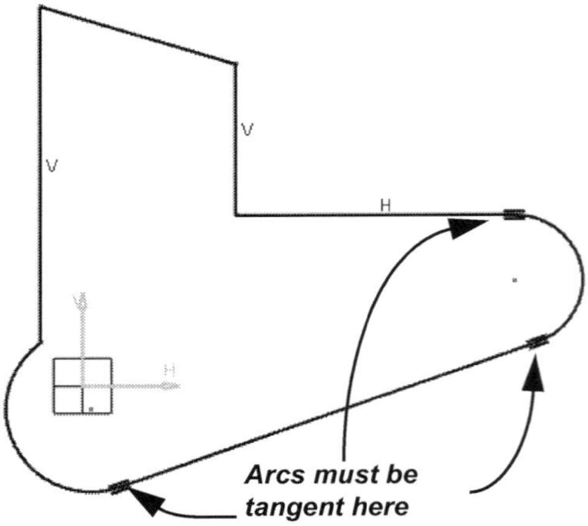

Figure 5–37

Task 3 - Perform a sketch analysis.

1. In the *Analysis* section of the Action Bar, click  (Sketch Solving Status). The Sketch Solving Status dialog box opens as shown in Figure 5–38.

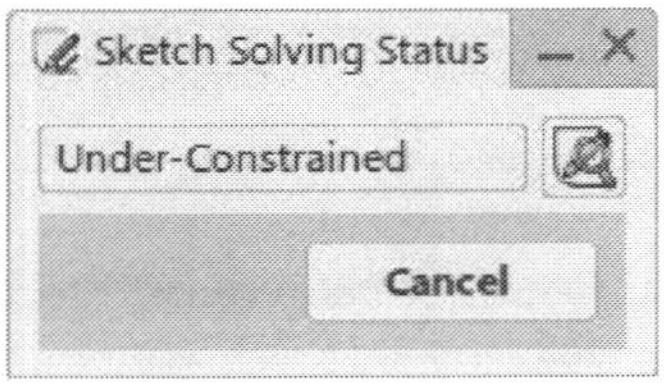

Figure 5–38

Design Considerations

The software reports that the section is under-constrained. Since no dimensions have been applied to the section, all entities are highlighted to indicate that they are under-constrained. You will apply dimensions to the section to constrain it in the part.

2. In the Sketch Solving Status dialog box, click (Sketch Analysis).

3. Select the *Geometry* tab. The Sketch Analysis dialog box opens as shown in Figure 5–39.

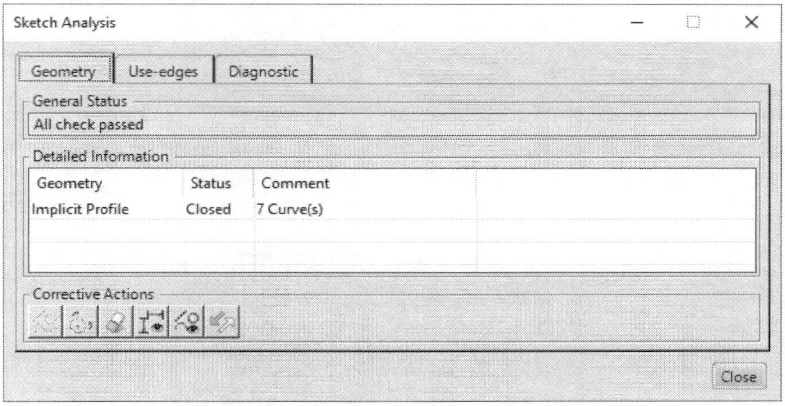

Figure 5–39

4. Verify that the software reports a closed status for the sketch and that only seven curves exist. If you receive a different result, verify that your section has been created correctly.

5. Close the Sketch Analysis dialog box.

Task 4 - Dimension the length of a straight line.

1. In the *Sketch* section of the Action Bar, click (Constraint) to start constraining.

2. Select the vertical line shown in Figure 5–40. Click the dimension to the left side of the line. Do not modify the default values of your sketch. You will adjust them later.

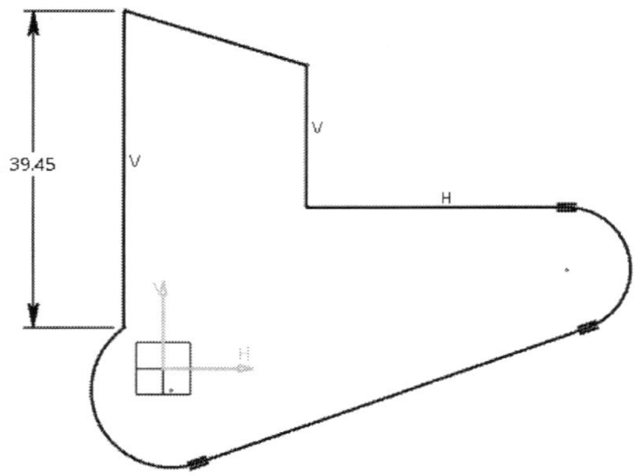

Figure 5–40

Task 5 - Dimension between parallel lines.

1. Note that 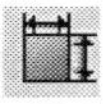 (Constraint) is no longer active. Select it again to create another dimension.

2. Select the short vertical line, as shown in Figure 5–41. A length dimension displays. You do not want this dimension. Select the long vertical line, and a dimension displays for the distance between the two lines.

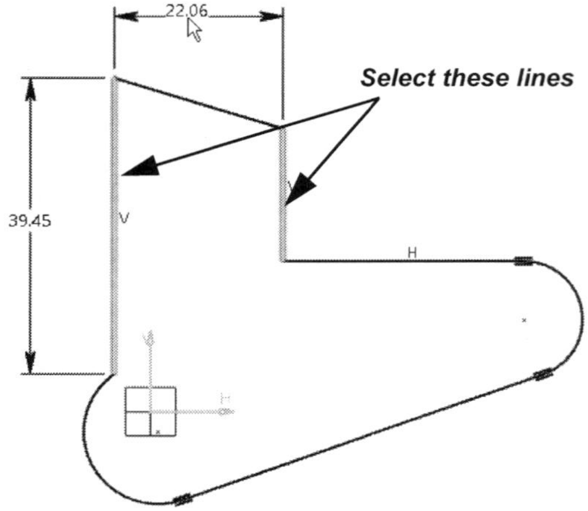

Figure 5–41

Task 6 - Enable continuous dimensioning and dimension the two arcs, one as a radius and one as a diameter.

1. Double-click on 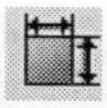 (Constraint) to enable continuous dimensioning. The icon remains enabled until you select another action.
2. Select the arc on the left side and click to place the radius dimension outside the sketch, as shown in Figure 5–42.
3. Select the other arc, and click  (Diameter Constraint) from the context menu, then click to place the dimension, as shown in Figure 5–42.

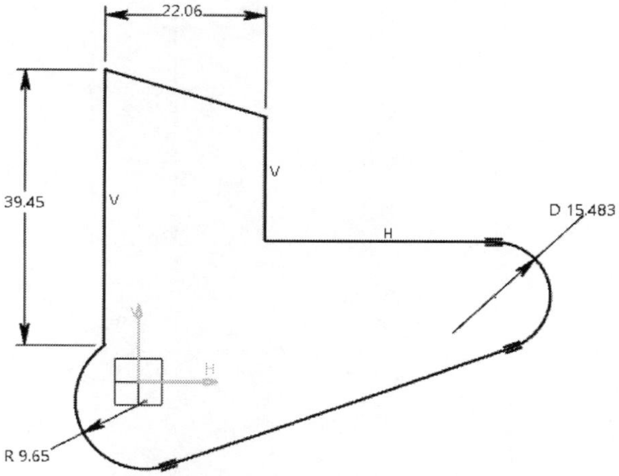

Figure 5–42

Task 7 - Change the radius dimension to a diameter dimension.

1. Click 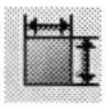 (Constraint) again to terminate dimension creation.
2. Double-click on the radius dimension.
3. In the Radius dialog box, using the Dimension drop-down list, select **Diameter**.
4. Click **OK** to complete the change.

Task 8 - Create an angle dimension.

1. Double-click on 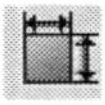 (Constraint).
2. Select the slanted line as the first element and the long vertical line as the second element, as shown in Figure 5–43. Before you place the dimension in its final location, move the cursor to other positions to preview the possible angle dimensions.
3. Place the angle dimension as shown in Figure 5–43.

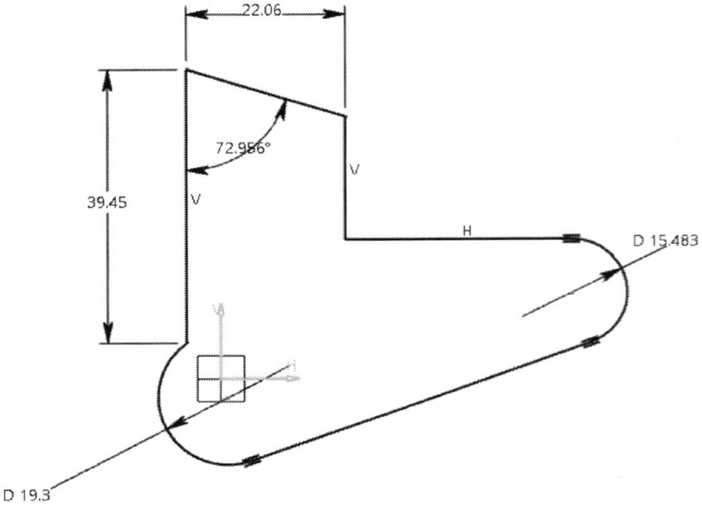

Figure 5–43

Task 9 - Create a horizontal dimension between the two arcs.

1. With 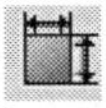 (Constraint) still be active, select each arc to initially create an absolute arc tangent dimension, but do not place the dimension.

2. Right-click and select **Horizontal Measure Direction**. The sketch displays as shown in Figure 5–44. Horizontal Measure Direction is also available in the context toolbar.

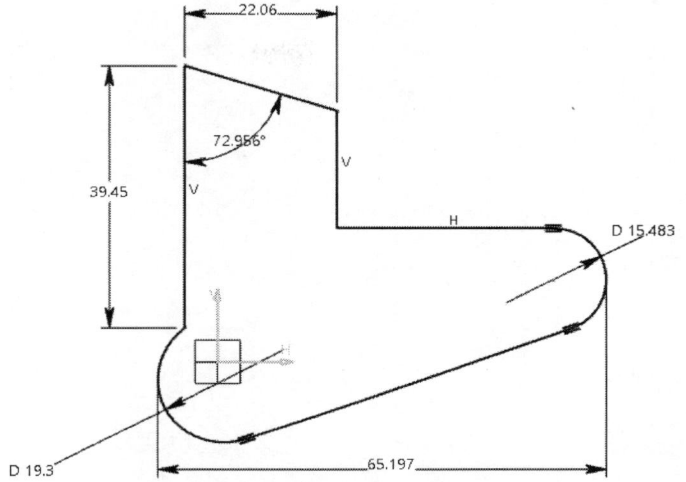

Figure 5–44

Task 10 - Create dimensions to fully constrain the sketch.

1. To finish constraining the shape of the sketch, create the two dimensions circled in Figure 5–45.

The 5.08 dimension is created by selecting the center point of the D51.664 arc and the 104.292 vertical line.

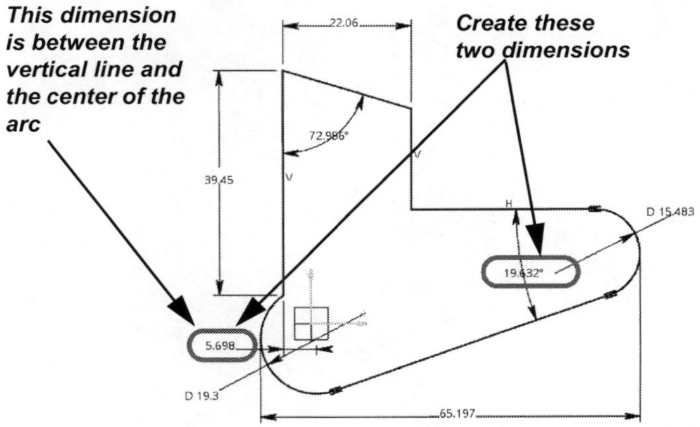

Figure 5–45

2. To constrain the location of the sketch relative to the datum planes, create the two dimensions circled in Figure 5–46. Create each dimension from the line to the horizontal or vertical axis.

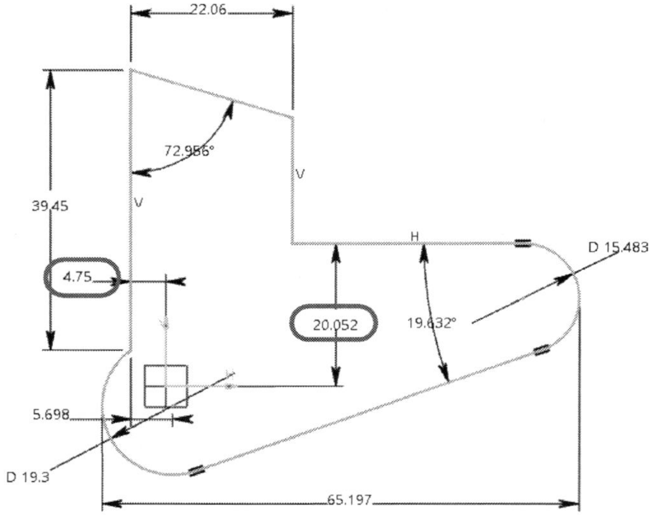

Figure 5–46

3. In the *Analysis* section of the Action Bar, click (Sketch Solving Status) to open the Sketch Solving Status dialog box, and verify that the section is fully constrained, as shown in Figure 5–47.

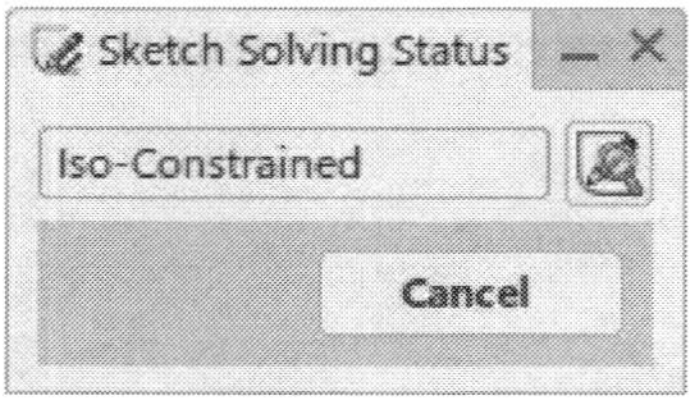

Figure 5–47

4. Click **Cancel** to close the dialog box.

Task 11 - Over-constrain the sketch.

1. Create a dimension for the length of the angled line, as shown in Figure 5–48.

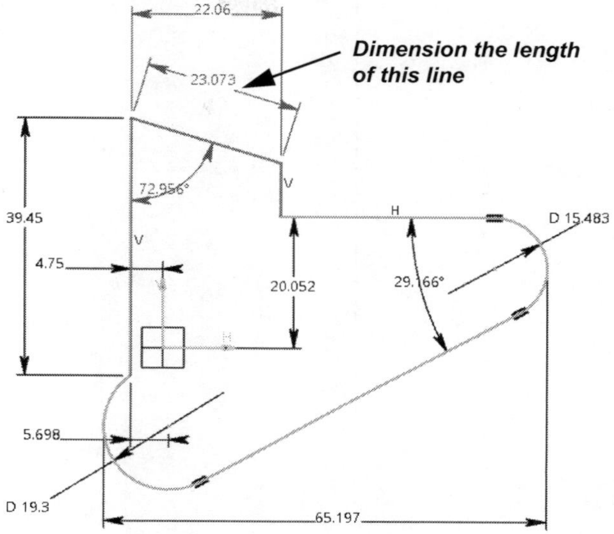

Figure 5–48

The sketch is now over-constrained, as indicated by the purple color of the affected sketch entities.

2. Click  (Sketch Solving Status). The software now reports that the sketch is over-constrained and highlights the three impacted sketch entities in light blue.
3. Close the Sketch Solving Status dialog box.

Remember that your dimensions will have different values.

4. Select the leader line of the **22.06** horizontal dimension, right-click and select **Delete**. If you select on the 22.06 number, it will attempt to change the number and not allow for the same right-click options. The sketch is again fully constrained (it will turn green).

Task 12 - Manipulate the dimensions.

1. Practice moving dimensions, as shown in Figure 5–49. Click the dimension's leader line to select the dimension it will turn light blue. Once selected, click and drag the number to move the dimension along the arrows. Click and drag the leader lines to move the dimension closer or farther from the sketch.

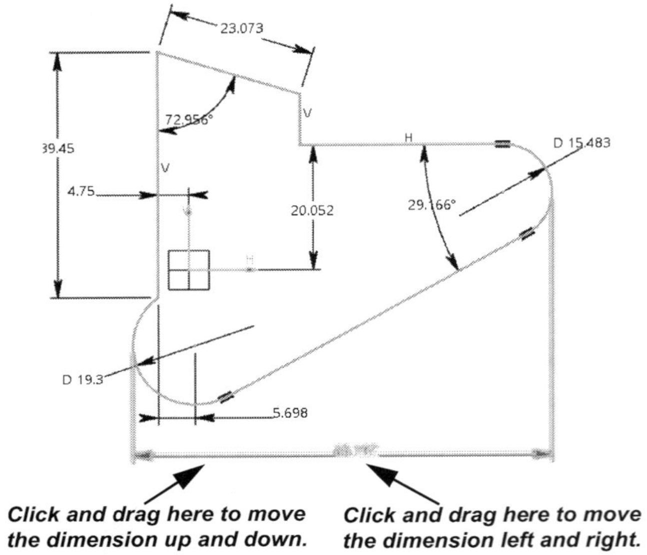

Figure 5–49

Task 13 - Modify the size of the dimensions.

1. Select the **72.956** angle dimension's number.
2. Set the *Angle* = value to **60.00** and press the **Enter** key.

3. Expand the (Constraint) fly-out and click (Edit Multi Constraint), as shown in Figure 5–50.

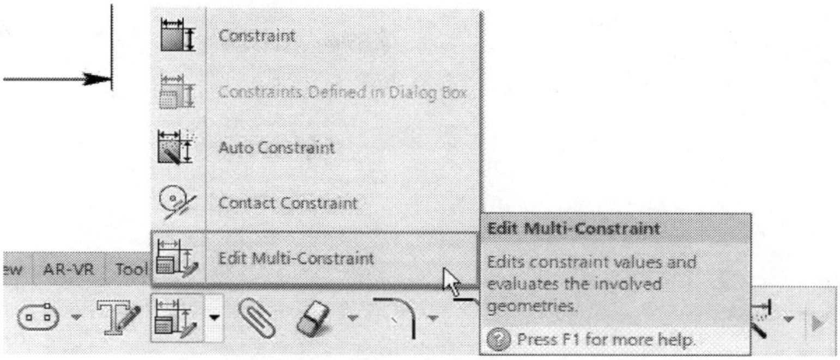

Figure 5–50

4. The Edit Multi-Constraint dialog box opens as shown in Figure 5–51. It contains all constraints in the sketch and their values.

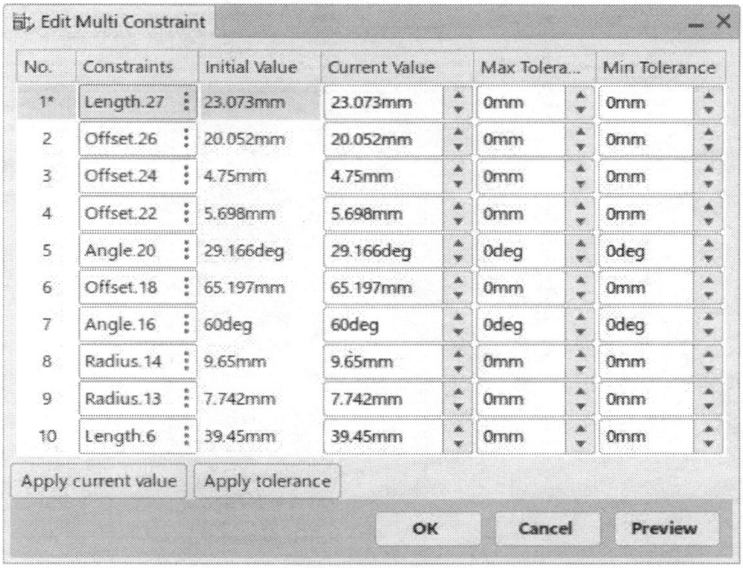

Figure 5–51

The constraint is highlighted in the sketch when you select it in the list.

Design Considerations

Be sure to enter half the diameter for the radius constraints, since both radius and diameter dimensions are represented using a radius.

Note that all entities are green, indicating that the sketch is fully constrained.

5. In the Edit Multi-Constraint dialog box, select each dimension and modify its value in the field below the list to the value shown in Figure 5–52.

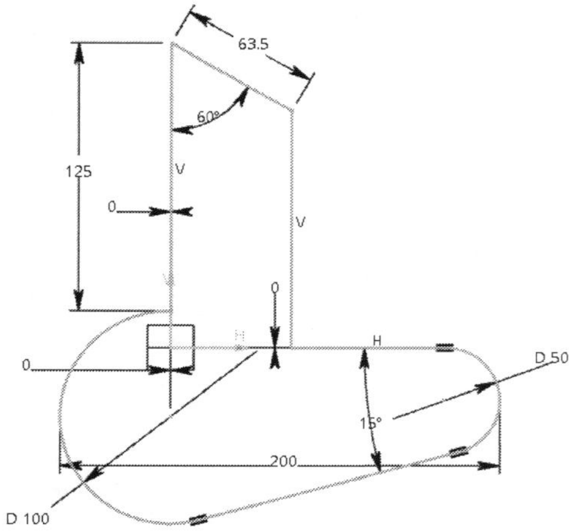

Figure 5–52

6. Click **Preview** to display the changes and then click **OK**.

Task 14 - Exit Sketcher and close the window.

1. Click (Exit App). The sketch displays as shown in Figure 5–53.

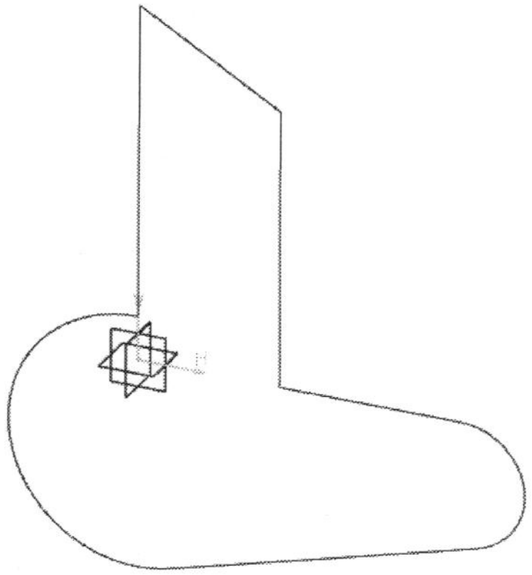

Figure 5–53

2. In the Top Bar, click (Share)>**Save** to save the part.
3. Close the *Constraints_1 A.1* tab.

Practice 5b

Constraints

Practice Objective

- Apply a variety of constraints to document the design intent of the sketch.

In this practice, you will create the sketch shown in Figure 5–54. You will gain an understanding of how geometrical constraints interact with one another. This practice will focus on driving the geometry through the use of constraints.

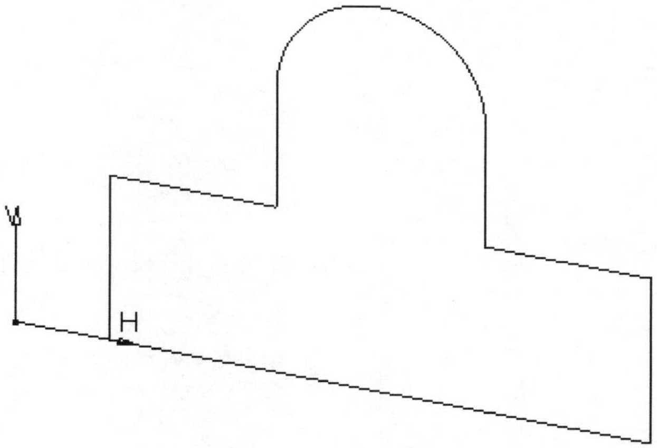

Figure 5–54

Task 1 - Create a new part and begin creating a sketch.

1. In the Top Bar, click  (Add)>**3D Part**.
2. In the 3D Part dialog box, enter **Constraints_2** as the *Title*.
3. Select the *3D Shape* tab and enter **Constraints_2** for the *Title*.
4. Select the *Characteristics* tab and ensure **Enable hybrid modeling** is disabled.
5. Click **OK**.
6. In the specification tree, select the YZ plane.
7. In the Action Bar, click  (Sketch).

Task 2 - Begin sketching the profile.

1. Ensure that the Sketch Action Bar is available.

2. Ensure that  (Geometrical Constraints) is selected, to enable automatic geometric constraints, as shown in Figure 5–55.

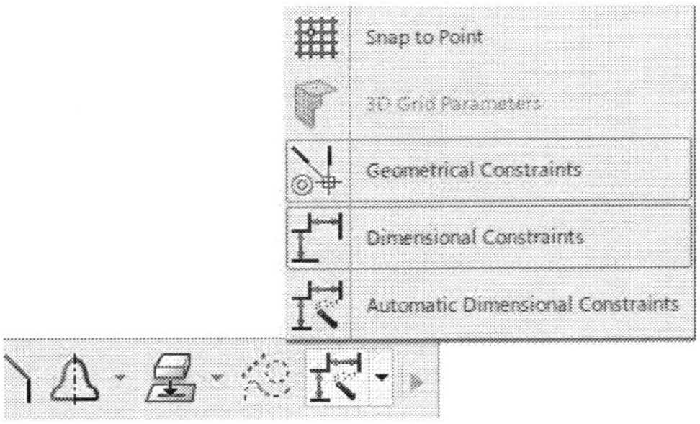

Figure 5–55

3. Sketch the profile and the axis, as shown in Figure 5–56.

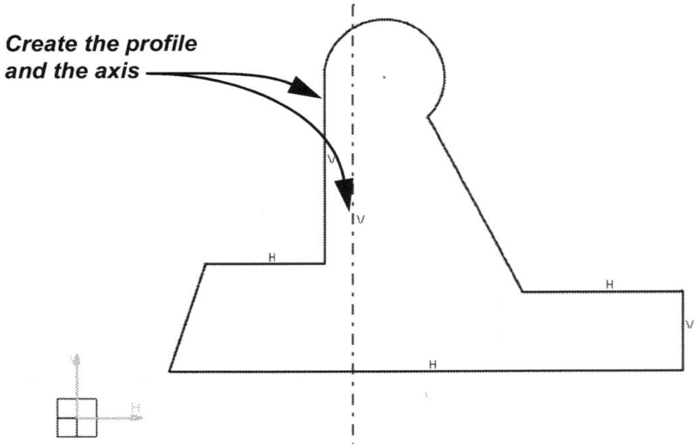

Figure 5–56

4. Use the Sketch Analysis to confirm that the section consists of one close profile that is constructed using 8 curves.

Task 3 - Make a slanted line vertical.

1. Select the slanted line shown in Figure 5–57 and click (Geometrical Constraints) to make the line vertical.

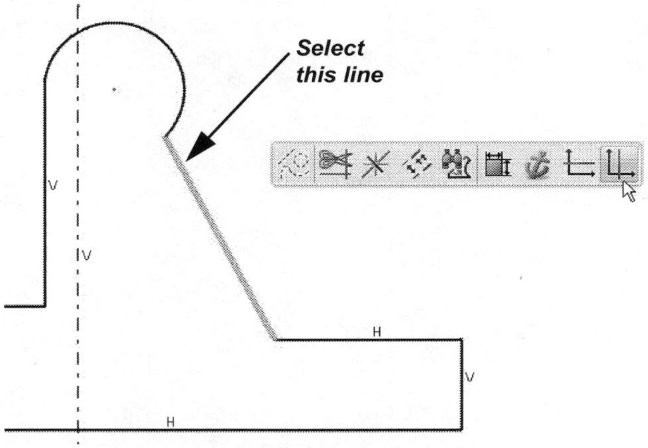

Figure 5–57

2. Click (Undo) to repeat the constraint another way.
3. Right-click on the line and select **Line.# object>Vertical**, as shown in Figure 5–58.

Figure 5–58

Design Considerations

This practice demonstrates the most efficient method of creating a geometric constraint in a sketch. Depending on the scenario, this might involve using a combination of icons and shortcut menu options. In each case, (Constraints Defined in Dialog Box) can be used instead. The corresponding option in the dialog box will be indicated in the margin. For example, the option for the **Horizontal** constraint displays as shown in Figure 5–59.

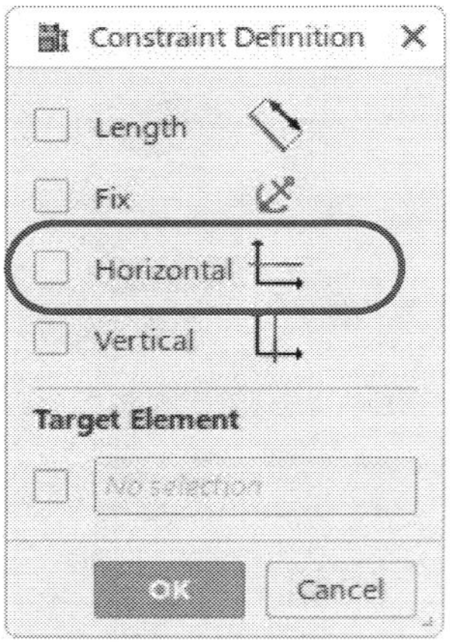

Figure 5–59

Task 4 - Make two lines coincident.

Enabling the Constraint icon also enables the Constraint context toolbar that appears on screen when selecting entities. If the toolbar does not appear, verify that the Constraint icon is active.

1. In the Action Bar, double-click on (Constraint) to define a series of constraints. Select the horizontal lines shown in Figure 5–60. This will begin the creation of a dimension between the two entities. Do not place the dimension.

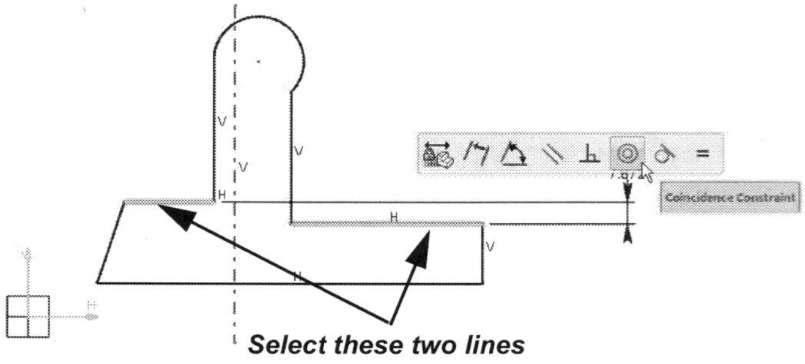

Figure 5–60

2. Click (Coincidence Constraint) in the Constraint toolbar.

Task 5 - Make two lines parallel.

1. Select the vertical lines shown in Figure 5–61.

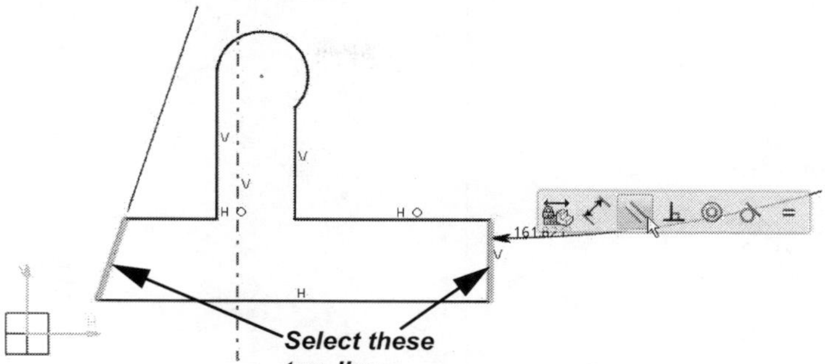

Figure 5–61

2. **Click**  (Parallelism Constraint) in the Constraint toolbar.
3. Place the parallel constraint using the left mouse button.

Task 6 - Make the arc tangent to the adjacent lines.

1. Select the arc and one of the adjacent straight lines as shown in Figure 5–62.

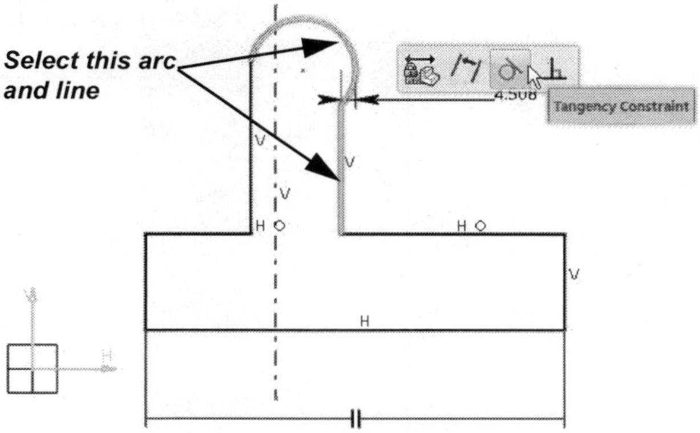

Figure 5–62

2. **Click**  (Tangency Constraint) in the Constraint toolbar.
3. Repeat this task for the arc and for the line on the other side.

Task 7 - Make arc center coincident with a sketched axis.

1. Select the sketched axis and the center of the arc shown in Figure 5–63.

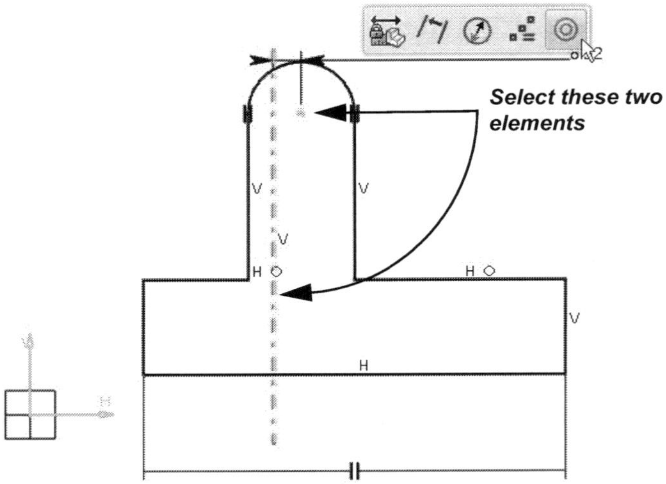

Figure 5–63

2. **Click**  (Coincidence Constraint) in the Constraint toolbar.

Task 8 - Make the sketch symmetrical about the sketched axis.

To make two elements symmetrical about an axis, start by selecting the elements to be made symmetrical (in this case, two vertical lines). Once you have identified the symmetry constraint, select the symmetry element (in this case, the vertical axis).

1. Select the two vertical lines shown in Figure 5–64.

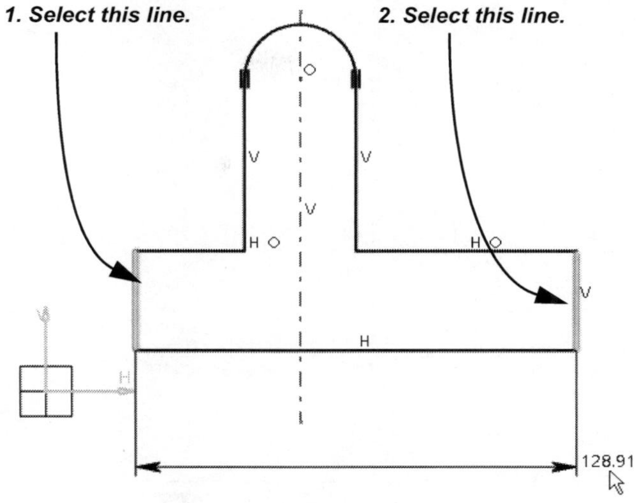

Figure 5–64

2. Right-click and select **Allow Symmetry Line**, as shown in Figure 5–65.

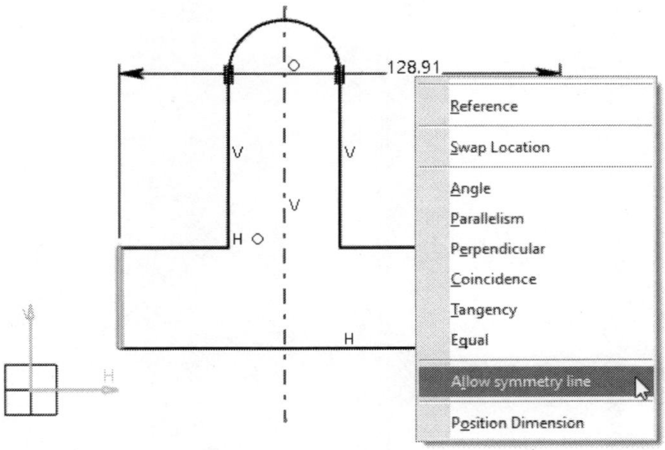

Figure 5–65

3. Select the axis shown in Figure 5–66 to complete the **symmetry** constraint.

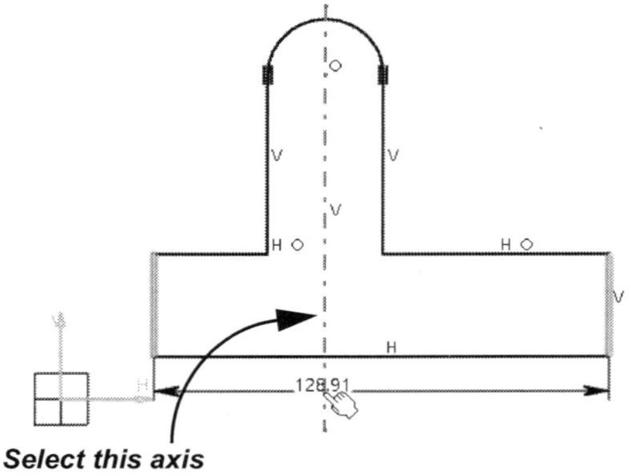

Figure 5–66

Task 9 - Constrain the sketch to the datum planes.

1. Create a (Coincidence Constraint) between the bottom horizontal line and the horizontal axis, as shown in Figure 5–67.

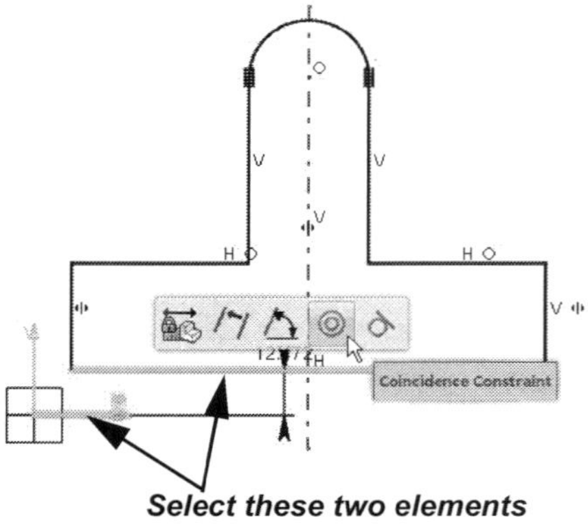

Figure 5–67

2. Click (Constraint) to clear it and to stop creating constraints.

Task 10 - Drag the sketch to test your constraints.

1. Select the vertical line on the far right side of the sketch and drag it left and right. The sketch updates to remain symmetrical.

2. Drag other elements to test your constraints, as shown in Figure 5–68.

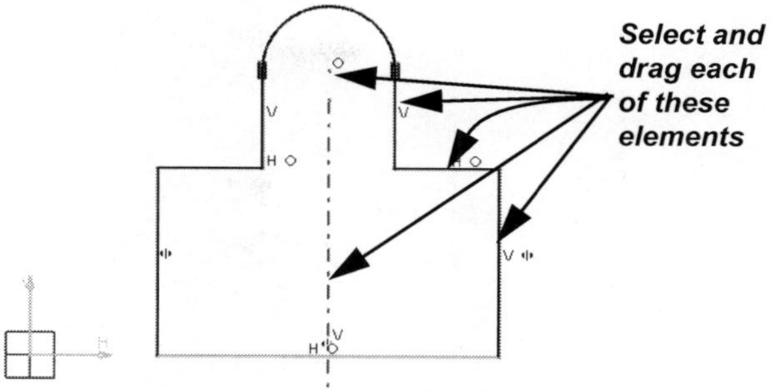

Figure 5–68

Task 11 - Dimension the section.

1. Add the dimensions and constraints shown in Figure 5–69. Adjust the dimension values accordingly.

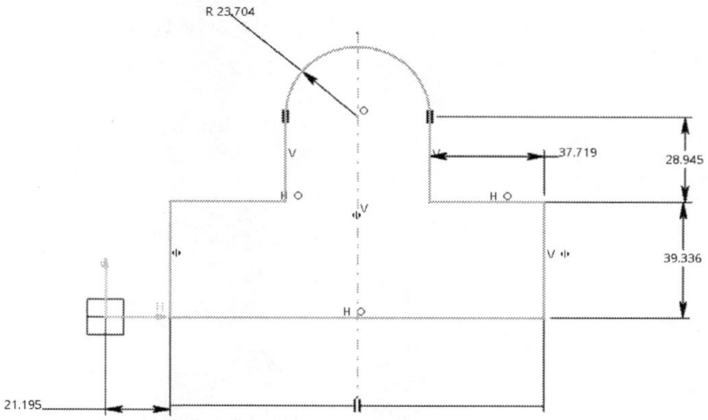

Figure 5–69

Task 12 - Exit the sketch and close the window.

1. Click (Exit App) to exit the Sketch app.

2. In the Top Bar, click (Share)>**Save** to save the part.

3. Close the *Constraints_2 A.1* tab.

Chapter Review Questions

1. You can create an unconstrained sketch.
    a. True
    b. False
2. When a sketch is fully constrained, what color are the sketched entities?
    a. Red
    b. White
    c. Green
    d. Purple
3. What tool can you use to edit more than one constraint at one time?
    a. **Edit**
    b. **Edit Multi-Constraint**
    c. **Modify Constraints**
    d. None of the above.
4. Geometric constraints can be added using which tools? (Select all that apply.)
    a. 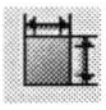 (Constraint)
    b.  (Edit Multi Constraint)
    c. 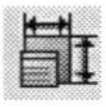 (Constraints Defined in Dialog Box)
    d. The shortcut menu.
5. What sketched entity must be present to create a revolved diameter dimension?
    a. An axis.
    b. A construction line.
    c. A line.
    d. The revolved diameter dimension can be created between any sketched entities.

6. Once created, how can you change a radius dimension to a diameter dimension?
    a. Right-click on the radius dimension and select **Diameter**.
    b. Double-click on the radius dimension and enter twice its value.
    c. Double-click on the radius dimension and select **Diameter** in the Dimension drop-down list.
    d. None of the above.
7. The **Sketch Analysis** tool can be used to perform corrective actions on sketches.
    a. True
    b. False
8. What displays in the Sketch Solving Status dialog box when a sketch is fully constrained?
    a. Fully Constrained
    b. Iso-Constrained
    c. Constrained
    d. None of the above.
9. How can an under-constrained sketch be identified?
    a. Sketch entities in a fully constrained sketch are, by default, green.
    b. When you use the **Sketch Solving Status** tool it reads Under-Constrained and highlights the affected entities on the sketch
    c. Use the **Sketch Analysis** tool. The *Diagnostic* tab indicates the status of each sketched entities.
    d. All of the above.

10. Select all of the following constraints that were used to sketch the geometry shown in Figure 5–70. (Select all that apply.)

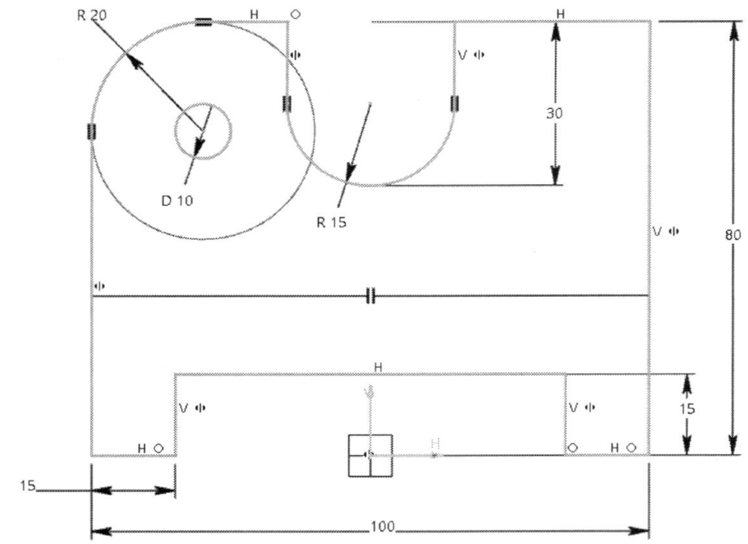

Figure 5–70

a. Tangent

b. Parallelism

c. Coincidence

d. Symmetry

e. Concentricity

f. Perpendicular

Answers: 1a, 2c, 3b, 4acd, 5a, 6c, 7a, 8b, 9d, 10abcde

Pad and Pocket Features

This chapter introduces the creation and modification of Pad and Pocket features, which serve as the foundation of your model. Understanding the various base features and the process of creating them helps you develop robust and flexible models. You learn how to create pads to add material and pockets to remove material. When creating sketches for features, you can have sketches that form a closed loop, or sketches that are open, depending on the existing geometry. You learn how to make changes to sketches.

Learning Objectives in This Chapter

- Use the various base features available.
- Use opened and closed sketches.
- Understand the basic process of creating a pad feature.
- Understand the restrictions on sketches used for pad features.
- Use the various options available for creating pad features.
- Understand the difference between a Pad and a Pocket.
- Understand the Limit options for the depth of Pad features.
- Learn how to use Open profiles.
- Learn about the types of changes that can be made to sketches, and the restrictions on those changes.

6.1 Base Features

When designing a new part, one of your first modeling decisions is to select which feature form to use as the Base feature. The Base feature is the first solid feature created in the model and it provides the foundation on which the entire model is constructed.

You can use one of the following features for your Base feature geometry:

- Pad
- Shaft
- Multi-sections Solid
- Rib

Figure 6–1 shows an example of a Pad feature.

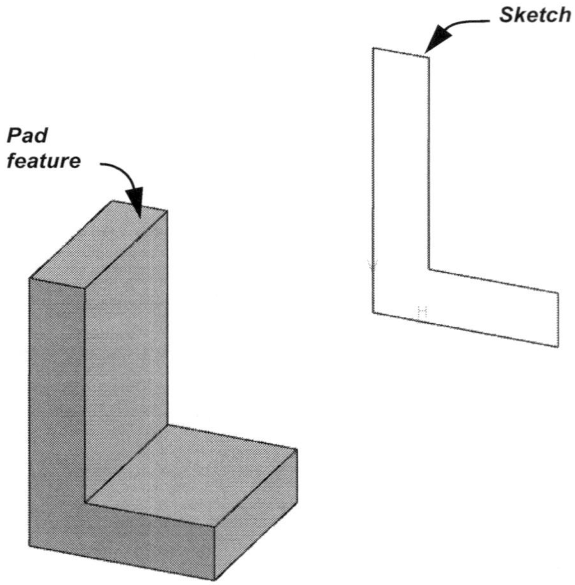

Figure 6–1

6.2 Creating a Pad Feature

With a Pad feature, an existing sketch is extruded a specified distance to define the solid geometry.

How To: Create a Pad Feature

1. Select a profile or surface. The shape of a Pad is determined by the profile that is used to create the feature. Select the sketch. Selected items display in blue by default, as shown in Figure 6–2.

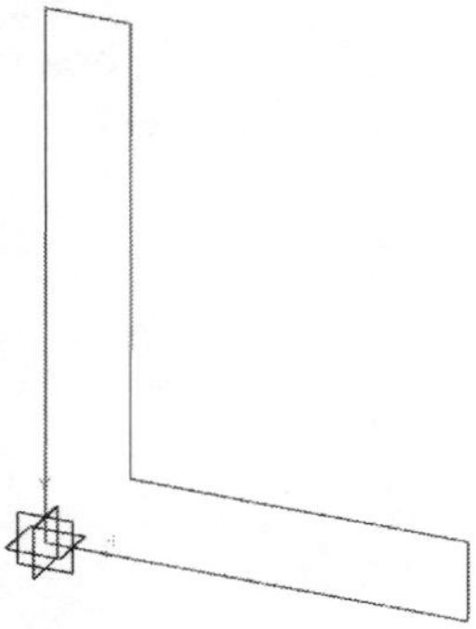

Figure 6–2

2. In the Action Bar, click  (Pad). The software initially constructs the Pad feature using the default values, as shown in Figure 6–3. The Pad Definition dialog box opens.

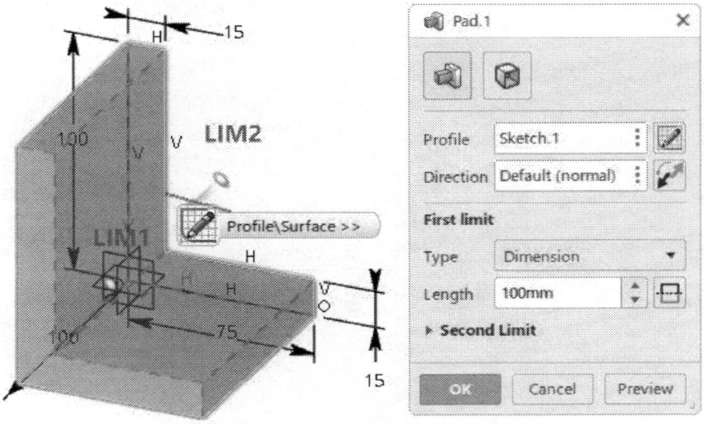

Figure 6–3

Additional limit types for Pad features are discussed later.

3. Specify Pad limit options.

   The distance that the sketch is extruded is known as the limit. The default limit type is dimension, which enables you to manually specify the extrusion distance. To specify the length of the feature, simply enter the distance in the *Length* field.

4. Click **Preview** to examine the geometry before completing the feature.
5. Click **OK** to complete the feature.

Mirrored Extent

You can select  (Mirrored extent) in the Pad Definition dialog box to create geometry on both sides of the sketch, as shown in Figure 6–4.

The total depth of a Mirrored extent Pad feature is twice the length value entered in the Pad Definition dialog box.

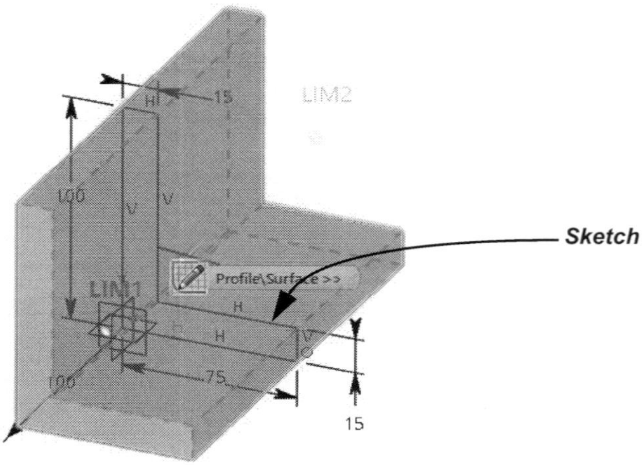

Figure 6–4

It is common practice to start a model with symmetrical geometry. This enables you to capture the design intent from the very beginning. Using this technique, additional features can be easily located relative to the center of the part and automatically remain centered, even when the size of the Base feature is changed.

Second Limit

Click **Second Limit** to fully expand the Pad Definition dialog box, as shown in Figure 6–5. By expanding the dialog box, you have access to options, such as the Type and Length in the Second Limit direction. By changing the value from the default *zero* to a new value, you can create asymmetrical geometry about the sketch. If the values are grayed out, ensure that the

 (Mirrored extent) icon is turned off.

- You can enter a negative value for the First or Second Limit.

As a reference, the software displays an arrow to indicate the direction of the First Limit.

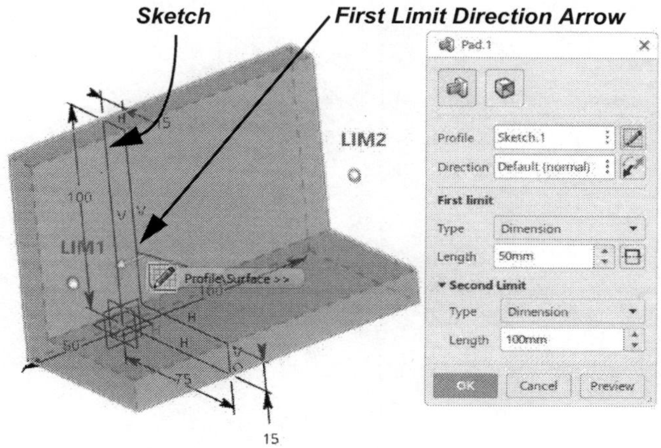

Figure 6–5

Sketch Restrictions for Pad Features

Not every sketch is valid for use with a Pad feature. Comparisons of valid and invalid sketches are described as follows:

Valid Sketch	Invalid Sketch	Description
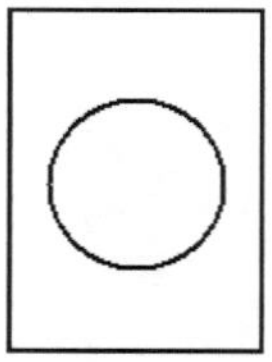	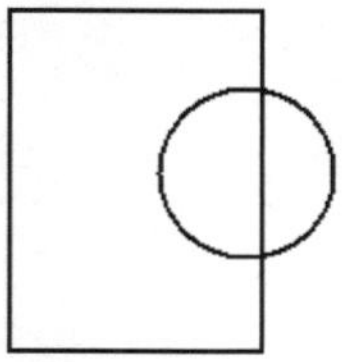	Multiple sections are acceptable, but they cannot intersect each other. You can use the trim function to eliminate the overlap condition.
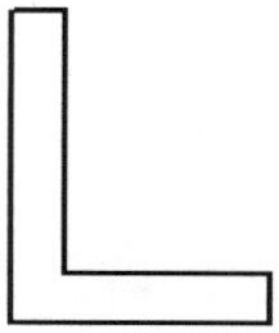		Open sections are not permitted for the first solid feature on the part unless the **Thick** option is used to create the Pad.

- If you try to create a Pad feature with an invalid section, an error message displays and you are not able to create the feature.

6.3 Pad Feature Options

To facilitate sketched feature creation, additional reference planes can be created at specific locations.

As features are added to a model, planar surfaces of existing geometry can be selected as sketching planes, as shown in Figure 6–6.

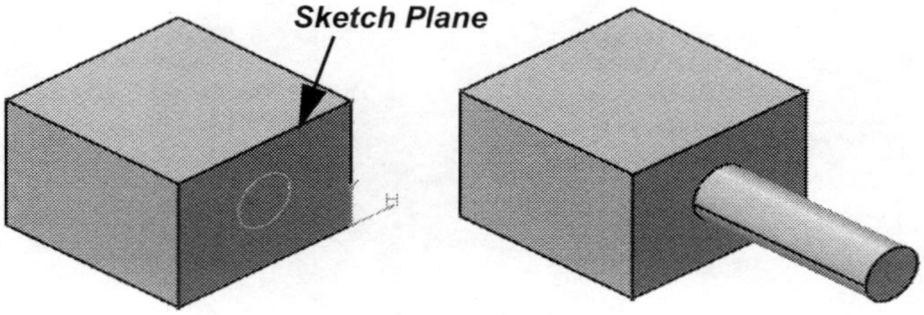

Figure 6–6

The following topics discuss several options available during Pad feature creation that help capture design intent.

Feature Depth Options

There are a number of methods that can be used to define the depth of a Pad feature. These options are shown in Figure 6–7.

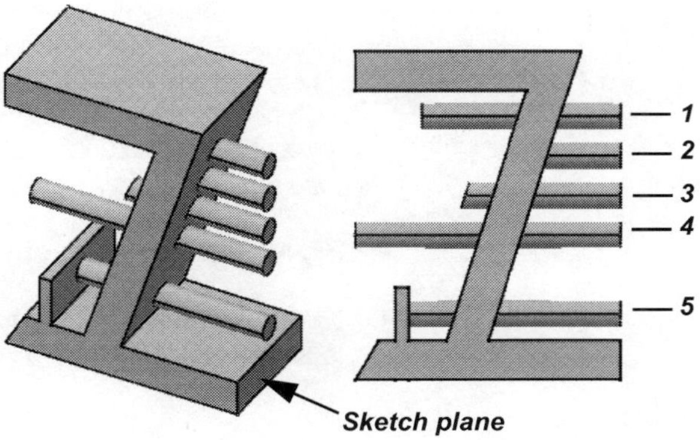

Figure 6–7

The depth options, set in the *Type* drop-down list of the Pad Dialog box, are described as follows:

Example	Option	Description
1	**Dimension**	Manually enter length of feature.
2	**Up to next**	Feature extruded to next solid surface that completely intersects sketch. You can use the **Offset** option which enables you to specify a positive or negative distance from that terminating plane.
3	**Up to last, with Offset**	Feature terminates at last solid surface that sketch completely intersects. Offset enables you to specify a positive or negative distance from that terminating plane.
4	**Up to plane**	Feature can be terminated at selected planar surface or reference plane.
5	**Up to surface**	Feature can be terminated at selected planar or non-planar surface that completely intersects sketch.

Second Limit Option

With Pad features, you can extrude the sketch on either side or both sides of the sketching plane. To access this functionality, click **More** in the Pad Definition dialog box.

For example, a circle is sketched on the planar surface of the Pad feature, as shown in Figure 6–8 and Figure 6–9.

- First limit type is **Dimension** with a length value of **20**.
- Second limit type is **Up to surface** and the cylindrical surface is selected.

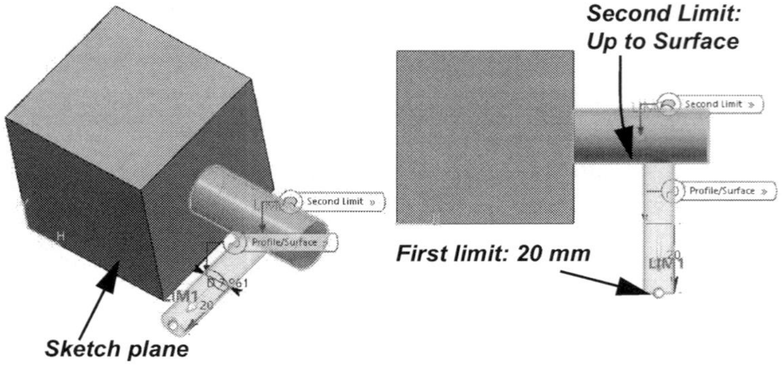

Figure 6–8

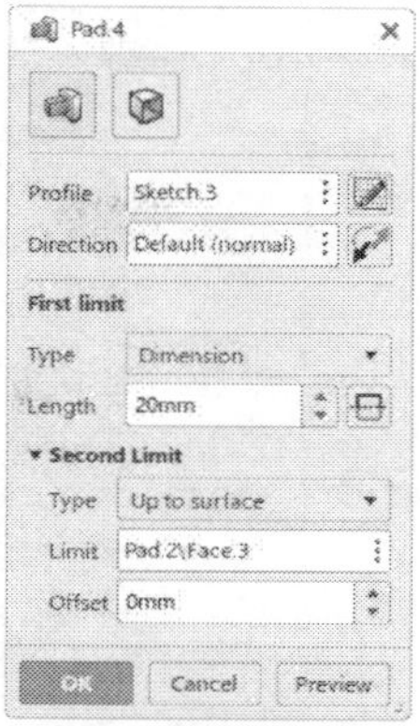

Figure 6–9

In simple cases, where you want to create a pad in one direction and with a dimensional depth, you can select a sketch and click  (Pad) in the context toolbar, as shown in Figure 6–10.

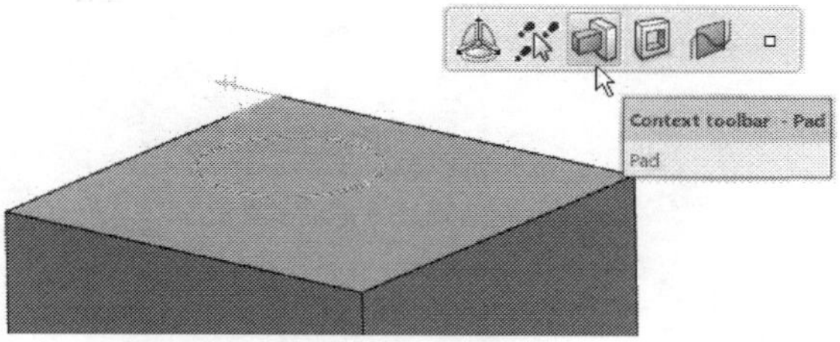

Figure 6–10

The pad immediately previews with a dimension dragger that allows you to drag to increase or decrease the depth dimension, as shown in Figure 6–11. When accessing the tool this way, you do not have access to the additional options found in the Pad Definition dialog box.

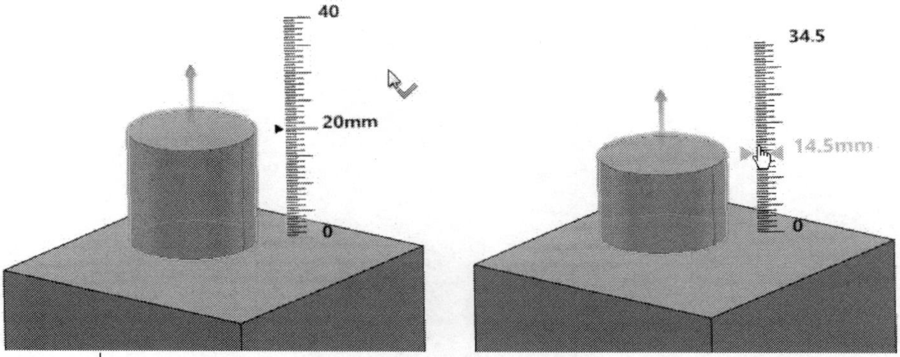

Figure 6–11

After entering the tool, if you realize that you do require the additional options, you do not have to restart the feature. Simply click (Pad) in the Action Bar, and the Pad Definition dialog box will open.

Non-Normal Direction

By default, Pads are extruded perpendicular (normal) to the sketch plane. You can choose an alternative direction by selecting in the *Direction* field, and then selecting a straight line or edge to define the feature direction.

In the example shown in Figure 6–12, note that the sketch does not extend the entire length of the Pad feature. This sketch is used to define the direction only; the length of the line is not important.

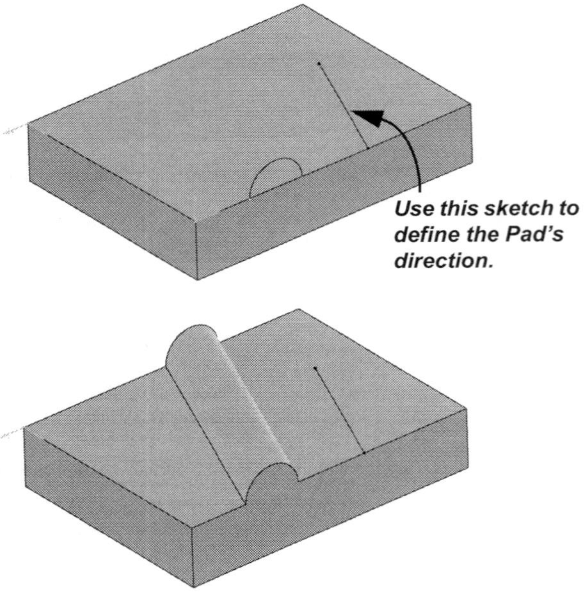

Figure 6–12

Open and Closed Sketches

Using open profiles for feature creation increases update time and introduces instability into the model. A closed profile should be developed whenever possible.

Your profile sketches do not have to form a closed loop. An open profile is acceptable under certain circumstances. However, the open end of the sketch must be bounded by existing geometry. This means the existing geometry must touch the open ends of the sketch at all times. If the Pad shown in Figure 6–13 is lengthened so that it extends off the part, the feature fails.

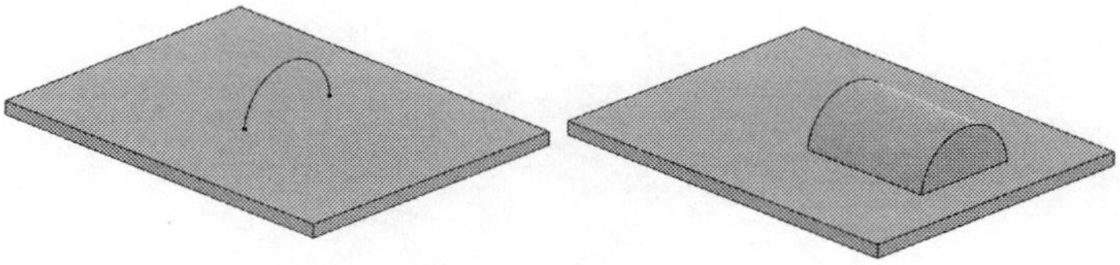

Figure 6–13

6.4 Pocket

A Pocket feature removes material by extruding a profile. It is similar to a Pad feature, except that a Pad adds material and a Pocket removes material, as shown in Figure 6–14.

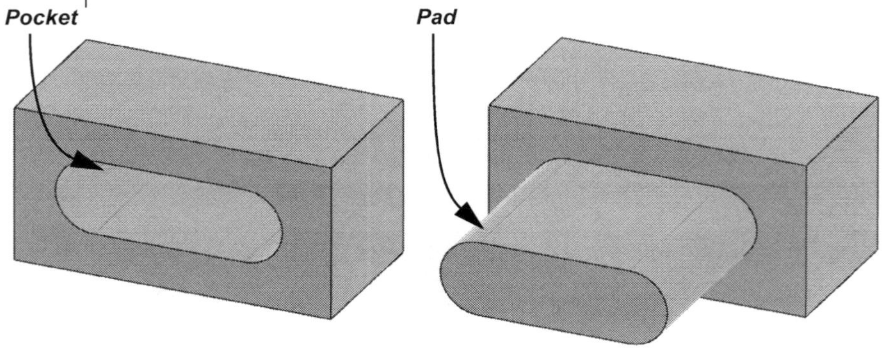

Figure 6–14

Limit Options

Several options are available to control the limits of a Pocket feature. These options are similar to those for the Pad feature, as shown in Figure 6–15.

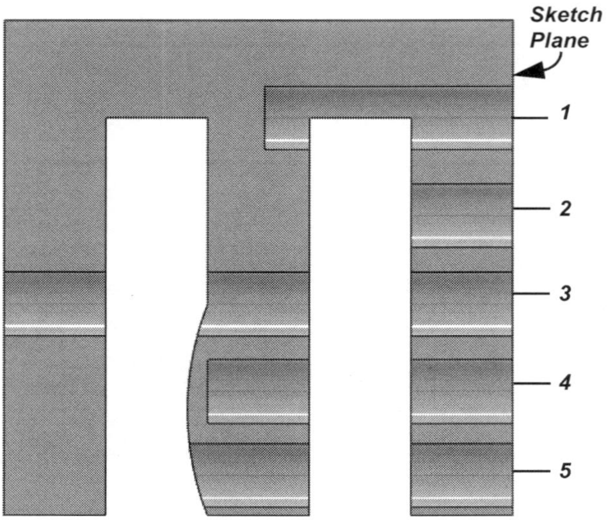

Figure 6–15

The limit options are described as follows:

Example	Option	Description
1	**Dimension**	Manually enter the depth of the Pocket.
2	**Up to next**	Sketch is extruded to the next surface that intersects the entire sketch. You can use the **Offset** option which enables you to specify a positive or negative distance from that terminating plane.
3	**Up to last**	Sketch is extruded through the entire model. You can use the **Offset** option which enables you to specify a positive or negative distance from that terminating plane.
4	**Up to plane**	Sketch is extruded to a specified plane. The sketch does not need to reside on the plane.
5	**Up to surface**	Sketch is extruded to a specified surface. The surface can be planar or non-planar. The surface must intersect the entire sketch.

All of the limit options, except for **Dimension**, have a default offset value of 0. You can change it to a positive value to extend the Pocket beyond the reference or change it to a negative value to pull it back from the reference, as shown in Figure 6–16.

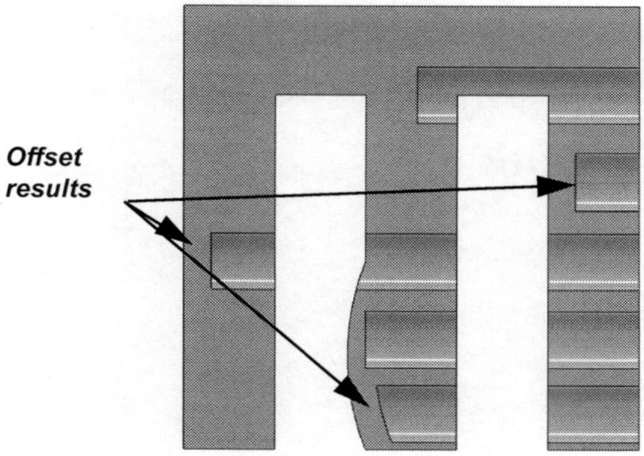

Figure 6–16

Open Profiles

When a Pocket feature uses an open profile sketch, the software only removes material from one side of the sketch to the boundaries of the model. Clicking (Reverse Side) in the dialog box enables you to remove material on the other side, as shown in Figure 6–17.

If the open ends of the sketch are not coincident with the sides of the part, the software automatically extends them, as shown in Figure 6–18.

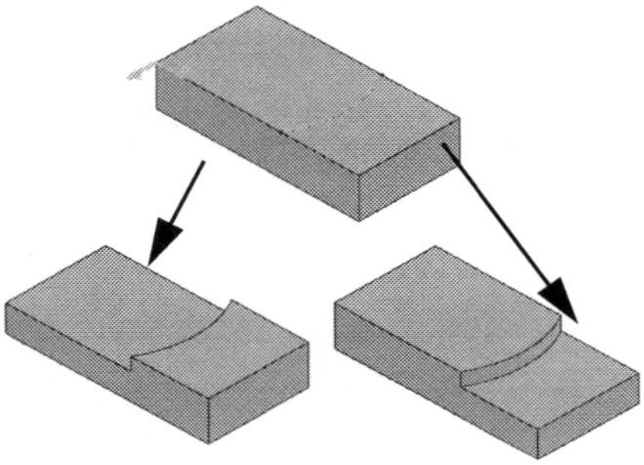

Figure 6–17

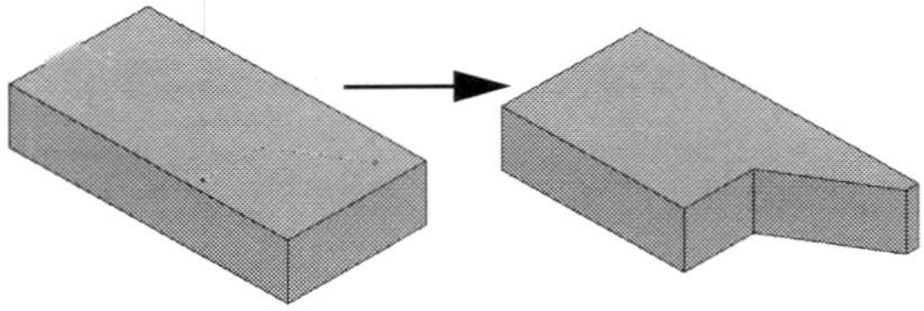

Figure 6–18

- Open profiles are subject to increased update time and introduce instability in the model. Avoid them whenever possible.

Other Feature Options

As is the case with Pads, Pocket features can have a unique second limit; they can be mirrored about the sketch and can be extruded in various ways, as shown in Figure 6–19.

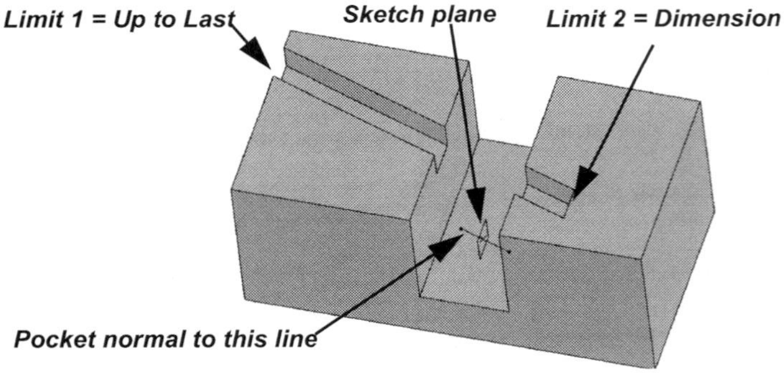

Figure 6–19

The Pocket Definition dialog box is shown in Figure 6–20.

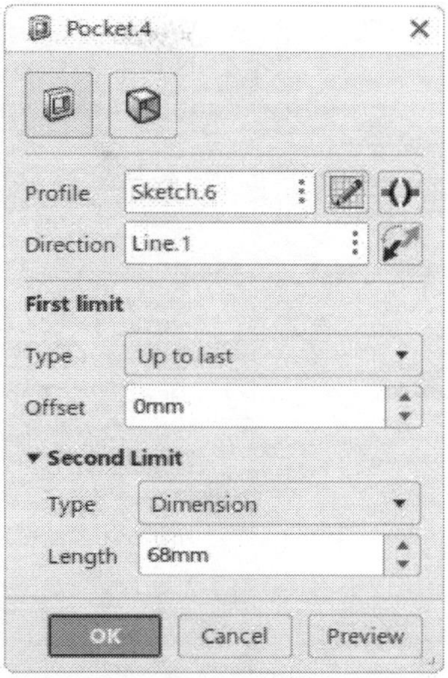

Figure 6–20

6.5 Making Changes to a Sketch

You can easily change the characteristics of a feature, such as the length, sketch dimensions, shape of the sketch, and attributes of the feature (e.g., Mirrored extent).

The following topics discuss these changes in more detail.

Dimensional Changes

How To: Change Dimensions

1. Double-click on a feature on the model to open its dialog box. The software also displays all dimensions of the feature, including the sketch dimensions.
2. Double-click the dimension to open the constraint's definition dialog box.
3. Enter a new value and click **OK** to complete the change. The software automatically updates the geometry, as shown in Figure 6–21.

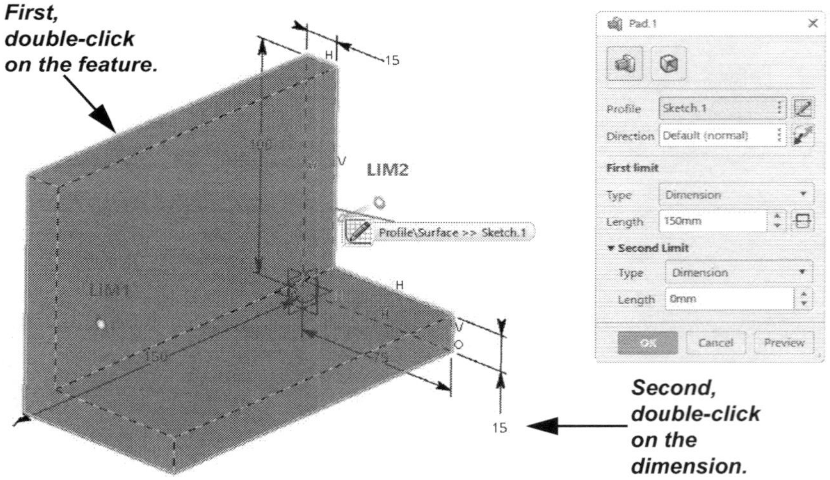

Figure 6–21

Changing the Sketch

The software automatically hides the sketch once you have used it for a Solid feature. To modify the sketch in the Sketch app, you can use one of the following methods:

- Double-click on the sketch in the specification tree. Even if the sketch is hidden from the display, it displays in the Sketch app.

- Click (Sketch) in the dialog box for the feature, as shown in Figure 6–22. You enter the Sketch app, where you can modify the sketch. When you exit Sketcher, you return to editing the feature in the Part Design.

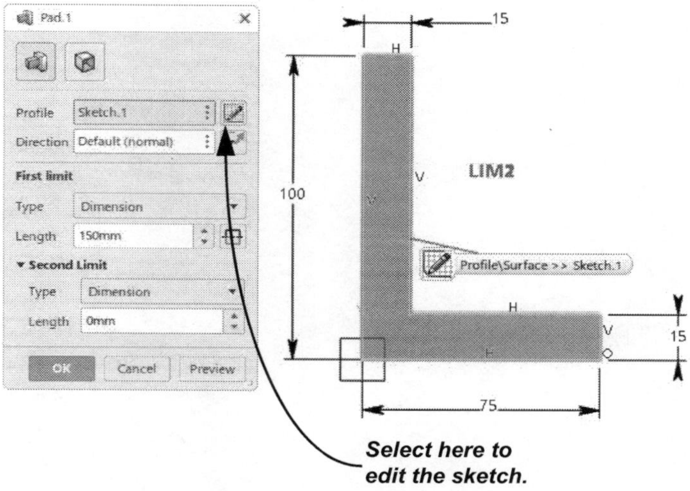

Figure 6–22

Deleting the Feature

Deleting a feature removes the geometry from the model. When a feature is deleted, the sketch remains. This enables you to use the sketch again, as required. Remember that you can use the (Undo) and (Redo) commands from the Action Bar to restore features that are accidentally deleted or changed.

You can delete a Pad or a Pocket feature in one of the following ways:

- Select the feature in the specification tree and press <Delete>.
- Select the feature in the specification tree, right-click and select **Delete**, as shown in Figure 6–23.

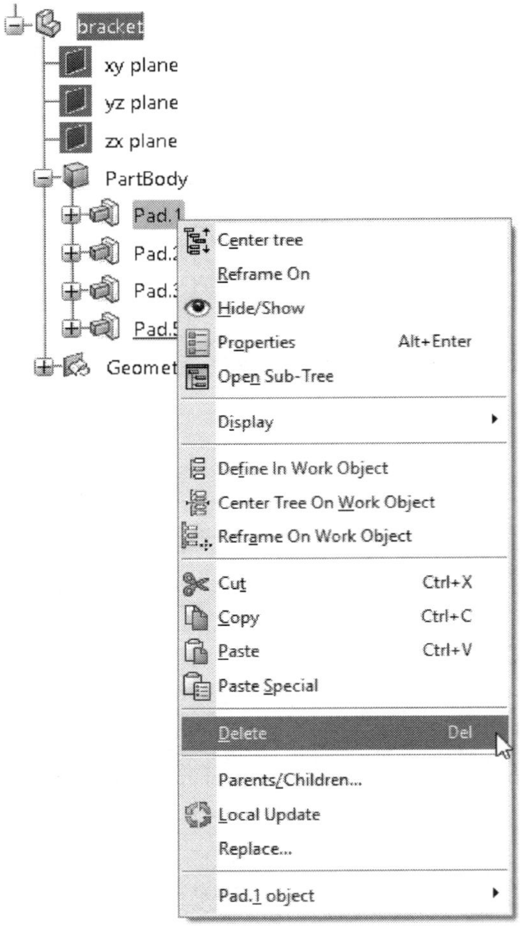

Figure 6–23

Change Restrictions

The only restriction to feature changes is on the feature form. You cannot change a Pad feature into a Pocket feature. You must delete the Pad feature, select the sketch, and then create a Pocket feature.

Practice 6a

Creating and Modifying Pad Features

Practice Objectives

- Create a sketch to create a Pad feature.
- Modify a Pad feature.

In this practice, you will create a Pad feature and modify it using the Pad Definition dialog box. You will create the part shown in Figure 6–24.

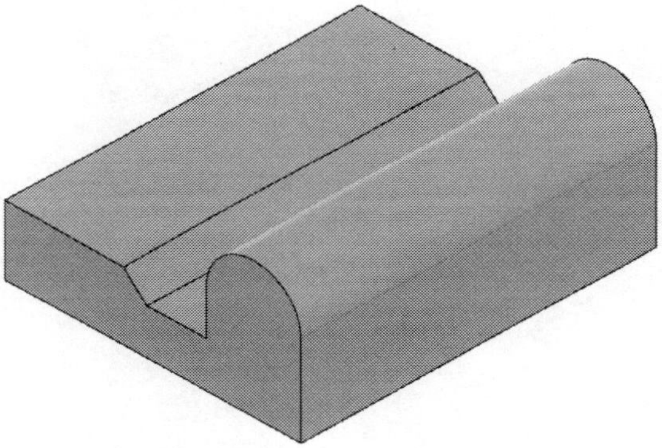

Figure 6–24

Task 1 - Create a new part.

1. In the Top Bar, click  (Add)>**3D Part**.
2. In the 3D Part dialog box, enter ***Your_Initials*_Pad_Sketch** as the *Title*.
3. Select the *3D Shape* tab and enter ***Your_Initials*_Pad_Sketch** as the *Title*.
4. Select the *Characteristics* tab and ensure **Enable hybrid design is disabled**.
5. Click **OK.**

6. Select the YZ plane as shown in Figure 6–25.

Figure 6–25

7. In the context toolbar, click (Sketch).

Task 2 - Sketch the profile.

1. Sketch and constrain the part profile, as shown in Figure 6–26.
   - 50 (1.969 in)
   - 60 (2.362 in)
   - 25 (4.921 in)
   - 125 (4.921 in)
   - 20 (0.787 in)
   - 45 (1.772 in)

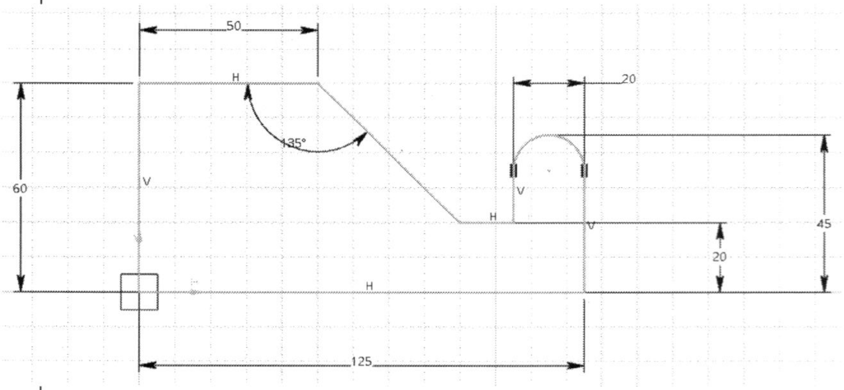

Figure 6–26

2. In the *Sketch* section of the Action Bar, click (Exit App) to exit the Sketch application.

Task 3 - Create a Pad feature from the sketch.

1. With the sketch highlighted, in the *Essentials* section of the Action Bar, click  (Pad).
2. The Pad Definition dialog box opens and the geometry previews, as shown in Figure 6–27.

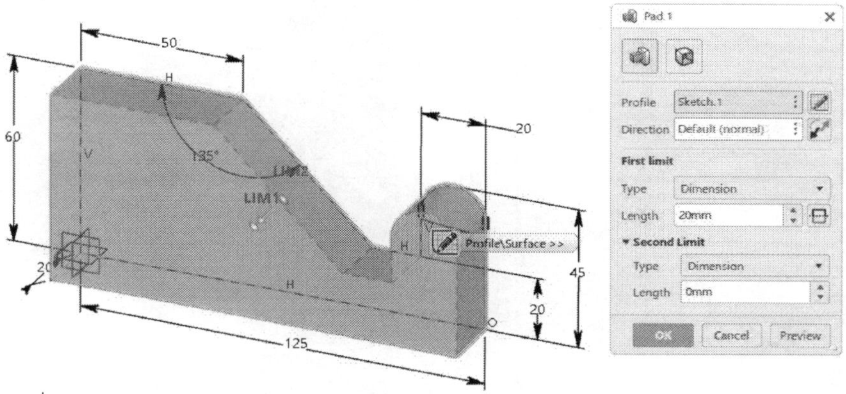

Figure 6–27

3. In the *Length* field, enter **75 (2.953 in)**.
4. Click **OK** to complete the feature. The resulting geometry displays as shown in Figure 6–28.

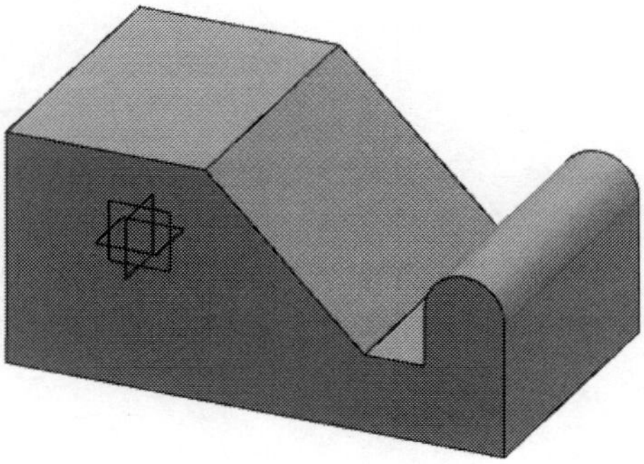

Figure 6–28

Task 4 - Make dimensional changes to the Pad feature.

1. Double-click on any face of the Pad feature. All of the dimensions of the feature are now displayed. The Pad Definition dialog box also opens.

2. Double-click on the *60* (2.362 in) dimension and change it to **30 (1.181 in),** as shown in Figure 6–29.

You can press <Enter> instead of clicking ***OK****.*

3. In the Constraint Definition dialog box, click **OK**.

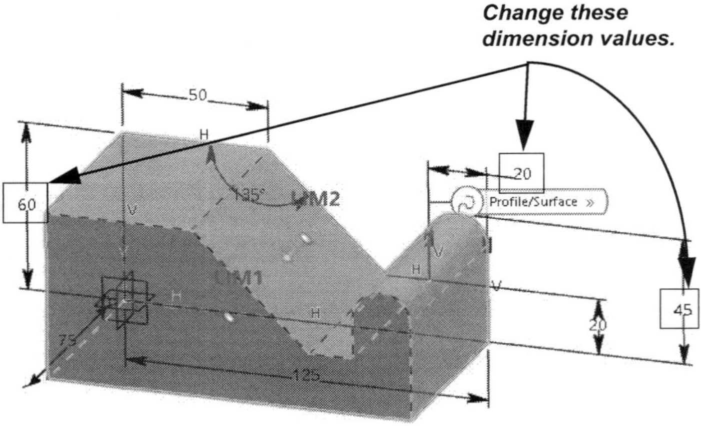

Figure 6–29

4. Repeat this process to change the *20* (0.787 in) dimension to **40 (1.575 in)** and the *45* (1.772 in) dimension to **60 (2.362 in)**.

5. Click **OK** in the Pad Definition dialog box to complete the dimensional changes and update the geometry. The resulting geometry displays as shown in Figure 6–30.

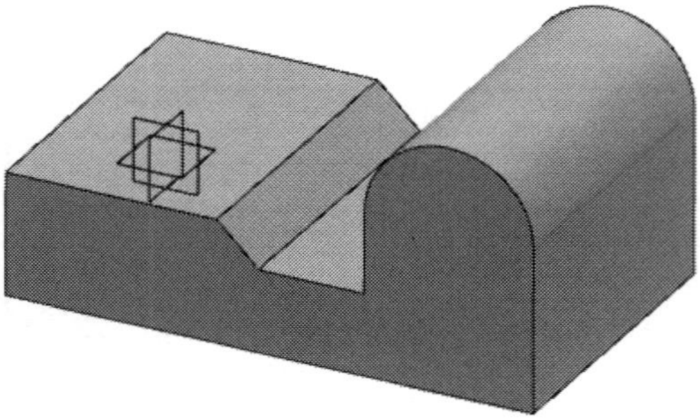

Figure 6–30

Task 5 - Change the attributes of the feature.

1. Double-click on the Pad feature again to open the Pad Definition dialog box.

2. Click (Mirrored extent). The software previews the geometry in wireframe, as shown in Figure 6–31. The geometry is symmetrical about the sketch and has a total length of 150 (5.906 in).

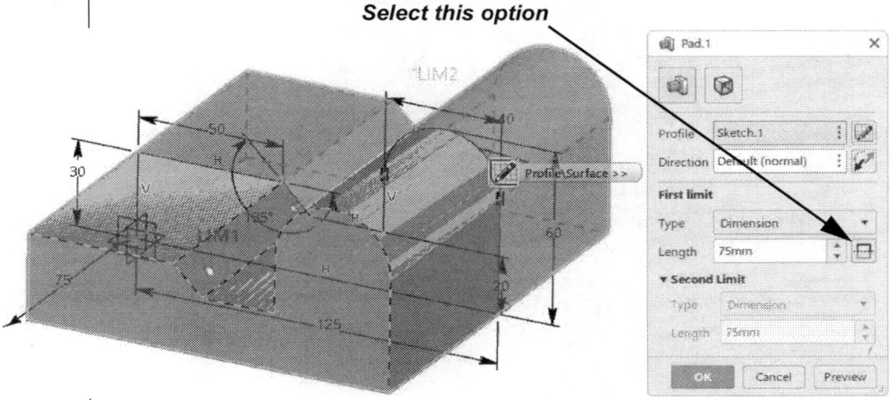

Figure 6–31

3. Clear the (Mirrored extent) icon.

4. Select **Second Limit** if it isn't already expanded. In the *First Limit* area, enter **50 (1.969 in)** for the length.

5. In the *Second Limit* area, enter **100 (3.937 in)** for the length. Click **Preview** and the resulting geometry displays, as shown in Figure 6–32.

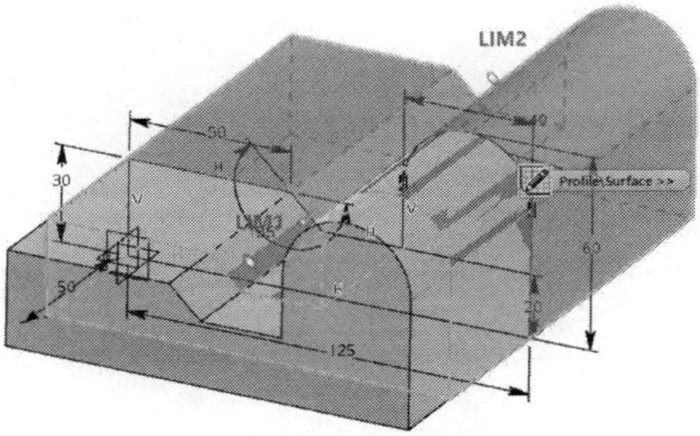

Figure 6–32

6. Click **OK** in the Pad Definition dialog box to complete the change and update the geometry.

Task 6 - Save the part and close the window.

1. In the Top Bar,click (Share)>**Save** to save the part.
2. Close the *Pad_Sketch A.1* tab.

Practice 6b

Creating Pocket Features

Practice Objectives

- Create a sketch to create a Pocket feature.
- Modify a Pocket feature.

In this practice, you will create and modify three Pocket features. The first feature will represent a hole with a keyway Groove to accept a Shaft. The second feature will create a cylindrical elongated hole cutout on the flange of the part. The completed model displays as shown in Figure 6–33.

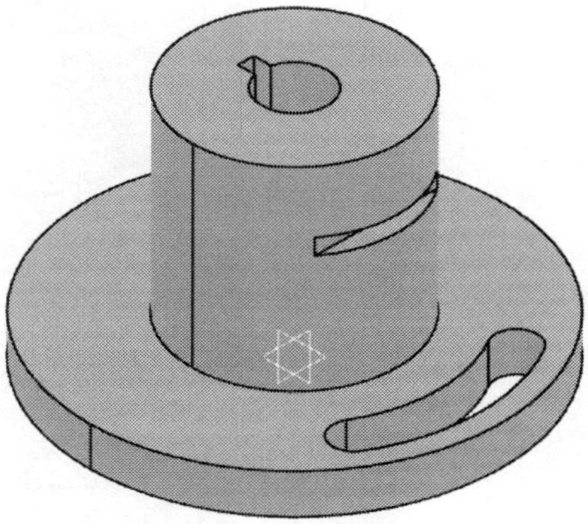

Figure 6–33

Task 1 - Open a model and create a profile on the top of it.

1. In the Top Bar, click (Add)>**Import**.
2. In the Import dialog box, click **(Open)**.
3. Select **Pockets.3dxml** and click **Open**.
4. Click **OK** in the Import dialog box.
5. Click **OK** in the Import Report dialog box.
6. You are currently in Explore mode. Right-click Pockets in the specification tree and select **Open**.

7. Select the top cylindrical face of the model and click (Sketch) in the Context toolbar, as shown in Figure 6–34.

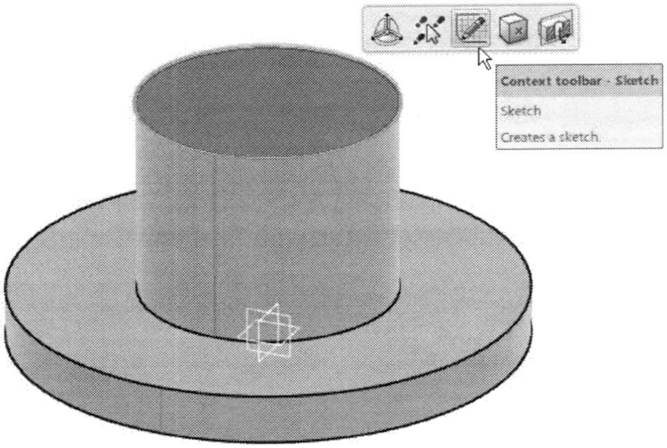

Figure 6–34

8. Sketch the profile as shown in Figure 6–35. Note that the arc is concentric with the cylindrical face and the keyway geometry is symmetrical about the vertical axis.

    - 4 (0.157 in)
    - 8 (0.315 in)
    - 12 (0.472 in)

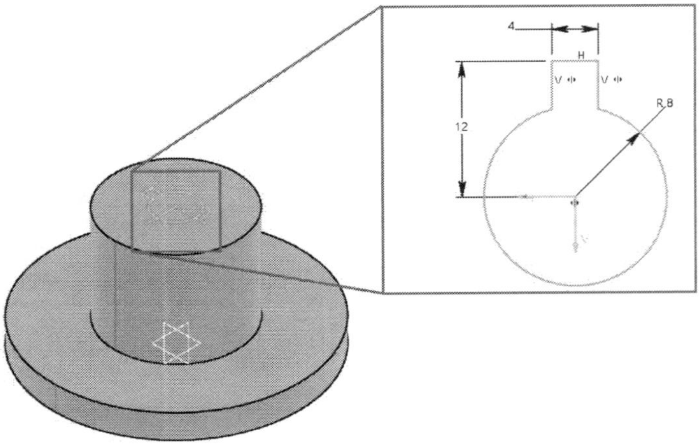

Figure 6–35

9. In the Action Bar, click (Exit App) to complete the sketch.

10. In the *Essentials* section of the Action Bar, click (Pocket) and select the sketch just created, if not already selected. The Pocket Definition dialog box opens as shown in Figure 6–36, indicating a *Depth* of **33 (1.299 in)**.

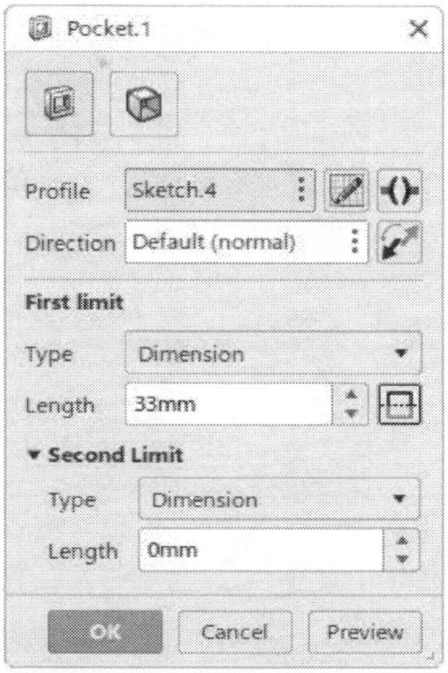

Figure 6–36

11. Verify that the arrow indicating direction points down into the part. Also confirm that the arrow indicating the material side, points toward the inside of the profile, as shown in Figure 6–37.

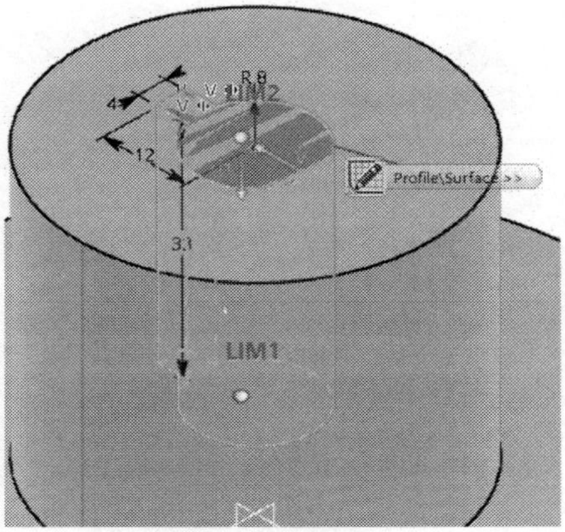

Figure 6–37

12. Enter a depth of **40 (1.575 in)** and click **OK**. The completed Pocket feature displays as shown in Figure 6–38.

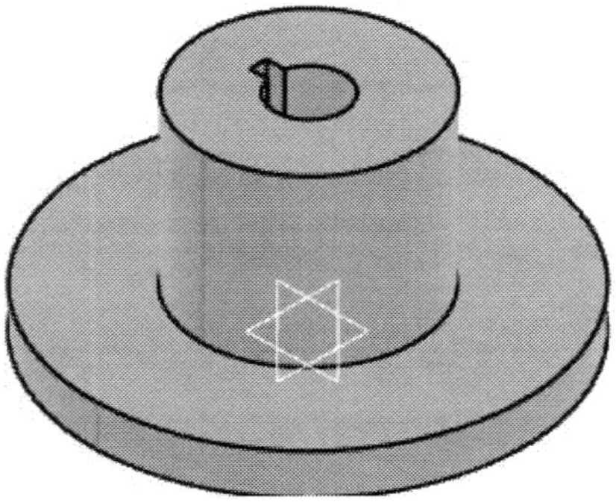

Figure 6–38

Task 2 - Modify the Pocket feature.

In this task, you will carry out a design change on the model. You will modify the depth of the cutout so that it will always extend up to the top face of the flange. This is done by modifying the depth options for the Pocket feature.

1. Locate the Pocket feature in the specification tree and double-click on it to open the Pocket Definition dialog box.

2. In the *First Limit* area, set *Type* to **Up to plane** and select the face as shown in Figure 6–39.

Since the section does not entirely intersect the selected face, the ***Up to surface*** *option cannot be used.*

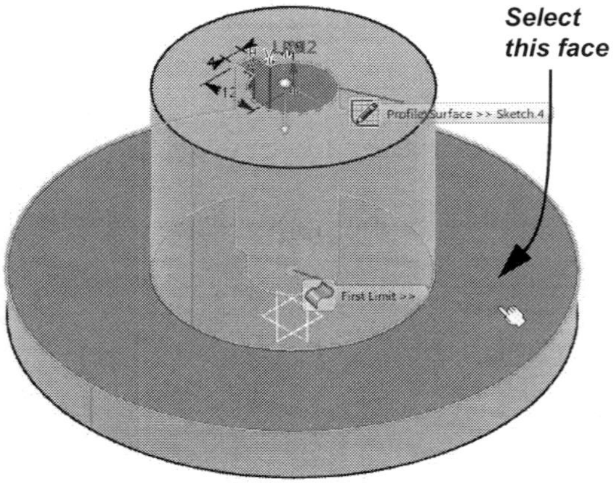

Figure 6–39

3. Click **OK** to complete the modification.

4. Using (ViewModes), select (Shading With Edges and Hidden Edges) to review the depth of the feature.

5. Modify the depth of Pad.1 from *40* (1.575 in) to **50 (1.969 in)**. Review the model to verify that the Pocket feature is reacting correctly (depth should still run to the previously selected surface).

6. Once complete, use (View Modes) to return the model to the (Shading With Sharp and Smooth Edges) display.

Task 3 - Create a second Pocket feature.

1. Select the face of the model as shown in Figure 6–40 and click (Sketch).

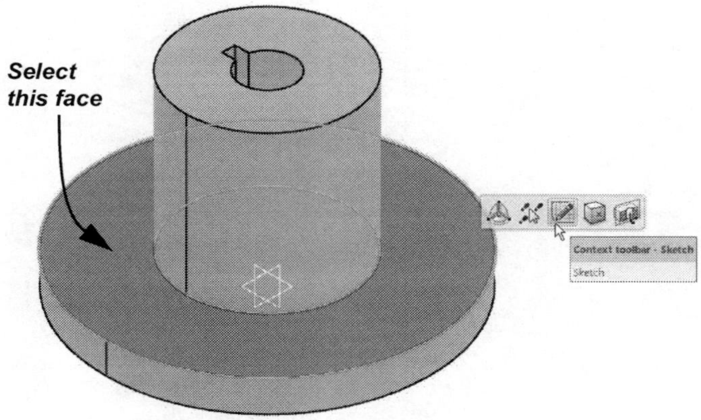

Figure 6–40

2. Sketch the profile as shown in Figure 6–41, using (Cylindrical Elongated Hole). To create the angle dimension, create two construction lines that are symmetrical about the vertical (**V**) axis and pass through the center of each arc.
   - 5 (0.197 in)
   - 40 (1.575 in)

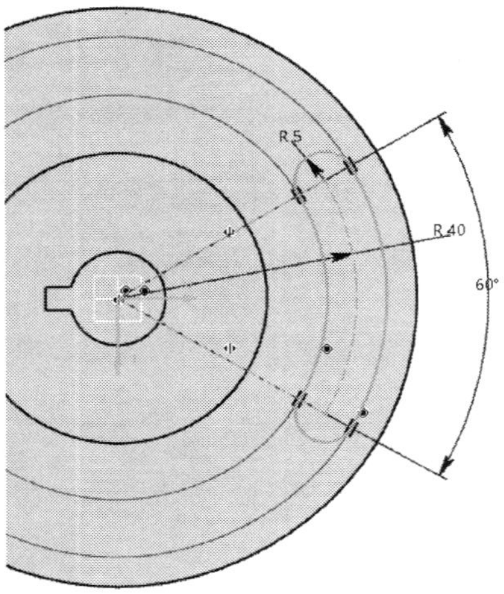

Figure 6–41

3. In the Action Bar, click (Exit App) to complete the sketch.

4. In the *Essentials* section of the Action Bar, click (Pocket) and select the sketch just created if not already selected. Define the depth using the **Up to last** option. The completed feature displays as shown in Figure 6–42.

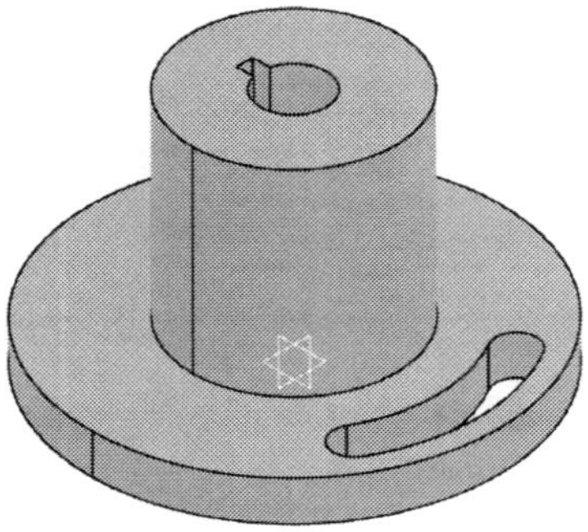

Figure 6–42

Task 4 - Create a Pocket using two limits.

In this task, you will sketch a profile for a Pocket feature on the YZ plane. Then you will create a Pocket feature that cuts material from both sides of the sketch plane.

1. Create a sketch on the YZ plane. Sketch the profile as shown in Figure 6–43.

   - 4 (0.157 in)
   - 10 (0.394 in)
   - 20 (0.787 in
   - 40 (1.575 in)

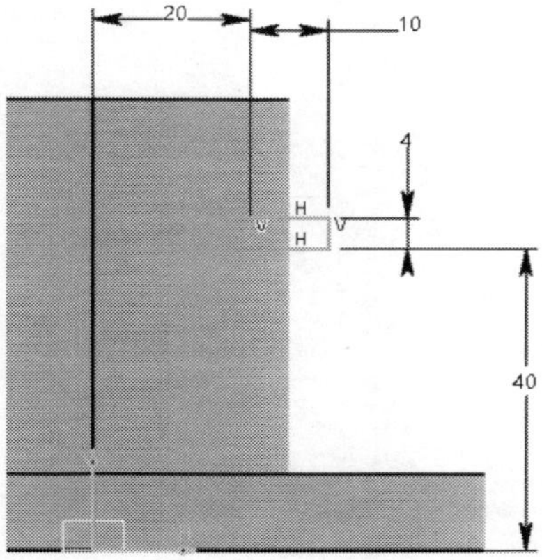

Figure 6–43

2. In the Action Bar, click  (Exit App) to complete the sketch.

3. In the *Essentials* section of the Action Bar, click  (Pocket) and select the sketch just created if not already selected.

4. Set the *First Limit* type as **Up to last**.

5. Click **Second Limit**. The Pocket Definition dialog box expands as shown in Figure 6–44.

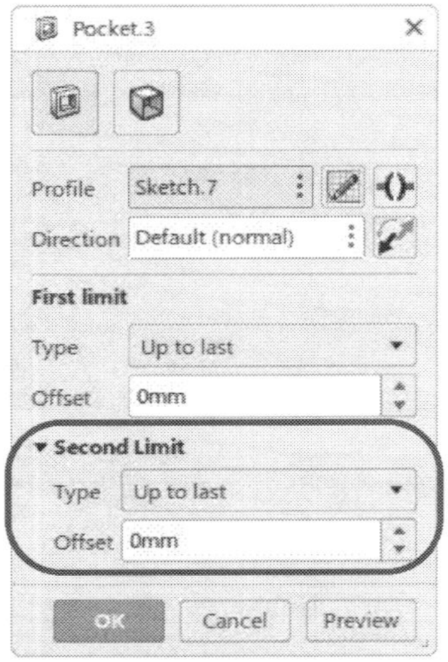

Figure 6–44

6. In the *Second Limit* area, set *Type* to **Up to last**.

7. Click **OK** to complete the feature. The model displays as shown in Figure 6–45.

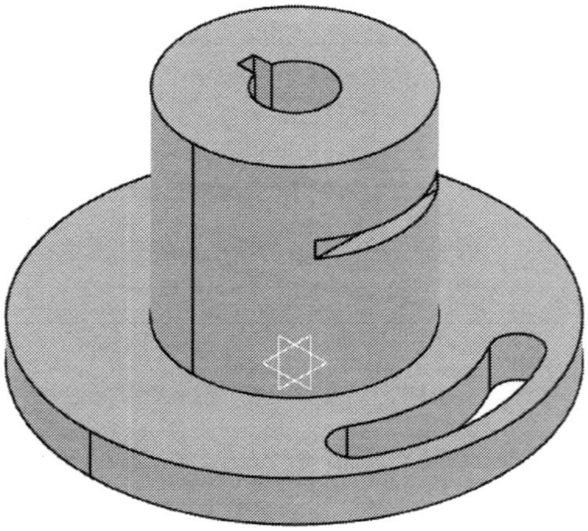

Figure 6–45

8. In the Top Bar, click  (Share)>**Save** to save the part.

9. Close the *Pocket A.1* tab.

Practice 6c

Working With Open Sketches

Practice Objectives

- Correctly sketch and constrain an open profile.
- Use an open sketch to create a Pad feature.

In this practice, you will add a Rib to a part, as shown in Figure 6–46. You will need to create an open profile sketch and use the Pad feature to create the Rib.

You can also use a stiffener to create the Rib geometry. Stiffeners are described later.

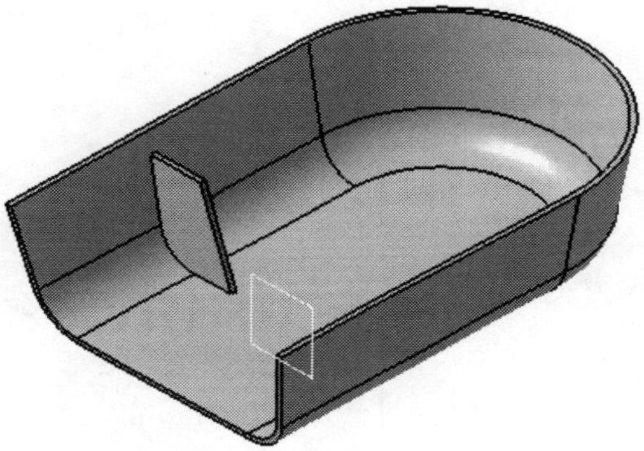

Figure 6–46

Task 1 - Create an open profile on the YZ plane.

1. In the Top Bar, click  (Add)>**Import**.
2. In the Import dialog box, click  **(Open).**
3. Select **Open_Sketch.3dxml** and click **Open**.
4. Click **OK** in the Import dialog box.
5. Click **OK** in the Import Report dialog box.
6. You are currently in Explore mode. Right-click **Part1** in the specification tree and select **Open**.
7. Select the YZ plane and click  (Sketch).

8. Sketch a horizontal and angled line as shown in Figure 6–47.

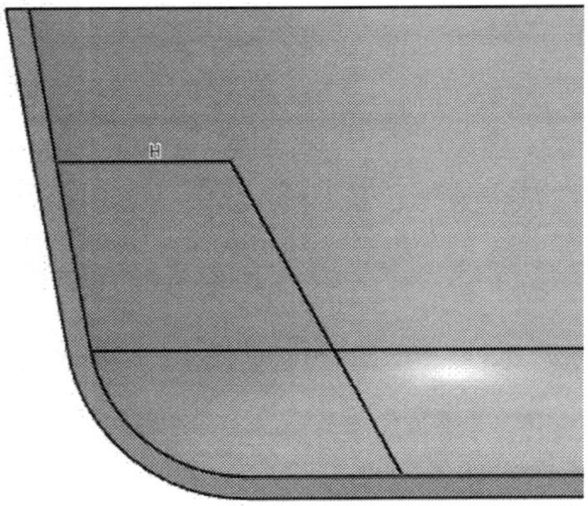

Figure 6–47

Design Considerations

To successfully use an open sketch as a Pad feature, the sketch must be fully constrained to other geometry. This way, CATIA knows how to extrude the open sections of the profile.

9. Press and hold <Ctrl> and select one of the open end points and the adjacent edge of the part, as shown in Figure 6–48.

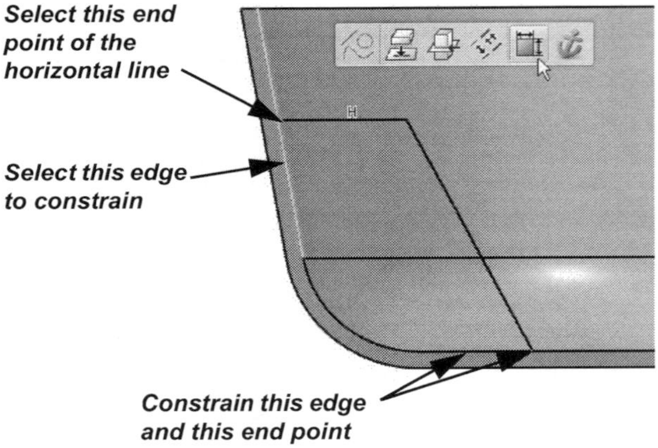

Figure 6–48

10. Click (Coincidence Constraint) in the context toolbar, as shown in Figure 6–49, or right-click and select **Coincidence**.

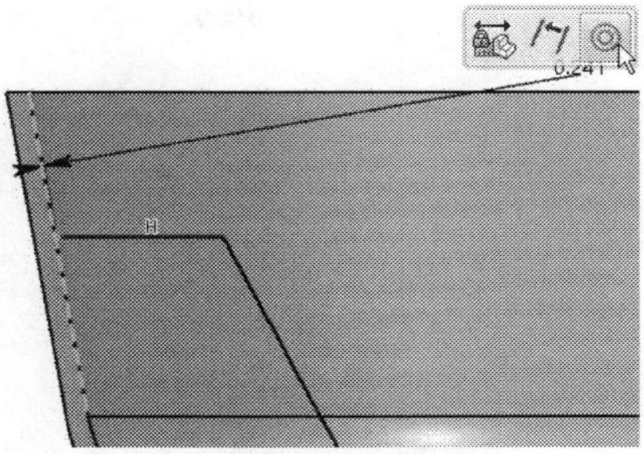

Figure 6–49

11. Repeat the previous three steps for the other open end.

12. Create the **12.5 (0.492 in)**, **32 (1.260 in)**, and **110** dimensions as shown in Figure 6–50.

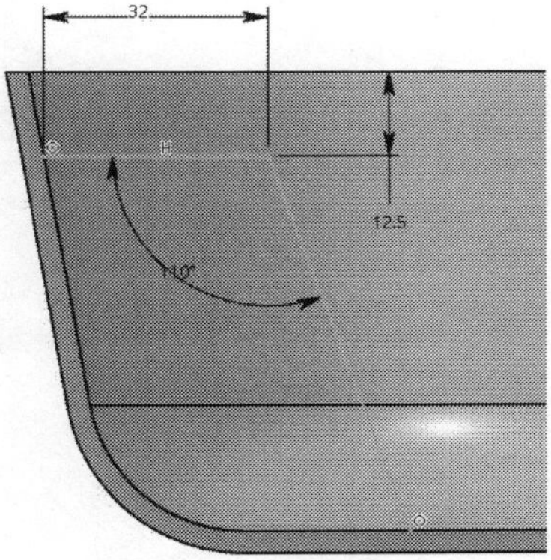

Figure 6–50

13. In the Action Bar, click (Exit App) to complete the sketch. The part displays as shown in Figure 6–51.

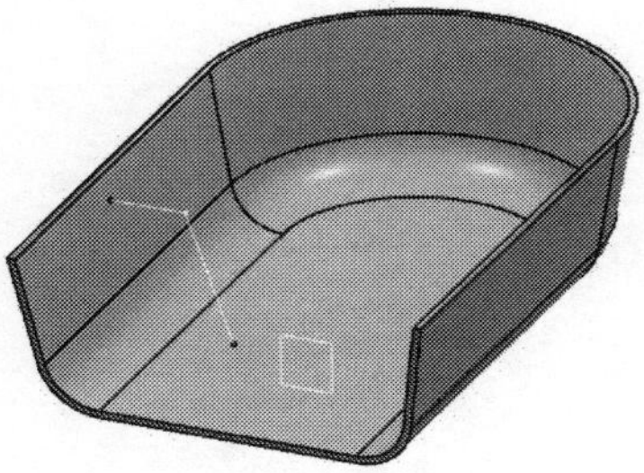

Figure 6–51

Task 2 - Create a Pad feature that represents the Rib's geometry.

1. Select the sketch and, in the *Model* section of the Action Bar, click (Pad).
2. Enter **1.60 (0.063 in)** for the length.
3. Select the (Mirrored extent) option to add material on both sides of the sketch plane.
4. Click **OK** to complete the feature. The part displays as shown in Figure 6–52.

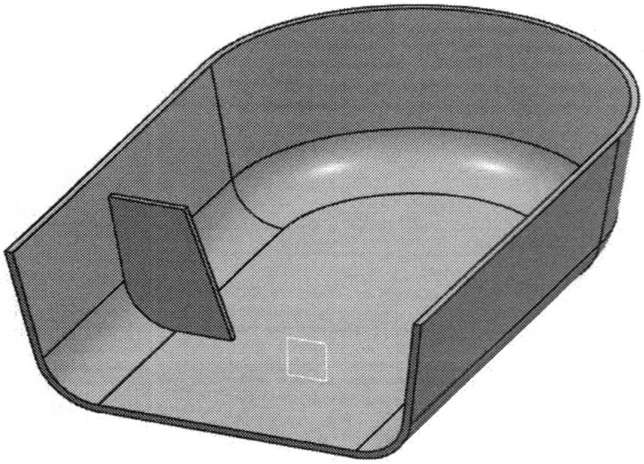

Figure 6–52

5. In the Top Bar, click (Share)>**Save** to save the part.
6. Close the *Part1* tab.

Practice 6d

Pad and Pocket

Practice Objective

- Create a Pad feature and a Pocket feature.

In this practice, you will create the model shown in Figure 6–53 using Pad and Pocket features.

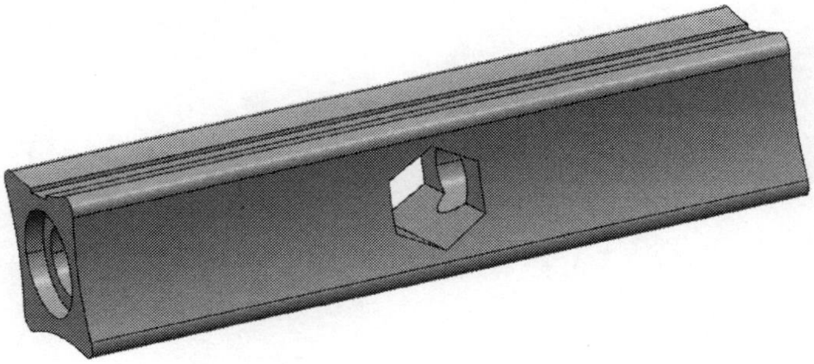

Figure 6–53

Task 1 - Create a Pad feature.

In this task, you will create a Pad feature to define the base feature for the model.

1. Create a new part.
2. In the 3D Part dialog box, enter ***Your_Initials*_Pad_Pocket** as the *Title*.
3. Select the *3D Shape* tab and enter **Pad_Pocket** as the *Title*.
4. Select the *Characteristics* tab and ensure **Enable hybrid design** is disabled.
5. Click **OK.**
6. Select the YZ plane and click  (Sketch).

7. To create the required profile, start by creating two centered rectangle construction squares, using dimensions of **80 (3.150 in)** and **100 (3.937 in)**, as shown in Figure 6–54.

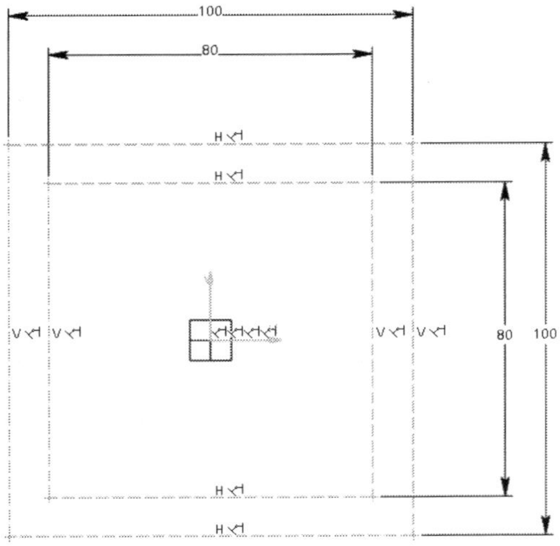

Figure 6–54

8. In the Action Pad, expand the circle flyout and click  (Three Point Arc).

9. Select the three points as shown in Figure 6–55 to create the arc.

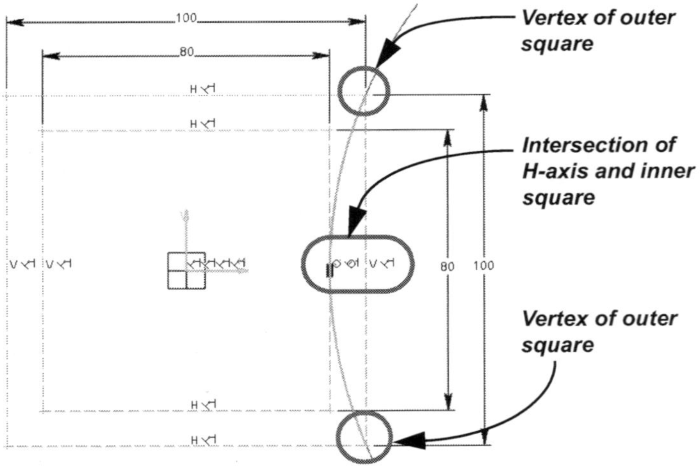

Figure 6–55

10. Create three more arcs using the method described in the previous step. The completed arcs display as shown in Figure 6–56.

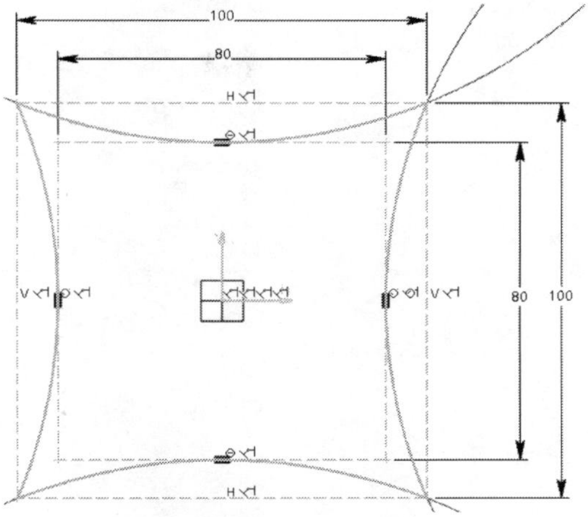

Figure 6–56

11. Select one of the arcs and click  (Auto Search).

12. In context toolbar, click  (Corner).

13. In the Tools Palette, enter **8 (0.315 in) for the radius**. The completed profile displays as shown in Figure 6–57.

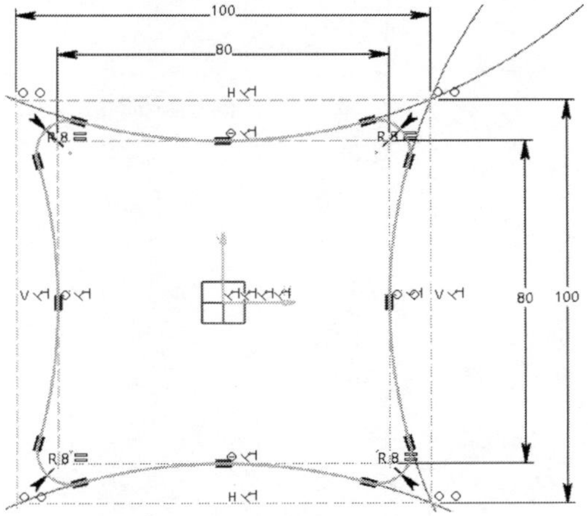

Figure 6–57

14. Exit the Sketch app to complete the sketch.

Task 2 - Create a Pad feature.

*If prompted to convert points to construction entities, click **Yes**.*

1. In the Action Bar, click  (Pad) and enter the following properties:
   - *Profile:* **Sketch.1**
   - *Length:* **400mm (15.748 in)**
2. Click **OK**.

Task 3 - Create a Pocket profile.

1. Create a sketch on the face as shown in Figure 6–58.
2. Sketch the **60 (2.362 in)** diameter circular profile as shown in Figure 6–59.

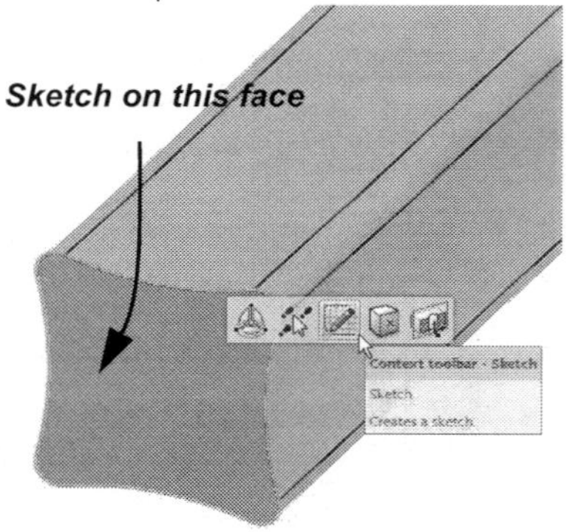

Figure 6–58

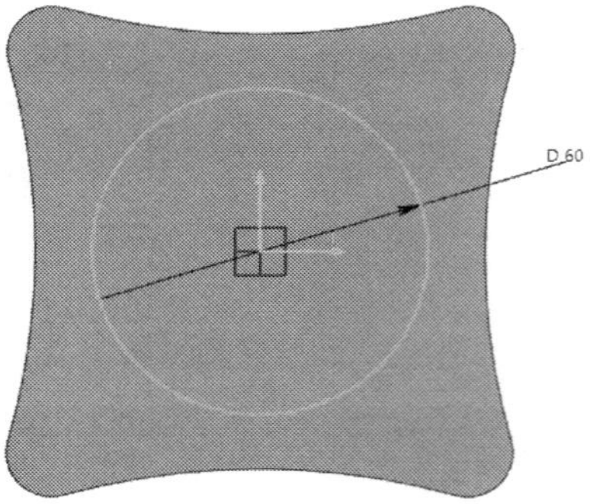

Figure 6–59

3. Exit the Sketch app.

Task 4 - Create a Pocket.

1. Create a Pocket feature using the profile just created. Enter a depth of **10 (0.394 in)**. The completed feature displays as shown in Figure 6–60.

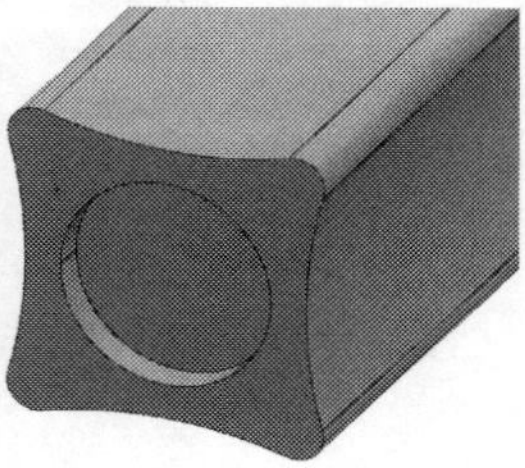

Figure 6–60

Task 5 - Create a through Pocket.

To create this Pocket, you will copy and paste a Sketch. This Sketch will act independently of the original profile.

1. In the specification tree, expand PartBody and Pocket.1, and then select **Sketch.2**. This is the 60mm diameter profile used to create the previous Pocket feature.
2. In the Action Bar, click  (Copy).
3. Select the face as shown in Figure 6–61.

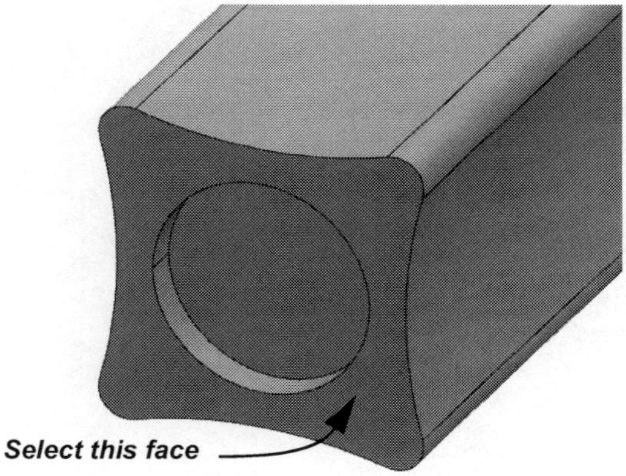

Figure 6–61

4. In the Action Bar, click  (Paste). The profile is pasted onto the part as **Sketch.3**, as shown in Figure 6–62.

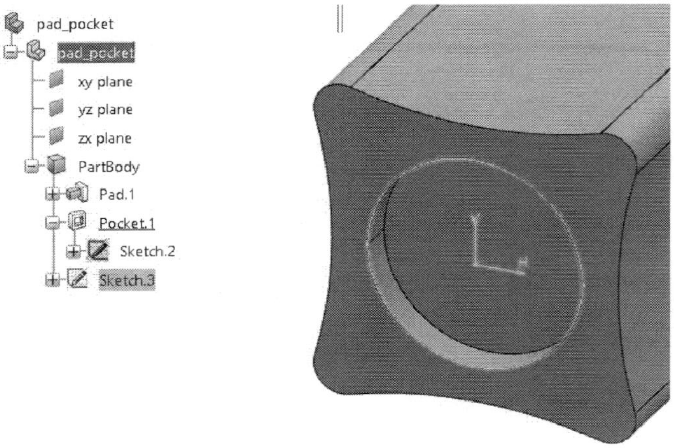

Figure 6–62

5. Double-click **Sketch.3** and change the diameter from *60* (2.362 in) to **40 (1.575 in)**. Do not exit Sketcher.

6. Sketch and dimension a rectangular profile, as shown in Figure 6–63. Verify that the rectangle is symmetrical about the vertical axis.
   - 10 (0.394 in)
   - 20 (0.787 in)
   - 38 (1.496 in)
   - 40 (1.575 in)

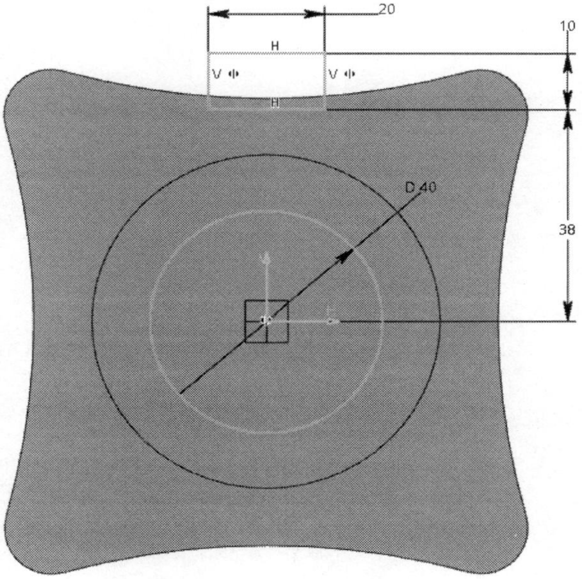

Figure 6–63

Design Considerations

Creating a profile that has more than one closed section has advantages and disadvantages. One advantage is that fewer sketched based features need to be created (in this case, one less sketch and Pocket will be created). However, the disadvantage is that the rectangular Pocket cannot be deactivated without deactivating the circular Pocket. Verify that you structure your model according to your design intent.

7. Create a Pocket feature using **Sketch.3**. Set the *First Limit Type* to **Up to last**. The model displays as shown in Figure 6–64.

Figure 6–64

Task 6 - Create a Pocket.

1. Create a sketch on the ZX plane. In the Action Bar, expand the 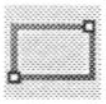 (Rectangle) flyout and click 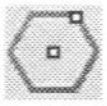 (Polygon). Place the sketch and use a dimension of **50 (1.969 in)**, as shown in Figure 6–65.

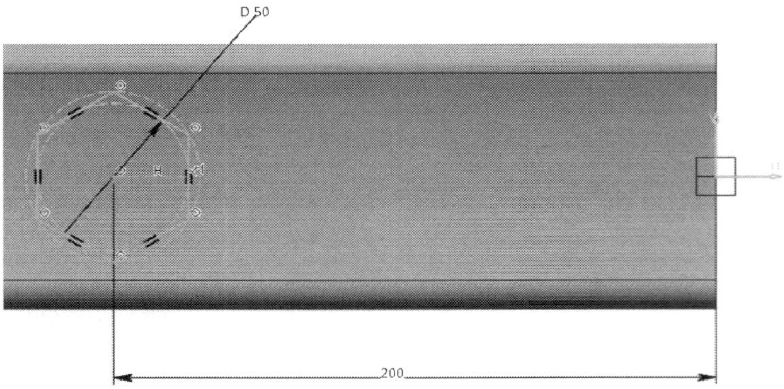

Figure 6–65

2. Create a Pocket feature that removes the hexagonal section from both sides of the sketch plane, using the **Up to last** option.

3. Hide the default reference planes. The completed model displays as shown in Figure 6–66.

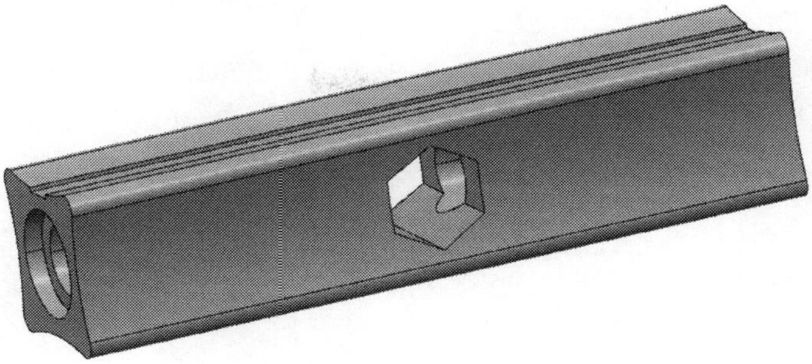

Figure 6–66

4. In the Top Bar, click  (Share)>**Save** to save the part.
5. Close the ***Pad_Pocket*** tab.

NOTE: Additional pad and pocket practices are found in Practice B3, Practice B4, and Practice B5 at the end of this guide.

Chapter Review Questions

1. What is the general term for the first solid feature in a model?
   a. Foundation feature
   b. Base Feature
   c. Sketch
   d. Reference plane
2. Multiple profiles can be used as a profile for a Pad feature.
   a. True
   b. False
3. A Pad feature can be converted to a Pocket by changing its direction.
   a. True
   b. False
4. What option is used to create a Pad that is symmetrical to the sketch support?
   a. **Symmetric**
   b. **Mirror**
   c. **Mirrored Extent**
   d. None of the above.
5. To use the **Up to Surface** depth option, the terminating surface must completely intersect the feature.
   a. True
   b. False
6. Which of the following are true, related to open sketches?
   a. An open profile can be used as the profile for a Pad when the open end of the sketch is bounded by existing geometry.
   b. Although you can use open profiles, it is good practice to create features using closed profiles wherever possible.
   c. Open profiles increase update time and introduce instability in the model.
   d. All of the above.

7. The sketch shown on the left side of Figure 6–67 is used to create a Pocket feature. What will the Pocket look like? Note the direction arrows in the image on the right side of Figure 6–67.

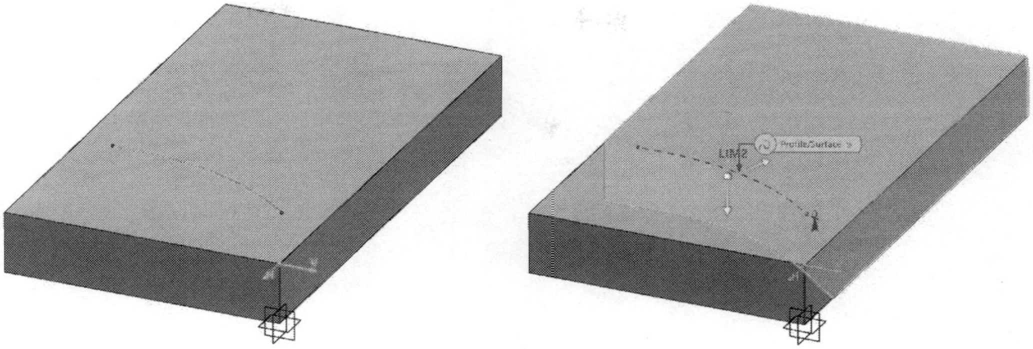

Figure 6–67

a. The Pocket feature would fail (No image).

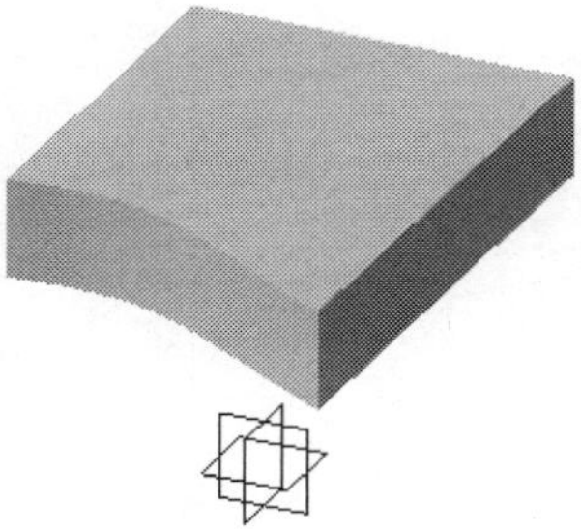

b. Resulting Geometry:

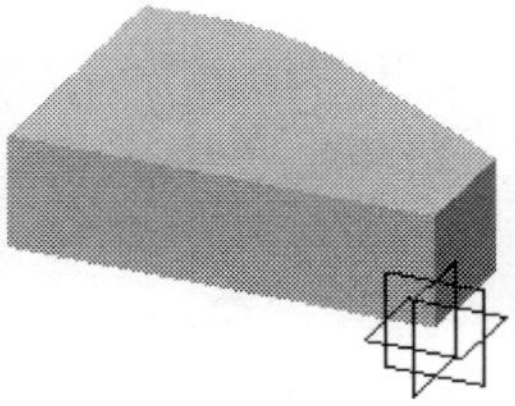

c. Resulting Geometry:

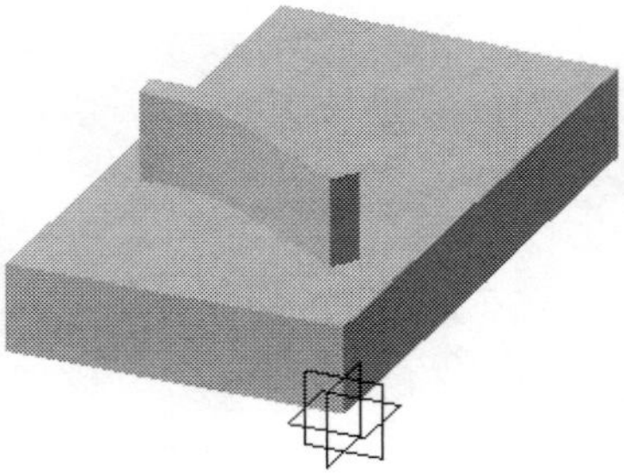

d. Resulting Geometry:

8. In the specification tree shown in Figure 6–68, if you delete **Sketch.1**, **Pad.1** fails because **Sketch.1** is listed under the **Pad.1** branch of the feature tree, meaning **Pad.1** uses **Sketch.1** as its profile.

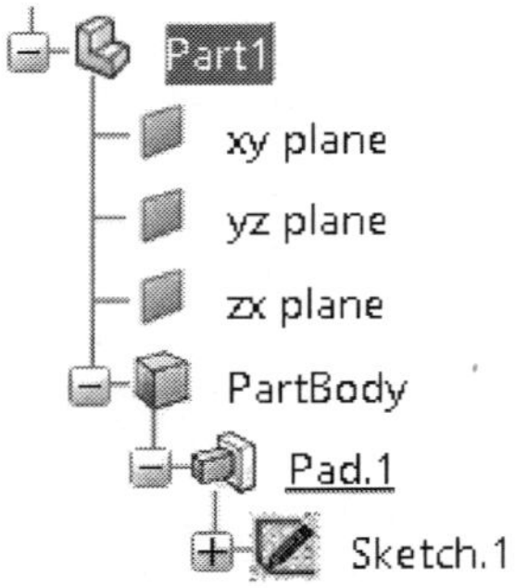

Figure 6–68

   a. True

   b. False

Answers: 1b, 2a, 3b, 4c, 5a, 6d, 7c, 8a

Sketcher Tools and Techniques

It is important to understand all of the elements of the Sketch app to work productively in CATIA. The Sketch app has many useful tools that can help save time when designing and making changes.

Learning Objectives in This Chapter

- Understand the difference between a standard sketch and a positioned sketch.
- Use imported geometry.
- Understand the various methods of projecting entities from existing geometry into the sketch.
- Learn about the available tools for editing sketch entities.
- Understand how the SmartPick tool can help in the creation of sketches.
- Use the Visualization to help clarify the display while sketching.

7.1 Positioned Sketch

In CATIA, you can create a sketch in two different ways:

- Standard Sketch
- Positioned Sketch

Positioned Sketch

In a standard sketch, the sketch axis is free to move on the sketch support if the 3D geometry is modified. A positioned sketch enables you to select references to define the origin and orientation of the sketch support. This method enables the designer to incorporate the design intent of the model into the sketch. If you need to move the sketch relative to a geometric reference, you can define it during the creation of a positioned sketch. This provides more predictable results when modifying the geometry downstream.

How To: Create a Positioned Sketch

1. In the *Essentials* section of the Action Bar, click (Positioned Sketch). The Sketch Positioning dialog box opens, as shown in Figure 7–1.

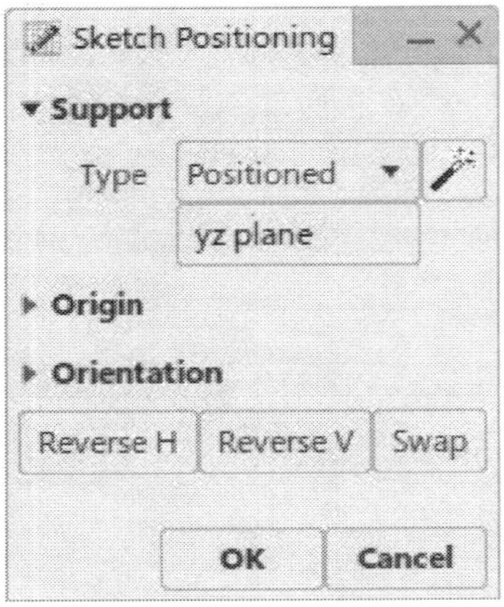

Figure 7–1

2. Ensure that (Smart Positioning) is currently **NOT** selected. (If it is selected, the *Type* field in the *Support* section will be grayed out and the Sketch Positioning window will close as soon as a support is selected.)
3. Verify that the **Positioned** option is selected in the Type drop-down list in the *Sketch Positioning* area. A default sketch support is selected.

4. Place your cursor over any planar surface or datum plane, and it highlights on the screen, as shown in Figure 7–2.

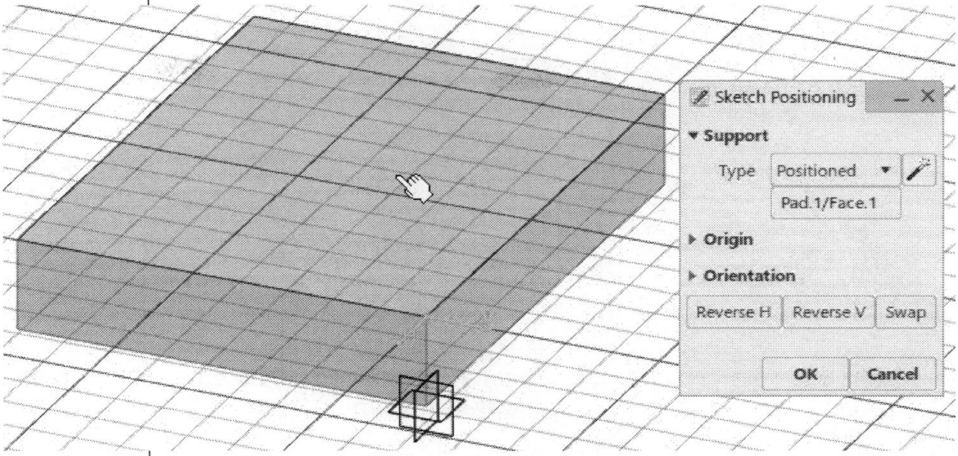

Figure 7–2

5. Select the required planar reference to define the sketch support. The sketch axis system displays on the part.
6. To define the location of the origin of the sketch axis system, in the *Origin* area, select an option in the Type drop-down list and select an appropriate reference, as shown in Figure 7–3.

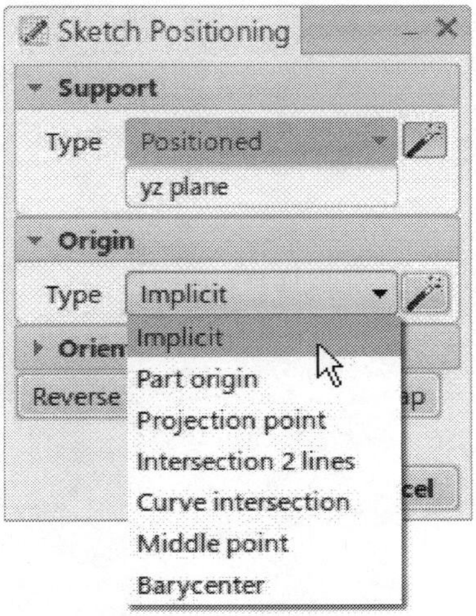

Figure 7–3

Some of the more commonly used options are described as follows:

Option	Description
Projection point	The origin of the sketch is located at the projection of a selected point or vertex onto the sketch support.
Intersection 2 lines	The intersection of two lines creates a point. The origin of the sketch is located at the projection of this intersection point onto the sketch support.
Barycenter	The origin of the sketch is located at the projection of the center of the area of the selected entity.

7. To define the orientation of the sketch axis system, in the *Orientation* area, select an option in the Type drop-down list and select an appropriate reference as shown in Figure 7–4.

*You can use the **Reverse H**, **Reverse V**, and **Swap** options at the bottom of the dialog box to re-orient the sketch axis system.*

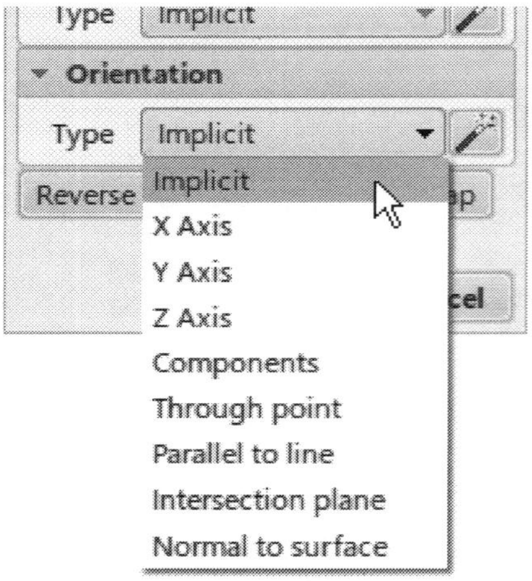

Figure 7–4

7.2 Copying and Importing Sketch Geometry

Copy and Paste

Copying and pasting a sketch is a quick way of duplicating sketch geometry between part models or in the same part model.

How To: Copy a Sketch from Another CATIA File into the Current File

1. Open the model that contains the sketch you want to copy.
2. Right-click sketch in the specification tree and select **Copy**, as shown in Figure 7–5. Alternatively, select the sketch and in the Action Bar, click  (Copy).

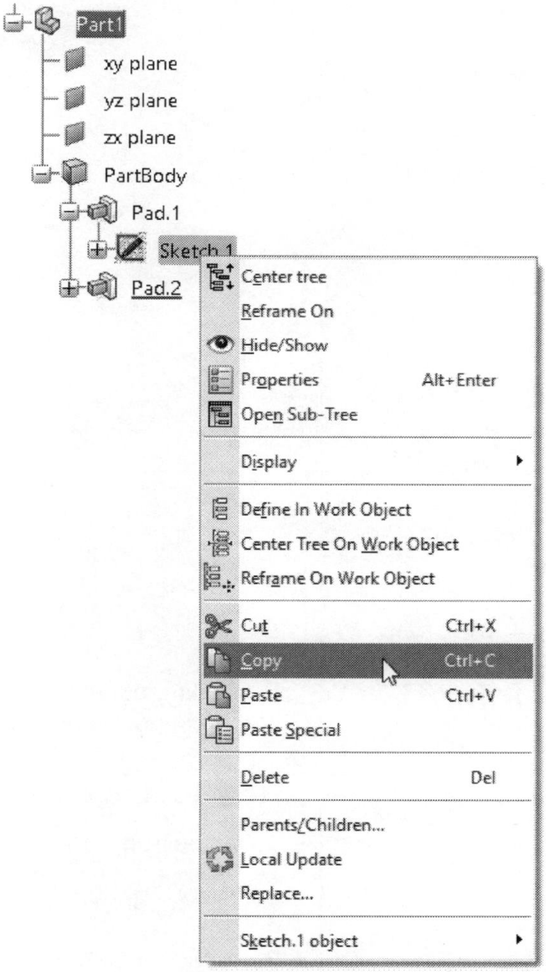

Figure 7–5

3. Activate the current file and select a plane or face as the support for the copied sketch. Right-click and select **Paste**, as shown in Figure 7–6. Alternatively, in the Action Bar, click (Paste). A copy of the sketch is created in the current model.

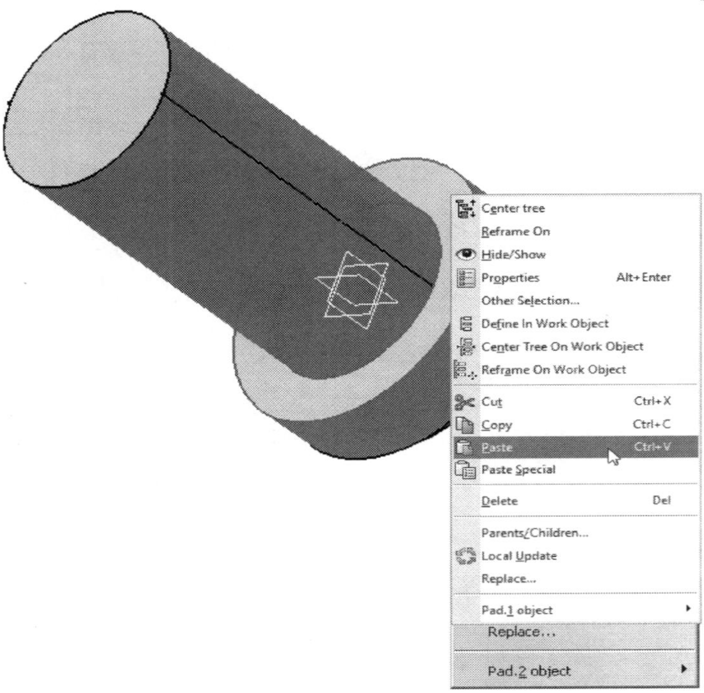

Figure 7–6

4. Verify that the sketch is correctly constrained by double-clicking on it in the specification tree to edit it and then using **Sketch Analysis** tool.

Import 2D Section

Sections created in other systems using formats such as DXF can be imported as sketches.

How To: Import a 2D Section

1. In the Top Bar, click (Add), and then click **Import**.
2. In the Import dialog box, select **DXF2d (*.dxf)** from the Format drop down list.
3. In the Filename field, click (Open), and navigate to the correct folder.

4. Select the **DXF** file.

5. Click **OK**.

6. A new window opens with the DXF sketch. Click **OK** in the Operation report dialog box.

7. On the left of the window, click to display the specification tree, if required.

8. In the specification tree, select **Main View**.

9. Right-click and select **Copy**, as shown in Figure 7–43.

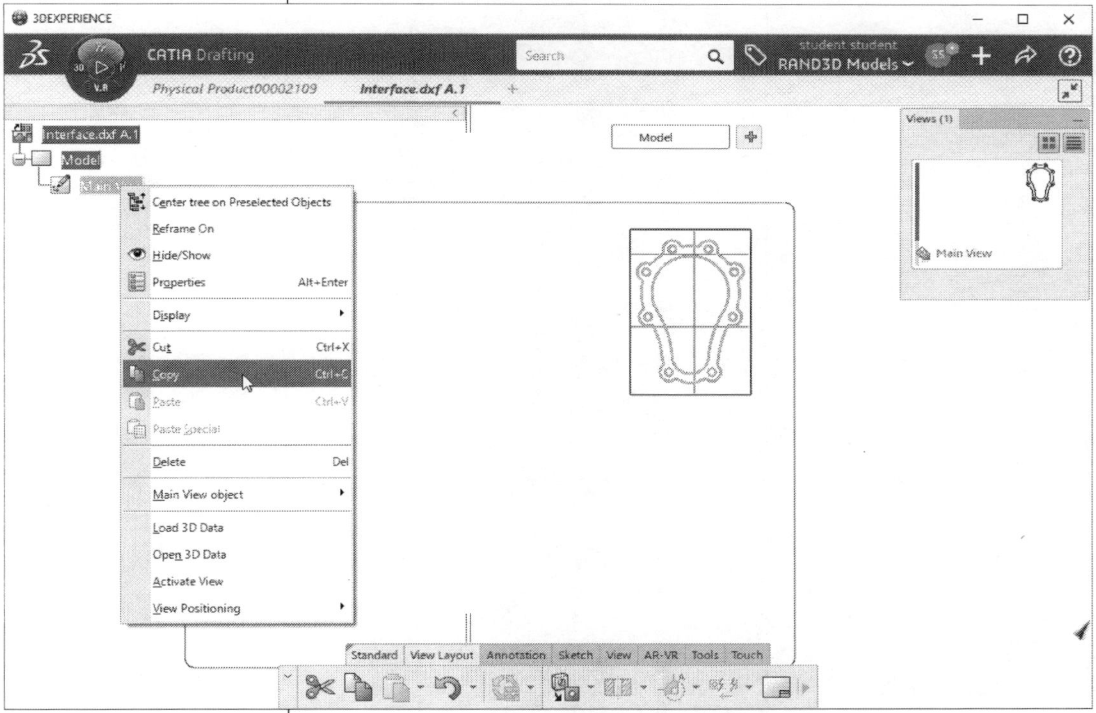

Figure 7–7

10. Select the tab of the part you are importing into to switch back to the 3D solid model.

11. Select a planar surface and paste the copied sketch geometry, as shown in Figure 7–44.

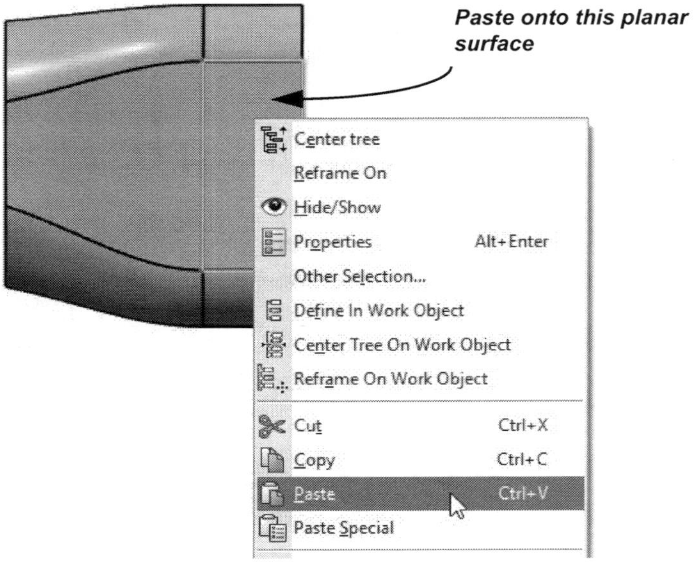

Figure 7–8

7.3 Projecting Geometry

The **3D Geometry** flyout options enable you to create sketches using existing 3D geometry. These options, found in the *Sketch* section of the Action Bar, are shown in Figure 7–9.

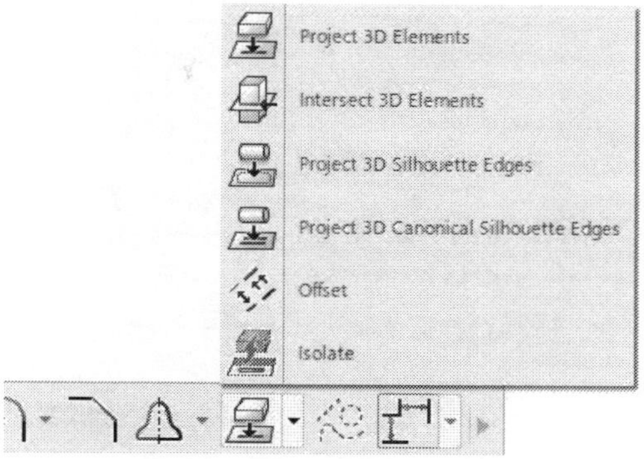

Figure 7–9

Project 3D Elements

 (Project 3D Elements) creates sketched geometry by projecting 3D entities such as edges and surfaces onto the 2D support. If the referenced geometry changes, the projected elements update accordingly. Projected entities display in yellow, indicating that they are locked in place. Locked entities cannot be translated, rotated, or scaled. However, they can be manipulated using the Relimitations toolbar options or by applying corners or chamfers.

If you select the curved surface of a cylindrical face, you can right-click and select **Select Boundary Edges** or **Select Axis**, as shown in Figure 7–10.

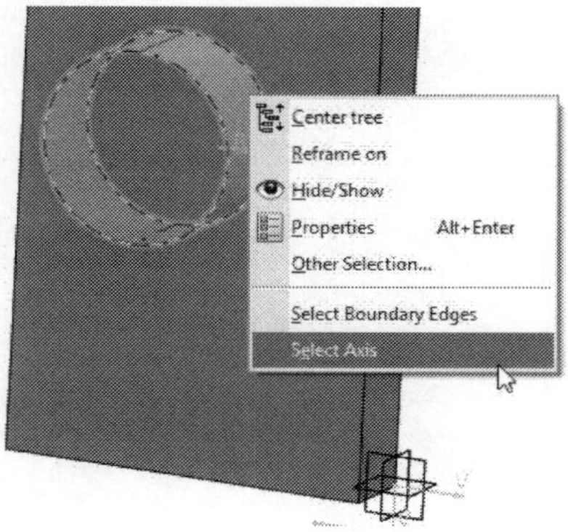

Figure 7–10

Intersecting 3D Elements

 (Intersect 3D Elements) creates a projected entity where the selected 3D entity intersects the support. Projected entities display in yellow, indicating that they are locked in place. As with projected 3D entities, you can still apply options from the Relimitation toolbar, corners, and chamfers to intersected 3D entities.

If you select the curved surface of a cylindrical face, you can right-click and select **Select Boundary Edges** or **Select Axis**.

Project 3D Silhouette Edges

 (Project 3D Silhouette Edges) projects all of the silhouette edges of a feature onto the support. For example, the edge along the Spherical feature and adjacent planar surface (shown in Figure 7–11) are required references for the new geometry.

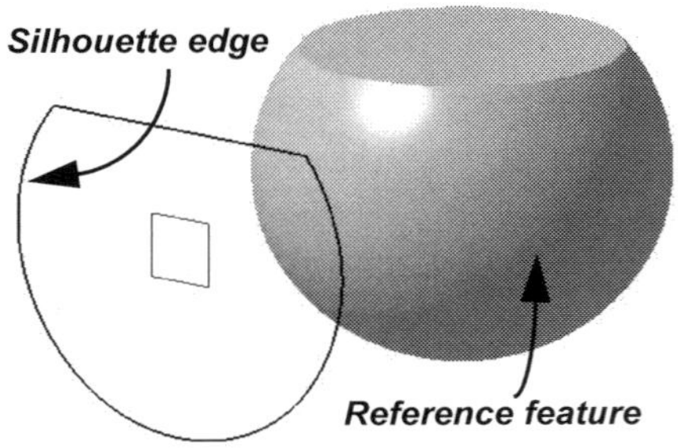

Figure 7–11

Project 3D Canonical Silhouette Edges

 (Project 3D Canonical Silhouette Edges) only projects the silhouette edges of curved surfaces onto the support. In the example shown in Figure 7–12, the edge along the Spherical feature is a required reference for the new geometry.

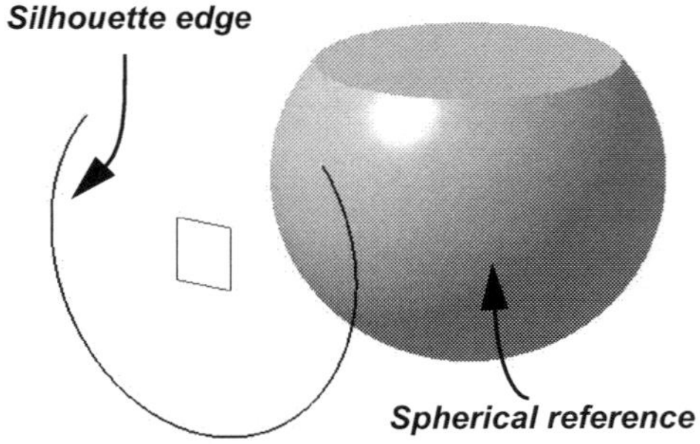

Figure 7–12

If the referenced geometry changes, the sketch also changes.

These four tools create a relationship between the sketched geometry and the referenced 3D geometry.

Sketch Analysis

To analyze and review the projections and intersections defined in a sketch, access the Sketch Analysis dialog box by clicking  (Sketch Analysis) in the *Analysis* section of the Action. The dialog box is shown in Figure 7–13. Select the *Use-edges* tab, which displays the status of all entities that are projected from existing geometry. The cylindrical Pad in the center of the rectangle was referenced for a hole in the center of the new sketch.

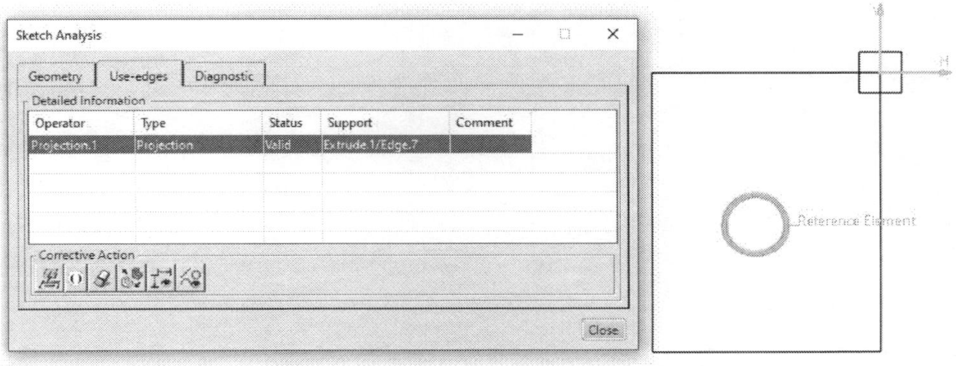

Figure 7–13

As with the *Geometry* tab, you can use the icons in the *Corrective Action* area of the dialog box to correct any problems with the referenced geometry. These icons are described as follows:

Icon	Description
	Isolates the entity such that it is no longer linked to or referenced to 3D geometry.
	Toggles off/on the highlighted constraint in the detailed information area.
	Removes the highlighted geometry from the sketch.
	Replaces highlighted referenced geometry with selected geometry on the screen.
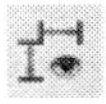	Toggles the display of constraints.
	Toggles the display of construction geometry.

7.4 Editing Tools

To modify sketched geometry, use the options found in the *Sketch* section of the Action Bar. Figure 7–14 shows the options available for editing the 2D elements in your sketch.

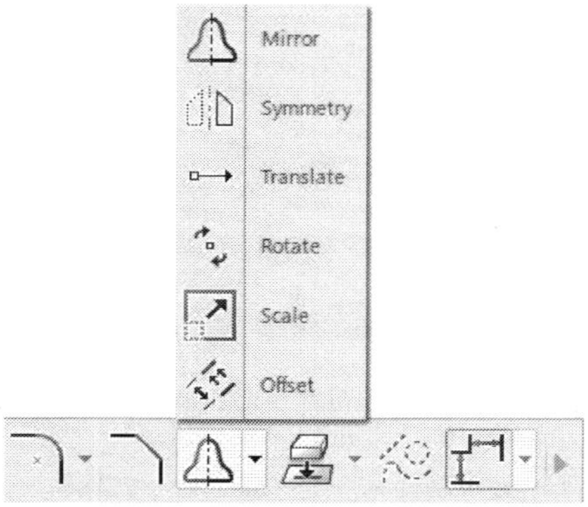

Figure 7–14

Mirror

Click (Mirror) to symmetrically mirror sketched geometry about a line or axis, as shown in Figure 7–15.

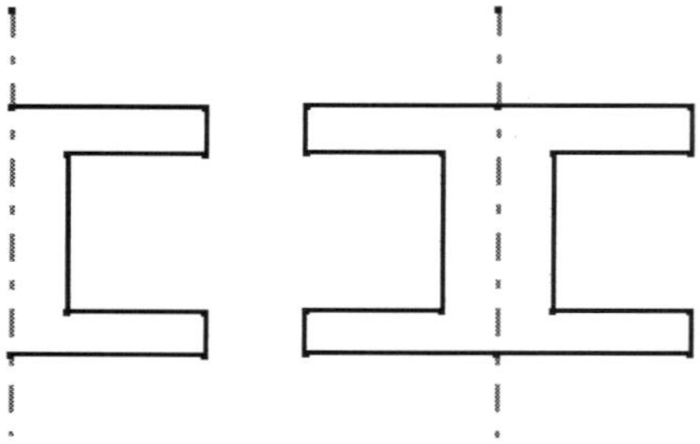

Figure 7–15

Symmetry

Click (Symmetry) to symmetrically transform the selected geometry about a line or axis, as shown in Figure 7–16.

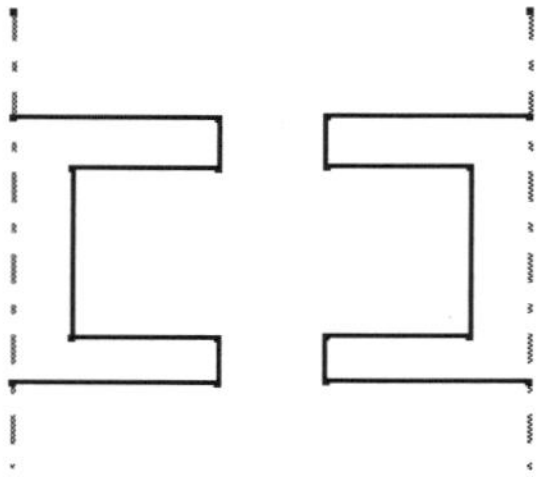

Figure 7–16

Translate

The **Translate** option moves sketched geometry you have selected along a translation vector.

How To: Translate Entities

1. Select the entities that you want to move, and click 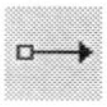 (Translate). The Translation Definition dialog box opens.
2. Select a location on the screen as the start point for the translation. The Translation Definition dialog box updates, as shown in Figure 7–17.

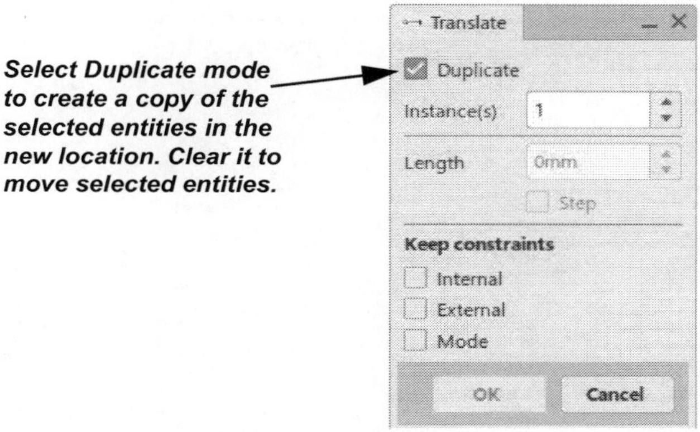

Figure 7–17

3. In the *Length* area, enter a specific value for the translation, or move the start point directly on the model to the required location.
   - If the **Step** option is selected, the cursor snaps in increments of the value entered in the *Value* field.
4. Select the **Duplicate** option to keep the original sketch and create a copy of it in the new location.
5. Click **OK** to complete the definition.

Rotate

 (Rotate) enables you to rotate sketched geometry using a method similar to that for translating.

How To: Rotate Entities

1. Select the entity or entities that you want to rotate, and click  (Rotate) to open the Rotation Definition dialog box.
2. Select a location for the center of rotation and the dialog box updates as shown in Figure 7–19.

If the Step option is selected, each element is rotated from the previous element by the angle value. For example, if the value of angle is 10, the entities would rotate in 10 degree steps.

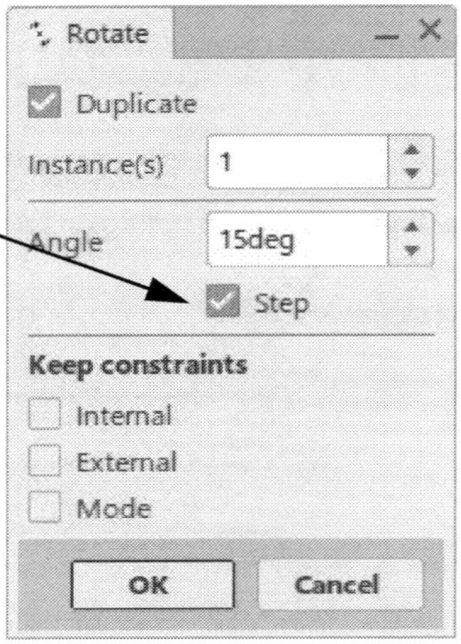

Figure 7–18

3. In the *Angle* area, enter a value for angle of rotation and click **OK**.
   - As with translation, selecting the **Duplicate** option keeps the original entities and rotates a copy of them to the new angle.

Scale

The **Scale** option resizes the selected sketched geometry using a scale factor.

How To: Scale Entities

1. Select the entities to edit and click  (Scale) to open the Scale Definition dialog box.
2. Select a location for the scaling centerpoint, and the Scale Definition dialog box updates, as shown in Figure 7–19.

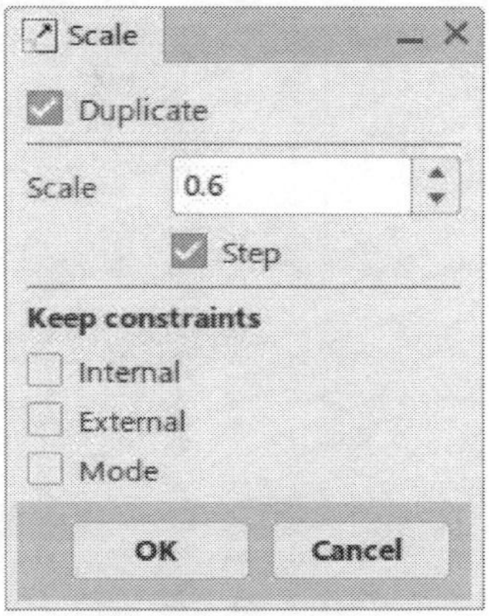

Figure 7–19

3. Enter the scale value and click **OK** to complete the definition.

For each of the Translate, Rotate, and Scale options, the following options apply:

Keep internal constraints	Preserves the internal constraints applied to the selected elements.
Keep external constraints	Preserves the external constraints applied to the selected elements.
Keep Mode	Preserves the original constraints applied to the selected elements. The constraints defined in the original geometry are driving constraints.
Step	Enter a value, and dragged entities will move in increments matching the value. For example, if you enter a value of 10 for the Angle when rotating entities, the entities will rotate in increments of 10 degrees.

Offset

The **Offset** option enables you to create sketched entities by offsetting from existing sketched entities or from the edges of 3D geometry. Click  (Offset) and select the entity that you want to offset. If offsetting from other sketched geometry, use the Sketch Tools toolbar options to define how to offset the entity. These options are described as follows:

Icon	Example	Description
 (No Propagation)	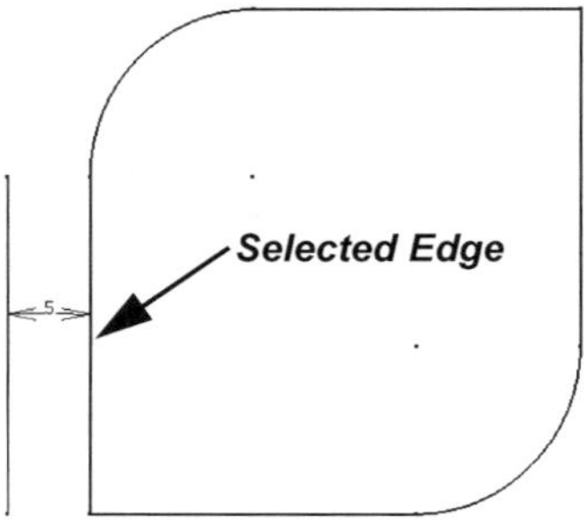	Offsets a single selected entity.
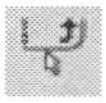 (Tangent Propagation)	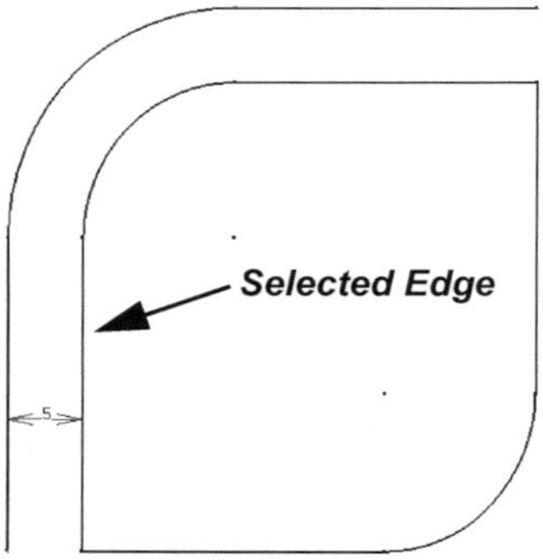	Offsets the selected entity and any entities that form a tangent chain with it.
 (Point Propagation)	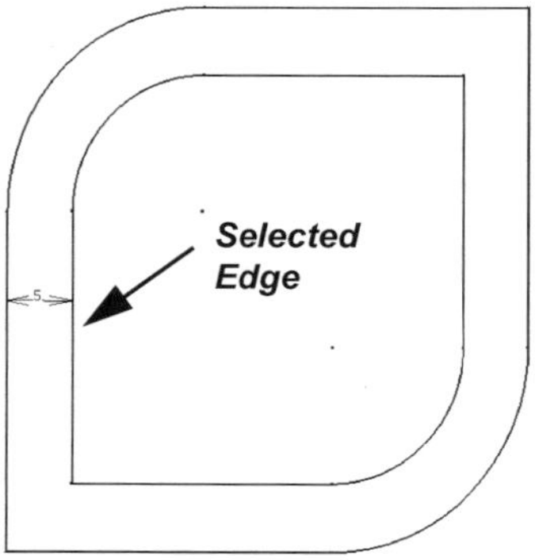	Offsets the selected entity and any entities that form a chain with it.

Additionally, you can offset in both directions by clicking 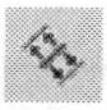 in the Sketch Tools toolbar. Offset in both directions can be applied to both sketched entities and edges of 3D geometry, as shown in Figure 7–20.

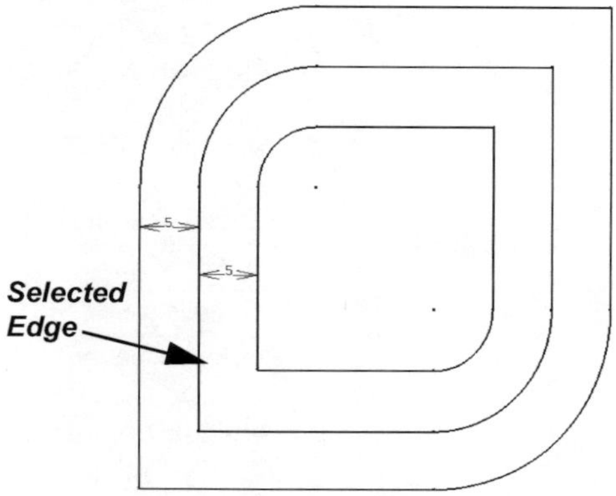

Figure 7–20

The offset can be repeated several times by entering the number of instances in the Sketch Tools toolbar. Each instance is offset from the previous one by the offset distance, as shown in Figure 7–21.

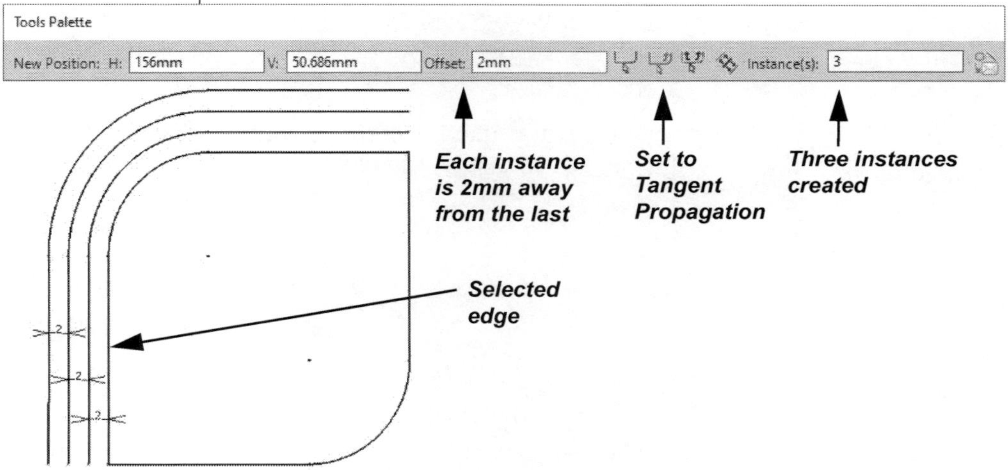

Figure 7–21

In addition to offsetting individual elements of a an existing 3D profile, you can offset an entire profile, provided it contains simple geometry such as lines, arcs and circles, and has no self-intersecting entities.

7.5 Sketch Using SmartPick

SmartPick is an automatic tool used to ease the creation of a sketch. SmartPick is active anytime you create new geometry in Sketcher. As you sketch with SmartPick, it dynamically detects entities and adds positional and geometrical constraints to the geometry being created. The constraints being added display as symbols on the screen.

SmartPick detects the following entity positions and constraints:

• Support line and circles	• Tangency
• Alignment	• Concentricity
• Parallelism	• Horizontal and vertical
• Perpendicularity	• Midpoint

SmartPick only detects references and adds constraints to geometry in the active sketch. It does not snap to previously created features or sketches. If a reference to a previous feature is required, you must either project the 3D elements you want to reference into the current sketch, or sketch the geometry, unconstrained, and then add the required geometric constraints.

When SmartPick is active, the cursor changes to a crosshair symbol. The **H** and **V** coordinates for the cursor location display on the screen and in the Sketch Tools toolbar. All constraints detected by SmartPick display on the screen and are indicated by a change in color, as shown in Figure 7–22.

- Entities used to create the constraint and the constraint added displays in blue.

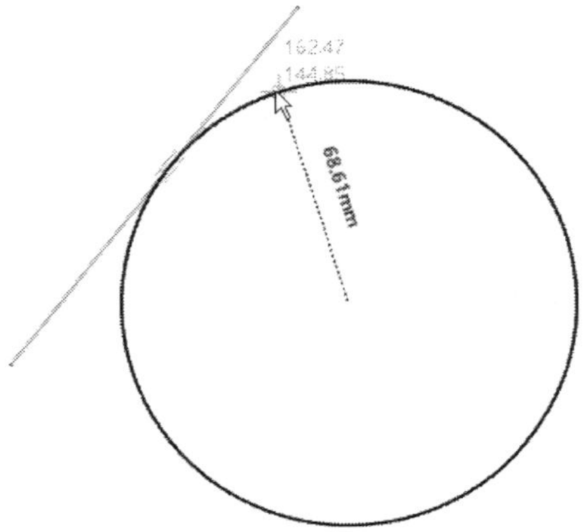

A circle being created tangent to a line with SmartPick.

Figure 7–22

Shortcut Menus

While sketching, the cursor becomes highlighted when moved over an existing sketched entity. Once highlighted, right-click on the entity to access its shortcut options.

For example, while creating a new line, the cursor is moved over an existing angled line. Right-click on the highlighted angled line to display the shortcut menu, as shown in Figure 7–23. The new line can be created so that it starts at the angled line's midpoint or its nearest end point.

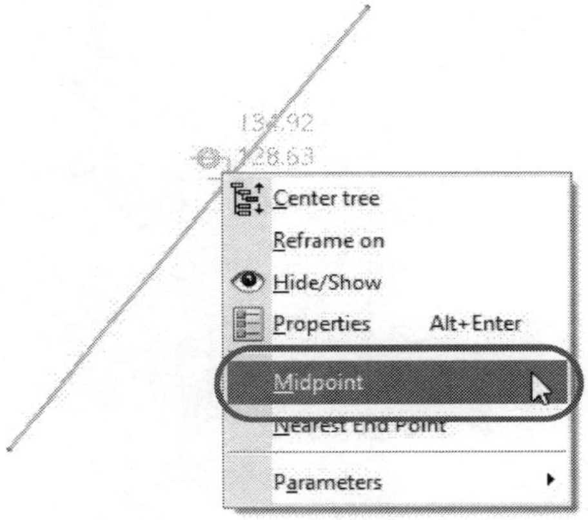

Figure 7–23

<Shift> and <Ctrl>

Use <Shift> and <Ctrl> to better control the creation of a constraint using SmartPick. If SmartPick detects a reference that is not required, you can temporarily deactivate the detection feature by pressing <Shift> as you sketch. You can also force the current constraint to snap using <Ctrl>. Once displayed, press <Ctrl> to keep the constraint snapped as you move the cursor.

SmartPick Options

You can control the type of constraints that SmartPick detects by changing the sketcher settings. The settings are accessed by selecting **Me** in the top bar, then clicking **Preferences> App Preferences>3D Modeling>3D Modeling Core>Sketcher>Constraint>SmartPick**. The available options are shown in Figure 7–24.

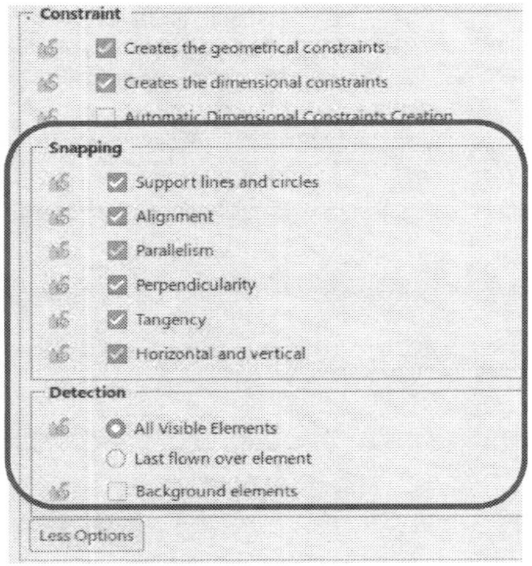

Figure 7–24

Constraint Tools

You can automatically generate geometric and dimensional constraints using the options shown in the *Sketch* section of the Action Bar, shown in Figure 7–25.

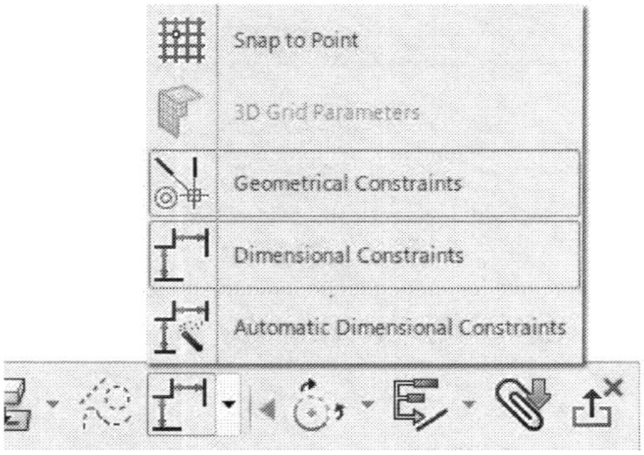

Figure 7–25

When you enable  (Geometrical Constraints), constraints detected are permanently added to the model.

- If the icon is toggled on (default setting), constraints are added to the sketch and updated when changes occur in the model.
- If the icon is toggled off, a permanent constraint is not added and does not update with changes to the model.

When you enable  (Dimensional Constraints), the software automatically creates dimensions for corner and chamfer elements. It also creates dimensions when you manually enter coordinates or manually specify feature size while you are sketching.

When you enable  (Automatic Dimensional Constraints), the software automatically creates dimensions as you sketch rectangles, circles, arcs, and ellipses.

7.6 Visualization Tools

Visualization tools display information about the internal geometry of a part or constraints of a sketch. They also simplify the display of a sketch by hiding information for complex sections. You can access these tools in the Visualization toolbar shown in Figure 7–26.

Figure 7–26

The icons are described as follows:

Option	**Description**
(Grid)	Toggle the sketch grid on and off.
(Diagnostics)	Select to enable/disable the display of constraint diagnostic colors for sketched entities.
(Display Dimensional Constraints)	Select to enable/disable the display of all dimensional constraints in the sketch.
(Display Geometrical Constraints)	Select to enable/disable the display of all geometrical constraints in the sketch.
(Lock Rotation View Point)	Select to Lock or Unlock rotation about the current view point.
(Cutting Plane)	Select to cut away the geometry in front of a sketch plane so that you can constrain the sketch to internal edges.
(Only Current Body)	This option displays the geometry of the current part body or open body only.

Visualization drop-down	This drop-down contains three icons that control the display of existing model geometry in Sketcher. This functionality simplifies the view of a sketch by displaying 3D geometry in low light or by hiding it, thereby displaying only sketched geometry.
 (Usual)	All modeling elements display in the sketch view.
 (Low light)	All solid and surface geometry displays in a low light gray color. All wireframe and sketch geometry displays normally. Elements cannot be selected from the model and must be selected from the specification tree.
 (No 3D Background)	Only sketched elements created in the current section display. For example, the edges of an existing solid that have been projected onto the sketch display, but the geometry that was referenced is not. Elements can still be selected from the specification tree.

Practice 7a

Projecting 3D Geometry

Practice Objectives

- Project 3D geometry elements into a sketch.
- Offset sketched elements.

In this practice, you will practice using several projection tools in the Sketch app. You will also offset some of these elements using a variety of methods. You are provided with existing solid and surface geometry and you will use these to create sketched elements. Upon completion, the model displays as shown in Figure 7–27.

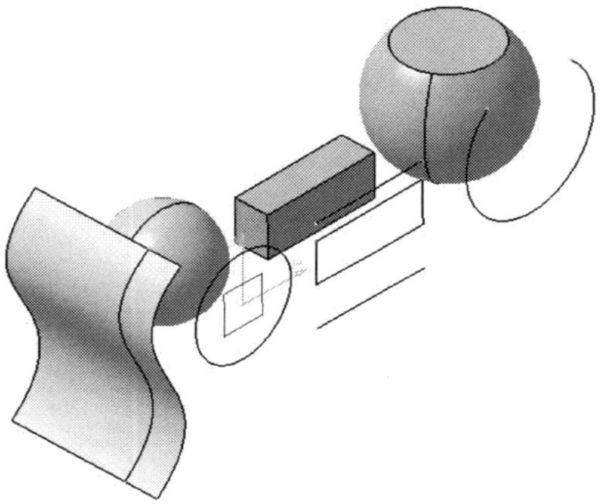

Figure 7–27

Task 1 - Open a part file and activate the Sketch app.

1. Import **SketchTools.3dxml**.
2. In the *SketchTools (Explore)* tab, right-click **SketchTools** in the specification tree and select **Open**.

3. Select the plane shown in Figure 7–28. Activate the Sketch app.

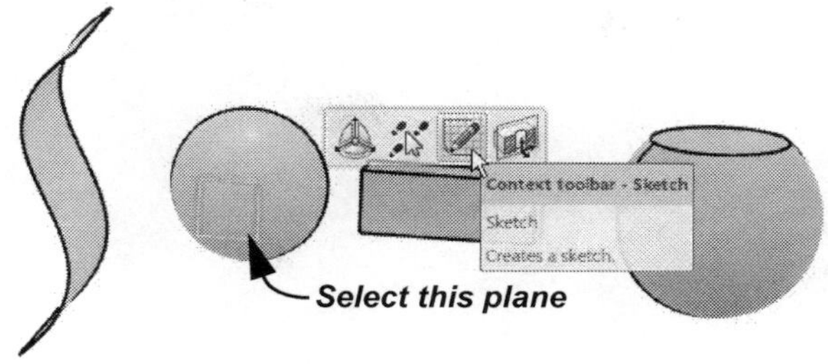

Figure 7–28

Task 2 - Project existing 3D geometry into the sketch.

In this task, you will project the edges of the rectangular Pad and the silhouette of the spherical surface onto the sketching plane. You will then create a sketcher entity at the intersection of the extruded surface and the sketch plane. The final geometry is shown in Figure 7–29.

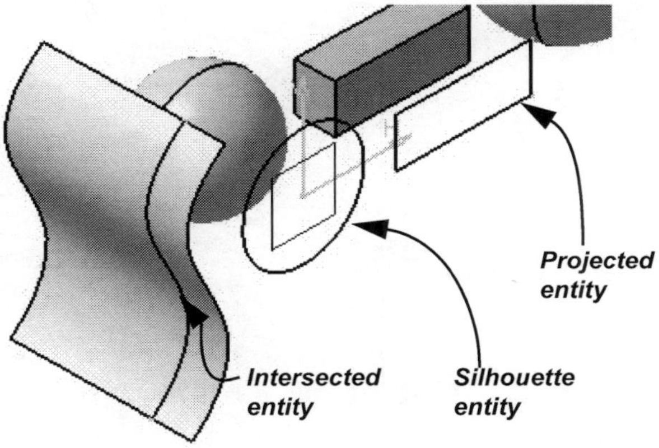

Figure 7–29

1. In the Action Bar, click  (Project 3D Elements).

2. Select the top edge of the rectangular Pad, as shown in Figure 7–30. In the Projection dialog box, click **OK** and select a space on the background. A yellow line displays, which represents the edge projected into the sketch.

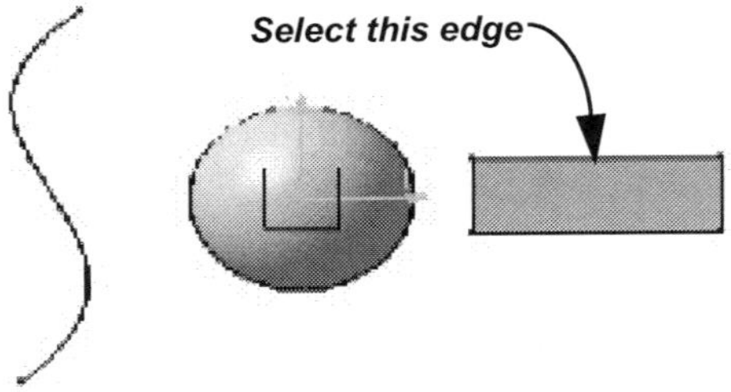

Figure 7–30

3. Click on (Project 3D Elements) and project the remaining three edges.

4. In the *View* section of the Action Bar, click (* iso). The view switches to Isometric, and the sketched elements display as shown in Figure 7–31.

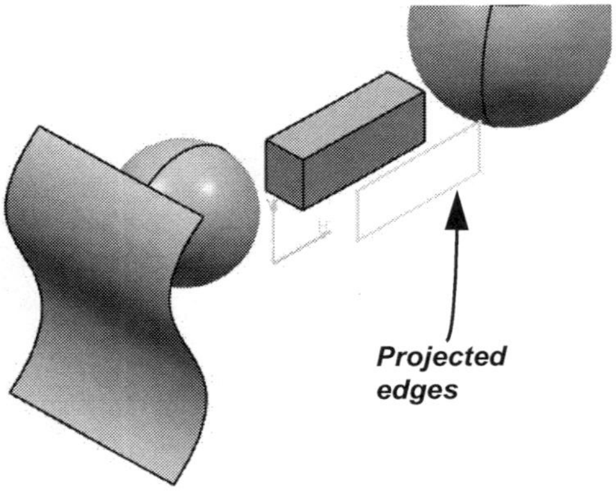

Figure 7–31

5. In the *Sketch* section of the Action Bar, click (Intersect 3D Elements).

6. Select the extruded surface and click **OK**. The element representing the intersection between the sketch plane and the Surface feature is created as shown in Figure 7–32.

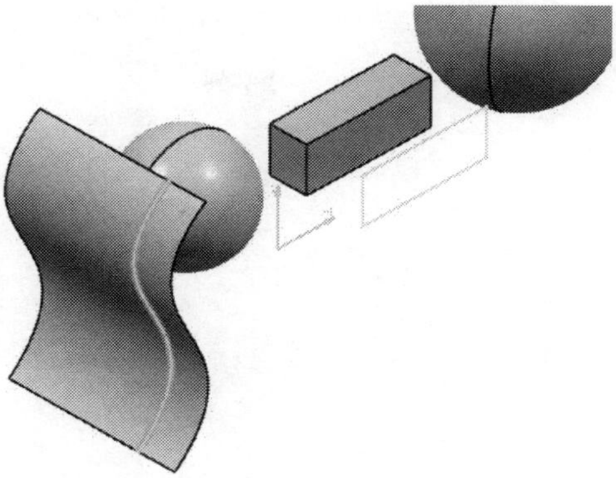

Figure 7–32

7. Select anywhere in the background to clear the selection of the intersection.

8. Click  (Project 3D Silhouette Edges).

9. Select the spherical surface. The silhouette edge of the surface is projected into the sketch plane as shown in Figure 7–33. Select in the background.

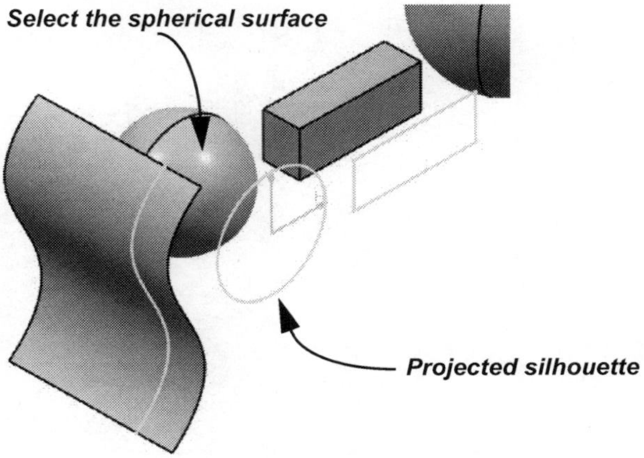

Figure 7–33

10. Click  (Project 3D Silhouette Edges).

11. Select the other spherical surface. The silhouette edges of the surface and adjacent edge are projected into the sketch plane as shown in Figure 7–34.

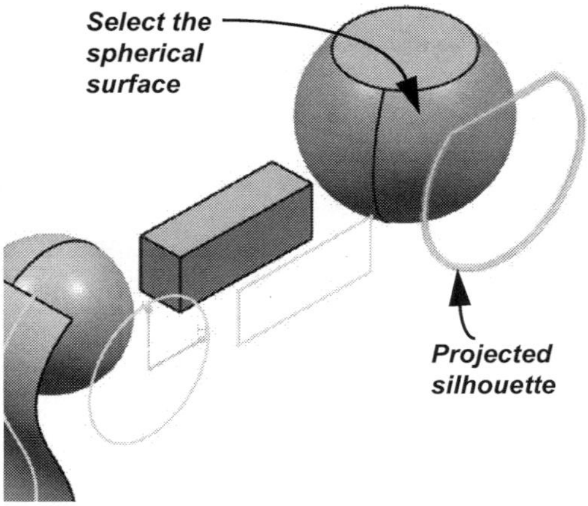

Figure 7–34

12. **Click** (Undo). If you clicked on the screen to accept the projection (if it turned yellow) you will have to click (Undo) twice.

13. Click (Project 3D Canonical Silhouette Edges).

14. Select the spherical surface. The silhouette edge of only the spherical surface is projected into the sketch plane as shown in Figure 7–35.

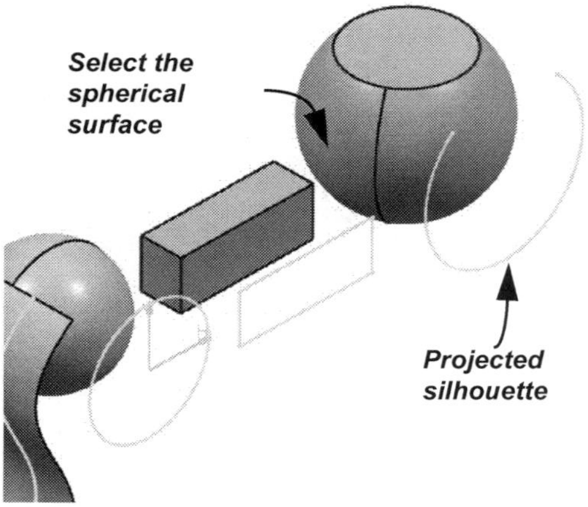

Figure 7–35

Task 3 - Create elements offset from the projected edges.

In this task, you will use the **Offset** option to make offset copies of the projected rectangle.

1. Click  (Normal View) to orient the model to the sketch view.
2. In the Action Bar, click  (Offset).
3. Select the top edge from the Pad. You may want to spin the model slightly so you select the edge and not the entity previously offset.
4. Move the cursor toward the middle of the rectangle. The location of the cursor when doing the next step will affect what direction the line goes in.
5. Edit the Offset value in the Tools Palette dialog box to **-10 (-0.394 in)**. The edge is offset to that location, as shown in Figure 7–36. Note: you can press Tab key multiple times to toggle through the fields in the Tools Palette. This allows you to type in values without needing to move the cursor.

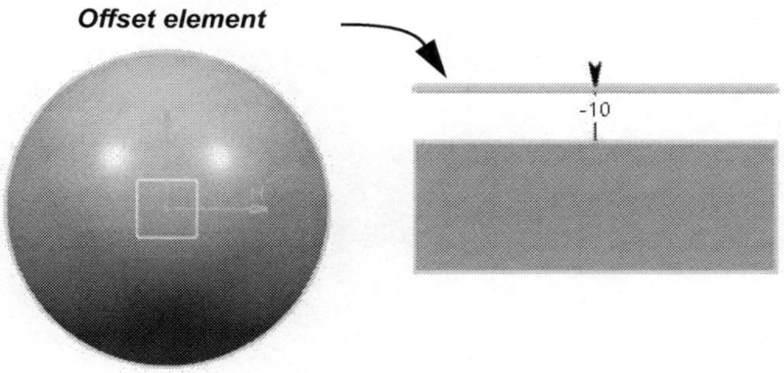

Figure 7–36

6. Click  (Offset) and select the bottom projected edge from the Pad. Move your cursor below the selected edge.

7. In the Sketch Tools toolbar, in the *Offset* field enter **30 (1.181 in)**, as shown in Figure 7–37.

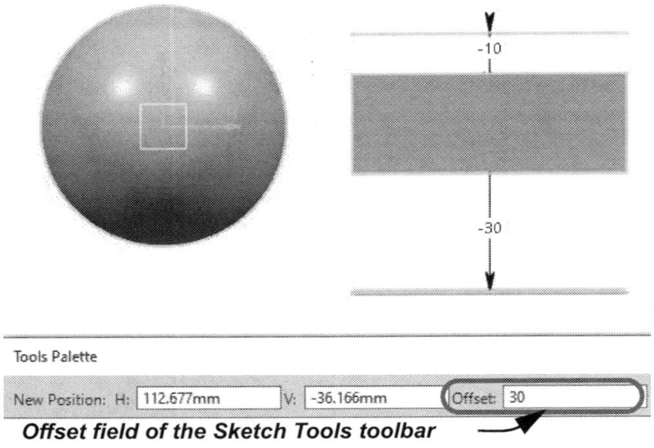

Figure 7–37

8. Press <Enter>. The sketch displays as shown in Figure 7–38.

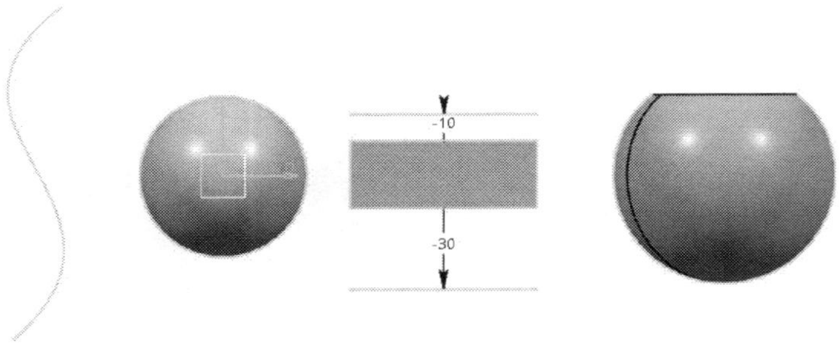

Figure 7–38

Task 4 - Analyze the sketch.

1. In the *Analysis* section of the Action Bar, click (Sketch Analysis). The Sketch Analysis dialog box opens as shown in Figure 7–39.

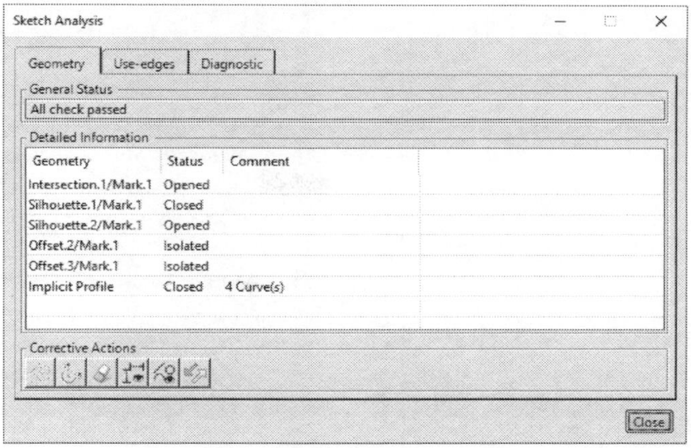

Figure 7–39

2. Investigate the open and closed sections listed under the *Status* column. They highlight as you select them in the display.

3. Select the *Use-edges* tab and note the projections listed as shown in Figure 7–40.

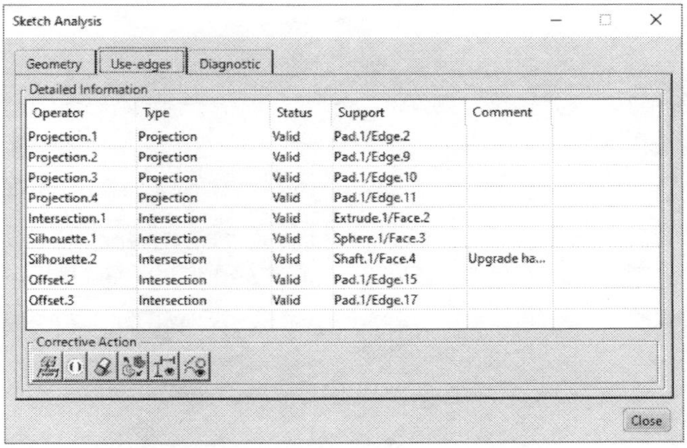

Figure 7–40

4. Click **Close**.

5. Exit the Sketch app.

6. Save the model and close the file.

Practice 7b Sketcher Techniques

Practice Objectives

- Create and transform sketched elements.
- Create base solid geometry.
- Import a DXF file into Sketcher.

In this practice, you will create a part with a Pad as the base feature. You will then use the **Copy**, **Import**, and **Analysis** tools to create the feature shown in Figure 7–41.

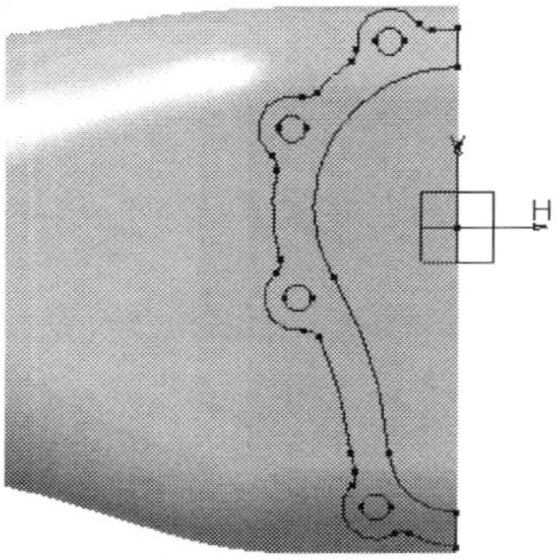

Figure 7–41

Task 1 - Import a DXF file.

1. Import **BlockLeft.3dxml.**
2. In the *1703 (Explore)* tab, right-click **1703** in the specification tree and select **Open**.
3. To switch the model orientation to the back view, click 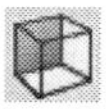 (* back) in the *View* section of the Action Bar, as shown in Figure 7–42.

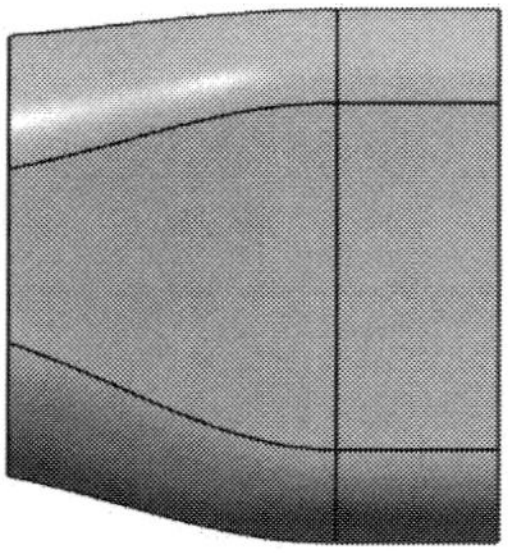

Figure 7–42

1. In the Top Bar, click (Add), and then click **Import**.
2. In the Import dialog box, select **DXF2D (*.dxf)** from the Format drop down list.
3. In the Filename field, click (Open), and select the **Interface.dxf** file.
4. In the Import dialog box, click **OK**. A new window opens with the DXF sketch.
5. Click **OK** in the Operation report dialog box.
6. On the left of the window, click to display the specification tree, if required.
7. In the specification tree, select **Main View**.
8. Right-click and select **Copy**, as shown in Figure 7–43.

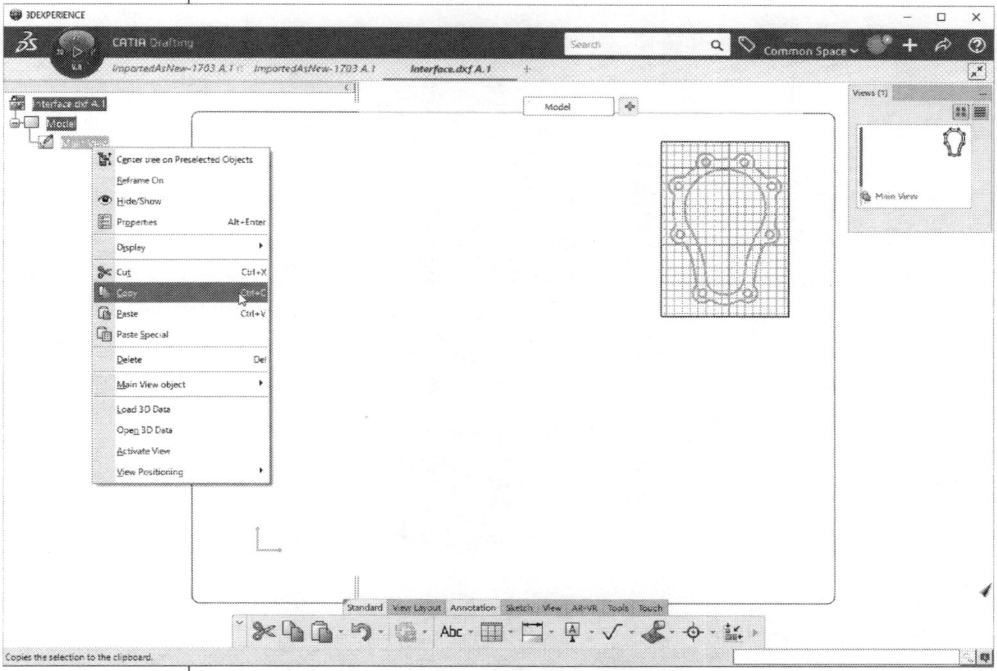

Figure 7–43

9. Select the ***1703* tab** to switch back to the 3D solid model.

10. Select the planar surface and paste the copied sketch geometry, as shown in Figure 7–44.

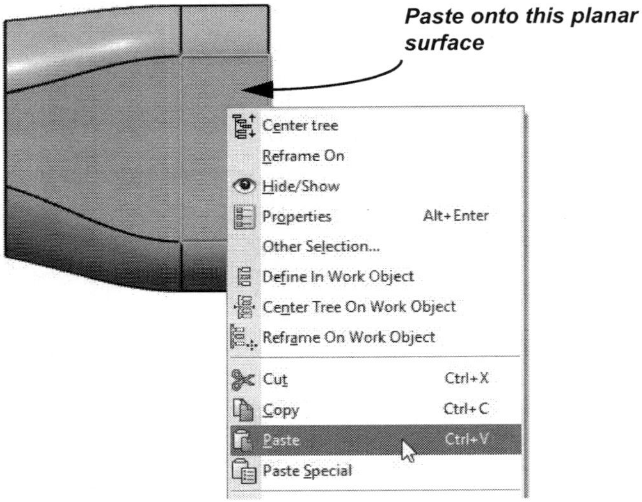

Figure 7–44

11. In the *View* section of the Action Bar, click  (Fit All In). The imported sketch displays as shown in Figure 7–45.

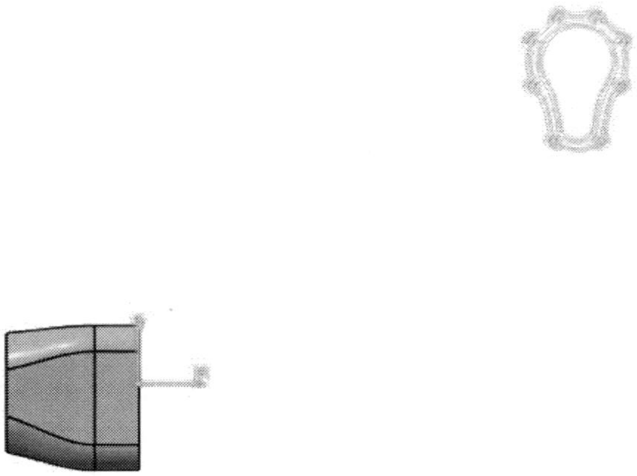

Figure 7–45

Task 2 - Modify the imported geometry.

1. Double-click on **Main View** sketch to activate the Sketch app. Zoom in on the imported sketch.

Zoom in to ensure that the vertical line is coincident with the outer profile of the import geometry at the top and bottom. A geometric constraint can be applied as required.

2. Only half of the sketch is required. Select **location 1** (just to the right of center), as shown in Figure 7–46. Hold the mouse button, drag the cursor to location 2, and release the mouse button. A selection trap is used to select all geometry in the rectangular trap.

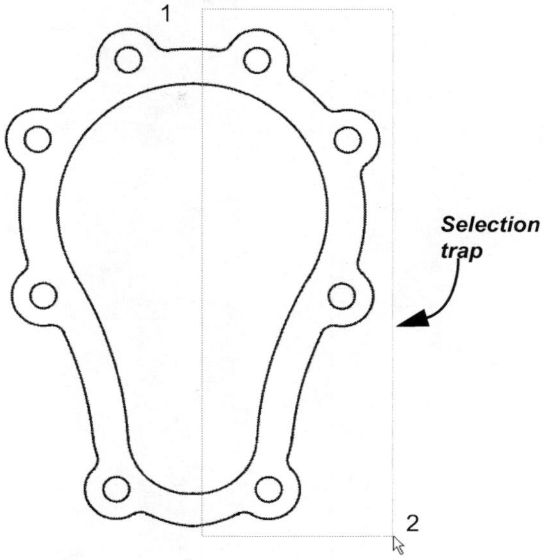

Figure 7–46

3. Press and hold <Ctrl> and select any entities not captured by the selection trap. The entities should be highlighted as shown in .

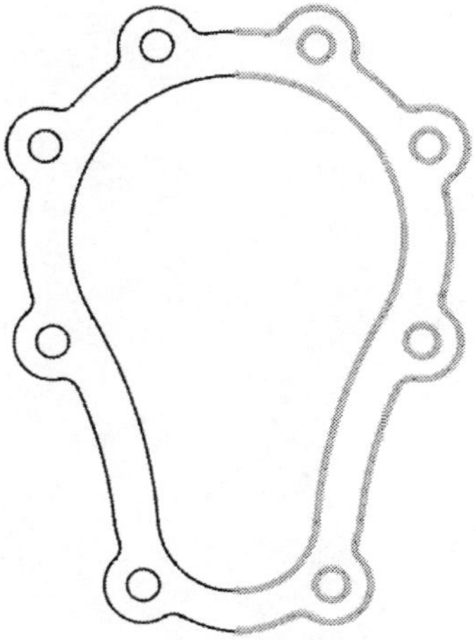

Figure 7–47

4. Press <Delete>. The sketch updates as shown in Figure 7–48.

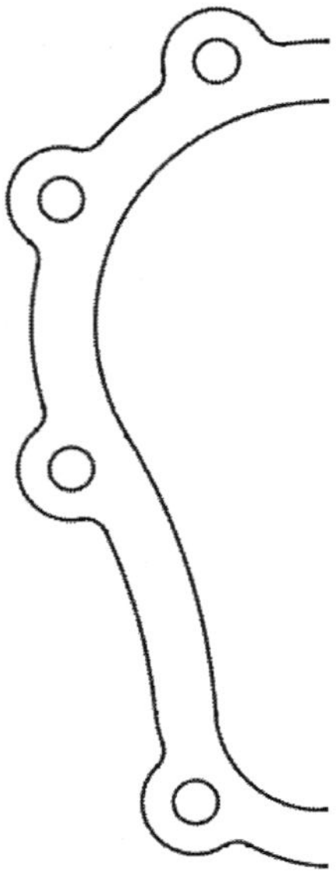

Figure 7–48

5. Sketch two lines to close the sketch, as shown in Figure 7–49. Apply Vertical constraints if necessary.

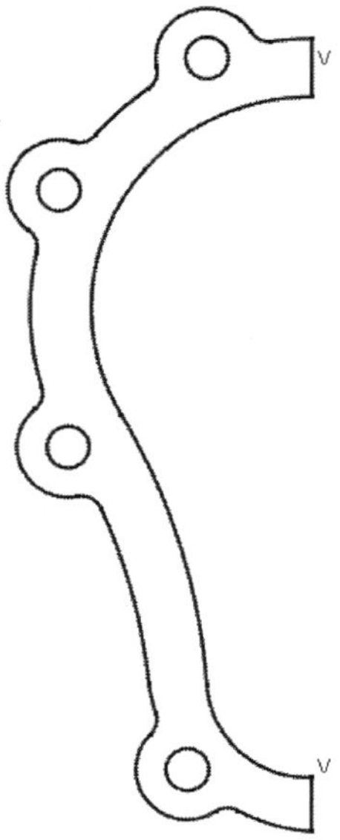

Figure 7–49

Task 3 - Analyze the sketch.

1. In the *Analysis* section of the Action Bar, click (Sketch Analysis). The Sketch Analysis dialog box opens as shown in Figure 7–50.

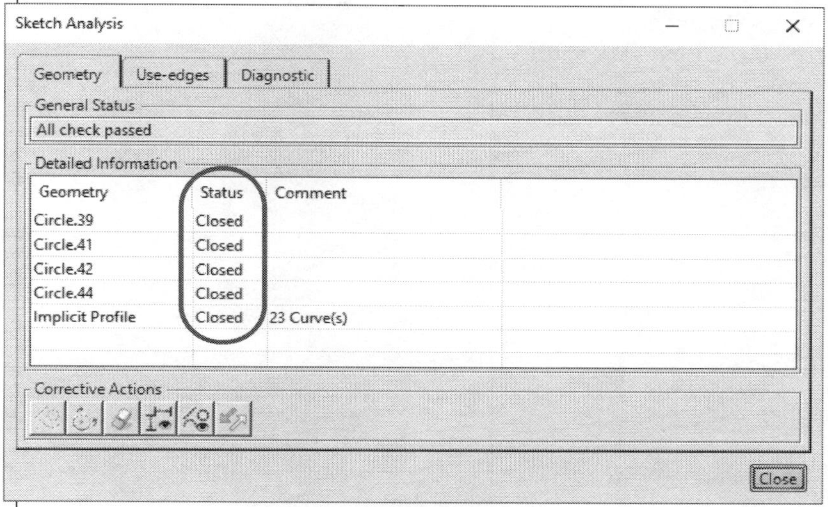

Figure 7–50

2. Ensure that the Status is set to **Closed** for all the geometry profiles that are listed in the dialog box. If it is not set to **Closed**, constrain the geometry to close all profiles.

3. Click **Close**.

Task 4 - Constrain the sketch.

1. Select the entire sketch using a selection trap.

You could have selected

(Group) from the context toolbar as well, but the Group Definition dialog bx would not have displayed.

2. In the *Sketch* section of the Action Bar, click (Group) to constrain the relative positions of the imported entities. The Group Definition dialog box opens as shown in Figure 7–51.

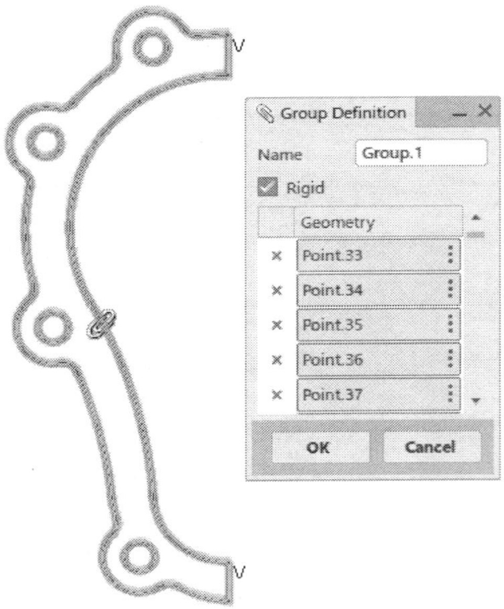

Figure 7–51

3. Click **OK**. The sketch updates as shown in Figure 7–52.

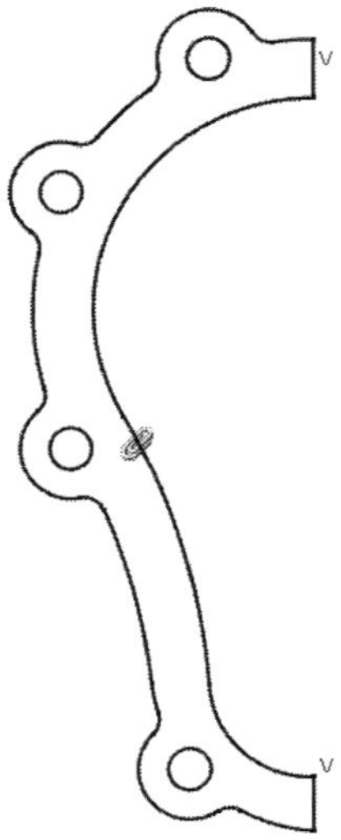

Figure 7–52

Task 5 - Position the imported sketch on the solid.

1. Drag the imported geometry closer to the solid by grabbing one of the elements in the sketch and holding the mouse button while you move the mouse.
2. Add a **Coincidence** constraint between the planar right face of the model and the lower vertical line of the imported geometry, as shown in Figure 7–53.
3. Add a dimension between the lower vertex of the imported geometry and the bottom vertex of the 3D model in the sketched view. The sketch updates as shown in Figure 7–54.

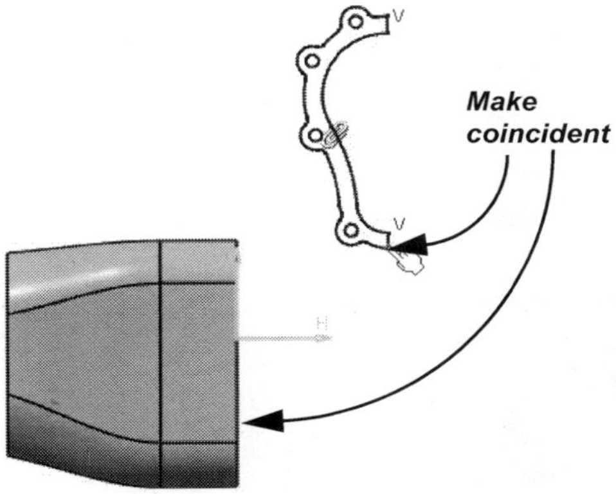

Figure 7–53

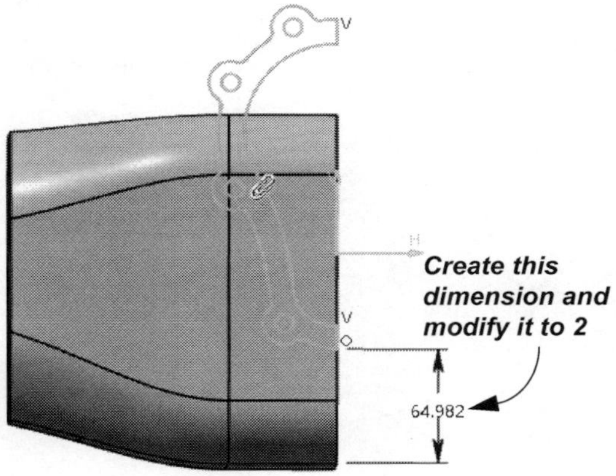

Figure 7–54

The model is shown without the auto-constraints for visual clarity.

4. Modify the value of the dimension to **2**. The model updates as shown in Figure 7–55.

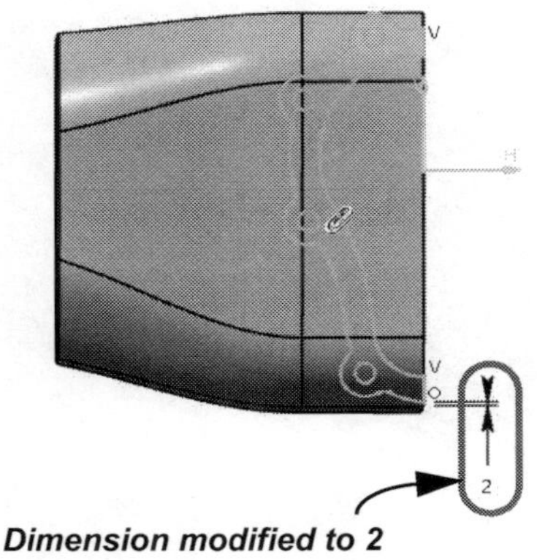

Figure 7–55

5. In the *Analysis* section of the Application Bar, click (Sketch Solving Status). Ensure that the message in the Sketch Solving Status dialog box indicates that the sketch is **Iso-Constrained**, as shown in Figure 7–56.

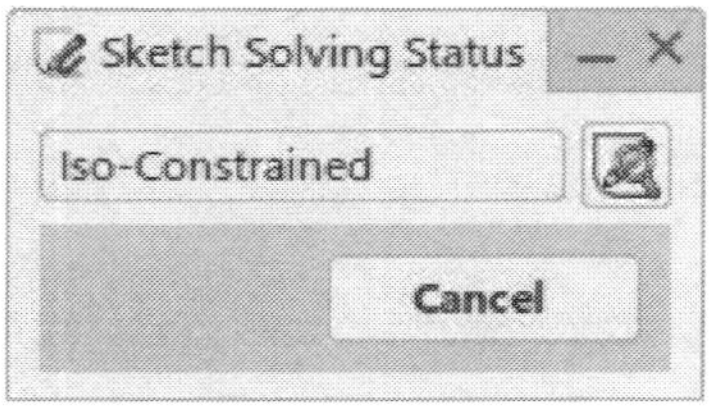

Figure 7–56

6. Click (Sketch Analysis) in the Sketch Solving Status dialog box.

7. Click (Hide Constraints) to hide the constraints. The sketch displays as shown in Figure 7–57.

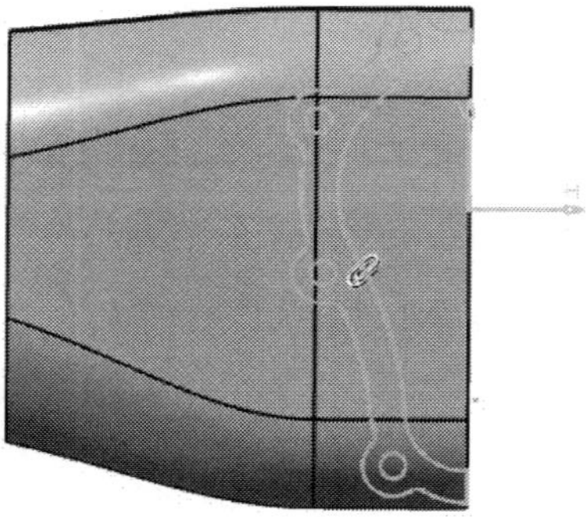

Figure 7–57

8. Click **Close**.

9. Exit the Sketch app.

Task 6 - Develop the transmission interface.

In this task, you will use the imported sketch to create a Pad for the transmission interface of the engine block.

1. Create a Pad feature using the sketch you just created. The Pad should extend up to the solid in one direction and extrude to a depth of **10** in the other direction. The completed part model displays as shown in Figure 7–58.

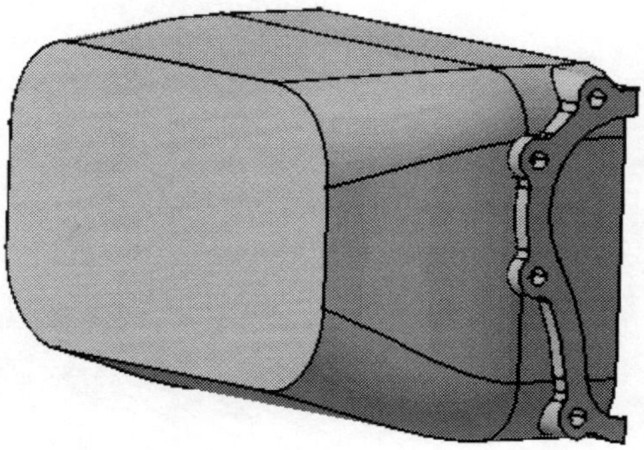

Figure 7–58

2. Save the model and close the window.

Practice 7c

Set Visualization and SmartPick

Practice Objectives

- Set visualization options.
- Manipulate SmartPick constraint creation.

In this practice, you will use the visualization options to control the display of existing solid geometry while in Sketcher. These options make sketching over existing geometry easier by dimming or hiding the model. You will also lock and disable SmartPick constraints to create the required sketched entities. The completed model displays as shown in Figure 7–59.

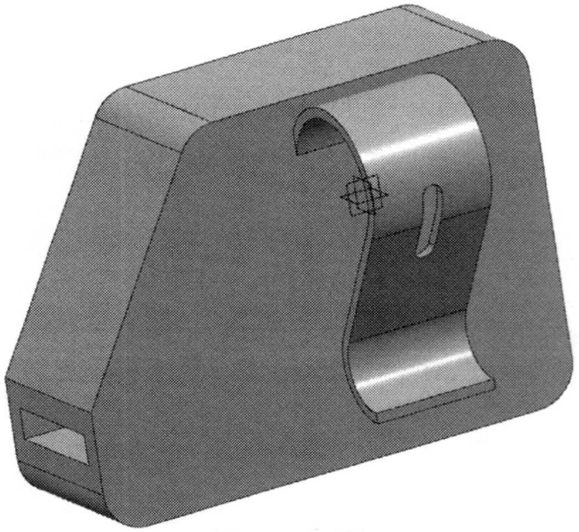

Figure 7–59

Task 1 - Create a new part and base feature.

1. Create a new 3D Part. Set the *3D Part* and *3D Shape* titles to ***Your_Initials*_Clip**. Ensure that **Enable hybrid design** is disabled in the *Characteristics* tab.

2. Select the ZX Plane and click (Sketch), as shown in Figure 7–60.

Figure 7–60

3. Create the sketch shown in Figure 7–61. Use the **Equivalent Dimension** tool to make all four radius dimensions equal.
   - 20 (0.787 in)
   - 55 (2.165 in)
   - 60 (2.362 in)
   - 150 (5.906 in)
   - 180 (7.087 in)
   - 240 (9.449 in)

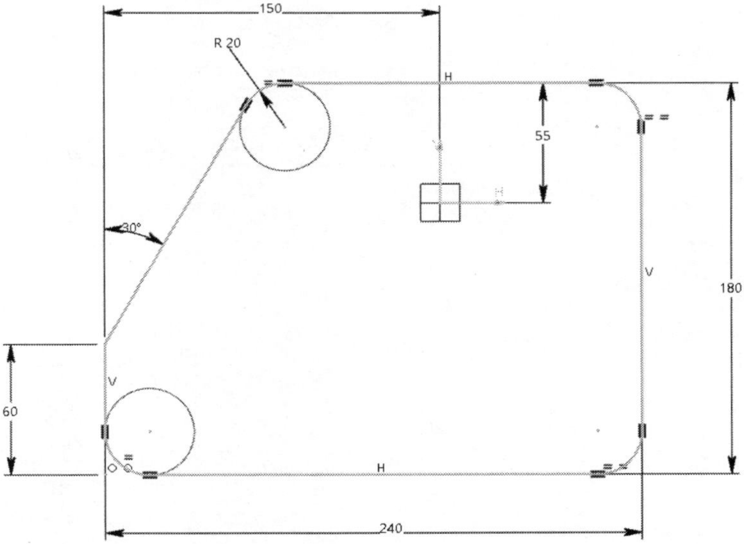

Figure 7–61

4. Exit the Sketch app and use the sketch to create a Pad **80 (3.150 in)** in length, as shown in Figure 7–62. To obtain the correct direction of the Pad, in the *View* section of the Action Bar, click (* front). The Absolute planes should be on the right side of the Pad.

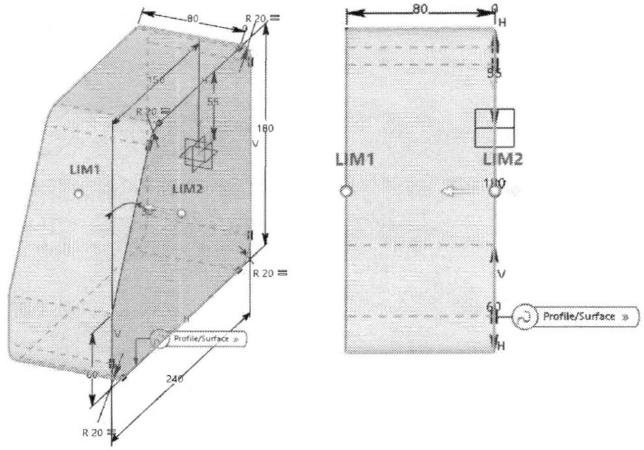

Figure 7–62

5. Click **OK**.
6. Set the display back to (* iso).

Task 2 - Create a pocket using formulas.

1. Select the surface of the part shown in Figure 7–63.

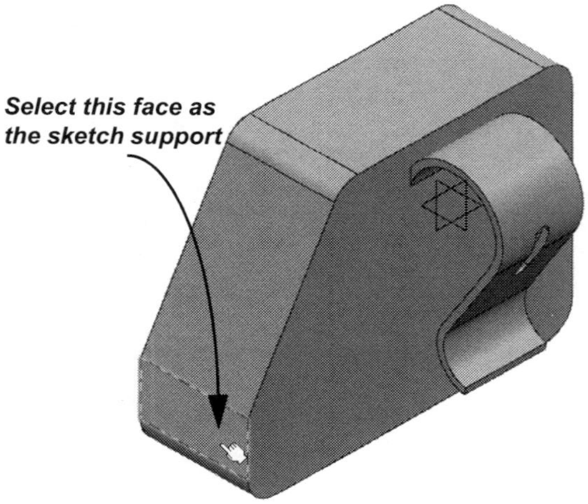

Figure 7–63

2. In the *Essentials* section of the Action Bar, click  (Positioned Sketch).

3. In the *Origin* area, select **Middle point**, as shown in Figure 7–64, and select the edge shown.

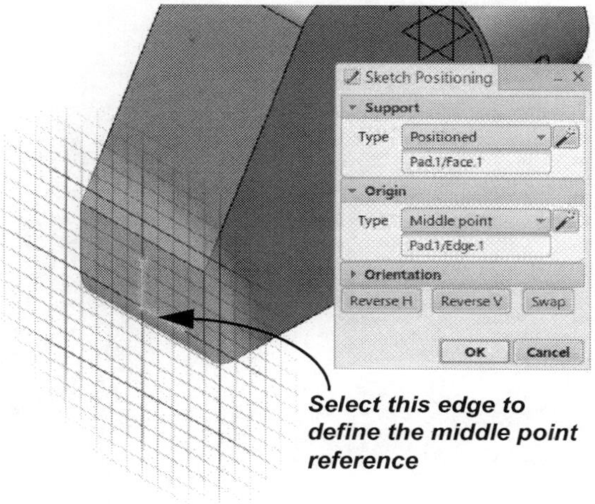

Figure 7–64

4. Click **OK** to access the Sketch app.

5. Create the sketch using the dimensions **12.5 (0.492)**, **15 (0.591 in)**, and **60 (2.362 in)**, as shown in Figure 7–65.

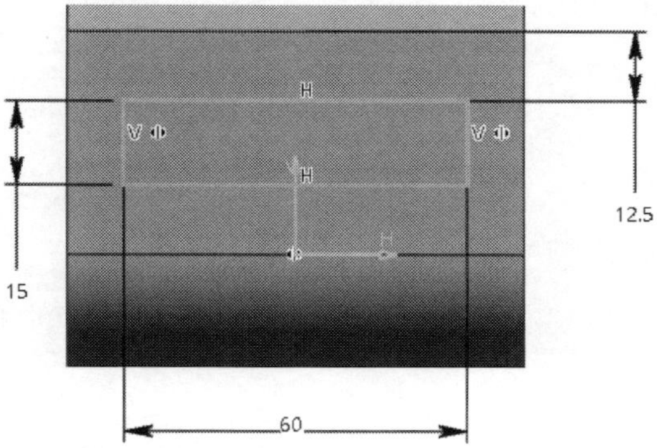

Figure 7–65

6. Exit the Sketch app.

7. Create a Pocket feature **100 (3.937 in)** deep. The model displays as shown in Figure 7–66.

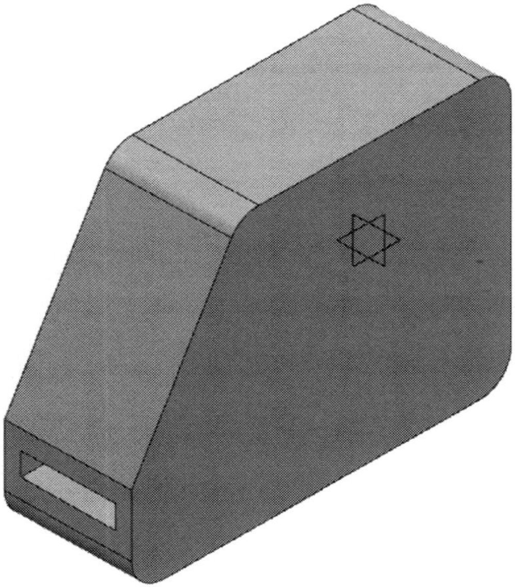

Figure 7–66

Task 3 - Modify the Visualization setting.

Design Consideration

In this task, you will create a sketch that will be used as the profile for the clip. This clip will be used in other models so it is important that unnecessary references are not used. In this situation, the design requirement is that the clip only references the three default reference planes.

1. Create a sketch on the YZ plane.

2. In the *View* section of the Action Bar, click  (Low light). The 3D geometry displays in a dark gray color, but you are not able to select it.

3. Click  (No 3D Background). The solid geometry is removed from the display. This setting ensures that the base feature is not selected when dimensioning the sketch. It also helps with clarity when creating the geometry.

Task 4 - Create the sketched geometry.

1. **Enable** 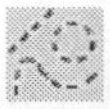 (Construction/Standard Element) and sketch the circles shown in Figure 7–67.

   - 5 (0.197 in)
   - 20 (0.787 in)
   - 37 (1.457 in)
   - 40 (1.575 in)
   - 64 (2.520 in)

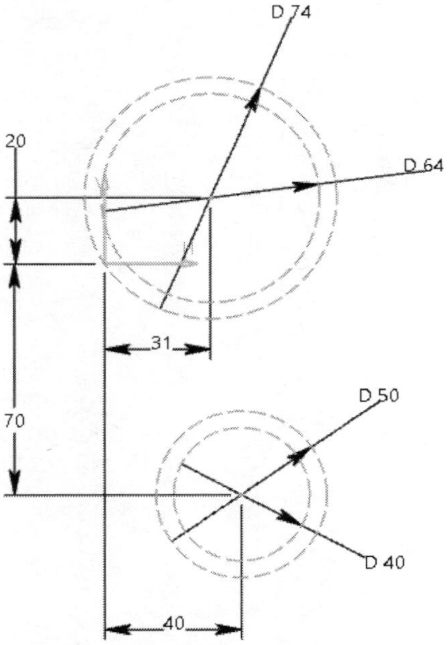

Figure 7–67

2. Sketch two lines using the  (Bi-Tangent Line) option, as shown in Figure 7–68.

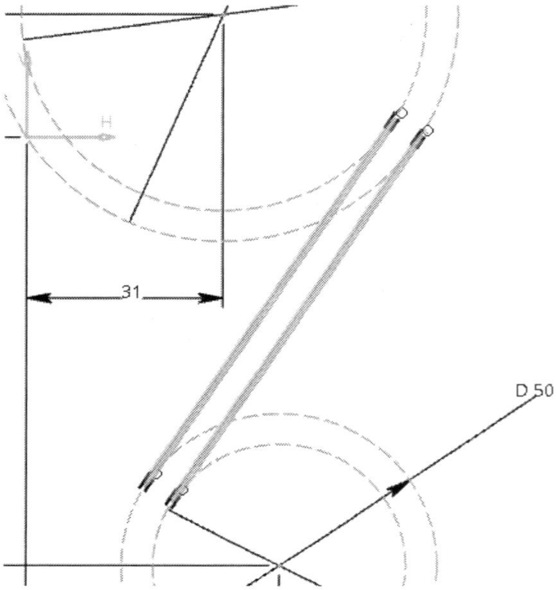

Figure 7–68

3. Sketch the vertical line shown in Figure 7–69. Ensure it is coincident with the Vertical axis and that it snaps to the two construction circles.

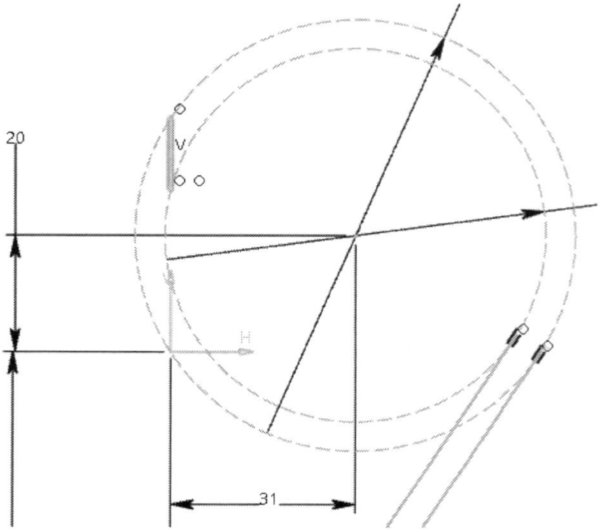

Figure 7–69

4. Sketch the two arcs shown in Figure 7–70. Each arc is centered on the construction circles, and runs tangent to the appropriate line.

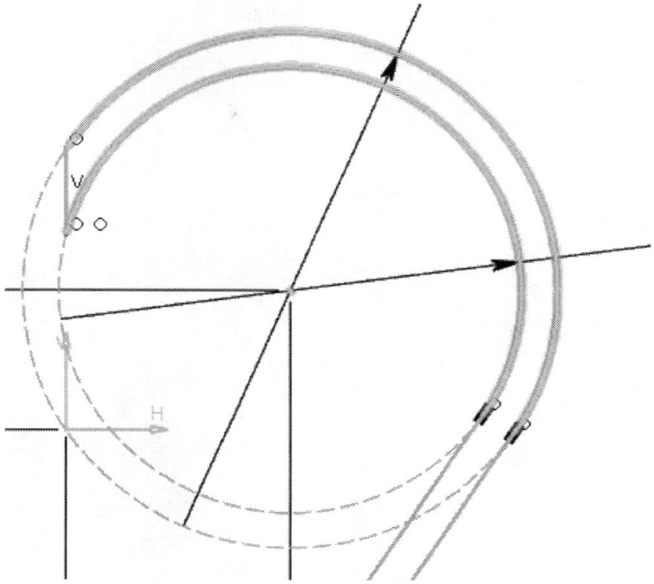

Figure 7–70

5. Sketch the two arcs and vertical line shown in Figure 7–71.

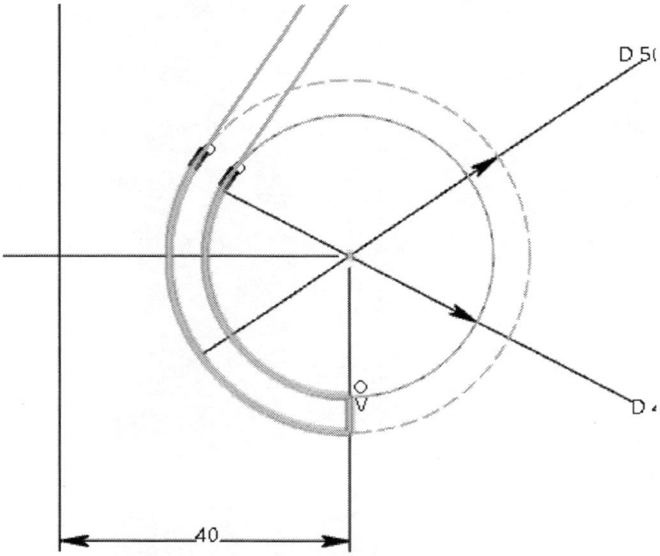

Figure 7–71

6. Exit the Sketch app.
7. Create a pad with a length of **30 (1.181 in)**. Select  (Mirrored extent). The model displays as shown in Figure 7–72.

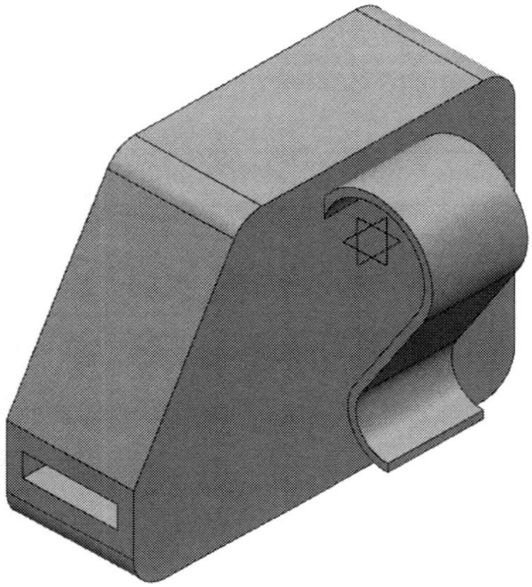

Figure 7–72

Task 5 - Create a pocket.

1. Create a sketch on the ZX plane.
2. Select the *View* section of the Action Bar and click  (No 3D Background).

3. Create the sketch using the dimensions **5 (0.197 in)**, **15 (0.591)**, and **30 (1.181 in)**, as shown in Figure 7–73.

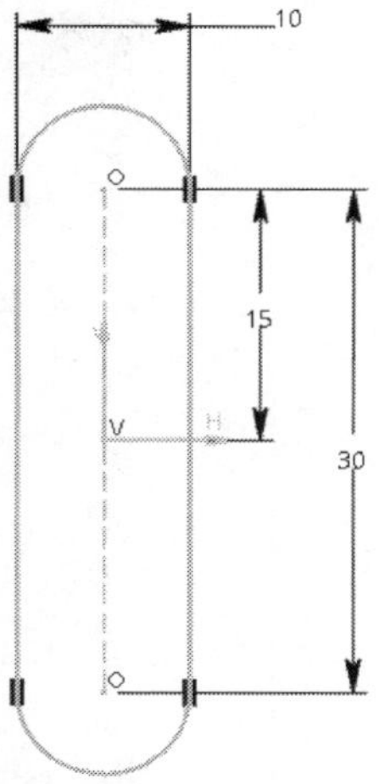

Figure 7–73

4. Exit the Sketch app.

5. Create a Pocket feature to cut through the clip. Use the **Up to Last** depth option. The pocket direction might need to be reversed.

6. The complete model displays as shown in Figure 7–74.

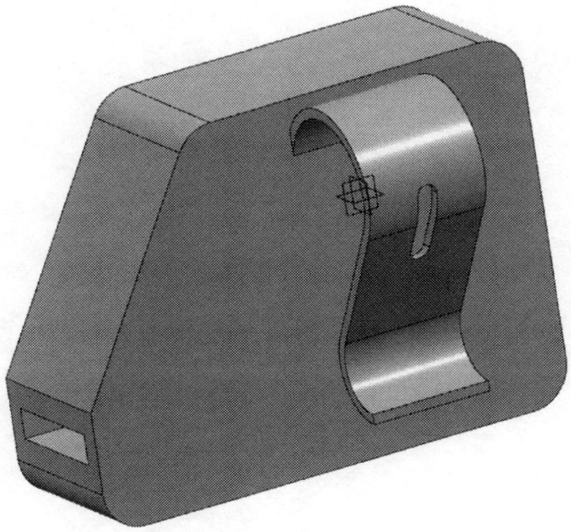

Figure 7–74

7. Save the file and close the tab.

Chapter Review Questions

1. The two types of sketches in CATIA are Standard and Positioned.
    a. True
    b. False
2. A sketch cannot be copied between part models.
    a. True
    b. False
3. Which tools can be used to copy sketched entities? (Select all that apply.)
    a. <Ctrl>+<C>
    b. 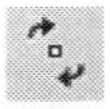 (Rotate)
    c.  (Translate)
    d.  (Scale)
4. Data imported into a sketch (i.e., from a DXF file) can be scaled, rotated, and translated.
    a. True
    b. False
5. Projected geometry can be scaled, rotated, and translated.
    a. True
    b. False
6. What does a sketched entity displayed in yellow indicate?
    a. The entity is over-constrained.
    b. The entity is under-constrained.
    c. The entity is locked.
    d. The entity has been imported from another file.

7. Which tool can be used to create the profile shown on the right side of Figure 7–75, from the entities shown on the left side of Figure 7–75?

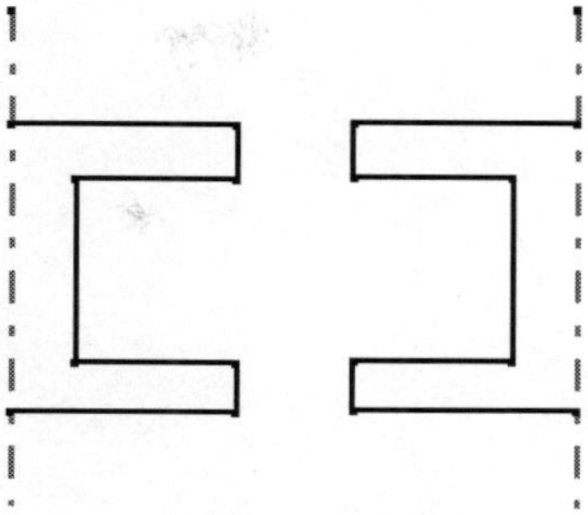

Figure 7–75

   a. 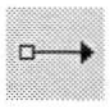 (Translate)

   b.  (Mirror)

   c.  (Symmetry)

   d.  (Scale)

8. Multiple instances can be created with a single offset.
   a. True
   b. False

Answers: 1a, 2b, 3abcd, 4a, 5b, 6c, 7c, 8a

Chapter 8

Reference Elements

References elements consist of points, lines, planes and axis systems. These items can be used as support elements to create complex sketches, pads, and pockets.

Learning Objectives in This Chapter

- Understand how features display in the specification tree.
- Create necessary sketch planes when none are available.
- Create axis systems as reference frames for modeling.
- Understand the various methods of creating points, lines, and planes.
- Define reference elements.

8.1 Reference Elements

Reference elements are non-solid points, lines, and planes that aid in geometry creation. They do not have any volume, area, or mass properties, and they do not cause interference at the assembly level.

Feature Structure

All solid geometry is grouped under the PartBody branch in the specification tree.

- System-defined reference features, such as default reference planes, are always the first features of a model.
- User-defined reference features are automatically grouped in the Geometrical Set branch, which is automatically created by the software and lists all non-solid features, as shown in Figure 8–1.

This feature structure enables efficient navigation when selecting features in the specification tree.

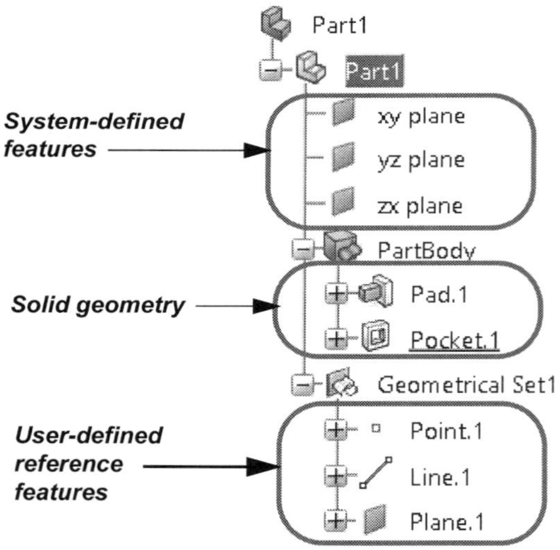

Figure 8–1

Sketch Plane Positioning

Figure 8–2 shows an example of a circular Pad Feature where the base feature geometry does not have a suitable planar face on which to sketch the circular profile. Additionally, the default reference planes are not in a suitable location. A reference plane can be created to provide the required sketching plane.

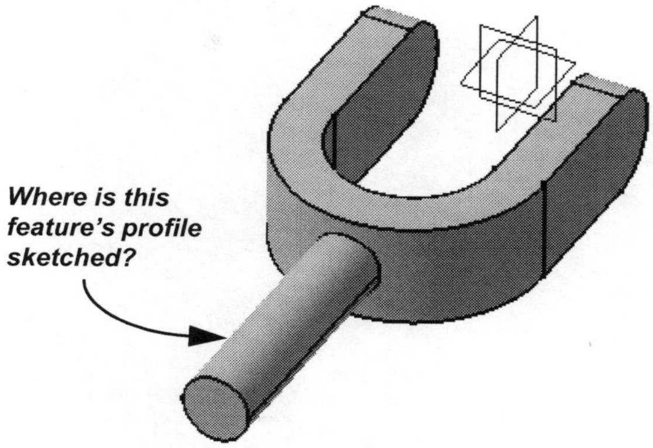

Figure 8–2

The creation of points and lines can also assist in the definition of a positioned sketch. The sketcher axis shown in Figure 8–3 was positioned using a point to locate the origin and a line to orient the vertical axis.

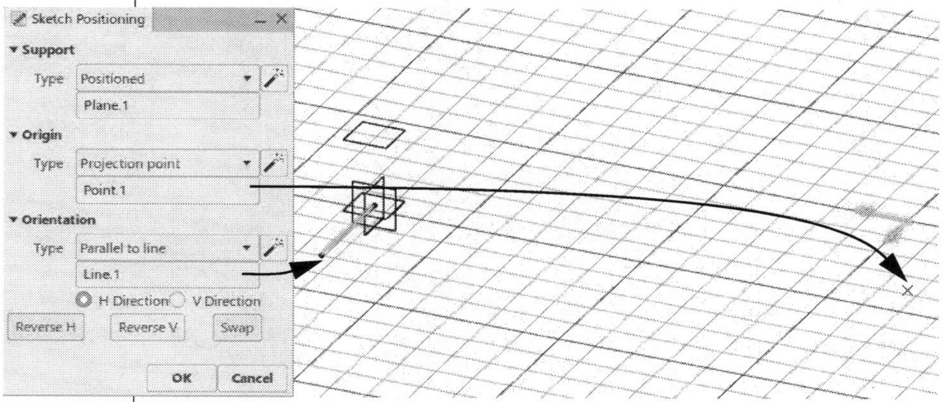

Figure 8–3

8.2 Axis Systems

An axis system is used to define a reference frame for a model, or portion of geometry in a part file. More than one axis system can be created for a model, as shown in Figure 8–4. The active axis system is shown with a solid line front and an orange color.

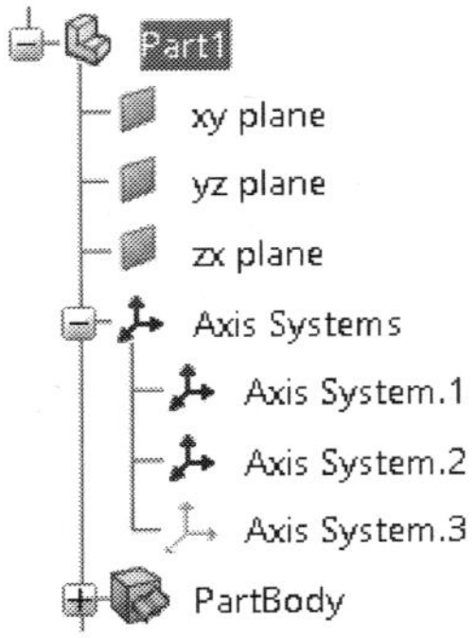

Figure 8–4

- To create an axis system, click  (Axis System) in the Tools toolbar. The Axis System Definition dialog box opens, as shown in Figure 8–5.
- The origin for each type of axis system is defined by selecting a point or vertex on the model. The origin can also be defined by right-clicking on the *Origin* field, as shown in Figure 8–6.

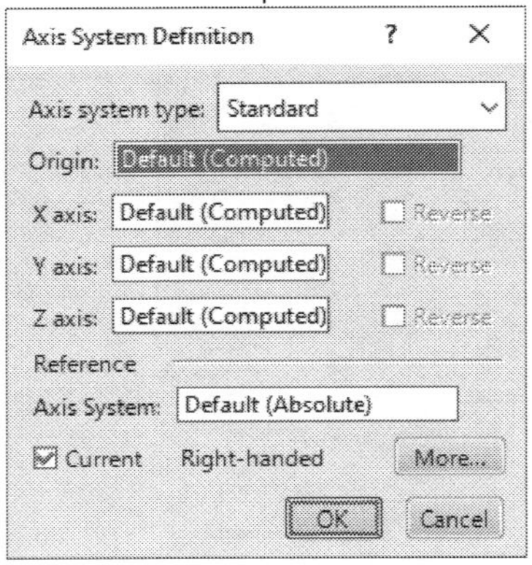

Figure 8–5

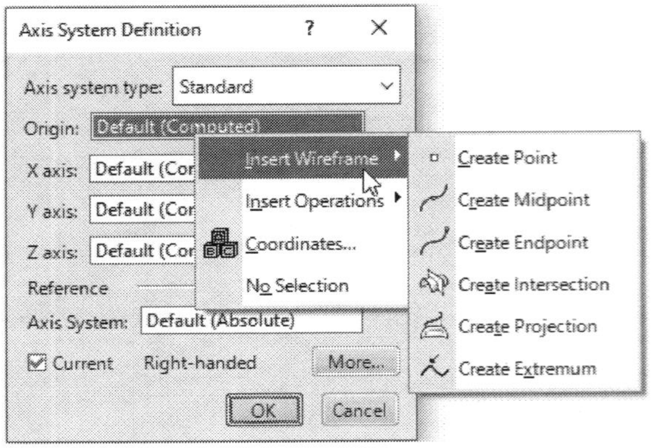

Figure 8–6

To introduce flexibility into the axis system, the origin is defined using the **Coordinates** option, which enables you to define the X-, Y-, and Z-coordinates relative to the part origin. The system can then be translated by modifying these coordinates.

All axis systems start in a default orientation about the origin and can be further defined by specifying the type and orientation references. These are described as follows:

Type	Orientation References
Standard	Select a reference to define the orientation of up to two axes (X, Y, Z). The orientation can be defined by selecting a point (the axis is oriented along a line between the point and the origin), a line, or a plane (defining a normal vector).
Axis rotation	Select a reference for the X-, Y-, or Z-axis. The axis system is then rotated about this axis by the specified angle measured from the specified reference.
Euler angles	Define the origin, and enter an angle to define the orientation of the X-, Y-, and Z-axes.

8.3 Point Creation Methods

Points mark a location on a model and can be referenced by subsequent features. The methods used to create a point are described as follows:

Point Type		**Description**
Coordinates		Enter the X-, Y-, and Z-distances from an existing reference point or the origin of the part. 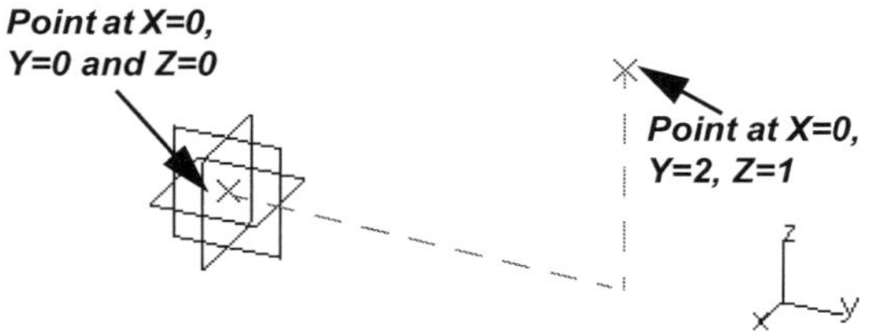 You can define the reference for the point using the following options:
	Point	The point's coordinates are measured from the selected point. By default, the coordinates are measured from the origin of the current local axis system.
	Axis System	The direction of the point's X-, Y-, and Z-coordinates are changed with respect to the selected axis system.
	Compass Location	If the compass is located on geometry, the X-, Y-, and Z-coordinates of the point can be set based on the compass location.
On Curve		Select to place the point on an edge of a solid feature, a segment of a sketch, or a line. 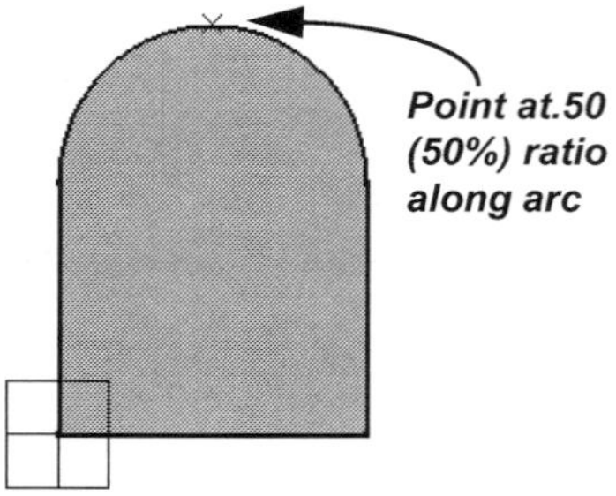 You can define the location of the point along the edge using the following options:

	Ratio	Percentage along curve.
	Geodesic Distance	Distance measured along curve.
	Euclidean Distance	Absolute distance from a reference.
		The **Repeat object after OK** option enables you to specify additional points spaced at an incremental distance. There is also an option to create planes through points that are normal to the curve.
On Plane		Select the location for the point on a planar surface and specify the horizontal and vertical distances for the point. By default, the distances are relative to the origin of the part. Optionally, another reference point can be selected. 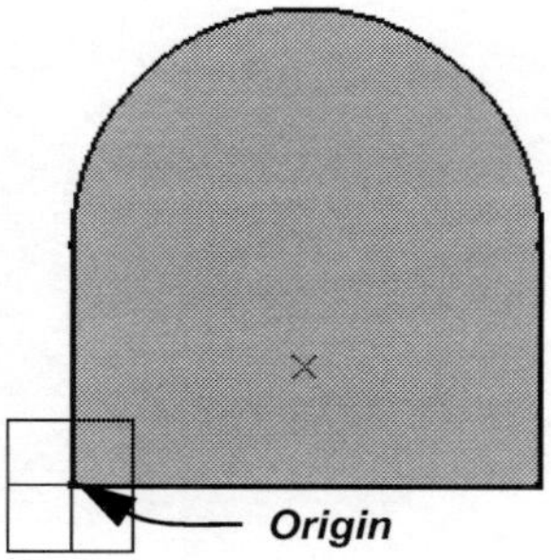
On Surface		Select the location for the point on a curved surface. By default, the point is created at the center of the surface. You can locate the point on the surface using one of the following: • An edge. • The surface normal of a plane. • Points X, Y, and Z values using the shortcut menu. 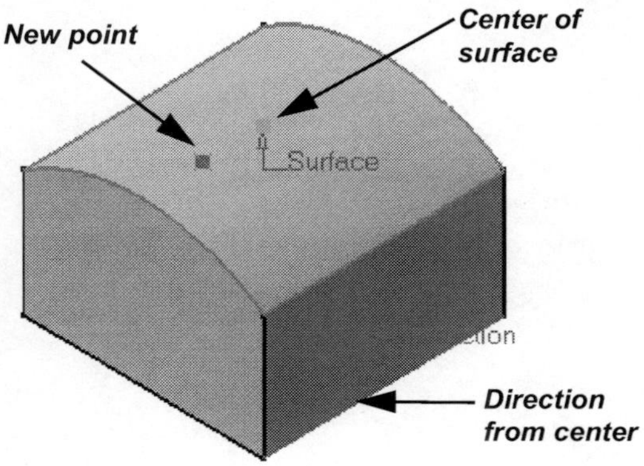

Circle/Sphere/ Ellipse Center	Locate a point at the center of a circle, sphere, arc, or ellipse. 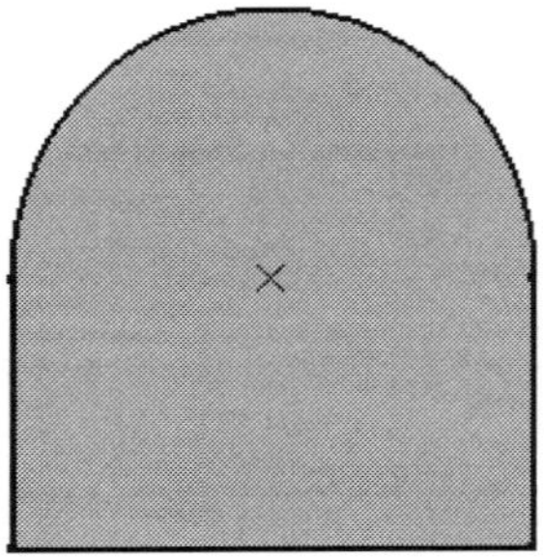
Tangent on Curve	Select a planar curve and a direction line. A point is placed at each tangent location relative to the direction line. 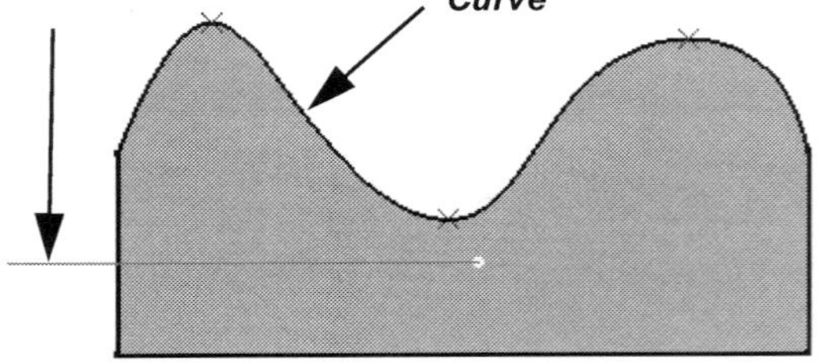
Between	Select two points and enter the ratio of the distance from the first point to the new point. You can use the  (Reverse Direction) option to specify the distance from the second point to the new point. If the ratio is greater than one, the point is located on a virtual line extended beyond the two points. 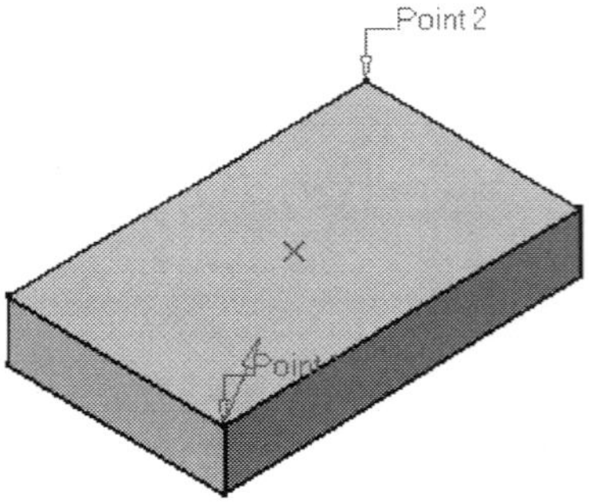

8.4 Line Creation Methods

Lines can define the axis of rotation for Shaft features, mark the center axis of cylindrical pads, and define the direction for non-normal pads. The methods you can use to create a line are described as follows:

Line Type	Description
Point-Point	Select two points or vertices for the line to connect. By default, a straight line between the two points or vertices is created. If required, you can select a support surface for the line to follow. 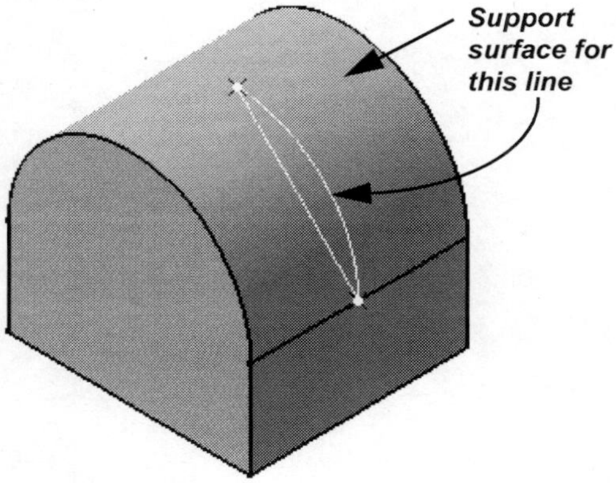 You can enter the distance for the start and end points of the line to extend beyond the two points.
Point-Direction	Select a starting point and an edge, line, or plane to define the line direction. Enter the length of the line. 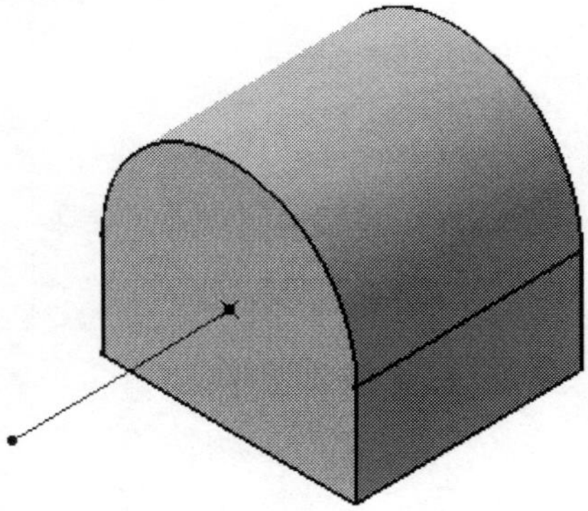

Angle/ Normal to curve	Select the start point for the line and a line or edge to measure the angle relative to. Select a plane that has both the point and the line, and enter the angle. 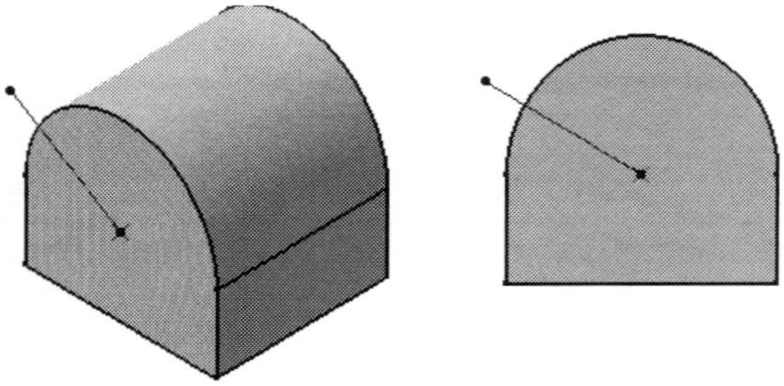 The **Repeat object after Validation** option enables you to create a number of additional lines spaced at the same angle. These lines are not related to each other after they are created. 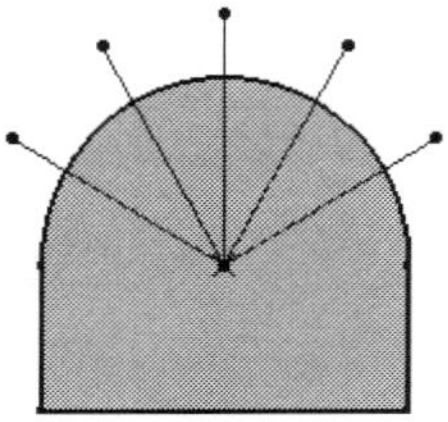
Tangent to curve	Select an edge for the line to be tangent to and a point for the start of the line. Enter the line length. 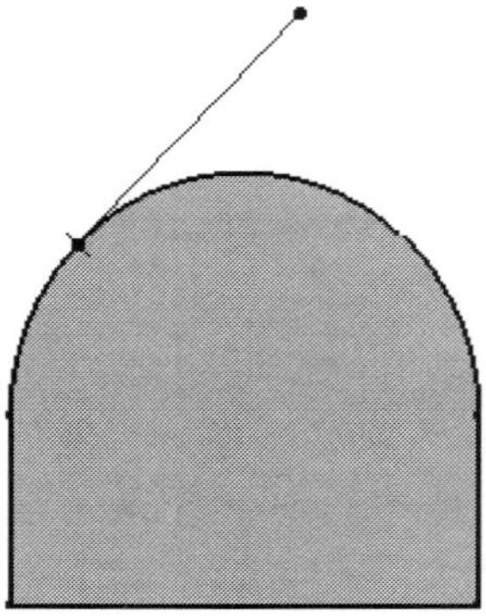

Normal to surface

Select a surface for the line to be perpendicular to and a starting point. Enter the length of the line.

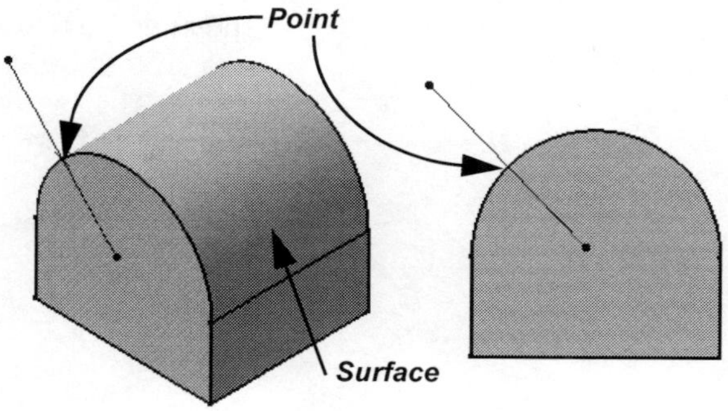

The (Mirror Extent) option constructs the line equally on each side of the point.

Bisecting

Select two lines or edges, and a new line is created that bisects them. If there is more than one solution, you can select the location for the bisecting line.

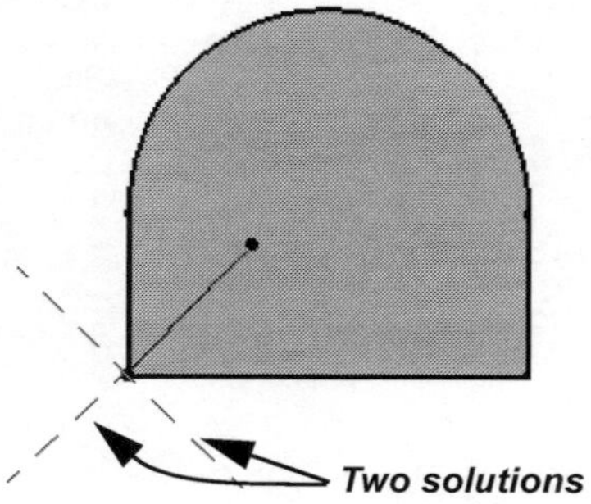

8.5 Plane Creation Methods

Planes can be used for sketch-based features, such as pads and shafts, and to provide a dimensional reference for other types of features. The methods you can use to create planes are described as follows:

Plane Type	Description
Offset from plane	Select a planar face on the model or a reference plane, and enter the offset distance. 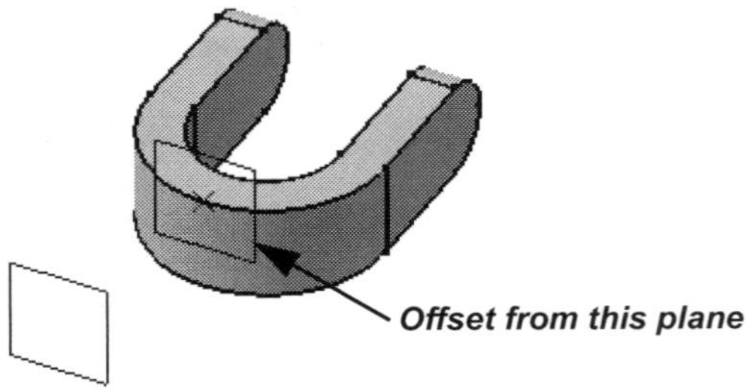
Parallel through point	Select a planar face on the model or reference plane for the new plane to be parallel to, and select a point for the new plane to pass through. 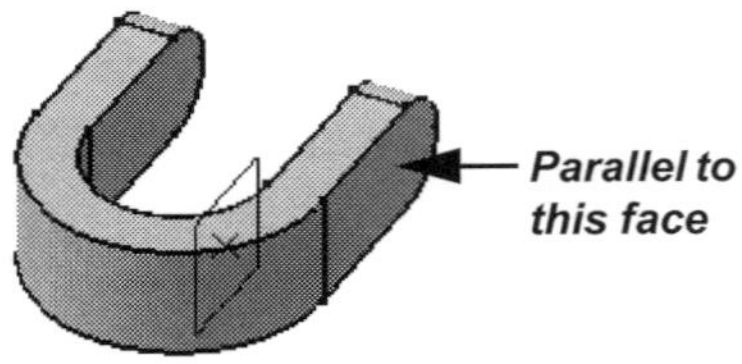
Angle/Normal to plane	Select a line, edge, or axis for the plane to pass through, and a planar reference for the angle to be measured relative to. 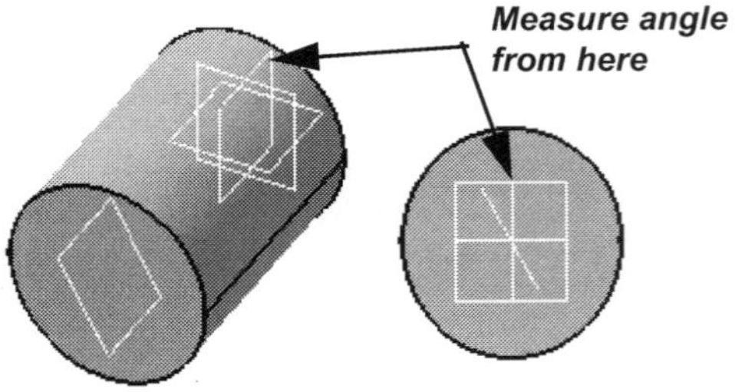

Through three points	Select three points or vertices for the plane to pass through. 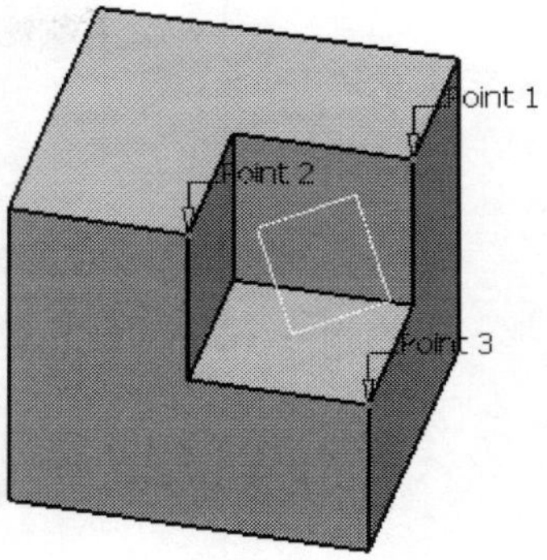
Through two lines	Select two lines, edges, or axes for the plane to pass through. 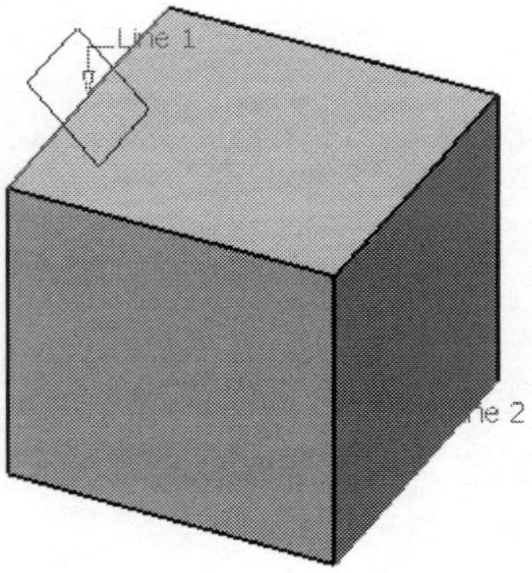
Through point and line	Select a point/vertex and a line/edge/axis for the plane to pass through. 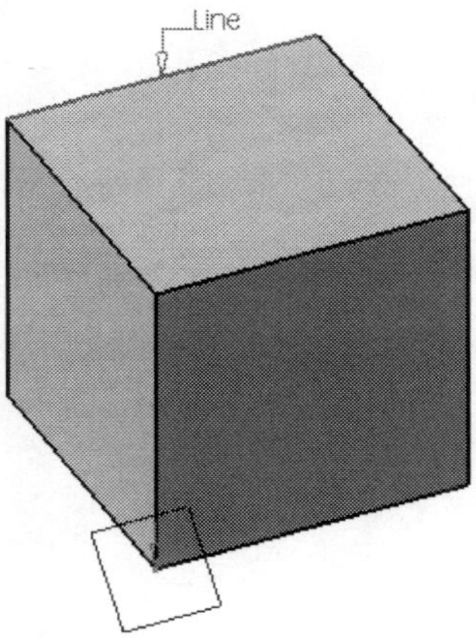

Through planar curve	Select a planar curve or sketched entity for the plane to pass through. 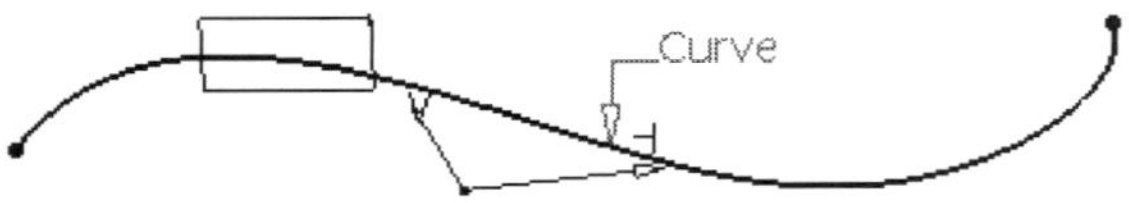
Normal to curve	Select a line, edge, or sketch segment for the new plane to be perpendicular to, and a point for the new plane to pass through. 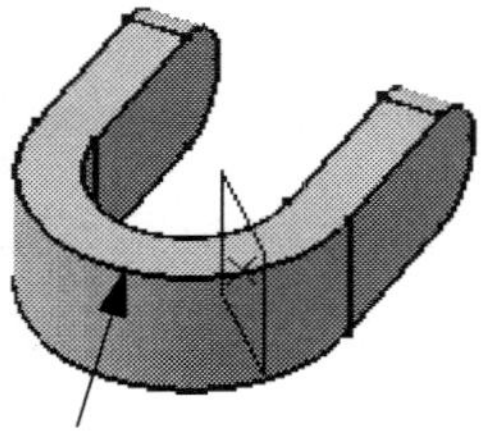
Tangent to surface	Select a point that the new plane passes through, and a surface the new plane is tangent to. 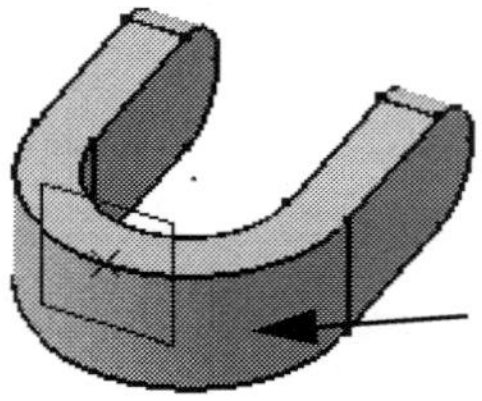
Equation	Select a point and enter values for A, B, and C. The point defines the location of the plane while the A, B, and C values define vectors in the X-, Y-, and Z-directions. For example, A=1, B=0, C=0 creates a plane that is perpendicular to the X axis. Use **Normal to Compass** and **Parallel to Screen** to orient the plane as required.
Mean through points	Select three or more points to define the orientation of the plane. When more than three points are selected, the system uses the additional points to influence the orientation of the plane.
Between	Select two parallel or non-parallel planes (**Element 1** and **Element 2**). An intermediate plane is created coplanar with the **Element 1**. A ratio value is entered to define the location of the intermediate plane relative to **Element 1**. For example, a ratio value of **0** is coplanar with **Element 1,** a ratio value of **1** is coplanar with **Element 2**, and a ratio value of **0.5** is a mid-plane between **Element 1** and **Element 2**.

8.6 Reference Element Definition

The following topics are common to the creation of point, line, or plane reference elements:

- Implicit Axis Selection
- Lock Reference Element
- Shortcut Menus

Implicit Axis Selection

By default, cylindrical features do not display their axes. To reference the axis of a cylindrical feature, press <Shift> while holding the cursor over the feature. The axis shown in Figure 8–7 is useful for creating a plane that is at an angle to a planar reference and passes through the axis.

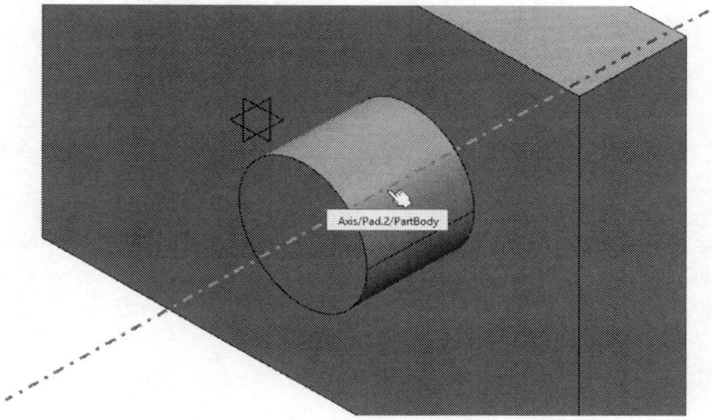

Figure 8–7

Lock Reference Element

If you need to create multiple instances of a type of reference element (e.g., point, line, or plane), you can lock the type of element you want to create.

- To efficiently create multiple offset reference planes, you can lock the **Offset from plane** Plane type, as shown in Figure 8–8.

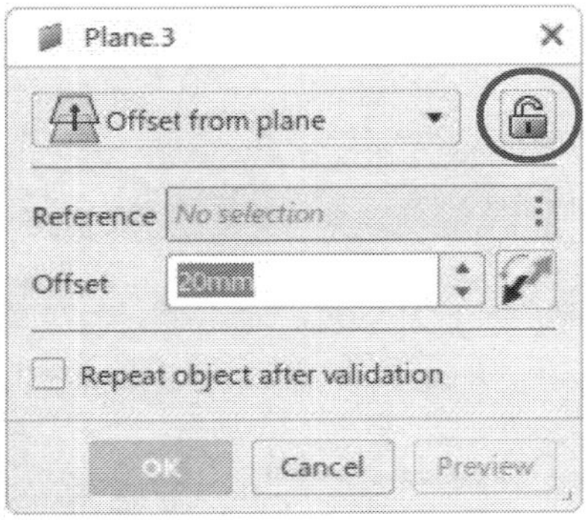

Figure 8–8

To lock the type, click . A locked type displays as , as shown in Figure 8–9.

The lock stays active while CATIA is in session. If you exit the application and launch CATIA, the setting resets to default.

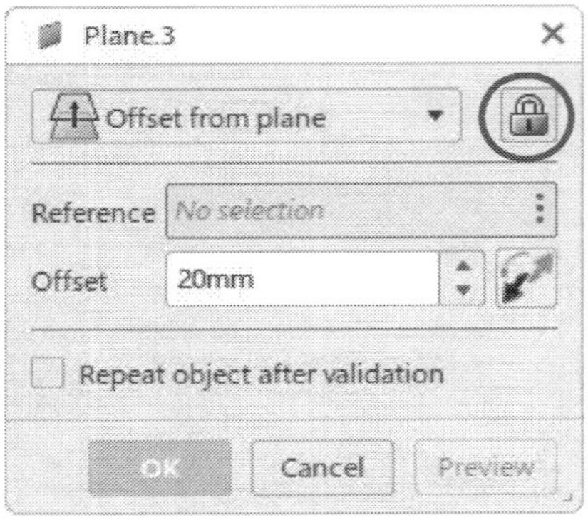

Figure 8–9

Shortcut Menus

The options available in the shortcut menu vary based on the type of input required.

You can access shortcut menu options when creating reference elements in the dialog boxes.

- To create a point on the fly while creating a **Parallel through point** reference plane on an edge, right-click in the *Point* field, as shown in Figure 8–10.

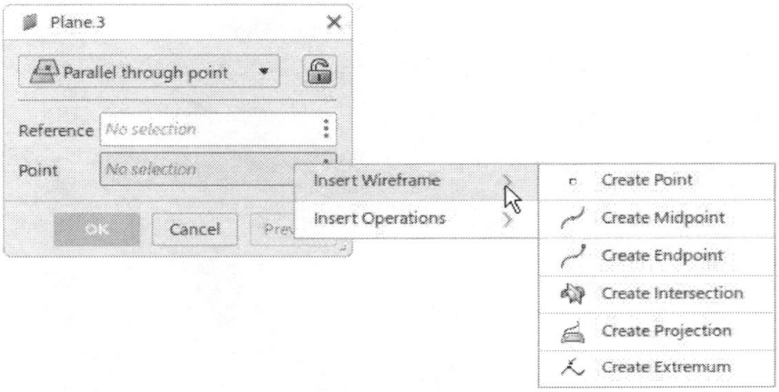

Figure 8–10

The creation of an element on the fly simplifies feature creation. It enables you to create required sub-elements without exiting the active feature.

- The element created on the fly is placed beneath the active feature in the specification tree. Figure 8–11 shows that the point created in the previous example is placed beneath the reference plane and hidden.

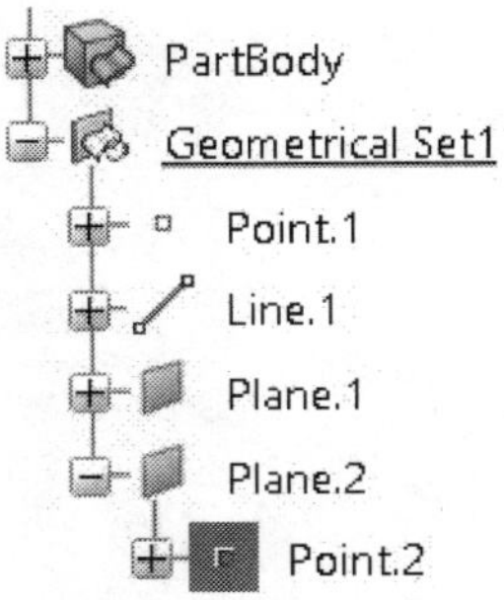

Figure 8–11

Practice 8a Working with Feature Limits

Practice Objective

- Specify a different limit setting for each side of a mirrored extent Pad.

In this practice, you will create the part shown in Figure 8–12. You will create reference elements and use a different limit setting for the Pad feature.

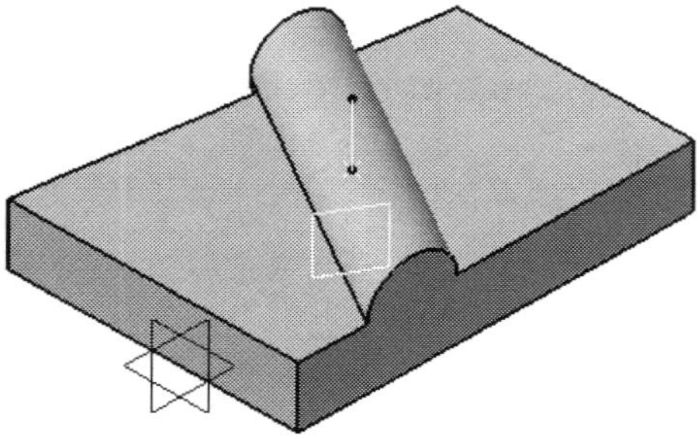

Figure 8–12

Task 1 - Open the part for use in this practice.

1. Import **Limit.3dxml**.
2. In the *Part1 (Explore)* tab, right-click **Part1** in the specification tree and select **Open**.
3. Note that the right side of the part is perpendicular to adjacent surfaces, and the left side is angled.

Task 2 - Create a point on the top face.

Design Considerations

This point will later be used as a reference point to constrain the profile sketch of a Pad feature. It will also be used as a starting point for a reference line.

1. In the *Essentials* section of the Action Bar, click (Point).
2. In the Point type drop-down list, select **On surface**.
3. Select the top surface of the block.
4. Enter **0** for the *Distance*.
5. In the *View* section of the Action Bar, click (* top).

6. Click **OK** to complete the feature. A point is created on the center of the face, as shown in Figure 8–13.

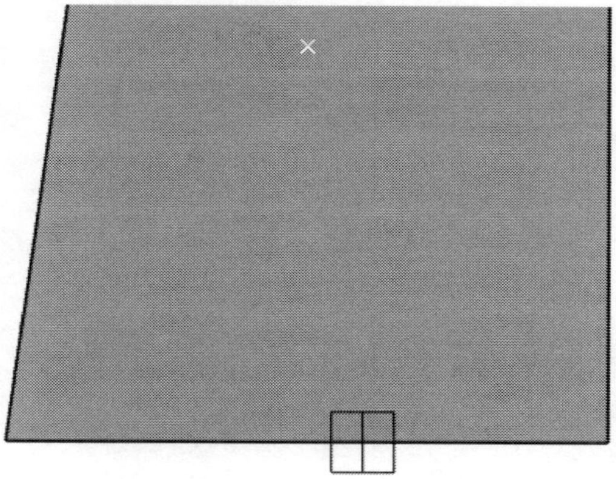

Figure 8–13

7. Click (* iso) to return to isometric orientation.

Task 3 - Create a line through the point and make it perpendicular to the top face of the part.

Design Considerations

This line will be perpendicular to the top face of the part and will pass through the point. It will be used as an axial reference for plane creation in later tasks.

1. In the *Essentials* section of the Action Bar, click (Line).
2. In the Line type drop-down list, select **Normal to surface**.
3. Select the top face as the surface that the line is perpendicular to, and select the point that the line will pass through, as shown in Figure 8–14.
4. Enter **20 (0.787 in)** for the *Line End - Offset* value. The length of the line is not important. It only needs to be long enough for you to see and easily select.

Click (Reverse Direction) to orient the line in a direction that suits your preference. The direction or length of the line will not impact later features.

5. Click **OK** to complete the feature. The part displays as shown in Figure 8–14.

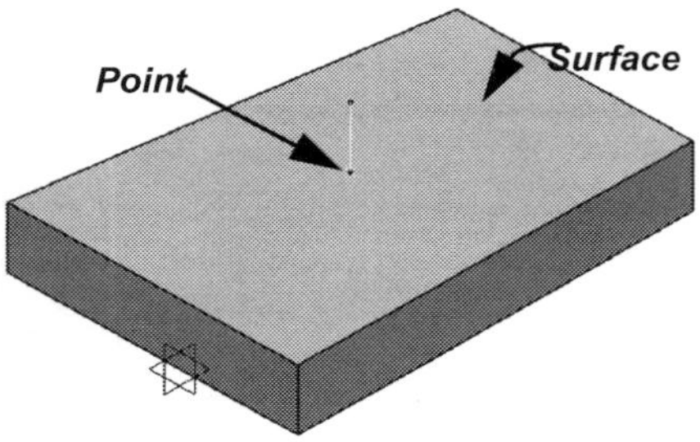

Figure 8–14

Task 4 - Create a plane through the line at an angle to the YZ plane.

Design Considerations

This angled plane will use a default datum plane and the line as references. It will be used as a sketching plane for the profile of a Pad feature in the next task.

1. Click (Plane).
2. In the Plane type drop-down list, select **Angle/Normal to plane**.
3. Select the line as the rotation axis.
4. Select the YZ plane as the angular reference.
5. Enter **-60** for the angle.
6. The part displays as shown in Figure 8–15.

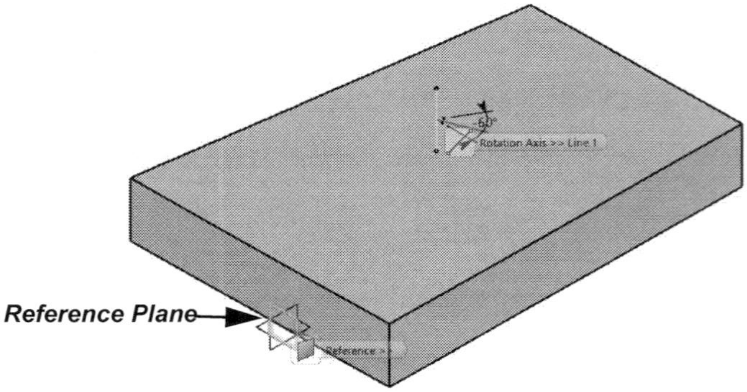

Figure 8–15

7. Click **OK** to complete the feature.

Task 5 - Sketch a profile on the angled plane.

1. Select the angled plane and click (Sketch) from the context toolbar.
2. Sketch a **25.0 (0.984 in)** diameter circle, as shown in Figure 8–16. Use the **Coincidence** constraint to constrain the center of the circle to the point.

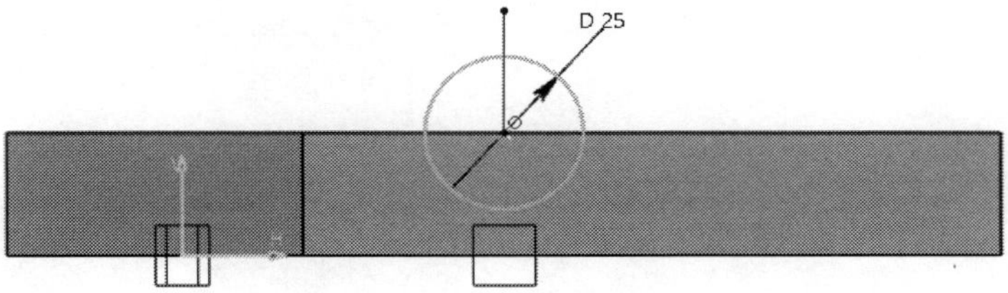

Figure 8–16

3. Click (Exit App) to complete the sketch.

Task 6 - Create a Pad feature using the circular sketch.

1. Select the sketch and click (Pad) from the *Essentials* section in the Action Bar. Use the following parameters, as shown in Figure 8–17:

    - Select **Up to plane** for the First Limit Type and select the planar surface.
    - Select **Up to plane** for the Second Limit Type and select the planar surface.
    - Enter **6.00 (0.236 in)** offset for Limit 2.

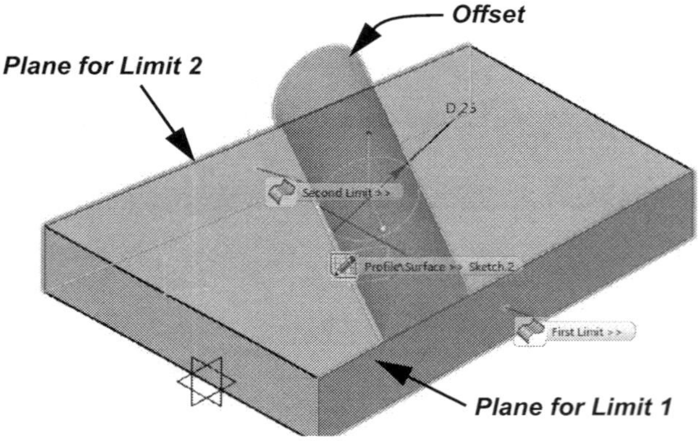

Figure 8–17

2. Click **OK** to complete the feature.

3. Save the part and close the tab.

Practice 8b

Reference Elements

Practice Objectives

- Create reference elements.
- Create solid features using reference elements.

In this practice, you will create the part shown in Figure 8–18. You will create reference elements to use as sketch planes. From these you will create the features.

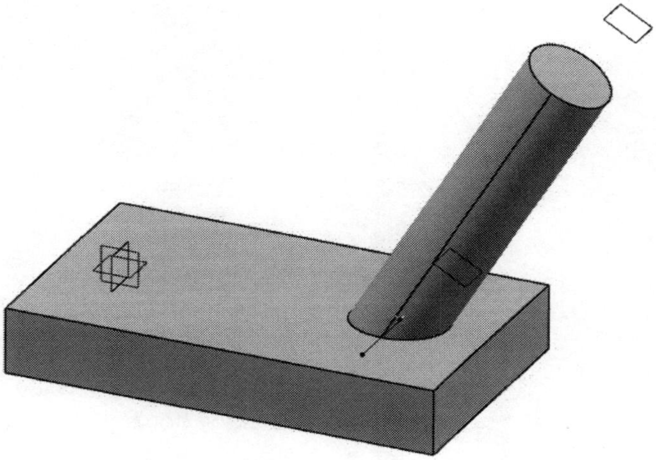

Figure 8–18

Task 1 - Open a model with an initial Pad feature.

1. Import **Ref_Elements.3dxml**.
2. In the *Part1 (Explore)* tab, right-click **Part1** in the specification tree and select **Open**.

Task 2 - Create a point at the center of the part.

Design Considerations

The point you create here is used later to constrain the profile of a Pad feature. It is also used as a starting point for a line, which will serve as an axial reference for reference planes.

1. Select the top face of the part as shown in Figure 8–19.

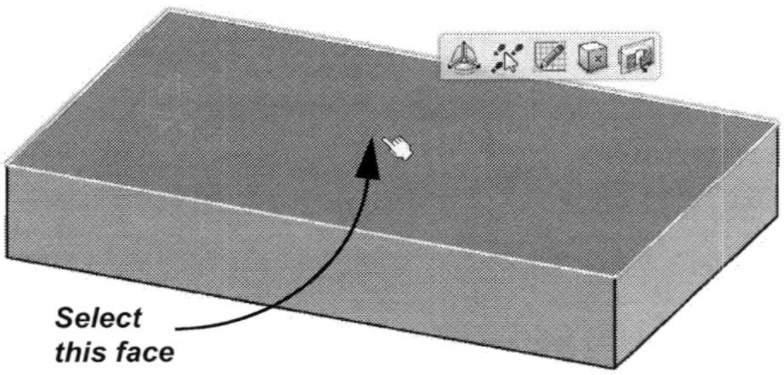

Figure 8–19

2. In the *Essentials* section of the Action Bar, click (Point) to create a point. The Point Definition dialog box opens.

3. The system has already selected **On Plane** in the *Point type*. Note the horizontal and vertical arrows on the model. They are located at the current origin of the model

4. Set the following, as shown in Figure 8–20:

   - *H* field: **38 (1.496 in)**
   - *V* field: **63.5 (2.500 in)**

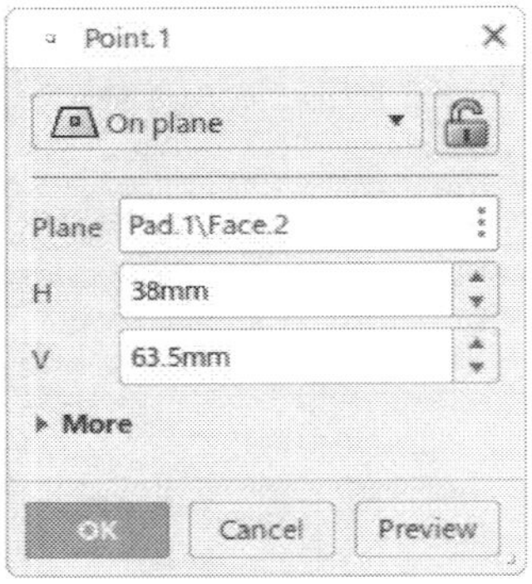

Figure 8–20

5. Click **OK**.

Task 3 - Create a line.

Design Considerations

This line will begin on the point you previously created. It is used as a pivot axis for several angled planes.

1. Click (Line) to create a line.
2. In the Line Definition dialog box, in the Line type drop-down list, select **Point-Direction.**
3. The **Point** field is now highlighted in the dialog box. Select the point you created in the previous task. The line begins at this point.
4. Ensure that the **Direction** field is now highlighted. In the specification tree or on the model, select the YZ plane. The line is perpendicular to this plane.
5. Ensure that the **Support** field is now highlighted. Select the top face of the part. The line resides on this plane.
6. Enter **25.00 (0.984 in)** in the *Line End-Offiset* field. The length of the line is not important. It only needs to be long enough for you to see and easily select.
7. Click **OK** to complete the line. The resulting part displays as shown in Figure 8–21.

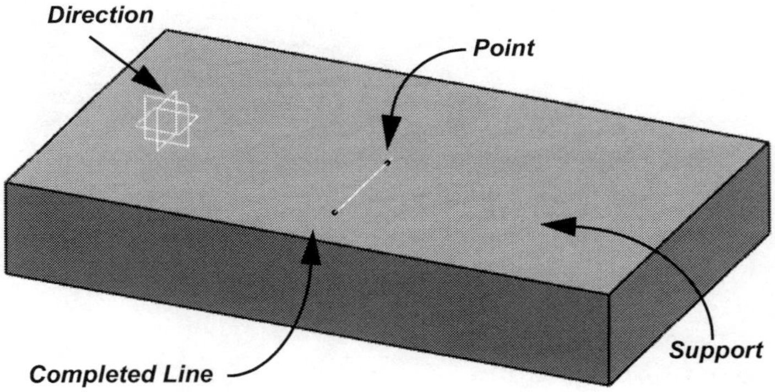

Figure 8–21

Task 4 - Create planes to locate a sketch.

Design Considerations

Using the previously created axis and one of the datum planes, you will create an angled plane. This plane will be used as a reference for the following plane that you will create.

1. Click  (Plane) to create a plane.
2. In the Plane Definition dialog box, in the Plane type drop-down list, select **Angle/Normal to Plane**.
3. The **Rotation Axis** field is now highlighted. Select the line created in the previous task. The new plane passes through this axis.
4. The **Reference** field is now highlighted. Select the ZX plane as the plane to measure the angle from.
5. Enter **-30** for the angle.
6. Click **OK** to complete the first plane. The resulting part displays as shown in Figure 8–22.

*You might need to enter **30** for the angle to obtain the result shown in Figure 8–22.*

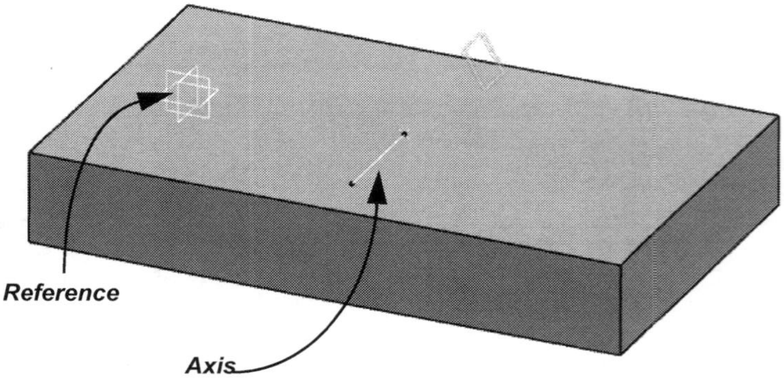

Figure 8–22

Design Considerations

The following plane will be used as a sketching plane for the profile sketch of a Pad feature. The plane will be offset from the angle plane.

7. Make the second plane offset from the first plane. You will use it as the sketching plane in the next task. Click  (Plane) again.
8. Select **Offset from plane** in the Plane type drop-down list.

9. Select the first plane as the reference and enter **50.00 (1.969 in)** as the offset distance.

10. Click **OK** to complete the creation of this plane. The resulting part displays as shown in Figure 8–23.

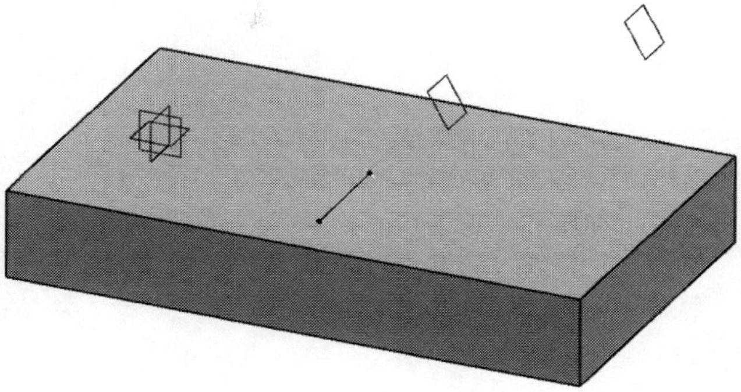

Figure 8–23

Task 5 - Create a sketch on the offset plane.

Design Considerations

This sketch will be used as a profile for a Pad feature. It is created on the offset plane and will be constrained to the point that you created earlier.

1. Select the offset plane and click  (Positioned Sketch) from the *Essentials* section of the Action Bar.

2. Expand the *Origin* section and in the Origin Type drop-down list, select **Projection Point**.

3. Select **Point.1**. The Sketch Positioning dialog box displays as shown in Figure 8–24.

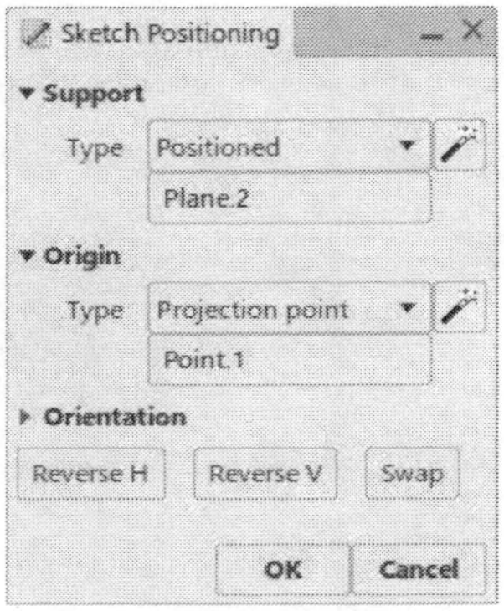

Figure 8–24

4. Click **OK** to enter the Sketch app.
5. Sketch a **25 (0.984 in)** diameter circle centered on the origin as shown in Figure 8–25.

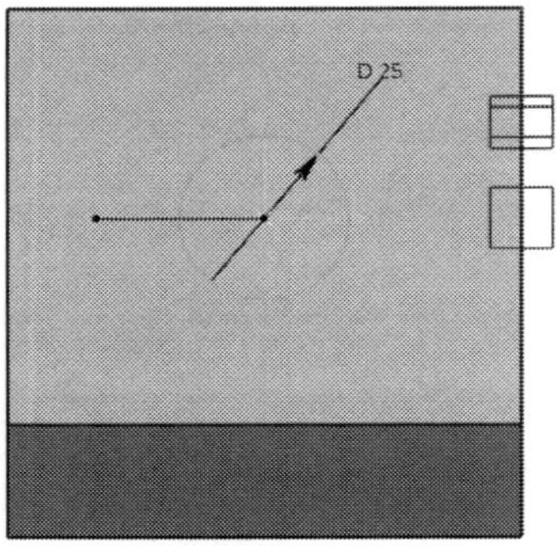

Figure 8–25

6. Click (Exit App) to complete the sketch and exit the Sketch app.

Task 6 - Create a Pad feature.

1. Select the sketch created in the last task and click (Pad) to create a Pad feature.
2. If required, click (Reverse Direction) to extrude the profile toward the existing geometry.
3. In the Pad Definition dialog box, in the *First Limit* area, select **Up to next** in the Type drop-down list.
4. Click **OK** to complete this feature. The resulting part displays as shown in Figure 8–26.

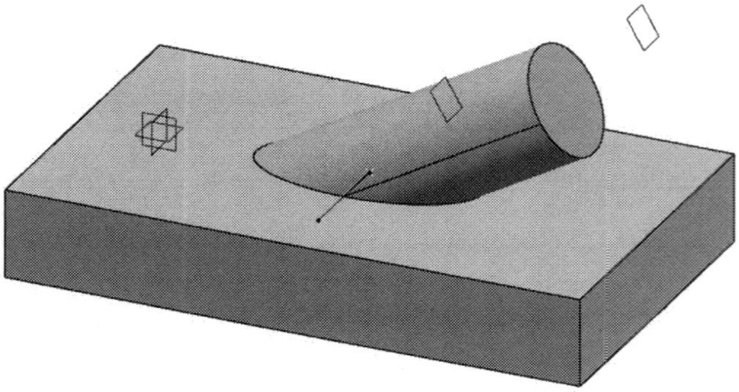

Figure 8–26

Task 7 - Modify the angle, offset distance, and location of the Pad feature.

1. Double-click **Plane.2** (the offset plane). Edit the offset value to **100.00 (3.937 in)** and click **OK**.
2. Double-click **Plane.1**. Edit the angle to **60.00** and click **OK**.
3. Double-click **Point.1**. Edit the dimensions to **63.5mm (2.500 in)** to **100.00 (3.937 in)** and click **OK**. The model displays as shown in Figure 8–27.

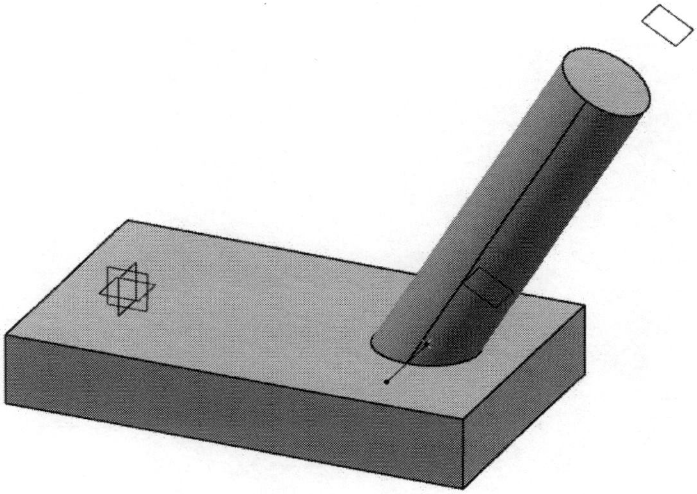

Figure 8–27

Task 8 - Rename the reference elements to more easily identify which features control the aspects of Pad.2.

1. In the specification tree, select **Point.1**, right-click, and select **Properties**.
2. In the *Feature Properties* tab, enter **Pad2: X&Y** as the *Feature Name*.
3. Repeat Step 2 and change the name of **Plane.1** to **Pad2: Angle**.

4. Repeat Step 3 and change the name of **Plane.2** to **Pad2: Offset**. The specification tree displays as shown in Figure 8–28.

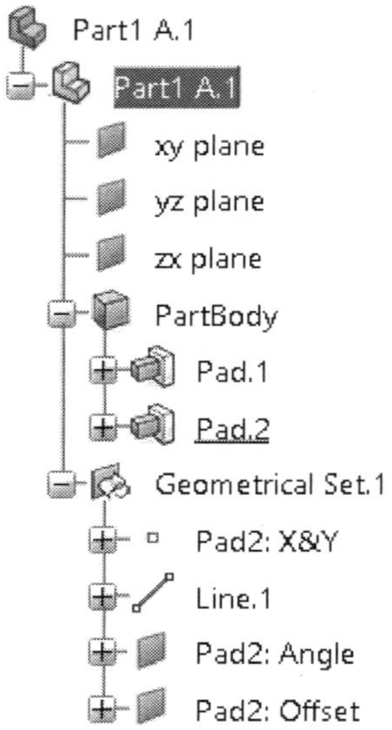

Figure 8–28

Task 9 - Save the part and close the window.

1. Save the part and close the tab.

NOTE: An additional reference element practice is found in Practice B6 at the end of this guide.

Chapter Review Questions

1. The default reference planes are the only reference planes that can exist in a model.
   a. True
   b. False
2. Which combination of constraints enables you to create the reference plane shown in Figure 8–29?

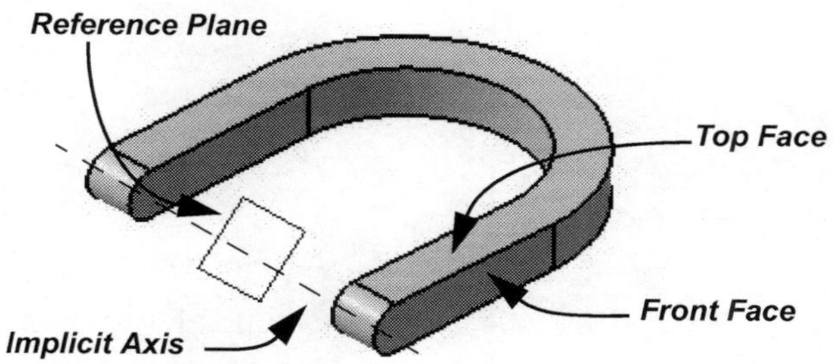

Figure 8–29

   a. Tangent to the Fillet and through the implicit axis of the Fillet.
   b. Through the implicit axis of the Fillet at an angle to the front face.
   c. Through the implicit axis of the Fillet at an angle to the top face.
   d. Through the top face at an angle to the front face.
3. Which of the following are valid constraint combinations to create a reference plane? (Select all that apply.)
   a. Through two edges.
   b. Offset from a surface.
   c. Parallel to a plane and through a point.
   d. Tangent to a surface and through a point.

4. Which of the following are valid constraint combinations to create a reference line? (Select all that apply.)
    a. At the intersection of two planes.
    b. Through the center of a circle.
    c. Through two points.
    d. Parallel to a line.

5. Which of the following statements is true regarding the specification tree shown in Figure 8–30?

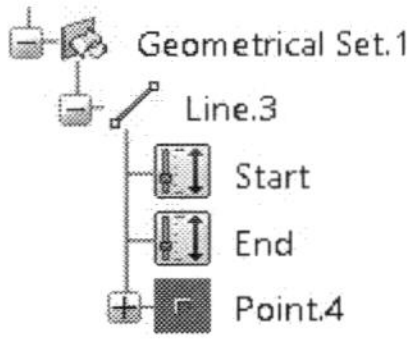

Figure 8–30

    a. A point was created first and then used to create the line.
    b. The point was created on the fly while creating the line.
    c. The point was automatically created by CATIA when the vertex of existing geometry is used as the point reference.
    d. A line was created and then a point.

6. Points, lines, and planes affect the mass properties of a model.
    a. True
    b. False

7. Where are user-defined reference features placed in the specification tree? (Assume that the **Hybrid** design option is not active).
    a. In the Geometrical Set branch.
    b. In the Annotations branch.
    c. In the Features branch.
    d. None of the above.

8. A Point-Point line type that lies on a support surface is always a straight line.
    a. True
    b. False

Answers: 1b, 2c, 3abcd, 4cd, 5b, 6b, 7a, 8b

Shaft and Groove Features

Shafts and Grooves are used to create revolved shapes and are set up similarly to Pads and Pockets. This chapter covers the requirements for sketches used in Shaft features. Additionally, you learn how to create grooves to remove material from the model and how you can create grooves on both planar and cylindrical surfaces.

Learning Objectives in This Chapter

- Learn the steps required to create a shaft feature.
- Understand the restrictions on sketches used for shaft features.
- Learn the steps required to create a groove feature.
- Create grooves on cylinders.

9.1 Shaft Feature

A Shaft feature consists of an existing sketch rotated about an axis. Figure 9–1 shows an example of a section rotated 360° about a sketched axis.

You can also use the vertical axis of the sketch.

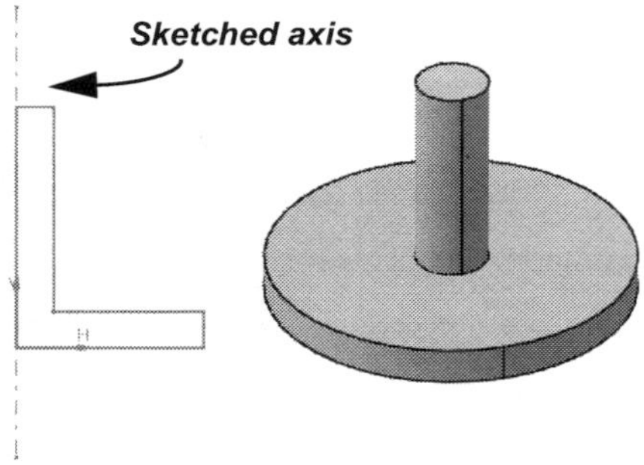

Figure 9–1

General Steps

Use the following general steps to create a Shaft feature:

1. Select a profile.
2. Initiate the creation of a Shaft.
3. Select a rotational axis.
4. Specify **Shaft limit** options.
5. Complete the Shaft feature.

Step 1 - Select a profile.

The shape of a Shaft is determined by the profile that is used to create the feature. An example is shown in Figure 9–2.

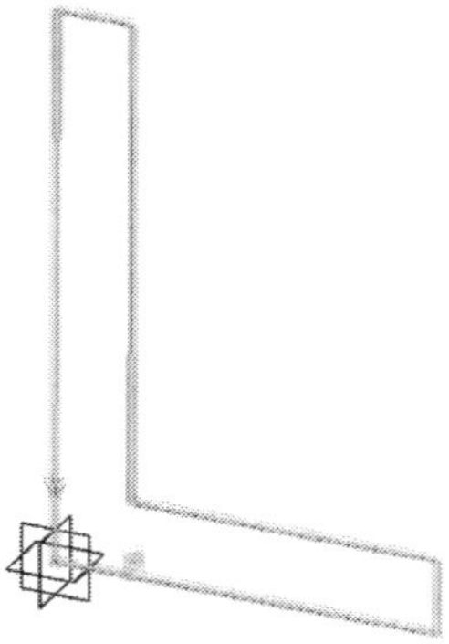

Figure 9–2

Sketch Restrictions

The sketch you select for a Shaft feature requires valid sketch geometry and an axis. The valid and invalid combinations of geometry and axis are described as follows:

Sketch	Shaft Geometry	Description
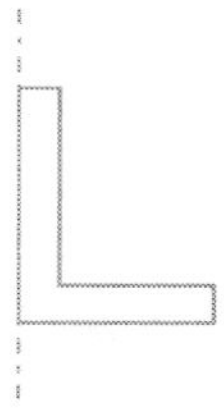	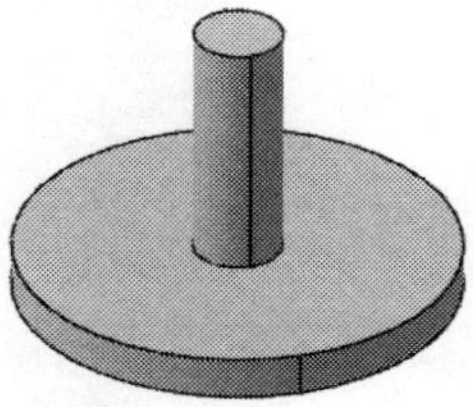	This is a closed sketch with the axis on the edge of the profile.
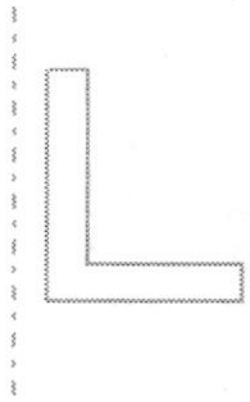	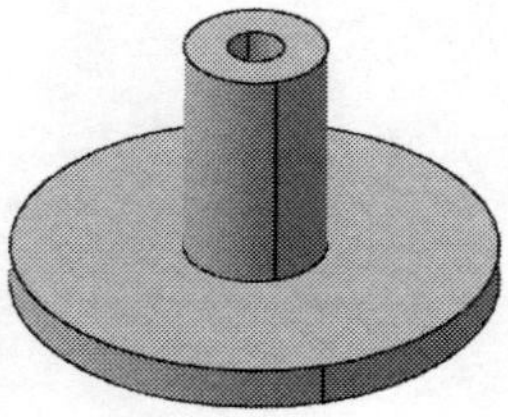	This is a closed sketch with the axis offset from the profile. The result is a hole in the Shaft.
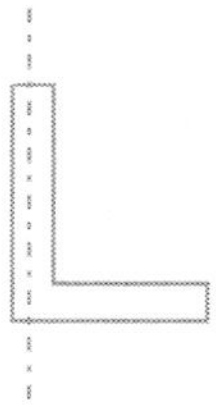	**Invalid**	This is a closed sketch with the axis inside the profile. A Shaft feature cannot sketch geometry on both sides of the axis of rotation, since the geometry would overlap.
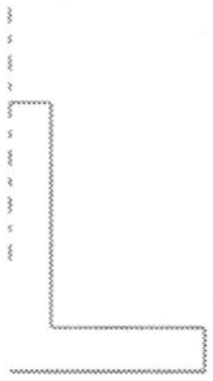	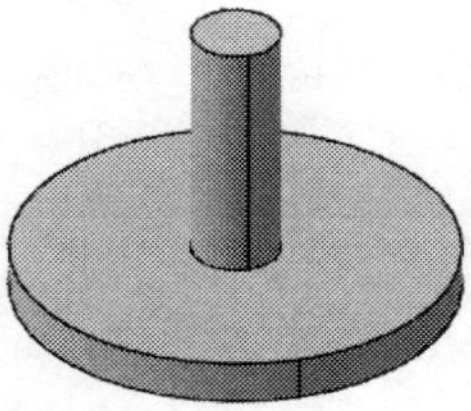	This is an open sketch with the axis coincident with the open ends of the profile. This sketch is valid, because the axis closes the sketch.
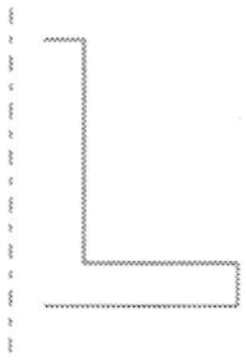	**Invalid**	This is an open sketch with the axis offset from the profile. This sketch is invalid, because no sketched geometry exists that generates a surface on the inside of the hole in the Shaft.

Step 2 - Initiate the creation of a Shaft.

To create a shaft, click (Shaft). The software initially creates the feature using the default values shown in the Shaft Definition dialog box in Figure 9–3

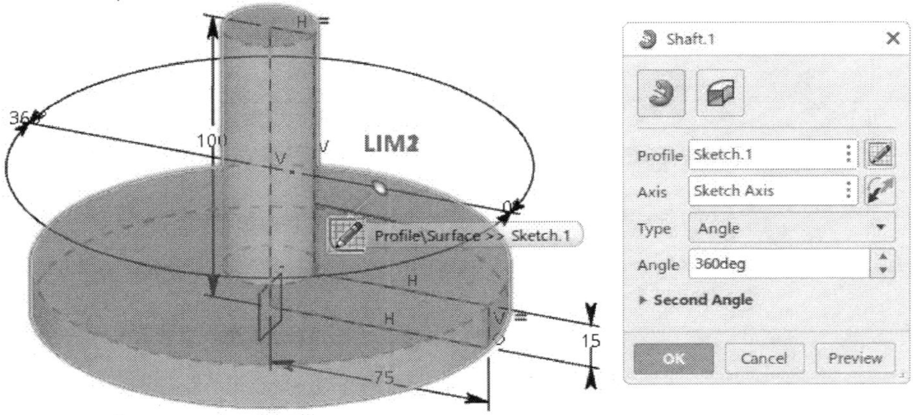

Figure 9–3

Step 3 - Select a rotational axis.

To create the Shaft feature, the rotational axis about which the profile is going to be revolved is required. By default, the software uses the first sketched axis created in the profile. If the sketch does not contain an axis, click (Sketch) in the Shaft Definition dialog box to alter the sketch without leaving the definition of this feature.

- While in the Sketch app, expand the (Line) flyout and click (Axis) to sketch an axis, as shown in Figure 9–4.

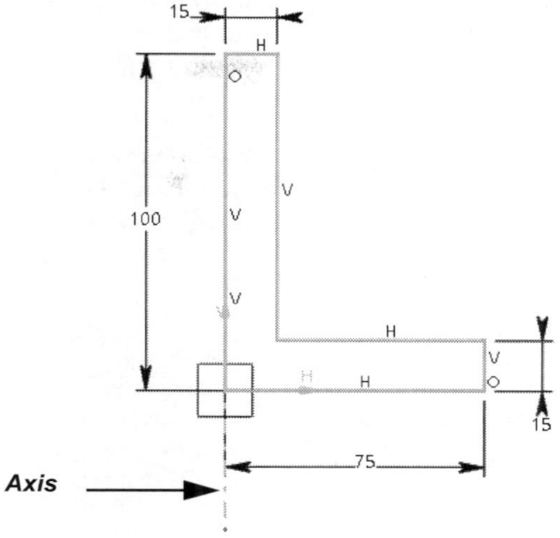

Figure 9–4

- Alternatively, you can select an existing edge, line, or axis. Figure 9–5 shows the selected vertical absolute axis of the sketch.

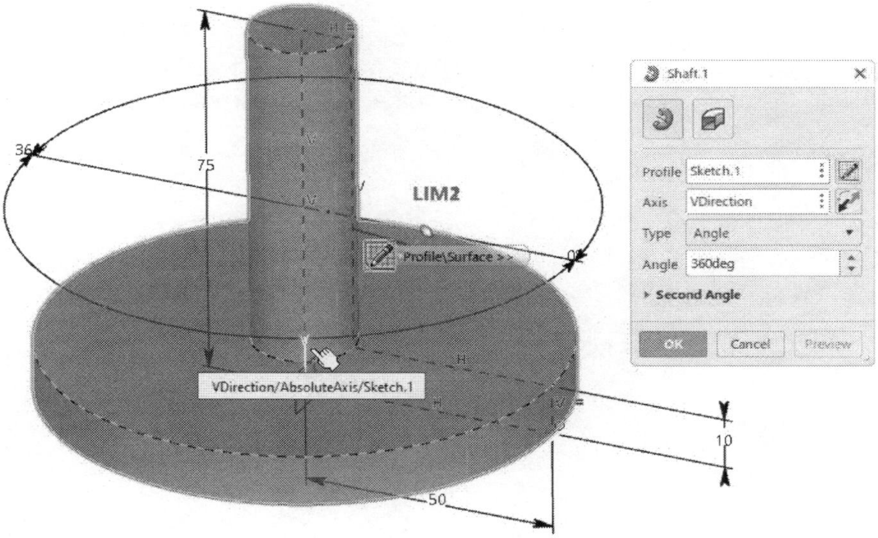

Figure 9–5

Step 4 - Specify Shaft limit options.

The angle that the sketch is rotated through is known as the limit. By default, the sketch is rotated 360° about the axis. This value can be changed, as required.

Rotation Angle

The default rotation angle is 360°. If you enter a smaller angle, the sketch is rotated in the direction indicated by the first angle direction arrow, as shown in Figure 9–6.

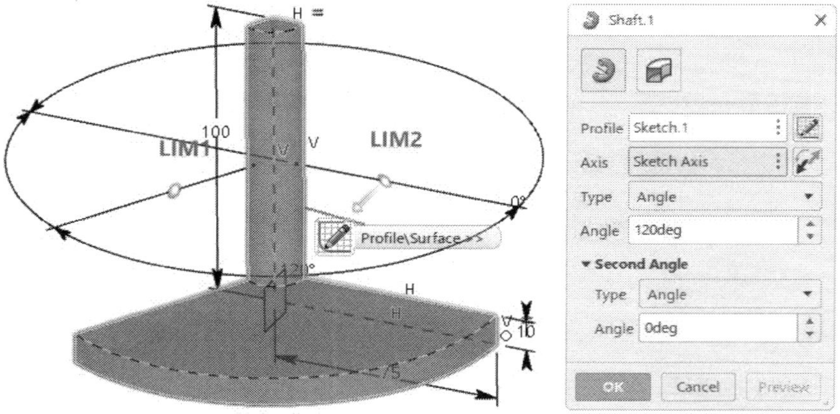

Figure 9–6

Entering a negative first angle value enables you to specify the angle of material to be removed from a 360° Shaft, as shown in Figure 9–7.

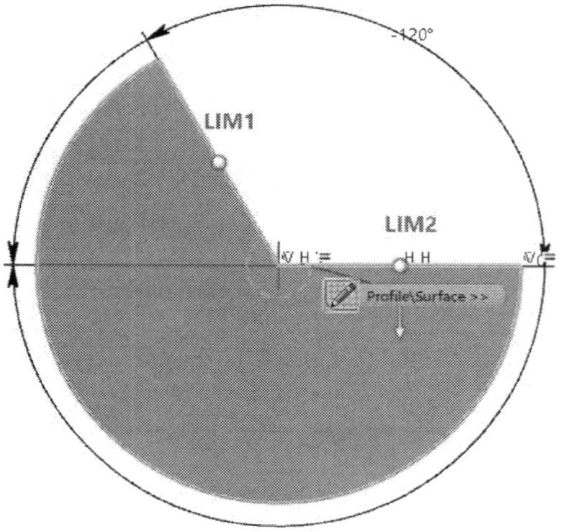

Figure 9–7

The sum of the first and second angles must be greater than zero and no more than 360°.

You can also change the default zero value of the second angle to rotate the sketch to the opposite side, as shown in Figure 9–8.

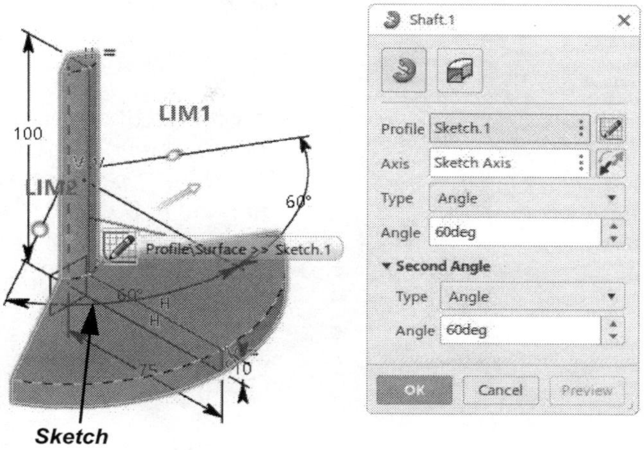

Figure 9–8

- Entering **0** for *Angle* and a value for the *Second angle* enables you to reverse the direction of the Shaft feature.
- Ensure that the sum of the two angles is 360° or less.
- To examine the geometry before you complete the feature, click **Preview**.

In addition to entering the *Angle* and *Second Angle* limits, you can apply any of the following limiting types, which are similar to those used for Pad and Pocket features:

- **Angle**: Creates a feature up to the defined angle value.
- **Up to next**: Creates a feature up to the next intersecting feature.
- **Up to last**: Creates a feature up to the last intersecting feature.
- **Up to plane**: Creates a feature up to the defined plane.
- **Up to surface**: Creates a feature up to the defined surface.

Step 5 - Complete the Shaft feature.

Click **OK** to complete the feature.

9.2 Groove Feature

A Groove feature removes material by rotating a sketch about an axis, as shown in Figure 9–9. It is similar to the Shaft feature, except that material is removed, instead of being added.

- As with the Shaft feature, you can accept the default value of 360° for the first limit and 0 for the second limit value. Figure 9–10 shows a model where the first limit value is changed to 90° and the second limit value is changed to 45°.

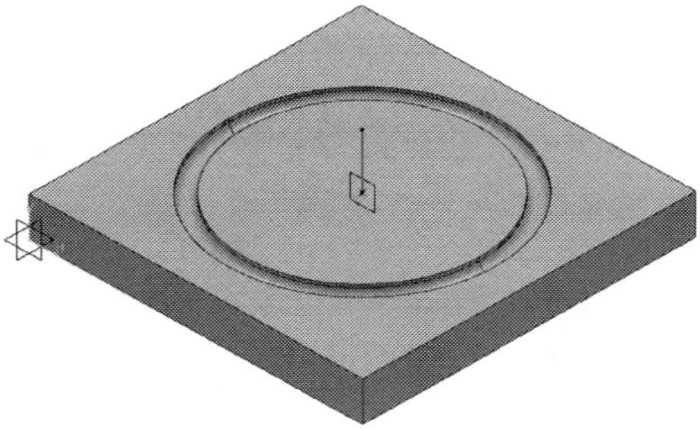

Figure 9–9

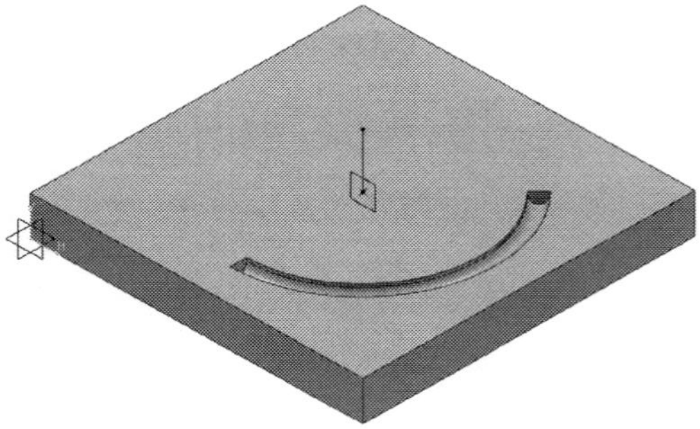

Figure 9–10

In addition to entering the *Angle* and *Second Angle* limits, you can apply any of the following limiting types:

- **Angle**: Creates a feature up to the defined angle value.
- **Up to next**: Creates a feature up to the next intersecting feature.
- **Up to last**: Creates a feature up to the last intersecting feature.
- **Up to plane**: Creates a feature up to the defined plane.
- **Up to surface**: Creates a feature up to the defined surface.

Requirements

To create a Groove feature, you must meet the following requirements:

- You must provide a rotation axis for the sketch. It can be a line, a sketched axis in the profile, or the implicit axis.
- Your profile must only be on one side of the axis.
- The section can be open or closed.

Grooves on Cylinders

To create a Groove feature on a cylindrical feature, a sketch plane must pass through the center of the cylindrical feature. If a suitable plane does not exist, you can use the **Angle/Normal to Plane** option when creating the reference plane. An axis must be selected as a placement reference.

- To select an implicit axis, hold <Shift> and place the cursor over the cylinder to highlight it, as shown in Figure 9–11. You can then select this axis as the rotation axis for the new plane.

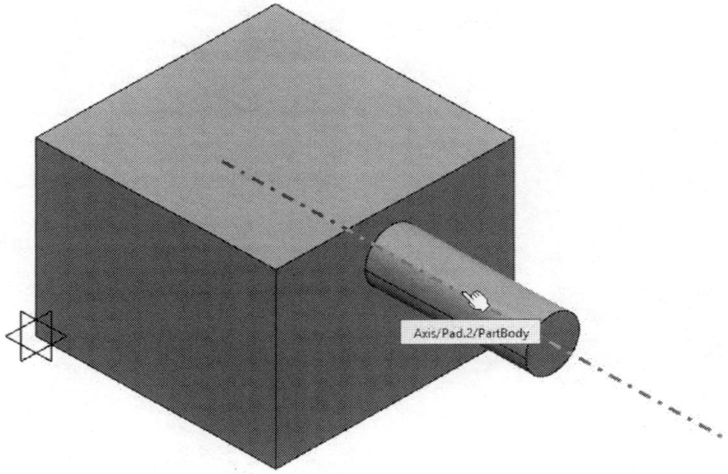

Figure 9–11

Rotation Axis

The implicit axis can be used to define the rotation axis for the Groove feature. This reduces the need to create additional line or sketched axis features.

Silhouette Edges

In some cases, you might need to constrain the sketch so that one or more sketched entities are coincident with the silhouette edge of the cylinder, as shown in Figure 9–12.

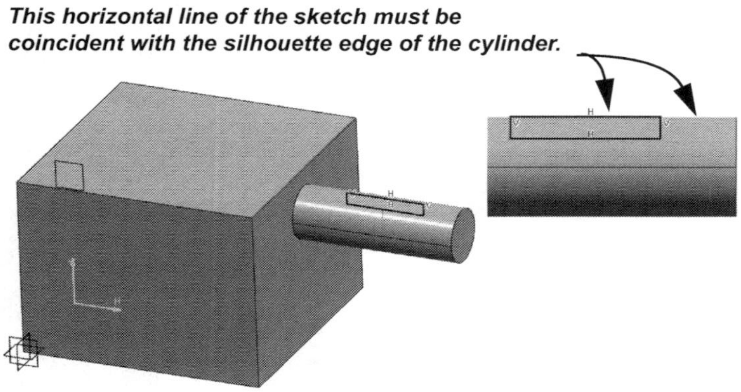

Figure 9–12

You cannot apply a coincidence constraint between the line and the silhouette edge. Therefore, click (Project 3D Canonical Silhouette Edges) and select the cylinder. This copies the top and bottom edges into the sketch, as shown in Figure 9–13.

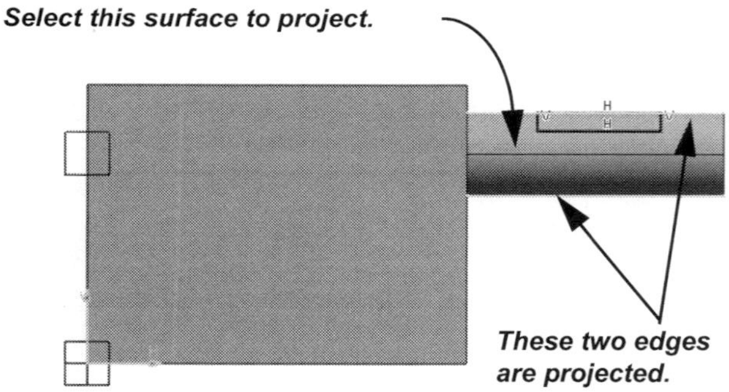

Figure 9–13

Once the silhouette edges are copied into your sketch, they display in yellow, which indicates projected geometry.

To complete your sketch, use one or a combination of the following methods:

- Delete the top or bottom silhouette edge that is not required.
- Convert the silhouette edge to construction geometry, and constrain your sketch to it.
- Leave the silhouette edge as a geometry element.

Dimension the Remaining Material Diameter

If the design intent is to control the diameter of a Groove feature, create a diameter dimension between the bottom of the sketch and the sketched axis, as shown in Figure 9–14.

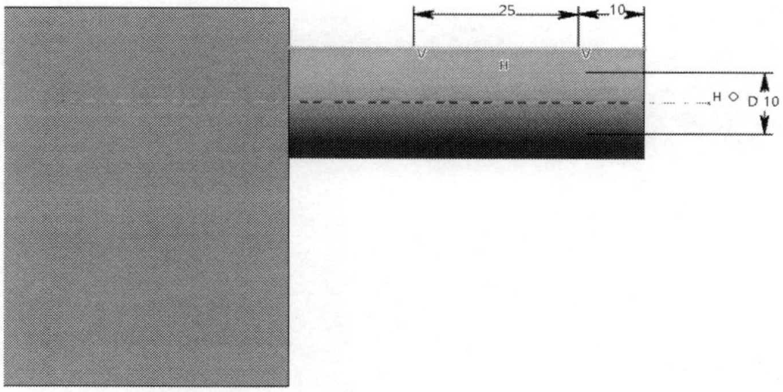

Figure 9–14

Practice 9a Shaft & Groove Features

Practice Objective

- Create a Shaft feature and a Groove feature.

In this practice, you will create the part shown in Figure 9–15. The base feature for the model is created using a Shaft feature by revolving a profile about the Y-axis. A Groove feature is then used to develop the lubrication grooves.

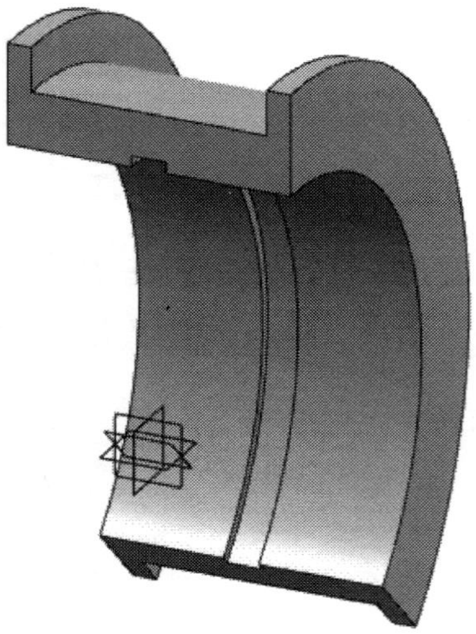

Figure 9–15

Task 1 - Create a new part.

1. In the Top Bar, click (Add)>**3D Part**.
2. In the 3D Part dialog box, enter **Bearing** as the *Title.*
3. Select the *3D Shape* tab and enter **Bearing** as the *Title.*
4. Select the *Characteristics* tab and ensure that **Enable hybrid** design is disabled.
5. Click **OK**.

Task 2 - Create a sketch.

1. Select the YZ plane as shown in Figure 9–16.

Figure 9–16

2. In the context toolbar, click (Sketch).
3. Sketch the horizontal axis, as shown in Figure 9–17. This will define the rotational axis of the Shaft feature.

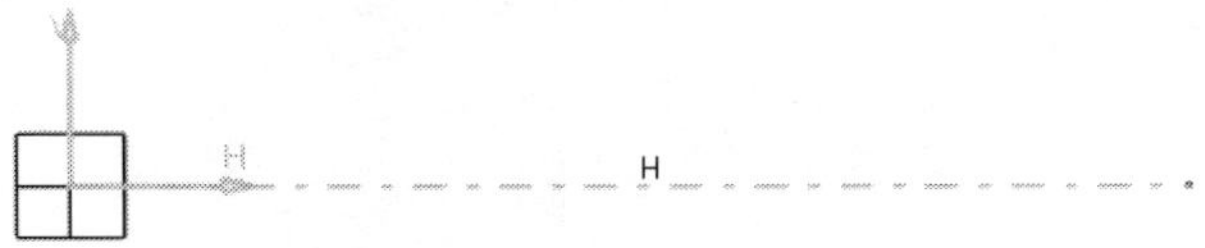

Figure 9–17

4. Sketch the profile as shown in Figure 9–18. Verify that the vertical elements are symmetrical about the vertical axis, and that the top horizontal elements are coincident.
   - 2 (0.079 in)
   - 5 (0.197 in)
   - 9 (0.354 in)
   - 24 (0.945 in)
   - 60 (2.362 in)

To create the diameter dimension, right-click and select ***Radius/ Diameter****.*

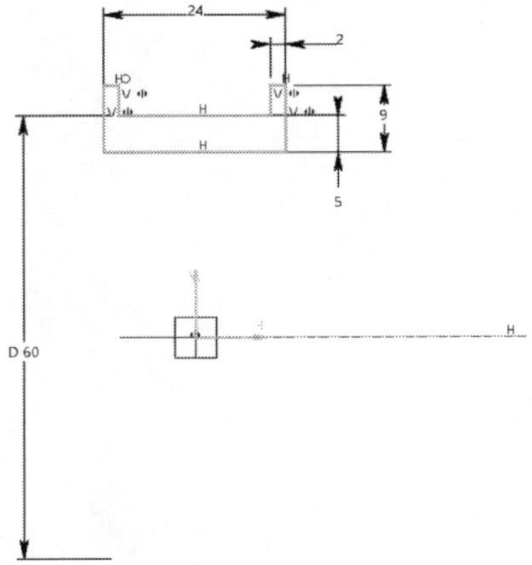

Figure 9–18

5. Click (Exit App) to exit the Sketch app.

Task 3 - Create a datum plane for use later in this practice.

1. In the *Essentials* section of the Action Bar, click  (Plane).
2. In the Plane Definition dialog box, in the Plane type drop-down list, select **Angle/Normal to plane**.
3. Right-click in the *Rotation axis* field and select **Insert Wireframe>Y Axis**, as shown in Figure 9–19.

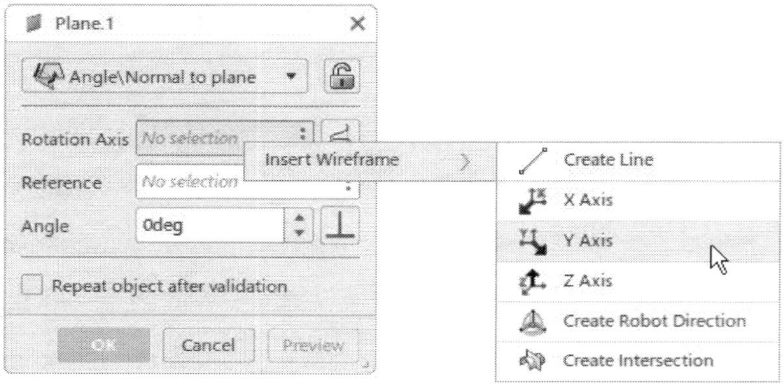

Figure 9–19

4. For the *Reference*, select **yz plane** in the specification tree.
5. Edit the angle to **100**, as shown in Figure 9–20.

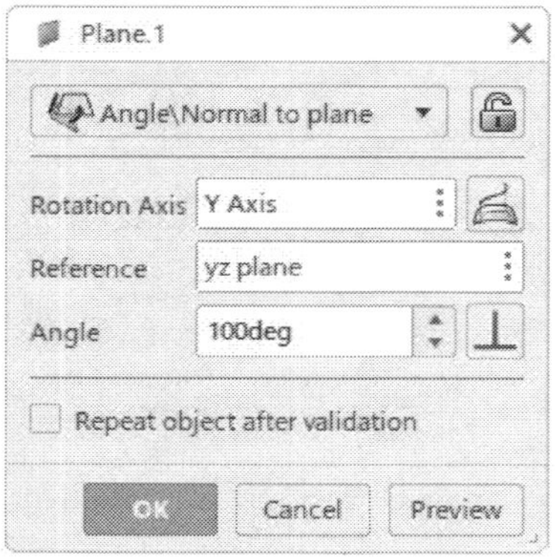

Figure 9–20

6. Click **OK** in the Plane Definition dialog box.

Task 4 - Create a Shaft feature.

Selecting (Shaft) will create a shaft with default settings. You want to access the Shaft Definition dialog box, so select (Shaft) from the Action Bar.

1. Select the sketch and click (Shaft) in the *Essentials* section of the Action Bar. The Shaft Definition dialog box opens as shown in Figure 9–21.

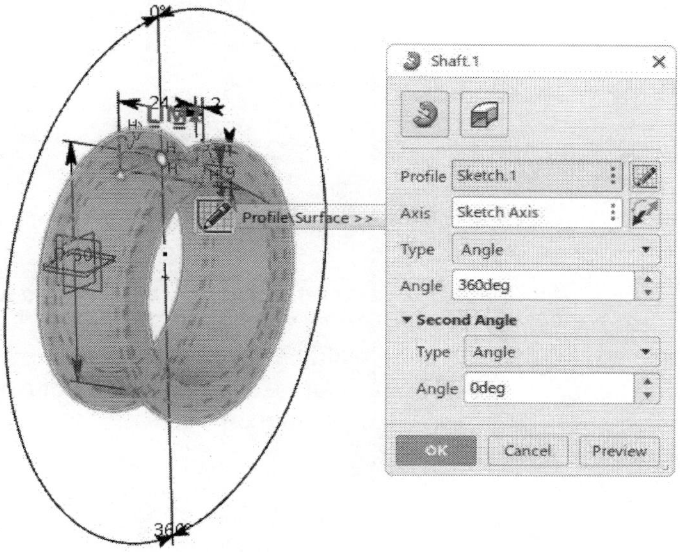

Figure 9–21

2. Enter the following parameters to define the Shaft feature:
   - *Angle:* **180deg**
   - *Second Angle-Angle:* **0deg**
   - Click *(Reverse Direction)*.

3. Click **OK**. The model displays as shown in Figure 9–22.

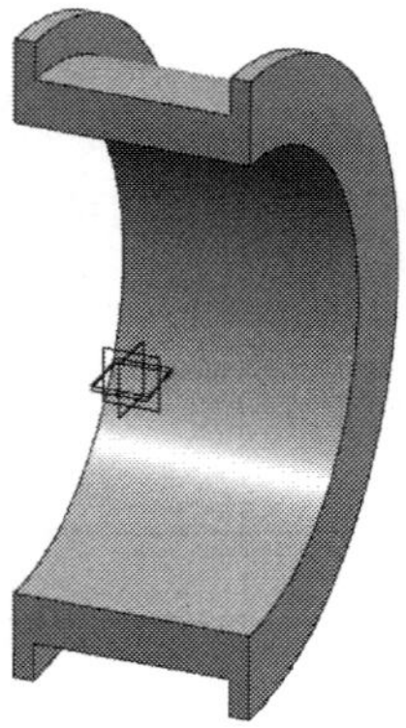

Figure 9–22

Task 5 - Create a Groove feature.

In this task, you will create a feature to represent the lubrication Groove on the inside diameter of the bearing. The completed feature displays as shown in Figure 9–23.

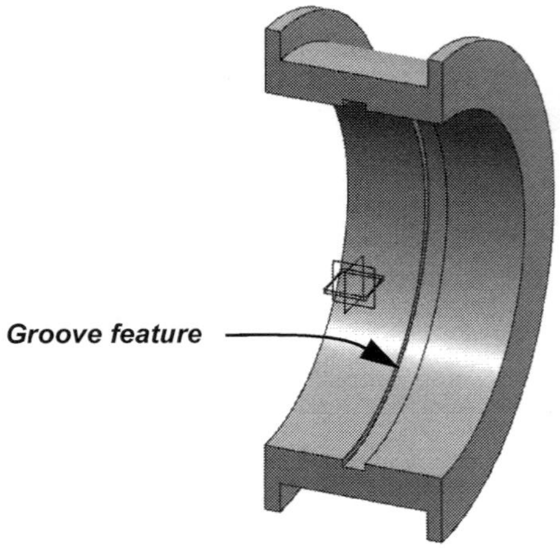

Figure 9–23

1. In the *Essentials* section of the Action Bar, click (Positioned Sketch). Create a positioned sketch on the YZ plane. To define the origin, use the **Middle Point** type and select the edge shown in Figure 9–24.

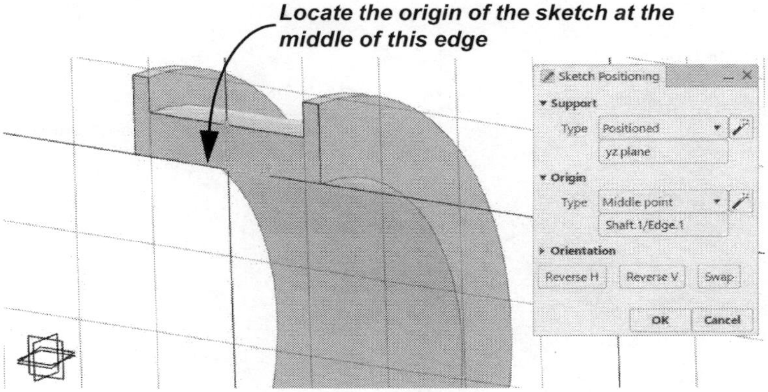

Figure 9–24

2. Click **OK**.

3. Sketch the profile shown in Figure 9–25, using the dimensions of **1 (0.039 in)** and **3 (0.118 in)**. Verify that the profile is symmetrical about the vertical sketch axis.

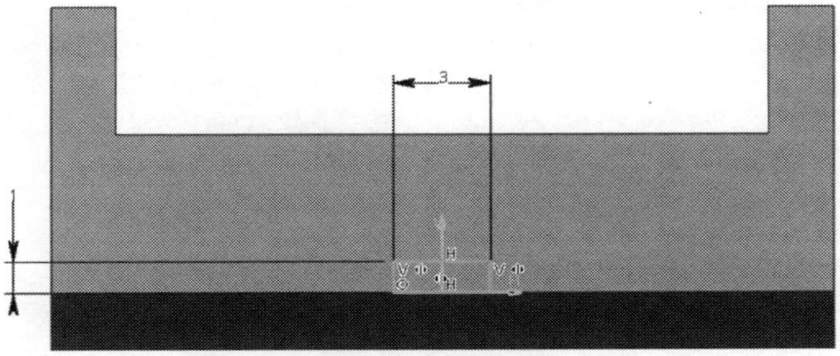

Figure 9–25

4. Click (Exit App).

5. With the sketch preselected, click  (Groove) in the *Essentials* section of the Action Bar. The Groove Definition dialog box opens as shown in Figure 9–26.

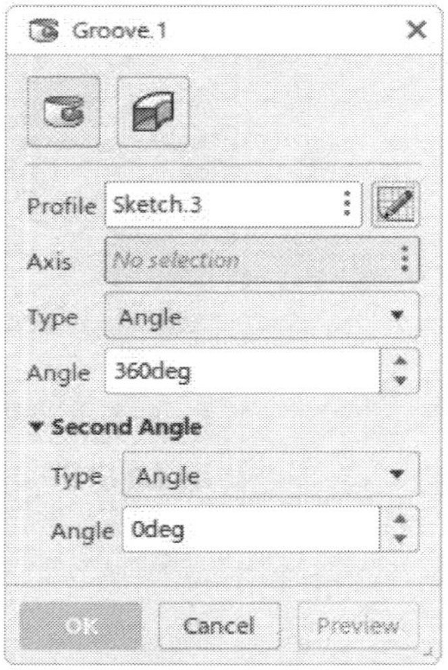

Figure 9–26

Design Considerations

Note how the **OK** and **Preview** buttons are grayed out. An axis was not sketched into the profile used for the Groove, so a rotation axis for the feature is not automatically defined.

6. Select the **Shaft.1** feature to select its axis. The Groove Definition dialog box updates as shown in Figure 9–27.

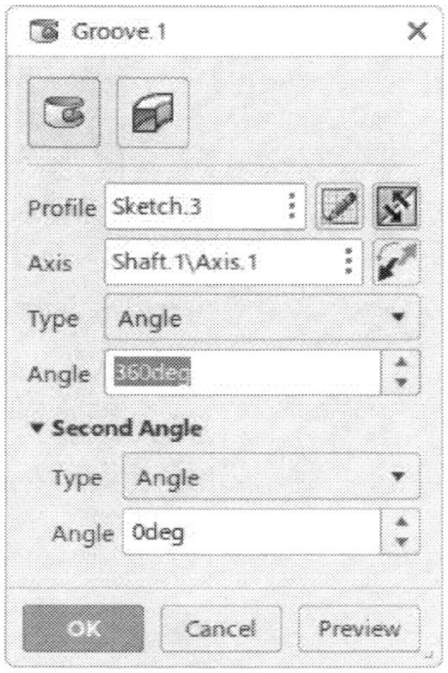

Figure 9–27

You might need to click ***Reverse Direction*** *to get the required result.*

7. Modify the options in the Groove Definition dialog box so that the resulting feature displays as shown in Figure 9–28.

Figure 9–28

Task 6 - Change the shaft to reference the datum plane.

1. In the specification tree, double-click on **Shaft.1**.
2. In the Shaft Definition dialog box, select **Up to plane** from the Limit drop-down list.
3. Select **Plane.1** in the specification tree.
4. Click **OK**.
5. In the Update Diagnosis Shaft.1 dialog box, click **Sub Elements**.

6. In the Sub Elements in Error dialog box, click **OK**. The model updates as shown in Figure 9–29.

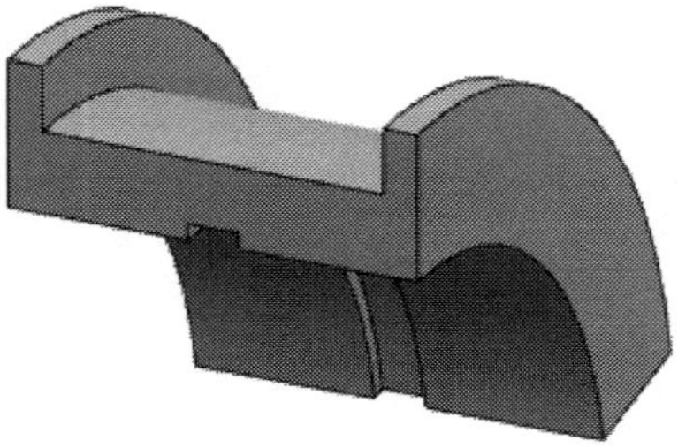

Figure 9–29

Task 7 - Edit the angle of the plane.

1. In the specification tree, double-click **Plane.1**.
2. Edit the *100* angle dimension to **45** and click **OK**.
3. The model updates as shown in Figure 9–30.

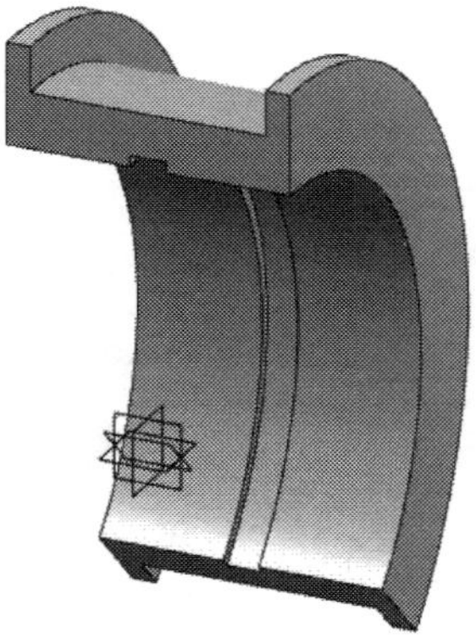

Figure 9–30

4. Save the model and close the tab.

Practice 9b Groove Features

Practice Objectives

- Create a Groove feature.
- Locate revolved sketches to cylindrical geometry.

In this practice, you will create the part shown in Figure 9–31. The part will consist of two Groove features. You will also use silhouette projections to locate a sketch onto cylindrical geometry.

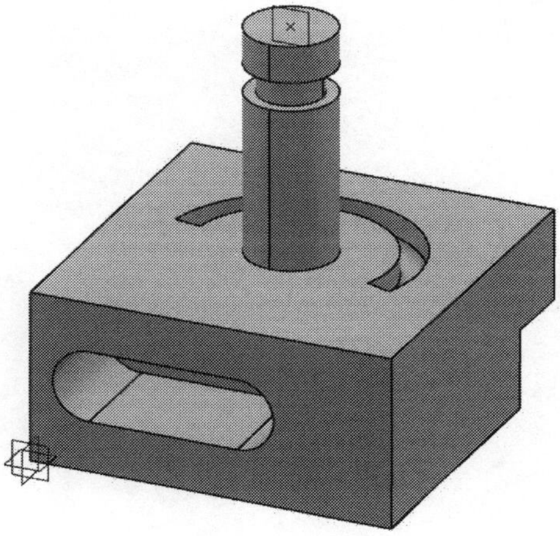

Figure 9–31

Task 1 - Create a point.

Design Considerations

This point will mark the center of the cylinder. It will be used as a reference for a plane, which will be used to create the two profiles in this task.

1. Import **Groove.3dxml**.
2. In the *Groove (Explore)* tab, right-click **Groove** in the specification tree and select **Open**.
3. Click (Point) in the Reference Elements toolbar.
4. Select **Circle/Sphere/Ellipse center** as the point type.

5. Select the circular edge on the top of the cylinder, as shown in Figure 9–32.

6. Click **OK** to complete the feature.

7. Click (Plane) and select **Parallel through point** as the plane type.

8. Select the YZ plane as the parallel reference for the new plane, and select the point to locate the plane.

9. Click **OK** to complete the feature. The new point and plane display as shown in Figure 9–32.

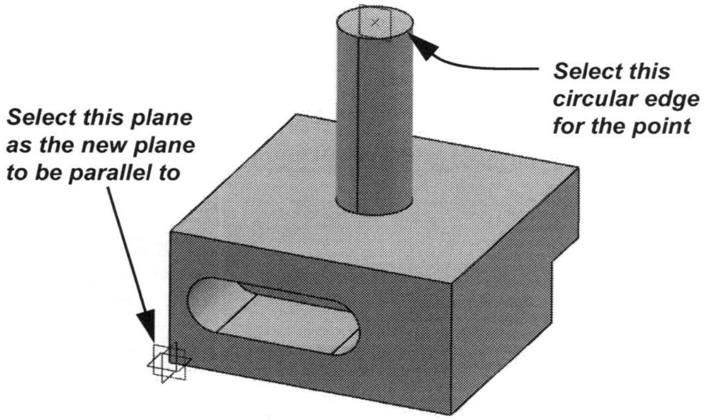

Figure 9–32

Task 2 - Create a sketch to be used for a Groove feature.

1. Create a positioned sketch on the newly created reference plane, using **Point.1** as the origin.

This sketched profile should be closed to avoid feature failure.

2. Click (Profile) to sketch the shape. Dimension the width and height of the shape, as shown in Figure 9–33.
   - 22.5 (0.886 in)
   - 32 (1.260 in)
   - 95 (3.740 in)

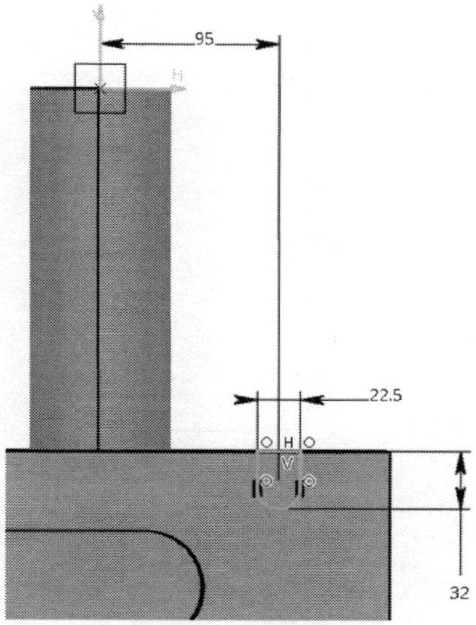

Figure 9–33

3. Constrain the horizontal line of the sketch with the horizontal edge of the part.
4. Dimension the center of the arc to the vertical sketcher axis.
5. When the sketch is fully constrained, click (Exit App).
6. With the sketch still highlighted, click (Groove) to create a Groove feature. The software does not automatically build a preview of the Groove because the sketch does not have an axis. Note that the axis selection box is active.

7. Place the cursor over the cylinder. The implicit axis displays. Select this axis and feature displays as shown in Figure 9–34.

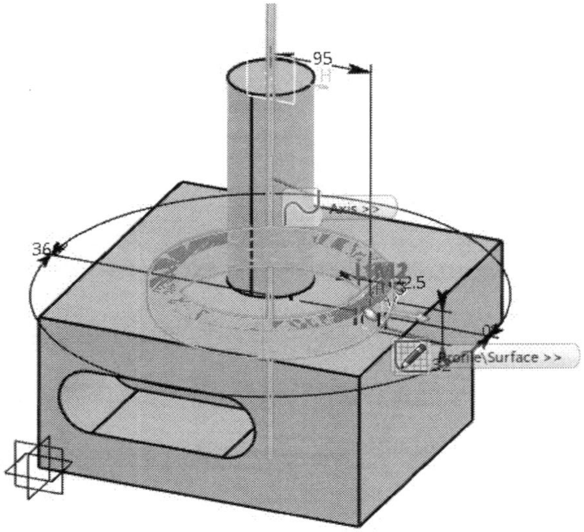

Figure 9–34

8. Set the *Angle* as **90** and set the *Second Angle-Angle* as **150.**
9. Click **Preview**. The part displays as shown in Figure 9–35.

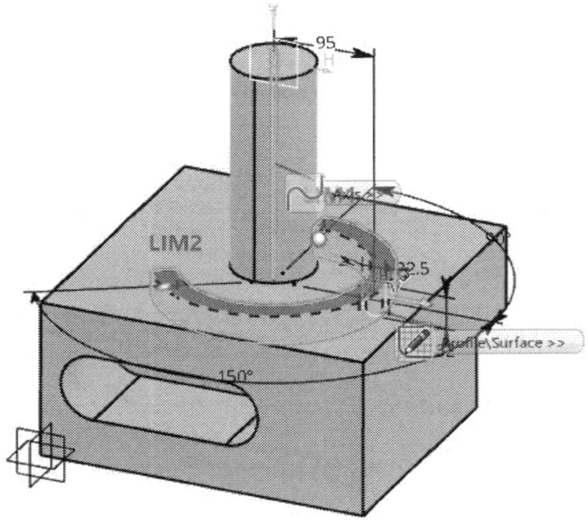

Figure 9–35

10. Select and drag the **LIM1** and **LIM2** tags of the Groove to dynamically modify the rotation angles.

11. When you have set the limits to an angle similar to that shown in Figure 9–36. Click **OK**.

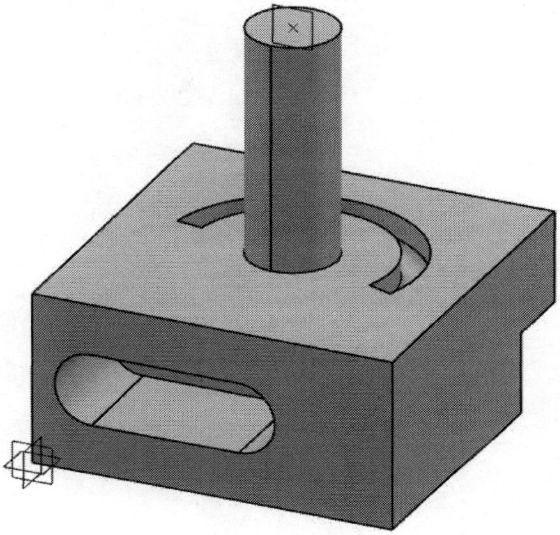

Figure 9–36

Task 3 - Create a sketch for a Groove feature on the cylinder.

1. Create a positioned sketch on the newly created reference plane using **Point.1** as the origin.
2. Select **View>Zoom Area** and zoom into the top of the cylinder by dragging a box around it.
3. Click  (Project 3D Canonical Silhouette Edges).
4. Select the cylinder. The warning message box opens, as shown in Figure 9–37.

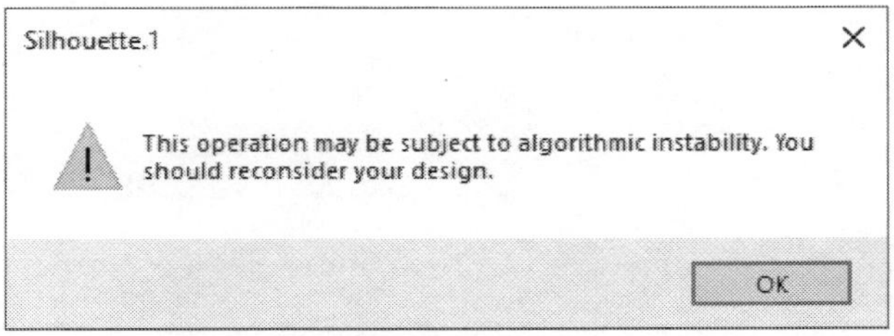

Figure 9–37

Design Considerations

The warning message displays to make you aware that features using silhouette edge projections in a sketch might become unstable. CATIA occasionally loses references to silhouetted edges. Use caution when using this type of projection in your models.

5. Click **OK** and two vertical lines display.

6. With the two silhouette projections selected, click 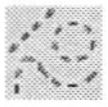 (Construction/Standard Element). The silhouette edges are now changed to construction lines.

7. Select the background area of the display to clear the geometry and click 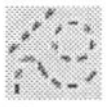 (Construction/Standard Element) to return to Standard Element creation.

8. Sketch and dimension the rectangle as shown in Figure 9–38. Verify that the right vertical edge of the rectangle is coincident with the construction line.

   - 25 (0.984 in)
   - 27 (1.063 in)
   - 32 (1.260 in)

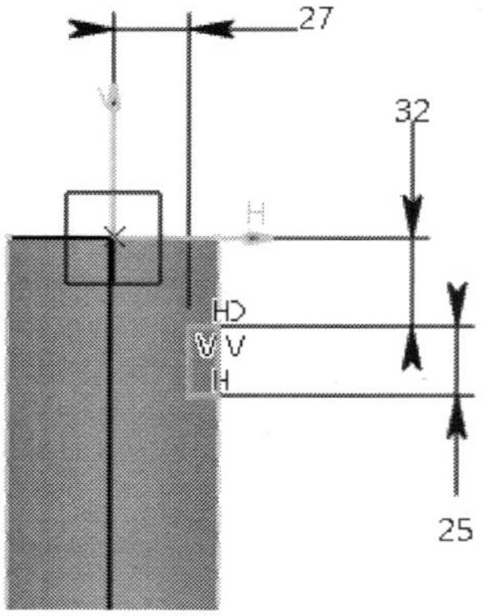

Figure 9–38

9. Sketch a vertical  (Axis) coincident with the vertical axis.

10. Exit the Sketch app.

11. With the sketch highlighted, click  (Groove). Note that the sketch axis is automatically selected as the rotational axis for the Groove feature.

12. Ensure the First Angle is set to **360deg** and the Second Angle is **0deg**.

13. Click **OK** to complete the feature. The part displays as shown in Figure 9–39.

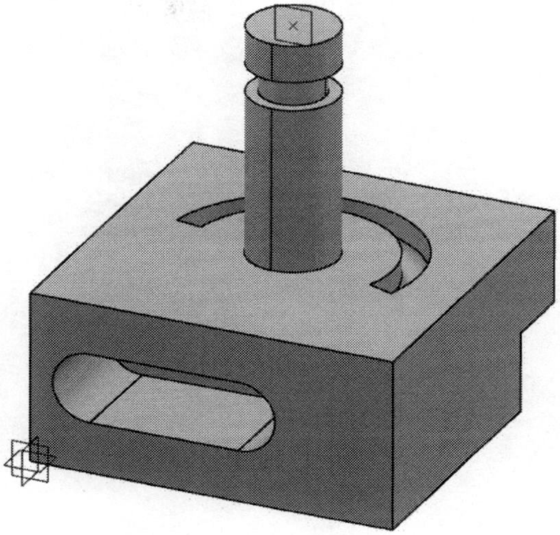

Figure 9–39

14. Save the file and close the tab.

NOTE: Additional shaft and groove practices are found in Practice B7 and Practice B8 at the end of this guide.

Chapter Review Questions

1. You mistakenly use a sketch to create a Pad feature, when you really intended to create a Shaft. What do you need to do to fix this?
   a. Right-click the pad and select **Convert to Shaft**.
   b. Right-click the Pad and select **Pad.object>Definition**. In the Pad Definition dialog box, select **Shaft**.
   c. Delete the Pad and use the sketch to create a Shaft feature.
   d. None of the above.
2. Which of the following profiles is not valid for use in creating a Shaft feature?
   a. 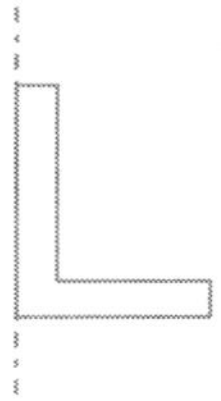
   b. 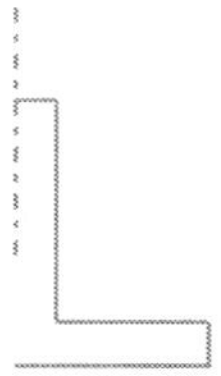
   c. 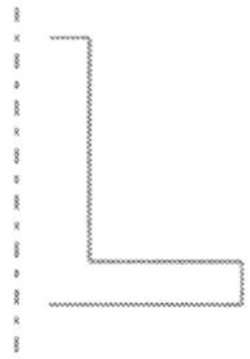
   d. 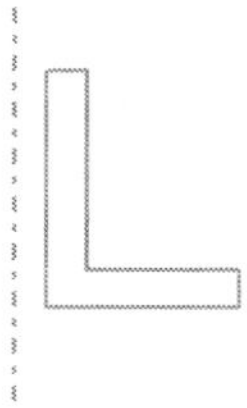

3. Which of the following are valid selections as an axis for a Shaft or Groove feature? (Select all that apply.)
    a. An axis created inside the sketch.
    b. An existing edge.
    c. The vertical absolute axis of a sketch.
    d. The implicit axis of an existing feature.
4. The profile for a Groove feature must lie completely to one side of the axis of revolution.
    a. True
    b. False
5. A Groove is required on the side of the cylindrical feature shown in Figure 9–40. What feature is required to aid in the creation of the Groove feature?

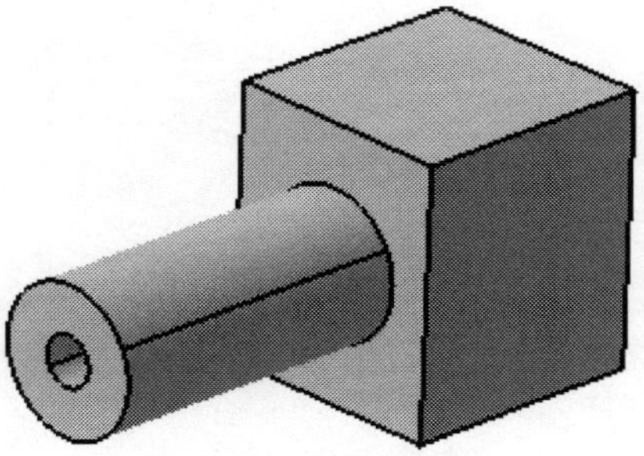

Figure 9–40

    a. A construction line.
    b. A sketch support.
    c. A point.
    d. None of the above.

6. What is going to be projected onto the sketch if the Cylindrical feature, shown in Figure 9–41, is projected using the **Project 3D Canonical Silhouette Edges** icon?

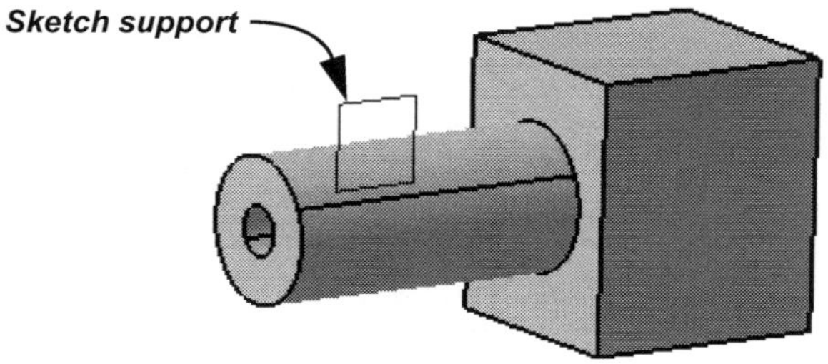

Figure 9–41

   a. The silhouette edges of the cylinder.
   b. The implicit axis of the cylinder.
   c. The edges of the hole in the cylinder.
   d. None of the above.

Answers: 1c, 2c, 3abcd, 4a, 5b, 6a

Chapter 10

Feature Management

CATIA provides several tools to simplify the display of your model. Three of these tools are Search, Hide/Show, and Activate/Deactivate. Using these tools will increase your overall efficiency. You can also use Selection Sets to quickly select groups of features at the same time.

Learning Objectives in This Chapter

- Use Search in complex models to find specific objects.
- Show and hide features to simplify the display and make working with complex models more efficient.
- Understand how hidden features display in the specification tree.
- Learn how to Activate and Deactivate objects.
- Learn how to group features using selection sets.

10.1 Search for Features

In complex models with a large number of features, locating specific features in the model might become difficult. The **Search** tool enables you to locate and select the feature in the specification tree using a variety of search parameters.

- Press *<Ctrl>+<F>* to perform a search. The Search dialog box opens and it displays the results of a sample search for a feature with a name containing the string **Rib,** as shown in Figure 10–1.

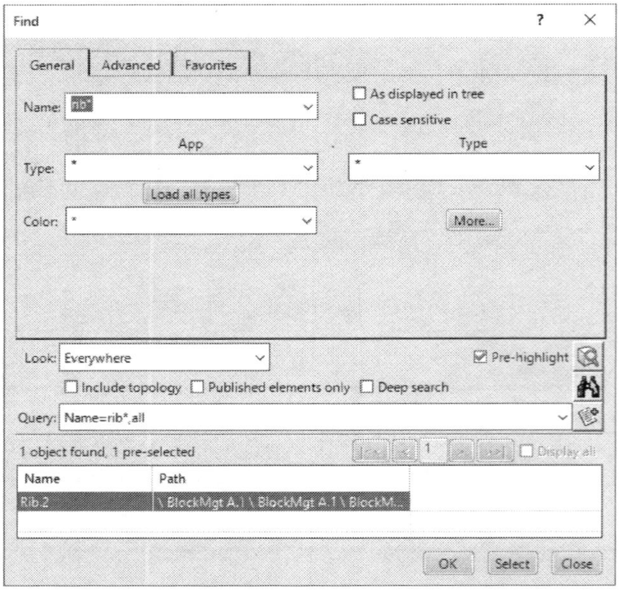

Figure 10–1

When you select the found objects, the features are highlighted in the main window and specification tree. The feature can be selected for use in the current operation by clicking **Select**.

- The *Advanced* tab provides options to define more search parameters.
- The *Favorites* tab provides access to search results that have been stored using  (Add to favorites).

10.2 Hide and Show

CATIA contains two default display spaces - invisible and visible. You have been working in visible space. As you create additional features and your models become more complex, the display area of the screen becomes cluttered. To simplify the display, the **Hide** and **Show** commands can be used to move features between the two spaces.

A model with all elements visible is shown in Figure 10–2.

Sketches are normally hidden after they are referenced by a feature. They are shown here for illustration purposes.

The display shows many elements that no longer need to be shown.

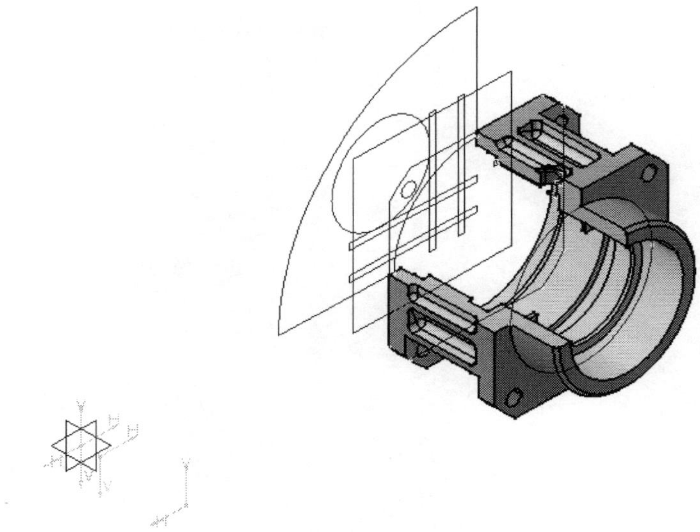

Figure 10–2

The model shown includes all of the sketches, lines, and reference planes. Individual features can be moved from the visible space to the invisible space by using one of the following methods:

- Select the feature in the display area or in the specification tree, right-click, and select **Hide/Show**. When a feature is switched to the invisible space, it no longer displays. However, the features still exist.

To select all elements of a particular type, select the top-level model, right-click and select **ModelTitle object**>**Show** or **Hide** then select the required element type, as shown in Figure 10–3.

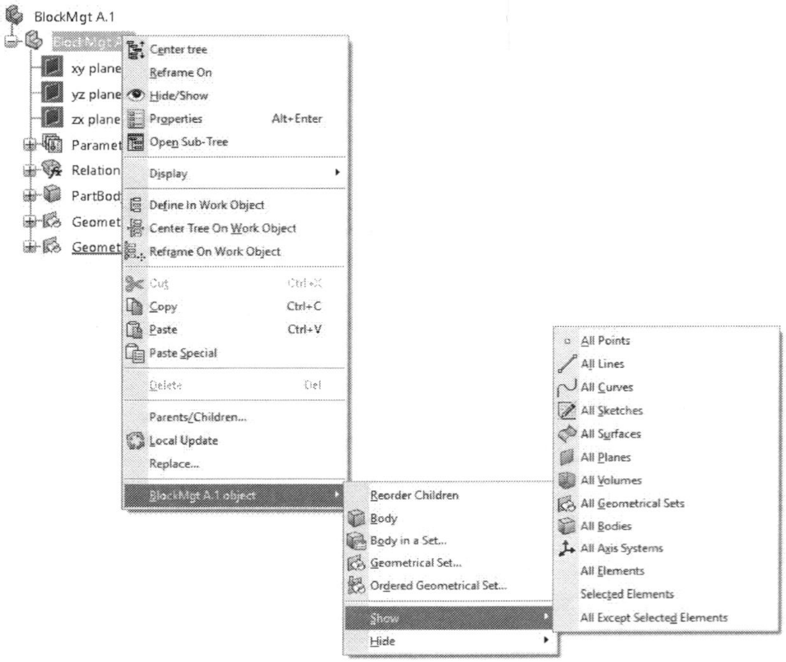

Figure 10–3

As a result, the display area is much less cluttered. Figure 10–4 shows the same model as the one shown in Figure 10–2, except that all sketches, planes, points, and axis systems are hidden from visible space.

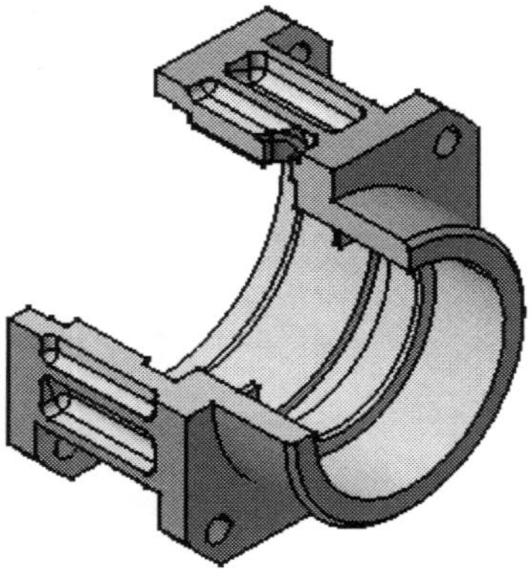

Figure 10–4

Indication of Hidden Features

The specification tree displays hidden features as faded or grayed icons, as shown in Figure 10–5.

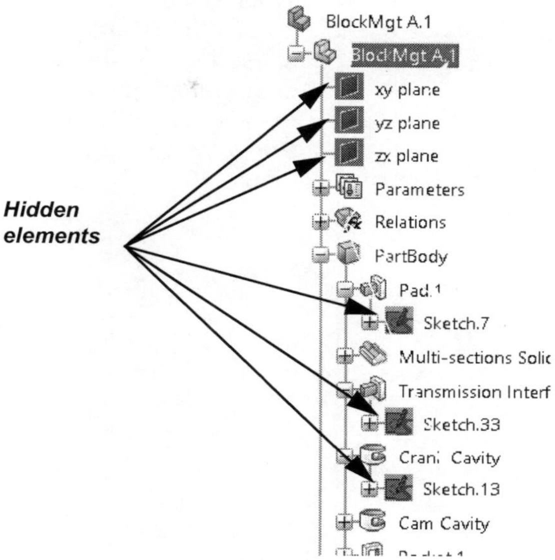

Figure 10–5

- To swap between the visible working space and invisible working space, click  (Swap Visible Space) in the lower-right corner of the graphics area. Hidden features are shown in a separate working space (i.e., invisible). Click the icon again to return to the visible working space.
- To make individual features visible after they have been hidden, select them in the specification tree, right-click and select **Hide/Show**.

Tips and Techniques

Use the **Hide/Show** command carefully. Although no real harm can be done to your model, the **Hide/Show** command can produce unexpected results if you select inactive features, or select the wrong types of features.

- A feature in the specification tree that affects the mass properties of the model cannot be hidden without hiding all solid features. To control the display of solid features independently, the feature must be deactivated.

10.3 Activate and Deactivate

If features are deactivated, the update sequence time decreases.

When features are added to the model, the software updates them with any changes made. When a change occurs that forces subsequent features to change drastically, the update can fail. To deactivate a feature and help solve an update failure, select the feature, right-click and select the feature object name (e.g., **Pocket.3 object**), and then select **Deactivate**, as shown in Figure 10–6.

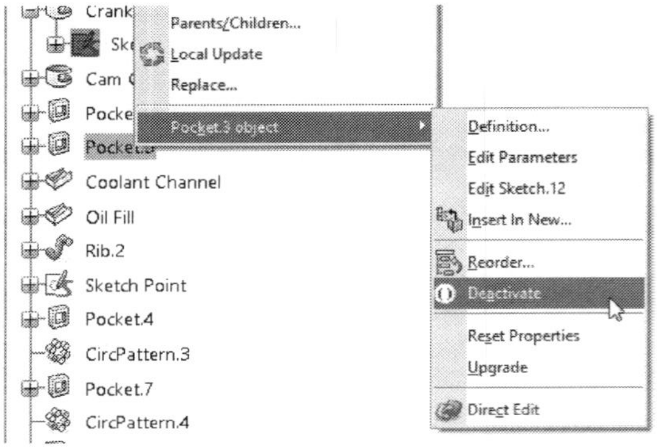

Figure 10–6

The **Deactivate** option temporarily removes the feature from the update sequence. This enables you to keep the feature as currently defined, without deleting it. The feature icon displays with a deactivation symbol in the specification tree, as shown for the **Hole.1** object in Figure 10–7.

Deactivation symbol

Figure 10–7

You can modify any previous features to help solve an update failure. Once solved, the feature can be returned to the update sequence by selecting it in the specification tree, right-clicking the feature object name, and selecting **Activate**.

Features should only be deactivated temporarily. If they are not required, they should be deleted from the model.

You can use the **Deactivate** option to:

- Reduce the chance of unwanted parent/child relationships.
- Make models run faster.
- De-feature the model for Finite Element Analysis purposes.
- Try alternative designs for a feature.

To avoid accidentally referencing a Fillet feature when creating additional features, deactivate the Fillet feature on your model, as shown in Figure 10–8. Deactivating fillets is one way to help CATIA run faster for modeling design and Finite Element Analysis.

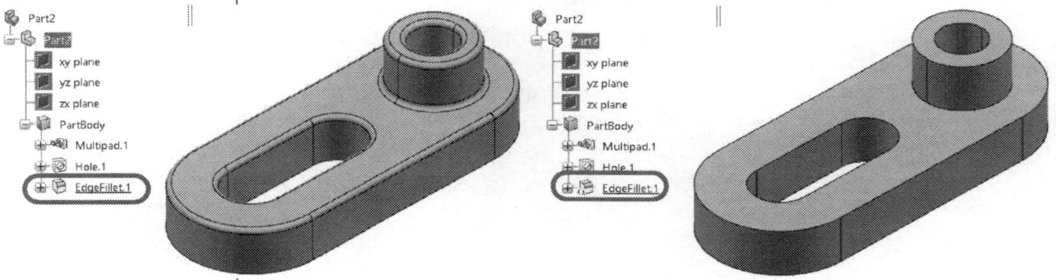

Figure 10–8

Once the design is finalized, it is recommended that you delete all unused features, rather than keep them deactivated in the model. If not deleted, these features can unnecessarily increase file size and cause confusion to someone else using this file at a later time.

Parent/Child Considerations

If a parent feature is selected for deactivation, its children must also be deactivated. Child features that are impacted by deactivating the parent are highlighted in the specification tree and the model. Figure 10–9 shows the **Hole.1** feature selected for deactivation and the Deactivate dialog box. The EdgeFillet feature on the edge of the hole is a child feature and would also have to be deactivated.

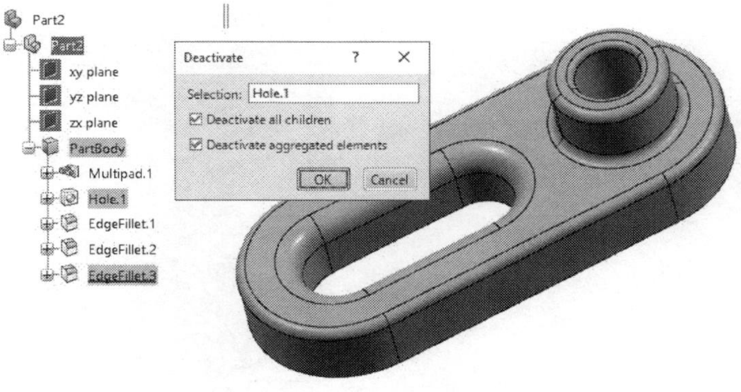

Figure 10–9

10.4 Creating Selection Sets

Selection sets enable you to define groups of features that can be quickly selected at the same time. This function is ideal for groups of features that are selected often. For example, you can quickly deactivate and activate fillet, chamfer, and other dress-up features by adding them to a selection set.

The Selection Sets options, found in the *Tools* section of the Action Bar, are shown in Figure 10–10. It can be hidden if you don't click the expand arrow.

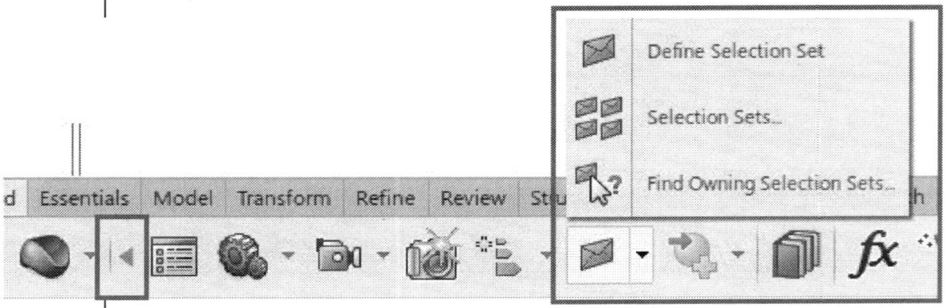

Figure 10–10

How To: Create a Selection Set

1. Click (Define Selection Set) to create a selection box. The Selection Sets Edition dialog box opens, as shown in Figure 10–11.

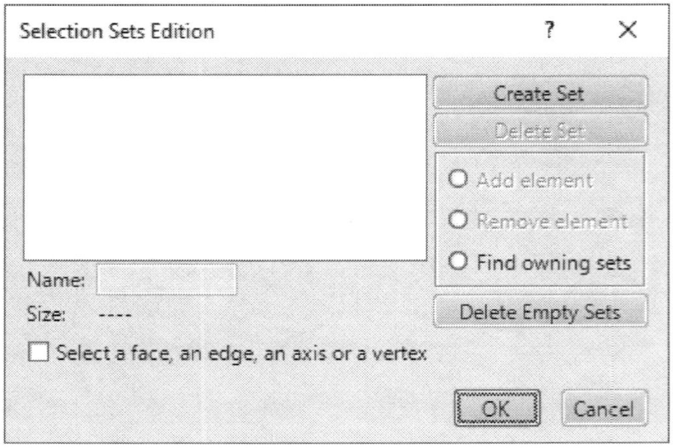

Figure 10–11

2. Click **Create Set** and enter a name for the set in the *Name* field.
3. With the new set highlighted, select the **Add element** option. Select features in the specification tree to add to the set. The **Select a face, an edge, an axis or a vertex** option, enables you to select geometry from the model.
4. Click **OK** to complete the creation of the set.
5. Click  (Selection Sets) to select a feature. The Selection Sets Selection dialog box opens, as shown in Figure 10–12.

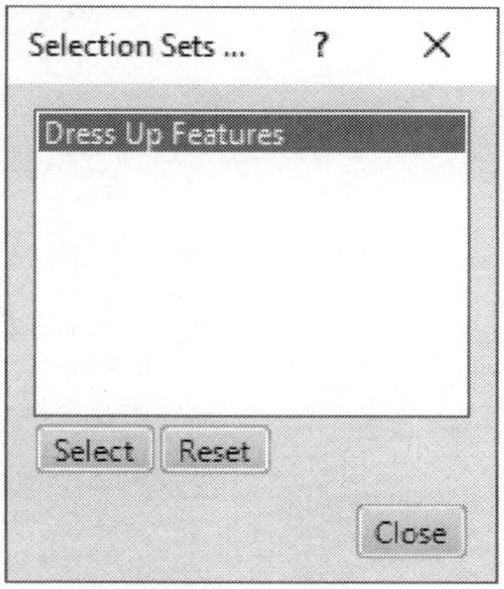

Figure 10–12

6. Select the set from the list and click **Select**. Close the dialog box to complete the selection.

Practice 10a Feature Management

Practice Objectives

- Simplify the model display using the **Hide/Show** commands.
- Activate and deactivate features.
- Create and use selection sets.

In this practice, you will use feature management techniques to modify a part. You will use the **Hide/Show**, **Activate/Deactivate** and **Selection Set** commands. In addition, you will learn the properties of these commands and how they affect the model display.

Task 1 - Hide reference geometry and sketch features.

Features are selected for visual clarity.

1. Import **BlockMgt.3dxml**.
2. In the *BlockMgt (Explore)* tab, right-click **BlockMgt** in the specification tree and select **Open**. Note that the reference elements and feature sketches are also displayed.
3. View the invisible space by clicking (Swap Visible Space) in the lower right corner of the graphics area. The background changes to the invisible space color. Some measurements are hidden in the model. Therefore, they display in the invisible space as shown in Figure 10–13.

Note the Invisible Space color in this example is gray. Your system may differ.

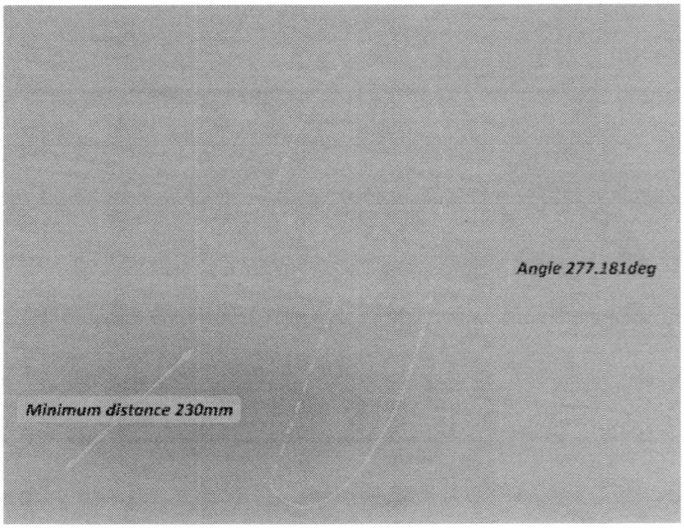

Figure 10–13

4. Return to the visible space by clicking (Swap Visible Space).

5. In the specification tree, using <Ctrl>, select the three default reference plane features.

6. Right-click over any of the selected planes and select **Hide/Show**. The planes are removed from visible space and added to invisible space.

7. The icons for the three planes display in the specification tree with grayed backgrounds, as shown in Figure 10–14.

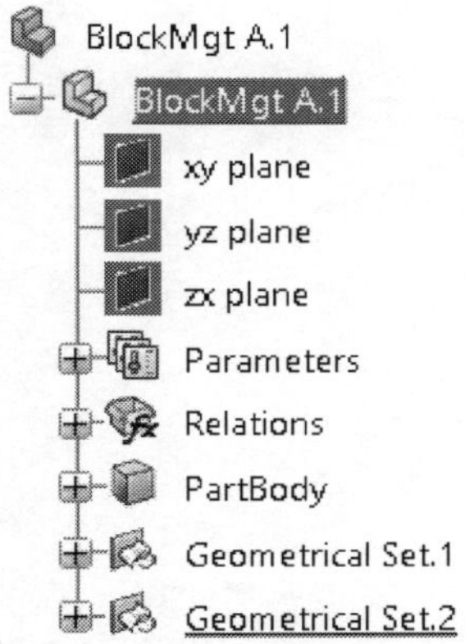

Figure 10–14

8. Click (Swap Visible Space) to switch to invisible space, and note that the planes are shown.

9. Click (Swap Visible Space) again to switch back to visible space.

10. By default, sketches that are used to create other features, such as pads, grooves, pockets, etc., are automatically hidden from display. Currently, they are all set to display. In the specification tree, **right-click BlockMtg A.1** and select **BlockMtg A.1 object>Hide>All Sketches** to remove all sketches from visible space. The model updates, as shown in Figure 10–15. If the part turns red without updating, you will need to select (Update) to update it.

Note that all hidden feature icons are grayed in the specification tree.

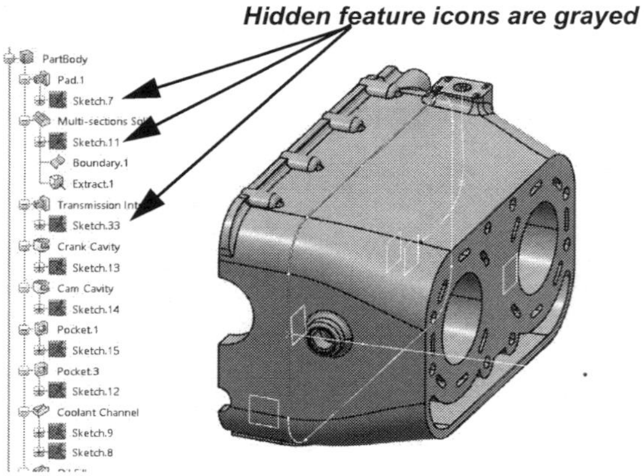

Figure 10–15

11. Reference geometry features are still set to display in visible space. Right-click on **Geometrical Set.1** and select **Geometrical Set.1 object>Hide Components**.

12. Click (Swap Visible Space) to switch to invisible space. The hidden space displays as shown in Figure 10–16.

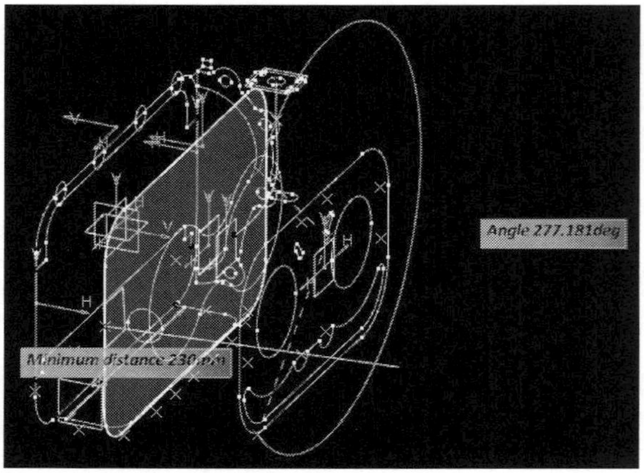

Figure 10–16

13. Switch back to visible space.

Task 2 - Attempt to hide a Hole feature.

1. Select the **Hole.5** feature in the specification tree, right-click and select **Hide/Show**. If you are unable to locate the feature in the specification tree, you can select any other solid feature to hide.

   Note that the contents of the PartBody switch to invisible space. Solid features cannot be hidden or shown independently from the rest of the PartBody solid features.

2. Select the **Hole.5** feature in the specification tree again, right-click and select **Hide/Show** to return PartBody to visible space.

Task 3 - Deactivate the Hole feature.

Design Considerations

As shown in Task 2, individual solid geometry features cannot be hidden independently. However, you can deactivate the individual solid features independently.

1. Right-click on the **Pad.8** feature in the specification tree and select **Pad.8 object>Deactivate**.

2. Note that since this feature has children, the **Deactivate all children** option is automatically enabled, as shown in Figure 10–17.

*Select the **Deactivate aggregated elements** option to deactivate all geometry grouped below the main element node being deactivated.*

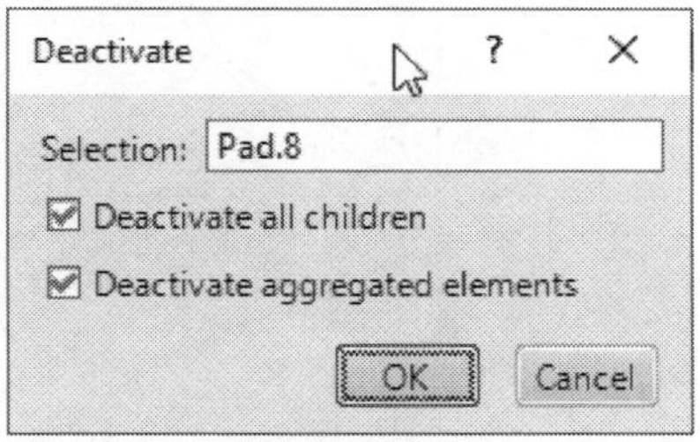

Figure 10–17

3. Click **OK** in the Deactivate dialog box.

The Pad.8 feature and its children are deactivated and removed from visible space, as shown in Figure 10–18.

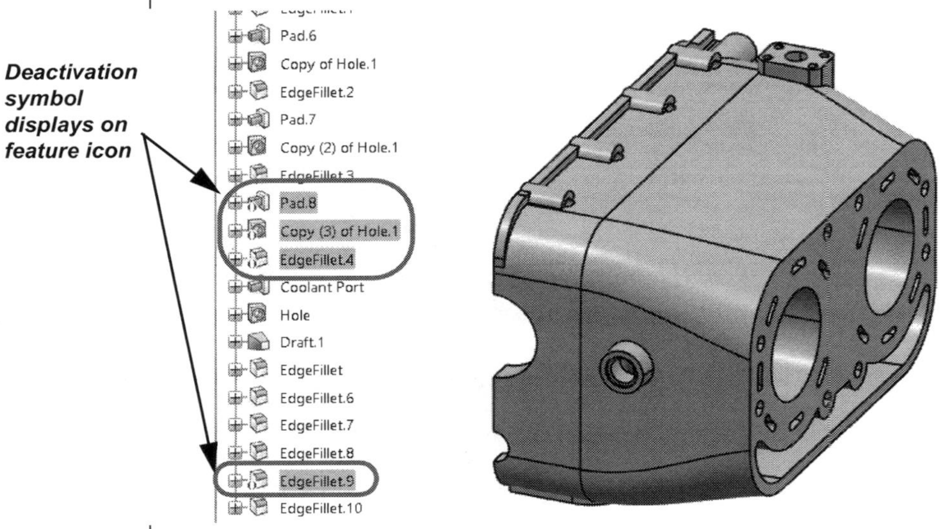

Figure 10–18

The feature is not switched to invisible space because it is deactivated and therefore no longer updates with the rest of the model. In the specification tree, select the deactivated **Pad.8** feature. Right-click, and select **Pad.8 object>Activate**.

4. The **Activate all children** and **Activate aggregated elements** options are enabled by default, as shown in Figure 10–19.

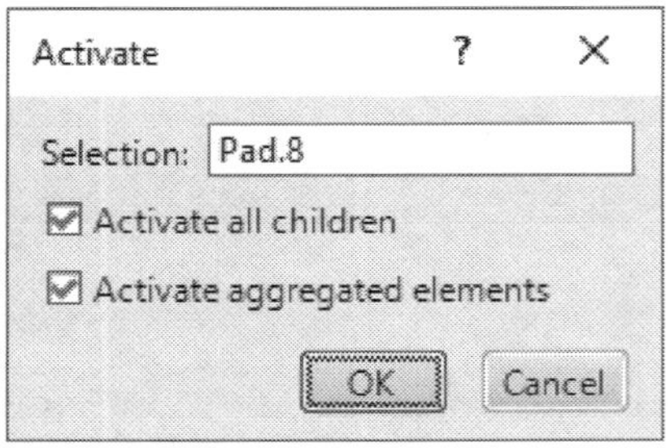

Figure 10–19

5. Click **OK** then click in the background to clear the selection. The model returns to the active state.

Task 4 - Deactivate the Fillet features.

1. Select the *Tools* section of the Action Bar.

2. Near the middle of the Action Bar, click .

3. The Action Bar expands as shown in Figure 10–20.

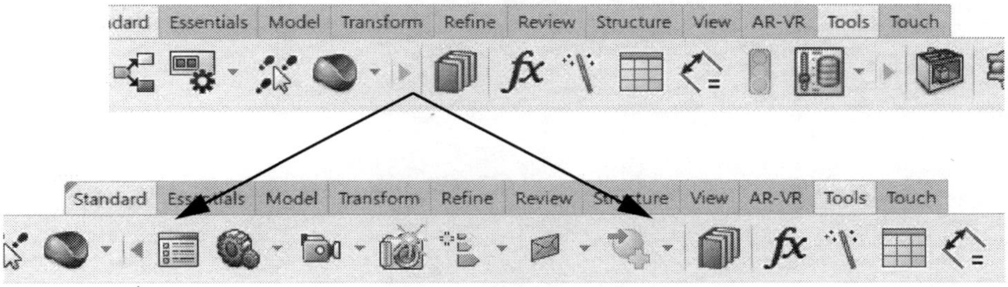

Figure 10–20

4. Click  (Define Selection Set). The Selection Sets Edition dialog box opens.

5. Click **Create Set**.

6. Enter **FilletSet** in the *Name* field. Select the **Add element** option as shown in Figure 10–21.

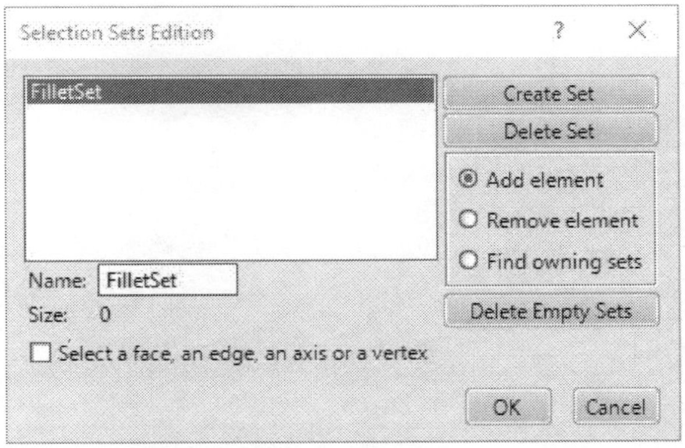

Figure 10–21

Design Considerations

You must perform a search operation to locate the Fillet features to add to the selection set. Searching is the most efficient way to locate and select all of the Fillet features in the model.

7. **Press <Ctrl> + <F>**. The Search dialog box opens.

8. In the App **Type** drop-down list, select **Part Design** and in the adjacent Type drop-down list, select **Fillet**. The Search dialog box opens as shown in Figure 10–22.

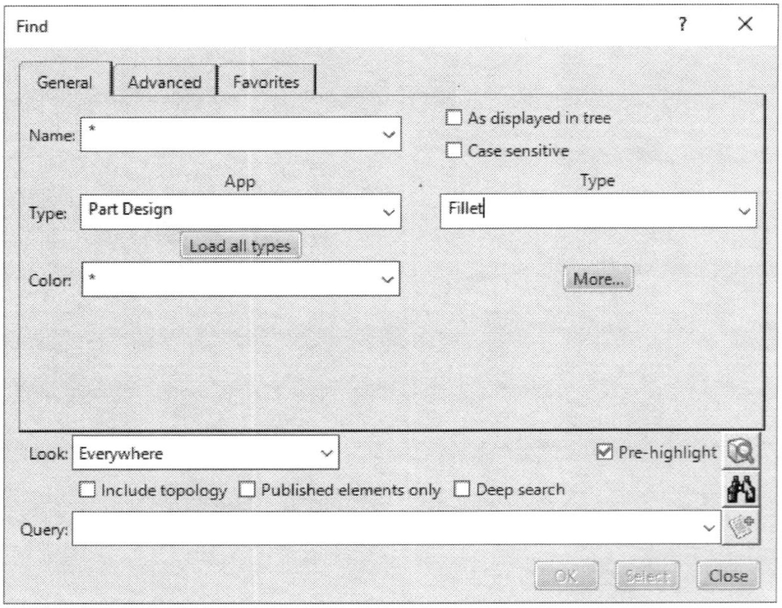

Figure 10–22

9. Click  (Find and Select) to start the search. The results of the search is shown in Figure 10–23.

10. In the Selection Sets Edition dialog box, *Size* updates to **10**, as shown in Figure 10–23.

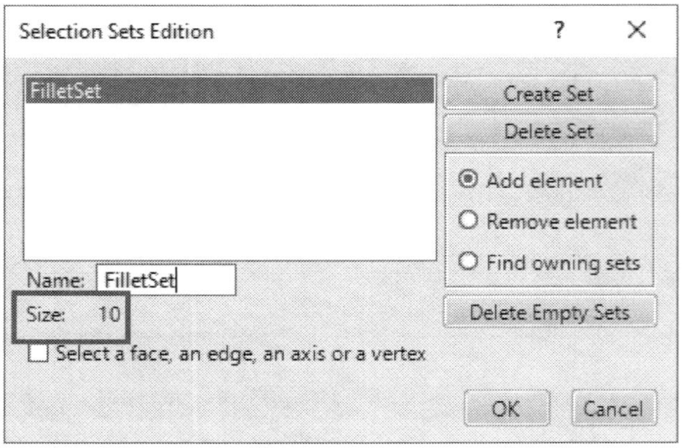

Figure 10–23

11. Click **OK** to close the Selection Sets Edition dialog box. The Fillet features should still be selected.

12. Right-click on any of the selected features in the specification tree and select **Selected objects>Deactivate**. The Fillet features are deactivated from the model, as shown in Figure 10–24.

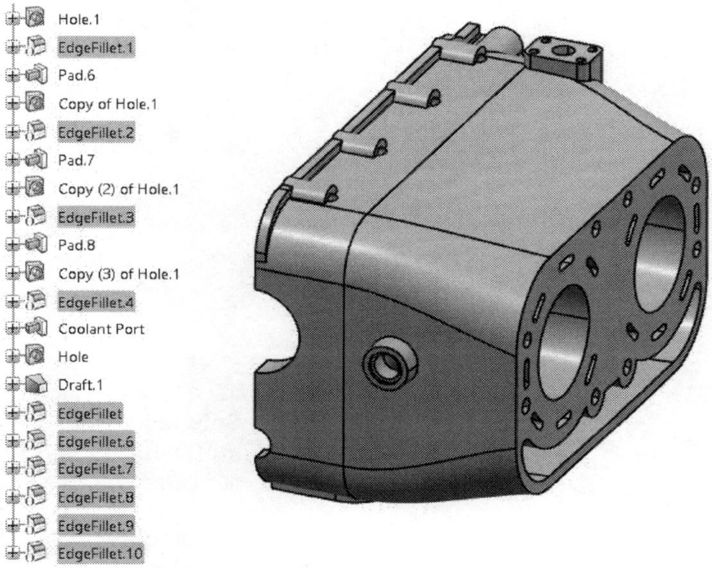

Figure 10–24

13. Clear the Fillet features by clicking in the background.

You can also click  *(Selection sets) to open the Selection Sets Selection dialog box.*

14. Click  (Find Owning Selection Sets). The Selection Sets Edition dialog box opens as shown in Figure 10–25.

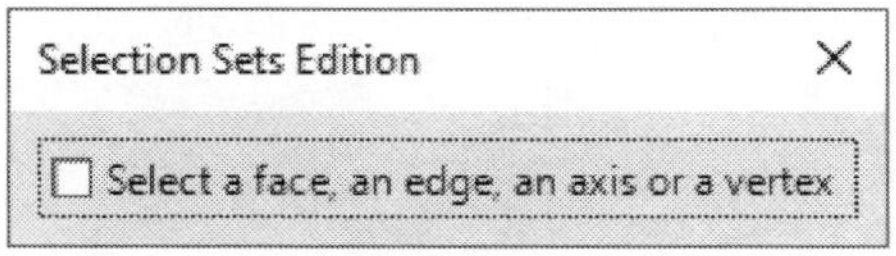

Figure 10–25

15. In the specification tree, select any of the Fillet features. The Selection Sets Selection dialog box opens as shown in Figure 10–26.

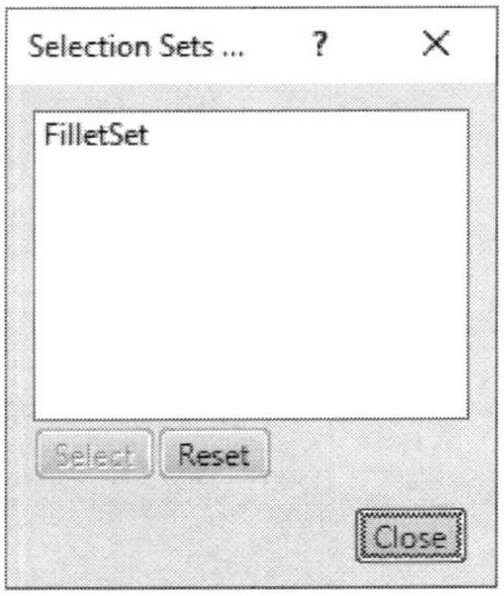

Figure 10–26

Design Considerations

When many unnamed or ambiguous selection sets (e.g., groups of fillets) exist and are difficult to distinguish, use **Find Owning Selection Sets** to locate the required set. Selection sets are accessed through the **Selection Sets** icon. Therefore, remember to name your selection sets meaningfully.

16. In the list, select **FilletSet** and click **Select**. Close the Selection Sets Selection dialog box to complete the selection. The Fillet features are highlighted in the specification tree.

17. Right-click on a Fillet feature in the specification tree and select **Selected objects>Activate**.

18. Save the file and close the tab.

Chapter Review Questions

1. Which of the following feature types are not visible on screen when hidden using the **Hide/Show** command? (Select all that apply.)
   a. Points
   b. Planes
   c. Sketches
   d. Pads
2. Deactivating a feature does not modify children of that feature.
   a. True
   b. False
3. When you deactivate a feature, it continues to be part of the update sequence.
   a. True
   b. False
4. Visible space contains any features that are shown. Invisible space shows features that have been hidden.
   a. True
   b. False
5. A selection set can be used to select individual edges.
   a. True
   b. False
6. By default, sketches that are used to create other features, such as Pads, are automatically hidden from display.
   a. True
   b. False

Answers: 1abc, 2b, 3b, 4a, 5a, 6a

Chapter 11

Introduction to Dress-Up Features

In this chapter, you are introduced to three basic types of dress-up features. You learn how to create these features and how to select appropriate references for them. Dress-up features enable you to create some of the finishing geometry on your models, such as fillets, chamfers, and holes.

Learning Objectives in This Chapter

- Review the three types of dress-up features.
- Create edge fillets and holes.
- Understand the various selection techniques for edge fillets.
- Understand the five types of holes.
- Learn about chamfer features.
- Understand the Reverse, Symmetric extents, and Corner Cap options.
- Review some best practices for working with dress-up features.

11.1 Dress-Up Features

Figure 11–1 shows the three types of dress-up features available:

- Edge fillet
- Chamfer
- Hole

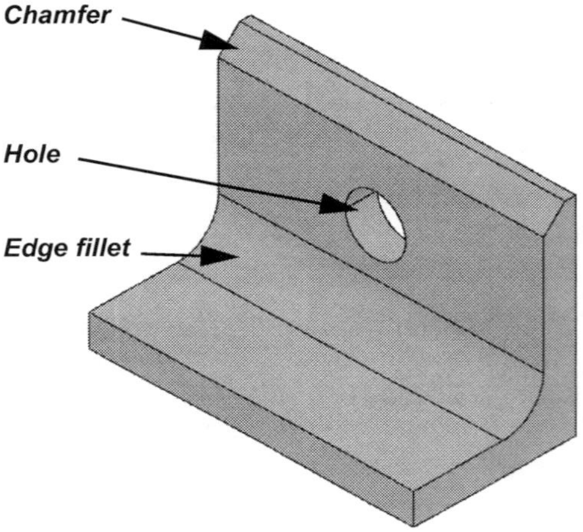

Figure 11–1

A dress-up feature does not require sketching. When you select a dress-up feature for creation, the software implies its shape and you select references, which locate the feature relative to existing geometry.

11.2 Creating Edge Fillets

An **Edge Fillet** is used to round a sharp edge. The software builds circular shaped geometry that is tangent to the two adjacent surfaces of the selected edge, as shown in Figure 11–2.

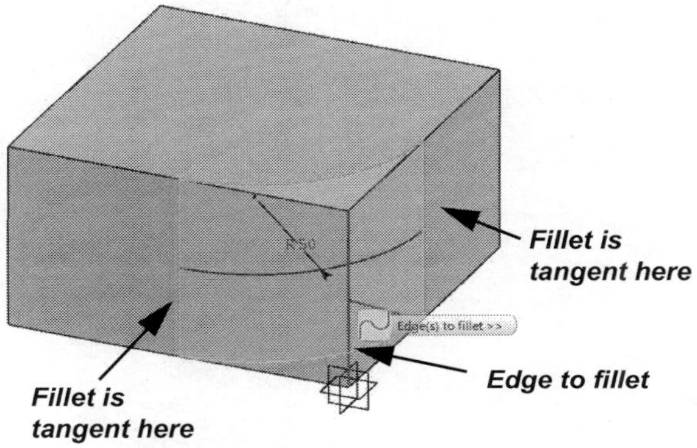

Figure 11–2

- A fillet can add or remove material in the model, as shown in Figure 11–3.

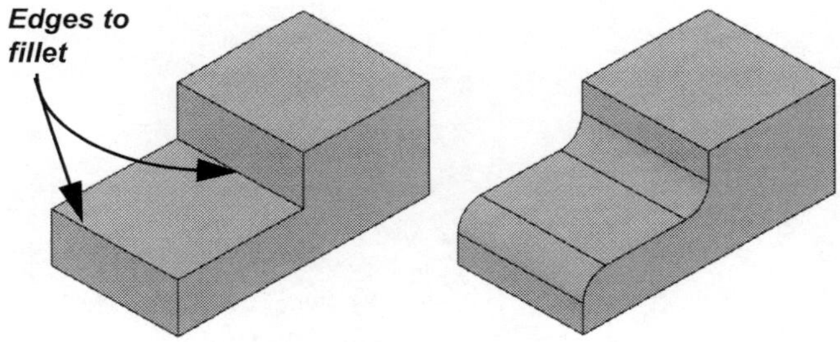

Figure 11–3

General Steps

Use the following general steps to create an edge fillet:

1. Identify the edges to be filleted.
2. Select a selection mode.
3. Specify the fillet radius.
4. Complete the feature.

Step 1 - Identify the edges to be filleted.

In the *Essentials* section of the Action Bar, click (Edge Fillet) to create a Fillet feature. The Edge Fillet Definition dialog box opens and the *Object(s) to fillet* field is activated. Select the edges and/or faces to fillet. The software adds the selected references to the dialog box, as shown in Figure 11–4.

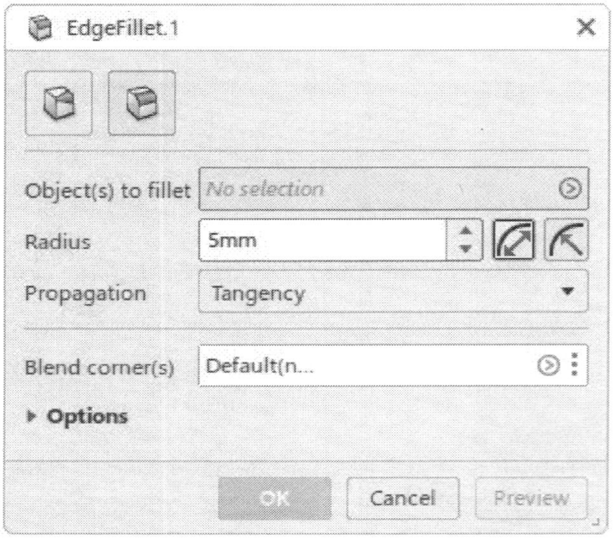

Figure 11–4

The references that have been selected can be reviewed by clicking to open the Objects to fillet dialog box shown in Figure 11–5. Use this dialog box to review, replace, and remove selected fillet references.

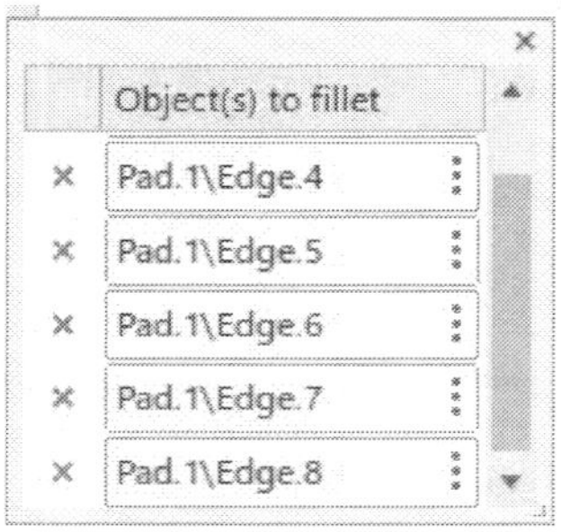

Figure 11–5

As an alternative creation method, you can select an edge or edges, and click  (Fillet) from the context toolbar, as shown in Figure 11–6.

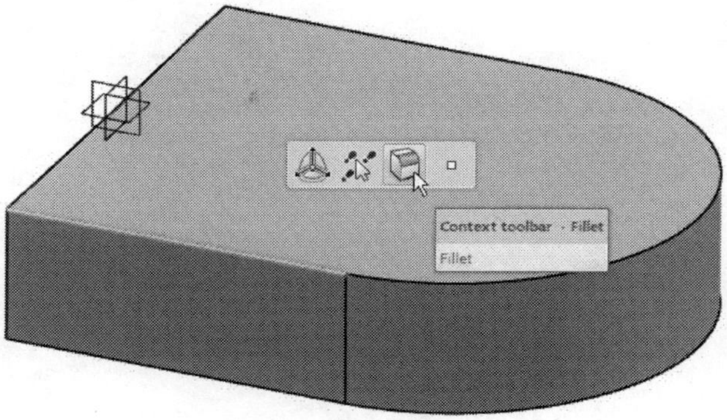

Figure 11–6

When using this method however, the Edge Fillet dialog box does not appear, so you do not have access to the additional options. Rather, you can only create a simple fillet driven by a radius, as shown in Figure 11–7.

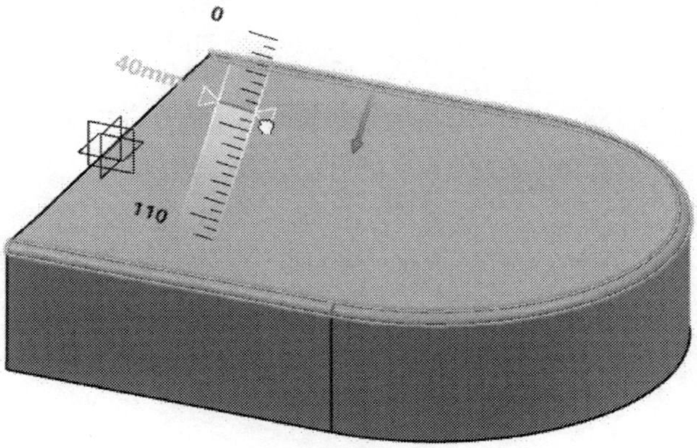

Figure 11–7

Edge Identification Methods

Individually Selecting Edges

You can select as many edges as required for one Fillet feature, as shown in Figure 11–8. When preselecting the edges, hold <Ctrl>. Each edge is highlighted in red as you select it. For hidden edges, you can spin the model to select them or set the display to show them.

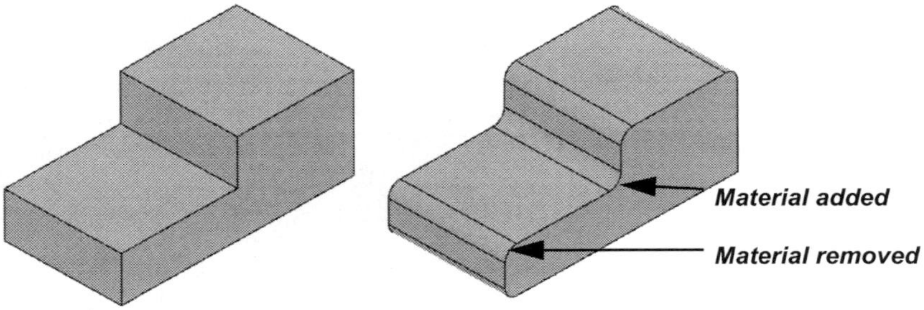

Figure 11–8

Selecting a Surface

When you select an entire surface for filleting, the software automatically highlights all of the edges on the surface's boundary and applies a fillet to each edge, as shown in Figure 11–9. If the surface contains inner edges, those are filleted as well, as shown in Figure 11–10.

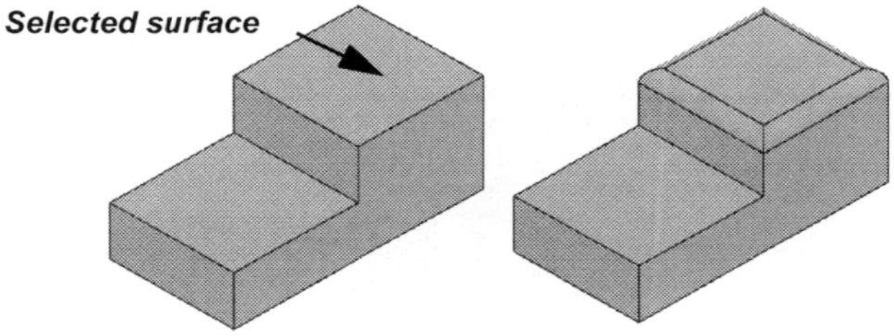

Figure 11–9

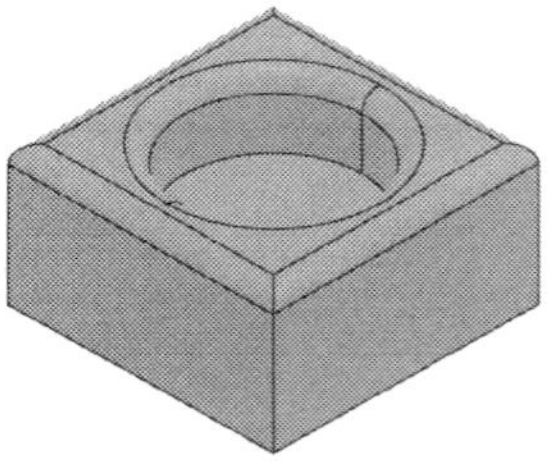

Figure 11–10

When you select a cylindrical surface for filleting, the software creates fillets on the edges at the top and bottom of the surface, as shown in Figure 11–11.

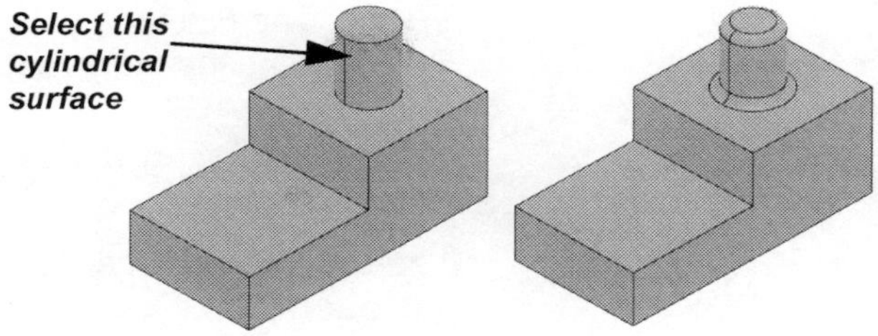

Figure 11–11

Selecting a Vertex

You can create a fillet on three adjacent edges by selecting a vertex. The software places a fillet on the three intersecting edges, as shown in Figure 11–12.

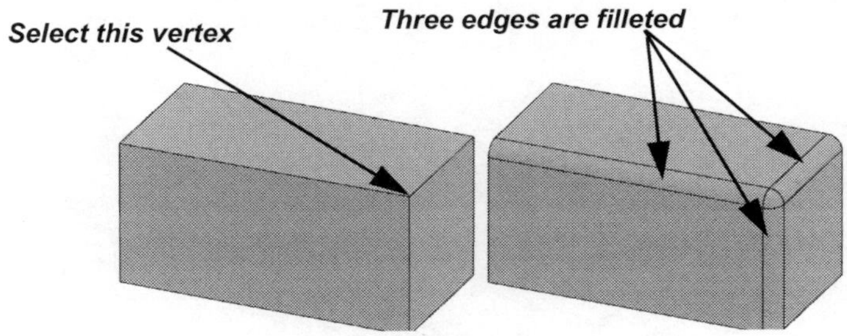

Figure 11–12

Combinations

Experiment with different combinations of edge identification methods until you can efficiently select the edges for filleting, as shown in Figure 11–13.

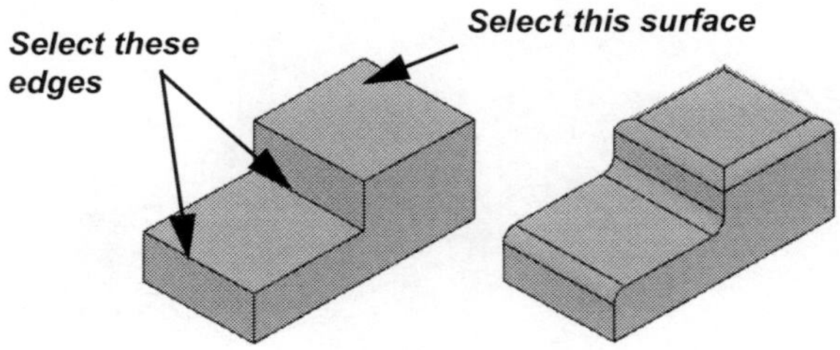

Figure 11–13

Clearing an Edge

To remove an edge or face from the feature at a later time, double-click on the Fillet feature and select the edge you want to remove. The first time you select an edge, it is included in the fillet. The second time you select it, it is removed from the fillet.

Step 2 - Select a selection mode.

When you select an edge to be filleted, the software automatically continues to fillet the adjacent edges that are tangent to your selected edge. This process, known as propagation, enables you to create fillets more efficiently, without manually select each edge along a continuous chain.

The Edge Fillet Definition dialog box provides options for controlling the selection mode. They are described as follows:

Setting	Description
Tangency	Fillet continues along adjacent edges of selected edge until non-tangency condition is encountered (default value).
Minimal	Disables propagation and only selected edge is filleted.
Intersection	Intersection edges of selected features with the current solid are filleted. In this selection mode, parts features are used instead of part edges.
Intersection with selected features	Intersection edges of selected features are filleted. Part features are used instead of part edges.

- Examples for Tangency and Minimal selection modes are shown in Figure 11–14.

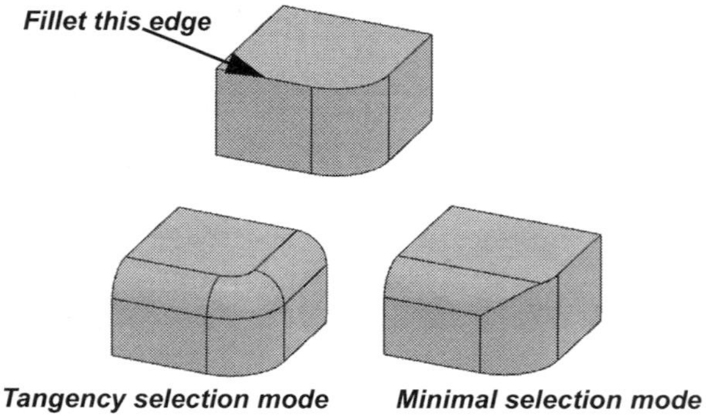

Figure 11–14

This option is only available when an edge has been selected.

Changing the option for selection mode (for Minimal and Tangency) only works for straight edges. When a curved edge is selected as the reference for a fillet, the software always continues the fillet to adjacent tangent edges.

- An example for Intersection selection mode is shown in Figure 11–15.

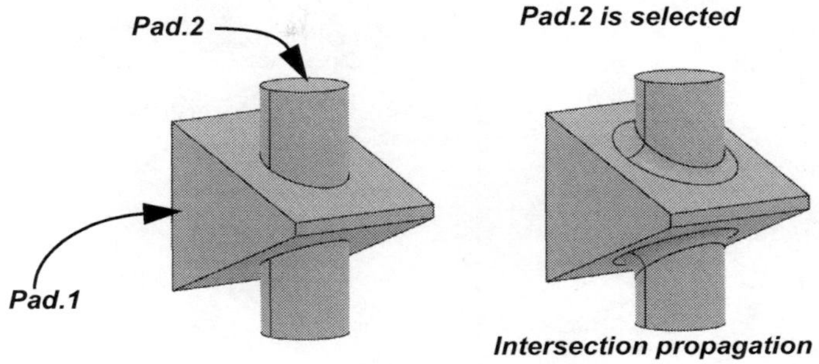

Figure 11–15

- An example for Intersection with selected features is shown in Figure 11–16.

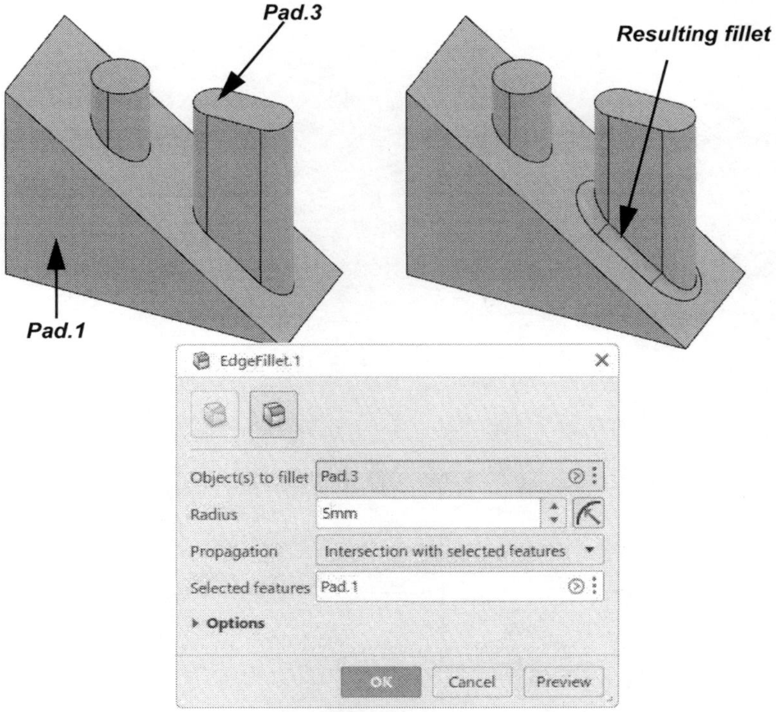

Figure 11–16

Step 3 - Specify the fillet radius.

The radius value entered is applied to all of the edge fillets created in the feature. If you want to have separate radius values for the edges, you must create them as separate fillet features.

Step 4 - Complete the feature.

Click **OK** to complete the Edge Fillet feature.

11.3 Creating Chamfers

A Chamfer feature creates a flat, beveled surface between two faces that are adjacent to an edge. Similar to Fillet features, chamfers behave in the following ways:

- They can add or remove material from the model, as shown in Figure 11–17.

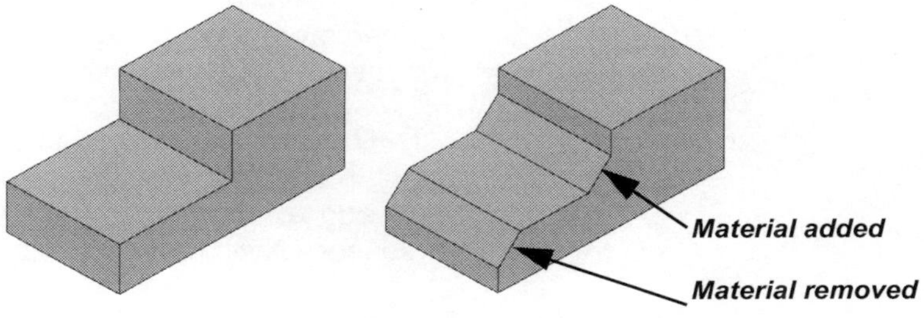

Figure 11–17

- You can select edges or surfaces to be chamfered. When you select a surface, all of the edges on the surface's boundary are chamfered.

- Chamfer features follow the same selection rules as Fillet features, as shown in Figure 11–18.

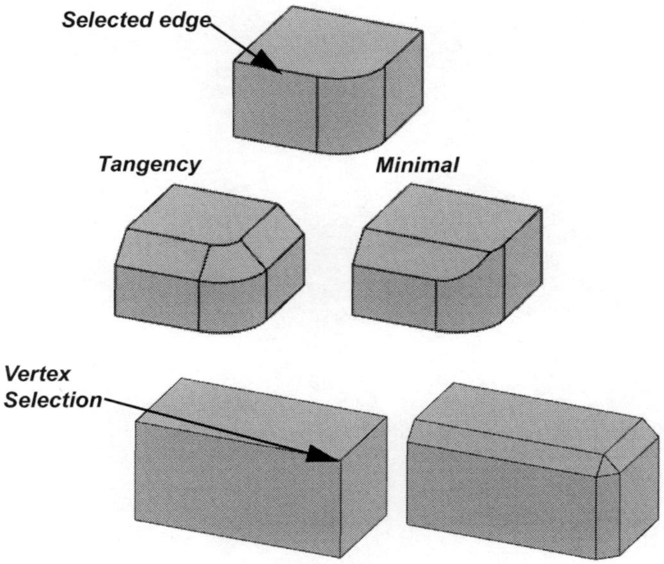

Figure 11–18

How To: Create a Chamfer Feature

1. In the *Essentials* section of the Action Bar, click  (Chamfer).

2. Select the edges to chamfer. Similar to Fillets, chamfer edges can be selected individually, or propagated by using propagation methods.

3. The Dimension mode for a chamfer can be defined in the Mode drop-down list in the Chamfer Definition dialog box. It dictates how the chamfer is dimensioned.

   The **Length1/Angle** option creates a chamfer where the length equals the distance from the edge to be chamfered to the edge of the bevel, as shown in Figure 11–19. The angle is measured with respect to **Length1**).

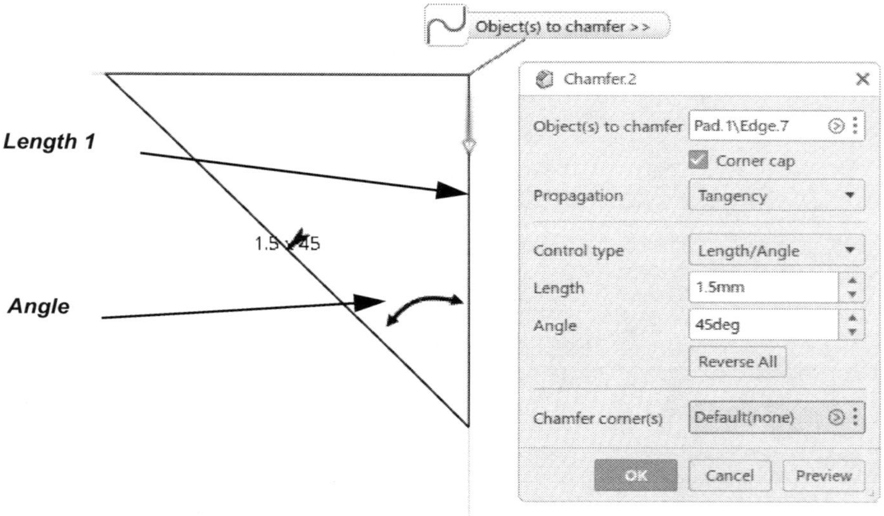

Figure 11–19

Another method of defining the size of the chamfer is to select **Length1/Length2** in the Mode drop-down list. You enter the distance from the edge to be chamfered to the edge of the bevel on each side, as shown in Figure 11–20.

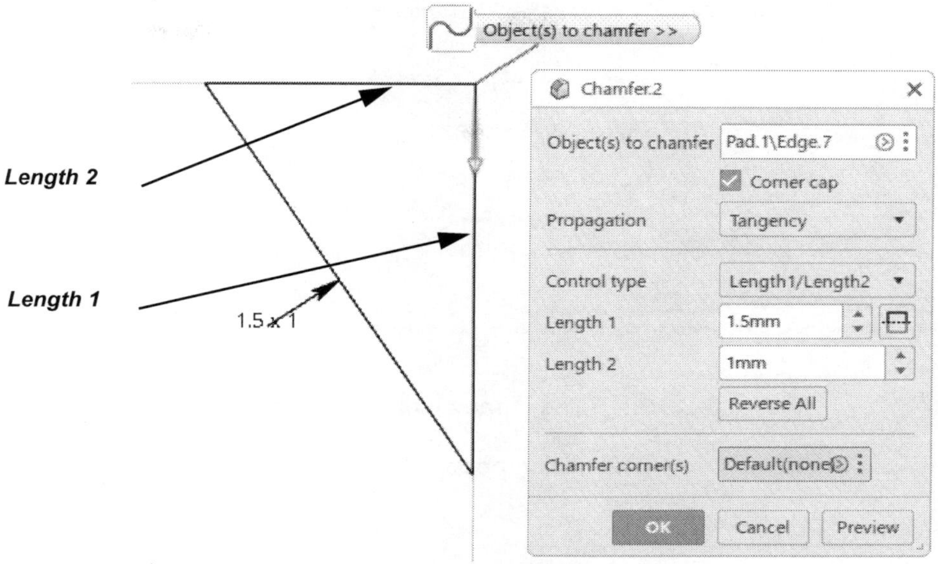

Figure 11–20

If you select the  *(Symmetric extent) option, Length 2 is set to match Length 1, and is then grayed out in the Chamfer Definition dialog box.*

4. Select the **Reverse All** option in the Chamfer Definition dialog box to flip the direction of the chamfer dimensions. The **Corner Cap** option creates a clean corner when more than two edges converge, as shown in Figure 11–21.

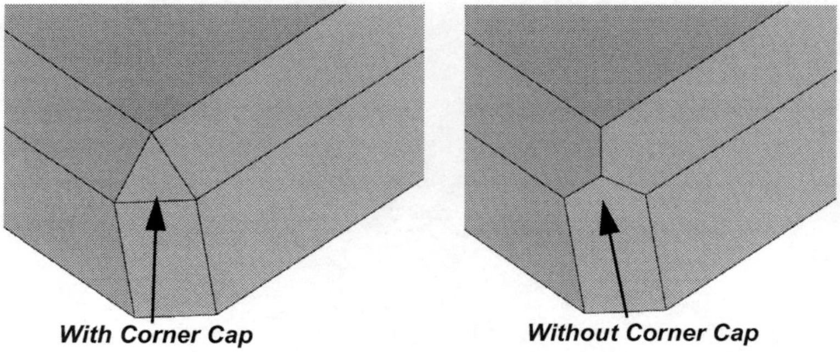

Figure 11–21

5. Click **OK** to complete the feature.

11.4 Creating Holes

You can create five types of holes, as shown in Figure 11–22.

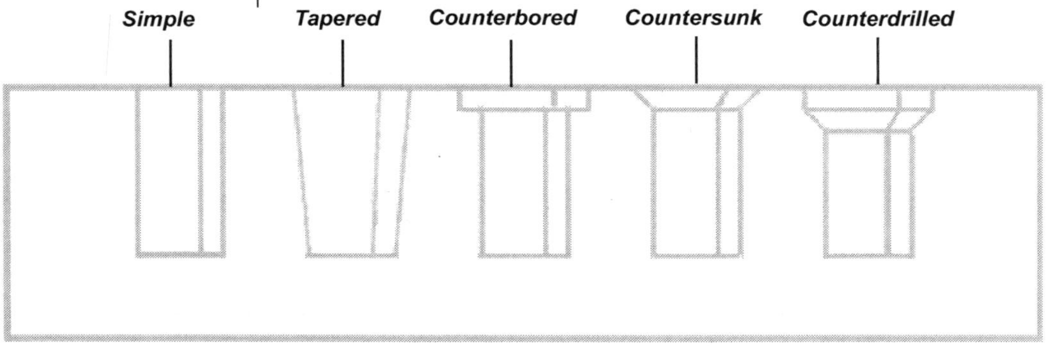

Figure 11–22

The parameters used to define the size of the holes change with each type. The parameter values are set in the Hole Definition dialog box as shown in Figure 11–23.

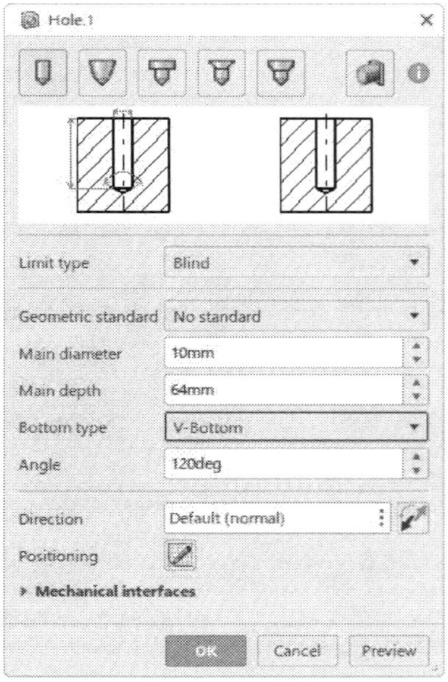

Figure 11–23

- With a simple hole, you must specify the hole diameter and the depth of the hole.
- With a countersunk hole, you must provide the diameter and depth of the hole, and the depth and angle of the countersink.

General Steps

Use the following general steps to create a Hole feature:

1. Select references for the hole.
2. Position the hole.
3. Specify **Hole** options.
4. Complete the feature.

Step 1 - Select references for the hole.

The dimension scheme is initially determined by the references you select. For example, if you select a face on which to locate the hole and two edges as references, the hole has a linear dimensioning scheme, as shown in Figure 11–24.

When selecting references, you must select an edge for locating the hole, not a surface or plane.

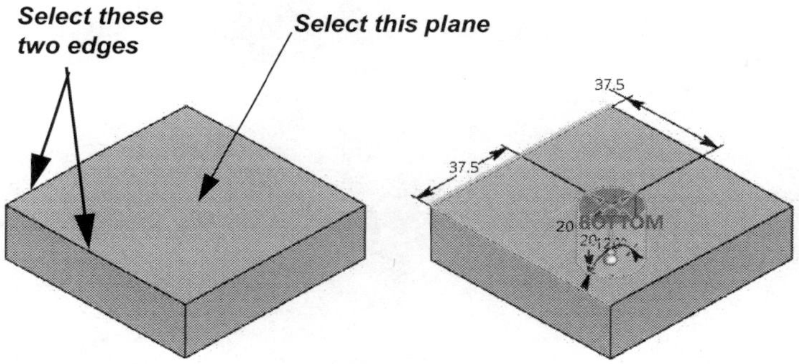

Figure 11–24

Selecting references to define the location of the hole is optional. You can select the placement plane for the hole and have the software locate the hole at the exact location you selected on the face.

You can also select the cylindrical surface as the reference for the coaxial hole.

- If you select a surface and a circular edge, the software locates the hole on the plane and coaxial to the center of the circular arc, as shown in Figure 11–25.

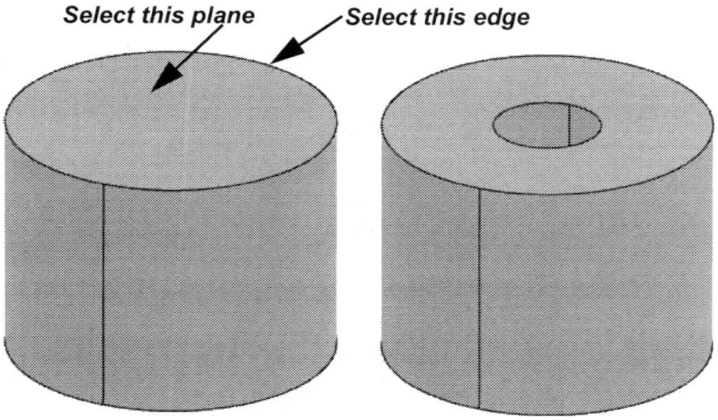

Figure 11–25

- If you preselect a face and a point, the software locates the hole on the plane and it is automatically constrained to the point, as shown in Figure 11–26.

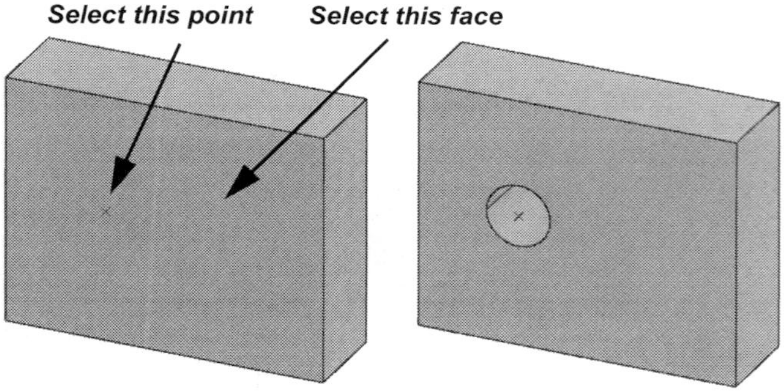

Figure 11–26

- If you preselect a cylindrical surface, the hole is placed at the selected location and normal to the cylindrical surface, as shown in Figure 11–27.

The location of the hole in the cylinder and the distance from the end of the cylinder are undefined.

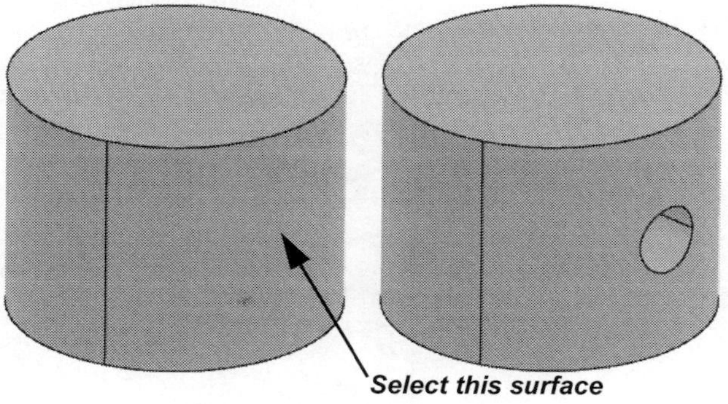

Figure 11–27

Step 2 - Position the hole.

If the dimensioning schemes described above do not capture your design intent, click (Sketch) in the Hole Definition dialog box to manually create dimensions that locate the feature. When you enter the Sketch app, the center of the hole is marked with an asterisk (*). You can drag the asterisk to a new location and create dimensions to the asterisk from edges, surfaces, or planes.

A positioning sketch is used to locate a hole in a circle with an angle dimension, as shown in Figure 11–28. A construction circle is used to define the diameter of the bolt circle, and an axis is used to locate the asterisk around the circle.

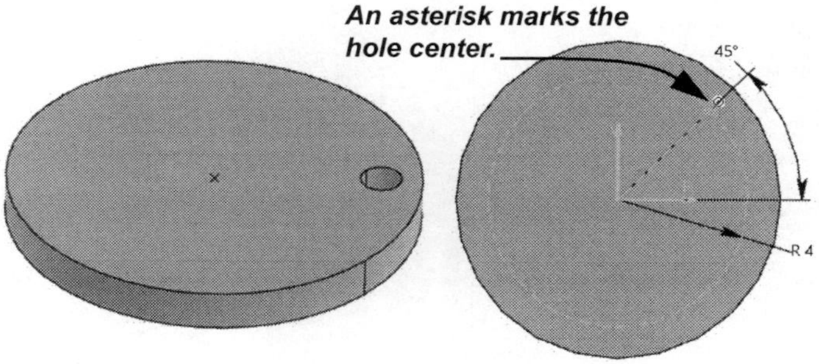

Figure 11–28

Figure 11–29 shows an example of a hole on a cylindrical face. If you want to precisely locate the hole, you can use the positioning sketch to dimension the asterisk vertically on the cylinder. You can also apply a coincidence constraint between the asterisk and a plane that passes through the center of the cylinder.

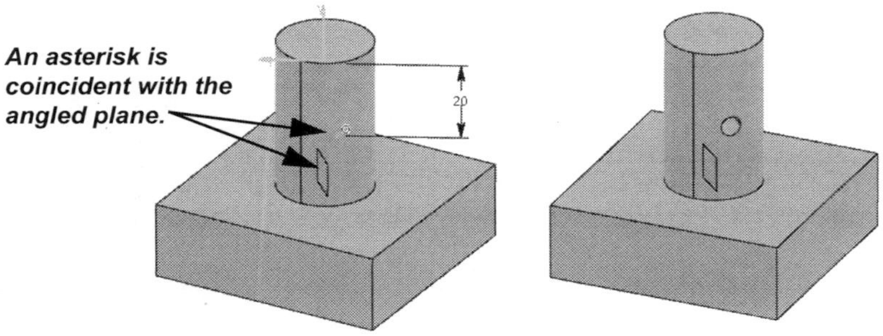

Figure 11–29

Positioning sketches can also be used to constrain holes that are initially created as unconstrained.

Step 3 - Specify Hole options.

Depth Options

*The **Blind** hole depth option is identical to the **Dimension** depth option for pads and pockets.*

Similar to previously discussed features, there are many options available for you to capture your design intent of the hole, as shown in Figure 11–30.

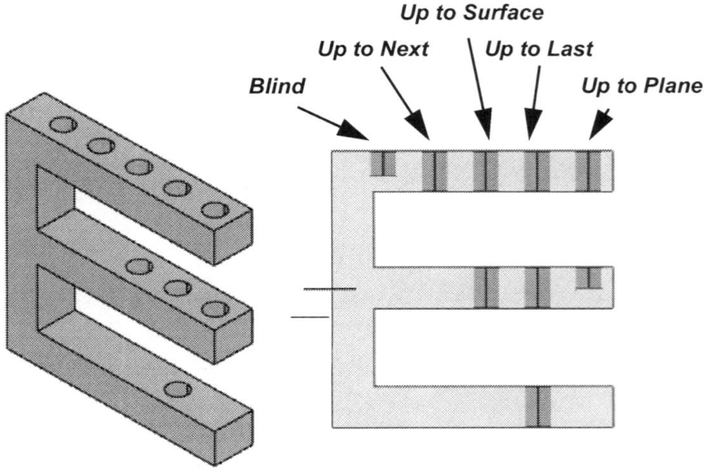

Figure 11–30

Hole features that have a depth option other than **Blind** can take advantage of the offset parameter, as shown in Figure 11–31. The default offset value of **0** can be changed to a positive value to extend the hole deeper or to a negative value to make the hole shallower.

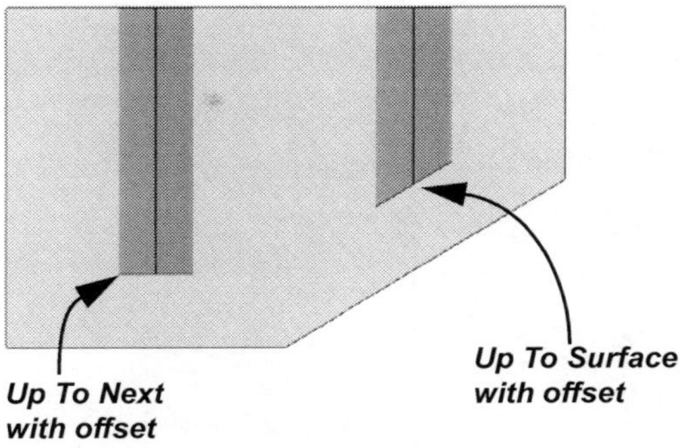

Figure 11–31

If you do not know the exact depth of a **Blind** hole, you can select the BOTTOM tag on the screen and dynamically drag the hole to a depth that suits your preferences, as shown in Figure 11–32.

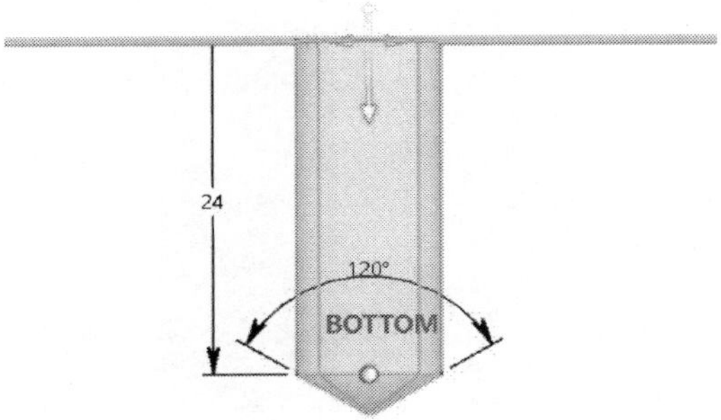

Figure 11–32

By default, the first **Blind** depth hole created will default to **V-Bottom**. You can specify an angle of the sharp point, as shown in Figure 11–33.

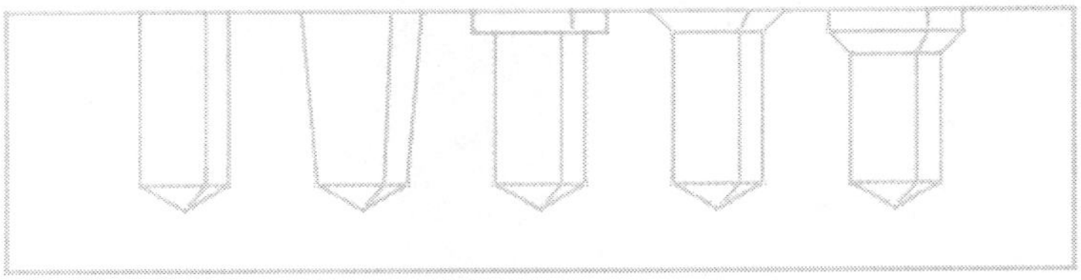

Figure 11–33

You can change the bottom option to **Flat**, resulting in a hole similar to that shown in Figure 11–34.

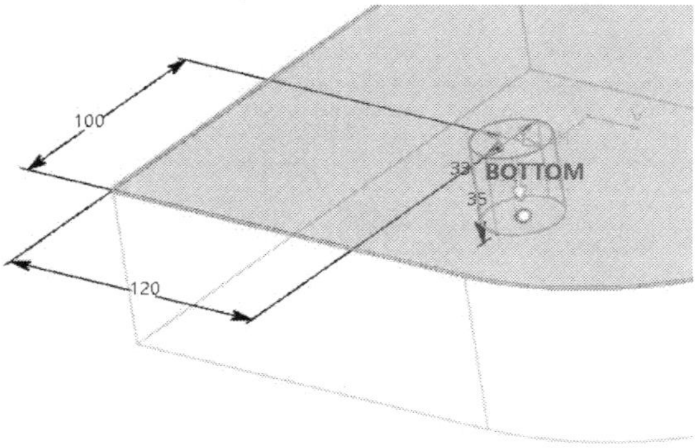

Figure 11–34

Any subsequent holes will default to the setting of the previously created hole.

Hole Direction

You can zoom in and drag the hole-to-edge dimensions outside the geometry for easier access.

When you select the planar face of an existing feature to create a hole, it removes material on one side of that plane only, as shown in Figure 11–35. Click  (Reverse Direction) in the Hole Definition dialog box to drill the hole in the opposite direction.

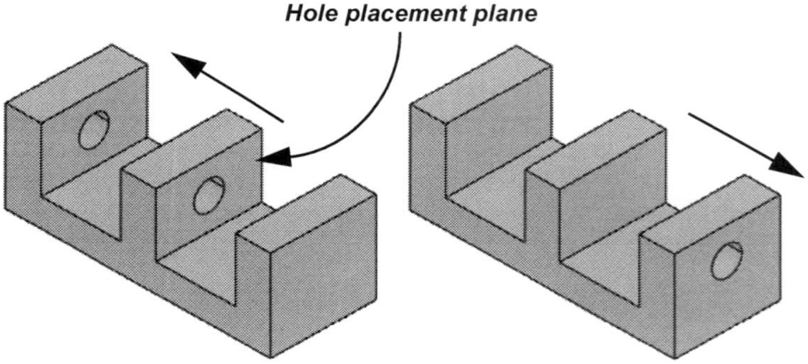

Figure 11–35

Step 4 - Complete the feature.

Click **OK** to complete the Hole feature.

11.5 Modeling Considerations

Use the following guidelines when working with dress-up features:

- Do not locate features on the tangent edges of fillets or the beveled edges of chamfers, as shown in Figure 11–36. This establishes a parent/child relationship between these features. If the parent feature (fillet or chamfer) is deleted from the model, the child feature fails and requires additional work to maintain the geometry over time.

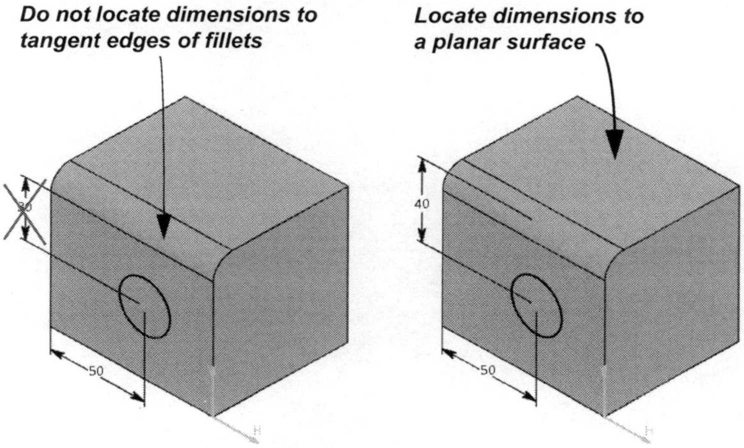

Figure 11–36

- When creating a dimension in the Normal view, the software creates a dimension to the first edge. Figure 11–36 shows the vertical dimension that was created to the tangent edge of the Fillet. It is recommended to orient the model in a 3D view and dimension from the circle's center to a planar surface.
- To prevent the above scenario, put fillets and chamfers into the model as late as possible in the design.

- Create holes, fillets, and chamfers as separate features instead of including them in one sketch for a Pad feature, as shown in Figure 11–37. This makes it easier for you to make changes to the model at a later time and enables you to create your sketches more quickly.

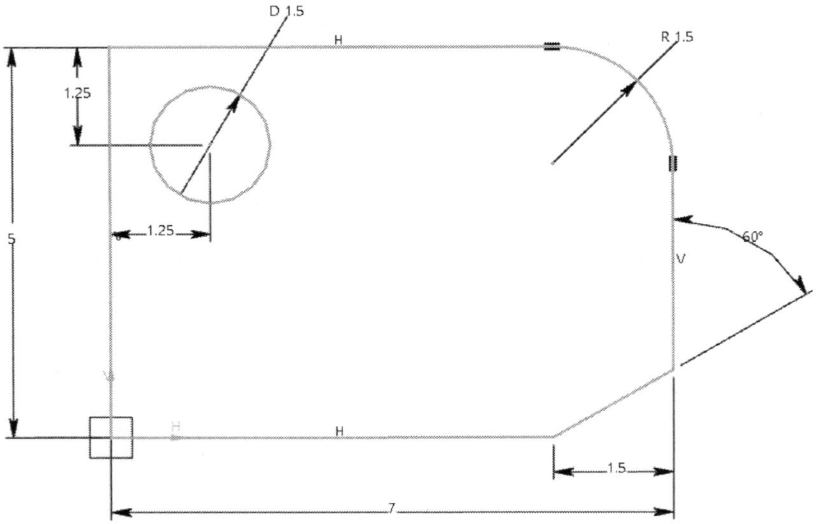

Figure 11–37

Practice 11a

Creating Holes, Fillets, and Chamfers

Practice Objectives

- Create a Fillet feature using several edge selection methods.
- Create and change Chamfer features.
- Create Hole features.

In this practice, you will add various dress-up features such as holes, fillets, and chamfers to a part, as shown in Figure 11–38. You will learn how different hole placement methods are affected as a model is modified, how different edge selection techniques can be used to create a Fillet feature, and how to create a Chamfer feature.

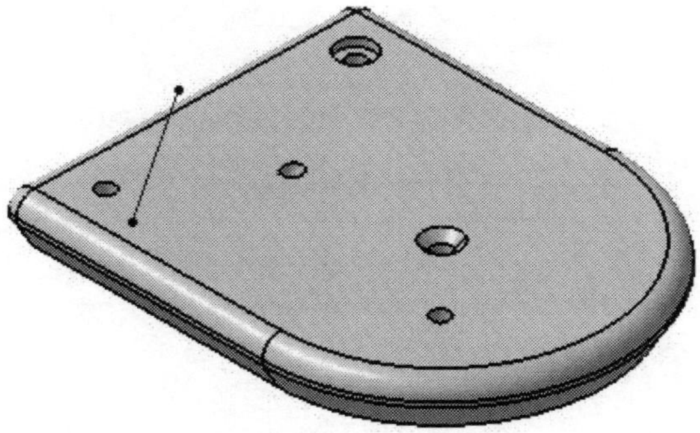

Figure 11–38

Task 1 - Create a hole that is located to two sides of the part.

1. Import **Dressup_Features.3dxml**.
2. In the *Part2 (Explore)* tab, right-click **Part2** in the specification tree and select **Open**.

Design Considerations

This hole will reference two edges of the part. By preselecting the face and two edges, the hole is automatically created on the face and references the two selected edges. This method enables the Hole feature to update with the edges if the part is modified. The hole will always remain a set distance from the edges.

3. Select the top face of the part, as shown in Figure 11–39.

4. Hold <Ctrl> and select the two edges, as shown in Figure 11–39. The selected edges highlight in red.

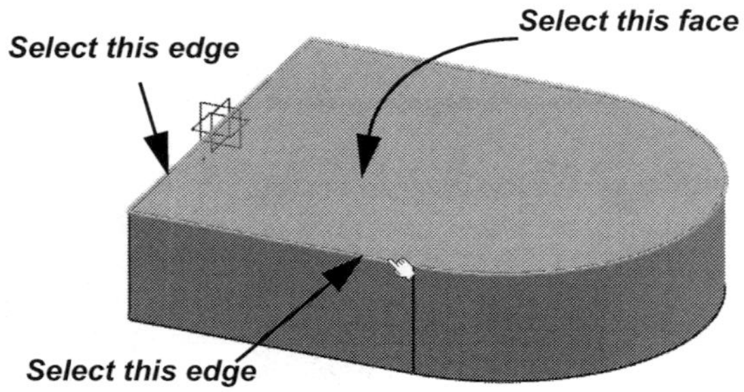

Figure 11–39

5. In the *Essentials* section of the Action Bar, click (Hole). A hole is placed in the exact location where you selected the face. The hole is also dimensioned to the two selected edges.

6. In the Hole Definition dialog box, set the following options, as shown in Figure 11–40.

   - *Depth*: **Blind**
   - *Diameter*: **25.00 (0.984 in)**
   - *Depth*: **63.50 (2.500 in)**
   - Bottom drop-down list: **V-Bottom**
   - *Angle*: **135**

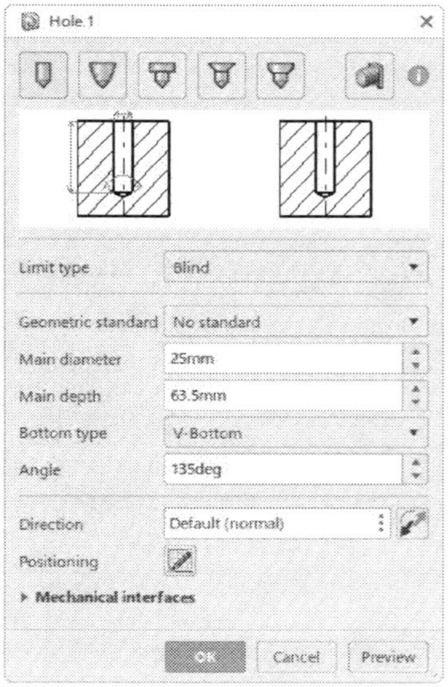

Figure 11–40

7. Double-click on the edge-to-hole dimensions in the model and set each value to **75.00 (2.953 in)**, as shown in Figure 11–41.

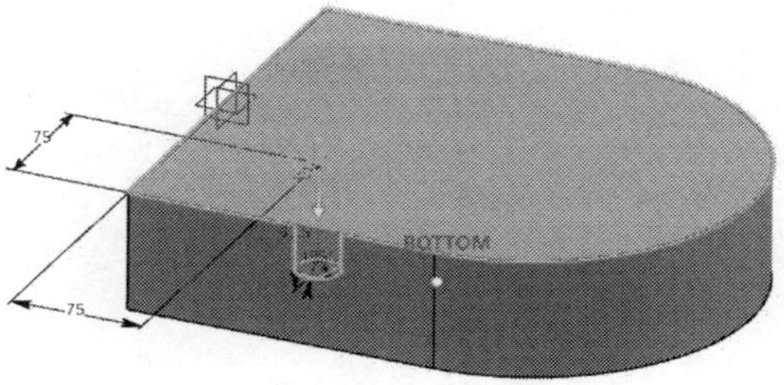

Figure 11–41

8. Click **OK** to complete the feature.

Task 2 - Create a hole at the center of an arc.

Design Considerations

By preselecting the face and arc, the hole is automatically created at the center of the arc. Using this method enables the Hole feature to remain centered on the part. If the arc radius is increased or decreased, the hole always remains at the center regardless of how far apart the edges move.

1. Select the top face of the part again, hold <Ctrl> and select the curved edge of the arc, as shown in Figure 11–42.

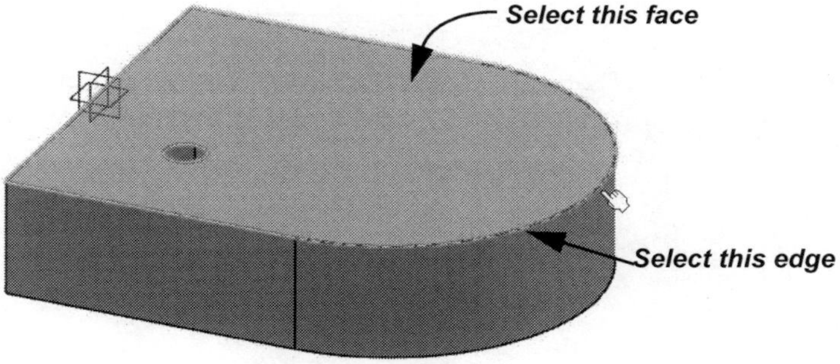

Figure 11–42

2. Click  (Hole). A new hole is placed at the center of the arc. Note that the hole has the same characteristics as the previous hole, such as *Diameter*, *Depth*, and *Bottom* settings.
3. Select **Up to Last** for the depth.
4. In the dialog box, select  (Counter sunk) for the hole.

5. Enter **12.50** (0.492 in) as *Depth* of the countersink, as shown in Figure 11–43.

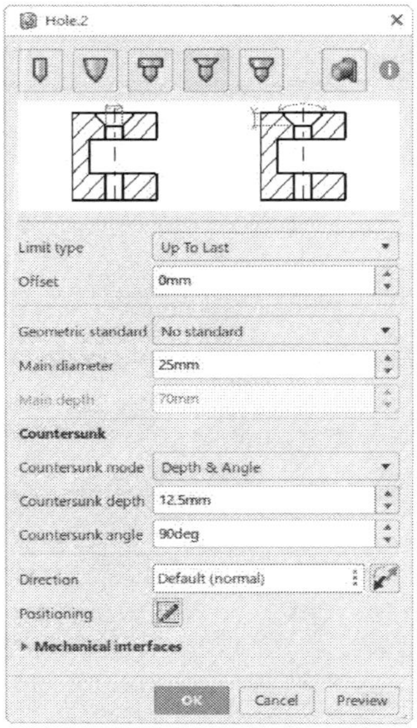

Figure 11–43

6. Click **OK** to complete the feature.

Task 3 - Create an under constrained hole.

Design Considerations

This hole will be placed on the surface of the part. It will not be constrained to any edges. If the part is modified, the hole's position will remain unaffected due to the lack of constraints.

1. Select the top face of the part and click (Hole). A Hole feature is placed at the exact location that you selected on the top face, as shown in Figure 11–44. Since you did not select any edges or surfaces to which the hole is located, its position is unconstrained.

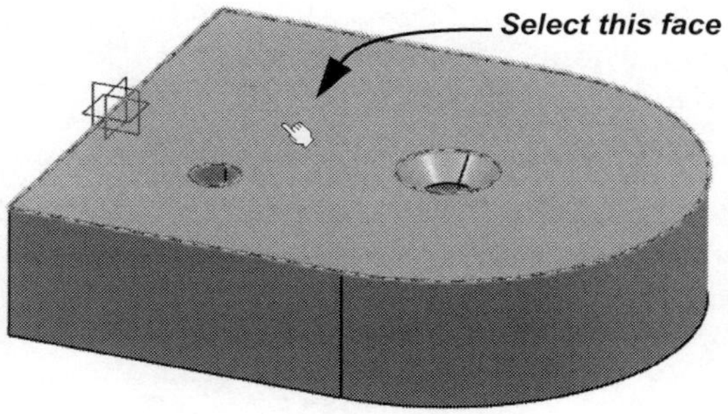

Figure 11–44

2. In the dialog box, select **Counterbored** for the hole.

3. Set the following:

   - *Diameter*: **50.00 (1.969 in)**
   - *Depth*: **12.50 (0.492 in)** (default value)

4. Click **OK** to complete the feature.

Task 4 - Make the part wider to see the impact of constrained and under-constrained features.

1. On the model or in the specification tree, double-click on the Pad feature to display the dimensional constraints.

2. Change the 250 *(9.843 in)* dimension as **380 (14.961 in)** and the 300 *(11.811 in)* dimension as **625 (24.606 in)**, as shown in Figure 11–45.

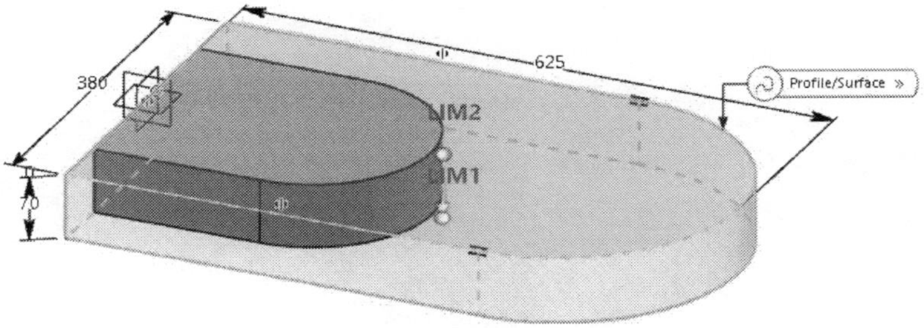

Figure 11–45

3. Click **OK** to complete the change. The first hole remains **75.00** (2.953 in) from each edge, as shown in Figure 11–46. The counter sunk hole remains coaxial with the center of the arc. The counterbored hole remains in the same location at which it was originally placed.

Your model will look slightly different depending on where you placed the third hole.

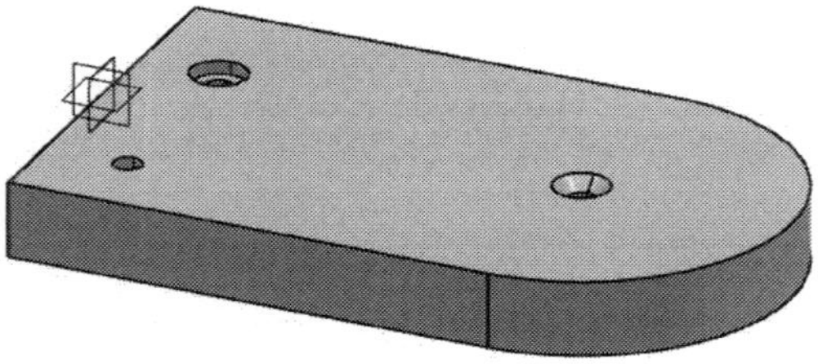

Figure 11–46

Task 5 - Change the counterbored hole to have dimensional constraints.

1. Double-click on the counterbored hole to begin the process of editing the feature.

2. In the Hole Definition dialog box, click (Sketch) to enter the Sketch app to dimension the location of the hole.

3. Select and drag the asterisk closer to the left side of the part and click (Constraint) from the context menu, as shown in Figure 11–47.

The asterisk (*) indicates the current location of the hole center.

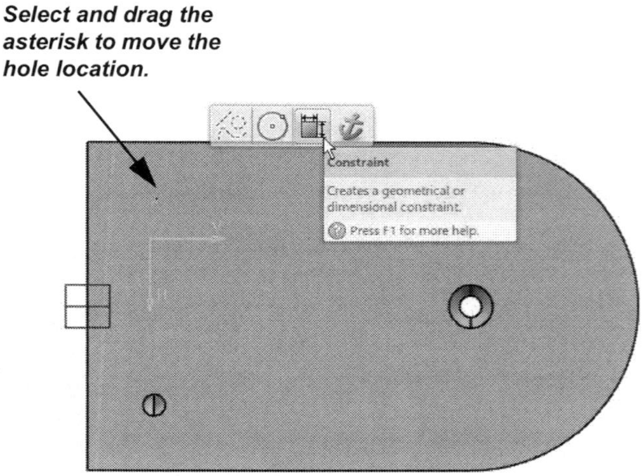

Figure 11–47

4. Create one of the dimensional constraints from the asterisk to the edge of the model, as shown in Figure 11–48.

5. Select the asterisk and click (Constraint) from the context menu to add the second dimension shown in Figure 11–48.

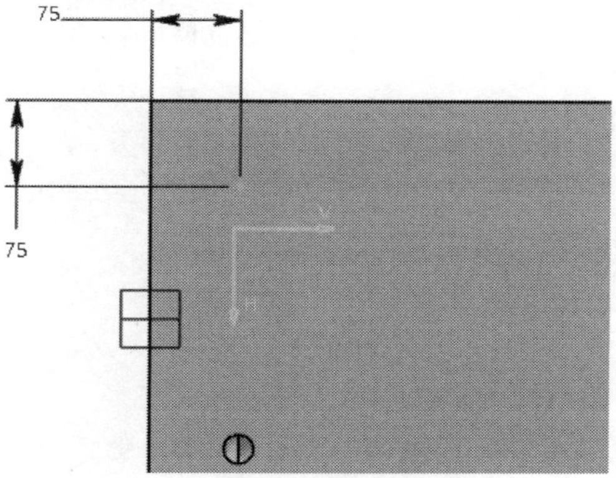

Figure 11–48

6. Set the values to **75.00 (2.953 in)** for each dimension.

7. Click (Exit App) to exit the sketching environment.

8. Click **OK** to complete the feature.

9. Change the width of the Pad feature from 380 (14.961 in) to **500 (19.685 in)** to verify that the counterbored hole works with the design intent. The part displays as shown in Figure 11–49.

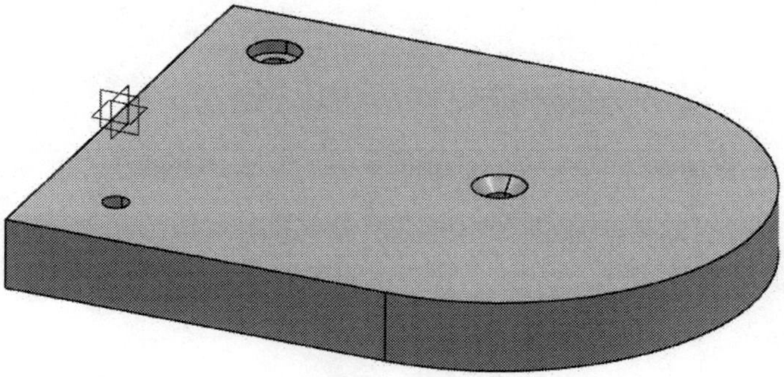
Figure 11–49

Task 6 - Create another simple hole.

Design Considerations

You will create this hole similar to the counterbored hole you previously created. However, you will use the positioning sketch function to develop a radial dimensioning scheme for the hole.

1. Select the top face of the part and click (Hole). Set the following:
   - *Depth type*: **Blind**
   - *Depth value*: **25.0 (0.984 in)**
   - *Bottom:* **Flat**
2. Select the *Type* tab and select **Simple** for the *hole type*.
3. Return to the *Extension* tab and click (Sketch).
4. Ensure that (Construction/Standard Element) in the *Sketch* section of the Action Bar is enabled.
5. Click (Circle) and sketch a construction circle that is approximately centered on the countersunk hole, as shown in Figure 11–50.

*Note the **H** and **V** axes will be in the location where you clicked on the screen, not necessarily as shown in the image.*

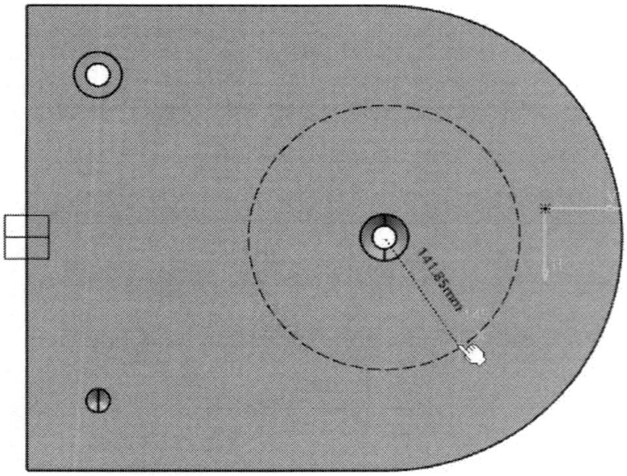

Figure 11–50

6. Select the construction circle, hold <Ctrl> and select the large arc of the Pad feature. Click (Constraint) from the context toolbar, as shown in Figure 11–51.

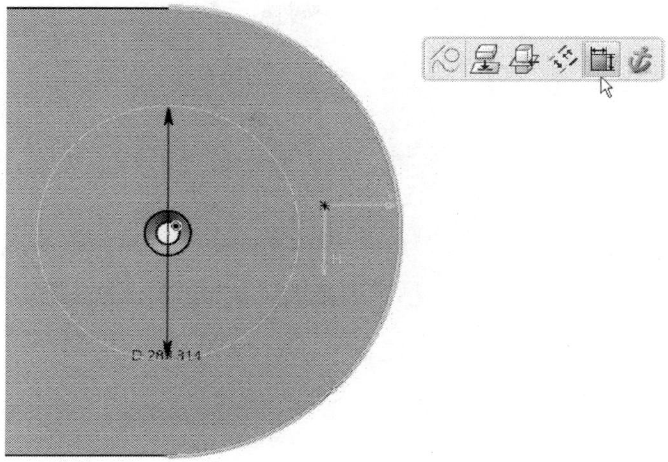

Figure 11–51

7. Select (Concentric Constraint) from the context toolbar, or right-click and select **Concentricity**.

8. Move the asterisk, located at the center of the H and V axes, to the approximate position shown in Figure 11–52.

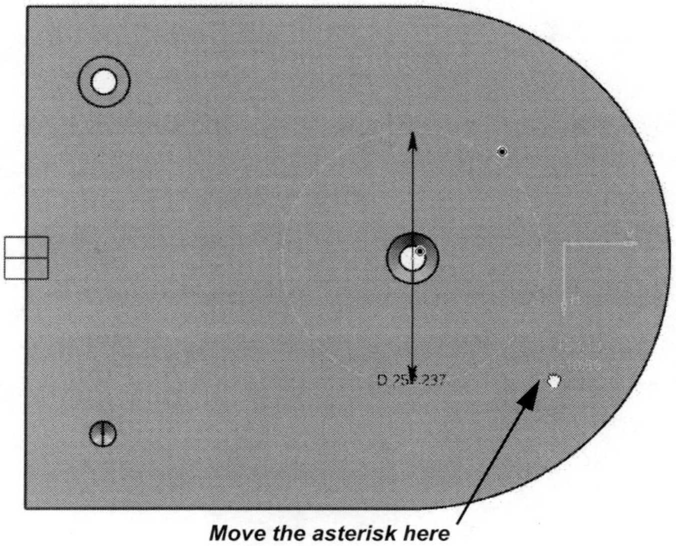

Figure 11–52

9. Select the construction circle, hold <Ctrl> and select the asterisk.

10. Select 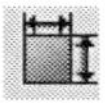 (Constraint) from the context toolbar, then select  (Coincidence Constraint).

11. Edit the *circle diameter* to **265 (10.433 in)**, as shown in Figure 11–53.

12. The final item required in the positioning sketch is an angle dimension for the location of the hole around the circle. Click  (Axis) to create an axis.

13. Sketch the axis such that it snaps to the center of the construction circle and the asterisk, as shown in Figure 11–53.

14. Create the angle dimension between the axis and the vertical plane.

15. Change the *Angle value* to **45**, as shown in Figure 11–53.

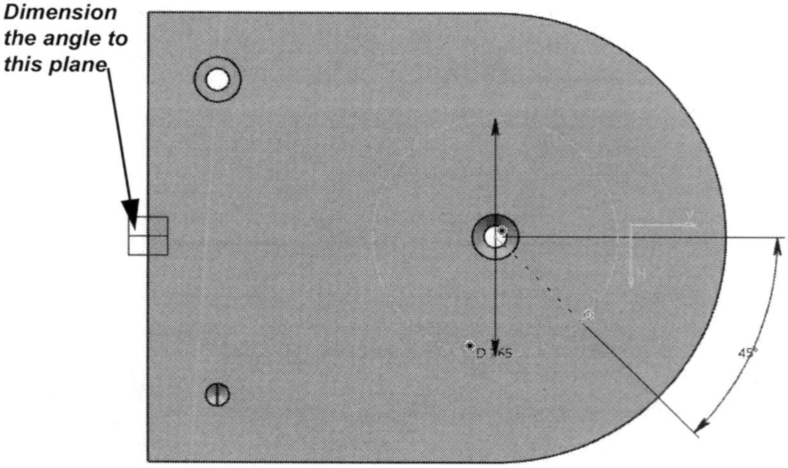

Figure 11–53

16. Click  (Exit App) to exit the sketching environment.

17. Click **OK** to complete the feature.

Task 7 - Create a Fillet feature on the top edge of the Pad.

1. In the *Essentials* section of the Action Bar, click  (Edge Fillet) to create a Fillet feature.

2. Select the straight edge of the Pad feature, as shown in Figure 11–54.

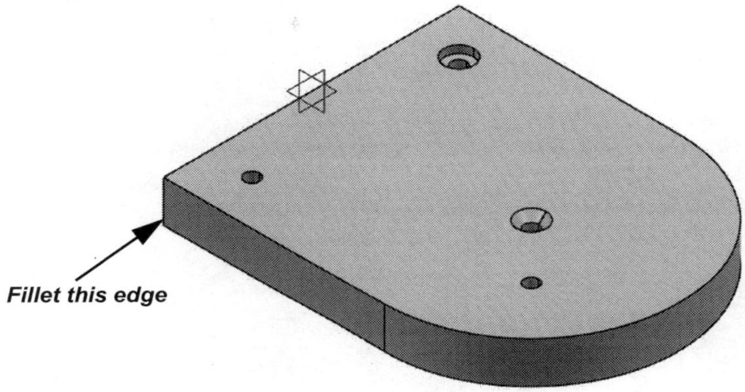

Figure 11–54

3. Enter **25.00 (0.984 in)** for *Radius* and click **Preview**. The fillet continues beyond the selected edge and stops when it reaches a sharp corner, as shown in Figure 11–55. This is a result of the default **Tangency** selection mode.

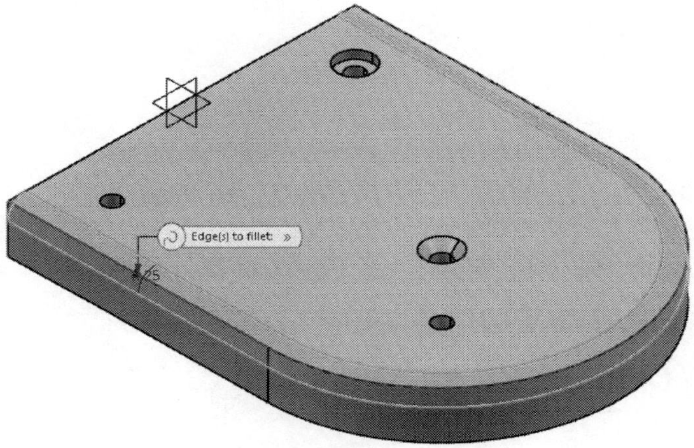

Figure 11–55

*When prompted with a warning that the edges will be replaced by normal edges, click **OK**.*

4. In the Propagation drop-down list, select **Minimal.** Click **Preview** again. Only the selected edge is filleted.

5. Return the selection mode to **Tangency**.

6. The *Object(s) to fillet* box lists one edge. Select the three additional edges to fillet, as shown in Figure 11–56. You can rotate the model or switch to hidden line display to select the hidden edge.

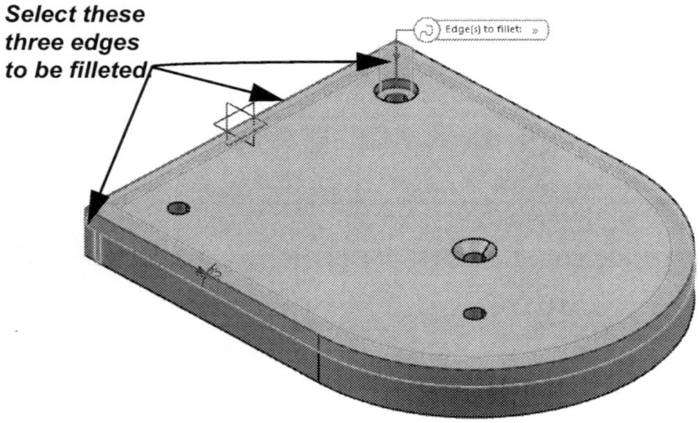

Figure 11–56

7. Click **OK** to complete the feature.

Task 8 - Create a Chamfer feature on the bottom edge.

---

1. In the *Essentials* section of the Action Bar, click

    (Chamfer) to create a Chamfer feature and select the bottom edge of the part, as shown in Figure 11–57.

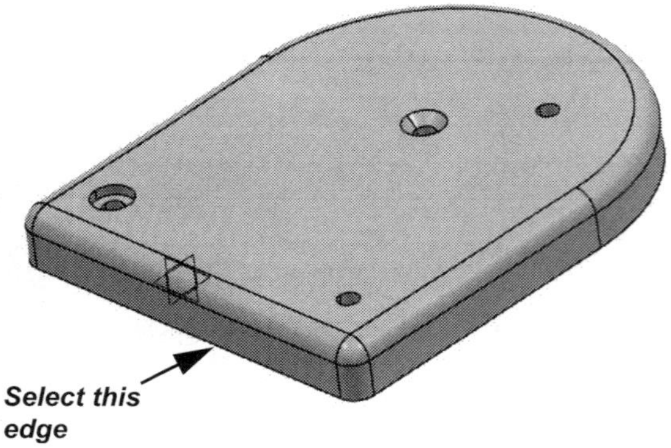

Figure 11–57

2. Set the following:

   - *Length 1*: **38.00 (1.496 in)**
   - *Angle:* **30**

3. In the *View* section of the Action Bar, click  (* front) and zoom in on the chamfered edge.

4. Select  (View Mode), and from within the window, select  (Wireframe).

5. Click the **Reverse All** option a few times and note that it enables you to flip the direction of the chamfer, as shown in Figure 11–58.

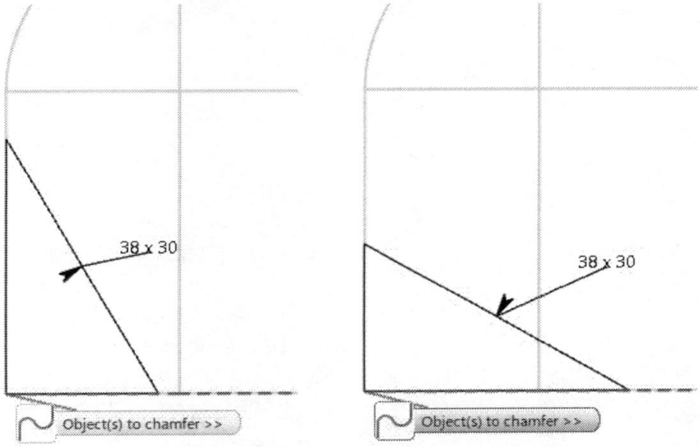

Figure 11–58

6. Toggle the **Reverse All** option till the 30° angle is at the bottom, and then click **OK** to complete the feature.

7. Select  (Shading With Edges) within the  (View Mode) command.

8. Click (* iso). The model displays as shown in Figure 11–59.

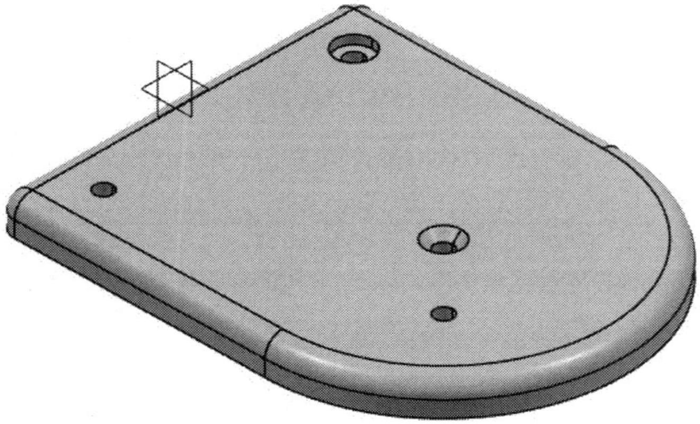

Figure 11–59

Task 9 - Create an angled hole.

In this task, you will create an angled hole. The angle of the hole will be controlled by a line you will create.

1. In the *Essentials* section of the Action Bar, click (Line).
2. In the Line type drop-down list, select **Angle/Normal to curve.** Right-click in each of the following fields and set the following options:
    - *Curve*: **Insert Wireframe>Z Axis**
    - *Support*: **Insert Wireframe>ZX plane**
    - *Point*: **Insert Wireframe>Create Point**

3. Using the **Coordinates** point type, create the point. Locate the point at **0, 0, 0**, as shown in Figure 11–60.

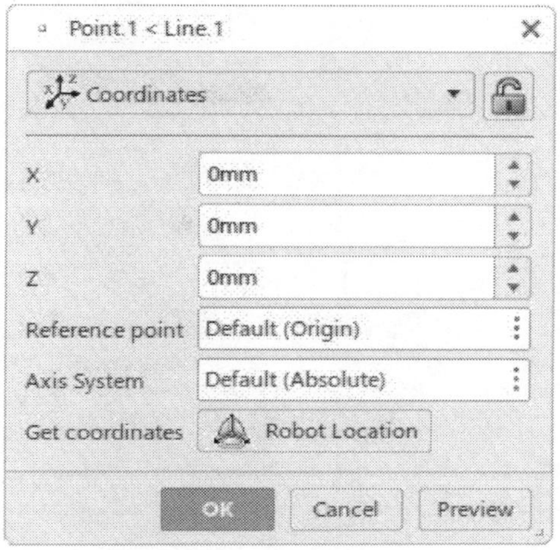

Figure 11–60

4. Click **OK** to create the point and return to the Line Definition dialog box. Set the following:
   - *Angle:* **135**
   - *End:* **150 (5.906 in)**
5. Click **OK** to complete the line. The line displays as shown in Figure 11–61.

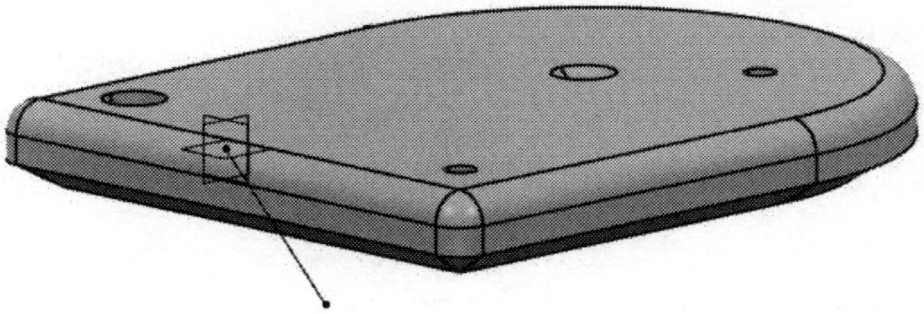

Figure 11–61

6. Create a new Hole feature anywhere on the top surface of the model. Set the following:
   - *Select* ***Simple***
   - *Main Diameter:* **25mm (0.984 in)**
   - *Main Depth*: **50mm (1.969 in)**

7. Set *Bottom* to **Flat**.

8. For the *Direction* field, select the line you just created, as shown in Figure 11–62.

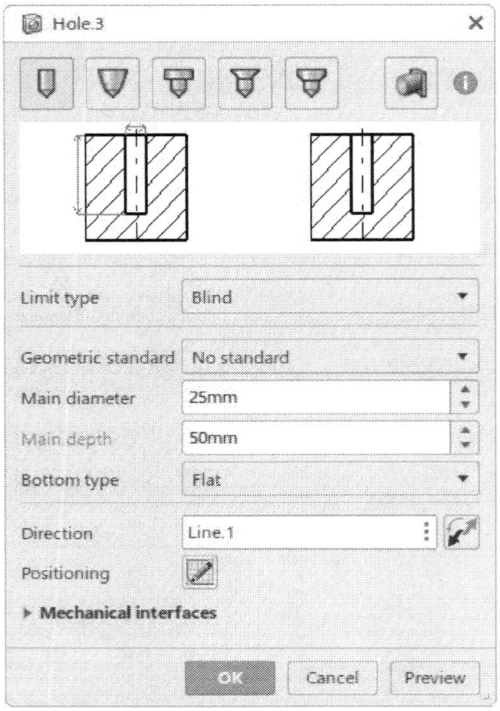

Figure 11–62

9. Complete the feature. The model displays as shown in Figure 11–63.

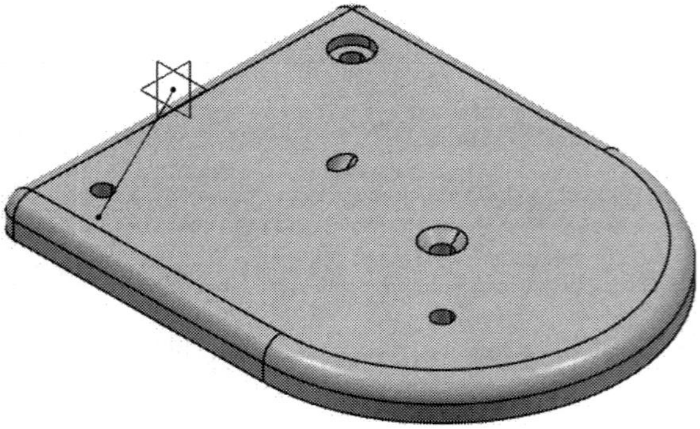

Figure 11–63

Task 10 - Modify the line angle.

Design Considerations

The angle of this Hole feature can now be controlled by modifying the Line feature used to define the direction.

1. In the *View* section of the Action Bar, click (*left) and within the (View Mode) command, select (Wireframe). The angled hole displays as shown in Figure 11–64.

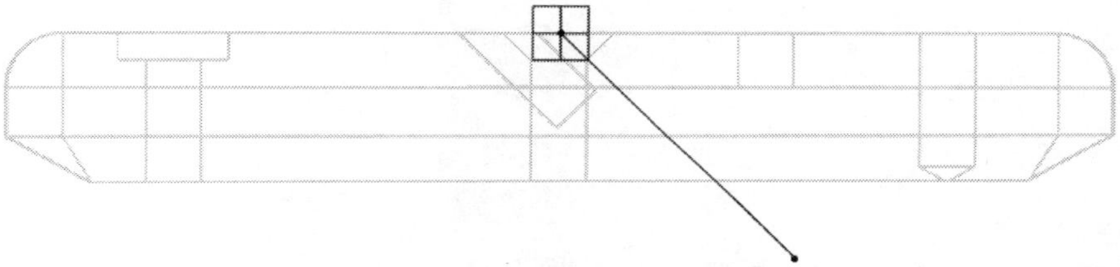

Figure 11–64

2. Change the *Angle* to **155**.
3. The angle of the hole updates as shown in Figure 11–65.

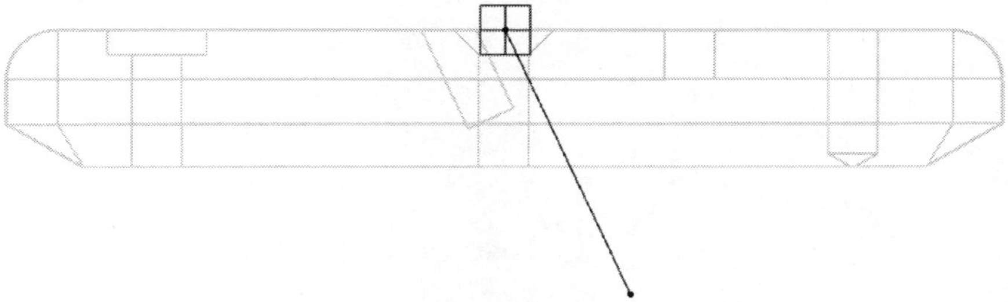

Figure 11–65

4. Save the file and close the tab.

NOTE: Additional dress up feature practices are found in Practice B9 and Practice B10 at the end of this guide.

Chapter Review Questions

1. ______________________ features represent features for which a shape is predefined.
   a. Sketched Features
   b. Solid Features
   c. Surface Features
   d. Dress-up features
2. Which feature type taught in this chapter creates a feature that is tangent to the adjacent faces of the resultant feature?
   a. Chamfer
   b. Fillet
   c. Hole
   d. None of the above.
3. Fillets on multiple edges can be controlled by one dimension.
   a. True
   b. False
4. Select the hole depth option that requires you to specify a dimension.
   a. Up to Surface
   b. Up to Next
   c. Up to Last
   d. Blind
5. Fillets can add or remove material.
   a. True
   b. False
6. Chamfer features always remove material.
   a. True
   b. False
7. You can create a coaxial Hole without entering the Sketch app by preselecting the planar surface and circular edge of the cylindrical feature.
   a. True
   b. False

8. Why is it considered bad practice to dimension to filleted or chamfered edges?
    a. Dimensioning to filleted or chamfered edges creates a parent/child relationship.
    b. If the fillet/chamfer is deleted, the child features are also deleted.
    c. It is better to dimension to stable features that are not likely to be removed or dramatically changed.
    d. All of the above.

Answers: 1d, 2b, 3a, 4d, 5a, 6b, 7a, 8d

Advanced Dress-Up Features

In this chapter, you learn how to work with various types of fillets to further refine your designs. Additionally, you learn how to effectively use dress-up features such as the Shell, Draft and Pocket features to modify and manipulate the geometry model to better fulfill the desired design intent.

Learning Objectives in This Chapter

- Use the various fillet types, such as Variable Radius, Tritangent, Face-face, and Chordal.
- Use a uniform wall thickness by creating a Shell feature.
- Select individual surfaces to shell with unique thicknesses.
- Create pad and pocket features that automatically contain draft and filleted edges.
- Learn how the order in which features are created affects the resulting geometry.
- Learn how to reorder features.

12.1 Additional Fillet Features

The Edge Fillet feature is the most basic of the fillet features. The four additional Fillet features are:

- Variable Radius
- Tritangent
- Face-face
- Chordal

Variable Radius Fillet

When using a **Variable Radius Fillet**, a different radius value can be entered at locations along the edge. To create a variable radius fillet, click  (Edge Fillet) to open the Edge Fillet Definition dialog box, then click  (Variable), as shown in Figure 12–1.

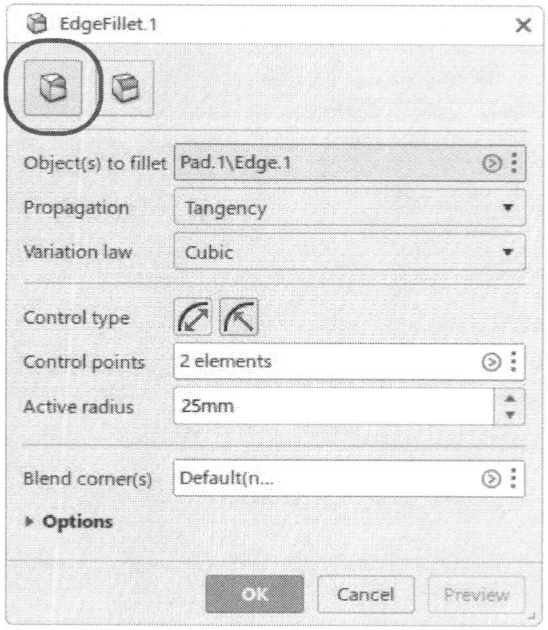

Figure 12–1

A Variable Radius fillet allows for varying radius values at the vertices and points along the selected edge, as shown in Figure 12–2.

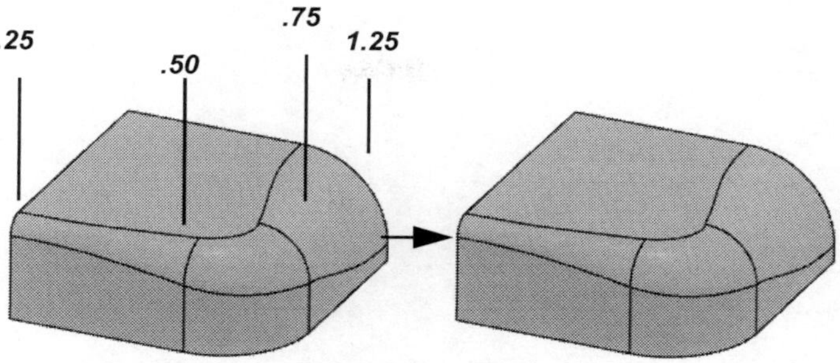

Figure 12–2

When you begin the creation of a variable radius fillet, the software assigns the entered *Radius* value to each end of the selected chain of edges, as shown in Figure 12–3. The points can each have a different radius value.

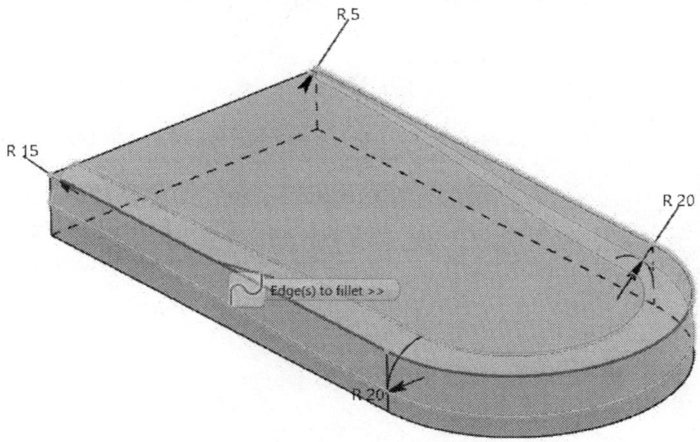

Figure 12–3

You can add or remove vertices or points along the edge in the *Points* field in the Variable Radius Fillet Definition dialog box, as shown in Figure 12–4. The software adds a radius value at that location. To change a radius value, double-click on it and enter a new value.

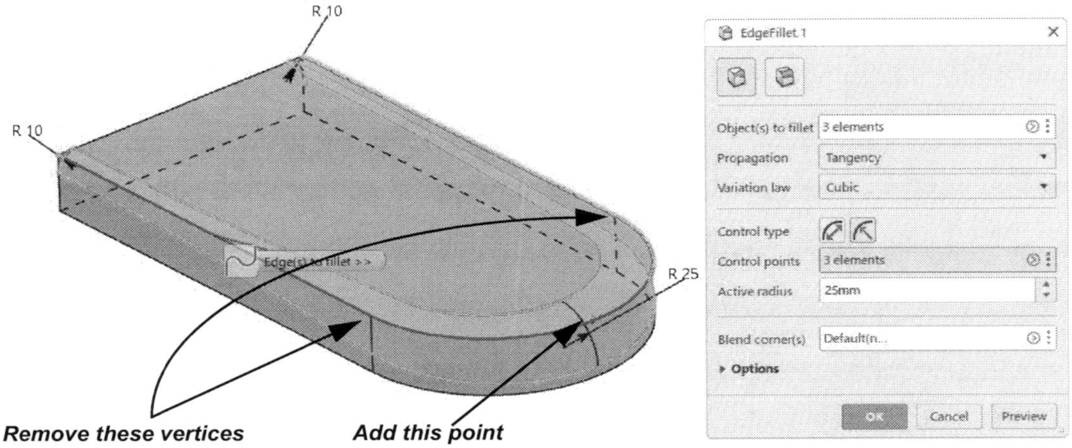

Figure 12–4

To remove a point or vertex, select the point near the dimension on the model. In addition, the icon can be clicked in the *Control Points* section of the Edge Fillet Definition dialog box to display a list of points, as shown in Figure 12–5. To remove a point from the Control Points dialog box, select the **x** next to the point. Close the Control Points window and click **Preview**.

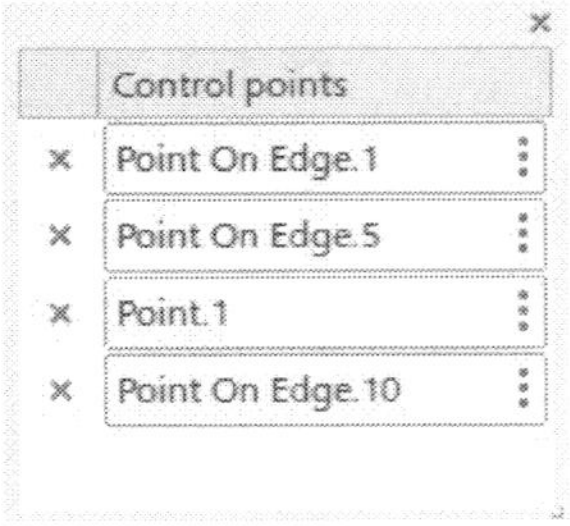

Figure 12–5

You can also use reference planes to identify where you want to control a variable radius fillet. The software intersects the plane with an edge and places a radius dimension at that location.

- To quickly edit all of the variable radius values, click  (Display Contextual Menu) to the right of the Control Points field, and then select **Edit Multiple Values** to open the Fillet Values dialog box, as shown in Figure 12–6.

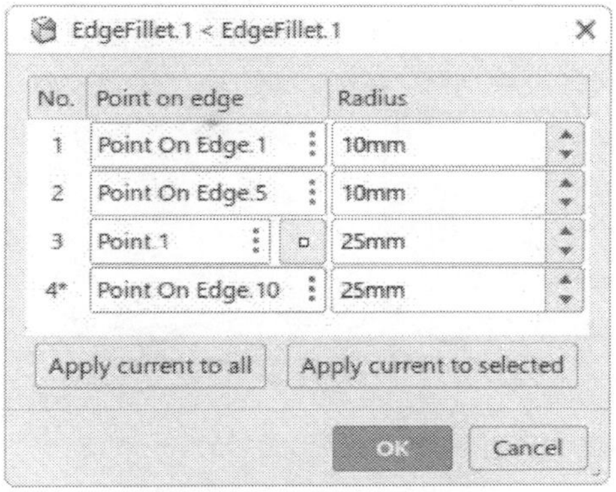

Figure 12–6

- **Apply current to all** enables you to edit individual radius values and set all of the values to be the same.
- **Apply current to selected** enables you to select several values and set them to be the same.

Note that you can change back to a constant radius fillet by clicking  **(Constant)** in the Edge Fillet Definition dialog box. If you added any additional radius points for a variable radius round however, they will be lost.

Tritangent Fillet

A **Tritangent Fillet** creates a fillet that is tangent to three surfaces, as shown in Figure 12–7.

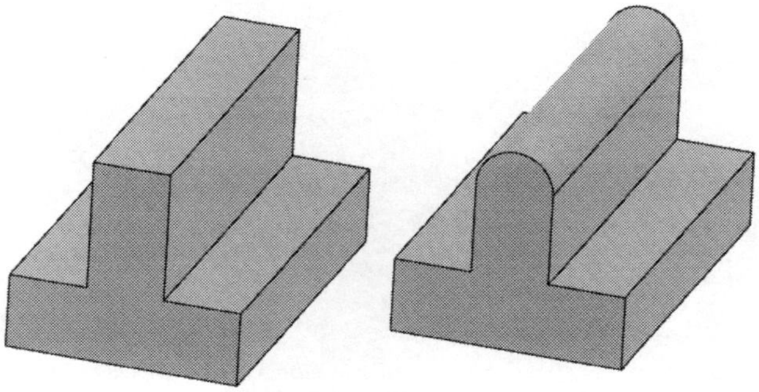

Figure 12–7

To create a tritangent fillet, click (Tritangent Fillet) in the *Refine* section of the Action Bar, and specify two faces to fillet and a face to be removed, as shown in Figure 12–8. Faces can also be preselected; however, you must select the two parallel faces to be filleted first and then select the face to be removed.

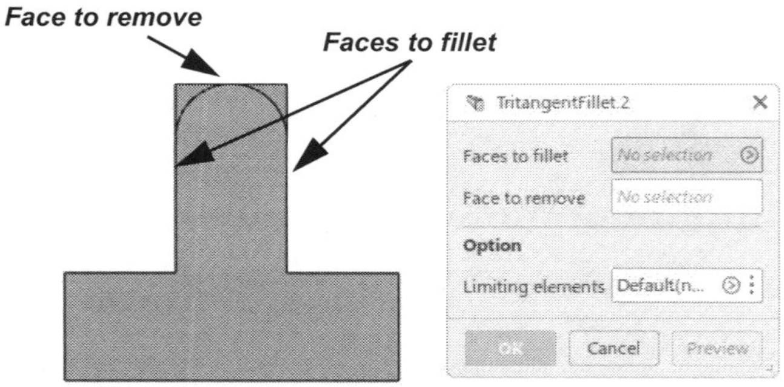

Figure 12–8

The three faces you specify for the tritangent fillet do not need to be planar or parallel, as shown in Figure 12–9.

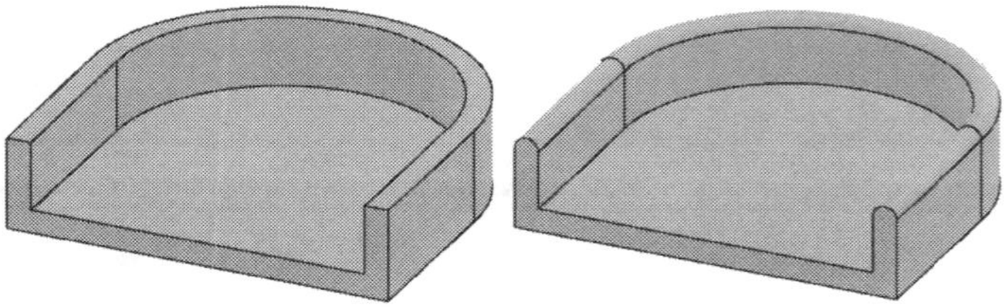

Figure 12–9

You can trim tritangent fillets to a plane, face, or surface by selecting the *Limiting element(s)* field, as shown in Figure 12–10.

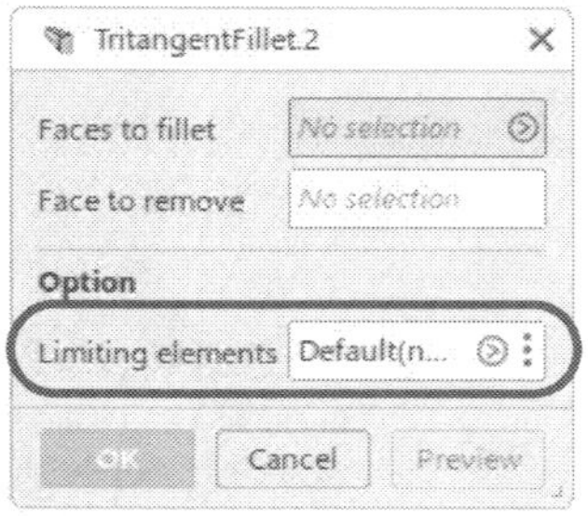

Figure 12–10

Then select the plane, face, or surface to limit the extend of the fillet.

Face-Face Fillet

A **Face-Face Fillet** is used when no intersection occurs between the surfaces that the fillet is tangent to, as shown in Figure 12–11.

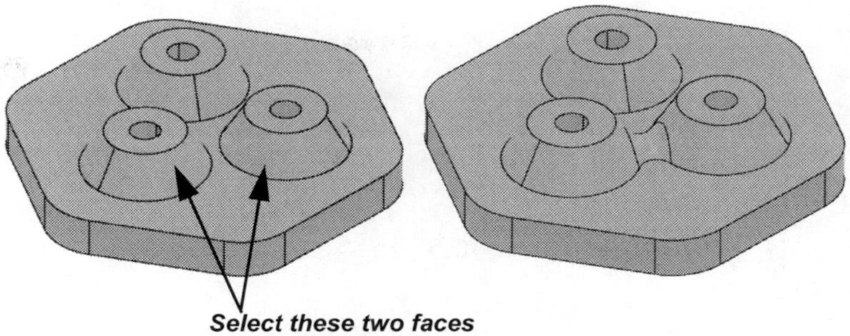

Figure 12–11

To create a face-face fillet, click  (Face-Face Fillet) in the *Refine* section of the Action Bar. A face-face fillet can also be used to fillet between the two surfaces shown in Figure 12–12.

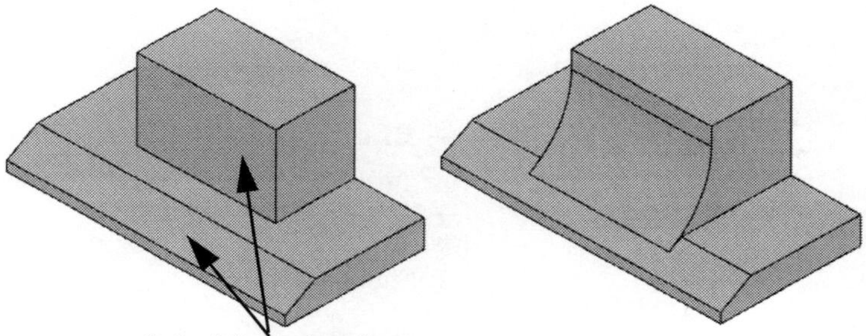

Figure 12–12

Face-face fillets fail to update if the radius value is not large enough to span between the surfaces, or if the radius is so large that it extends beyond the two faces.

Depending on the geometry, there can be circumstances in which the selection of two surfaces could result in more than one possible fillet. For example, the selection of the rounded surface and the base surface shown in Figure 12–13 could result in a fillet to one side or the other of the upper pad feature.

You can use the **Near Point** option in the Face-Face Fillet Definition dialog box to select the nearest point to the side on which you want the round to be created, as shown in Figure 12–14.

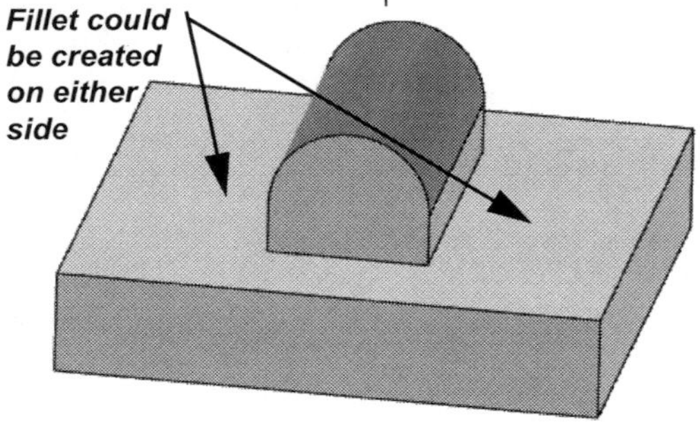

Figure 12–13

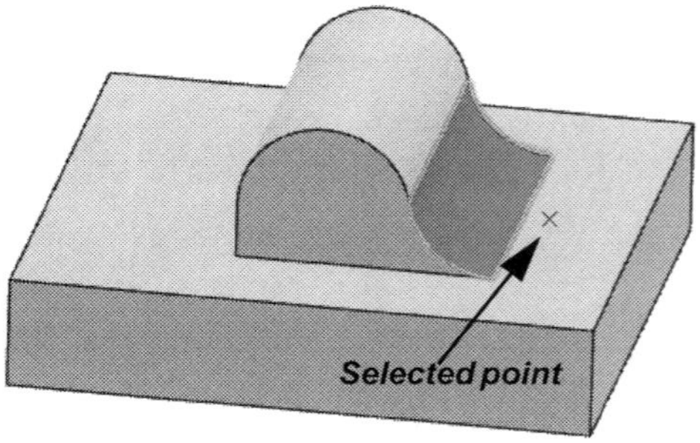

Figure 12–14

Chordal Fillet

A **Chordal Fillet** creates a fillet that is measured by a chord length, rather than radius value. Figure 12–15 shows an example of a cross-section of a chordal fillet. The measurements show what a chord looks like in comparison to a radius measurement.

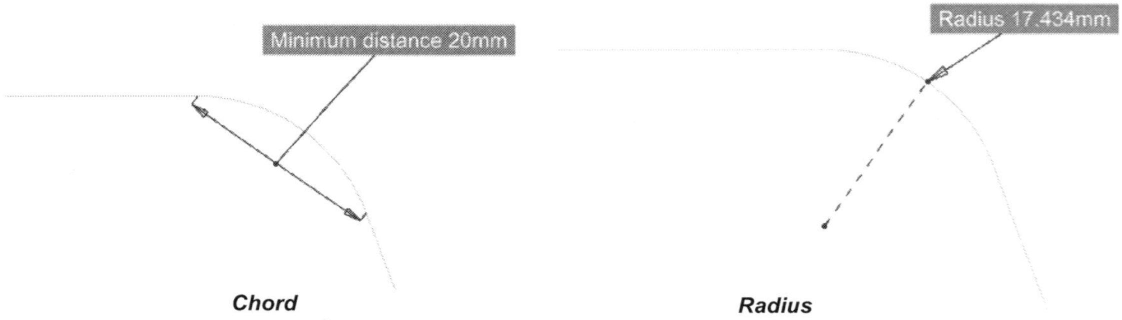

Figure 12–15

To create a chordal fillet, click (Edge Fillet) to open the Edge Fillet Definition dialog box, then click **(Chordal)** and specify the edges to fillet. Complete the fillet by entering a *Chordal length* value, as shown in Figure 12–16.

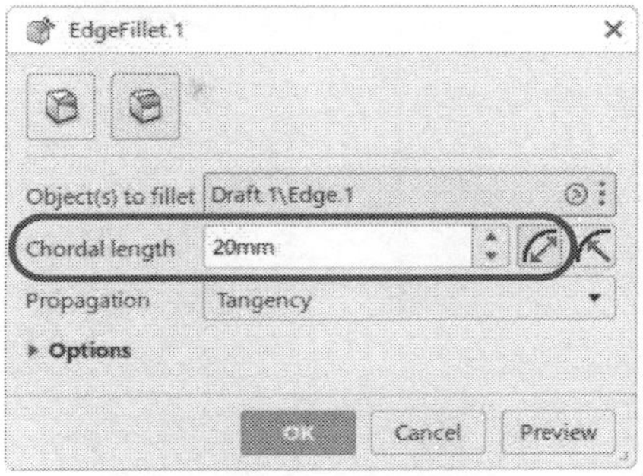

Figure 12–16

Variable Chordal Fillet

By default, chordal fillets use a constant chordal length. However, different chordal lengths can be defined at selected points by clicking (Variable). You can add or remove vertices or points along the selected edge in the *Points* field in the Edge Fillet Definition dialog box. The software adds a chordal length value at each location. To change the value, double-click on it and enter a new value.

To remove a point or vertex, select the point near the dimension on the model, or click the icon, then select the **x** next to the point in the Control Point dialog box to remove it.

12.2 Draft Feature

The Draft feature adjusts the surface of existing geometry. Draft is typically required for injection molded parts and castings to enable the part to be released from the mold. It should not be used to make angled cuts on features unless the intent is to mold the part. Figure 12–17 shows an example of a Draft feature.

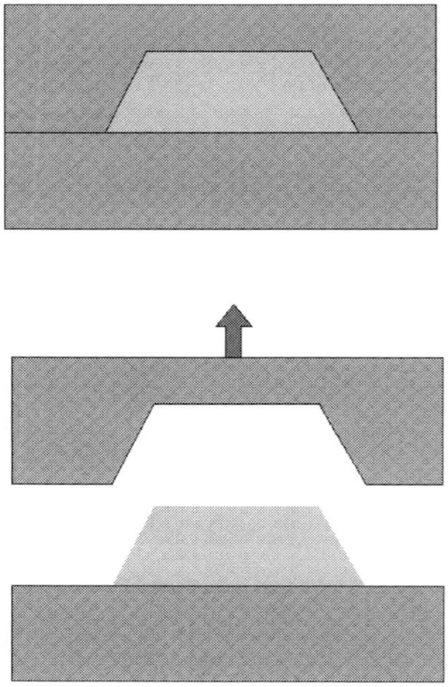

Figure 12–17

When you create a Draft feature, you are required to specify the following information:

- Neutral element
- Pull direction

General Steps

Use the following general steps to create a Draft feature:

1. Start the creation of the Draft feature.
2. Select the faces to draft.
3. Select a neutral element.
4. Specify a pull direction.
5. Complete the feature.

Step 1 - Start the creation of the Draft feature.

Click (Draft) in the *Essentials* or *Refine* section of the Action Bar to create a Draft feature. The Draft Definition dialog box opens as shown in Figure 12–18.

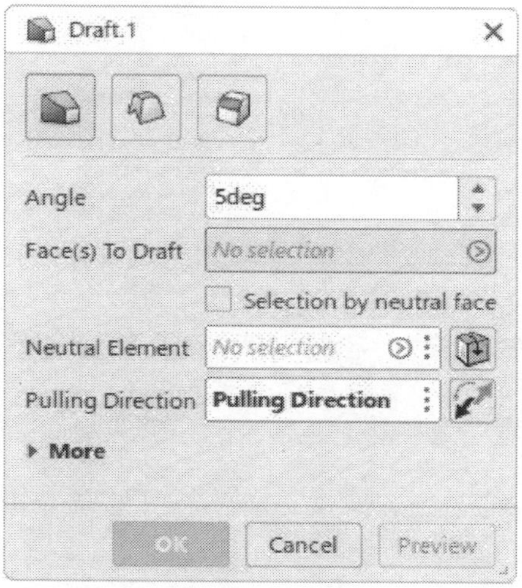

Figure 12–18

Note that three types of drafts can be defined in this dialog box.

-  (Constant) defines a constant draft feature.
-  (Variable) defines a variable draft feature. A variable draft feature enables you to define multiple draft angles for a single draft surface, as shown in Figure 12–19. The angles are defined at points or vertices on the model.
-  (Reflect) defines a draft face using the natural reflect lines of a rounded surface. Adjusting with the draft angle that is used.

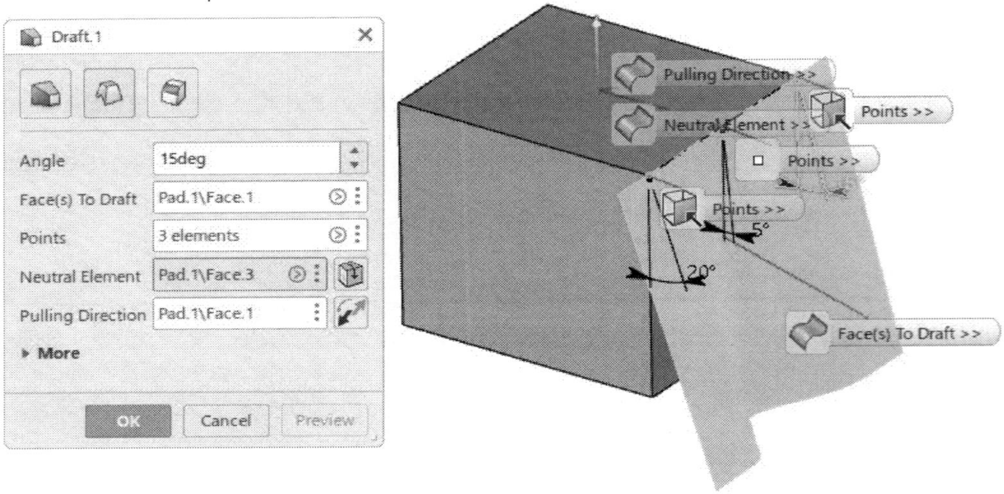

Figure 12–19

Step 2 - Select the faces to draft.

Specify the faces to draft by selecting them on the model.

Selection By Neutral Face

The **Selection by neutral face** option enables you to automatically select the faces to draft, based on the selected neutral element. Any face that is bounded by the neutral element is drafted, as shown in Figure 12–20.

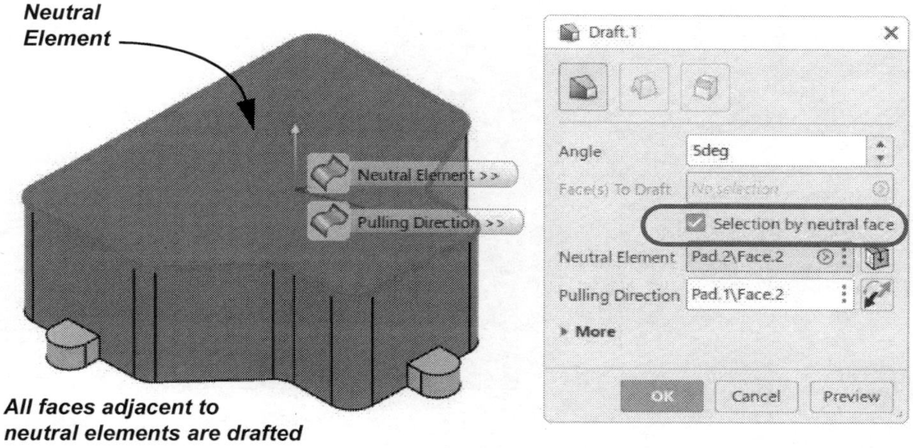

Figure 12–20

If this option is selected, the *Face(s) to draft* field is grayed out and the faces are determined by the selection of the neutral element.

Step 3 - Select a neutral element.

The neutral element defines where the part maintains its original size. For example, the part shown in Figure 12–21 is initially **5.50** units wide.

Three different neutral element scenarios are shown in Figure 12–21, where the model maintains the **5.50** value at the neutral element location. The pulling direction for each instance is upward.

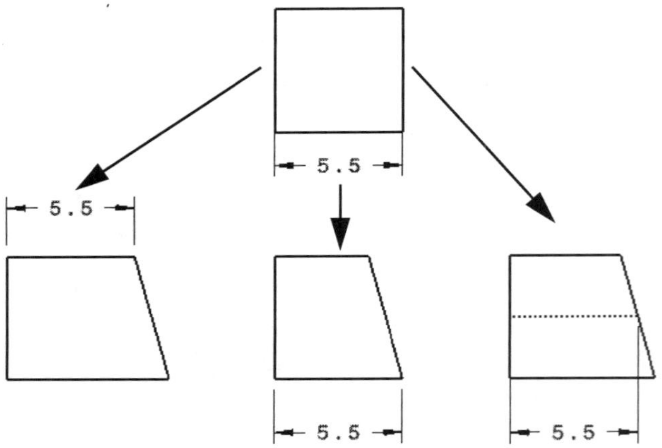

Neutral element is top face

Neutral element is bottom face

Neutral element is reference plane at middle of part

Figure 12–21

The implicit edge between the neutral element and the faces being drafted defines the start point of the draft. This edge can be developed from a planar or non-planar neutral element.

Consider the drain cap model shown in Figure 12–22. The curved end surface of the model is used as the neutral element because it provides the required start point for the draft angle.

Due to the shape of the neutral element face, the pulling direction cannot be determined automatically and must be manually defined by selecting a planar or linear reference. In this example, the YZ plane is selected.

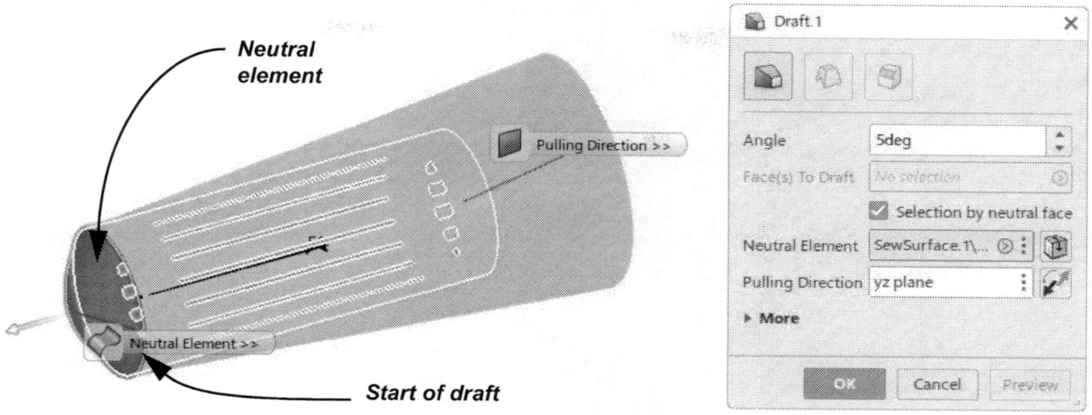

Figure 12–22

Draft Form

Click **More** for additional options to control the Draft feature, as shown in Figure 12–23. The Draft Form drop-down list enables you to refine the details of the draft.

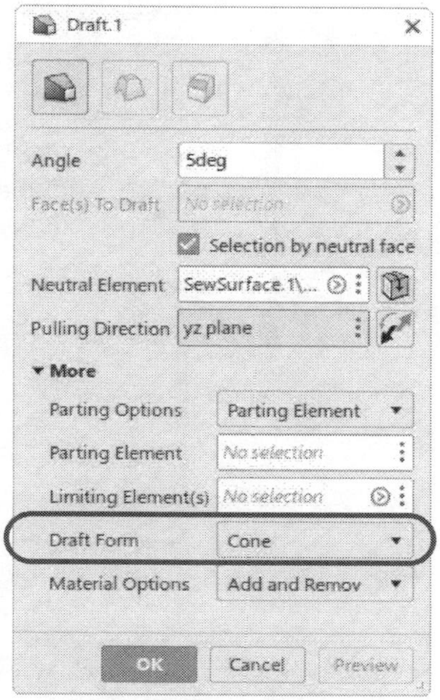

Figure 12–23

- **Cone** is the default value in the Draft Form drop-down list. With this option selected, a standard or non-radial Draft is created.

- With the **Square** option, a radial Draft is created that adds curvature to the resulting face, as shown on the right side of Figure 12–24.

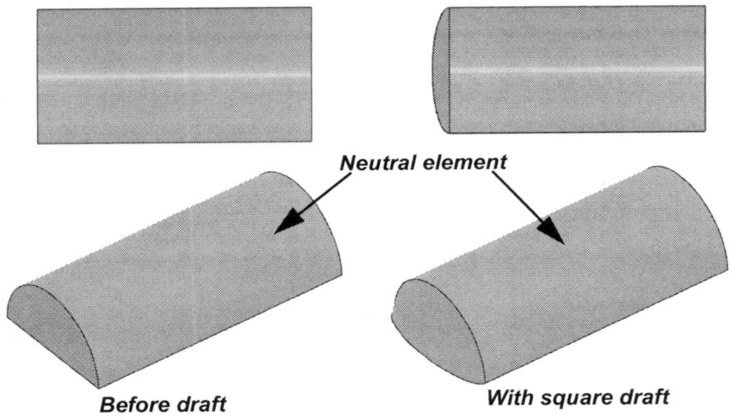

Figure 12–24

Step 4 - Specify a pull direction.

The pull direction defines the positive Draft direction. Select a planar surface as the reference for the pull direction. The normal vector of the surface reference defines the direction the mold is pulled apart. Clicking on the pull direction arrow to change its direction. The results of selecting different surfaces for the pull direction are shown in Figure 12–25.

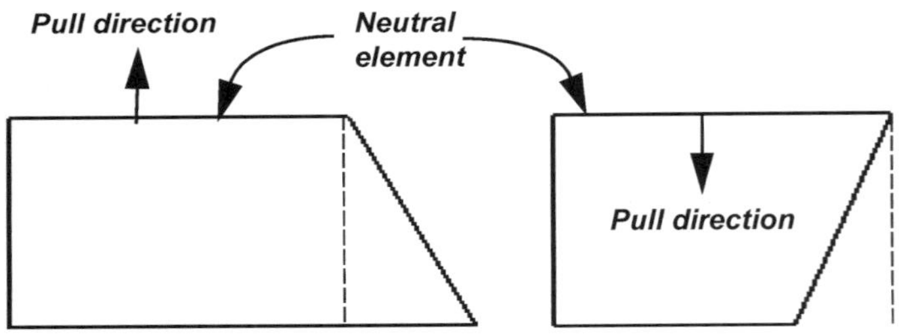

Figure 12–25

Step 5 - Complete the feature.

Click **OK** to complete the feature.

12.3 Creating Shell Features

The Shell feature removes selected surfaces from the model. It leaves a hollowed out solid of a specified wall thickness, as shown in Figure 12–26.

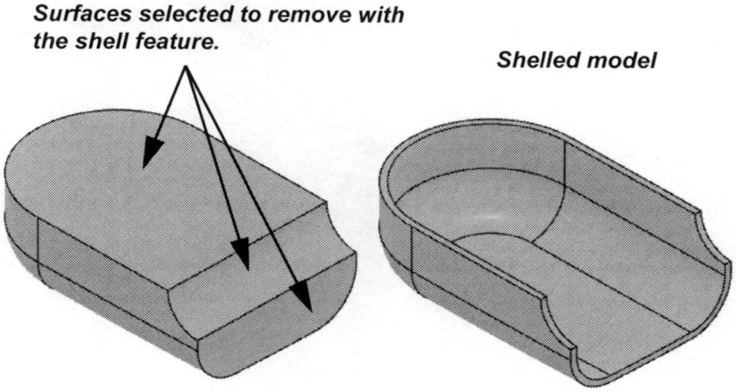

Figure 12–26

How To: Create a Shell Feature

1. Click  (Shell) to create a Shell feature. The Shell Definition dialog box opens as shown in Figure 12–27.

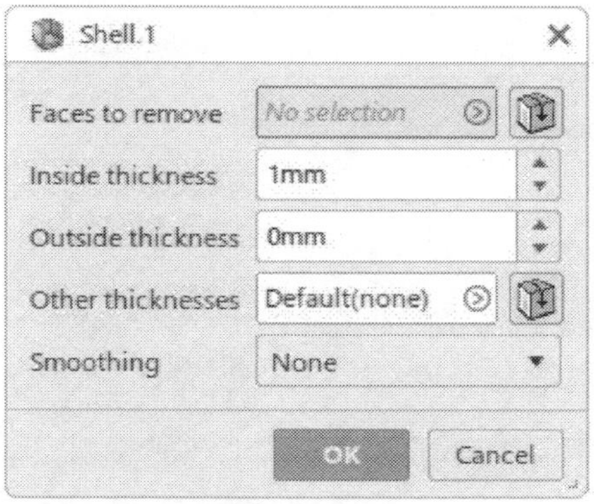

Figure 12–27

2. Select the surfaces to remove. Surfaces to be removed can be selected before or after clicking the **Shell** icon. Selected faces are shown in Figure 12–28. In CATIA, selected surfaces display in magenta.

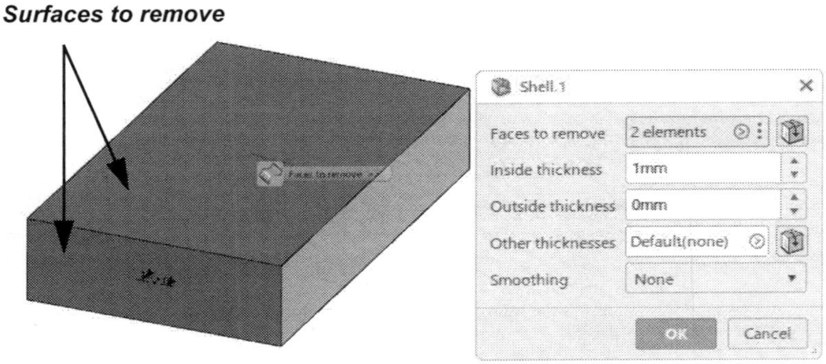

Figure 12–28

3. Use the Shell Definition dialog box to define the wall thickness. The wall thickness value can be offset from the inside and/or outside of the model. Different combinations of inside and outside thickness are shown in Figure 12–29.

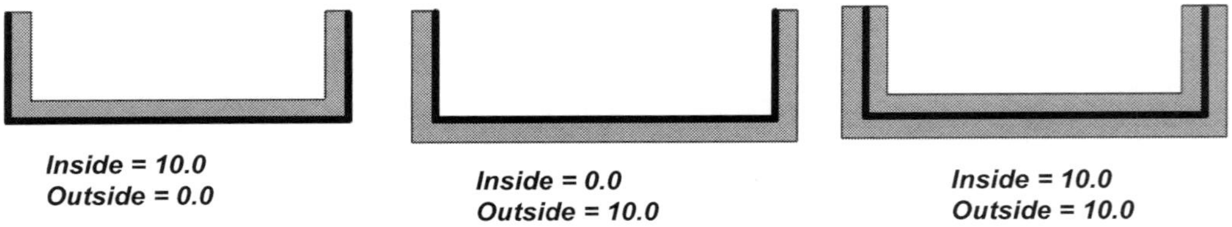

Figure 12–29

You can select additional surfaces to specify a different wall thickness, as shown in Figure 12–30.

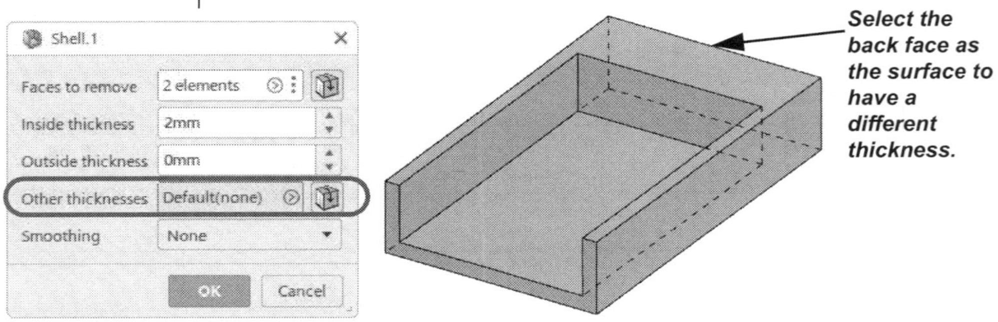

Figure 12–30

4. Click **OK** to complete the Shell feature.

12.4 Drafted Filleted Pad and Pocket Features

Drafted Filleted Pad Feature

A drafted filleted Pad enables you to quickly create a Pad feature that is drafted and has three different sized edge Fillets, as shown in Figure 12–31.

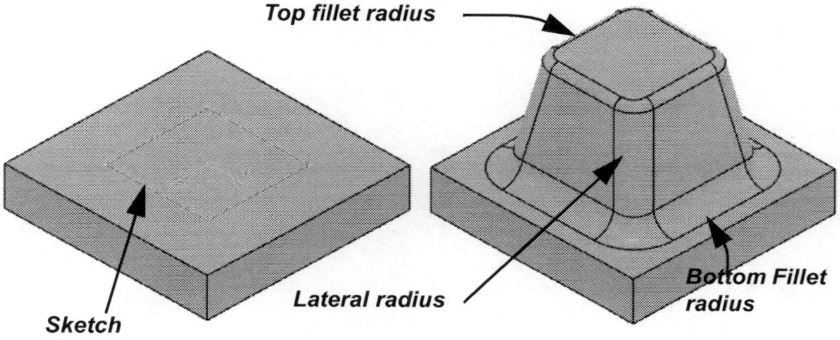

Figure 12–31

- Click (Drafted Filleted Pad) from the toolbar and select the sketch to be used for the Pad feature. The Drafted Filleted Pad Definition dialog box opens, as shown in Figure 12–32.

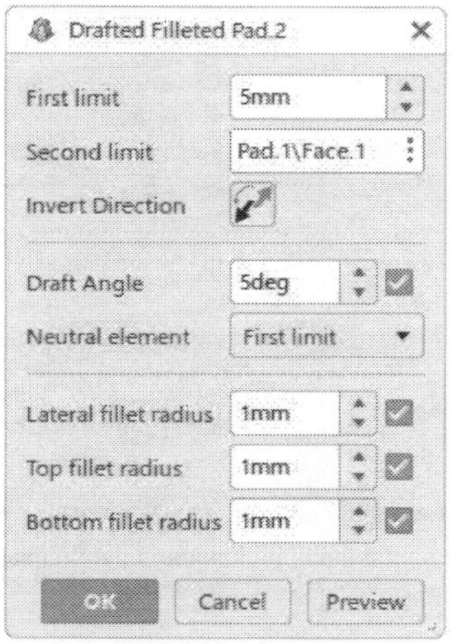

Figure 12–32

Note the options for the Draft and the three Radius features. Clearing these options eliminates them from the feature. You can create a drafted filleted Pad feature without a second limit radius.

Creating a drafted filleted Pad feature is a quick way to initially create the five features.

Once the drafted filleted Pad feature is created, all five features are listed separately in the specification tree, as shown in Figure 12–33. From this point, any changes to the features must be performed on the individual features.

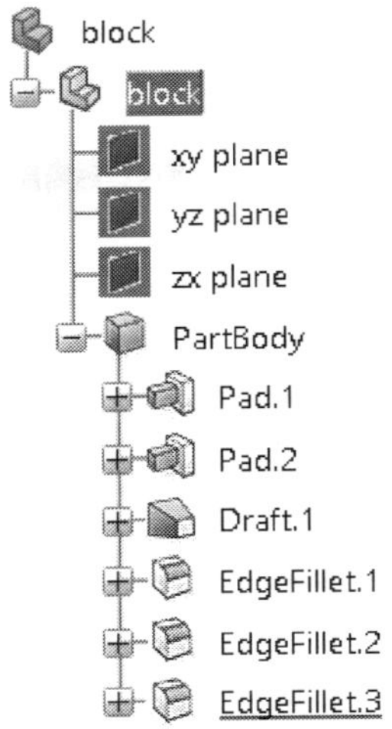

Figure 12–33

Drafted Filleted Pocket Feature

A drafted filleted Pocket is similar to the drafted filleted Pad, except that material is removed instead of being added, as shown in Figure 12–34.

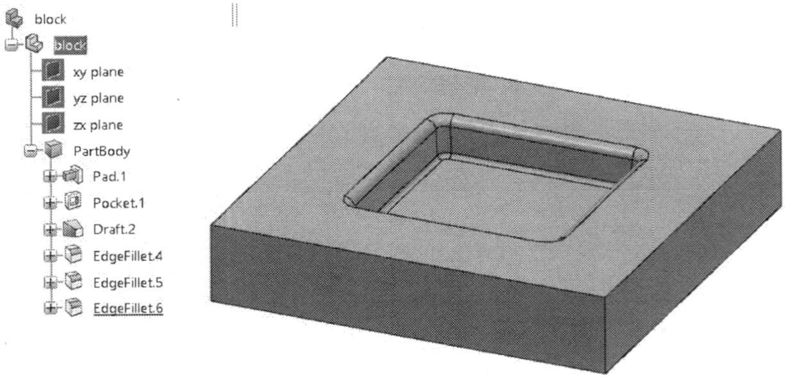

Figure 12–34

12.5 Impact of Feature Order on Geometry

CATIA is a feature-based solid modeler. The order in which the features are created is important and can have a dramatic impact on the resulting geometry. Figure 12–35 shows an example of a model that consists of two Pad features and a Shell feature. Note the order of feature creation in the specification tree.

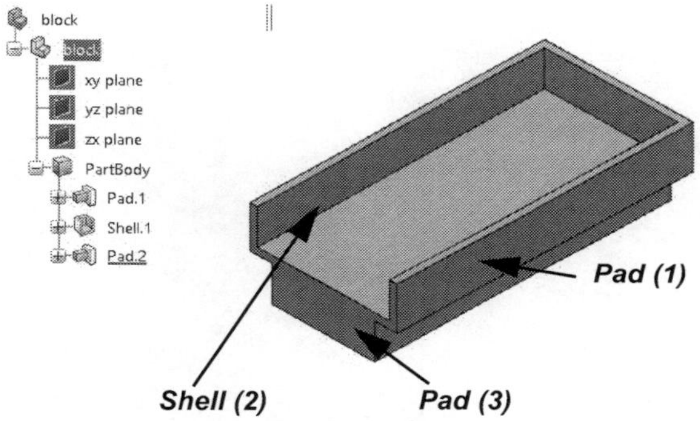

Figure 12–35

Figure 12–36 shows the same three features in a different order, as shown in the specification tree.

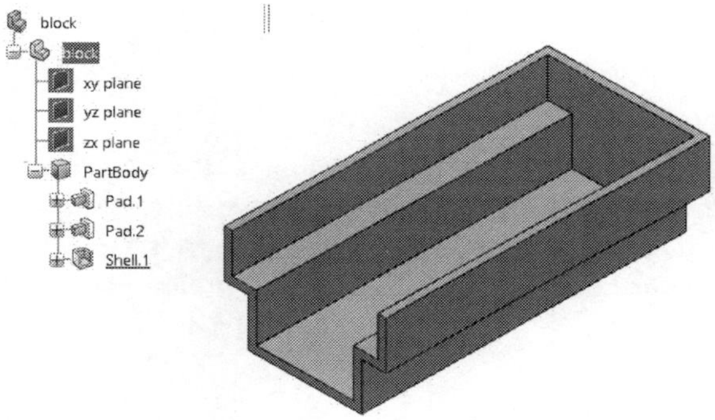

Figure 12–36

Feature Reorder

An advantage of feature-based solid modeling is that features can be easily reordered to change their sequence in the model. This saves time since you do not have to delete several features and recreate them in a new sequence.

How To: Reorder a Feature

1. Select the feature to be reordered in the specification tree. Right-click and select **Shell.# object>Reorder**, as shown in Figure 12–37.

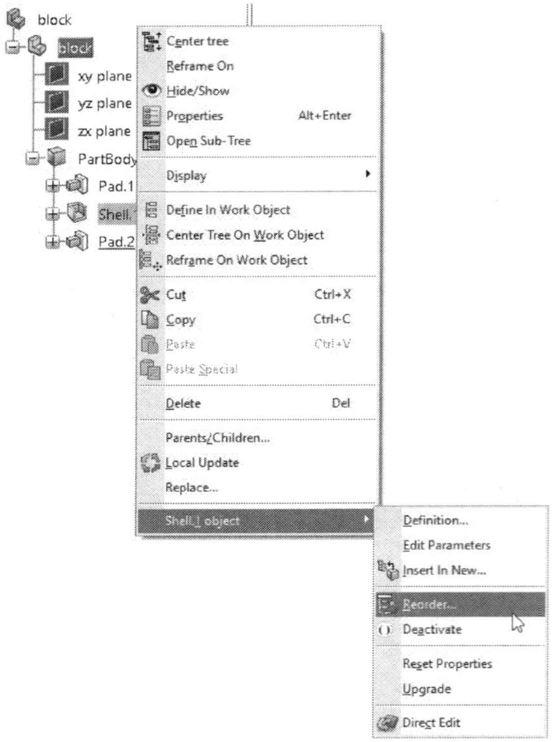

Figure 12–37

*When **Inside** is selected, the feature is positioned at the bottom of the selected body or geometrical set.*

2. Specify the new location of the feature. You can reorder a feature **Before** the selected feature, **After** the selected feature, or **Inside** a body or geometrical set, by selecting the appropriate option in the Reorder drop-down list, as shown in Figure 12–38.

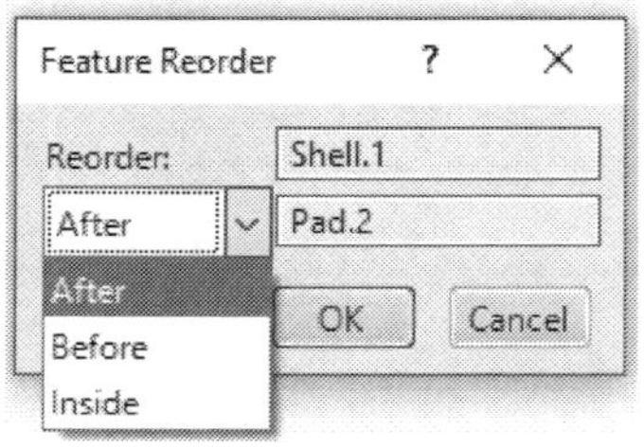

Figure 12–38

3. Click **OK** to complete feature reorder.

Define in Work Object

By default, when features are added to a model, they are added at the end of the feature list. The **Define in Work Object** option is used to insert new features between existing features. To access this option, select the feature in the specification tree, right-click and select **Define In Work Object**.

Figure 12–39 shows an example model that consists of a Pad feature and a Hole feature.

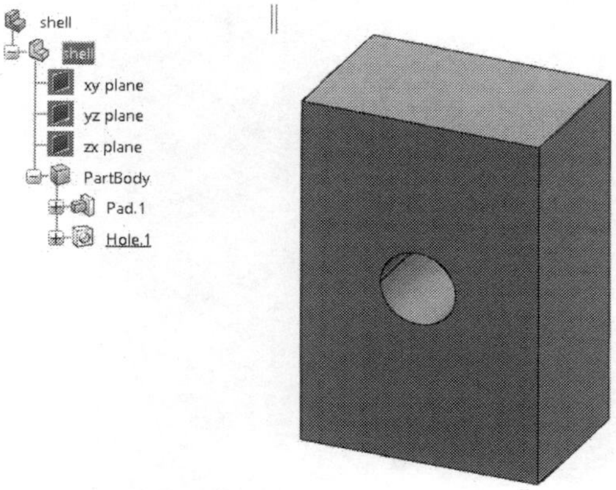

Figure 12–39

A Shell feature added to the model would be placed as the last feature in the specification tree and it would include the surface of the Hole. To insert the Shell before the Hole (or after the Pad), select **Pad.1**, right-click and select **Define In Work Object**. The **Hole.1** feature is removed from display, as shown in Figure 12–40. **Pad.1** is underlined, indicating that it is the work object.

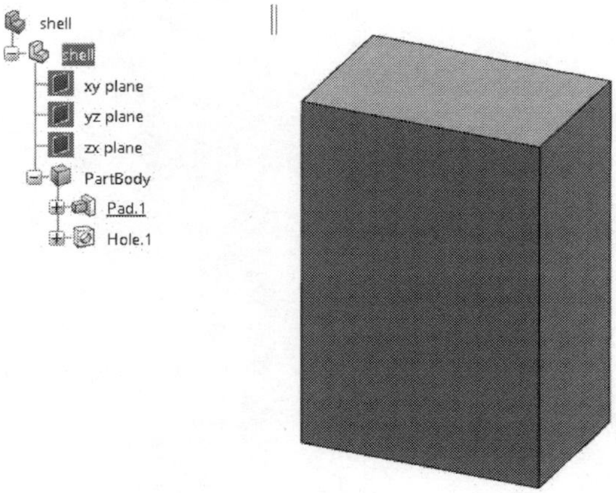

Figure 12–40

New features are added between the Pad and Hole features, as shown in Figure 12–41. To restore all features, select **PartBody**, right-click and select **Define In Work Object**, as shown in Figure 12–42.

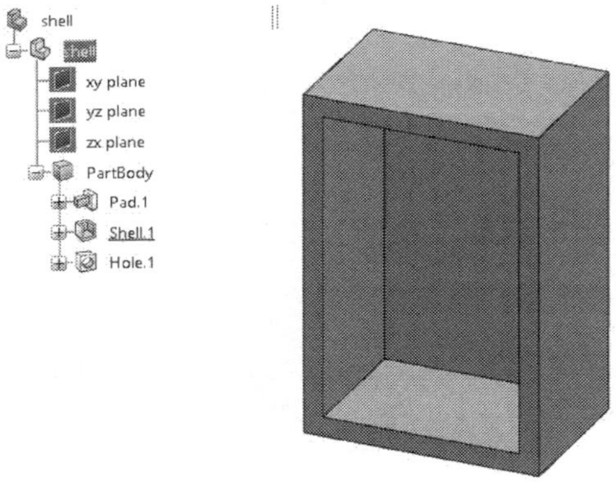

Figure 12–41

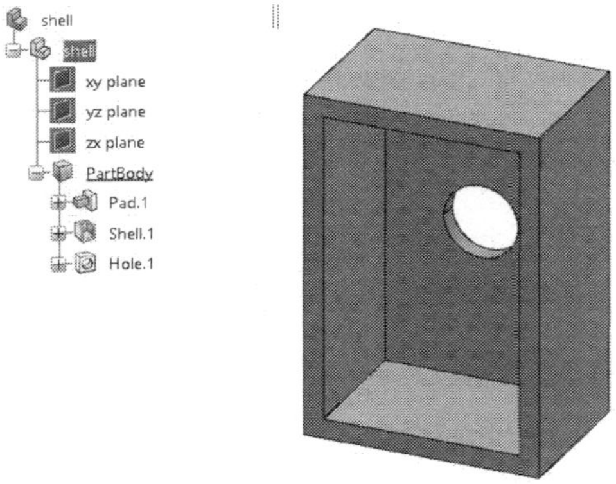

Figure 12–42

Restrictions

If one feature references another, a parent/child relationship is established between the two features. This means one feature is dependent on the other for an aspect of its definition and the software does not enable you to reorder the child feature before the parent feature. Figure 12–43 shows an example where the elongated Hole feature is dimensioned to the circular Hole feature.

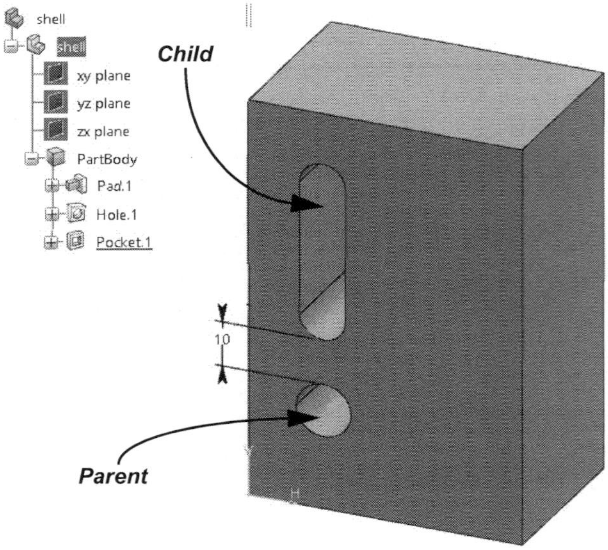

Figure 12–43

Practice 12a

Creating Additional Dress Up Features

Practice Objectives

- Create a Tritangent and Variable Fillet.
- Create a Draft and a Drafted Filleted Pad.
- Create a Shell.

In this practice, you will create the part shown in Figure 12–44. Since many features are used to create the part, you will use the **Reorder** function to rearrange the features to achieve the final design. When using the Shell feature, the creation order of features is important. Remember that incorrect ordering of features that are to be shelled can cause the creation of undesirable geometry.

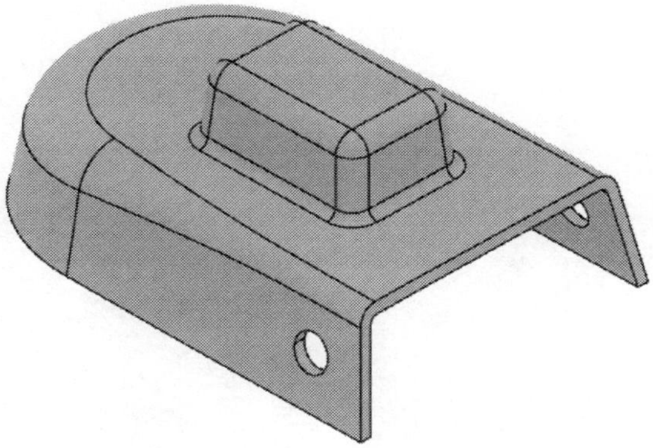

Figure 12–44

Task 1 - Create the base feature.

1. In the Top Bar, click (Add)>**3D Part**.
2. In the 3D Part dialog box, enter ***Your_Initials*_Cover** as the *Title.*
3. Select the *3D Shape* tab and enter **Cover** as the *Title.*
4. Select the *Characteristics* tab and ensure **Enable hybrid design is disabled**.
5. Click **OK**.

6. Create a sketch on the XY plane with the dimensions **75 (2.953 in)** and **120 (4.724 in)**, and constraints shown in Figure 12–45. Note the symmetry constraint.

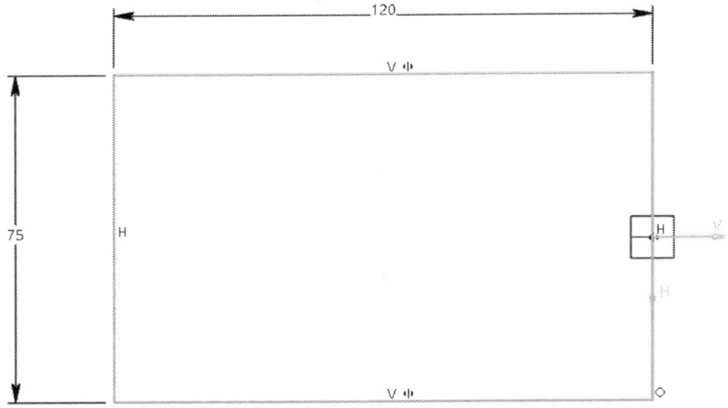

Figure 12–45

7. Create a Pad feature with a *length* of **30.0 (1.181 in)**, as shown in Figure 12–46.

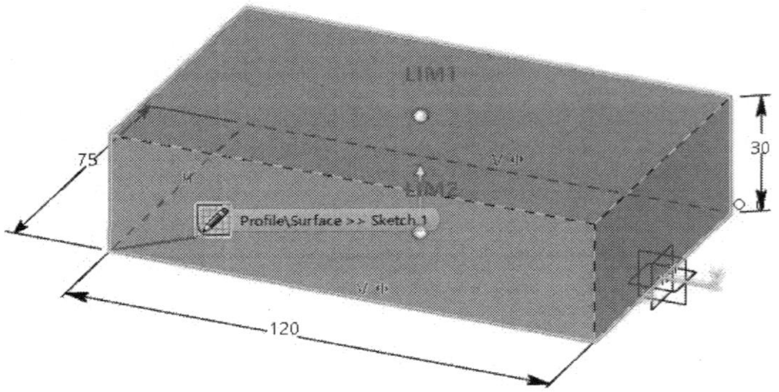

Figure 12–46

Task 2 - Create a sketch for use with a drafted filleted Pad feature.

1. In the specification tree, press and hold <Ctrl>, select the three default reference planes, right-click and select **Hide/Show**.

2. Create a positioned sketch using the following parameters:

   - *Sketch Positioning Reference:* Top face of the part
   - *Origin Type:* **Middle point**

- *Origin Reference:* Top, right edge of the part

The model displays as shown in Figure 12–47.

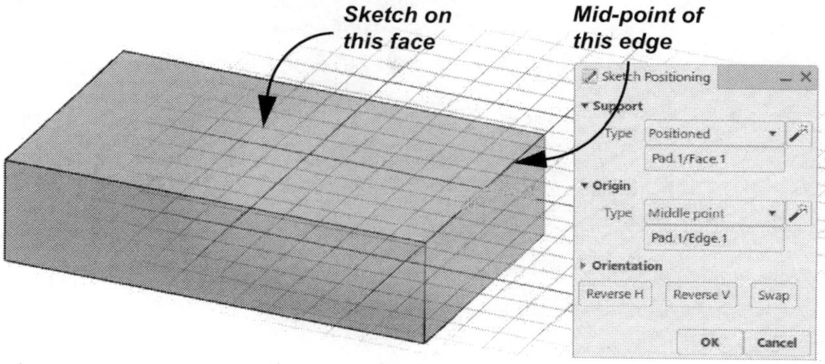

Figure 12–47

3. Sketch a rectangle approximately in the center of the top face.

Since the YZ plane is hidden, select it in the specification tree.

4. Add a symmetry constraint to center the rectangle about the YZ plane.
5. Create the dimensions shown in Figure 12–48.
   - 25 (0.984 in)
   - 30 (1.181 in)
   - 45 (1.772 in)

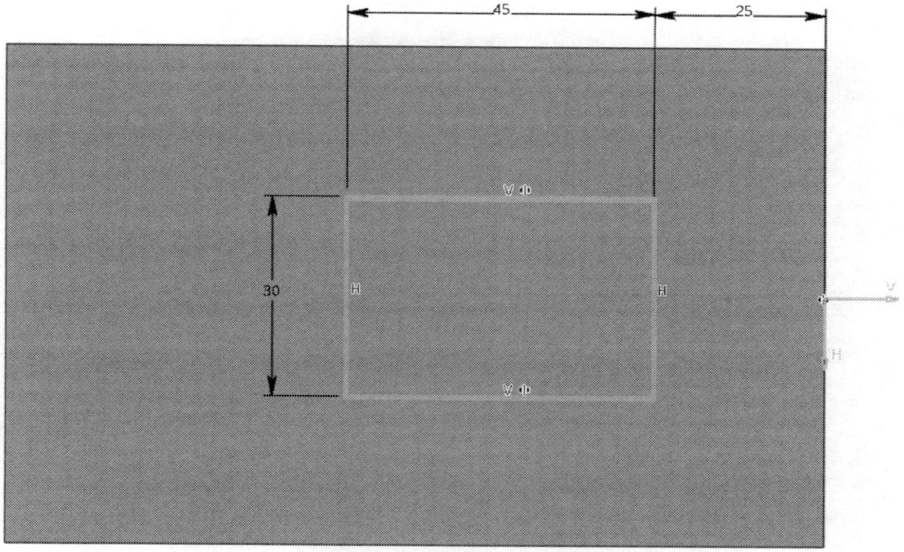

Figure 12–48

6. Exit the Sketch app.

7. With the sketch still highlighted, click  (Drafted Filleted Pad) in the *Model* section of the Action Pad. The Drafted Filleted Pad Definition dialog box opens.

8. Enter **20.0 (0.787 in)** for the *length*.

9. Select the *top face* of the part as the second limit.

10. Enter the values shown in Figure 12–49.

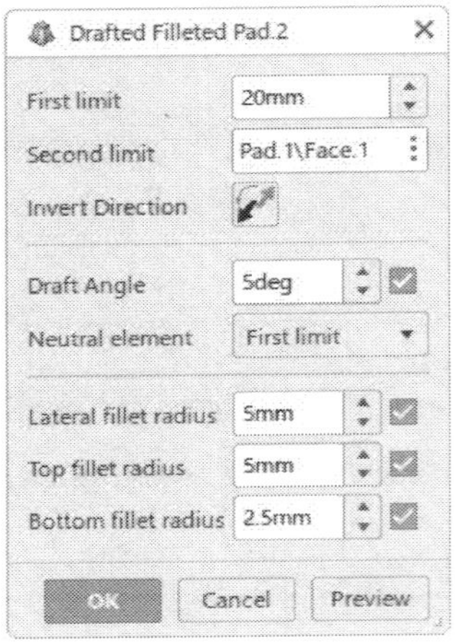

Figure 12–49

11. Click **OK** to complete the feature. The model displays as shown in Figure 12–50.

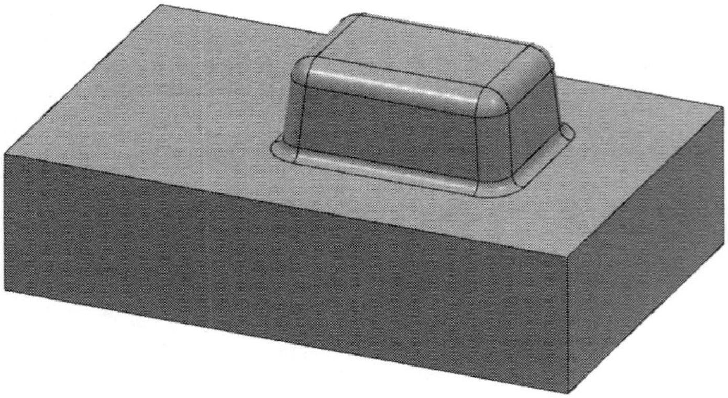

Figure 12–50

Task 3 - Create a Tritangent Fillet feature.

1. In the *Refine* section of the Action Bar, click  (Tritangent Fillet) to create a Tritangent Fillet. The Tritangent Fillet Definition dialog box opens as shown in Figure 12–51.

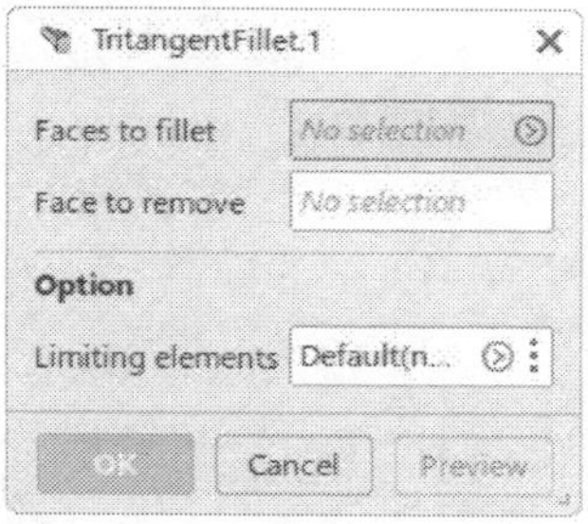

Figure 12–51

2. Make the following selections shown in Figure 12–52:

   - *Faces to fillet:* Select the two long faces of the bottom pad
   - *Face to remove:* Select the face of the bottom pad furthest from the top pad

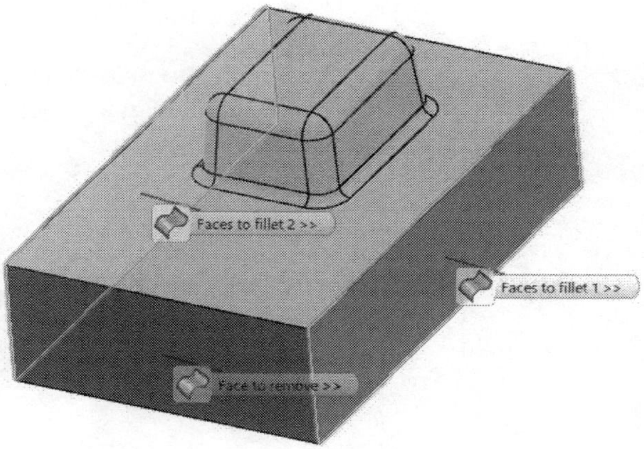

Figure 12–52

3. Click **OK** to complete the feature.

Task 4 - Create a Hole feature.

Design Considerations

The following Hole feature demonstrates the importance of feature order. You will draft the vertical faces of the part. If the Hole is created after the Draft feature, the Hole will be perpendicular to the drafted surface. To maintain the design intent of the part, you create the Hole before the Draft so that it is extruded perpendicular to the vertical face.

1. Create a Hole feature in the location shown in Figure 12–53 by preselecting the appropriate face and edges.

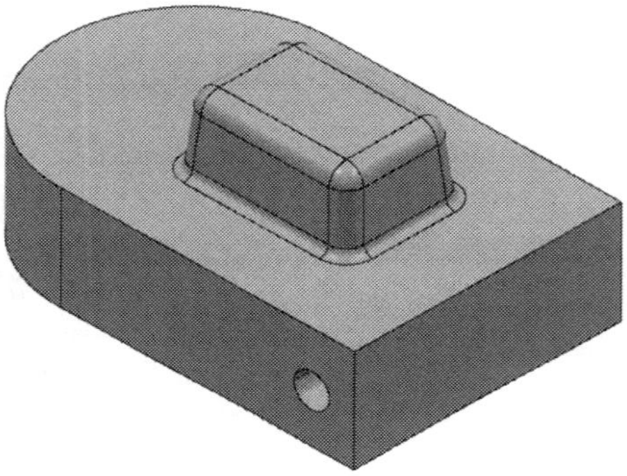

Figure 12–53

2. Modify the hole dimensions to **12 (0.472 in)** and **16 (0.630 in)**, as shown in Figure 12–54.

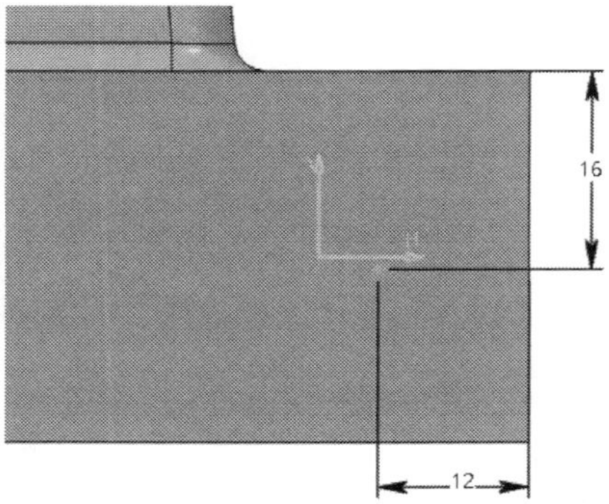

Figure 12–54

3. Set the following:

   - *Depth option:* **Up To Last**
   - *Main Diameter value*: **10.00 (0.394 in)**

Task 5 - Create a Draft feature.

1. In the *Essentials* section of the Action Bar, click (Draft). The Draft Definition dialog box opens.
2. Select the two surfaces shown in Figure 12–55. The draft surfaces turn maroon as a visual indicator.

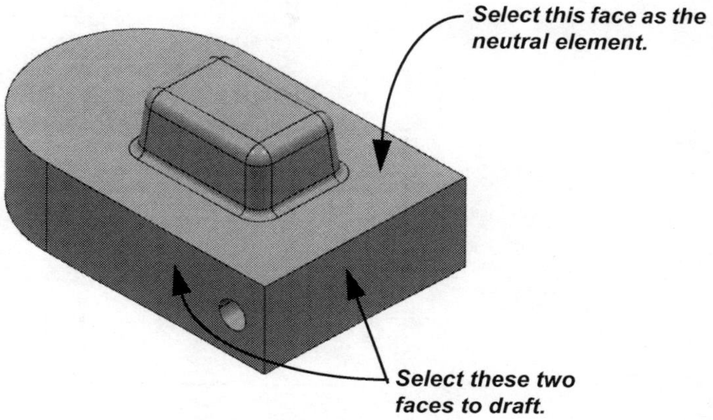

Figure 12–55

3. Click the selection box in the *Neutral Element* area and select the top face as the neutral element.The Draft Definition dialog box opens as shown in Figure 12–56.

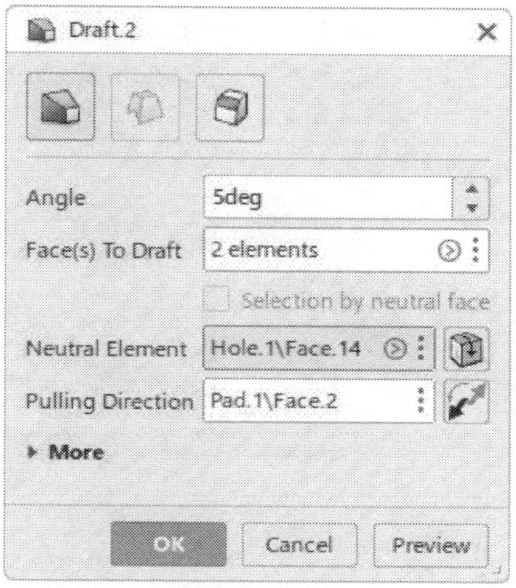

Figure 12–56

4. Ensure the pulling direction arrow faces up, as shown in Figure 12–57. Click the arrow head to flip it, if necessary.

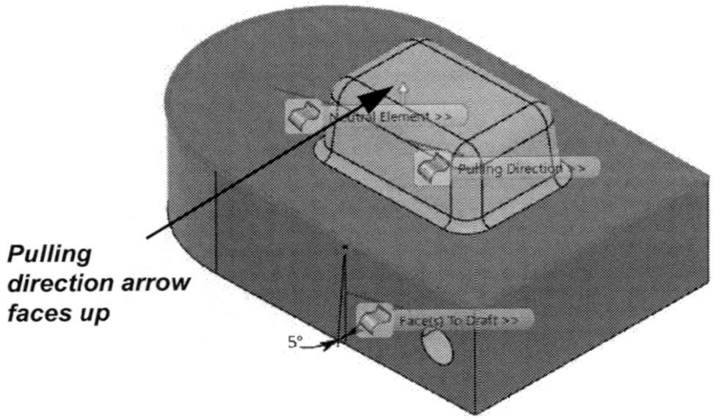

Figure 12–57

5. Enter **10** in the *Angle* field.

6. Click **OK** to complete the feature.

Task 6 - Create a point to mark the middle of the arc at the top of the part.

Design Considerations

This point will be positioned at the center of the arc on the part. It will be used to define a radius in a Variable Radius Fillet feature that you create in this task.

1. In the *Essentials* section of the Action Bar, click (Point) and select **On Curve** as the *point type*.

2. Select the arc edge as the curve reference and click (Middle point) to locate the point at the midpoint of the arc, as shown in Figure 12–58.

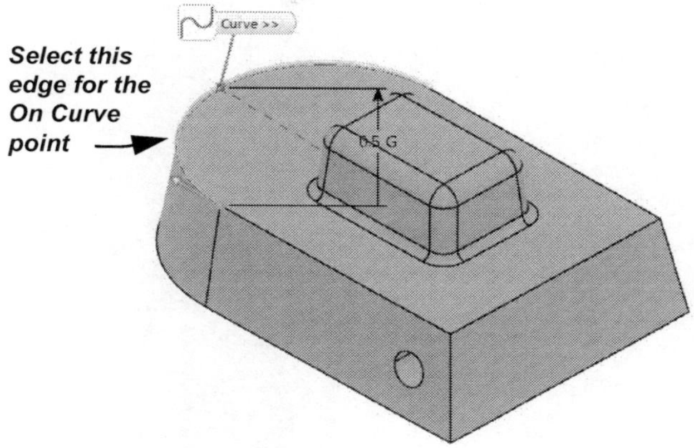

Figure 12–58

Task 7 - Create the variable Radius Fillet feature.

1. Click (Edge Fillet) to open the Edge Fillet Definition dialog box, then click (Variable) to create a variable radius fillet.
2. Select the edge as shown in Figure 12–59.

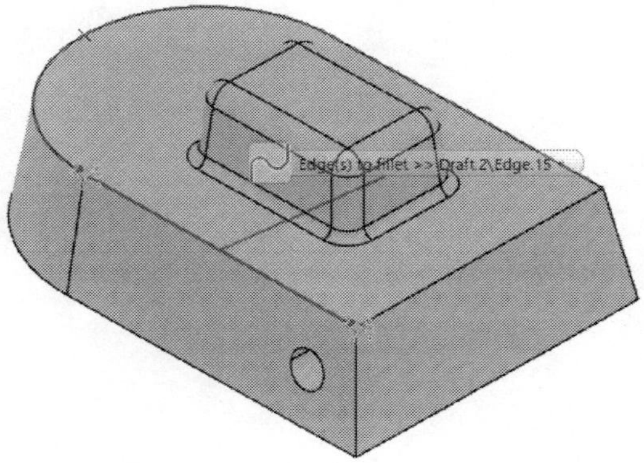

Figure 12–59

3. Enter **5.0 (0.197 in)** for the *radius*.

Small points display at each vertex along the chain of edges. Note the number of vertices listed in the Points field in the Variable Edge Fillet Definition dialog box.

4. Select the *Points* field to activate it and select the point you previously created, to add it to the location in which you are specifying a radius value.

5. Enter **15.0 (0.591 in)** for the *radius* (double-click on the 5.0 (0.197 in) value at the point). The Parameter Definition dialog box opens for you to enter a new value, as shown in Figure 12–60.

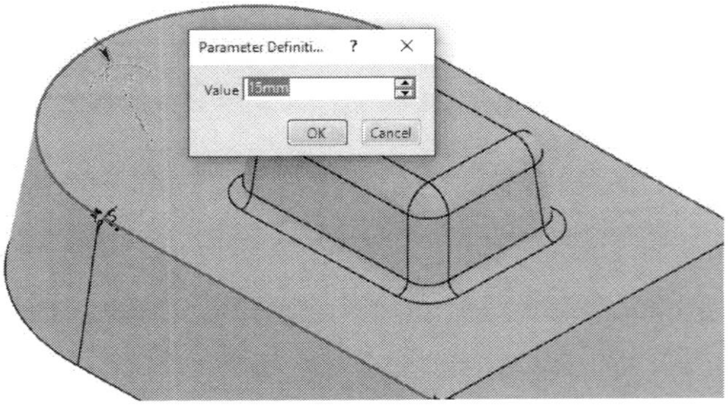

Figure 12–60

6. Click on the indicated vertices to add the back corner vertex as a point location and remove the front vertex as shown in Figure 12–61.

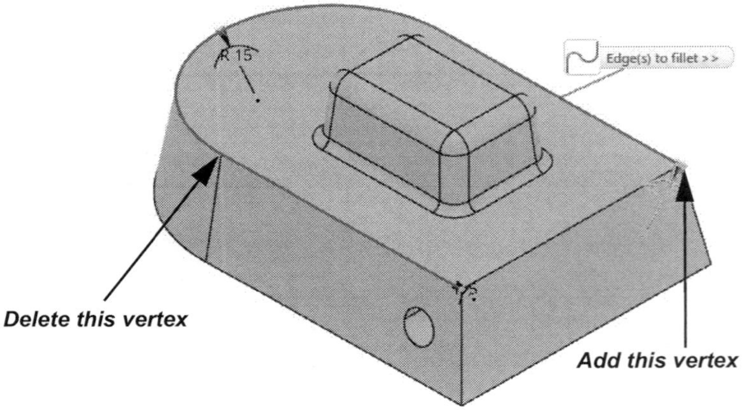

Figure 12–61

7. Double-click the dimension for the new vertex and edit it to **5.0 (0.197 in)**.

8. Click **Preview** to verify that the geometry is created in the required manner.
9. Click **OK** to complete the feature.
10. Hide the Point feature from display. The part displays as shown in Figure 12–62.

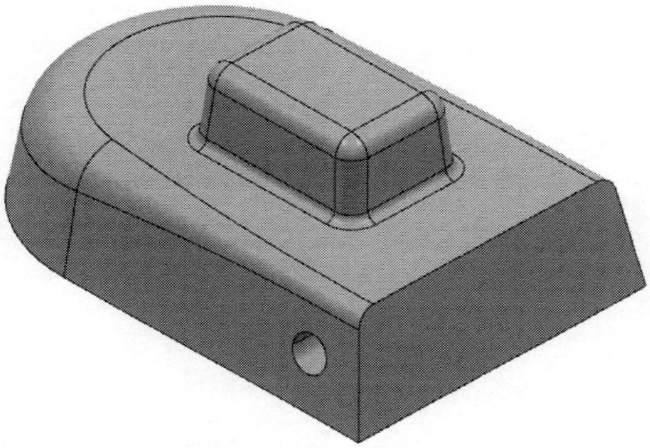

Figure 12–62

Task 8 - Create a Shell feature to hollow out the model.

1. Click  (Shell) to add a Shell feature.
2. Select the two surfaces shown in Figure 12–63.

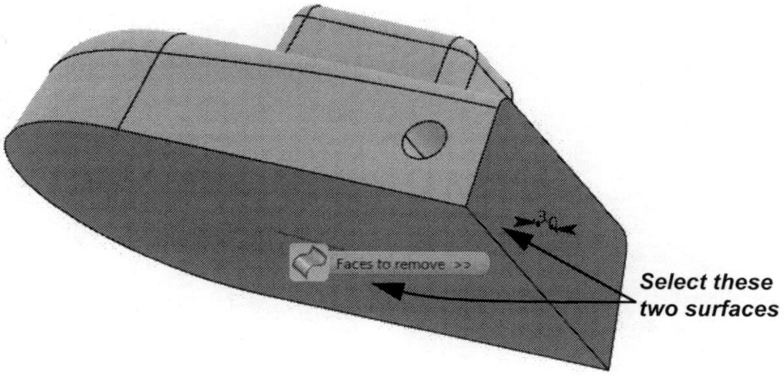

Figure 12–63

3. Enter **3.0 (0.118 in)** for the *inside thickness*.

4. Click **OK** to complete the feature. The feature hollows out around the hole, as shown in Figure 12–64.

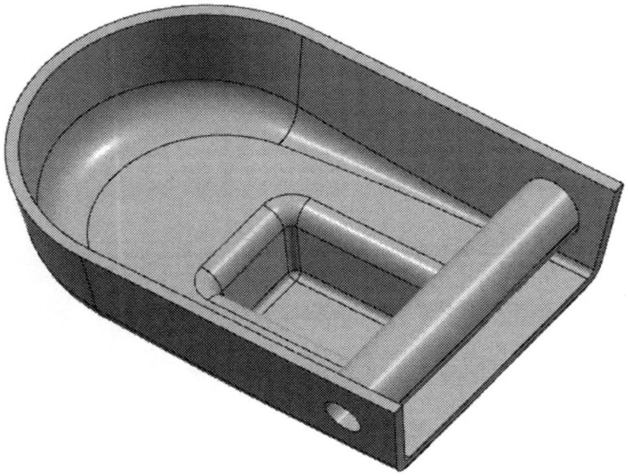

Figure 12–64

Task 9 - Reorder the Hole feature after the Shell feature.

Design Considerations

In the previous task, the Shell feature removed material around the hole, leaving a column of material. This geometry is not required in the final part. Reordering the Hole feature after the Shell feature eliminates this problem. Now that there are no features intersecting the part, the shell removes all the inside material. The hole then removes material from only the two side walls.

1. Right-click on the Hole feature in the specification tree and select **Hole.1 object>Reorder**.
2. By default, the Hole feature will be located **After** the selected feature. Leave this as the default option.
3. In the specification tree, select **Shell.1** and click **OK** in the Feature Reorder dialog box.

4. The Hole feature might not currently be the active object (indicated by an underline in the specification tree), so the model may not appear complete. Right-click on the PartBody in the specification tree and select **Define In Work Object**. The model displays as shown in Figure 12–65.

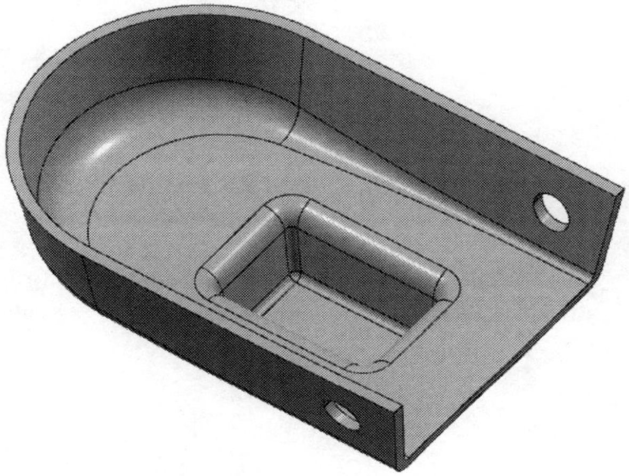

Figure 12–65

5. Save the file and close the tab.

Practice 12b Phone Cover

Practice Objectives

- Create a Draft with a non-planar neutral element.
- Create a Fillet.

In this practice, you will create Draft features in a mold-injected telephone cover so that it can be easily removed from its manufacturing die, as shown in Figure 12–66. To preserve the required profile for the top of the phone cover, a non-planar neutral element must be used for one of the Draft features. When a non-planar neutral element is used, a pulling direction should be specified, as the default might no longer fulfill your design intent. Remember that the direction of pull is perpendicular to the pulling direction plane.

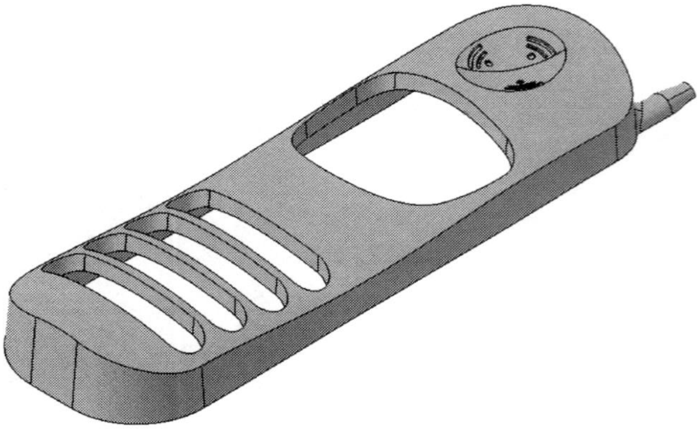

Figure 12–66

Design Considerations

This plastic part will be manufactured using injection molding. For the part to be easily separated from the manufacturing die, some of its faces must be drafted. Consider which faces should be drafted to optimize the manufacturing time of the part.

Task 1 - Create a draft on the exterior surfaces.

1. Import **PhoneCover.3dxml**.
2. In the *Part2 (Explore)* tab, right-click **Part2** in the specification tree and select **Open**.
3. Click  (Draft).
4. Enter **8deg** for the *draft angle*.

5. Select the face shown in Figure 12–67 as the face to draft.

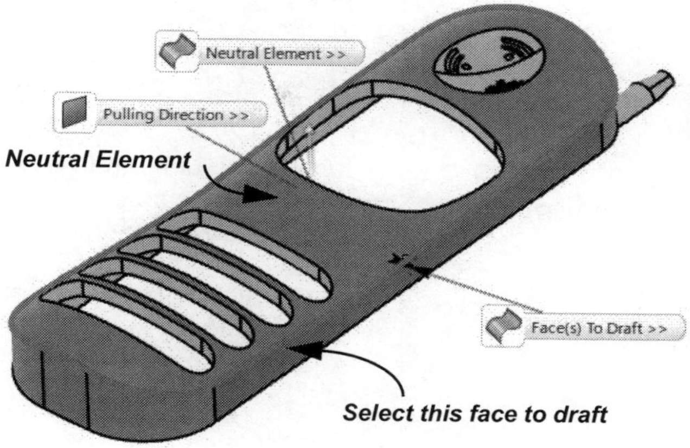

Figure 12–67

Design Considerations

The Draft Angle feature uses tangency propagation to automatically select tangent faces and reduce the amount of time consumed by selecting individual faces to draft.

6. Select the top face of the phone cover as the Neutral Element, as shown in Figure 12–67.

7. Select the XY plane as the pulling direction if not selected by default.

8. Verify that the direction of the arrow defining the pulling direction will enable the part to be removed from the die.

   The Draft Definition dialog box displays as shown in Figure 12–68.

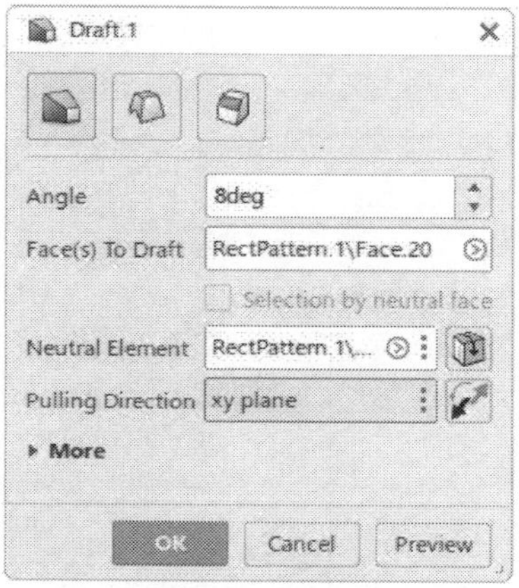

Figure 12–68

9. Click **OK** to complete the feature.

10. Rename the newly created draft feature as **Exterior**.

Task 2 - Create a draft on the interior surface.

Design Considerations

To maintain uniform thickness of the phone cover wall, the interior body surface must be drafted at the same angle as the exterior body surface.

1. Rotate the part to reveal the interior body surface, as shown in Figure 12–69.

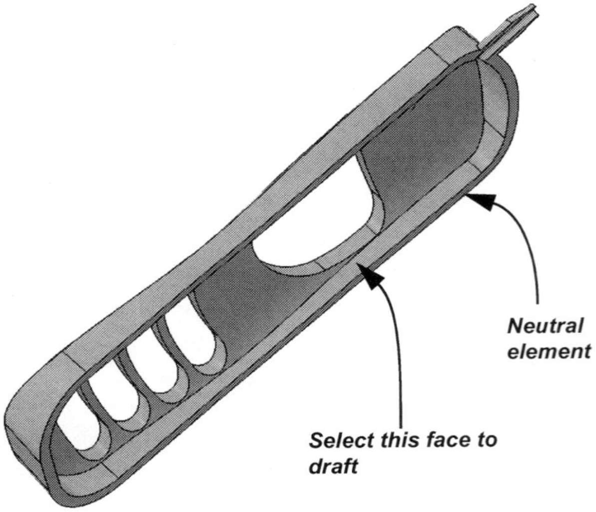

Figure 12–69

2. Click  (Draft).

3. Enter **8deg** as the *draft angle*.

4. Select the interior side surface as the face to draft, as shown in Figure 12–69.

5. Select the flat bottom face of the phone cover as the Neutral Element.

6. Select the XY plane as the pulling direction if not selected automatically, and click the arrow head to change the direction so that it points toward the bottom of the phone.

7. Click **OK** to complete the feature.

8. Rename the newly created Draft feature as **Interior**.

Task 3 - Create a draft on the end of the antenna silo.

1. Click  (Draft).
2. Enter **8deg** as the *draft angle*.
3. Select the end surface of the antenna silo as the face to draft the curved surface of the **multi-sections solid** feature as the Neutral Element, as shown in Figure 12–70.

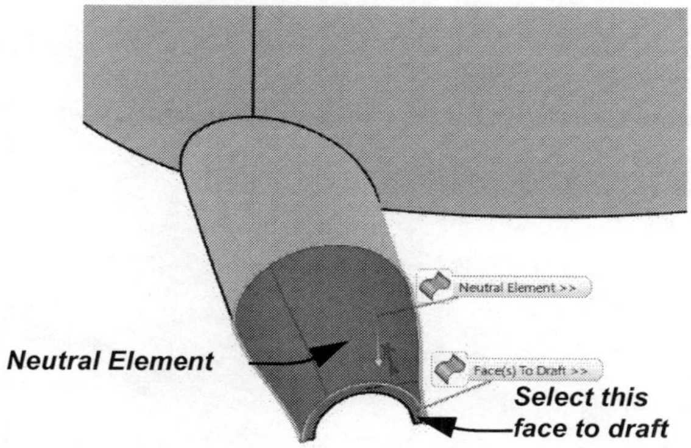

Figure 12–70

4. Select **Preview** and note the Feature Definition Error message, as shown in Figure 12–71.

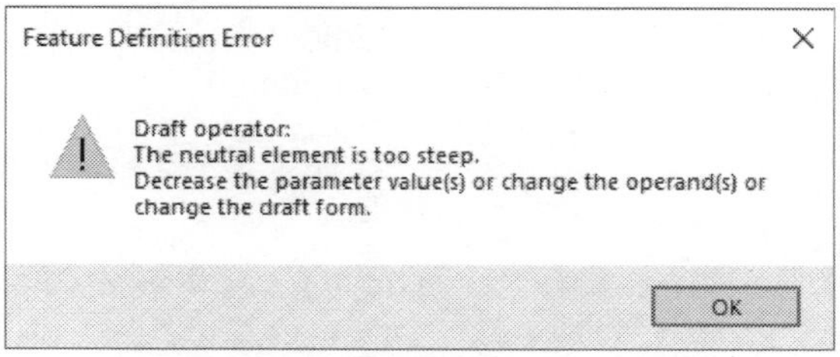

Figure 12–71

5. Click **OK**.

Design Considerations

Because the end face of the antenna silo is radial, the default conic draft form cannot be used because parts of the face will be parallel (tangent) to the pulling direction. The square draft form type must be used to create a draft on a radial surface.

6. Click **More**. In the Draft Form drop-down list, select **Square.**
7. Click **OK** to complete the feature.
8. Rename the newly created draft feature as **Antenna**.

Task 4 - Create a draft on the keypad and LCD display cutouts.

1. In the *View* section of the Action Bar, click (* iso).
2. Click (Draft).
3. Enter **4deg** as the *draft angle*.
4. Select the faces shown in Figure 12–72 as the faces to draft.

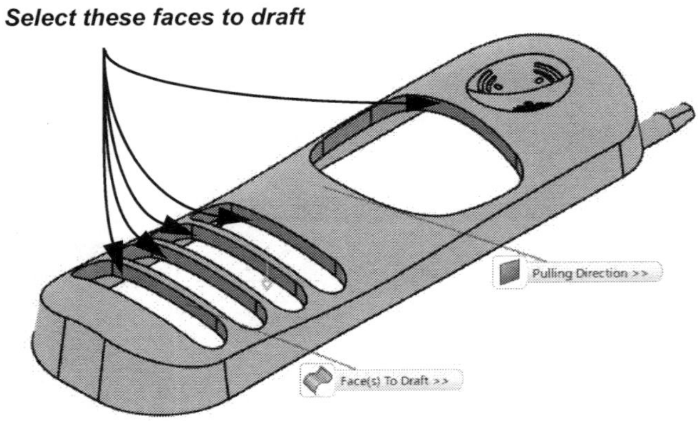

Figure 12–72

5. Select the XY plane as the pulling direction, if not selected by default.
6. Select the top face of the phone cover as the Neutral Element.
7. Click **OK** to complete the feature.
8. Rename the newly created Draft feature as **Keypad&LCD**.

Task 5 - Create a draft on the speaker holes.

1. Click (Draft).
2. Enter **10deg** as the *draft angle*.

3. Zoom in on and select the faces shown in Figure 12–73 as the faces to draft for all three instances of the speaker holes pattern.

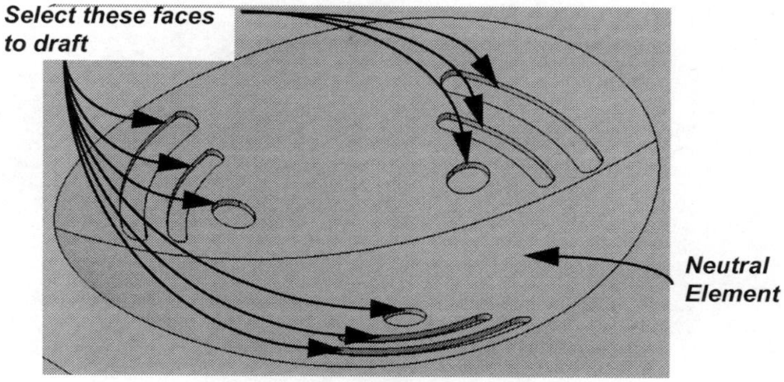

Figure 12–73

4. Select the indented speaker surface as the Neutral Element.
5. Select the XY plane as the pulling direction and ensure that the arrow is pointing above the phone. Select  (Reverse Direction) if needed to flip the arrow.
6. Click **OK** to complete the feature.
7. Rename the newly created Draft feature as **SpeakerHoles**.

Task 6 - Fillet the antenna to the exterior body surface.

Design Considerations

The Fillet feature is used to remove sharp edges and corners. With this injection-molded plastic part, leaving the corner between the antenna and cover body sharp creates a stress riser. Adding a fillet acts as a stiffener and aids in fulfillment of the design intent (in the case of a telephone, this might be the user requirement of durability).

1. Select one of the two parts of the edge joining the antenna to the exterior body surface and click  (Edge Fillet) in the context toolbar, as shown in Figure 12–74.

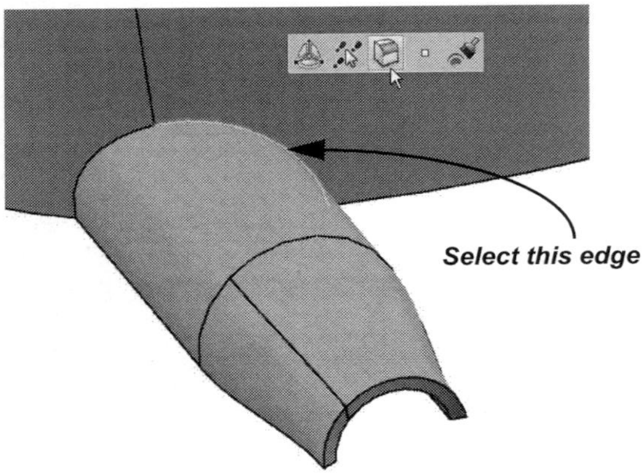

Figure 12–74

2. Enter **2.8 (0.110 in)** as the *Radius*.
3. Click **on** the screen to complete the feature.
4. Rename the feature as **Fillet-2.8mm**.
5. Save the model and close the tab.

Design Considerations

Make a habit of creating Edge Fillets as your final design features. Edge Fillets interfere with the implementation of other dress-up features, such as Chamfer and Draft Angle. Although advanced features, such as a Reflect Line Draft enables you to draft filleted geometry, they should only be used as a last resort. The increased complexity of advanced features unnecessarily increases model size and system resource consumption.

NOTE: Additional advanced dress up feature practices are found in Practice B11 and Practice B12 at the end of this guide.

Chapter Review Questions

1. The wall thickness of a Shell is always a constant thickness.
   a. True
   b. False
2. A child feature can be reordered above its parent in the specification tree.
   a. True
   b. False
3. A radius value of **0** is acceptable when creating a variable radius Fillet.
   a. True
   b. False
4. Which tool is used to create the model shown on the right side of Figure 12–75?

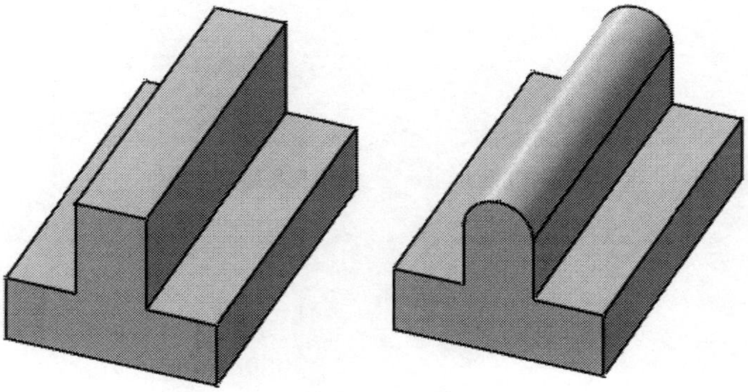

Figure 12–75

   a. Tritangent fillet
   b. Variable Radius fillet
   c. Face-Face Fillet
   d. Edge Fillet

5. Which tool is used to create a Fillet where no intersection between the surfaces to be filleted exists?
    a. Tritangent fillet
    b. Variable Radius fillet
    c. Face-Face Fillet
    d. Edge Fillet
6. Which of the following statements is true regarding the creation of a draft? (Select all that apply.)
    a. Multiple surfaces can be selected for drafting.
    b. Multiple faces can be selected when defining the pull direction.
    c. A planar surface is required as the reference for the pull direction.
7. The pull direction used to create the Draft shown in pull direction to produce the Draft shown in Figure 12–76 is _____.

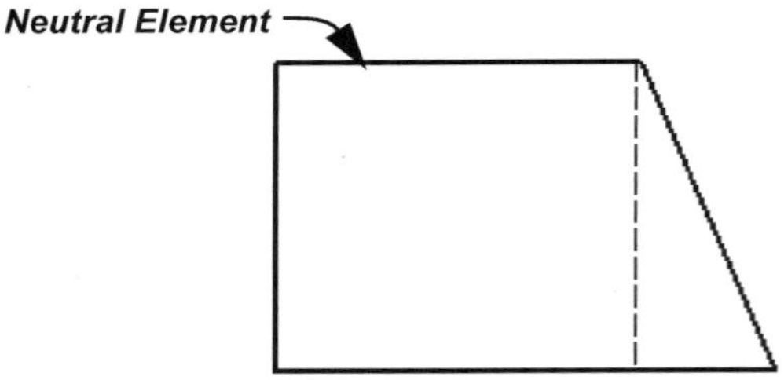

Figure 12–76

    a. Leftward
    b. Rightward
    c. Upward
    d. Downward
8. A Drafted Filleted Pad feature creates a single feature in the specification tree.
    a. True
    b. False

Answers: 1b, 2b, 3a, 4a, 5c, 6ac, 7c, 8b

Formulas and Parameters

In this chapter, you learn how to create and manipulate parameters both directly and through formulas. Using formulas enables you to control the design intent in the sketch. You can also control the design intent by assigning equivalence between entities, so that changing one dimension will change multiple entities.

You can also control design intent using formulas at the part level to ensure the model behaves as expected when changes are made.

Learning Objectives in This Chapter

- Create formulas to control design intent.
- Understand system parameter names and how to use them to create formulas.
- Learn to display formulas and parameters in the specification tree.
- Edit and delete formulas and user-defined parameters.
- Use and create various types of parameters, including user-defined parameters.
- Use formulas to control dimensional constraints in sketches, to ensure that your design intent is maintained.
- Use the Equivalent Dimension tool to establish a relationship between dimensions.

13.1 Equivalent Dimensions

The **Equivalent Dimensions** tool is another method of creating a relationship between two or more dimensions. This tool enables you to drive any number of sketcher dimensions with one base dimension. It is useful for constraining a number of identically sized geometric elements, such as the four corners of the sketch shown in Figure 13–1.

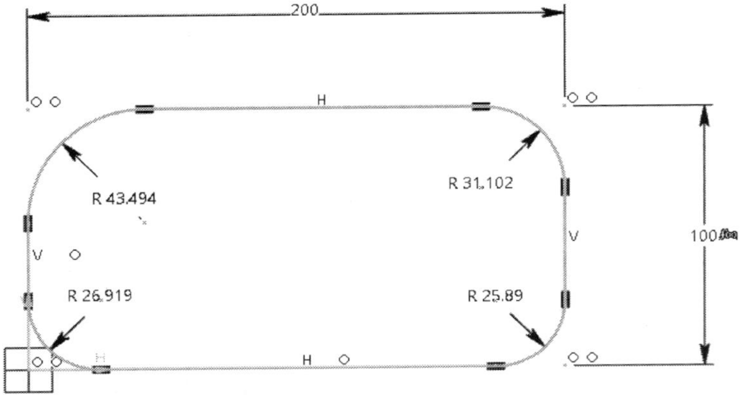

Figure 13–1

How To: Use the Equivalent Dimensions Tool

1. Click  (Equivalent Dimensions) in the *Tools* section of the Action Bar, as shown in Figure 13–2. The Equivalent Dimensions dialog box opens, as shown in Figure 13–3.

Figure 13–2

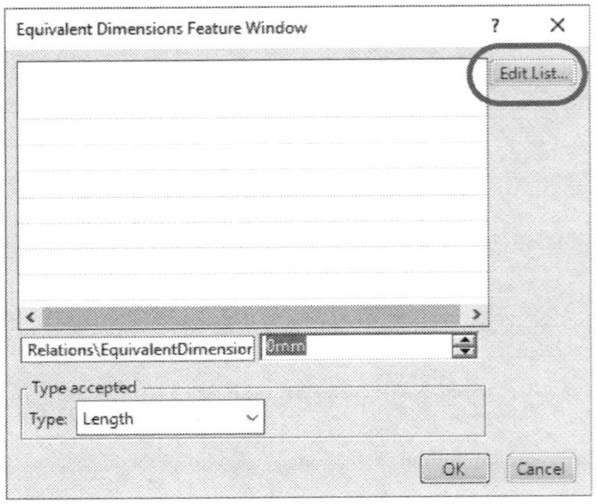

Figure 13–3

2. Click **Edit List** to add dimensions to the Equivalent Dimensions dialog box. A dialog box opens that lists all modifiable dimensions, as shown in Figure 13–4.

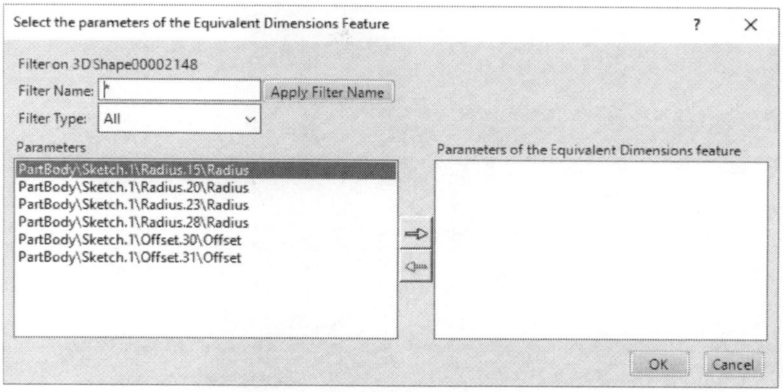

Figure 13–4

3. To add dimensions, highlight them (using <Ctrl> to multi-select) and then click  to move them to the *Parameters For Equivalent Dimensions feature* area. All radius dimensions are added, as shown in Figure 13–5.

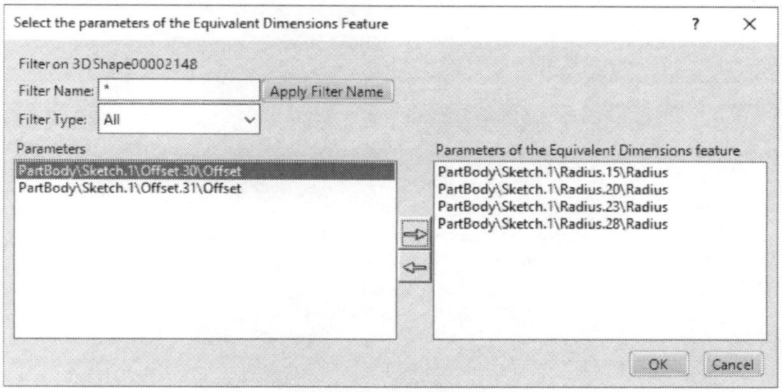

Figure 13–5

4. Click **OK** to return to the Equivalent Dimensions dialog box. Enter the equivalent dimension value in the field indicated in Figure 13–6. All dimensions are set to **10mm**.

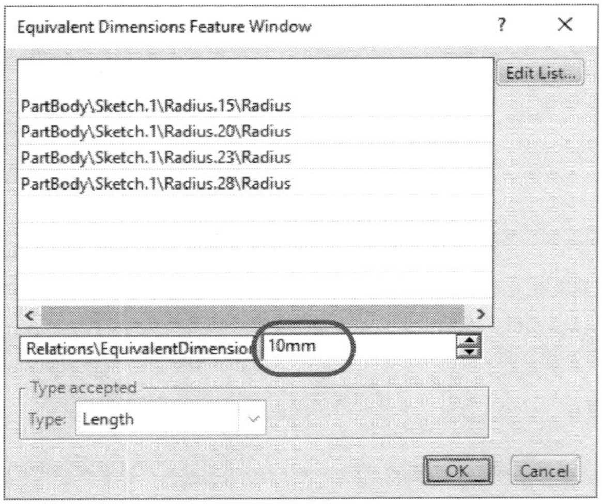

Figure 13–6

5. Once complete, click **OK** to return to Sketcher. The sketch updates with the equivalent dimensions, as shown in Figure 13–7. Note that a new branch has been added to the specification tree.

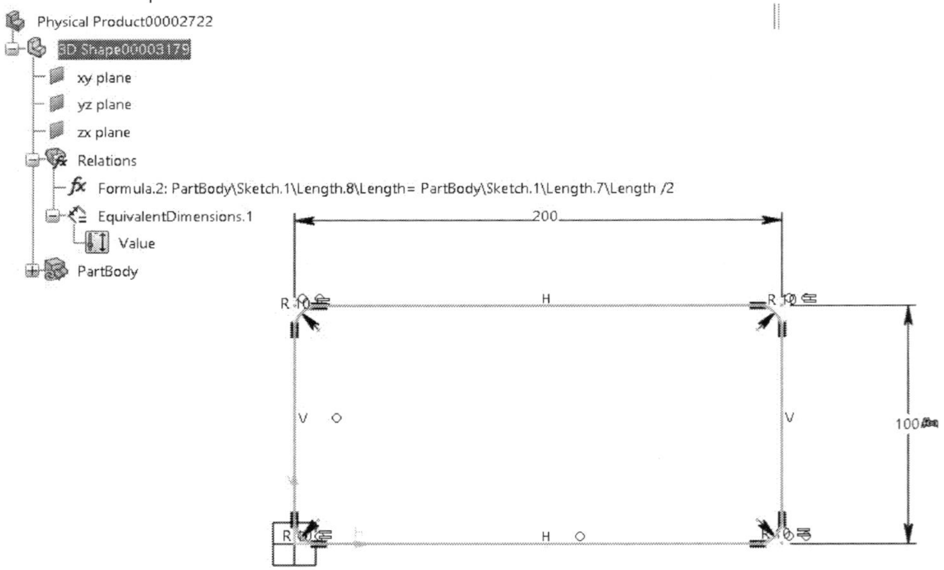

Figure 13–7

13.2 Sketch Formulas

To correctly convey the design intent, create a relationship between two or more dimensions in your sketch.

In the example shown in Figure 13–8, the design intent of the rectangular profile is that the height should always be half of the width. This can be achieved using the Formula Editor.

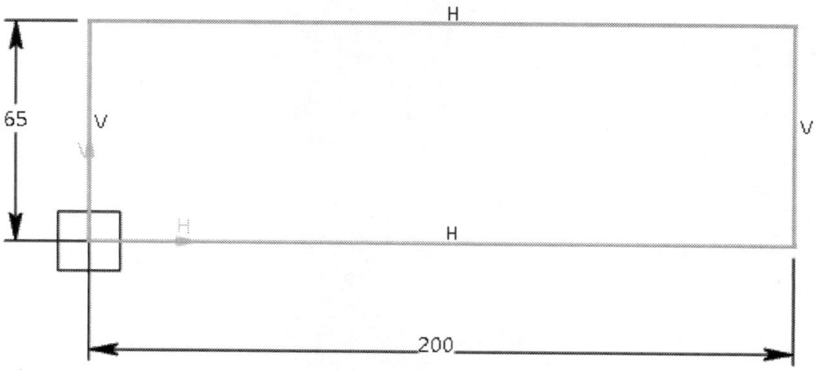

Figure 13–8

Before creating a formula, you must edit the dimension that you want to drive with the formula, called the base dimension. Drive the height of the rectangle by editing the 65mm dimension.

Select a dimension and click  (Formula) from the context toolbar, as shown in Figure 13–9.

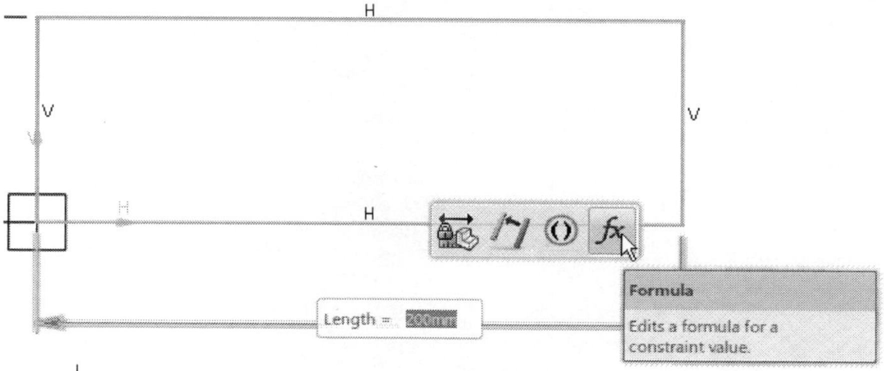

Figure 13–9

The Formula Editor dialog box opens. It lists the driven parameter in the field at the top (in this case, **PartBody\Sketch.1\Length.5\Length**) and enables you to enter the formula in the field shown in Figure 13–10.

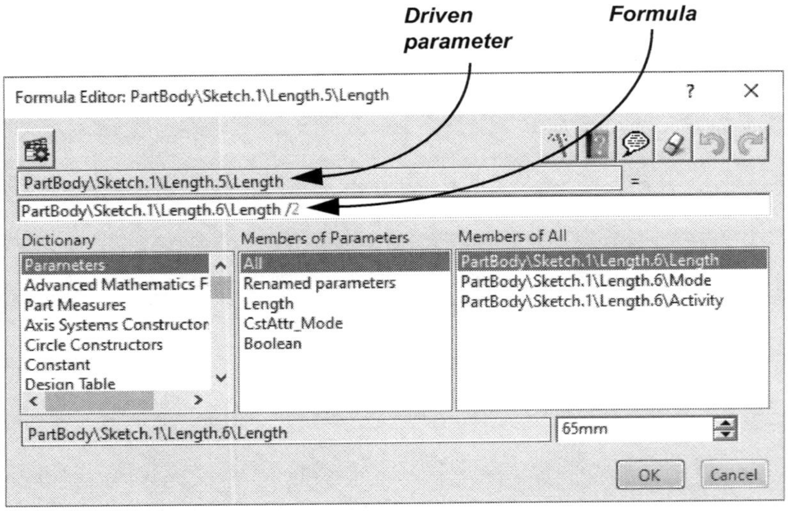

Figure 13–10

You can either type the formula directly into the dialog box or locate the driving dimension (**200mm**). By double-clicking the dimension, it is added to the formula editor. This method ensures that no syntax errors are in the formula.

In this example, the **200mm** dimension is selected and added to the dialog box, as shown in Figure 13–11. The formula shown in the previous figure would make the two dimensions equal. In this case, the design intent is Height = Width/2, so a ***/2*** is added to the end of the formula, as shown in Figure 13–12.

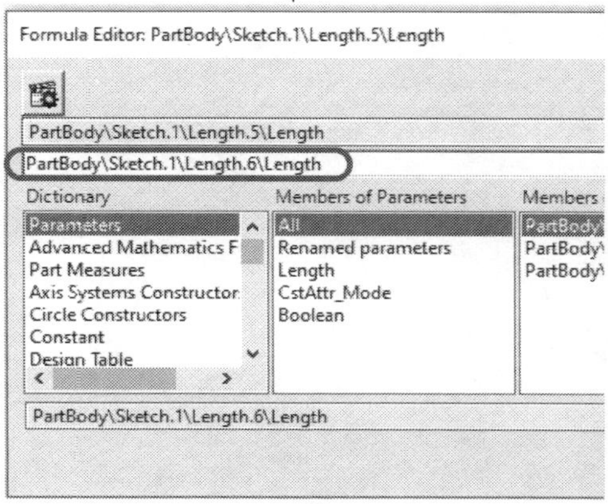

Figure 13–11

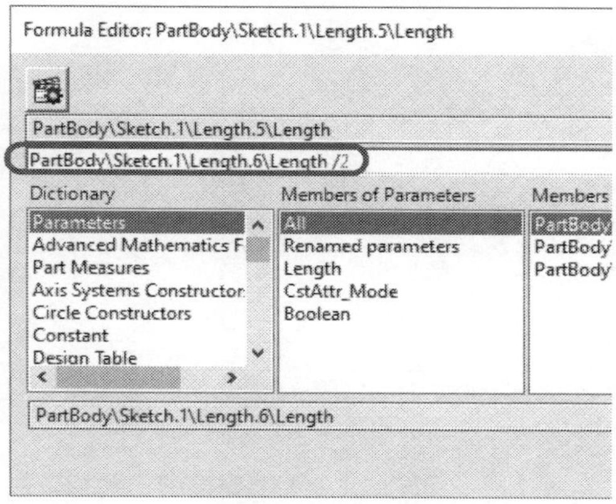

Figure 13–12

Once the formula has been entered, click **OK**.

The sketch updates automatically with the new height value of 100mm, and an icon displays next to the dimension to indicate that it is driven by a formula, as shown in Figure 13–13.

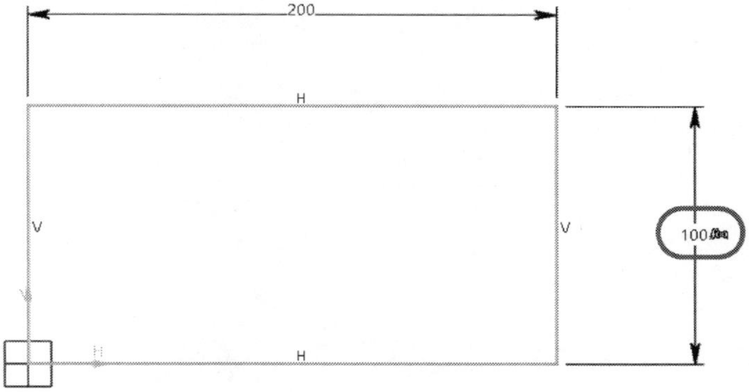

Figure 13–13

You cannot click the dimension and edit the value now that it is driven by the formula. You can select the dimension and click

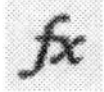 (Formula) in the context toolbar to edit the formula.

Alternatively, if you double-click the dimension, the Constraint Definition dialog box opens. The *Value* field in the Constraint Definition dialog box is grayed out, as shown in Figure 13–14, indicating it is driven by a dimension. You can use  (Formula) here to access, which can be used to edit the formula.

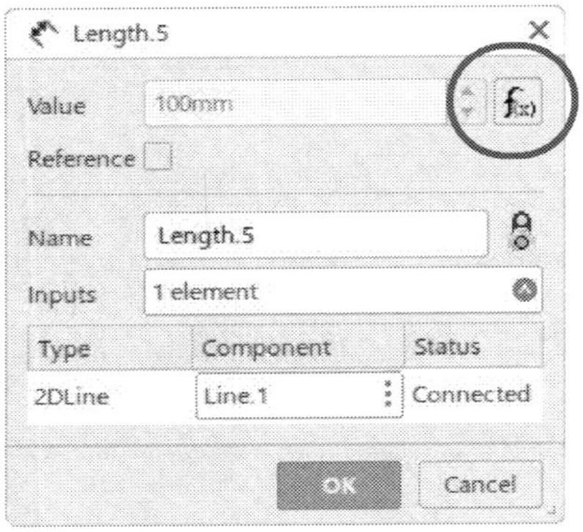

Figure 13–14

The only way to change the height of the rectangle now is to:

- Change the value of the width dimension.
- Edit the formula using  (Formula).
- Delete the formula by clearing the field in the Formula Editor dialog box.

13.3 Part Formulas

A CATIA model can consist of one or many features, known as the intrinsic properties of the model. The software creates a system-defined parameter for every intrinsic property of a model. System- and user-defined parameters can be used in a formula.

Formulas are features that define or constrain a parameter. Using formulas enables you to fully capture the design intent of the model.

Figure 13–15 shows an example of a model whose design intent is model is to ensure that the hole feature is centered on the block even if the size the block changes in the future. A formula can be defined to capture this intent.

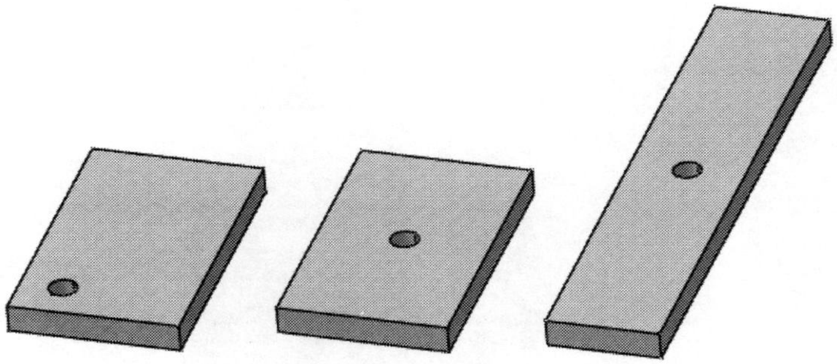

Figure 13–15

A formula is a relation that uses operators and functions to perform operations on parameters. An example of a formula is shown in Figure 13–16.

f(x) Formula.1: PartBody\Sketch.1\Length.5\Length=PartBody\Sketch.1\Length.6\Length *2

Figure 13–16

The left side of a relation is the parameter to be constrained and the right side is the statement used to control the feature.

13.4 Formulas Dialog Box

To create a formula (or function), click (Formula) in the *Tools* section of the Action Bar. The Formulas dialog box opens as shown in Figure 13–17. The Formulas dialog box enables you to perform the following actions:

- Display the list of parameters.
- Create parameters and formulas.
- Import external files.

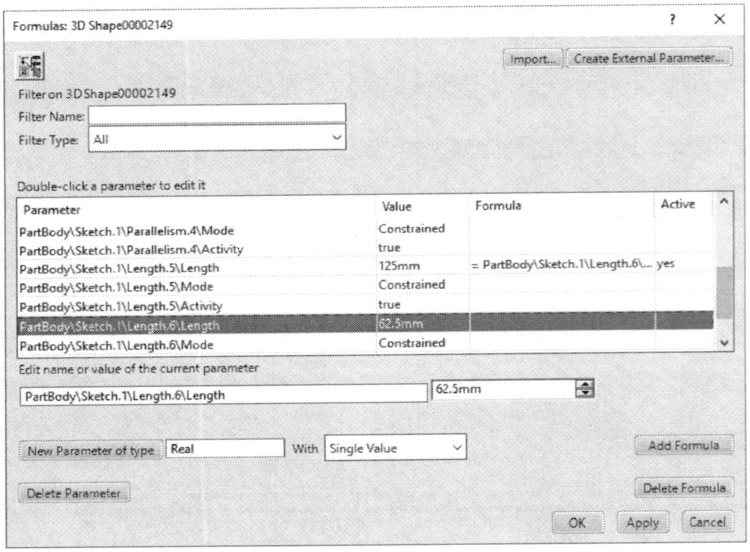

Figure 13–17

To access system or user-defined parameters, select a feature in the specification tree or from the model display and click (Formula). By default, all the parameters associated with that feature display in the *Parameter* area.

Parameter Area

The *Parameter* area lists all of the parameters associated with the selected feature, as shown in Figure 13–18. If a feature is not selected before opening the Formulas dialog box, all model parameters display by default.

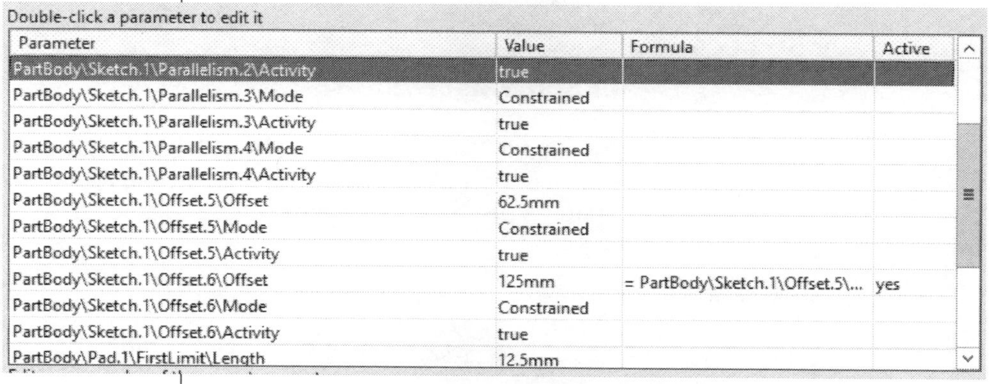

Figure 13–18

Edit Name or Value of Current Parameter

The *Edit name or value of the current parameter* box displays the selected parameter, as shown in Figure 13–19. The value box on the right side is not available if this parameter is already constrained by a formula.

Figure 13–19

Right-clicking on the value box opens a shortcut menu that enables you to redefine the parameter, as shown in Figure 13–20.

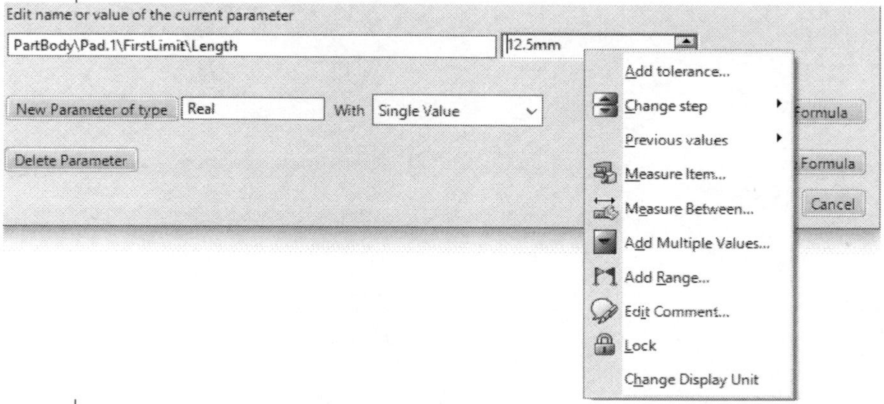

Figure 13–20

Filter Area

The *Filter* area in the Formulas dialog box enables you to narrow the parameter list using the following types of filters:

- Incremental option
- Filter Name
- Filter Type

Incremental Option

By default, (Incremental Mode) is not selected. When this option is not selected, the *Parameter* area lists the first level of features below the selected feature, as shown in Figure 13–21.

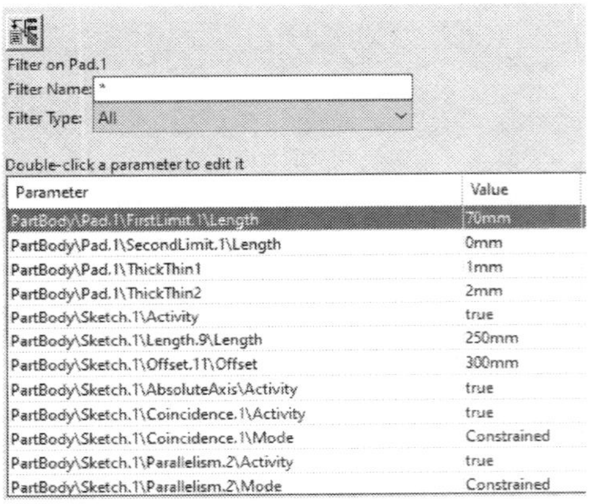

Figure 13–21

If you click (Incremental Mode), the *Parameter* area only lists one feature below the selected feature, as shown in Figure 13–22.

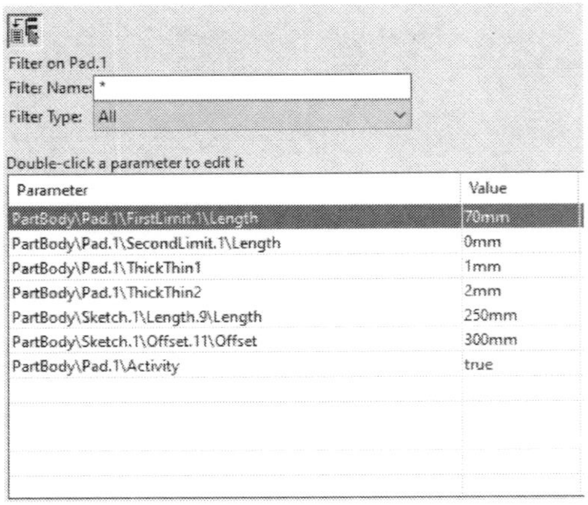

Figure 13–22

Filter Name

The *Filter Name* field enables you to specify a feature name to narrow the list of parameters displayed. Figure 13–23 shows the parameter list before entering a filter name value.Figure 13–24 shows the parameter list after **pad** has been entered in the *Filter Name* field. The software displays only the parameters containing the word "pad".

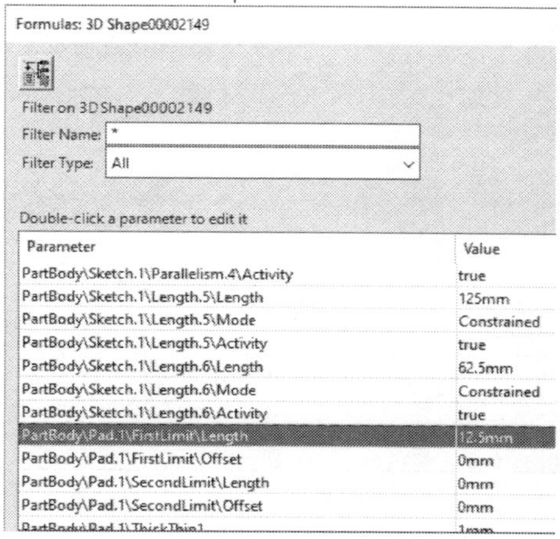

Figure 13–23

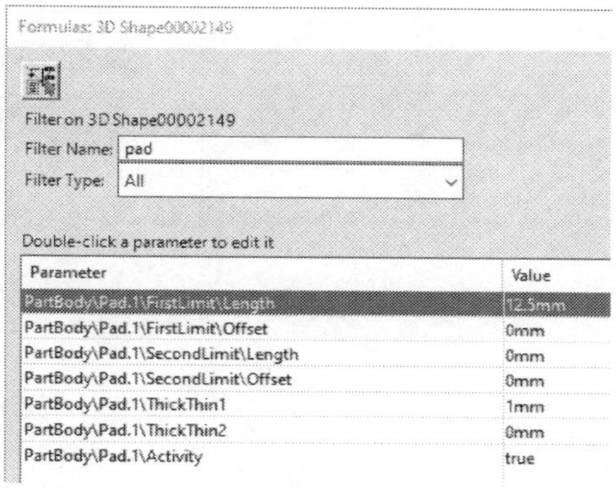

Figure 13–24

Filter Type

The value entered for filter name is not case-sensitive.

The *Filter Type* field enables you to specify the parameters to be displayed based on the type of parameter selected, as shown in Figure 13–25. Figure 13–26 shows the parameter list after *Filter Type* has been set to **Length**.

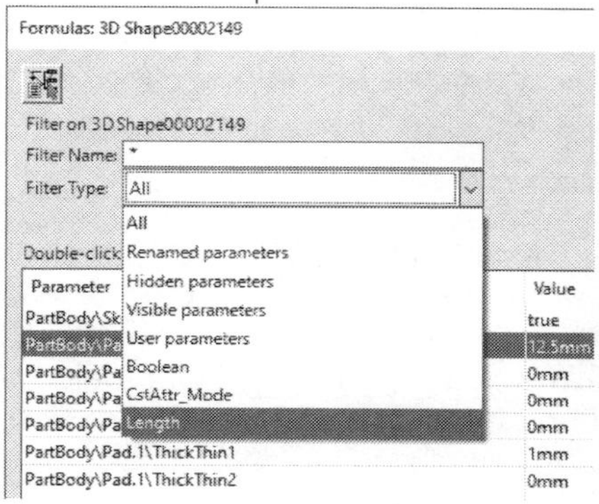

Figure 13–25

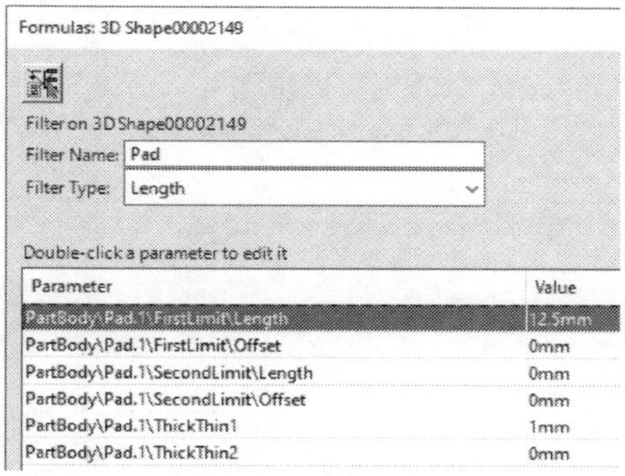

Figure 13–26

13.5 Create a Formula

Determining System Parameter Names

When in the Sketch app, you can place the cursor over a dimension to display a note with the name of the system-defined parameter. If you double-click an existing feature, the dimensions will display on the model, and the same behavior occurs. The dimension types and their corresponding parameter names are described as follows:

Dimension Type	Intrinsic Parameter Name
Radius Dimension	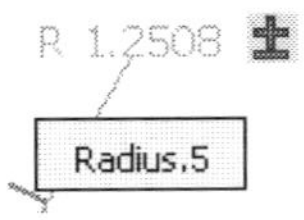
Line Length	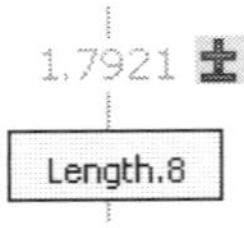
Distance Between Two Parallel Lines	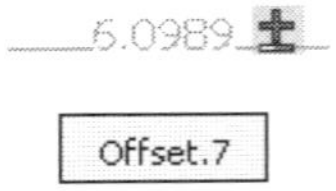
Angle Between Two Lines	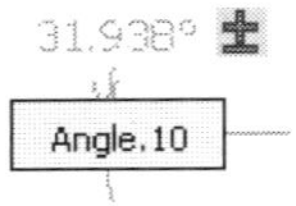

Creating a Formula

How To: Create a Formula

1. In the *Tools* section of the Action Bar, click  (Formula). The Formulas dialog box opens.
2. Select one or more feature(s) on the model to display their dimensions.
3. Select an intrinsic parameter name from the parameter list or select a dimension on the display. The formula drives this dimension.
4. Click **Add Formula**. The Formula Editor dialog box opens. Enter a formula and/or select another dimension to relate.
5. Click **OK** in the Formula Editor dialog box.
6. Click **OK** in the Formulas dialog box. The function symbol 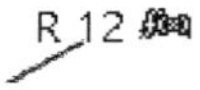 displays next to driven dimension.

13.6 View and Edit Formulas

Displaying in the Specification Tree

To display formulas and parameters in the specification tree, select **Me** in the top bar, then click **Preferences>Common Preferences> Object Properties>3D Shape> Display** and navigate to the *Display in Tree* section. Select the options to toggle the display of features on or off in the specification tree, as shown in Figure 13–27.

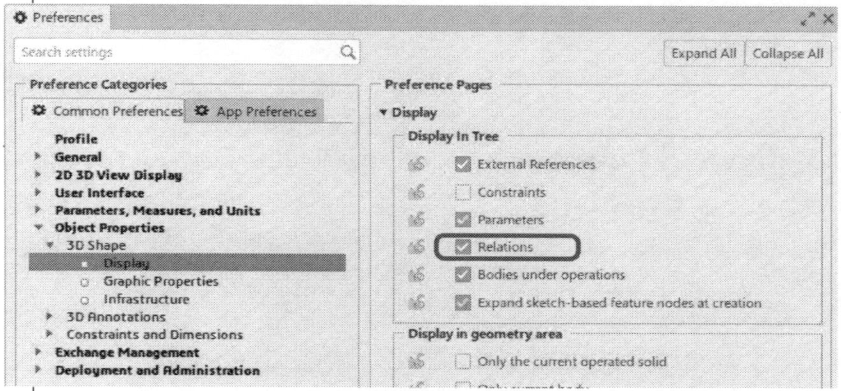

Figure 13–27

Figure 13–28 shows the specification tree with the relations display option enabled.

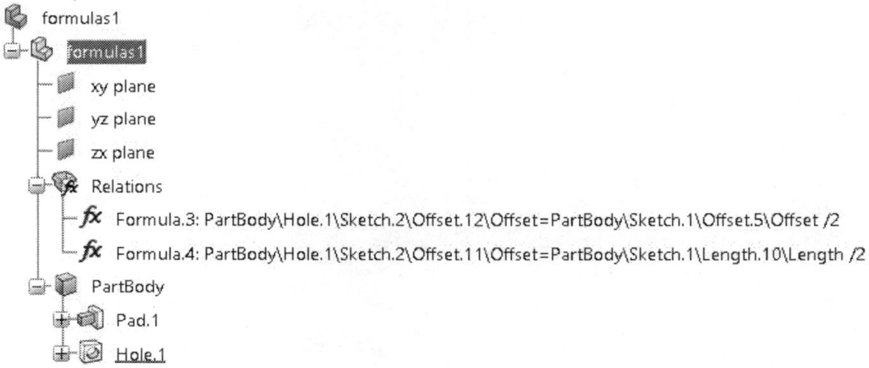

Figure 13–28

To display the full text of a formula, select **Me** in the top bar, then click **Preferences>Common Preferences>User Interface>Spec Tree**, then navigate to the *Tree Item Size* section. The number of characters can be set to text-dependent (shows all text) or to a maximum number of characters, as shown in Figure 13–29.

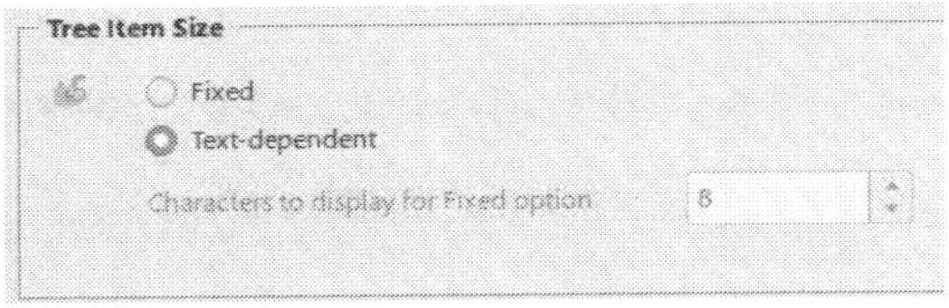

Figure 13–29

Edit and Delete a Formula

How To: Edit a Formula

1. Expand the relations branch in the specification tree.
2. Double-click on the relation to be edited.
3. Make changes using the Formula Editor dialog box, as shown in Figure 13–30.

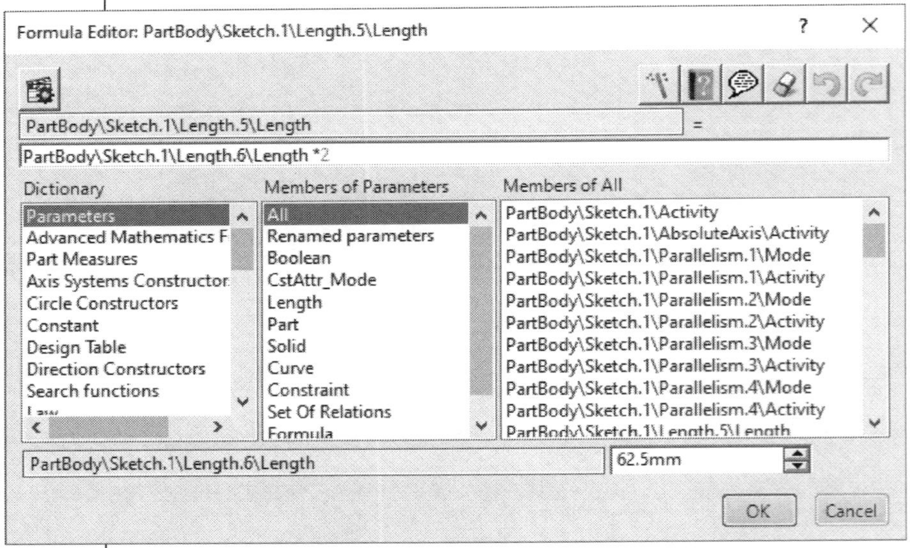

Figure 13–30

4. Click **OK** to complete editing the formula.

How To: Delete a Formula

1. Select the formula in the specification tree.
2. Press <Delete> or right-click and select **Delete**.

13.7 Create User-Defined Parameters

A user-defined parameter created in CATIA consists of a parameter name and a parameter value, which enable you to incorporate additional information into the model. Like system-defined parameters, they can be constrained by relations and used as an argument in a relation.

Types of Parameters

A few common parameter types include the following:

- Real Number
- Integer
- String

How To: Create a User-Defined Parameter

1. Click *fx* (Formula). The Formulas dialog box opens, as shown in Figure 13–31.

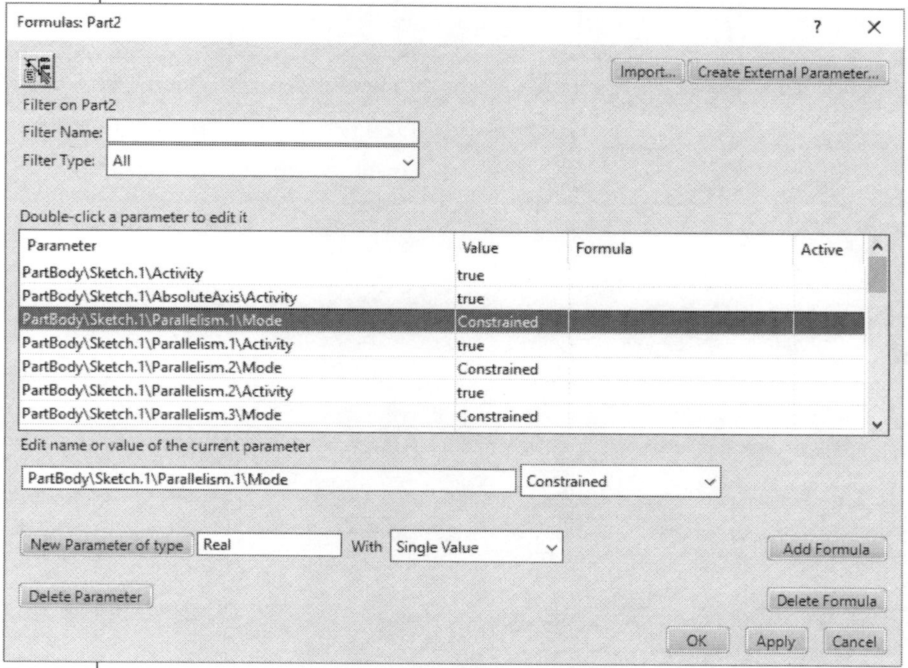

Figure 13–31

2. In the New Parameter of type drop-down list, select the type of parameter as shown in Figure 13–32.

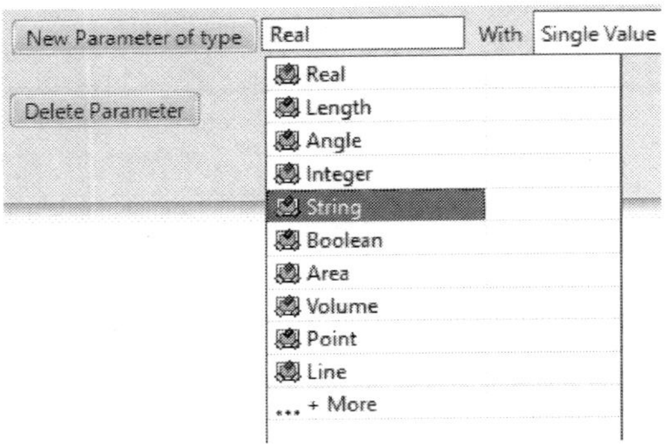

Figure 13–32

3. Click **New Parameter of type**. The dialog box updates with the additional input fields.
4. Enter a name and a value for the parameter, as shown in Figure 13–33.

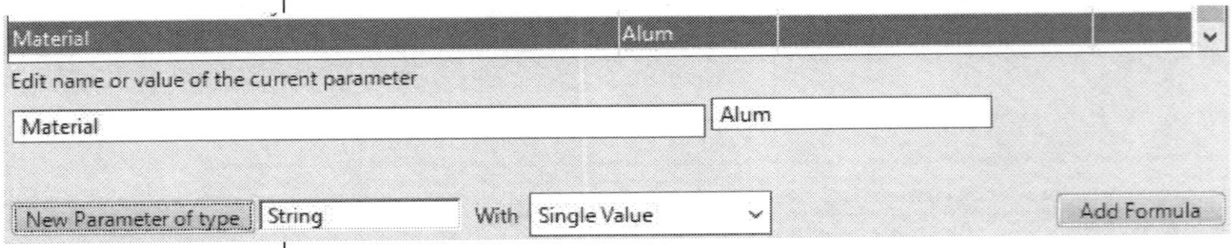

Figure 13–33

5. Click **Apply** to add the new parameter to the parameter list.
6. Click **OK**.

13.8 View and Edit User-defined Parameters

Displaying Parameters

To display the user-defined parameters in the specification tree, select your user icon in the top bar, then click **Preferences>Common Preferences> Object Properties> 3D Shape> Display** and navigate to the *Display in Tree section*. Select the **Parameters** option, as shown in Figure 13–34.

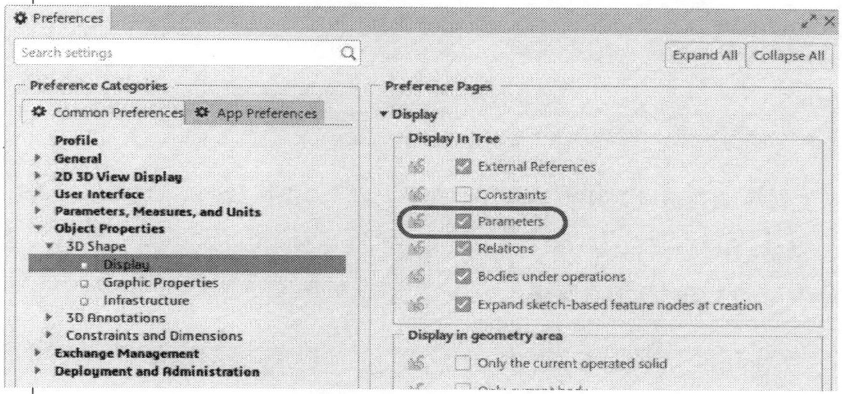

Figure 13–34

To display the user-defined parameter value in the specification tree, select your user icon in the top bar, then click **Preferences>AppPreferences>3D Modeling>Multi Discipline Automated Engineering> Basics** and navigate to the *Parameters tree view* section. Select the **Display value** option, as shown in Figure 13–35.

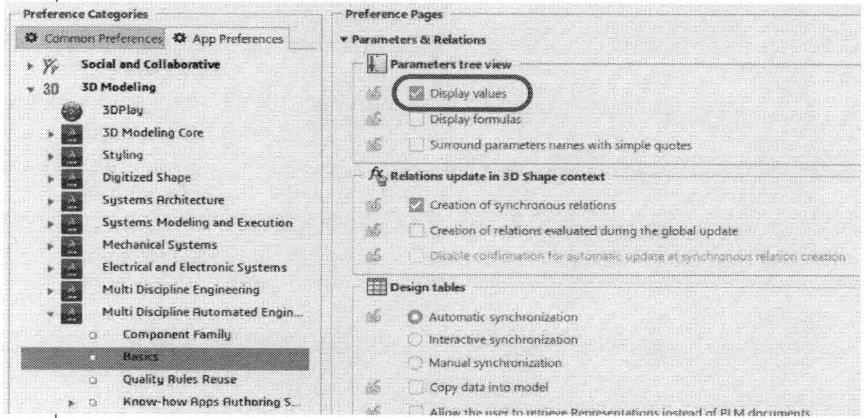

Figure 13–35

The specification tree is shown in Figure 13–36 listing a user-defined parameter of type string named material, which has a value of **Alum**.

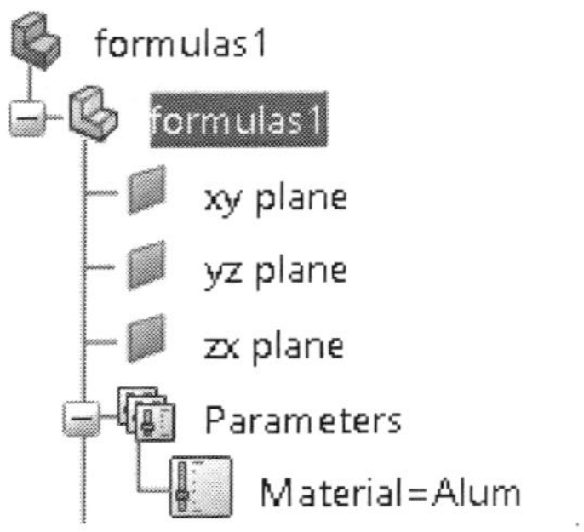

Figure 13–36

Edit and Delete a User-defined Parameter

How To: Edit a User-Defined Parameter

1. Double-click on a parameter in the specification tree.
2. The Edit Parameter dialog box opens as shown in Figure 13–37.

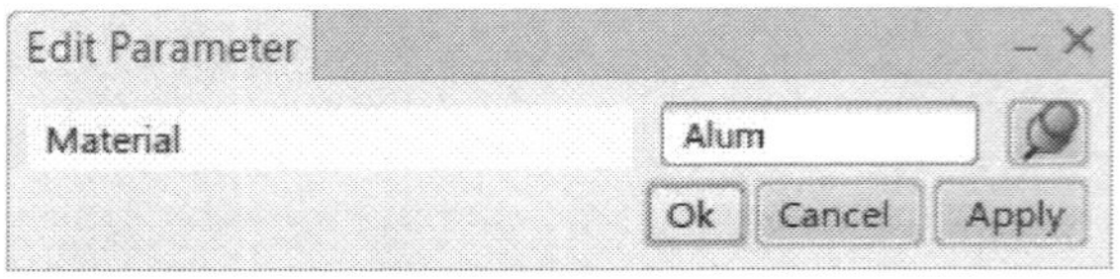

Figure 13–37

3. Make the changes as required.

How To: Delete a User-Defined Parameter

1. Select the parameter in the specification tree.
2. Press <Delete> or right-click and select **Delete**.

- You can also edit and delete parameters and formulas using the Formulas dialog box by selecting the parameter or formula and clicking fx (Formula).

Practice 13a Sketch Relations

Practice Objectives

- Create a relation in the sketcher using a formula.
- Create equivalent dimensions.

In this practice, you will create the sketch shown in Figure 13–38. The design requires the value of the dimension labeled A to be 1/2 of dimension B. It also requires that the three dimensions labeled X stay equal, and that the two radii labeled Y stay equal when changes occur. You will capture this design intent through the use of formulas and equivalent dimensions.

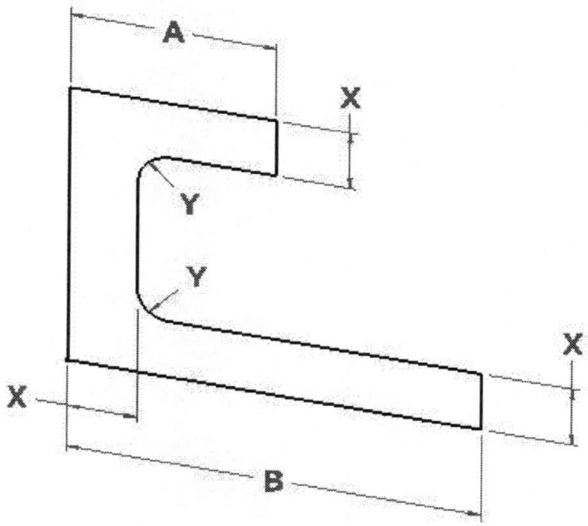

Figure 13–38

Task 1 - Create a new part model and rough sketch.

1. In the Top Bar, click (Add)>**3D Part**.
2. In the 3D Pat dialog box, enter ***Your_Initials*_ChannelSketch** as the *Title.*
3. Select the *3D Shape* tab and enter **ChannelSketch** as the *Title*.
4. Select the *Characteristics* tab and ensure **Enable hybrid design** is disabled.

5. Click **OK**.
6. Select the YZ plane as shown in Figure 13–39.

Figure 13–39

1. In the context toolbar, click (Sketch). Sketch the rough profile, as shown in Figure 13–40.

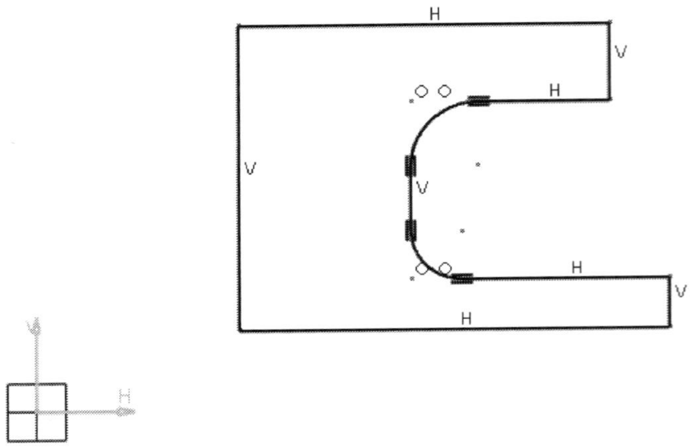

Figure 13–40

2. Constrain the lower left corner of the sketch to the sketch origin. Add dimensions and edit their values to those shown in Figure 13–41. Do not exit Sketcher.

- 10 (0.394 in)
- 15 (0.591 in)
- 20 (0.787 in)
- 25 (0.984 in)
- 80 (3.150 in)
- 100 (3.937 in)
- 120 (4.724 in)

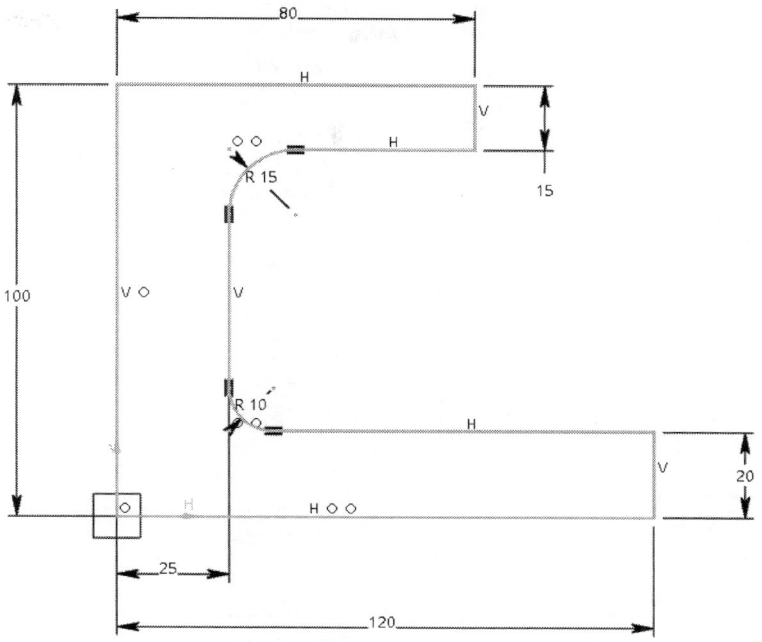

Figure 13–41

Task 2 - Add a formula to make the top length of the channel 1/2 of the bottom.

1. Select the **80 (3.150 in)** length dimension from the sketch and click (Formula) from the context toolbar. The Formula Editor dialog box opens, as shown in Figure 13–42.

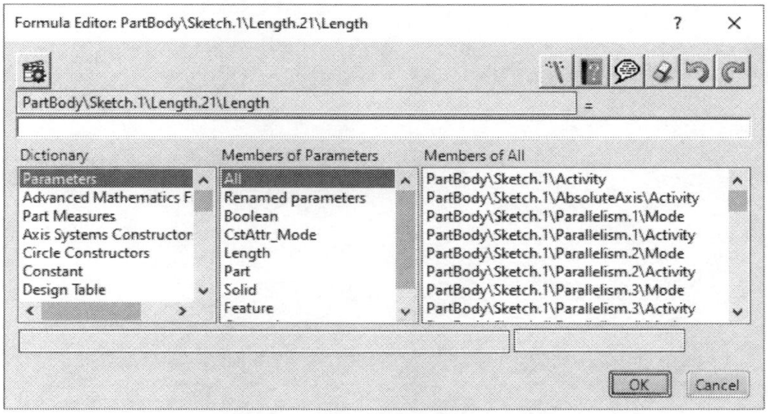

Figure 13–42

2. Double-click the **120 (4.724 in)** length dimension from the screen. In the Formula Editor dialog box, enter **/2** in the field, as shown in Figure 13–43. This sets the dimension of the top of the channel to be **1/2** of the bottom length of **120 (4.724 in)**.

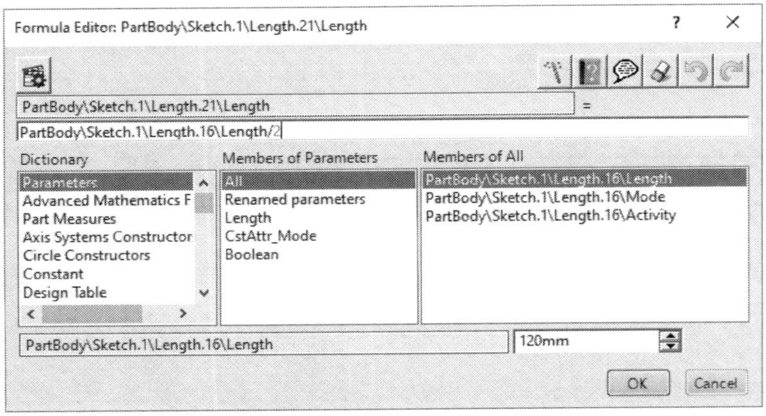

Figure 13–43

3. Click **OK** to exit the Formula Editor.The model will update to reflect the newly created formula.

Task 3 - Investigate the formula in the model.

1. Double-click on the **60 (2.362 in)** dimension to modify its value. This dimension is now driven by the formula and cannot be modified, as shown in Figure 13–44.

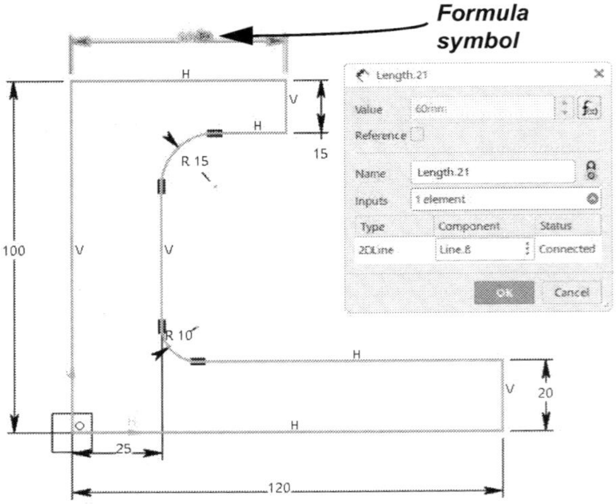

Figure 13–44

2. Click **OK** in the Constraint Definition dialog box.

3. Double-click on the **120 (4.724 in)** dimension and enter **140 (5.512 in)** as the new value. Note the updated values.

Task 4 - Add a formula to make the fillet radii equal.

1. Click on the **R15mm (0.591 in)** dimension for the top arc and click fx (Formula) from the context toolbar, as shown in Figure 13–45.

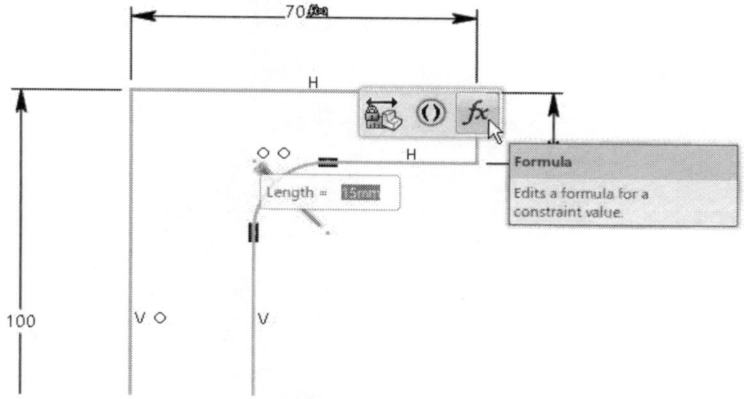

Figure 13–45

2. The Formula Editor dialog box opens. Double-click the **R10 (0.394 in)** dimension.

3. Click **OK** to close the Formula Editor dialog box. Note the change in dimension values.

4. In the Constraint Definition dialog box, click **OK** to complete the relation.

5. Modify the parent radius dimension (on the bottom arc) to **5 (0.197 in)** and note the updated changes.

6. Modify the radius back to **10 (0.394 in)**.

Task 5 - Create an equivalent dimension for the thickness of the channel.

1. In the Action Bar, select the *Tools* section.

2. Click  (Equivalent Dimensions). The Equivalent Dimensions feature Edition dialog box opens, as shown in Figure 13–46. Note that *Type* is set to **Length**.

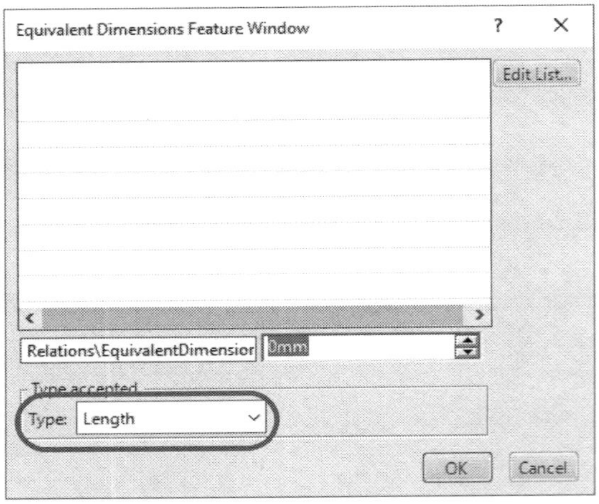

Figure 13–46

3. In the dialog box, click **Edit List**. A list of all sketch length dimensions display.

4. On the model, select the **20 (0.787 in)** dimension that represents the thickness of the lower flange. This dimension will be highlighted in the dialog box.

5. Click  to move the dimension to the right side of the dialog box.

6. Repeat Steps 4 and 5 for the two other flange thickness dimensions (**25 (0.984 in)** and **15 (0.591 in)**). The dialog box updates, as shown in Figure 13–47.

Note that the numbers for each element (Length.32 for example) may differ on your system, depending on how the sketch was created.

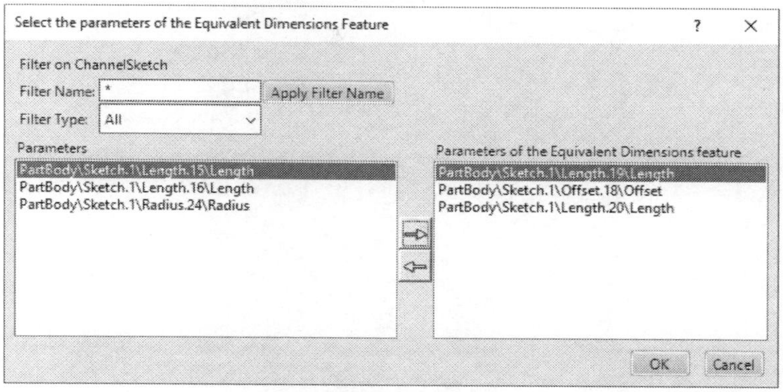

Figure 13–47

7. Click **OK**. The selected dimensions display as shown in Figure 13–48. The dimensions are driven by value at the bottom of the dialog box.

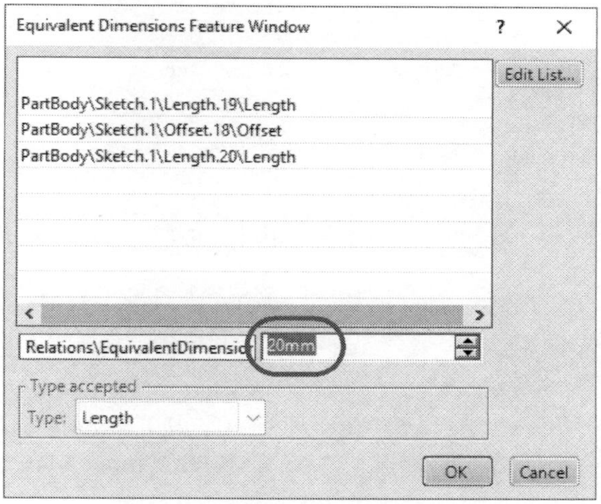

Figure 13–48

8. In the *Value* field, enter **10 (0.394 in)** and click **OK** to update all three dimensions. The profile displays as shown in Figure 13–49.

    - 10 (0.394 in)
    - 70 (2.756 in)
    - 100 (3.937 in)
    - 140 (5.512 in)

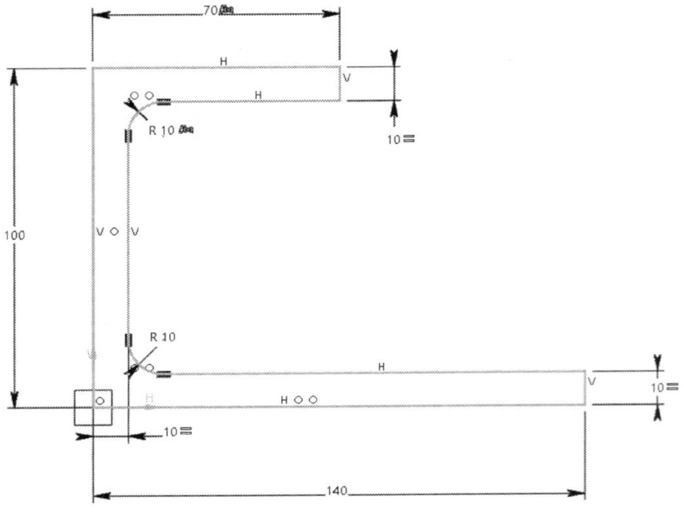

Figure 13–49

Task 6 - Edit an equivalent dimension.

1. Double-click on any of the three dimensions that drive the thickness of the channel. Note the icon that displays next to the *Value* field, as shown in Figure 13–50. This means that this dimension value is linked to other dimensions. If required, it can be used to change the definition of which dimensions are set as being equivalent.

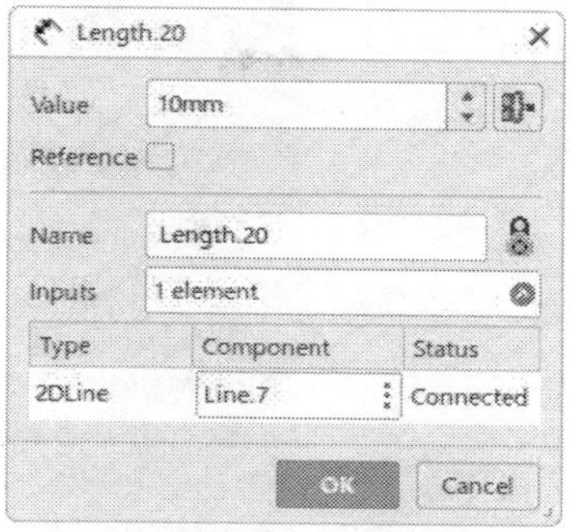

Figure 13–50

2. Enter **25 (0.984 in)** as the new value. All equivalent dimensions update, as shown in Figure 13–51.

   - 10 (0.394 in)
   - 25 (0.984 in)
   - 70 (2.756 in)
   - 100 (3.937 in)
   - 140 (5.512 in)

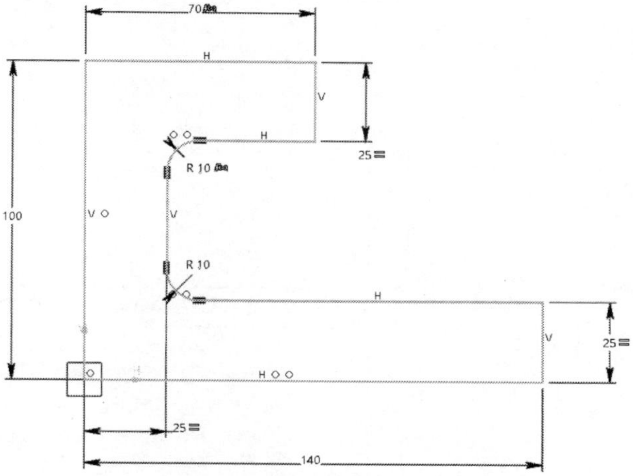

Figure 13–51

3. Click (Exit App).

4. Save the model and close the tab.

Practice 13b Relations I

Practice Objective

- Create a relation using formulas.

In this practice, you will create the part shown in Figure 13–52. The design requires the hole feature to remain located at the center of the part, regardless of changes to the main part. You will use formulas to constrain the hole feature to the center of the part.

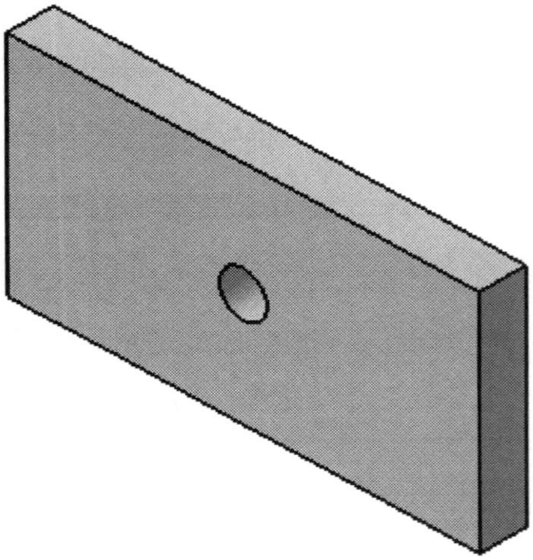

Figure 13–52

Task 1 - Create a new part model.

1. Create a new **3D Part** file. In the 3D Part dialog box, set the *3D Part* Title and *3D Shape* Title to ***Your_Initials*_Formulas1**. Ensure that *Enable hybrid design in the Characteristics* tab is disabled.

2. Create a sketch with the dimensions and constraints, as shown in Figure 13–53. Select the YZ plane as the sketching plane.

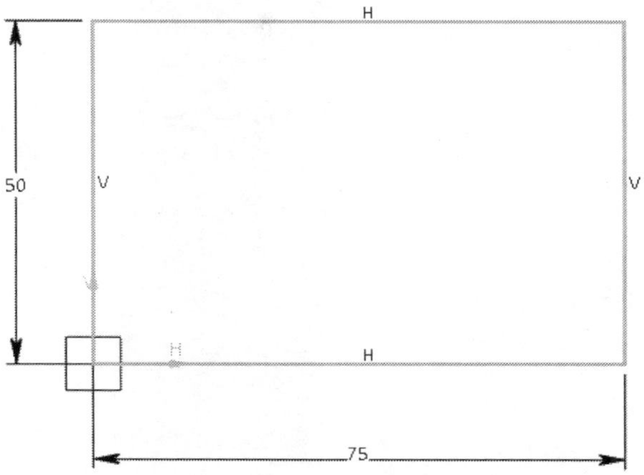

Figure 13–53

3. Create a pad feature that is **12.5** in length.

4. In the *View* tab, click  (* iso) so that the model displays as shown in Figure 13–54.

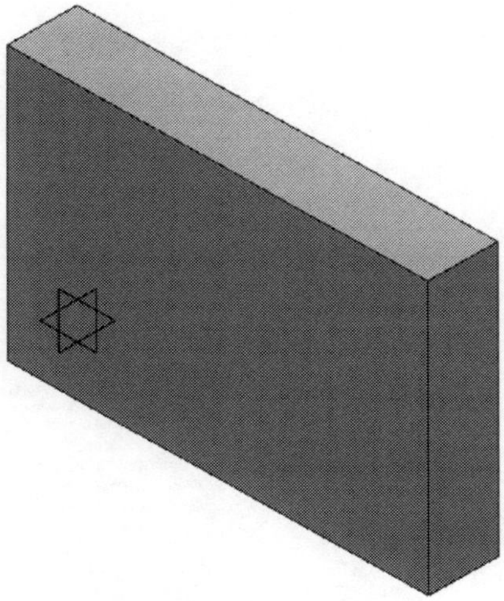

Figure 13–54

Task 2 - Create a relationship using a formula.

1. Click (Formula) from the *Tools* section of the Action Bar. The Formulas dialog box opens, listing all the system parameters.

2. In the specification tree, select **Sketch.1**. The dimensions used to constrain the sketch display.

3. In the Formulas dialog box, in the Filter Type drop-down list, select **Length** as shown in Figure 13–55.

Note the order in which the dimensions display will depend on how the sketch was created.

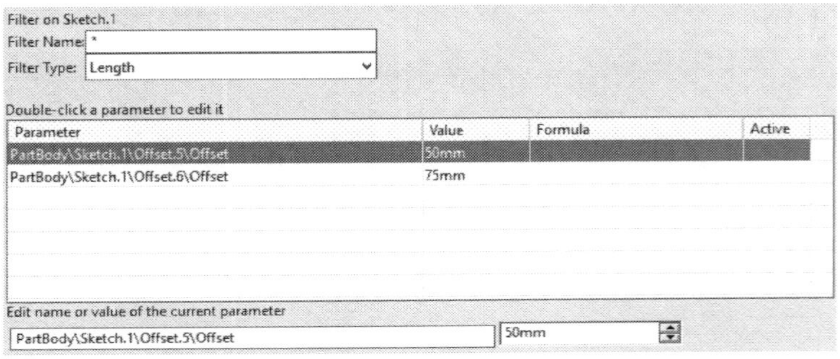

Figure 13–55

4. Select the **75 (2.953 in)** parameter.

5. Click **Add Formula**.

6. The Formula Editor dialog box opens, as shown Figure 13–56.

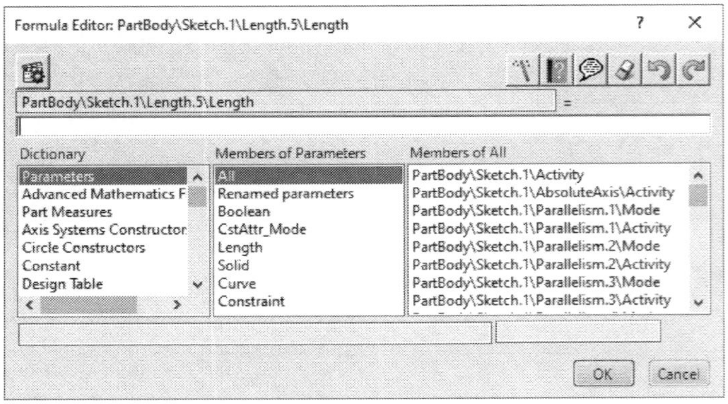

Figure 13–56

7. Double-click the **50 (1.969)** dimension.

8. Enter ***2** in the field, as shown in Figure 13–57.

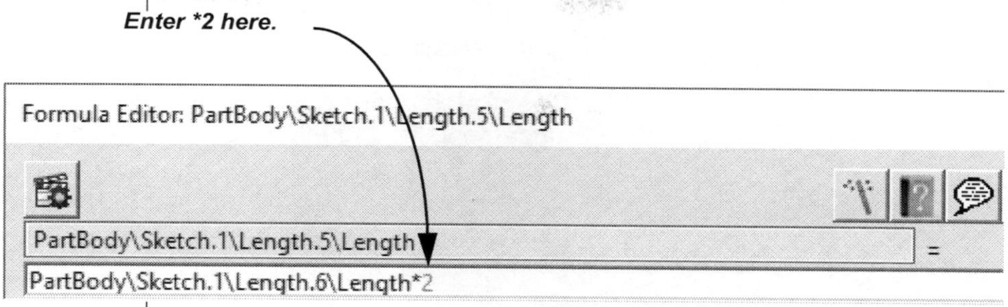

Figure 13–57

This sets the **75 (2.953 in)** parameter to be two times the **50 (1.969)** parameter.

9. Click **OK**.

10. Click **Apply** and **OK**.

11. The model updates to reflect the newly created formula, as shown in Figure 13–58.

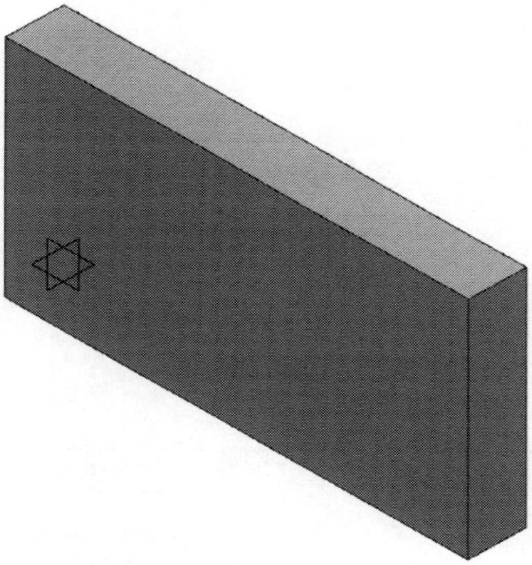

Figure 13–58

Task 3 - Investigate the formula in the model.

1. In the specification tree, double-click on **Sketch.1**.
2. The sketch opens as shown in Figure 13–59. Note the updated value (**100.00 (3.937in)**) and the appearance of the formula symbol.

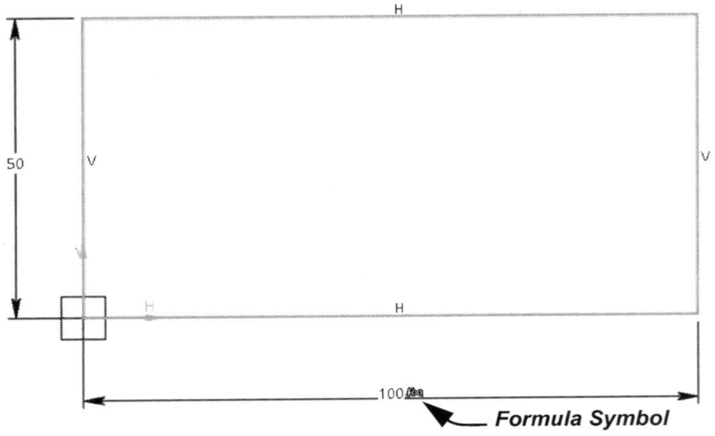

Figure 13–59

3. Double-click on **100.00 (3.937in)** dimension to modify its value. Note that this dimension is now driven by the formula and cannot be modified.
4. Click **OK**.
5. Click the **50.00 (1.969 in)** dimension and enter **62.5 (2.461)** as the new value. Note the updated values.
6. Exit the Sketch app and save the model.

Task 4 - Create a hole feature.

1. Create a Hole feature with a **12.5 (0.492 in)** diameter, using the **Up To Next** depth option.

2. Dimension the hole as shown in Figure 13–60.

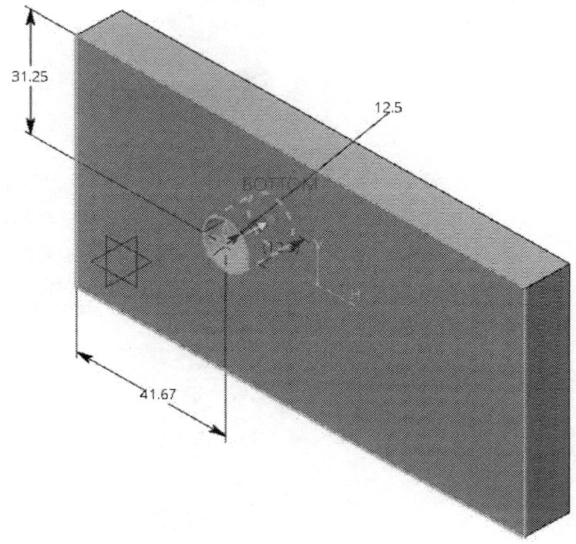

Figure 13–60

The design intent of this part is to keep the Hole feature centered on the height and 1/3 of the way along the part. Using the above dimensions, that requirement is fulfilled.

3. Modify the 41.67 (1.641 in) dimension of **Hole.1** to **75.00 (3.937in)**. Did the hole feature remain at a position of 1/3 the length of the part? Click  (Undo) to undo the modification.

Task 5 - Create a formula to locate the hole feature.

Design Considerations

Create a formula to ensure that the hole always remains 1/3 of the length of the part regardless of the part dimensions. Without a formula, the hole will not remain in the center if the part is modified. If we add a formula where the hole remains at the midpoint of the length and the midpoint of the width of the part, the hole will remain centered as the part is updated.

1. In the *Tools* section of the Action Bar, click  (Formula). The Formulas dialog box opens.
2. Select the Hole feature. The dimensions for the Hole feature display.
3. Select the **41.67 (1.641 in)** dimension of the Hole feature.

4. Click **Add Formula**. The Formula Editor dialog box opens.

5. In the specification tree, select **Pad.1**. The sketch dimensions of **Pad.1** display.

6. Double-click the **125.00 (4.921)** dimension.

7. Add **/3** to the pad Length parameter, as shown in Figure 13–61.

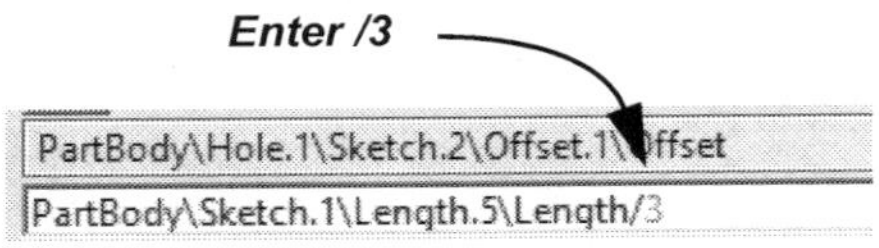

Figure 13–61

8. Click **OK**.

9. Repeat Steps 3 to 8 for the **31.25 (1.230 in)** dimension of the hole and the **62.5 (2.461 in)** dimension of **Pad.1**, but use **/2** instead of **/3**.

10. Click **OK** and **Apply** to complete the definition of the formula.

11. Modify the 62.5 dimension of **Pad.1** as **75.0 (3.937in)**.

12. Has the design intent of this part been captured? Which dimensions can be directly modified? Which dimensions cannot be directly modified?

Task 6 - Display the relation features in the specification tree, if not already displayed.

1. Select select **Me>Preferences>Common Preferences> Object Properties>3D Shape> Display** and navigate to the *Display in Tree section*.

2. Expand the *Display* section if needed and select **Relations**. Click **OK**. The specification tree updates to display the relation features you have created.

3. Change the text displayed for the relation features by selecting select **Me>Preferences>Common Preferences>User Interface>Spec Tree>Tree Appearance**, then navigate to the *Tree Item Size* section.

4. Ensure that the **Text-dependent** option is enabled and click **OK**. Note the changes in the specification tree.

5. **Save** the file and **close** the tab.

Practice 13c Relations II

Practice Objectives

- Create formulas to control geometry.
- Create user-defined parameters.

In this practice, you will modify an existing part by creating formulas and relations. The design require the wall thickness remain at one-eighth of the height, regardless of changes to the height. You will create a relation between the wall thickness and the height of the part to achieve the design intent.

Task 1 - Open an existing model.

1. Import **Shell_Relation.3dxml**.
2. In the *Part2 (Explore)* tab, right-click **Part2** in the specification tree and select **Open**.
3. Investigate the features in the specification tree that make up this part.

Task 2 - Create a relation to capture the design intent.

A structural analysis of this part indicates that a relationship between the height of the part and the wall thickness must exist. To maintain the structural integrity of the part, the wall thickness must be a function of the height by a factor of 0.125.

1. Click *fx* (Formula). In the specification tree, select the **Shell.1** feature. Select the shell thickness dimension **1.60 (0.063 in)** as the dimension to be driven.
2. Click **Add Formula**.
3. Select **Pad.1**.
4. Double-click the **9.5** (0.374 in) length (height) dimension on **Pad.1** and multiply the parameter by **0.125**. Apply the formula to complete the formula definition.
5. Flex the model by modifying the height value from 9.5 (0.374 in) to **12.50 (0.492 in)**.
6. Modify the height value again to **25.0 (0.984 in)**. Note the wall thickness of the shell updates.

Task 3 - Add a relation using the Constraint Definition dialog box.

1. Double-click on **Pad.1**. The dimensions for **Pad.1** display.

2. Double-click on the **38 (1.496 in)** dimension. The Constraint Definition Dialog box opens.

3. Right-click on the value field and select **Edit Formula** as shown in Figure 13–62.

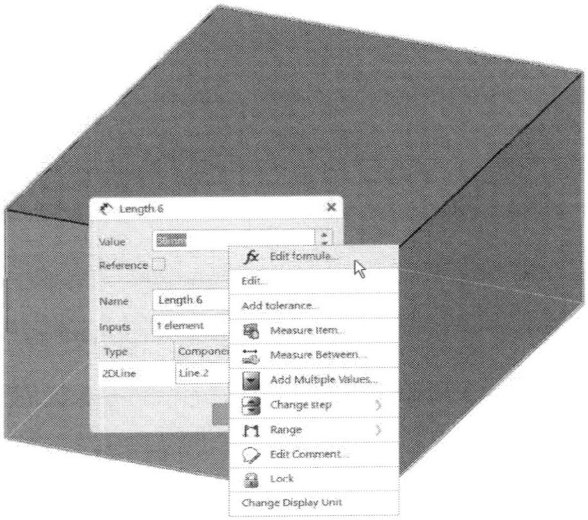

Figure 13–62

4. The Formula Editor dialog box opens. Select pad and double-click the **50 (1.969 in)** dimension.

5. Add **/2** to the parameter.

6. Click **OK** in the Formula Editor dialog box.

7. Click **OK** in the Pad Definition dialog box. The model updates and displays as shown in Figure 13–63.

Figure 13–63

Task 4 - Create a user-defined parameter.

1. Click (Formula).
2. In the New parameter of type drop-down list, select **String** as shown in Figure 13–64.

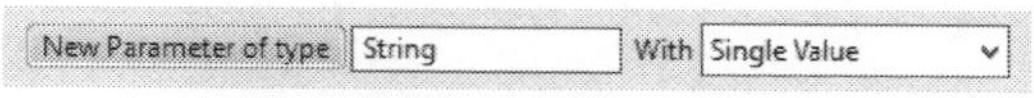

Figure 13–64

3. Click **New Parameter of type**.
4. Enter **Material** as the name and **6061 Alum** as the value as shown in Figure 13–65.

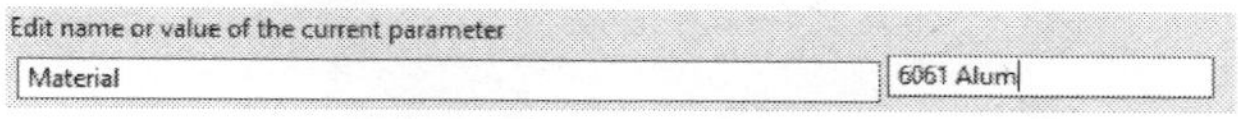

Figure 13–65

5. Click **OK**.

Task 5 - Display the parameter and its value in the specification tree.

1. Select **Me>Preferences>Common Preferences> Object Properties>3D Shape> Display** and navigate to the *Display in Tree section*. Select **Parameters**, if not already enabled.
2. Click **OK**. The specification tree updates to display the user-defined parameter feature you have created.
3. Display the parameter value in the specification tree by selecting **Me>Preferences**>**AppPreferences>3D Modeling>Multi Discipline Automated Engineering> Basics** and navigate to the *Parameters tree view* section.
4. Select the **Display value** option, and then click **OK**.
5. The specification tree updates to display this information, as shown in Figure 13–66.

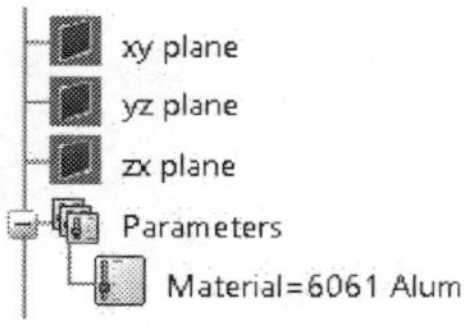

Figure 13–66

6. Save the file and close the tab.

Chapter Review Questions

1. Review the profile shown in Figure 13–67. How many dimensions are driven by formulas?

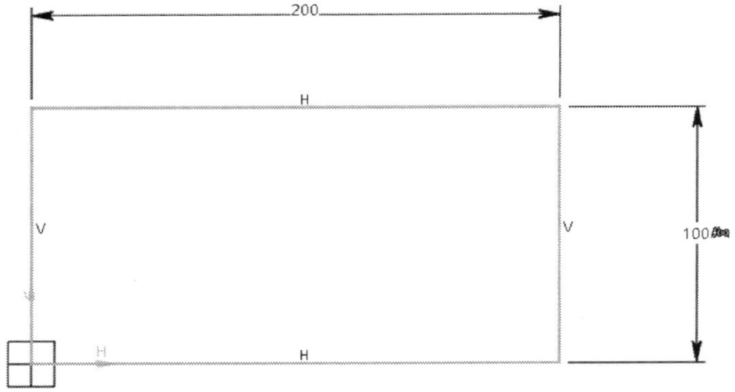

Figure 13–67

   a. 0
   b. 2
   c. 1
   d. It is impossible to tell.

2. The formulas: A = B, D = B/2, and C = A/2 can be created to center the hole and ensure that the length (dimension A) and width (dimension B) are equivalent as shown in Figure 13–68.

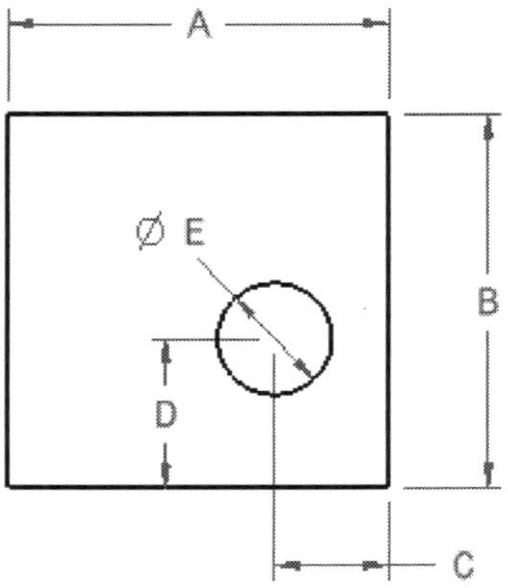

Figure 13–68

   a. True
   b. False

3. How can you tell that equivalent dimensions have been added to a model? (Select all that apply.)
    a.  displays next to dimensions that are equivalent.
    b.  displays next to the *Value* field in the Constraint Definition dialog box.
    c. A branch is added under the **Relations** branch in the specification tree.
    d. A branch is added under the **Sketch** branch in the specification tree.
4. You can change the dimension value of a driven dimension.
    a. True
    b. False

Answers: 1.c, 2.a, 3.bc, 4.b

Chapter 14

Feature Duplication

In this chapter, you learn how to duplicate features using patterns or the Copy/Paste command. You also learn how to use the Mirror command to mirror selected parts of an assembly. Using these tools will increase your modeling efficiency and help you build robust models.

Learning Objectives in This Chapter

- Create rectangular and circular patterns.
- Copy, paste, and mirror features.
- Understand user patterns for creating non-uniform patterns.

14.1 Pattern Features

Patterns are used to quickly duplicate geometry. Once the initial feature(s) is created, several instances of the same geometry can be patterned by a specified dimensional increment. The pattern can be created as a rectangular or circular pattern. If any dimension changes in the original feature, the instances update to the new dimensions.

Step 1 - Specify the reference direction.

Rectangular Pattern

When creating a rectangular pattern, features can be patterned along an edge in one or two directions. The initial Hole feature shown in Figure 14–1 is duplicated using a rectangular pattern in the first direction only. The direction of the pattern is defined by the part edge. This edge is selected as the reference element in the Pattern Definition dialog box.

Using the *Second Direction* tab in the dialog box, the hole can be patterned in a second direction, as shown in Figure 14–2.

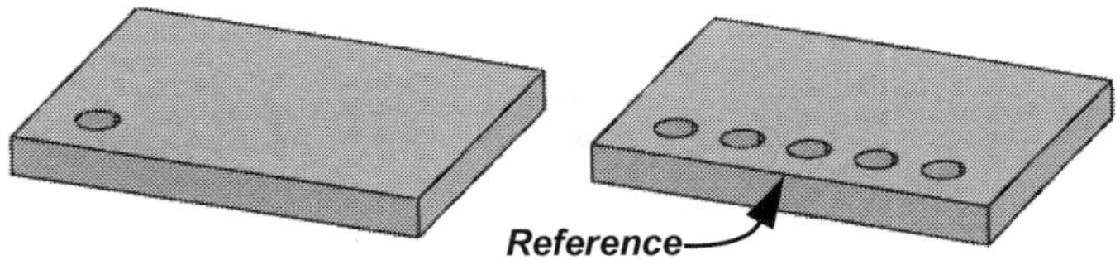

Figure 14–1

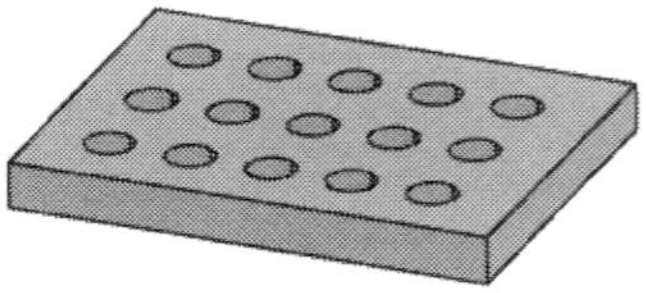

Figure 14–2

After defining the second direction, the  (Identical instances in both directions) option is made available. If selected, the pattern is created with the number of instances provided in the **Instance(s)** box in the First Direction tab, The number of instances in the second direction is set to match that of the first direction. If you change the number of instances in the first direction, the instances in the second direction automatically update.

Circular Pattern

When creating a circular pattern, features can be patterned by a set angle. Select a feature or a line to serve as an axial reference for the circular pattern. The Hole feature shown in Figure 14–3 is patterned about an axial reference defined by the center Pad.

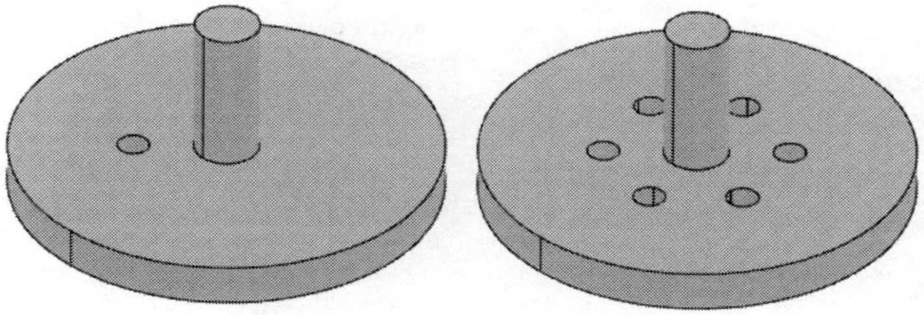

Figure 14–3

Step 2 - Specify the reference parameters.

Rectangular Pattern

Rectangular patterns can be defined by selecting one of the following combinations:

- Instance(s) & Spacing
- Instance(s) & Length
- Spacing & Length
- Instance(s) & Unequal Spacing

Circular Pattern

The dialog box updates according to the selected parameter type. Selecting the appropriate parameter scheme establishes the appropriate driving dimensions.

Circular patterns can be defined by selecting one of the following parameter options:

Option	Description
Instance(s) & Angular Spacing	Define the pattern by the number of instances and the spacing between the instances. 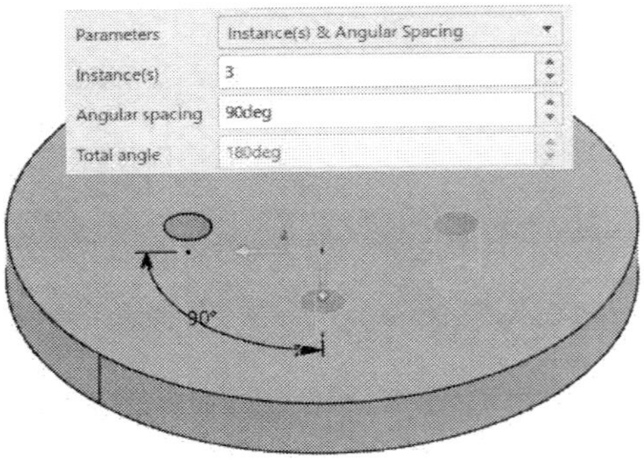
Instance(s) & Total Angle	The spacing between the instances is calculated by dividing the total angle by the number of instances. 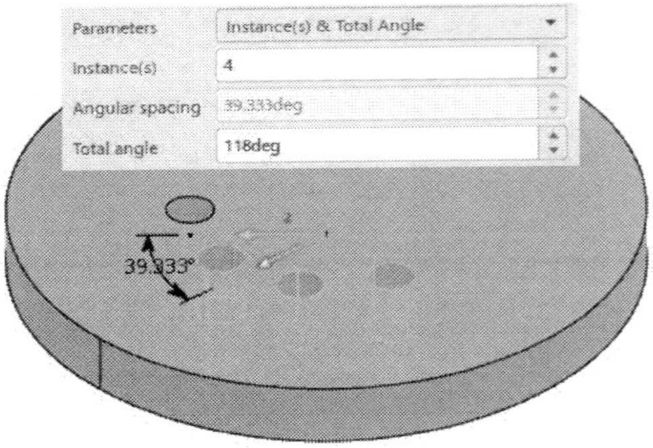

<table>
<tr><td>Angular Spacing & Total Angle</td><td>The number of instances is calculated by dividing the total angle by the angular spacing between the instances. The calculated value for the number of instances is always rounded up.
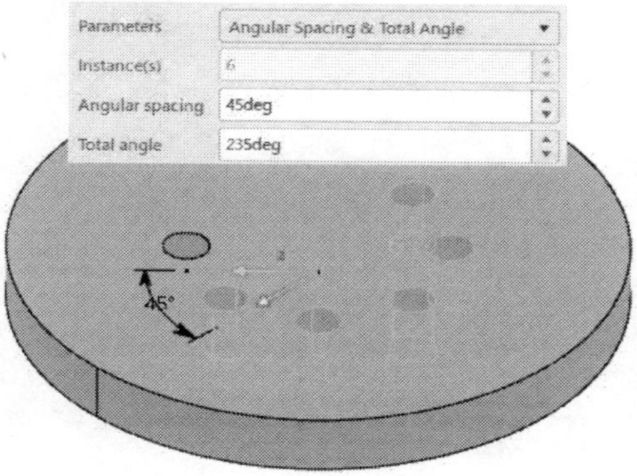
</td></tr>
<tr><td>Complete Crown</td><td>The angular spacing between instances is calculated by dividing the complete crown (i.e., 360 deg) by the number of instances.
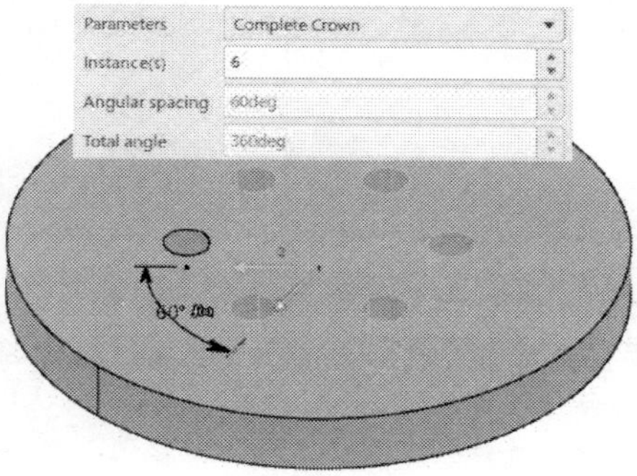
</td></tr>
<tr><td>Instance(s) & Unequal Angular Spacing</td><td>You can specify different angular values between different instances.
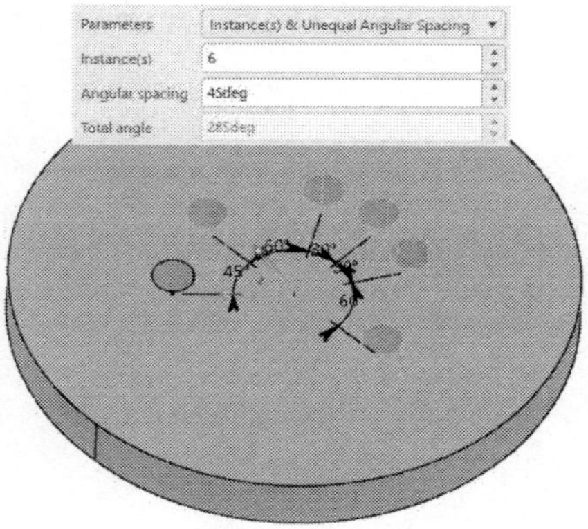
</td></tr>
</table>

The pattern can also be defined by defining parameters in the *Crown Definition* tab in the Circular Pattern Definition dialog box. A crown definition creates an additional circle pattern, as shown in Figure 14–4.

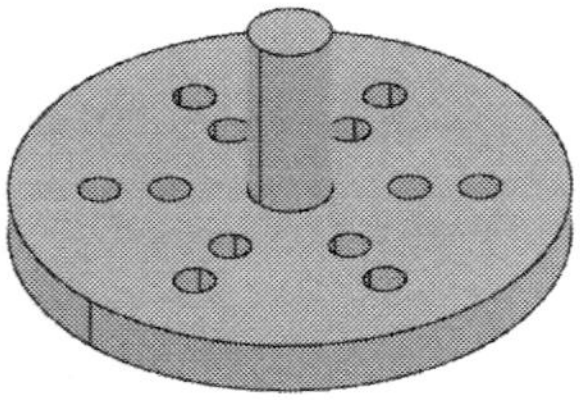

Figure 14–4

The dialog box updates according to the selected parameter type. Selecting the appropriate parameter scheme establishes the appropriate driving dimensions.

Crown definition patterns can be defined by selecting one of the following parameter options:

Option	Description
Circle(s) & Circle Spacing	The additional pattern rows are defined by entering the number of circles (including the original) and the spacing between rows. 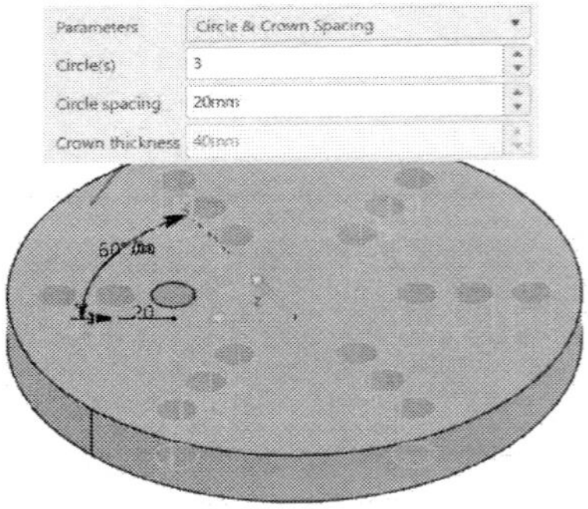

<table>
<tr>
<td>Circle(s) & Crown Thickness</td>
<td>The additional pattern rows are defined by entering the number of circles (including the original) and the distance to the last row.

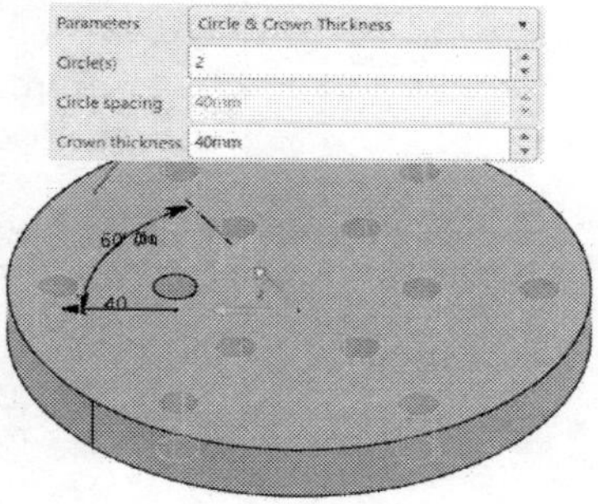

</td>
</tr>
<tr>
<td>Circle Spacing & Crown Thickness</td>
<td>The number of additional pattern rows is calculated by dividing the distance to the last row by the spacing between the rows. The calculated value is always rounded up.

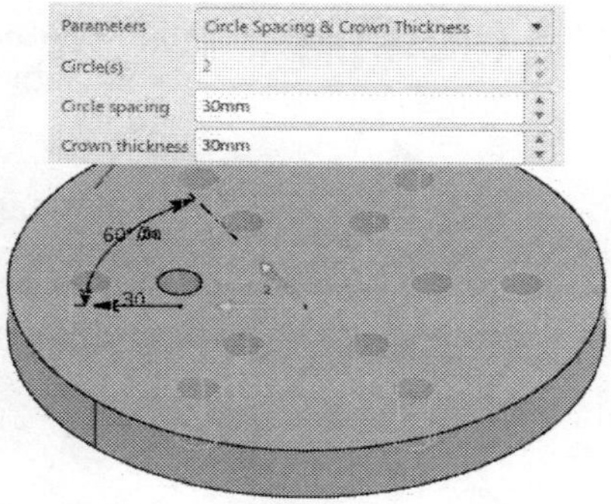

</td>
</tr>
</table>

Step 3 - Remove instances, if required.

While creating the pattern, you can easily remove an instance by selecting it while the Pattern Definition dialog box is active. The wireframe outline of the instance to be deleted is removed. All other instances remain in their offset position. The rectangular pattern shown in Figure 14–5 has the interior instances removed.

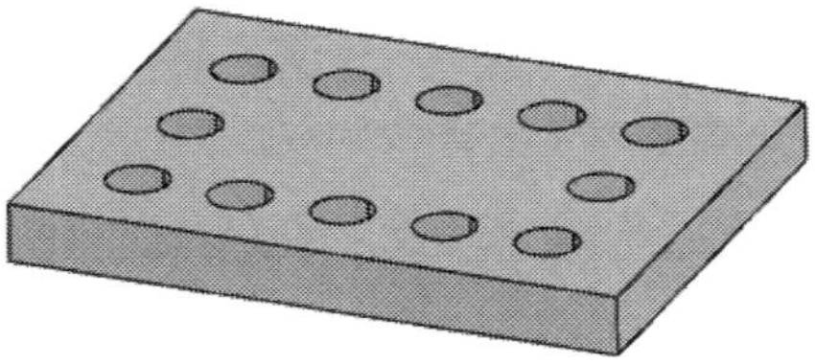

Figure 14–5

Pattern Multiple Features

In previous examples, only one feature is selected for duplication. You can also create a pattern using multiple features. To pattern multiple features, preselect the features at the same time using <Ctrl>, then click  (Rectangular Pattern) or 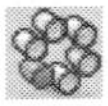 (Circular Pattern). Figure 14–6 shows an example of patterning multiple features. The circular pad, draft, and hole are all patterned in one operation.

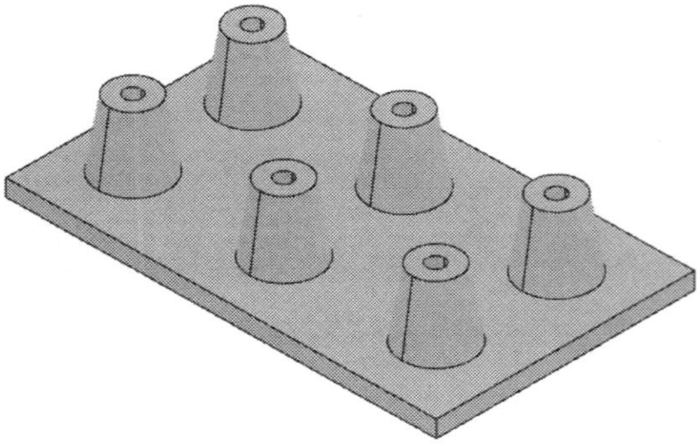

Figure 14–6

14.2 Creating User Patterns

User patterns allow custom pattern positions beyond rectangles and circles.

How To: Create a User Pattern

1. Select features for a user pattern as you would for the other types of patterns. Click (User Pattern) to open the User Pattern Definition dialog box, as shown in Figure 14–7.

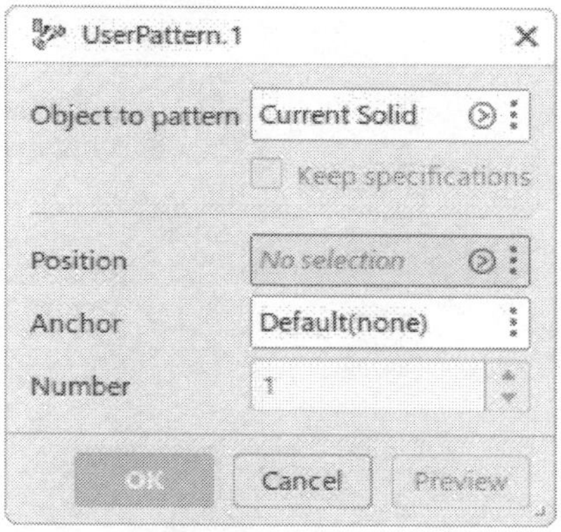

Figure 14–7

   Specify positions to place the instances. *Positions* controls the location of instances in a user pattern. Typically, this is done by placing points inside of a sketch, but point features in a geometrical set can be used as well.

   Alternatively, you can right click in the *Position* field then select Insert> (Create Sketch) and sketch a set of points.

2. Change the position of the anchor, if required.

   The anchor is the point on each instance where the position marker is located. By default, CATIA uses the center of gravity (center of the feature) of each instance. If this position is not correct, you can change it by changing the anchor location. To change the anchor location, select the *Anchor* field and then select a point on each instance to act as the new anchor.

- The anchor shown in Figure 14–8 is left as the center of gravity.
- The anchor shown in Figure 14–9 is set to the top of the feature.

Location of position marker

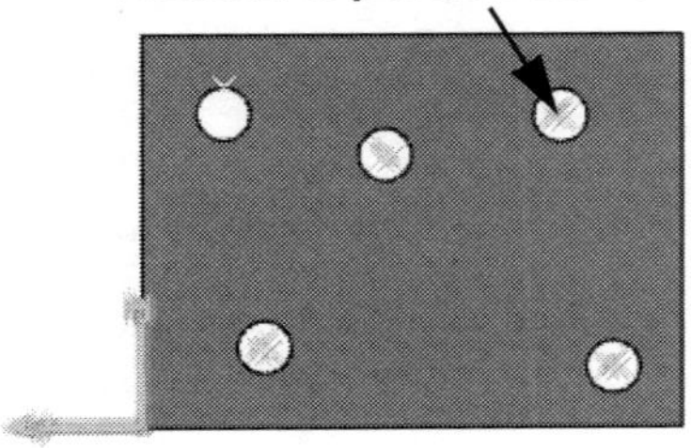

Figure 14–8

Location of position marker

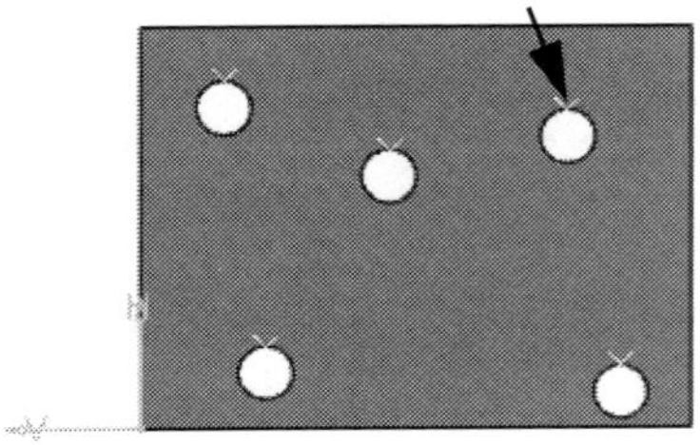

Figure 14–9

3. Remove instances and validate the pattern. You can remove instances from the pattern by selecting the position marker (anchor) of the instance while in the User Pattern Definition dialog box. The instance is removed from the display. Select the position marker again to return the instance to the display.
4. Click **OK** once you complete the pattern.

Patterns on the Fly

If you are creating a feature that you know will be patterned, you can create it on the fly in the Pattern dialog box. Click  (Rectangular Pattern), 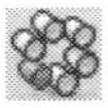 (Circular Pattern) or  (User Pattern), then, in the Pattern Definition dialog box, right-click on the *Object* field and select Insert PartDesign Feature and select the feature type you want to create, as shown in Figure 14–10.

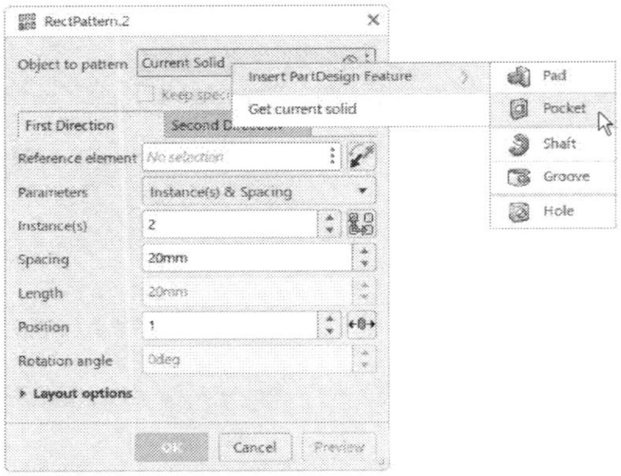

Figure 14–10

Once the feature is created, continue the pattern definition using the techniques previously described.

14.3 Copy Features

The **Copy/Paste** command is another way to duplicate features. The original circular pad is copied to new positions, as shown in Figure 14–11.

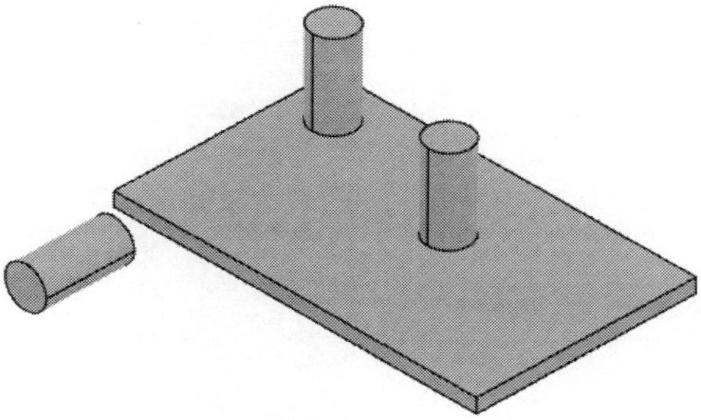

Figure 14–11

The pasted feature is placed directly on top of the original feature if the same placement plane is used. To change the position of the copied feature, the sketch must be redefined. The copied feature remains independent of the original feature.

You can also use <Ctrl>+<C> to copy and <Ctrl>+<V> to paste.

- To copy a feature, select the feature(s), right-click and select **Copy**. Select the new reference pad, right-click and select **Paste**.

14.4 Mirror Features

The **Mirror** command enables you to mirror selected features about a specified surface or reference plane. To use the **Mirror** command, select the features to be mirrored and click

 (Mirror) in the *Essentials* section of the Action Bar. Complete the feature by selecting the mirroring plane or surface.

Figure 14–12 shows a symmetrical part that can be created by designing only a portion of it. In this example, the part is mirrored twice.

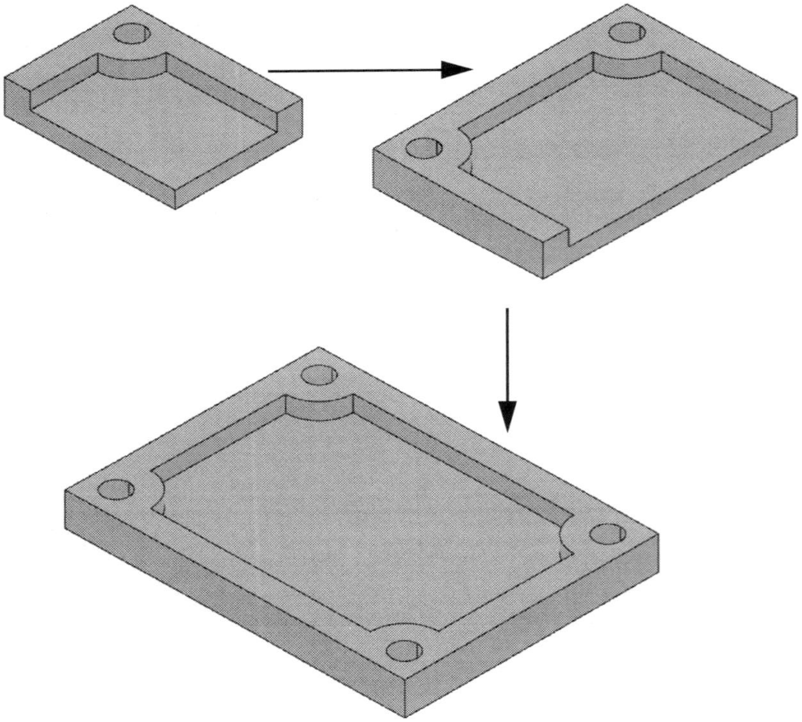

Figure 14–12

14.5 Using the Robot for Duplication

The Robot can be used to tweak parts and features in a variety of ways. In general, it can be used to adjust faces to new lengths and new angles. Items can be copied and moved. Patterns can be created. Features can be set to use the same dimensions and values.

Translating and Rotating Faces

1. Click the face to be modified, as shown in Figure 14–13.

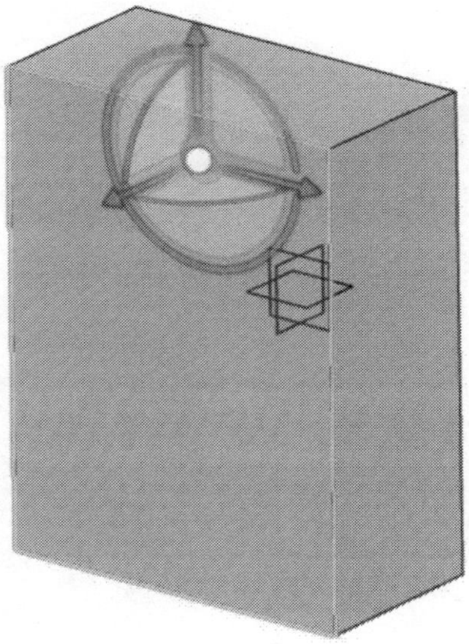

Figure 14–13

2. Verify Robot settings in the context toolbar (shown in Figure 14–14). Typically, Create Features Mode and Local Mode will be used to modify the part.

Figure 14–14

3. Translate and rotate the compass until the face is in the desired position, as shown in Figure 14–15.

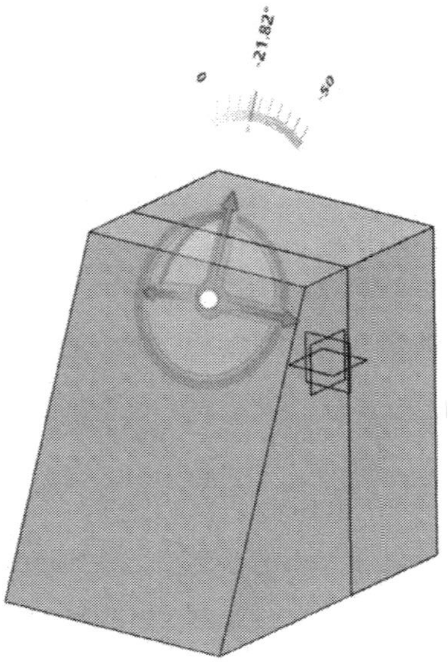

Figure 14–15

4. Click in the background to complete the change.

Reusing Feature Specifications

1. Select a dress-up feature, such as a hole, fillet, or chamfer, as shown in Figure 14–16.

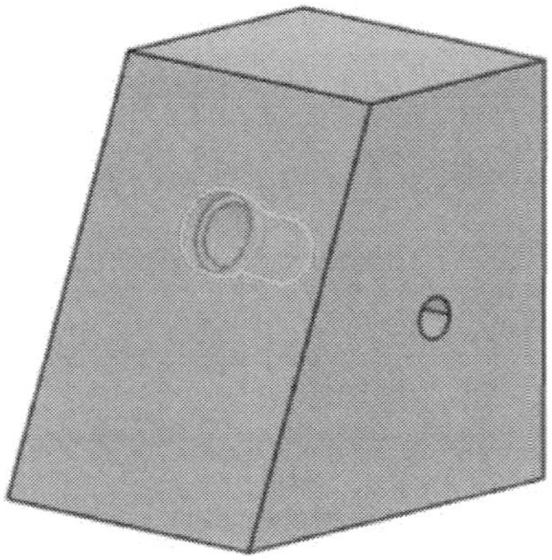

Figure 14–16

2. In the Robot context toolbar, pick Semantic Painter, as shown in Figure 14–17.

Figure 14–17

3. Select the target feature to *paint* as shown in Figure 14–18.

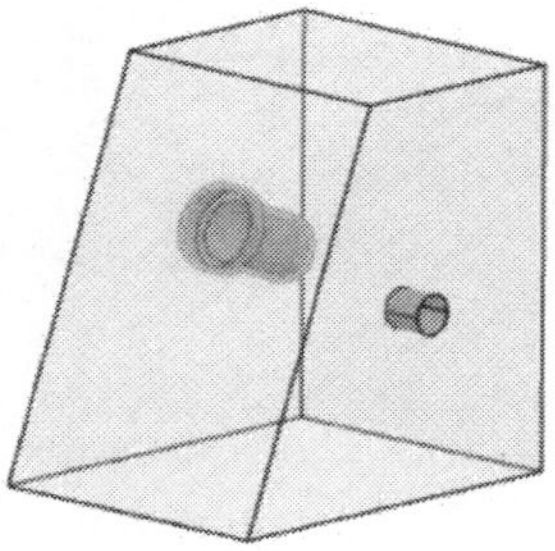

Figure 14–18

4. The targeted feature will now use the size and values of the original feature, as shown in Figure 14–19.

Figure 14–19

Duplicating and Patterning Items with the Robot

1. Set the Robot context menu to Create Features Mode, Global Mode, and Same Dimension.
2. Drag the selected item, in this case a Hole, along an axis while holding <Ctrl>, as shown in Figure 14–20.

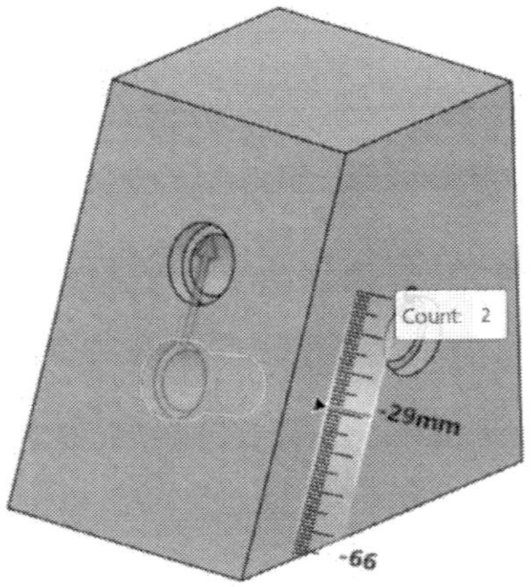

Figure 14–20

3. Enter the number of items in the *Count* field.
4. Click in the background to finish the pattern, as shown in Figure 14–21.

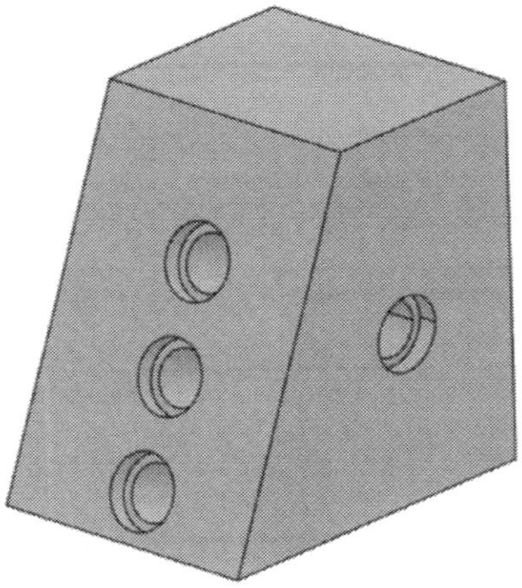

Figure 14–21

Practice 14a Patterning

Practice Objectives

- Duplicate a feature using a rectangular and circular pattern.
- Modify circular and rectangular patterns.

In this practice, you will create patterns on the two parts shown in Figure 14–22. The patterns are later modified, and some patterned instances are removed from the patterns manually.

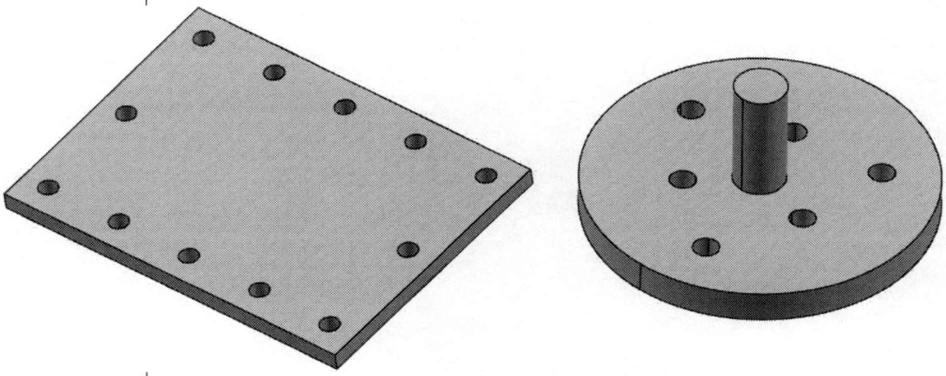

Figure 14–22

Task 1 - Open the part pattern1.

1. Import **Pattern_Rect.3dxml**.
2. In the *Part1 (Explore)* tab, right-click **Part1** in the specification tree and select **Open**.
3. Select **Hole.1** and in the *Essentials* section of the Action Bar, click (Rectangular Pattern). The Rectangular Pattern Definition dialog box opens.

4. Set the following, as shown in Figure 14–23:
    - *Parameters:* **Instance(s) & Spacing**
    - *Instance(s)*: **5**
    - *Spacing*: **25 (0.984 in)**

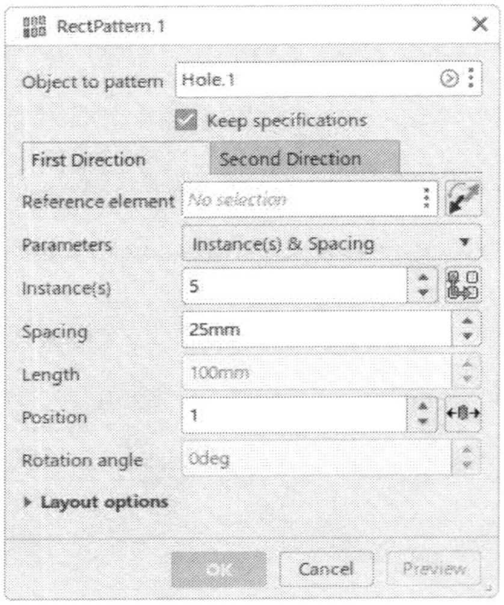

Figure 14–23

5. Select the *Reference element* field, and select the front edge as the reference direction, as shown in Figure 14–24.
6. Click **Reverse**, if required, to position the holes on the plate.

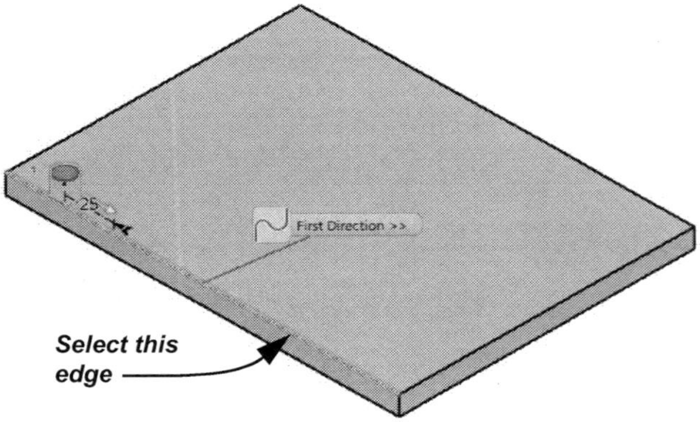

Figure 14–24

7. Click **OK** to finish the pattern definition. The pattern is not evenly spaced about the plate.

Task 2 - Modify the pattern for equal spacing.

1. Double-click one of the instances of the pattern (not the original hole). The Rectangular Pattern Definition dialog box opens.
2. Select **Instance(s) & Length** in the Parameters drop-down list.
3. The original hole is located 15mm (0.591 in) from the part edges and the part is 200mm (7.874 in) long in this direction. Change the length to **170 (6.693 in)**.
4. Click **OK** to display the new pattern, as shown in Figure 14–25.

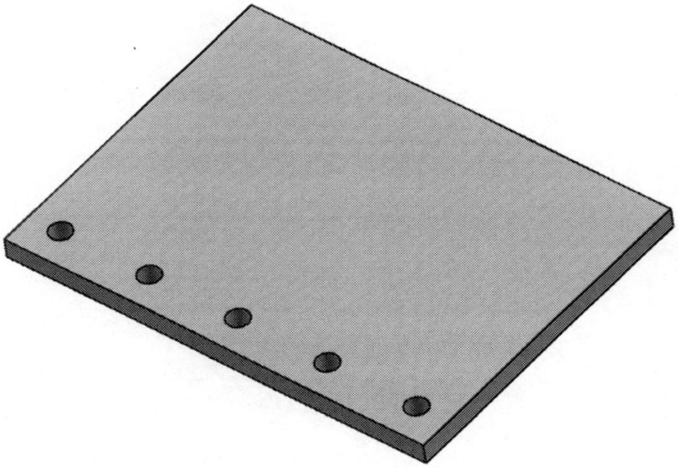

Figure 14–25

Task 3 - Modify the pattern for two directions.

1. Double-click on the pattern in the specification tree.
2. Select the *Second Direction* tab.

3. Position three instances of the holes centered on the Pad, as shown in Figure 14–26. The holes are 15mm (0.591 in) from the Pad edge and the part is 150mm (5.906 in) long in this direction. Click  (Reverse Direction) if the instances run off the part.

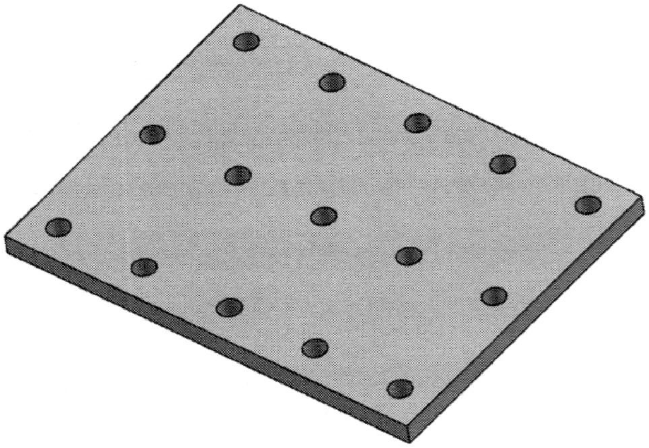

Figure 14–26

Task 4 - Remove the three holes in the center.

1. Double-click on **the pattern**.
2. Select the small dots at the center of the three holes that are in the center of the Pad.
3. Click **OK**. The model displays as shown in Figure 14–27.

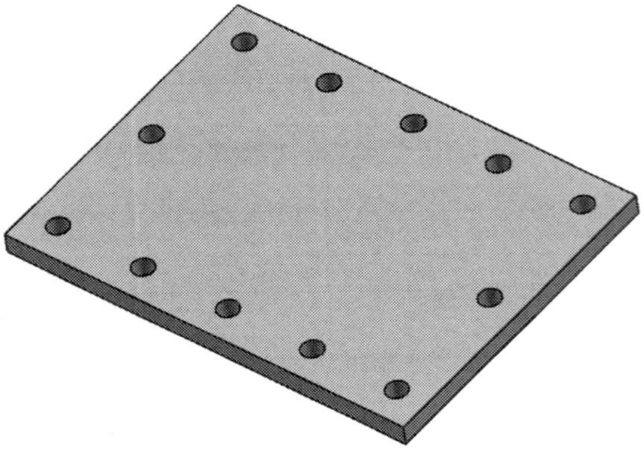

Figure 14–27

4. Save the model and close the tab.

Task 5 - Open the part Pattern_Circ.

1. Import **Pattern_Circ.3dxml**.
2. In the *Part1 (Explore)* tab, right-click **Part1** in the specification tree and select **Open**.
3. Select **Hole.1**.
4. In the *Essentials* section of the Action Bar, click  (Circular Pattern). The Circular Pattern Definition dialog box opens.
5. In the Parameters drop-down list, select **Complete crown** and enter **6** in *Instance(s)*.
6. Click in the Reference element field and select the cylindrical surface of the flange.
7. The **Pattern** tool will use the implicit axis as the reference element. The Circular Pattern Dialog box displays as shown in Figure 14–28.

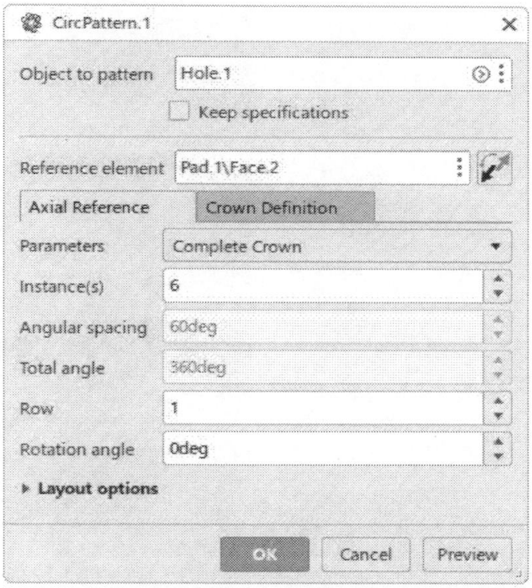

Figure 14–28

8. Click **OK** to finish the pattern creation. The part displays as shown in Figure 14–29.

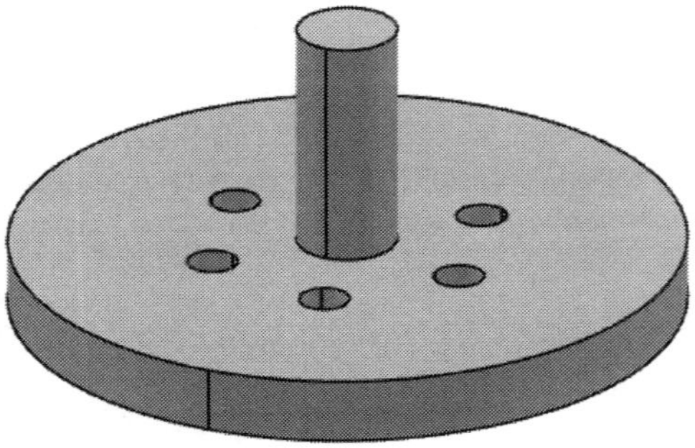

Figure 14–29

Task 6 - Add a second direction for the circular pattern.

1. Double-click **an instance of the pattern** (not the original hole).
2. Select the *Crown Definition* tab and set the following:
   - *Circle(s):* **2**
   - *Circle Spacing*: **25 (0.984 in)**
3. Click **OK** to finish the pattern creation. The model displays as shown in Figure 14–30.

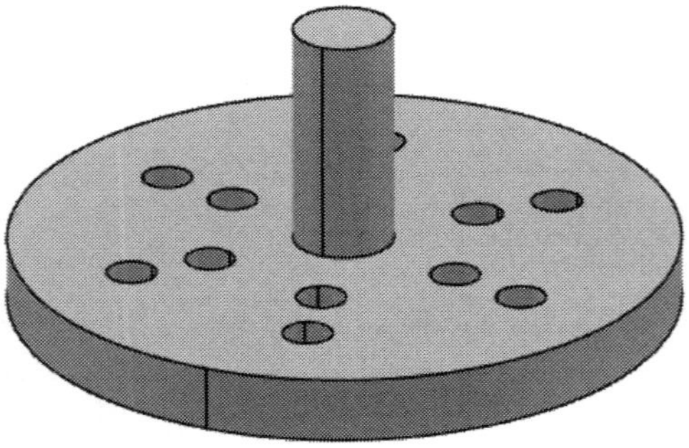

Figure 14–30

Task 7 - Remove instances from the pattern.

1. Redefine the pattern and remove instances so that the model displays as shown in Figure 14–31.

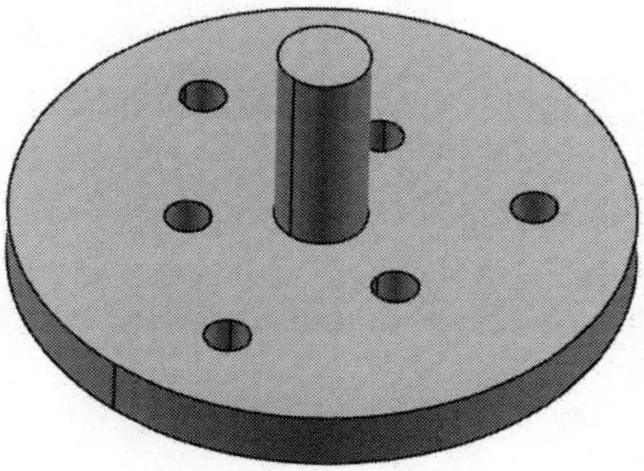

Figure 14–31

Task 8 - Create a Pocket using two limits.

In this task, you will sketch a profile for a Pocket feature on the YZ plane. Then you will create a Pocket feature that cuts material from both sides of the sketch plane.

1. Create a sketch on the YZ plane. Sketch the profile as shown in Figure 14–32.

    - 10 (0.394 in)
    - 10 (0.394 in)
    - 5 (0.197 in
    - 75 (2.953 in)

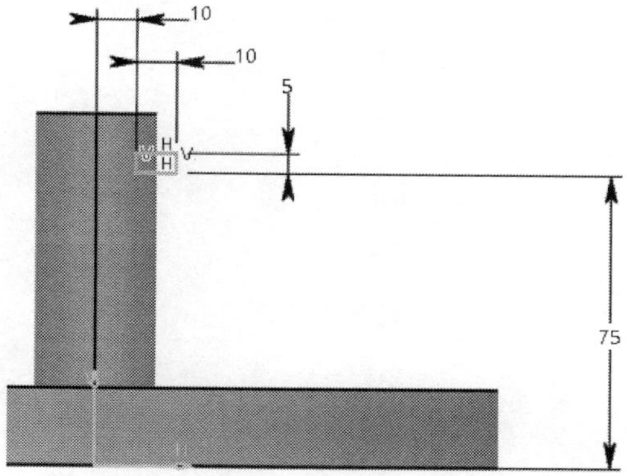

Figure 14–32

2. In the Action Bar, click (Exit App) to complete the sketch.

3. In the *Essentials* section of the Action Bar, click (Pocket) and select the sketch just created if not already selected.

4. Set the *First Limit* type as **Up to last**.

5. Click **Second Limit** to expand it if needed. The Pocket Definition dialog box expands as shown in Figure 14–33.

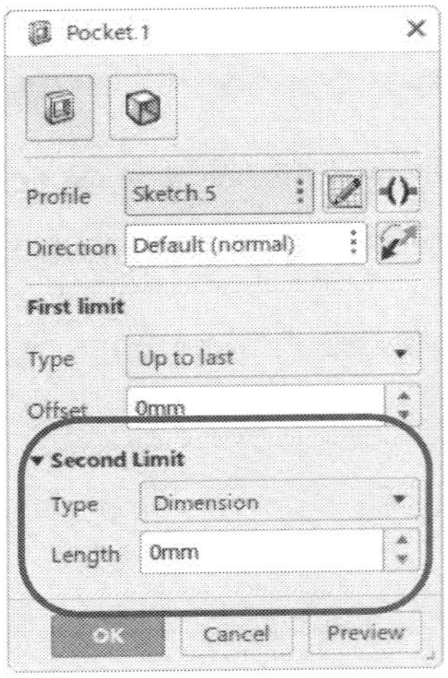

Figure 14–33

6. In the *Second Limit* area, set *Type* to **Up to last**.

7. Click **OK** to complete the feature. The model displays as shown in Figure 14–34.

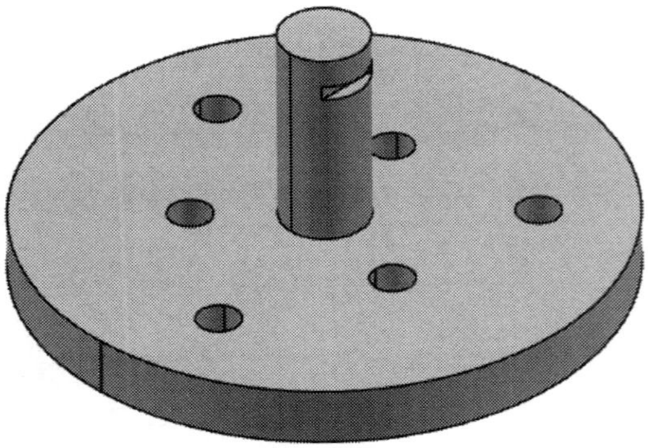

Figure 14–34

Task 9 - Use the robot to duplicate the pocket just created.

1. Select the pocket you just created, then select  (Use Robot) from the context toolbar, as shown in Figure 14–35.

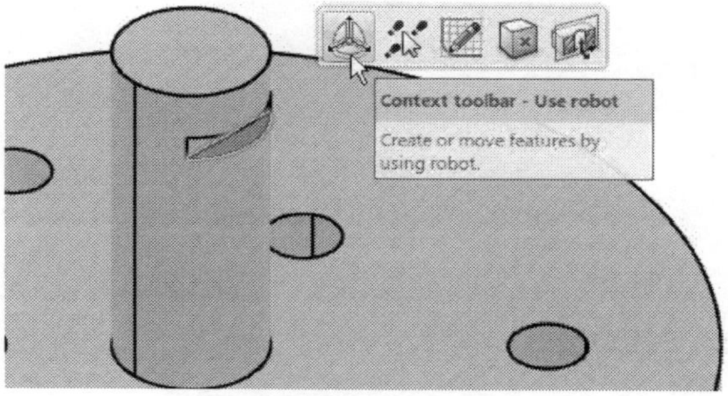

Figure 14–35

2. Ensure that the secondary context toolbar that opens has the options enabled as shown in Figure 14–36.

Figure 14–36

3. Select the robot axis running parallel to the axis of the cylinder and hold <Ctrl> and drag the center of the robot until the scale displays as shown in Figure 14–37.

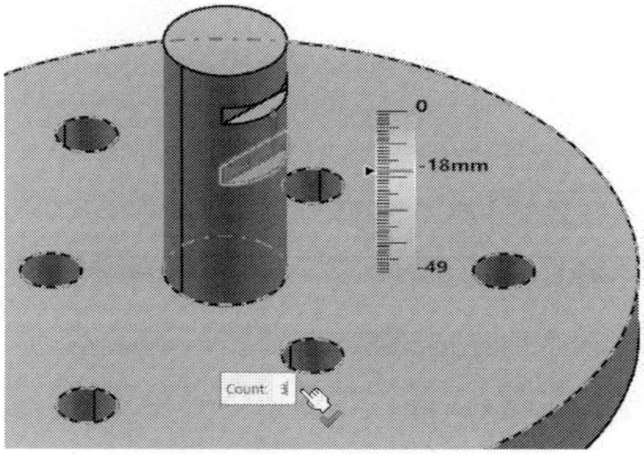

Figure 14–37

4. Edit the Count to **3** and click on the screen to complete the pattern.

5. In the specification tree, double-click **RecPattern.1**, and the Rectangular Pattern Definition dialog box opens as shown in Figure 14–38.

*Note the number of instances and spacing values. Also note that the Reference element is listed as **RobotDirection**.*

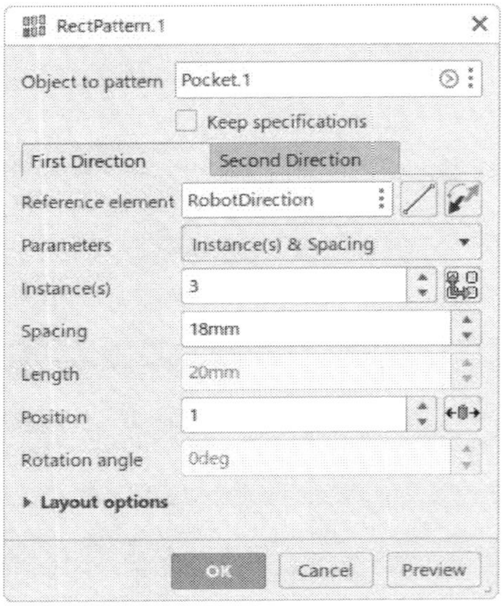

Figure 14–38

*If **-20** puts the instances off the model use **20** instead.*

6. Edit the Spacing to **-20** and click **OK**.

7. The model updates as shown in Figure 14–39.

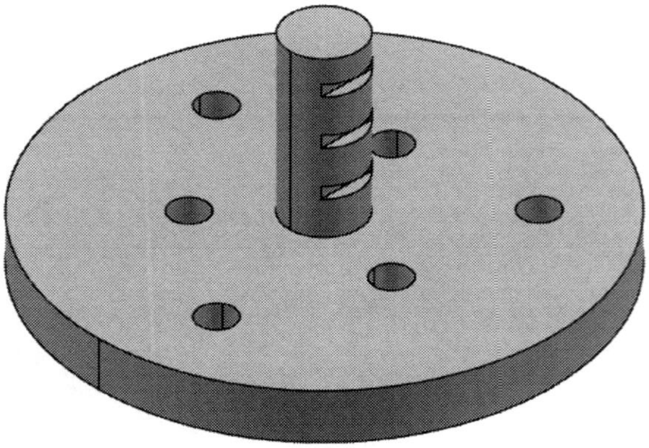

Figure 14–39

8. Save the model and close the window.

Practice 14b User Patterns

Practice Objective

- Create a user pattern.

In this practice, you will create a user pattern of multiple features to create the boss for the screws and to hold the two halves of the tape measure together. The completed model with a user pattern of three screw boss instances is shown in Figure 14–40.

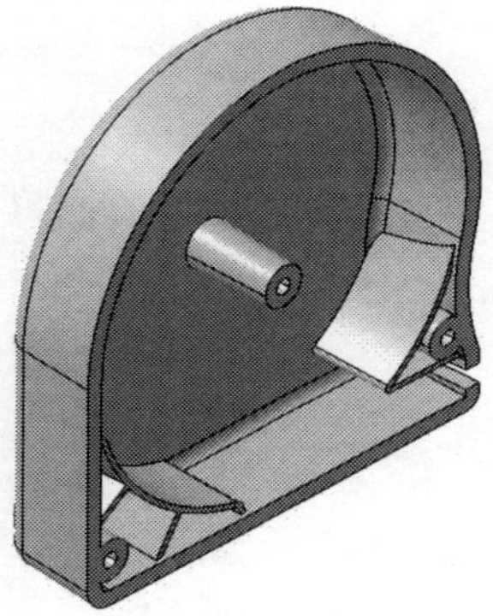

Figure 14–40

Task 1 - Create a user pattern.

1. Import **TapeMeasureBack.3dxml**.
2. In the *833599 (Explore)* tab, right-click **833599** in the specification tree and select **Open**.
3. Preselect the following three features, as shown in Figure 14–41:
   - **Pad.2**
   - **Hole.1**
   - **Draft.3**

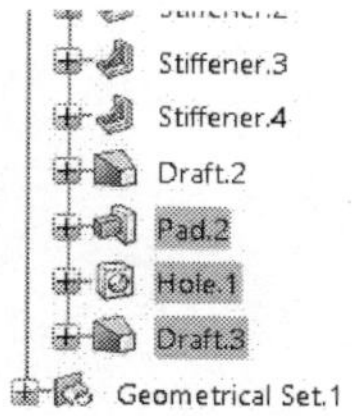

Figure 14–41

4. Click  (User Pattern). A warning message opens as shown in Figure 14–42.

5. Click **Yes** to open the User Pattern Definition dialog box shown in Figure 14–43.

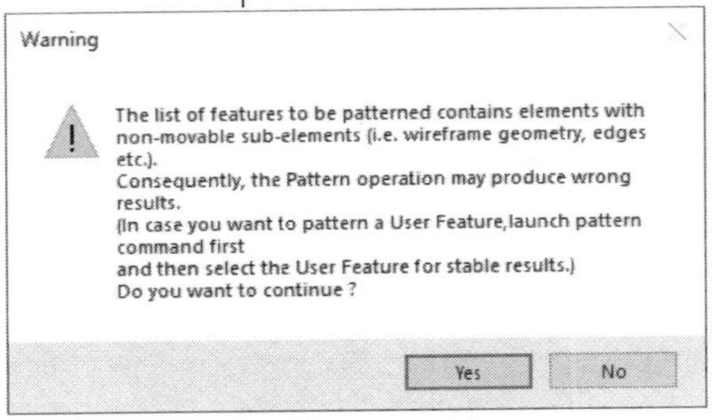

Figure 14–42

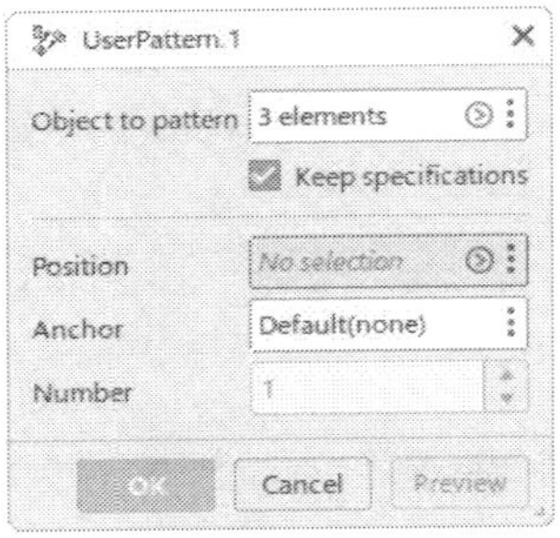

Figure 14–43

6. **Right Click** in the *Positions* field and select **Insert Wireframe>**  (Create Sketch). Select the **ZX** plane in the specification tree and then click **OK**.

7. Sketch and dimension the 3 points shown in Figure 14–44. Use the following dimensions:

   - 28 (1.102 in)
   - 36 (1.417 in)
   - 38 (1.496 in)

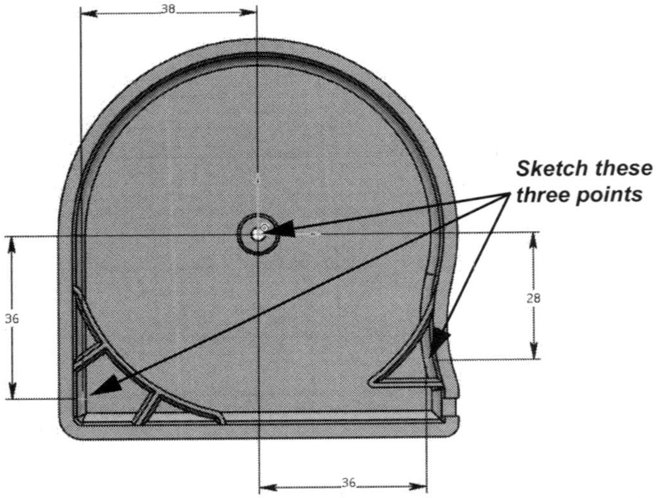

Figure 14–44

8. Exit the Sketch app.

9. Click **OK** in the User Pattern Definition dialog box. The model updates as shown in Figure 14–45.

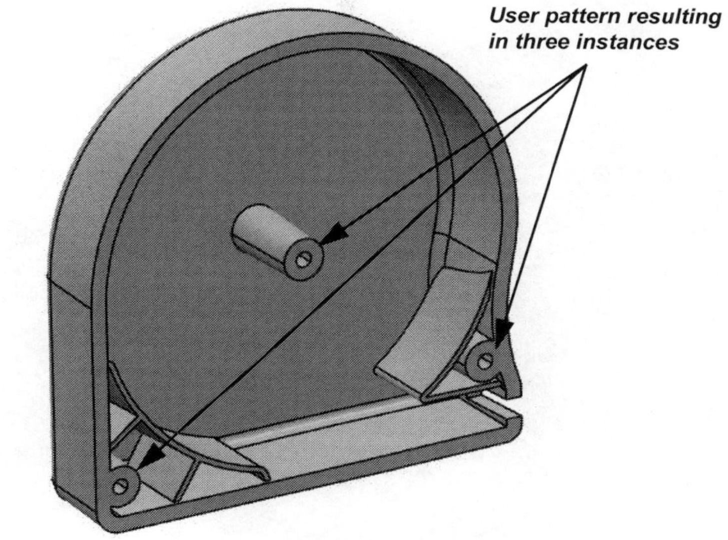

Figure 14–45

Task 2 - Create a Pocket feature.

1. Create a positioned sketch on the planar surface as shown in Figure 14–46.

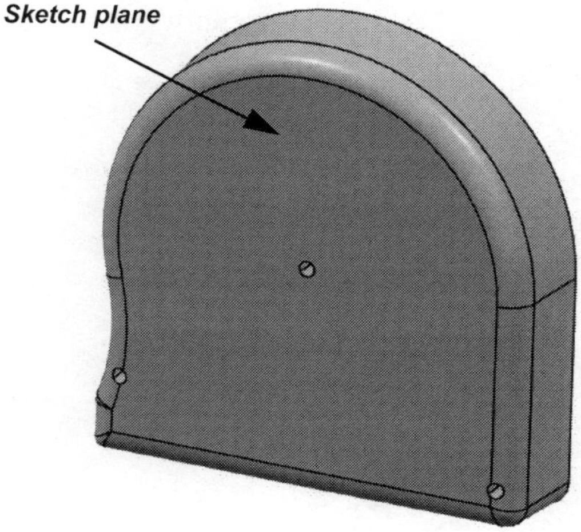

Figure 14–46

2. Create a sketch by offsetting the circular edge of the existing hole by **1.5 (0.059 in)**, as shown in Figure 14–47.

3. Exit the Sketch app.

4. Click  (Pocket) and define the Pocket by setting the *depth* to **1.5 (0.059 in)**.

   The completed Pocket is shown in Figure 14–48.

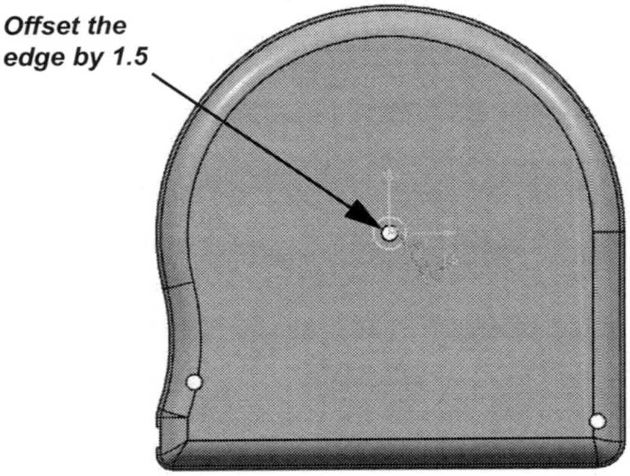

Figure 14–47

Figure 14–48

Task 3 - Create a user pattern.

1. Select the Pocket you just created and click  (User Pattern).

2. In the specification tree, select **Sketch.13**, which was established when creating the pattern for the Pad, Hole, and Draft.

3. Click **OK** and the completed Pocket user pattern displays as shown in Figure 14–49.

4. Click (* iso) and save the model. The model displays as shown in Figure 14–50.

Figure 14–49

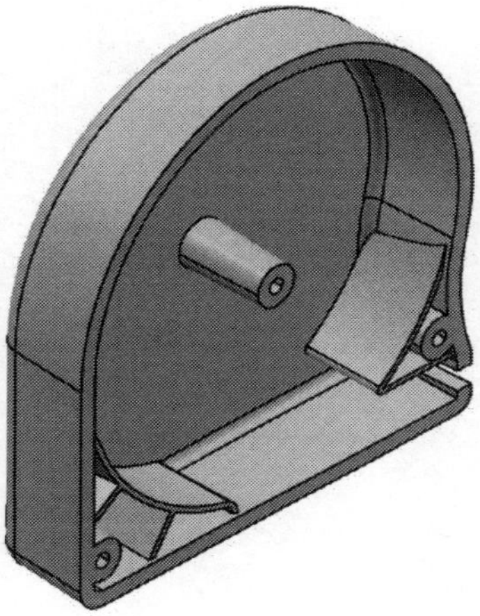

Figure 14–50

Design Considerations

A user pattern enables you to pattern multiple features and use the same positioning sketch multiple times as shown in Figure 14–51.

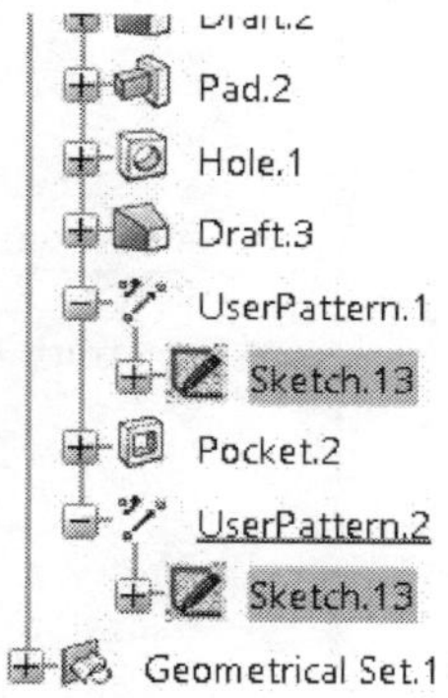

Figure 14–51

5. Save the model and close the tab.

Practice 14c Mirror

Practice Objectives

- Mirror features.
- Create patterns.

In this practice, you will create the part shown in Figure 14–52, which will consist of mirrored and patterned features. In some cases, you will copy a feature into a mirrored feature and then pattern the copied feature.

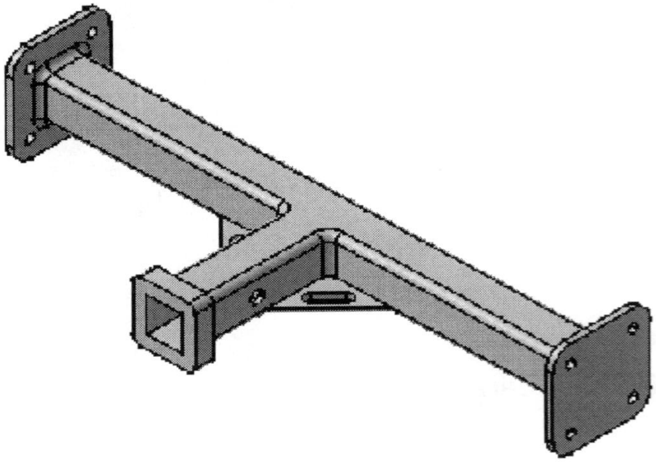

Figure 14–52

Task 1 - Open T_Support.

1. Import **T_Support.3dxml**.
2. In the *Support (Explore)* tab, right-click **Support** in the specification tree and select **Open**.

3. Create the rectangular pattern of **Hole.2**, as shown in Figure 14–53. Enter **89.2 (3.512 in)** for the *spacing*.

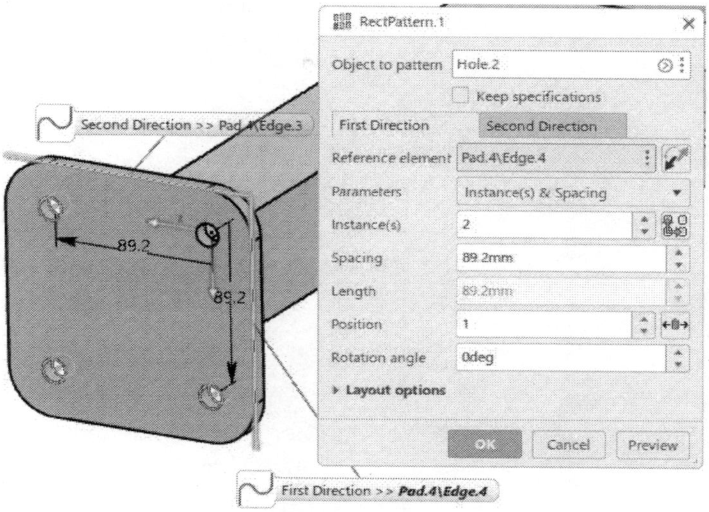

Figure 14–53

Task 2 - Mirror the mounting area to the other side.

1. Using <Ctrl>, select **Pad.4** and **EdgeFillet.3**.
2. Click  (Mirror). If a warring message pops up, select **Yes**.You are prompted for the mirroring element.
3. In the specification tree, select plane **ZX** and click **OK**. The model displays as shown in Figure 14–54.

Figure 14–54

Task 3 - Copy a Hole feature.

1. Select **Hole.2** in the specification tree.
2. In the Action Bar, click  (Copy).

3. Select the mirrored Pad surface, as shown in Figure 14–55 and click  (Paste).

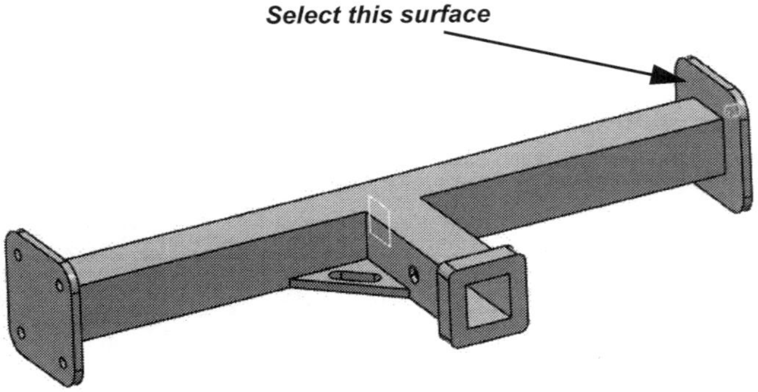

Figure 14–55

4. Create the rectangular pattern for **Hole.3**, as shown in Figure 14–56.

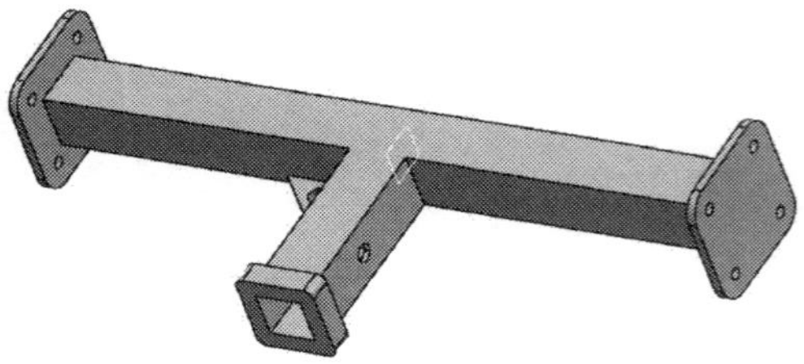

Figure 14–56

Task 4 - Mirror the stiffener and Pocket features.

1. In the specification tree using <Ctrl>, select **Stiffener.1** and **Pocket.1**.

2. Mirror the features about plane ZX, as shown in Figure 14–57.

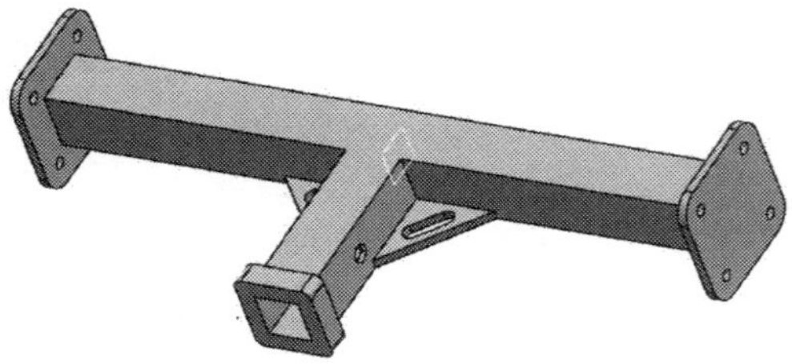

Figure 14–57

Task 5 - Finish the model.

1. Finish the model by adding **9.525 (0.375 in)** edge fillets where required. Use Figure 14–58 as a reference.

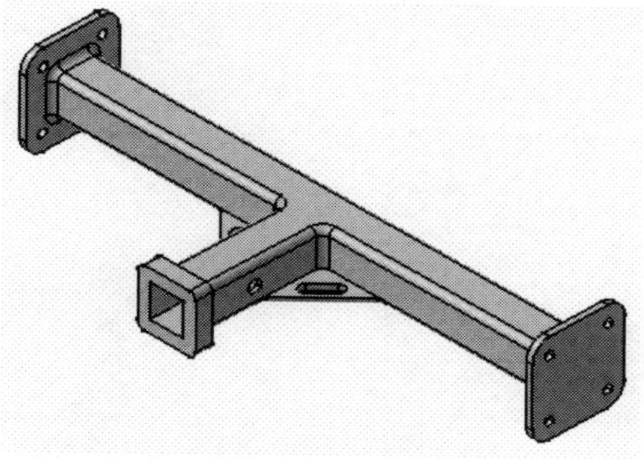

Figure 14–58

2. Save the model and close the window.

NOTE: Additional sketching practices are found in Practice B13 and Practice B14 at the end of this guide.

Chapter Review Questions

1. The model shown in Figure 14–59 has a rectangular pattern of holes created in one direction. What was the number of pattern instances defined in the dialog box?

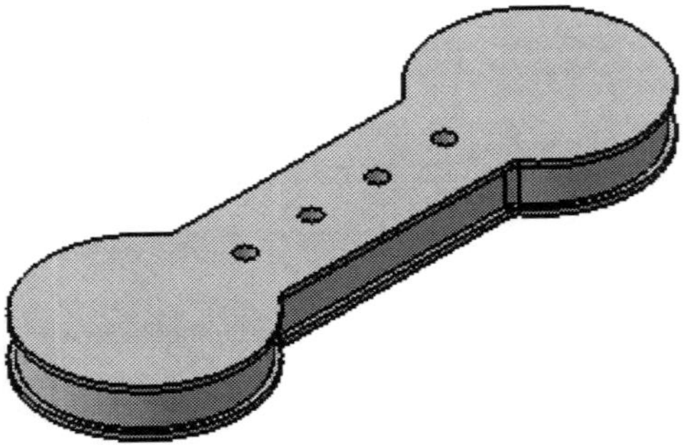

Figure 14–59

   a. 1
   b. 3
   c. 2
   d. 4

2. Which reference element(s) can be used as a reference for mirroring features?
   a. Plane
   b. Point
   c. Axis

3. You can mirror individual features or the entire part body.
   a. True
   b. False

4. When you delete a pattern, all occurrences of the Pattern feature are deleted including the original feature?
   a. True
   b. False

5. Multiple features can be Patterns at the same time.
   a. True
   b. False

6. To create the pattern shown in Figure 14–60, you could create a rectangular pattern in two directions and toggle off the instances that are not required.

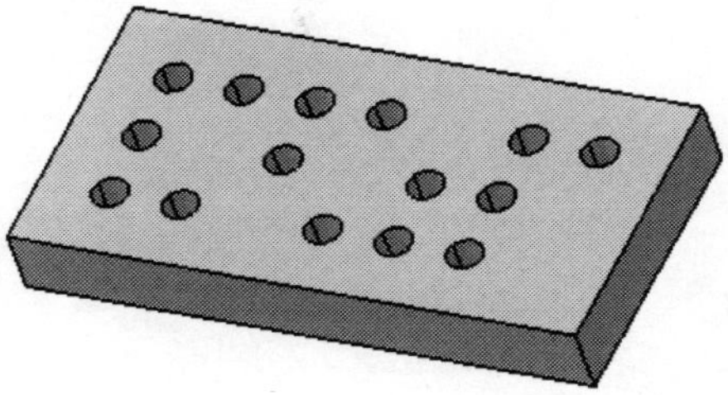

Figure 14–60

    a. True
    b. False

7. Copied features remain dependent on the source feature.
    a. True
    b. False

8. A PartBody contains five features. If the entire current solid is mirrored, how many features are listed in the specification tree?
    a. 5
    b. 10
    c. 6
    d. 11

9. A mirrored feature is dependent on the source geometry.
    a. True
    b. False

Answers: 1d, 2a, 3a, 4b, 5a, 6a, 7b, 8c, 9a

Thin Features

This chapter introduces solid features that enable the use of thin cross-sections by prompting you to input a thickness value.

Learning Objectives in This Chapter

- Create pads and pockets from open or closed sections using the **Thick** option.
- Learn how to quickly add stiffeners to a model.

15.1 Thin Pads and Pockets

Pad and Pocket features are created from sketches whose entities are closed, or otherwise closed by existing geometry. Solid material is either added to or subtracted from the enclosed area of the sketch.

Using the  (Thick) option, you can apply solid material to one or both sides of an open sketch. Solid material can also be applied to the inside or outside area of a closed sketch. The  (Thick) option offsets a section and adds or removes material between the original sketch and the offset section.

Thin Pads

To create a thin Pad, select  (Thick) in the Pad Definition dialog box, as shown in Figure 15–1.

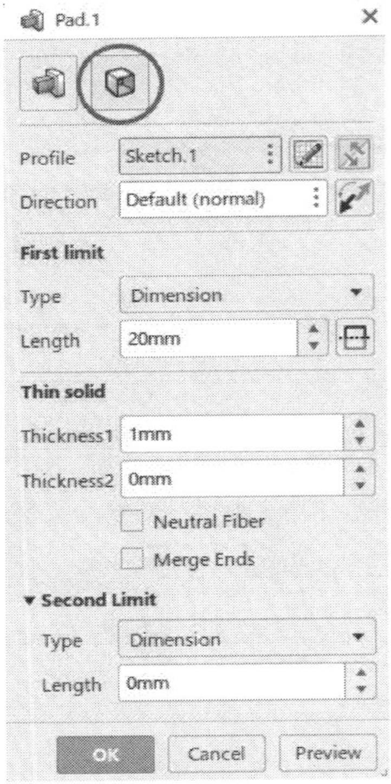

Figure 15–1

The base feature shown in Figure 15–2 has a constant thickness applied to one side of the open section sketch.

A thickness can be applied to both sides of the sketch.

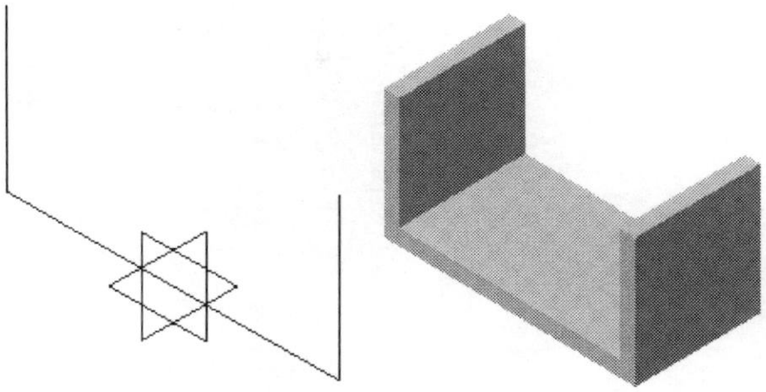

Figure 15–2

Thin Pockets

The (Thick) option can also be applied to a Pocket feature. Figure 15–3 shows a sketch that can be used to create a thin Pocket. The result of the offset displays with and without the **Merge Ends** option selected.

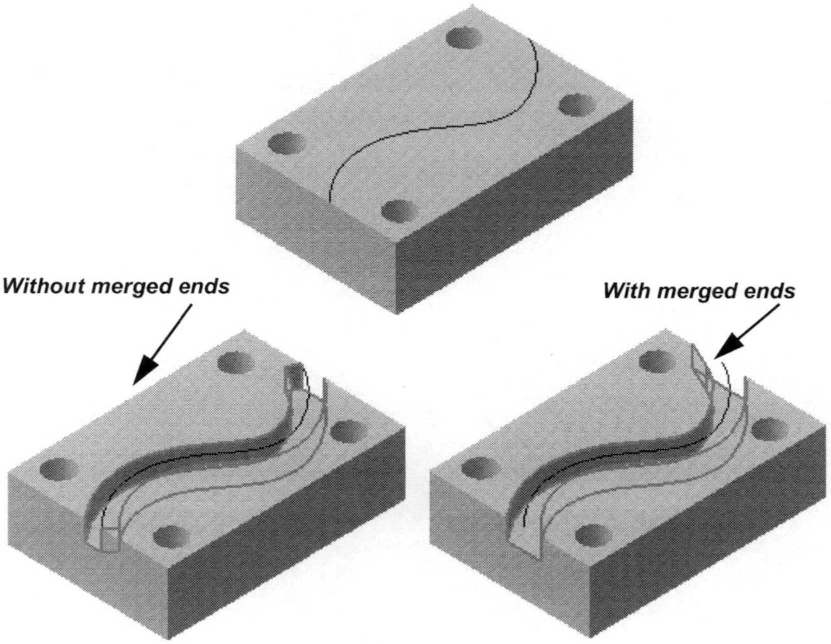

Figure 15–3

15.2 Stiffeners

A Stiffener feature adds material to your model. The Stiffener is used for two main reasons:

- Provides extra rigidity on a thin wall, as shown in Figure 15–4.
- Increases structural integrity, as shown in the example of the screw boss in Figure 15–5.

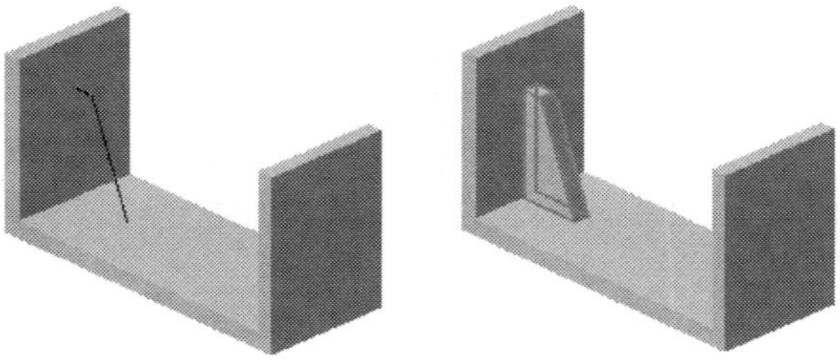

Figure 15–4

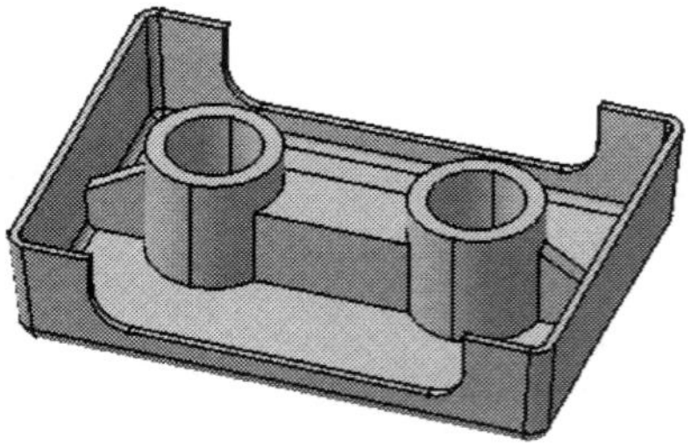

Figure 15–5

Stiffeners are created from open sections, whose end points are coincident with part edges.

How To: Create a Stiffener Feature

1. Click  (Stiffener). The Stiffener Definition dialog box opens as shown in Figure 15–6.

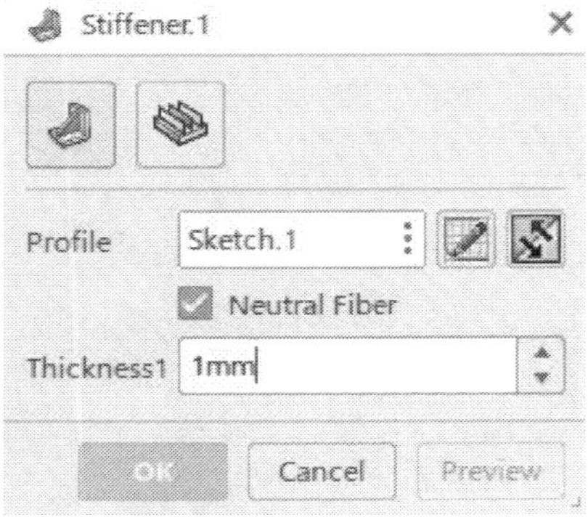

Figure 15–6

Applying thickness in both directions is limited, depending on the geometry present.

2. Select the sketch and apply the thickness in one or both directions using the fields in the dialog box.

3. Specify the mode. The  option creates the Stiffener parallel to the sketch plane, as shown in Figure 15–7. The  option creates the Stiffener perpendicular to the sketch plane, as shown in Figure 15–8.

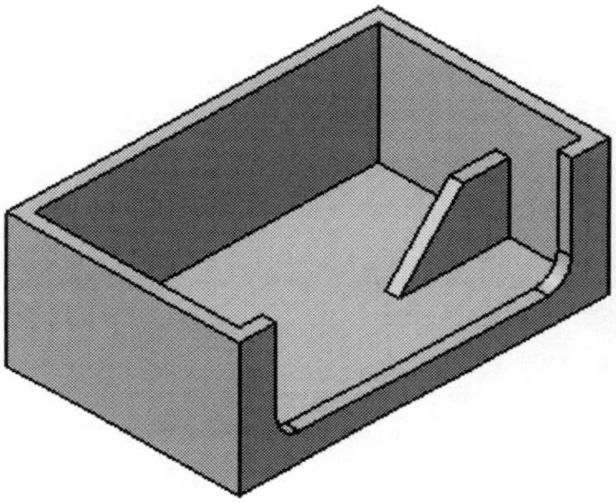

Figure 15–7

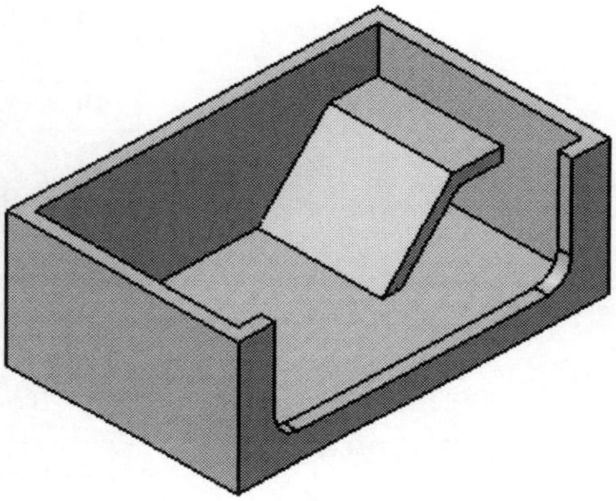

Figure 15–8

Practice 15a Creating Additional Features I

Practice Objective

- Create a thin Pad and a thin Pocket.

In this practice, you will add features to an electrical plug for a computer monitor.

Task 1 - Create a sketch for a thin Pad.

1. Import **Plug.3dxml**.
2. In the *Part1 (Explore)* tab, right-click **Part1** in the specification tree and select **Open**.

Design Considerations

The top face of the model requires a raised surface. Create two rectangular Pads for this purpose. The sketch profile will be used to create a thin Pad, which will then be patterned to create the second Pad.

3. Select the top face of the part and click (Sketch) in the context toolbar.
4. Sketch and dimension the rectangle shown in Figure 15–9.
    - Add a symmetry constraint to center the rectangle on the horizontal axis.
    - 3.125 (0.123 in)
    - 6.25 (0.246 in)
    - 25 (0.984in)

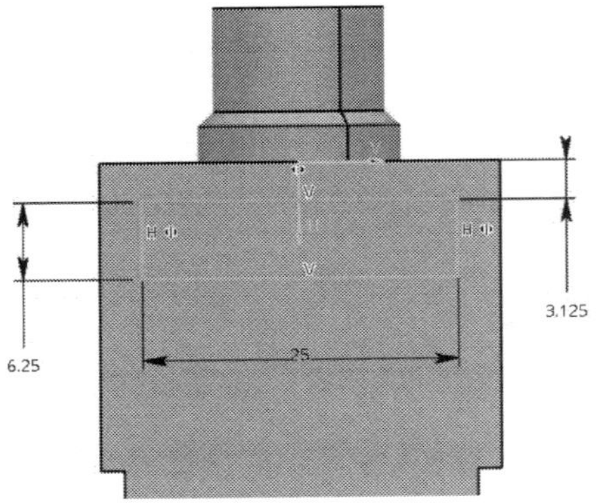

Figure 15–9

5. Click (Exit App) when the sketch is completed.

Task 2 - Create a thin Pad.

1. With the sketch still highlighted, click  (Pad) to create a Pad. The Pad Definition dialog box opens.
2. Set the *Length* to **1.600 (0.063 in)**.

*Thin Pads can add material to either side of the cross-section. **Thickness1** indicates the thickness of material added to the inside of the section, while **Thickness2** determines the thickness of the material added to the outside.*

3. In the *Profile/Surface* area, select 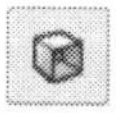 (Thick). The Pad Definition dialog box expands and the *Thin solid* section opens.
4. To add material to the inside of the section, set the following:
   - *Thickness1*: **1.600 (0.063 in)**
   - *Thickness2:* **0**

   The Pad Definition dialog box is shown in Figure 15–10.

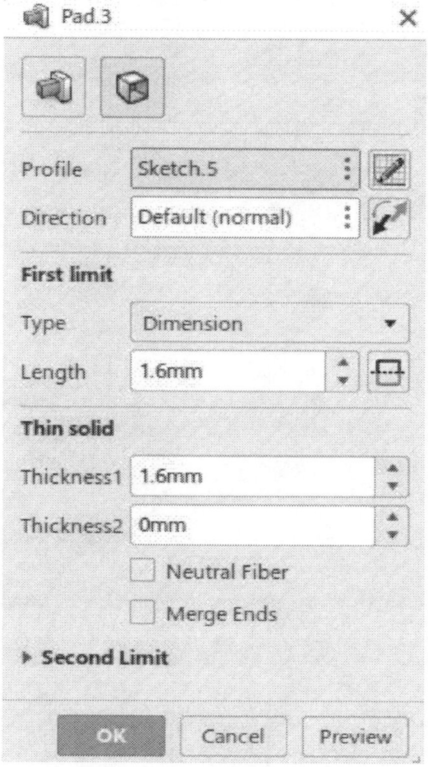

Figure 15–10

5. Click **OK** to complete the feature. The model displays as shown in Figure 15–11.

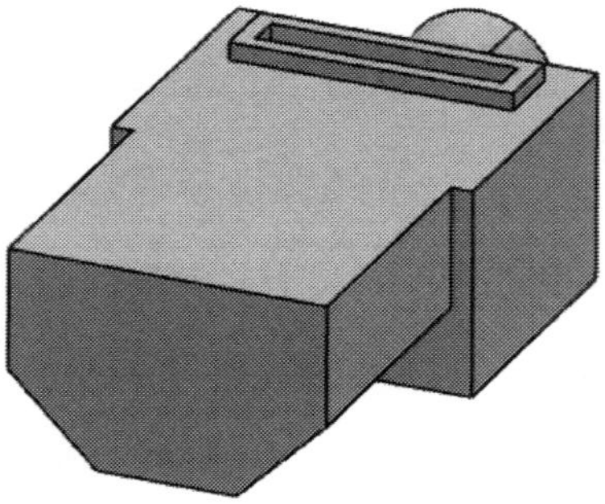

Figure 15–11

Task 3 - Pattern the thin Pad.

1. Select the thin Pad and click  (Rectangular Pattern) to pattern the feature. Set the following:
   - *Number of instances*: **2**
   - *Spacing*: **12.5 (0.492 in)**
2. Select the *Reference element* box and select the side of the thin Pad, as shown in Figure 15–12.

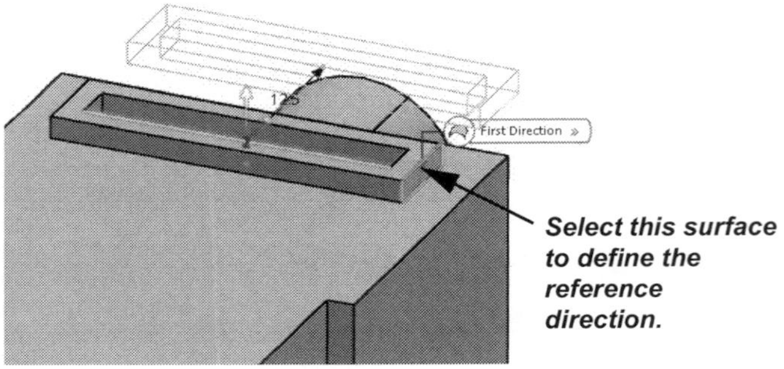

Figure 15–12

3. If required, click  (Reverse) so that the pattern lies on the part.
4. Click **OK** to complete the pattern. The model displays as shown in Figure 15–13.

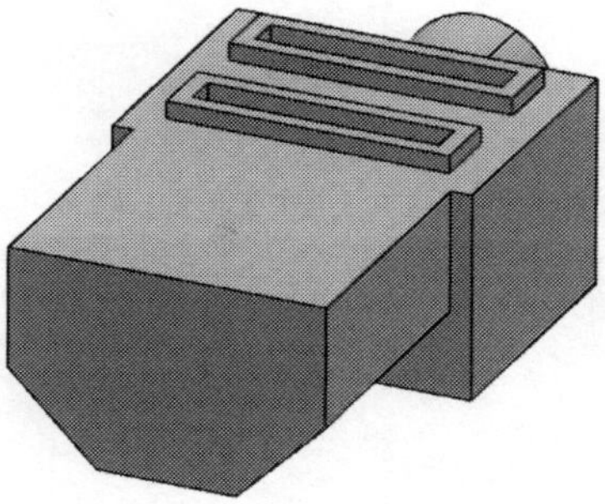

Figure 15–13

Task 4 - Create a sketch for a thin Pocket.

Design Considerations

Create the three thin Pockets for the plug sockets. The individual lines will be used as profiles for thin Pocket features.

1. Select the face shown in Figure 15–14 and click (Sketch).

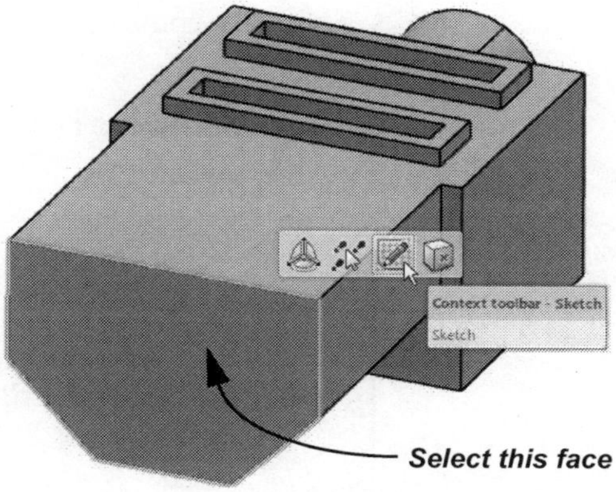

Figure 15–14

2. Sketch the section shown in Figure 15–15. The section consists of three vertical lines.
   - Make the upper two lines symmetrical about the vertical axis, and the end points coincident with the Horizontal axis.
   - Dimension the section as shown in Figure 15–15 using the dimensions of **6.25 (0.246 in)**, **3.8 (0.150 in)** and **19 (0.748 in)**.

- Use the (Equal) constraint to make all three lines equal length.

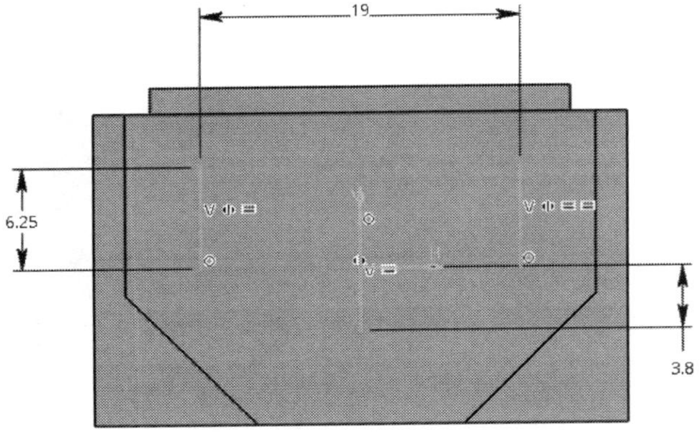

Figure 15–15

3. Click (Exit App) when the sketch is completed.

Task 5 - Create the thin pocket.

1. With the sketch highlighted, click (Pocket) to create a Pocket.
2. The Feature Definition Error dialog box opens as shown in Figure 15–16. Click **Yes** to continue to the Pocket Definition dialog box.

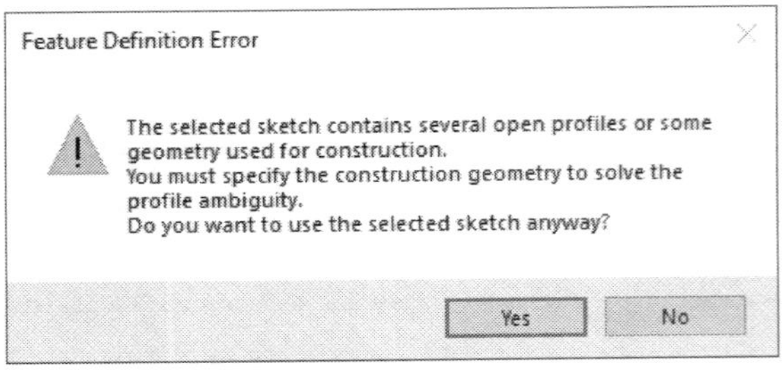

Figure 15–16

3. Set the *First* limit dimension to **19.00 (0.748 in)**.
4. Select the (Thick) option. The dialog box expands and the *Thin solid* area displays.
5. Select the **Neutral Fiber** option and enter **3.2 (0.126 in)** in the *Thickness1* field. The total thickness of the thin pocket is set to 3.2mm (0.126 in).

6. Click **OK** to create the thin Pocket. The model displays as shown in Figure 15–17.

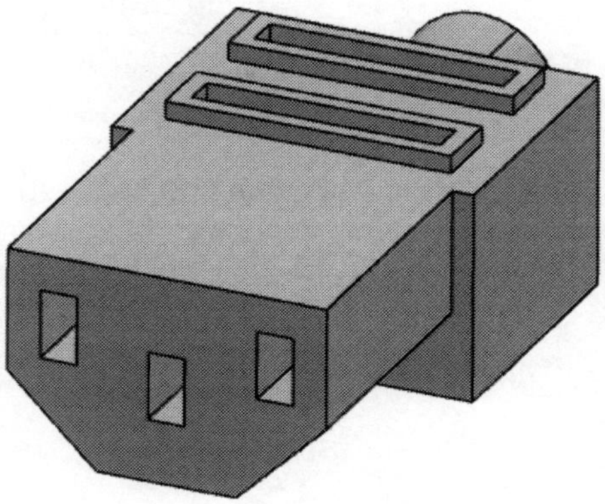

Figure 15–17

7. Save the model and close the tab.

Practice 15b Creating Additional Features II

Practice Objectives

- Create a thin Pad.
- Create a Tap, a Thread, and a Stiffener.

In this practice, you will add two bosses to a part using thin Pad features. These bosses will require support, so you will also create Stiffener features, as shown in Figure 15–18. Since the Stiffeners are created from open profiles, you will use the **Project 3D Silhouette Edges** tool to project the edges of the bosses features.

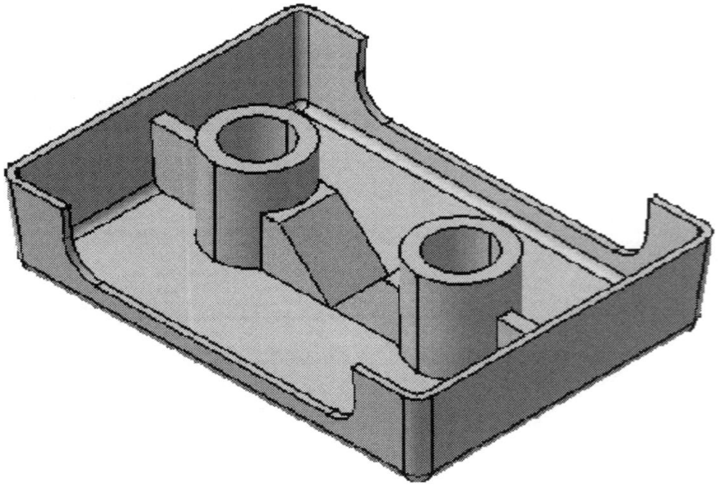

Figure 15–18

Task 1 - Create a sketch for a thin Pad.

1. Import **Lid.3dxml**.
2. In the *Part1 (Explore)* tab, right-click **Part1** in the specification tree and select **Open**.

Design Considerations

The following profiles will be constrained to the datum axis. They will be used to create thin Pads.

3. Select the surface shown in Figure 15–19 and click (Sketch).

4. Sketch the section shown in Figure 15–19 using the dimensions of **38 (1.496 in)** and **90 (3.543 in)**. Make the two entities coincident with the vertical axis and symmetrical about the horizontal axis.

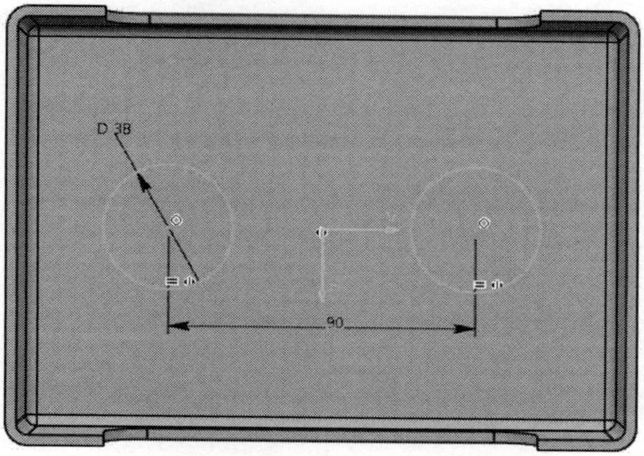

Figure 15–19

5. Click (Exit App) when the sketch is completed.

Task 2 - Create the thin Pad.

1. With the section highlighted, click (Pad).
2. Enter a *length* of **38.00 (1.496 in)**.
3. Select the (Thick) option.
4. Select the **Neutral Fiber** option and enter **6.4 (0.252 in)** in the *Thickness1* field. The total thickness is now 6.4mm (0.252 in).

5. Click **OK** to complete the feature. The model is shown in Figure 15–20.

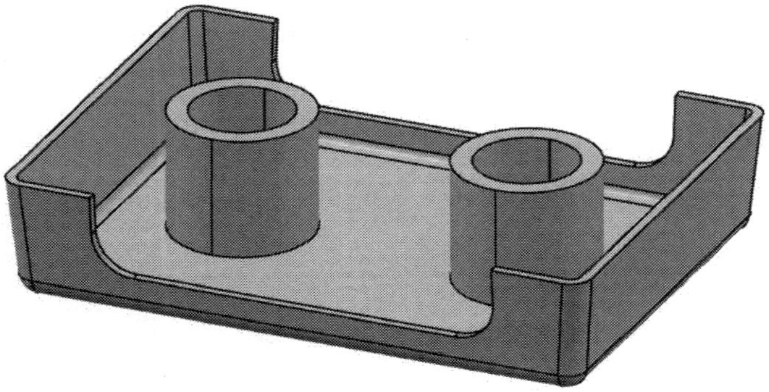

Figure 15–20

Task 3 - Create a sketch for the stiffener.

In this task, you will define the profile of a Stiffener feature using a positioned sketch. The origin of this sketch will be located on the inside face of the lid so that the stiffener profile can snap to this surface. You will start creating a point that defines the origin.

1. Select the three default planes in the specification tree, right-click and select **Hide/Show**.
2. Create a reference point using the **On plane** option. Select the inside face of the lid and enter an *H* and *V offset* of **0mm**, as shown in Figure 15–21.

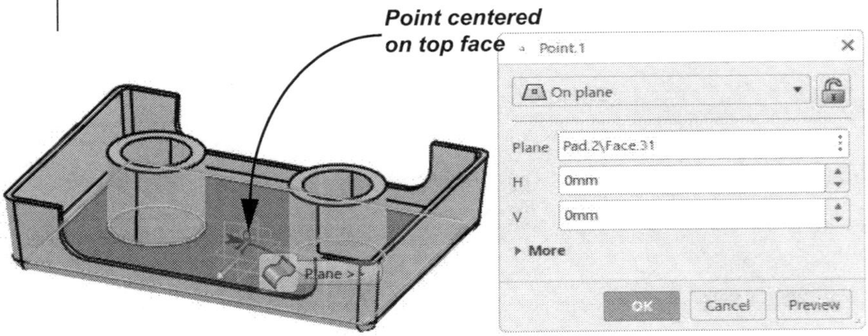

Figure 15–21

3. Create a positioned sketch on the YZ plane. Locate the origin using the **Projection point** option and select the point just created.

Design Considerations

A Stiffener is created from an open section, whose end points are coincident with two surfaces on the part. To help constrain the section, *Projections* and *Cut Part By Sketch Plane* will be used to create reference geometry. Projections should be converted to construction elements so that they are not used in the profile of the Stiffener.

- In the sketch you are about to create, you will need to project the edges of the cylinder and the lid onto the sketch plane.

  This is done by clicking (Project 3D Canonical Silhouette Edges) and selecting the cylinder.

- Additionally, you can select edges from the sketch plane of the part by clicking (Cutting Plane). Note that edges selected using the **Cutting Plane** tool are not projected onto the sketch. However, constraints made to the edges are constrained in the sketch plane.

Figure 15–22 shows the resulting silhouette projection and cut part when the edge of the sketch plane is selected.

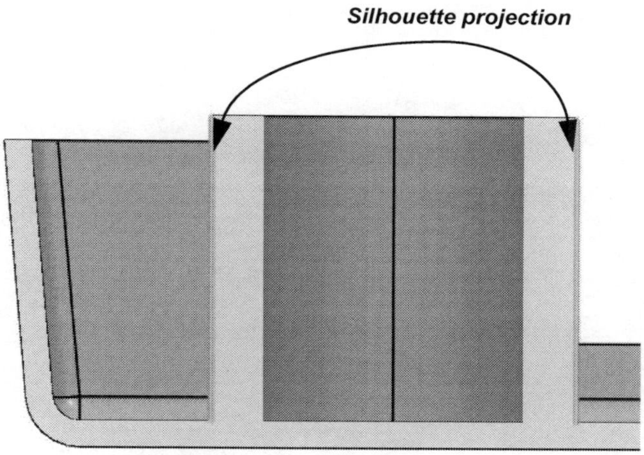

Figure 15–22

4. Sketch the two lines shown in Figure 15–23, using the dimensions **3.2 (0.126 in)** and **19 (0.748 in)**. Use the projection methods discussed in the Design Considerations to correctly constrain the section.

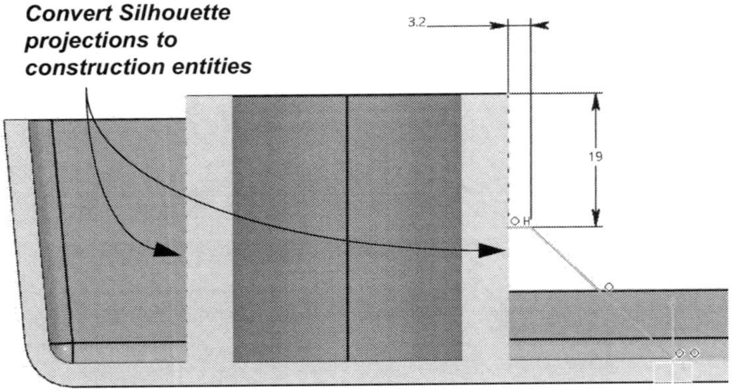

Figure 15–23

5. When the sketch is completed, click (Exit App).

Task 4 - Create a stiffener.

Design Considerations

Unlike a Pad feature, when the Stiffener is created, it does not extrude the open profile in two directions. The Stiffener feature will follow the curvature of the cylindrical part which it supports.

1. With the sketch preselected, in the *Essentials* section of the Action Bar, click (Stiffener). The Stiffener Definition dialog box opens as shown in Figure 15–24. Make the following selections:

   - *Mode:*
   - *Thickness1:* **3.2mm (0.126 in)**
   - Select **Neutral Fiber**.

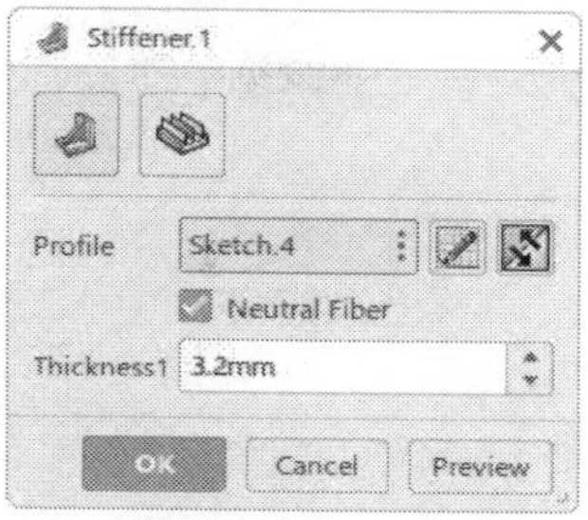

Figure 15–24

2. Click **OK** to complete the feature. The model displays as shown in Figure 15–25.

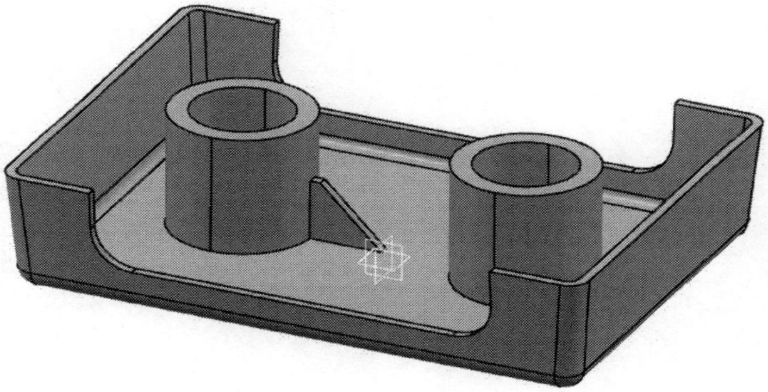

Figure 15–25

Task 5 - Modify the depth of the stiffener.

1. In the specification tree, double-click on the Stiffener feature.
2. Modify *Thickness1* to **25.00 (0.984 in)**.

3. Click **OK** to update the feature. The model displays as shown in Figure 15–26. Note that the Stiffener adapts to follow the cylindrical face that its section is aligned.

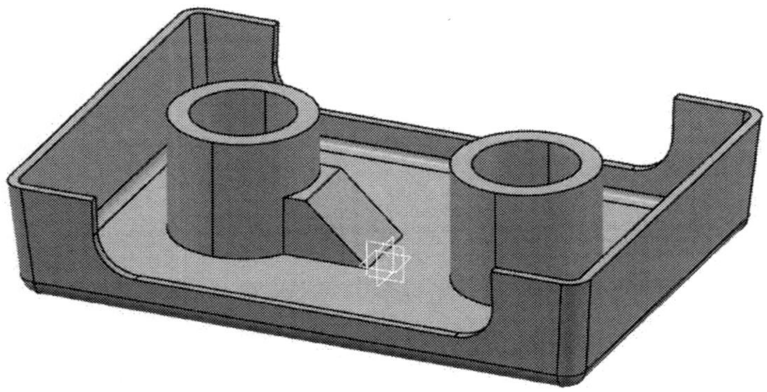

Figure 15–26

Task 6 - Create additional stiffeners (optional).

1. Create a sketch on the YZ plane. Sketch the profile shown in Figure 15–27, using a dimension of **12.5 (0.492 in)**. Remember to use 3D projections and intersections to correctly constrain the profile.

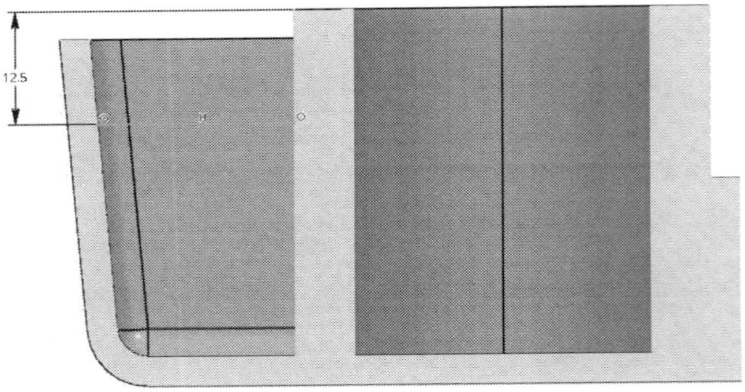

Figure 15–27

2. Create a second Stiffener feature with a *Width* of **6.25 (0.246 in)**.

3. Hide the three default planes and the point you created. The model displays as shown in Figure 15–28.

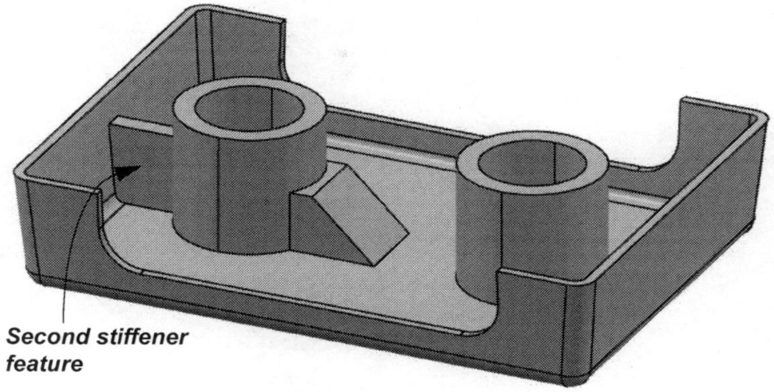

Figure 15–28

4. Create two additional Stiffener features on the YZ plane to support the right cylindrical boss. Use the dimension scheme and values used to create the stiffeners supporting the left cylindrical box. The finished model displays as shown in Figure 15–29.

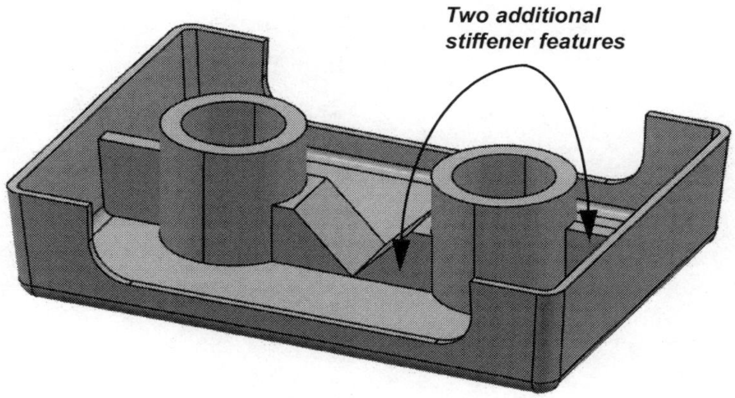

Figure 15–29

5. Save the model and close the tab.

NOTE: An additional thin features practice is found in Practice B15 at the end of this guide.

Chapter Review Questions

1. A closed profile cannot be used to create a thin Pad.
   a. True
   b. False
2. Using the  (Thick) option, where can material be added?
   a. One side of the profile only.
   b. One or both sides of the profile.
   c. Both sides of the profile only.
   d. None of these.
3. A Stiffener can be an open or closed profile.
   a. True
   b. False
4. The end points of a Stiffener profile must be coincident with an existing part edge.
   a. True
   b. False
5. The thickness of a Stiffener is always applied symmetrically about both sides of the profile.
   a. True
   b. False
6. Which Stiffener mode creates a Stiffener that is parallel to the sketch plane?
   a. 
   b. 

7. Which option is used to apply solid material equally to both sides of an open sketch?
   a. Neutral Plane
   b. Neutral Fiber
   c. Symmetric
   d. None of the above.

Answers: 1b, 2b, 3a, 4b, 5b, 6a, 7b

Chapter 16

Parent/Child Relationships

Parent/Child relationships are an important aspect of CATIA, as they control how features interact with one another. In this chapter you learn how to create and modify parent/child relationships and how to use them to your advantage.

Learning Objectives in This Chapter

- Understand the impact of Parent/Child relationships.
- Understand the various ways in which Parent/Child relationships can be created.
- Investigate Parent/Child relationships.
- Learn how to change existing Parent/Child relationships.
- Use the **Replace** command to replace features with Parent/Child relationships.
- Investigate feature failures.

16.1 Establishing Parent/Child Relationships

A parent/child relationship is the dependency of one feature on another. The independent feature is referred to as the parent and the dependent feature is referred to as the child.

- Modifying a parent feature can also affect the children of that feature. For example, if a child feature is dimensioned to an edge of a parent feature and modifying the parent moves this edge, the child feature moves accordingly. If the parent feature is deleted, the system no longer contains enough information to update the child feature's location. In this case, the child feature must be edited.

There are a several ways of establishing parent/child relationships that can help you capture design intent.

Sketch Plane

Default reference planes are automatically created by the software and are used as a sketch plane for the base feature, as shown in Figure 16–1. Additionally, default reference planes cannot be deleted or modified, so they make stable parent references.

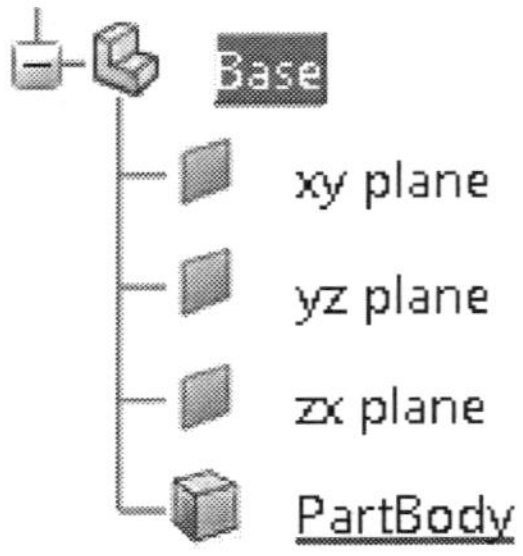

Figure 16–1

The references used to constrain additional reference features, such as reference points, lines, and planes become parents to these features, as shown in Figure 16–2.

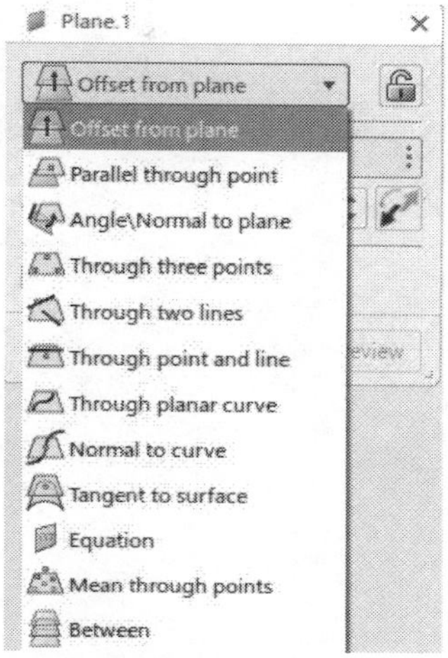

Figure 16–2

If a user-defined reference plane is used as a sketch plane, these references become parents to the sketch and the resulting geometry.

Planar surfaces of existing geometry can be selected as a sketch plane, as shown in Figure 16–3. This surface becomes a parent to the new sketch and subsequent geometry.

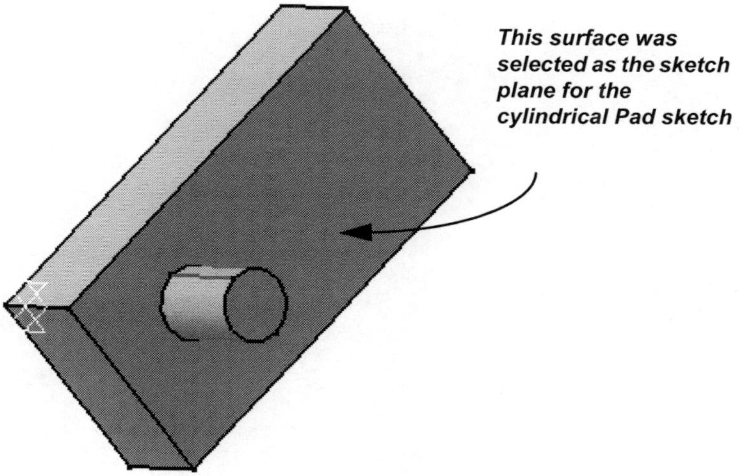

Figure 16–3

Sketch

The sketch from which sketched features derive their geometry are parents to the solid geometry, as shown in Figure 16–4.

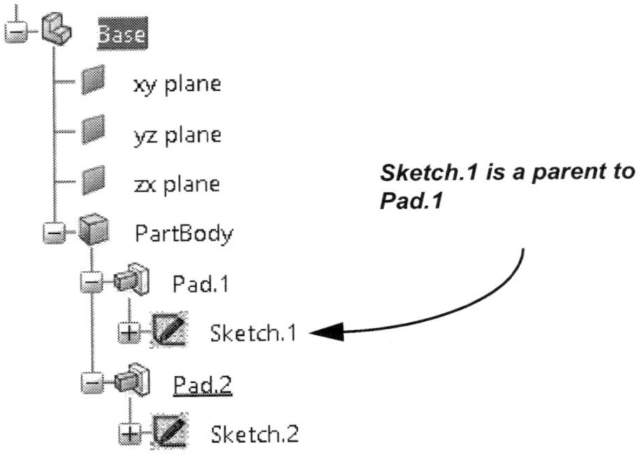

Figure 16–4

Sketch Constraints

Constraints meant for the creation of sketch geometry can create a dependency between features, as shown in Figure 16–5.

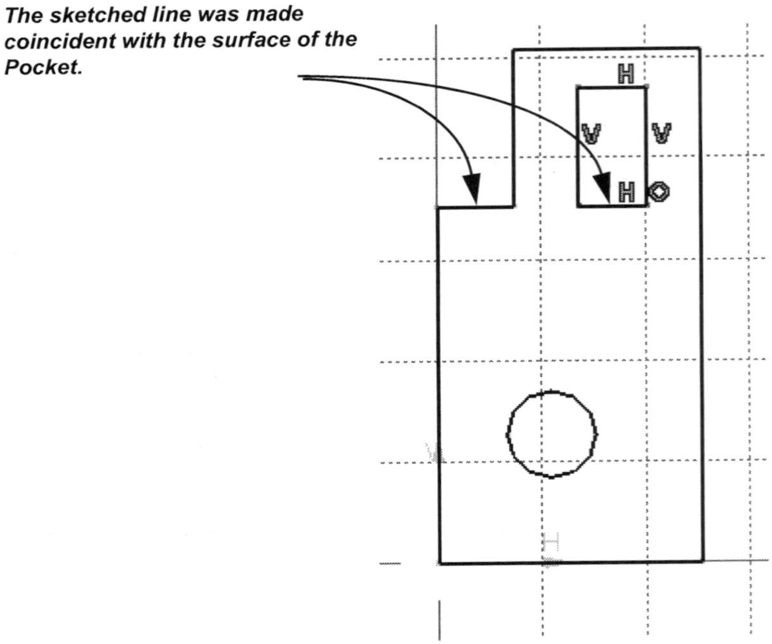

Figure 16–5

The resulting geometry is shown in Figure 16–6.

If modifications are made to the referenced Pocket feature, the coincident constraint maintains the design intent, as shown in Figure 16–7.

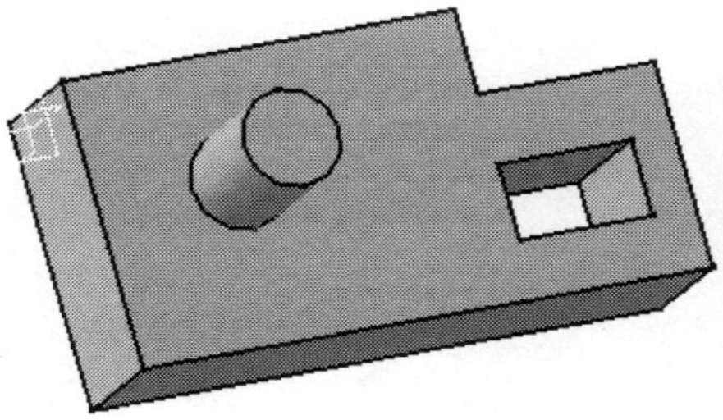

Figure 16–6

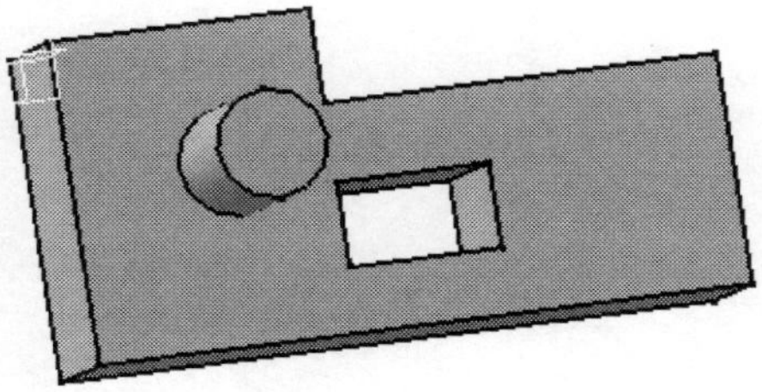

Figure 16–7

Dimensioning References

When dimensioning sketches to existing geometry, a parent/child relationship is established between the sketch and the geometry it is dimensioned to. If dimensions have not been specified to locate the sketch, the software automatically positions the sketch relative to the system-defined AbsoluteAxis, as shown in Figure 16–8.

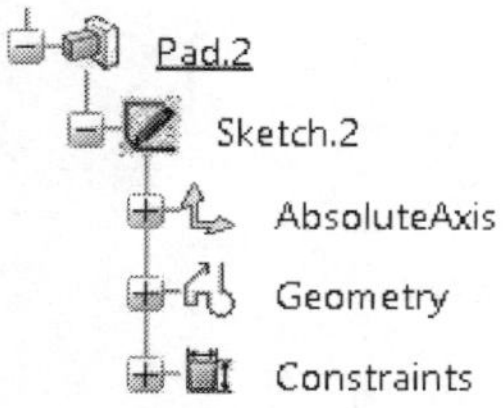

Figure 16–8

Note the relative coordinate values of initial sketch geometry, as shown in Figure 16–9.

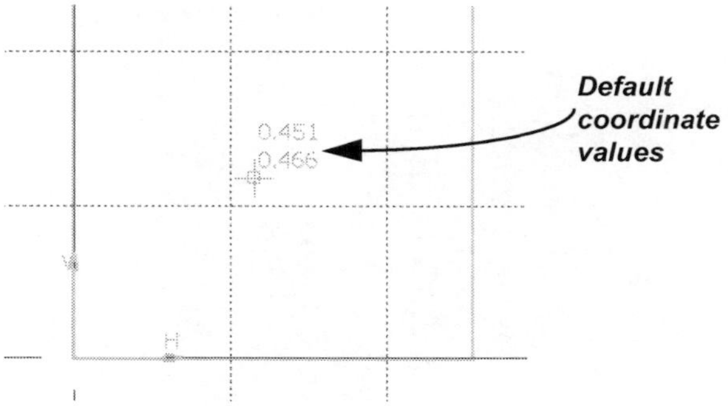

Figure 16–9

Projection of 3D Geometry

If the projected 3D geometry tools shown in Figure 16–10 are used to create sketch geometry, a parent/child relationship is established between the sketch and the existing geometry being projected.

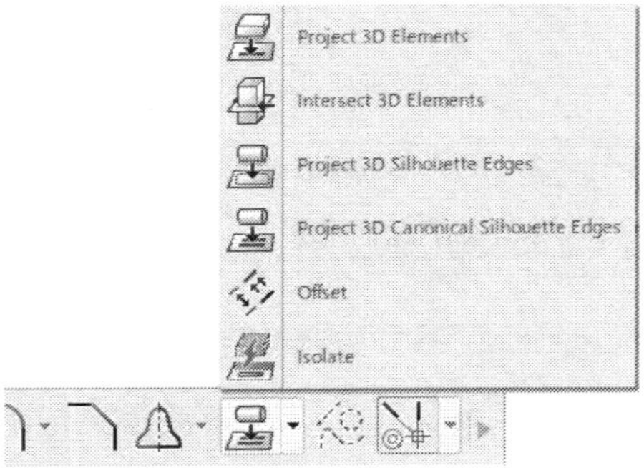

Figure 16–10

In Figure 16–11, the horizontal sketched line is dependent on the cylindrical Pad features.

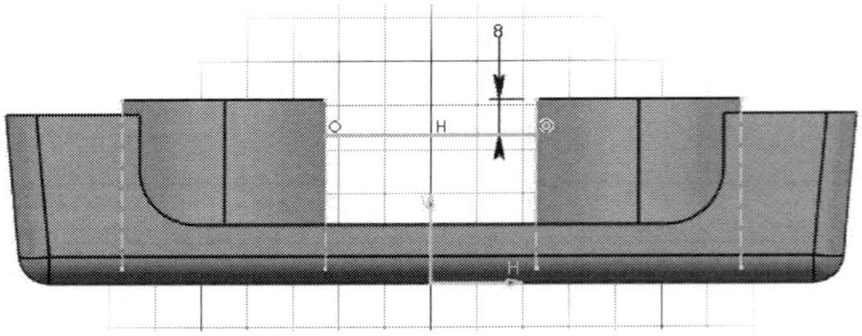

Figure 16–11

Depth Options

Consider the **Up to plane** option used in the example, as shown in Figure 16–12. Note the effect of modification to the parent feature, as shown in Figure 16–13.

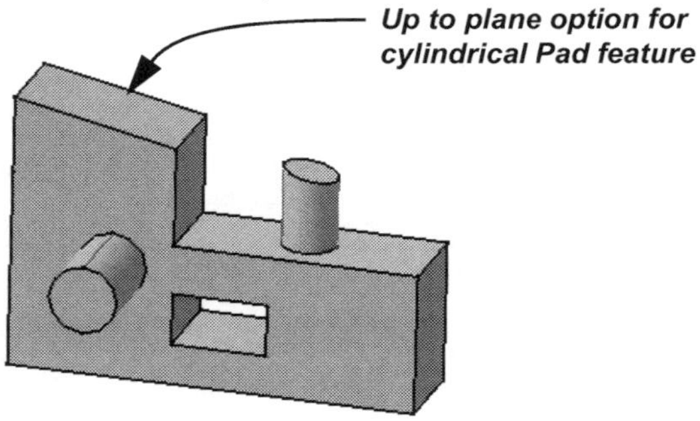

Figure 16–12

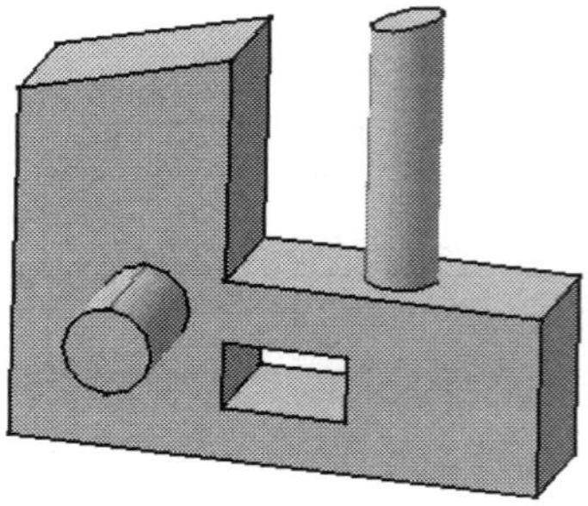

Figure 16–13

16.2 Investigating Parent/Child Relationships

The **Parent/Children** tool displays information about the parents and children of a selected feature. To activate the **Parent/Children** tool, select a feature in the specification tree or on the screen, right-click and select **Parents/Children**, as shown in Figure 16–14.

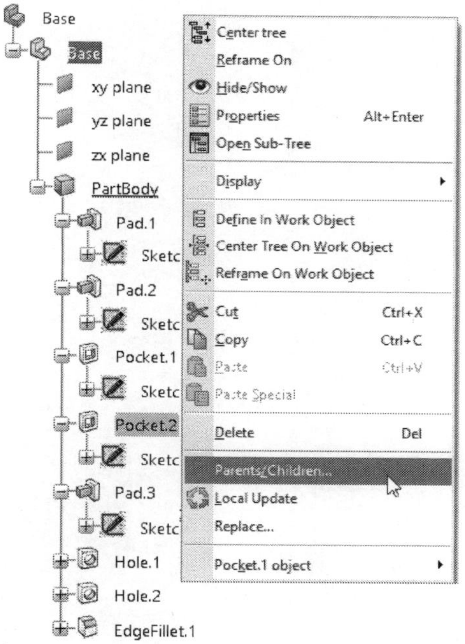

Figure 16–14

The Parents and Children dialog box opens as shown in Figure 16–15.

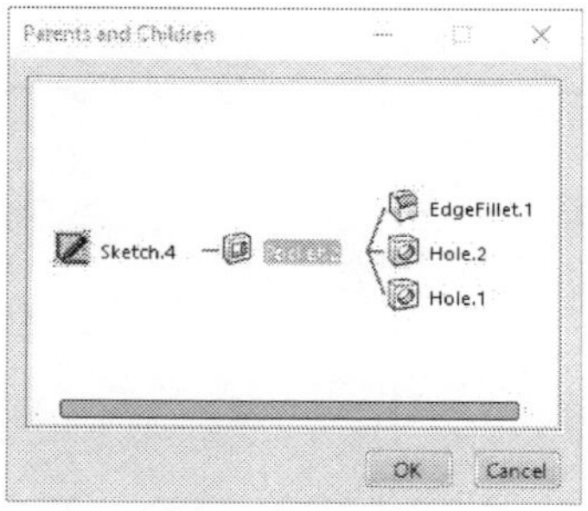

Figure 16–15

Double-clicking on the sketch item lists the parents and children of that item, as shown in Figure 16–16 for the model in Figure 16–17.

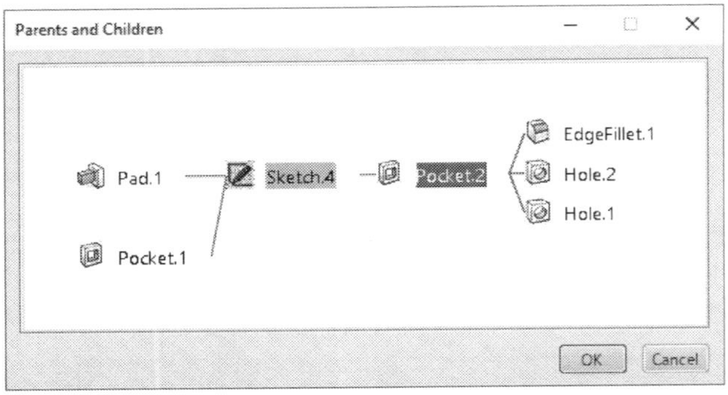

Figure 16–16

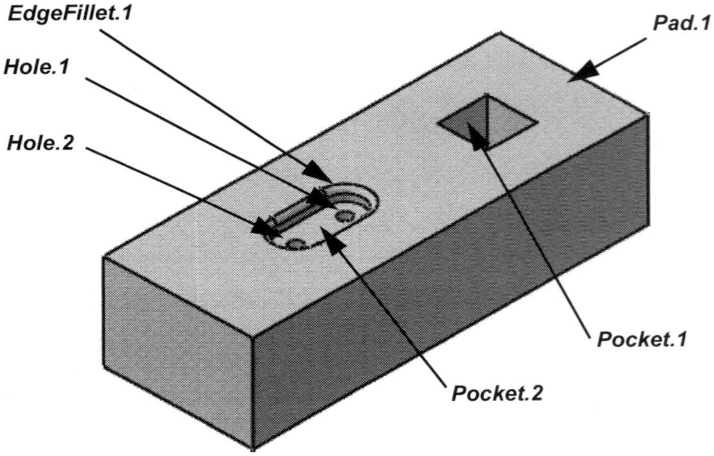

Figure 16–17

16.3 Changing Parent/Child Relationships

Changing the Sketch Plane

If the sketch plane of a sketched feature is changed, the solid geometry derived from that sketch follows the location of the sketch. To change the sketch plane reference of a sketch, select it from the specification tree, right-click and select **Sketch.# object>Change Sketch Support**, as shown in Figure 16–18.

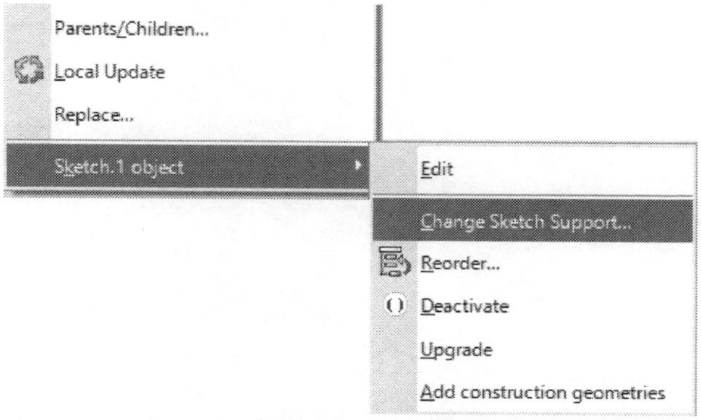

Figure 16–18

The Sketch Positioning dialog box opens as shown in Figure 16–19. The AbsoluteAxis for the sketch displays.

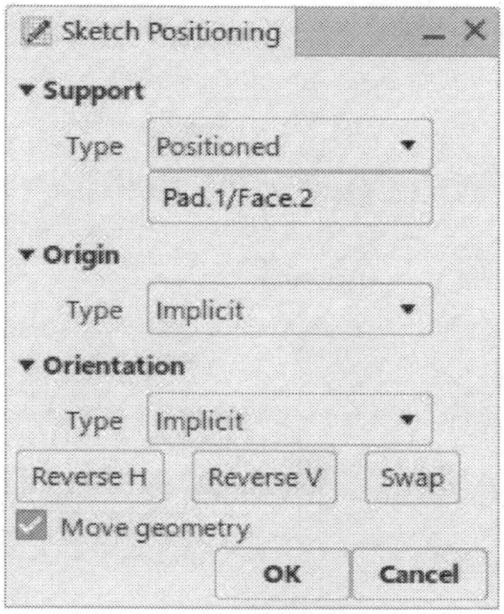

Figure 16–19

The sketch support type can be defined as either **Sliding**, **Positioning**, or **Isolated**, as shown in Figure 16–20.

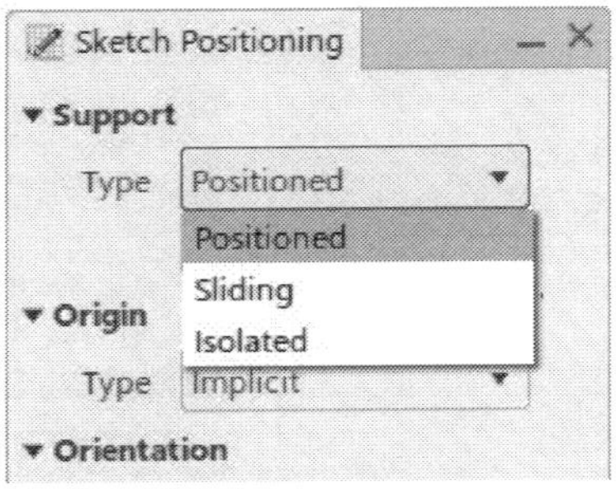

Figure 16–20

Sliding	Maintains the original orientation of the AbsoluteAxis sketch.
Positioning	Enables you to change the origin and direction of the H and/or V direction of the AbsoluteAxis.
Isolated	Breaks all absolute axis links with the AbsoluteAxis.

Sketch Dimensions

The parent/child relationships created by a dimensioning scheme can be changed by editing the sketched feature and deleting dimensions while in the Sketch app.

Sketcher Constraints

A parent/child relationship created through the use of constraints can be changed by editing the sketched feature and deleting the constraints while in the Sketch app.

Depth Option

The Depth option of a solid geometry feature can be changed by editing the Pad or Pocket and selecting a different depth option reference or a different depth option.

Replace

The **Replace** command enables you to replace a feature that has parent/child relationships. This option is not available for solid elements, but can be accessed in sketches and wireframe and surface designs.

For example, consider a Pocket with a fillet child. If you need to change the section of the Pocket, modifying the sketch using **Cut** and **Paste** causes the fillet to fail. Instead, create a new section and replace the section.

How To: Replace the Parent/Child Relationships of a Sketched Entity

1. Create the replacing entity.
   - In this example, the hexagonal section of the Pocket is replaced with a rectangular section. An edge fillet references the Pocket feature and fails if the geometry of the section is deleted and re-created. Therefore, the rectangular section is created in a new sketch and used to replace the hexagonal sketch.
2. In the specification tree, select the hexagonal sketch feature, right-click and select **Replace**.
3. In the specification tree, select the rectangular sketch to replace the hexagonal sketch. The Replace dialog box opens as shown in Figure 16–21. Depending on the references selected for the feature being replaced, you might have to go through each edge in the list and manually specify from the sketch which edge to replace it with.

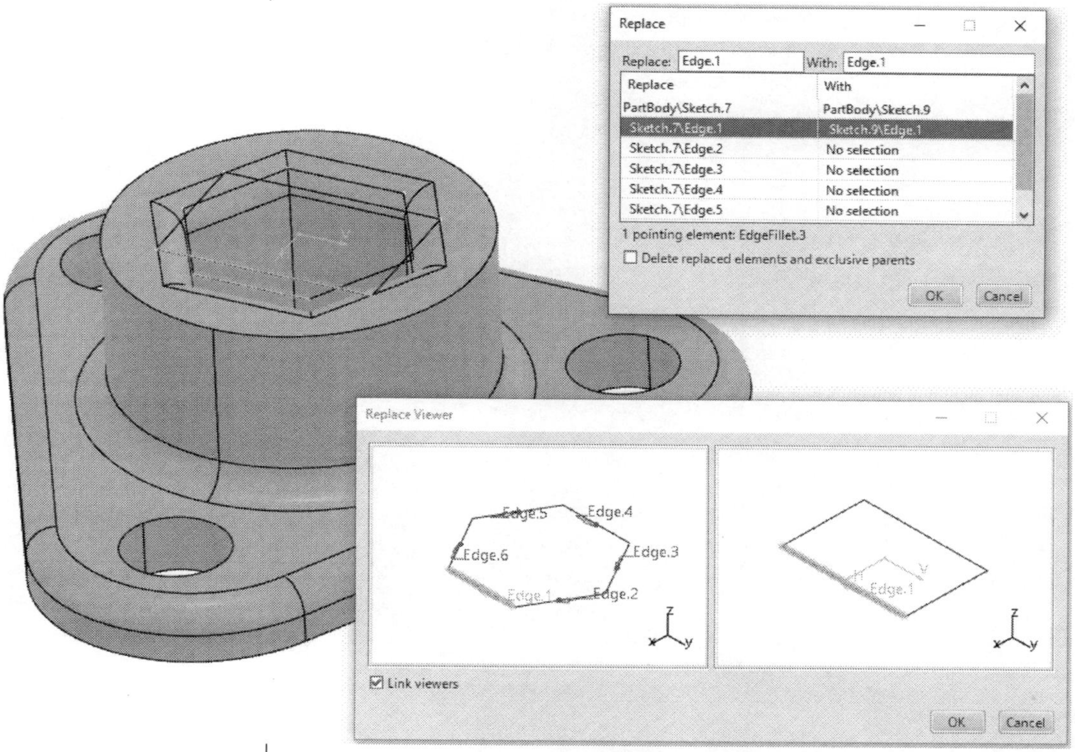

Figure 16–21

4. Click **OK** to replace the section. The feature updates to reflect the change. The replacement is shown in Figure 16–22.

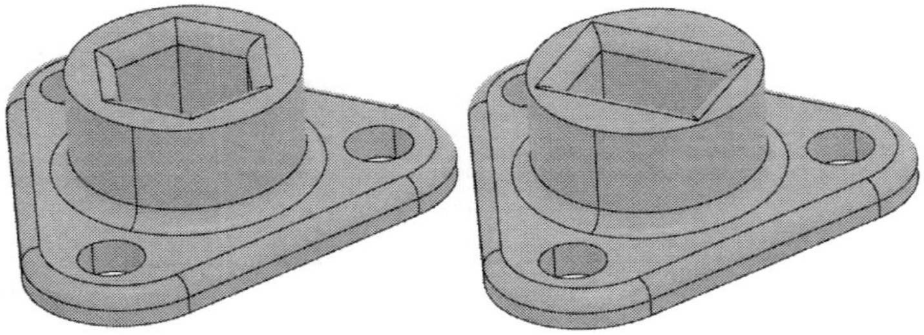

Before Replace ***After Replace***

Figure 16–22

You can also use the **Replace** command if you need to replace a section (with a parent/child relationship) that was automatically constrained to the origin. In this case, copying and pasting the sketch causes the children features to fail. However, you can maintain parent/child relationships by replacing the section with a duplicate sketch.

16.4 Feature Failure

Modifications to the part model are common during the course of product design. Depending on the magnitude of the changes, subsequent features might fail as a result of parent/child relationship disruption. When a feature fails, the Update Diagnosis dialog box opens and provides troubleshooting options, as shown in Figure 16–23. The **Update Diagnosis** tool is used to repair parent/child relationships when the **Replace** command cannot be used.

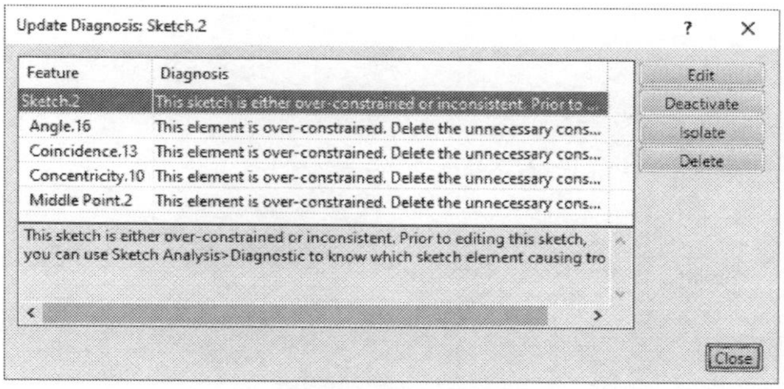

Figure 16–23

The feature failure troubleshooting options available in the Update Diagnosis dialog box are described as follows:

Option	Description
Edit	Activates the Failed Feature dialog box so that modifications can be made to resolve the failure.
Deactivate	Deactivates the failed feature.
Isolate	Deletes all inconsistent parent/child relationships.
Delete	Deletes the selected failed feature.

The type of feature that has failed determines the options available in the Update Diagnosis window. For example, a failed dress-up feature (fillet, draft, or shell) cannot be isolated because dress-up features are dependent on solid body parent elements.

Two common feature failure types and solutions are available:

- Draft Angle Failure
- Fillet Failure

Draft Angle Failure

Figure 16–24 shows an example of a drafted Pad. The rectangular profile sketch is changed to a semi-circle so that three drafted faces are removed.

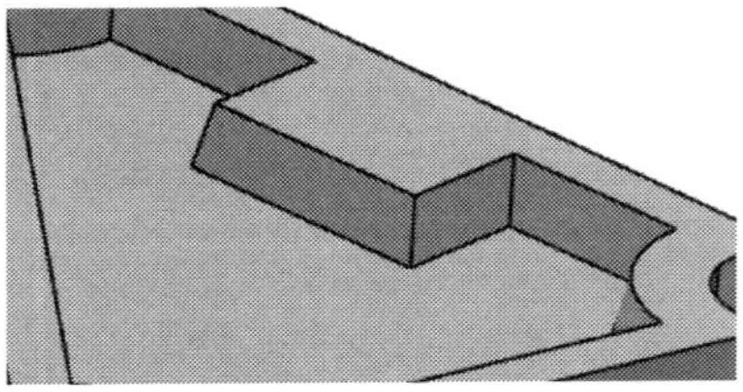

Figure 16–24

The Update Diagnosis dialog box opens as shown in Figure 16–25.

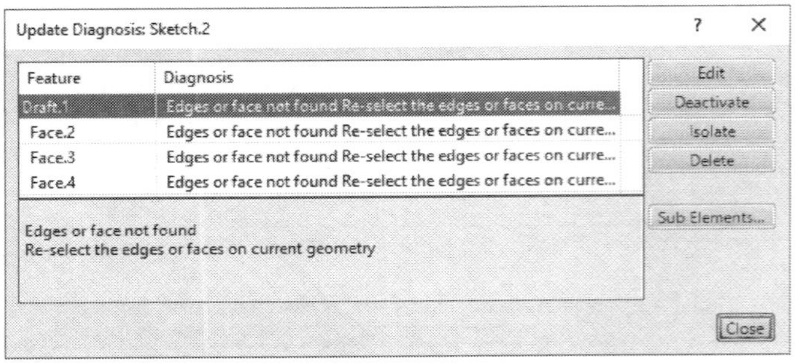

Figure 16–25

Since the Draft.1 feature is a child of the Pad feature, the three faces that were removed with the original Pad are no longer recognized and prevent the model from updating. The Draft feature cannot be isolated because it is driven by existing geometry. Deactivating the Draft feature toggles it off temporarily, but does not resolve the issue. **Delete** removes the feature from the model.

When selecting **Edit**, the Feature Definition Error opens, as shown in Figure 16–26. The three faces specified in the Update Diagnosis dialog box cannot be used because they no longer exist.

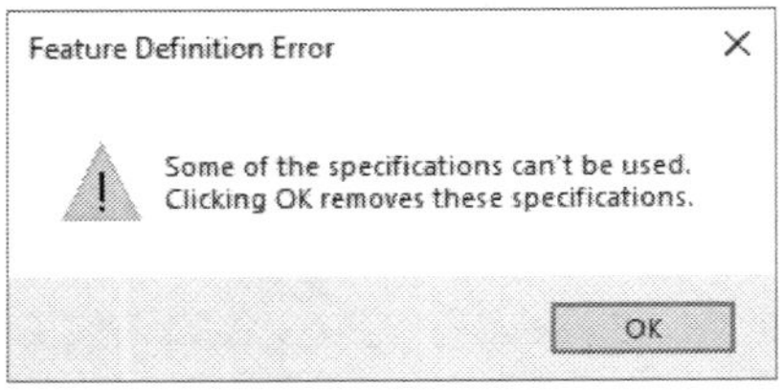

Figure 16–26

After closing the Feature Definition Error dialog box, the Draft Definition dialog box opens, as shown in Figure 16–27. The three faces removed during the creation of the semi-circular Pad are highlighted in the model display. The new semi-circular Pad face can be added as a face to draft. The model updates when the Draft Definition dialog box is closed.

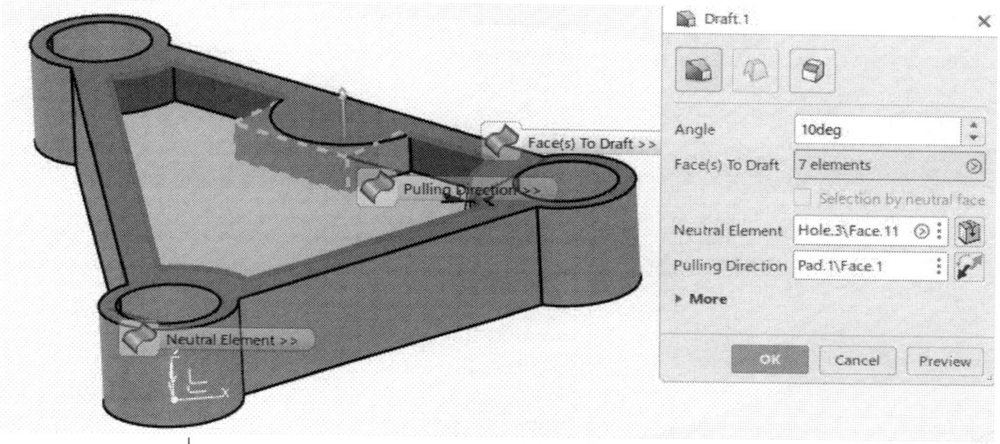

Figure 16–27

Fillet Failure

It is not recommended to create constraints using the edges of a fillet. If improper fillets result from poor design technique or designer oversight, they can be repaired. Figure 16–28 shows an example of a wedge Pad.

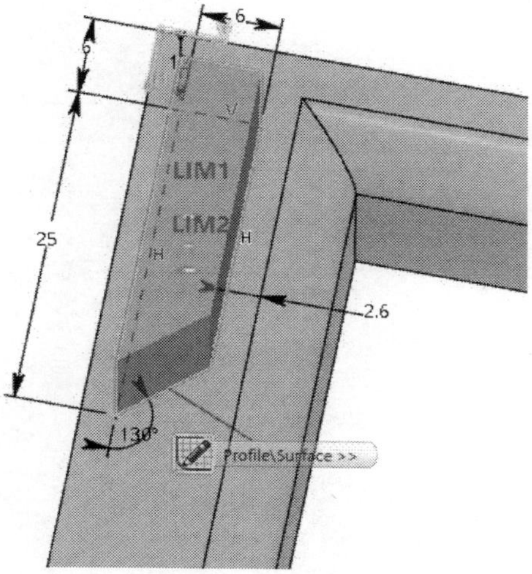

Figure 16–28

The wedge is constrained to the edge of a fillet by the 2.6mm dimension. When the Fillet feature is removed from this edge, the Update Diagnosis dialog box opens as shown in Figure 16–29. This indicates that a parent/child relationship has failed and that the constraint is no longer recognized.

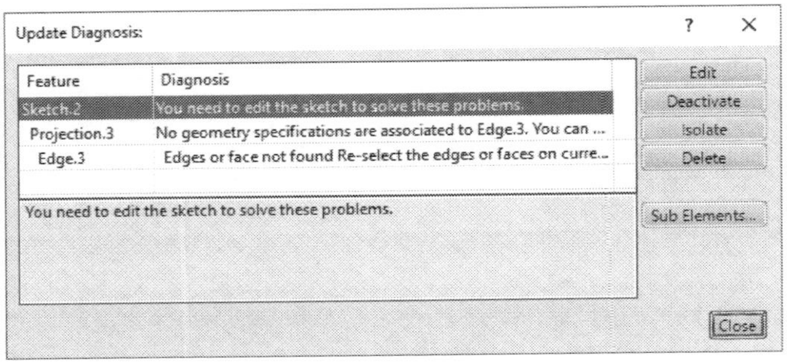

Figure 16–29

By isolating the sketch feature, the failed constraint is removed and **Sketch.3** becomes under-constrained. The former constraint edge is saved as an external reference (construction) line in the sketch.

- Select the **Edit** option to repair the parent/child relationship issue. The part automatically enters the Sketch app and the damaged constraint can be reconnected to the non-filleted edge by selecting **component**, as shown in Figure 16–30.
- The parent/child relationship has been reconciled, and the part updates when you exit the Sketch app.

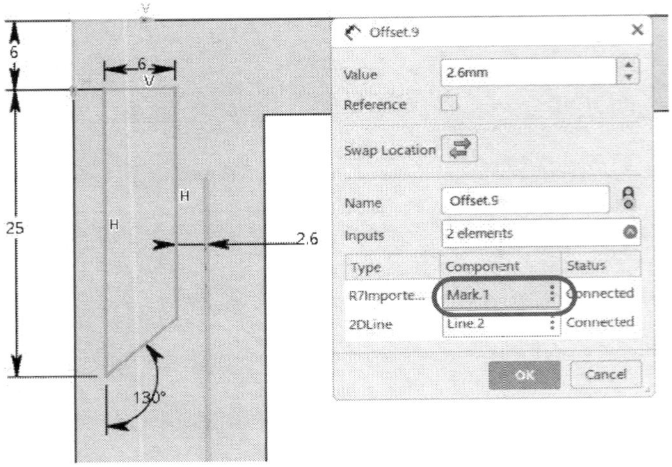

Figure 16–30

Practice 16a Parent/Child Relationships

Practice Objectives

- Edit parent/child relationships.
- Resolve feature failure.

In this practice you will import a model and modify it to create the part. You will analyze and edit parent/child relationships and resolve feature failure. In addition, you will observe the importance of correctly referencing features. The final part model displays as shown in Figure 16–31.

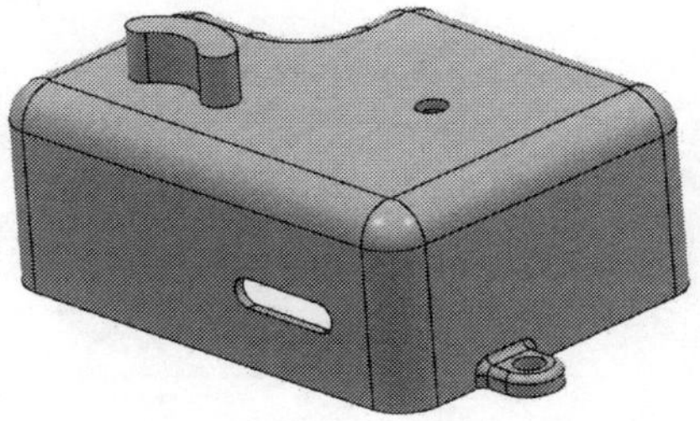

Figure 16–31

Task 1 - Investigate the part.

1. Import **Enclosure.3dxml**.
2. In the *Part1 (Explore)* tab, right-click **Part1** in the specification tree and select **Open**.
3. Note the location of the hole on the top of the part. The hole is centered between the two side surfaces, as shown in Figure 16–32.

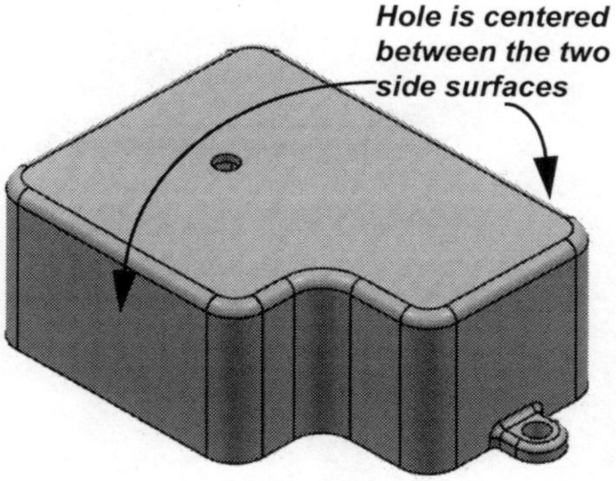

Figure 16–32

4. Change the *radius* of the top Fillet feature to **15mm (0.591 in)**. The model displays as shown in Figure 16–33. The hole is no longer positioned in the middle of the part.

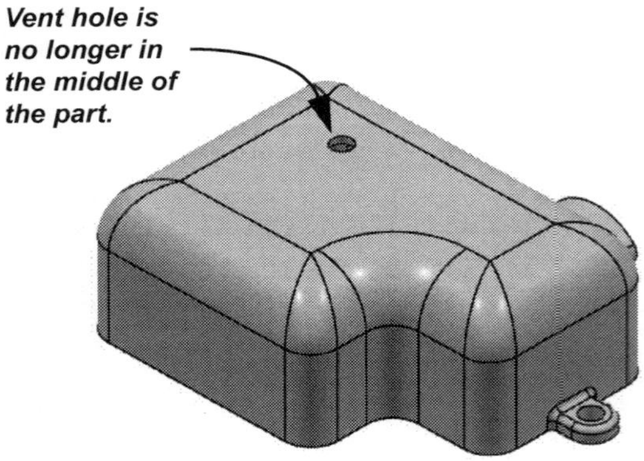

Figure 16–33

Task 2 - Investigate the Vent Hole feature.

1. In the specification tree, expand the Vent feature, right-click on the Sketch Vent sketch and select **Parents/Children**. The Parents and Children dialog box opens as shown in Figure 16–34.

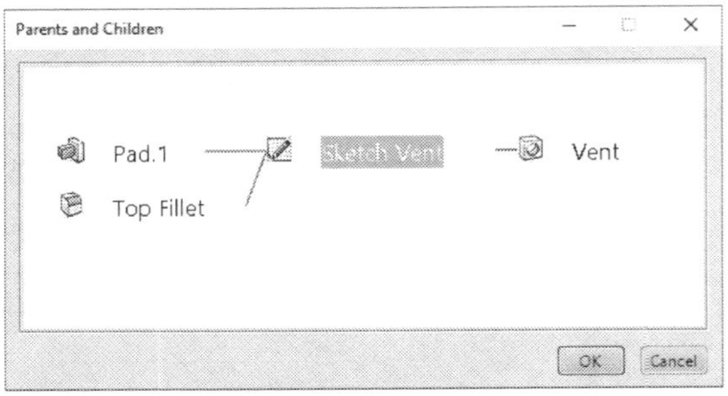

Figure 16–34

   - Pad.1 and Top fillet are parents to the Vent hole. When the fillet radius changed, the hole moved because of this relationship.

2. Close the Parents and Children dialog box.

Task 3 - Change the parent/child relationship of the Vent hole.

1. Double-click on the Sketch Vent sketch feature in the specification tree to modify it. Note the 34.5 (1.358 in) dimension to the edge of the Fillet feature, as shown in Figure 16–35.

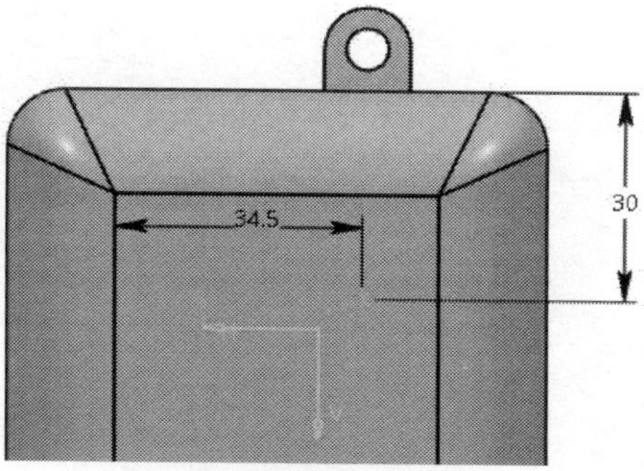

Figure 16–35

2. Delete the 34.5 (1.358 in) dimension.

3. Create a new dimension from the hole center to the left side surface of the part. Modify the *value* to **34.5 (1.358 in)**, as shown in Figure 16–36.

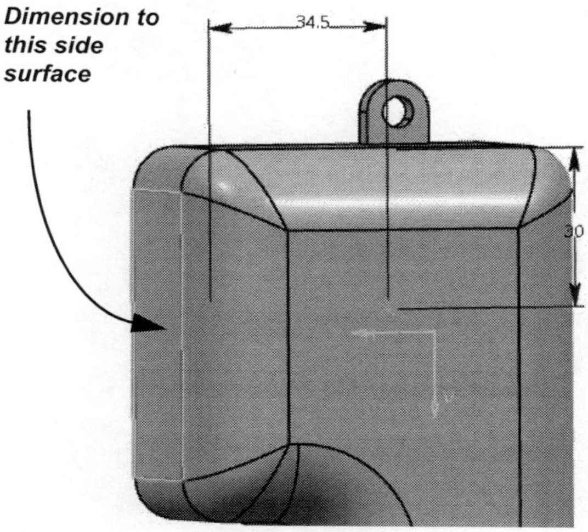

Figure 16–36

4. Exit the Sketch app.

5. Modify the *Top fillet* to **7.5 (0.295 in)**. The model displays as shown in Figure 16–37. Note that the position of the Vent hole remained in its intended position.

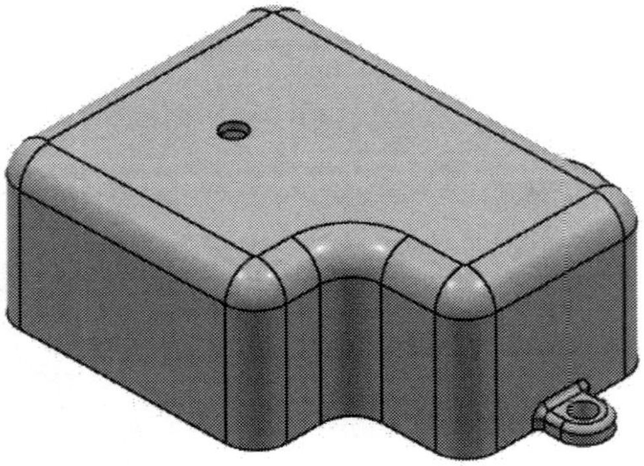

Figure 16–37

6. Investigate the parent/child information of the Sketch Vent feature again. Note that the top **Fillet** feature is no longer a parent of the Vent Hole feature, as can be seen in Figure 16–38.

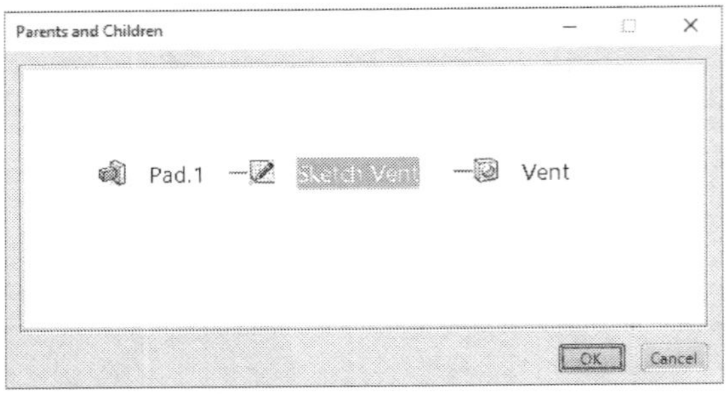

Figure 16–38

Task 4 - Change the sketch plane reference of a feature.

In this task, you will incorporate the design change shown in Figure 16–39.

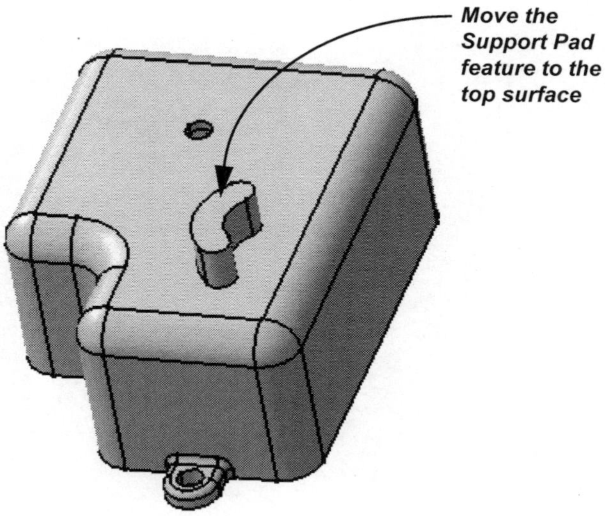

Figure 16–39

1. In the specification tree, expand Support and select the Sketch Support sketch feature. Right-click and select **Sketch Support object>Change Sketch Support**. The Sketch Positioning dialog box opens, as shown in Figure 16–40.

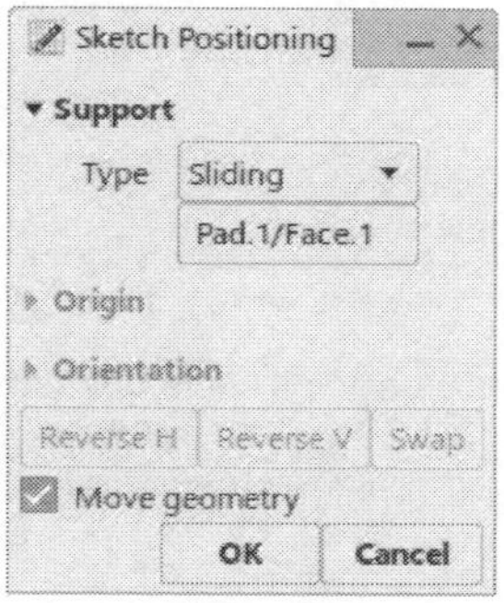

Figure 16–40

2. To change the sketching plane, select the top surface shown in Figure 16–41.

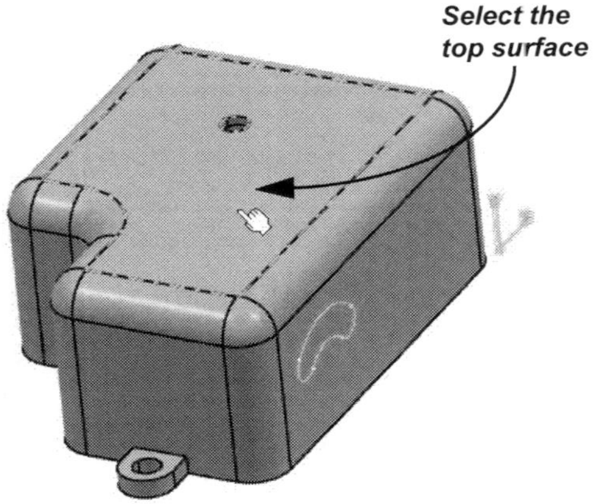

Figure 16–41

3. Click **OK** to accept the modification. The model displays as shown in Figure 16–42.

Figure 16–42

4. In the specification tree, double-click on Sketch Support to activate the Sketch app.

5. Drag a box around the sketch to select the entire sketch, as shown in Figure 16–43.

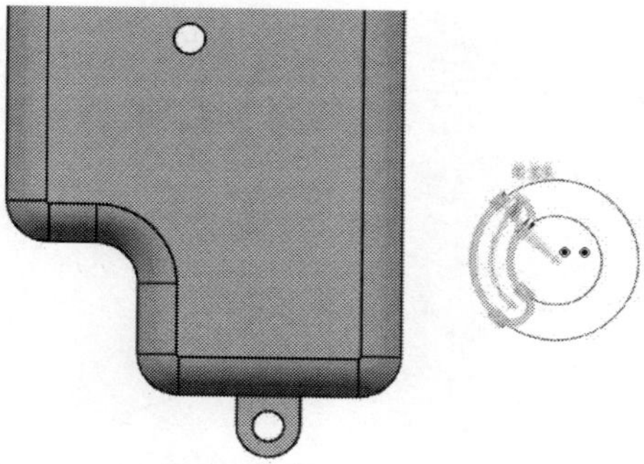

Figure 16–43

6. Drag the sketch to a location similar to the one shown in Figure 16–44.

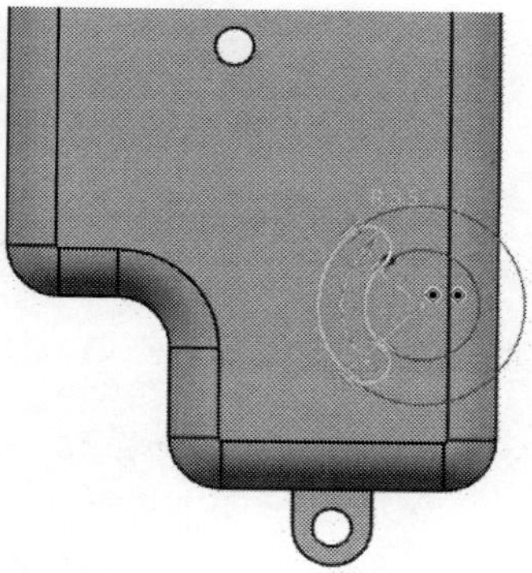

Figure 16–44

7. Exit the Sketch app. The model displays as shown in Figure 16–45.

Figure 16–45

Task 5 - Resolve a feature failure.

Design Considerations

In this task, you will cause a feature failure by changing the sketch support of the Pocket feature, as shown in Figure 16–46. Then you will resolve this feature failure.

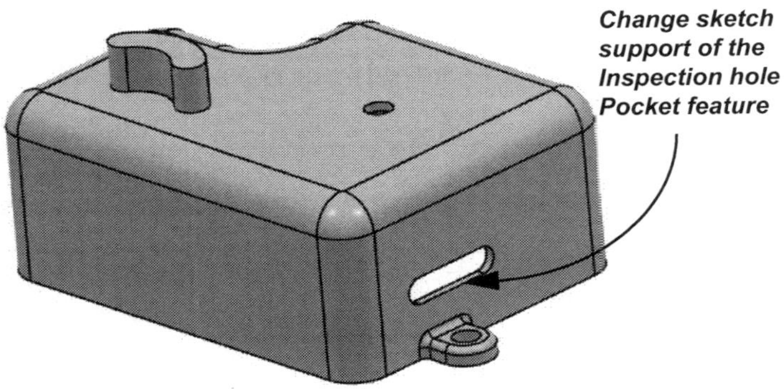

Figure 16–46

1. Investigate the sketch before it is moved by expanding Inspection Hole in the specification tree and double-clicking the Sketch Inspection sketch. The sketch is now activated in the Sketch app.

2. Note the dimensions (3 (0.118 in), 15 (0.591 in), and 18 (0.709 in)) and constraints that were used to place the sketch in Figure 16–47. Which dimensions and/or constraints locate the sketch vertically? Horizontally?

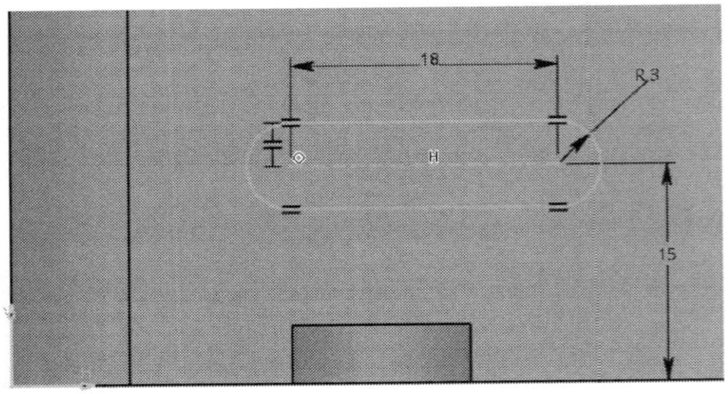

Figure 16–47

3. Exit the Sketch app without making any changes.

4. Select the Sketch Inspection sketch in the specification tree. Right-click and select **Sketch Inspection object>Change Sketch Support**.

5. Click **OK** to accept the warning.
6. Select the surface shown in Figure 16–48.

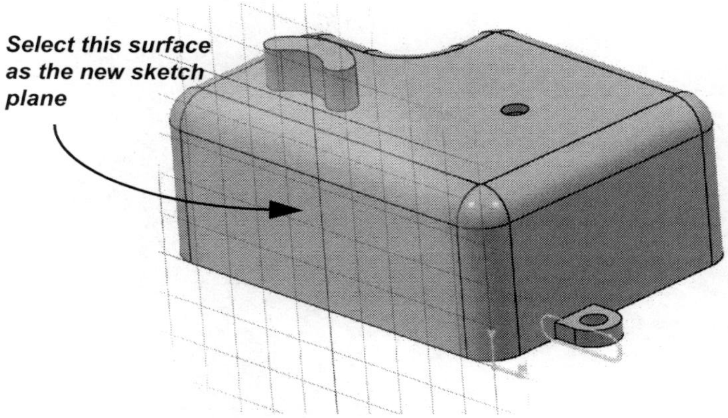

Figure 16–48

7. Click **OK** in the Sketch Positioning dialog box.
8. The Update Diagnosis dialog box opens as shown in Figure 16–49. It indicates that a feature failure has occurred.

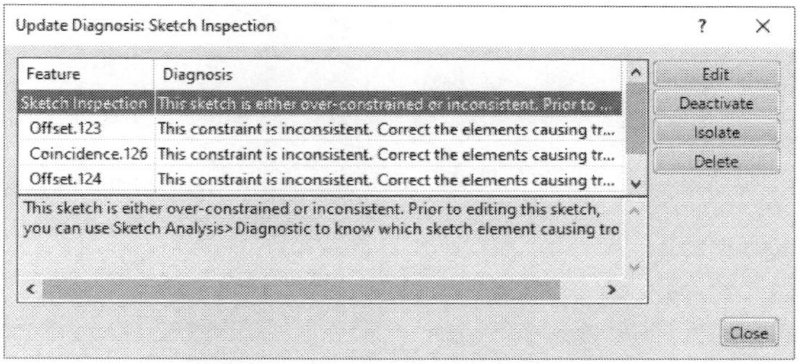

Figure 16–49

9. Click **Edit**.

10. The failed sketch feature activates, as shown in Figure 16–50. Note the resulting 15 (0.591 in) dimension. Drag the cursor over the dimensions if they are too dark to see on the screen.

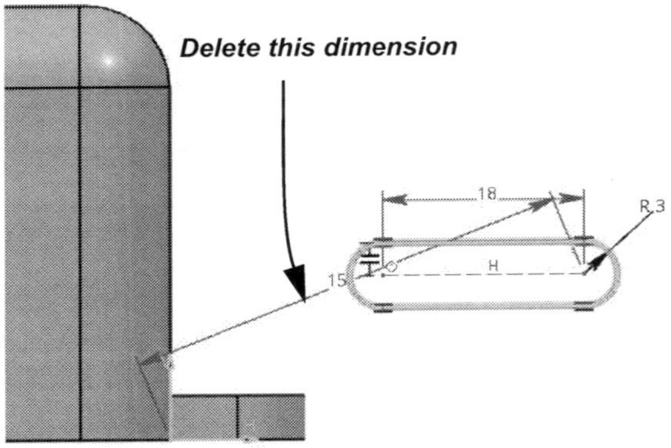

Figure 16–50

11. Delete the 15 (0.591 in) dimension.

12. Select the entire sketch and attempt to move it to the left onto the model. Note that it moves up and down but not left or right.

13. Delete the **Coincident** constraint between the sketch and the geometry below the sketch, as shown in Figure 16–51.

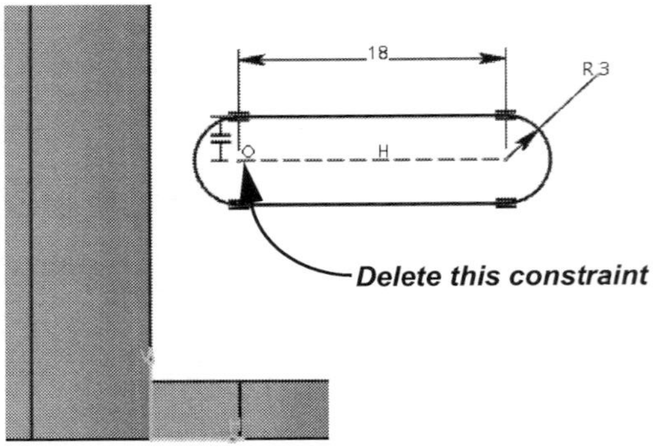

Figure 16–51

14. Select the entire sketch again and move it onto the model, as shown in Figure 16–52.

15. Using the correct values, add the dimensions **15 (0.591 in) 20 (0.787 in)**, as shown in Figure 16–52. Remember to dimensions to surfaces, not entities such as fillet edges.

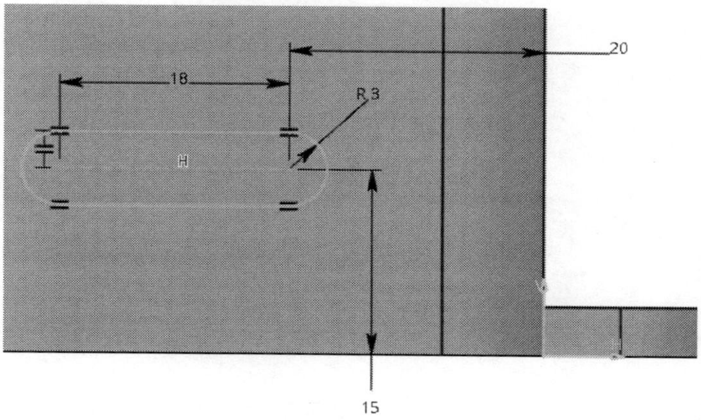

Figure 16–52

16. Exit the Sketch app. The model displays as shown in Figure 16–53.

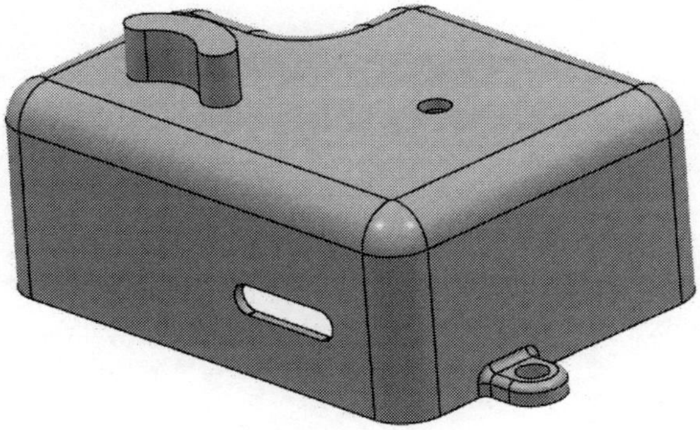

Figure 16–53

17. Save the file and close the tab.

Practice 16b Resolving Failed Features

Practice Objectives

- Edit a sketch profile.
- Resolve Draft and Fillet feature failure.

In this practice, you will modify the profile of a sketch that controls Pocket, Draft, and Fillet features as shown in Figure 16–54. After the profile has been modified, you will resolve feature update failures resulting from the modification of the sketch, which is a parent feature.

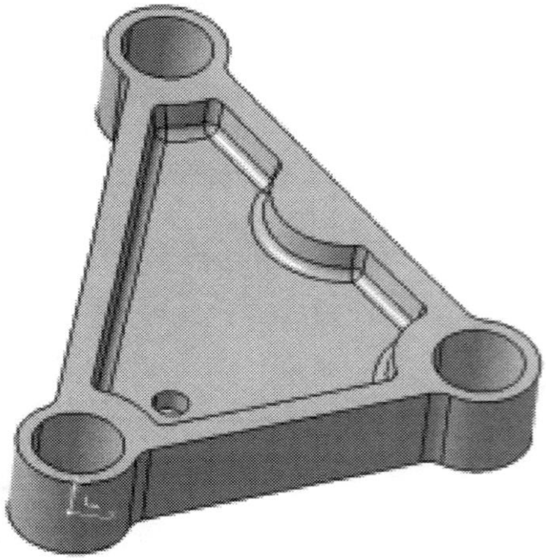

Figure 16–54

Task 1 - Investigate the part.

In this task, you will use the **Parents/Children** tool to locate and edit the sketch that drives the main Pocket feature.

1. Import **FeatureResolve.3dxml**.
2. In the *Resolve (Explore)* tab, right-click **Resolve** in the specification tree and select **Open**.

3. Right-click on the face shown in Figure 16–55. Select **Parents/Children**.

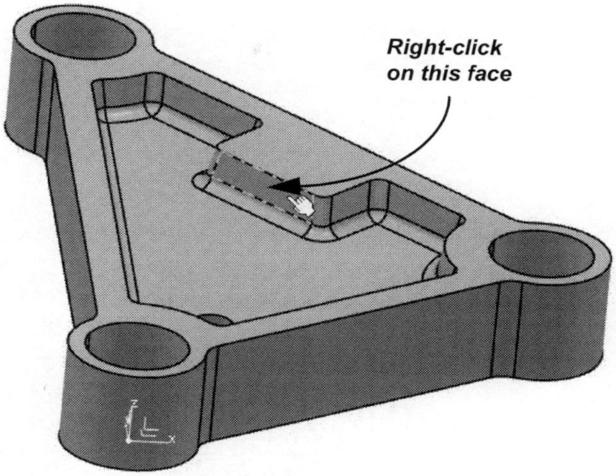

Figure 16–55

- The Parents and Children dialog box opens as shown in Figure 16–56. Note that the feature selected was **Draft.1**. The software shows the parents of the Draft feature, which are **Pocket.1** and **Pad.1**.

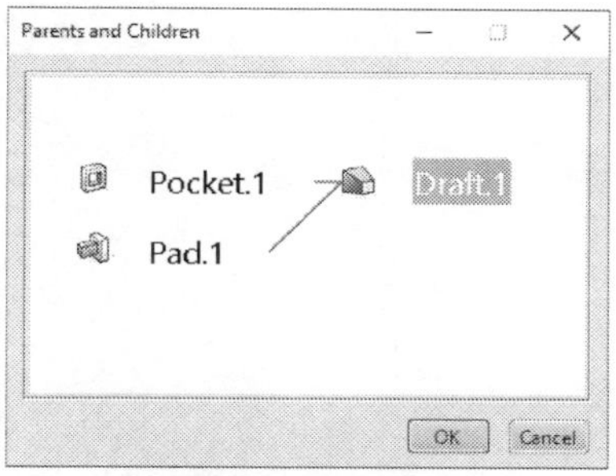

Figure 16–56

4. Locate the sketch that is parent to the **Pocket.1** feature in the Parents and Children dialog box. To do this, double-click on **Pocket.1**.

5. Right-click on the **Sketch.2** feature and select **Edit**, as shown in Figure 16–57. The Sketch app is activated.

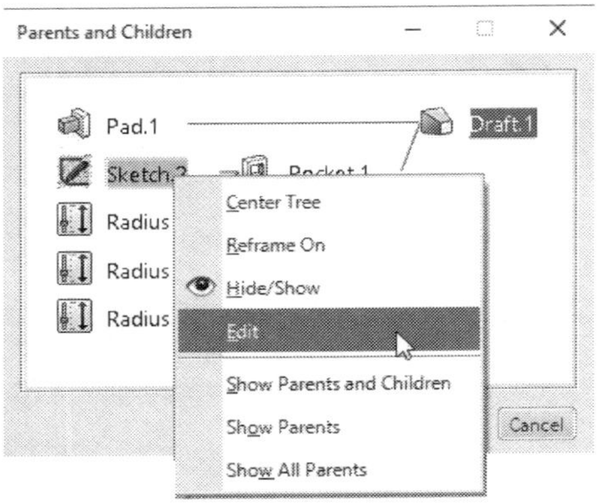

Figure 16–57

Task 2 - Modify the sketch.

1. In the sketch profile, delete the three lines shown in Figure 16–58.

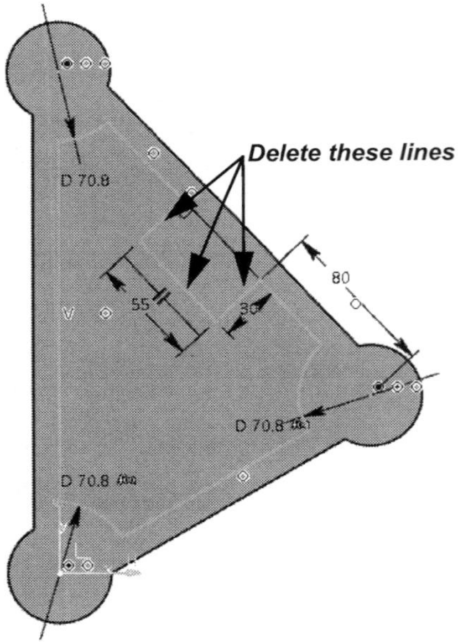

Figure 16–58

2. Add an arc of radius **30.0mm (1.181 in)** in place of the three deleted lines, as shown in Figure 16–59. Trim as required.

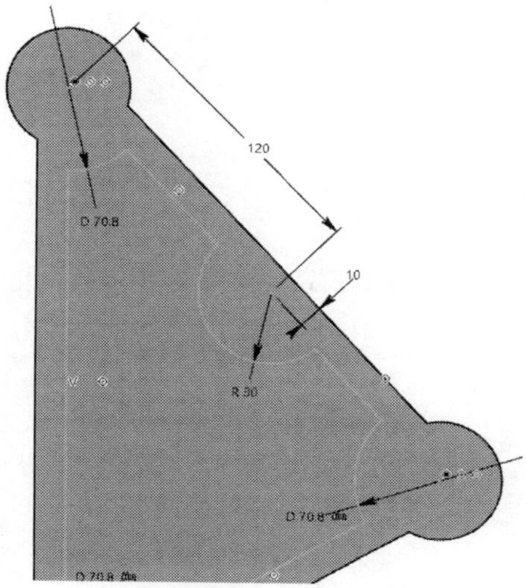

Figure 16–59

3. Exit the Sketch app.

Task 3 - Resolve the update error of the Draft.1 feature.

The Update Diagnosis dialog box opens, as shown in Figure 16–60.

Design Considerations

During the modification of the Sketch.2 profile, the three faces driving the **Draft.1** feature were removed, along with the three sketched lines. When working with complex parts, check the parent/child relationships of a sketch feature before modifying its profile. Analyze whether it is more efficient to repair resultant failures or to create a new sketch and subsequent dress-up features.

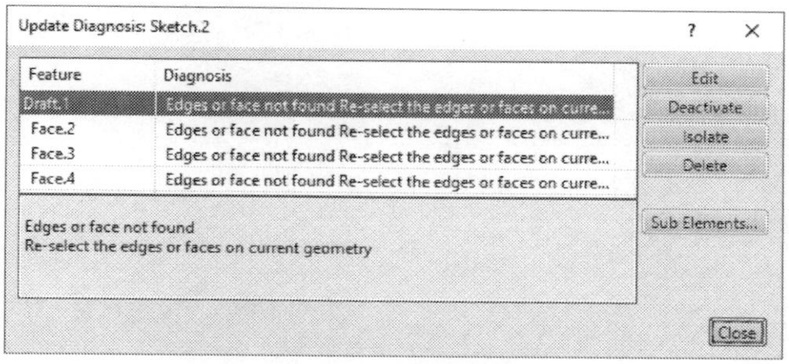

Figure 16–60

1. In the Update Diagnosis dialog box, select **Draft.1.** Click **Edit**. The Feature Definition Error dialog box opens, along with a graphical representation of the unrecognized faces, as shown in Figure 16–61.

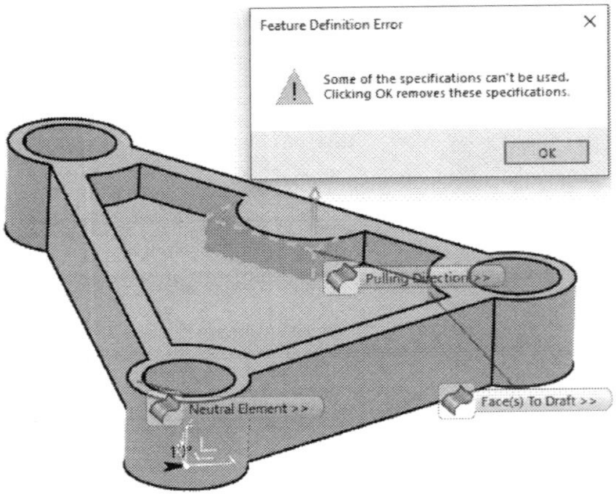

Figure 16–61

2. In the Feature Definition Error dialog box, click **OK** to remove the three faces from the draft definition. The Draft Definition dialog box opens, as shown in Figure 16–62.

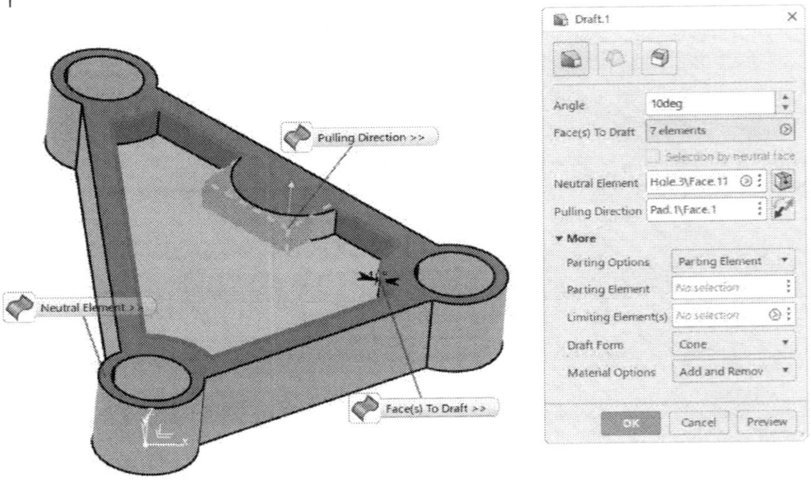

Figure 16–62

3. Select the *Face(s) to draft* field and then select the newly created cylindrical face, as shown in Figure 16–62.

4. Click **OK** to finish resolving the **Draft.1** feature failure.

Task 4 - Resolve the update error of the EdgeFillet.1 feature.

The modification of **Sketch.2** has also affected the EdgeFillet.1 feature. The Update Diagnosis dialog box reports that four edges are no longer recognized, as shown in Figure 16–63.

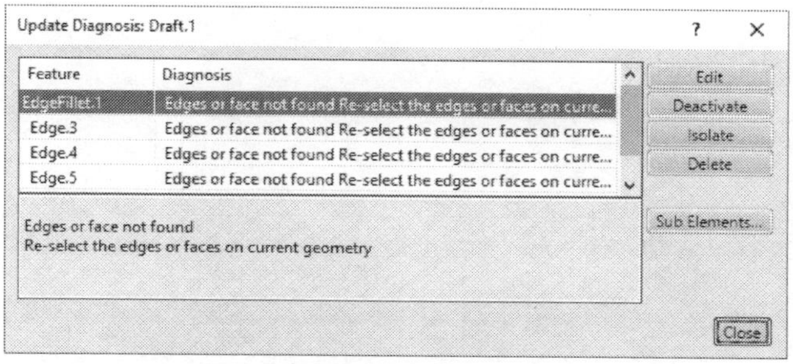

Figure 16–63

1. Select the **EdgeFillet.1** feature in the Update Diagnosis dialog box. Click **Edit** to begin resolving the feature failure.
2. The Feature Definition Error dialog box opens, along with a graphical representation of where the filleted edges used to be, as shown in Figure 16–64. Click **OK** in the Feature Definition Error dialog box to remove the four edges from the fillet definition.

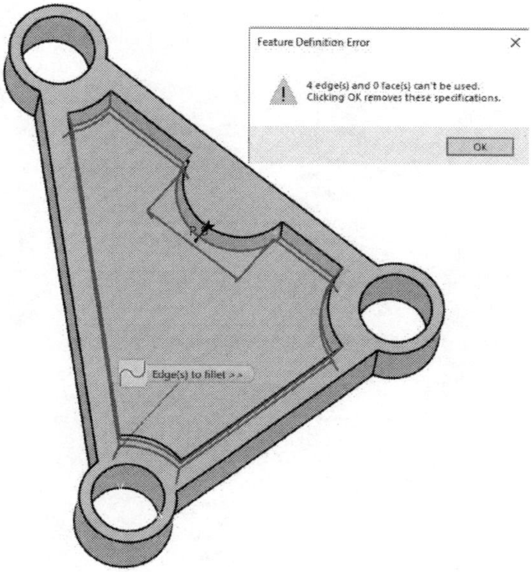

Figure 16–64

3. The Edge Fillet Definition dialog box opens. Select the *Object(s) to fillet* field and select the two edges shown in Figure 16–65.

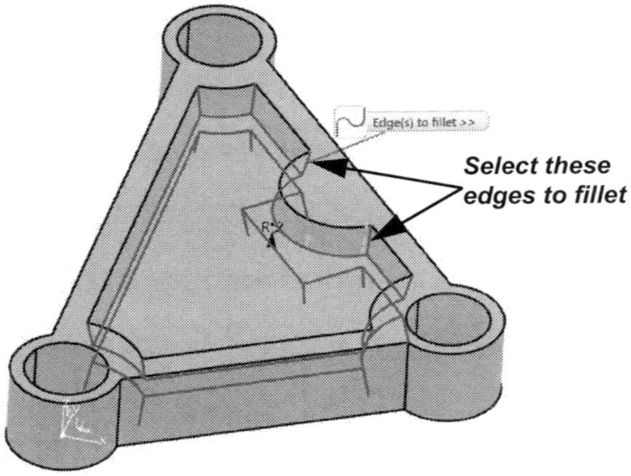

Figure 16–65

4. Click **OK** to finish resolving the **EdgeFillet.1** definition. The updated part displays as shown in Figure 16–66.

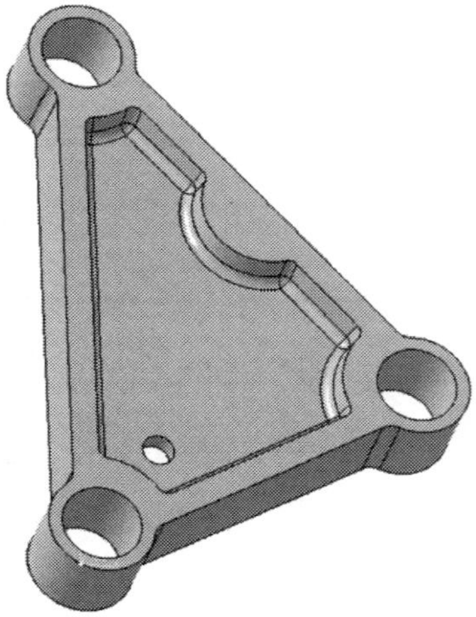

Figure 16–66

5. Save and close the file.

Chapter Review Questions

1. Which of the following actions create feature relationship when sketching a feature? (Select all that apply.)
   a. Selecting the Sketch support.
   b. Dimensioning the length of a line.
   c. Projecting an existing edge to create a new entity.
   d. Trimming two entities in the new sketch.
   e. Aligning a new entity with an existing entity.
   f. Dimensioning new entities to existing geometry.
   g. Selecting the **Dimension depth** option.
   h. Selecting the **Up to Surface depth** option.
2. A plane can be a parent of another plane.
   a. True
   b. False
3. Default reference planes cannot be deleted or modified.
   a. True
   b. False
4. In Figure 16–67, **Pad.1** and **Pocket.1** are parents of **Sketch.4,** and **Sketch.4** is a parent of **Pocket.2**. **Hole.2**, **Hole.1**, **EdgeFillet.1** are in turn, children of **Pocket.2**.

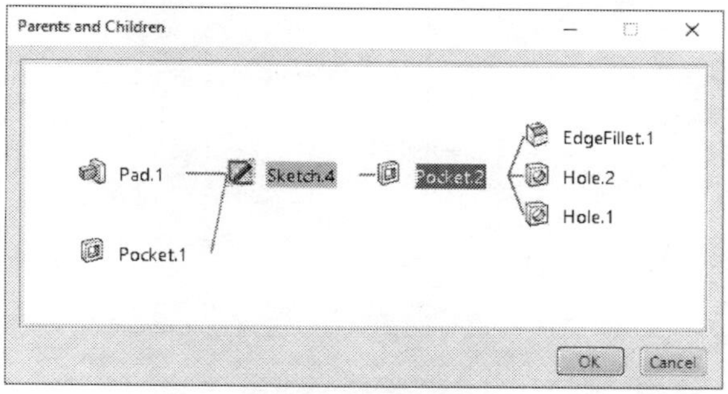

Figure 16–67

   a. True
   b. False

5. In Figure 16–67, deleting **Pocket.1** will not affect **Pocket.2**.
    a. True
    b. False
6. Which of the following depth options will not create a parent/child relationship? (Select all that apply).
    a. Up to Surface
    b. Up to Last
    c. Up to Plane
    d. Dimension
7. You can isolate a Fillet.
    a. True
    b. False
8. A feature is deleted from a model. The Update Diagnosis dialog box opens and indicates that a Fillet and a Pocket feature have both failed. You deactivate both features, which means you have resolved the failure.
    a. True
    b. False

Answers: 1acefh, 2a, 3a, 4a, 5b, 6d, 7b, 8b

Chapter 17

Part Information

CATIA provides you with several tools that can be used to obtain information about a part's measurements and inertia. You can also use the feature investigation tools to determine how the model was constructed.

Learning Objectives in This Chapter

- Use measure entities.
- Update measurements that result from a model modification.
- Learn how to measure between items.
- Understand Standard, Chain, and Fan modes.
- Apply material to a model.
- Measure 2D and 3D inertia.
- Position a section plane to visualize a 3D section of the model.

17.1 Measuring Items

Click (Measure Item) in the *Tools* section of the Action Bar, to open the Measure In Part dialog box, as shown in Figure 17–1.

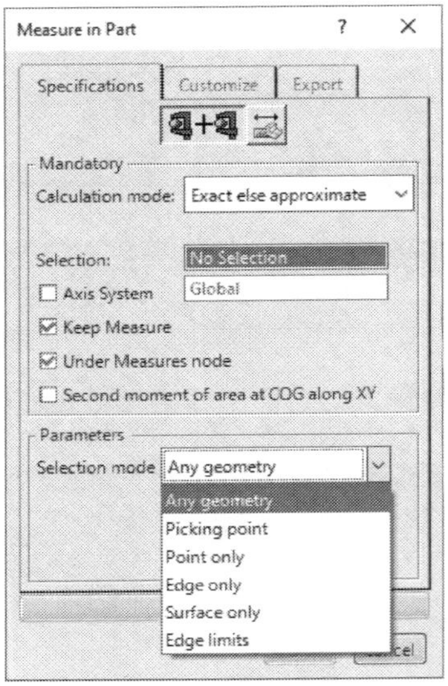

Figure 17–1

The **Measure In Part** tool is a one-click measurement tool that enables you to select one of the following items in the specification tree or on screen to measure:

- **Any geometry**: (Default) Enables measurement between any geometric entities.
- **Picking point:** Measures distance between points selected on defined geometric entities.
- **Point only:** Measures distance between points. Dynamic highlighting is limited to points.
- **Edge only:** Measures distance and angles between edges. Dynamic highlighting is limited to edges. All edge types are supported.
- **Surface only:** Measures distance and angles between surfaces. Dynamic highlighting is limited to surfaces.
- **Edge limits:** Measure the distance to edge extremity points.
- **Thickness:** Measure body thickness at any location.

The calculated results depend on what you select and what result settings are in place. The results for a curved surface are shown in Figure 17–2.

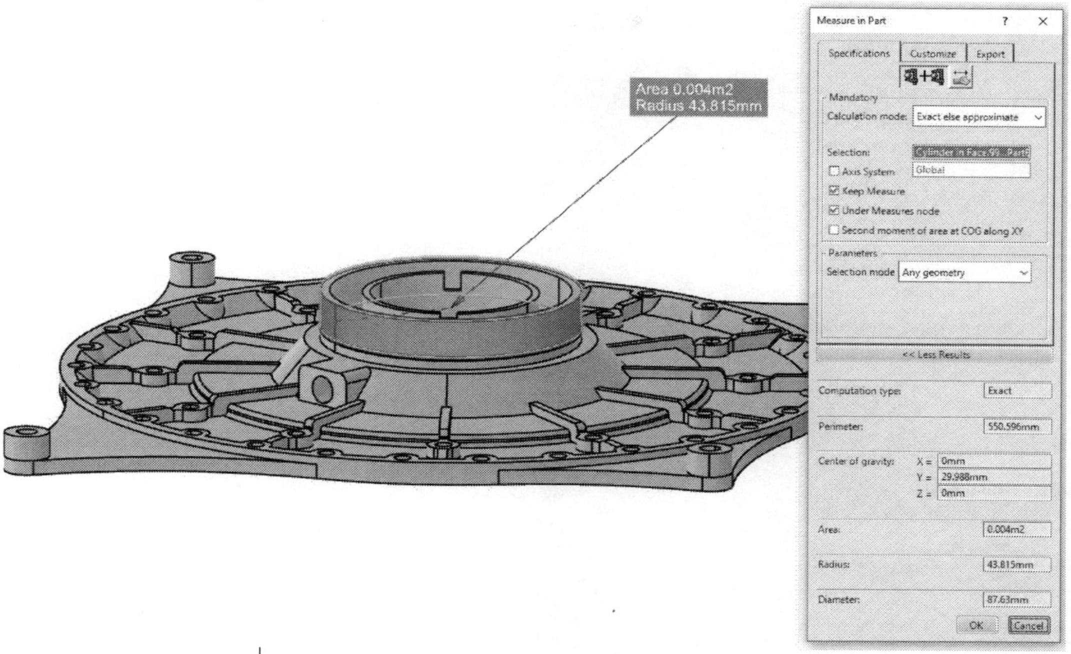

Figure 17–2

The measure item results can be customized for the selected item by selecting the *Customize* tab. The Measure Item Customization dialog box opens as shown in Figure 17–3.

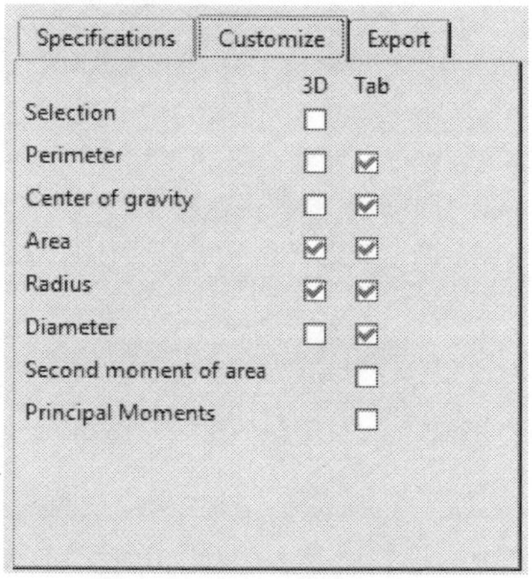

Figure 17–3

You can use the Measure in Part dialog box to create single measures or multiple measures. To create multiple measures, click 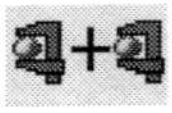 as shown in Figure 17–4.

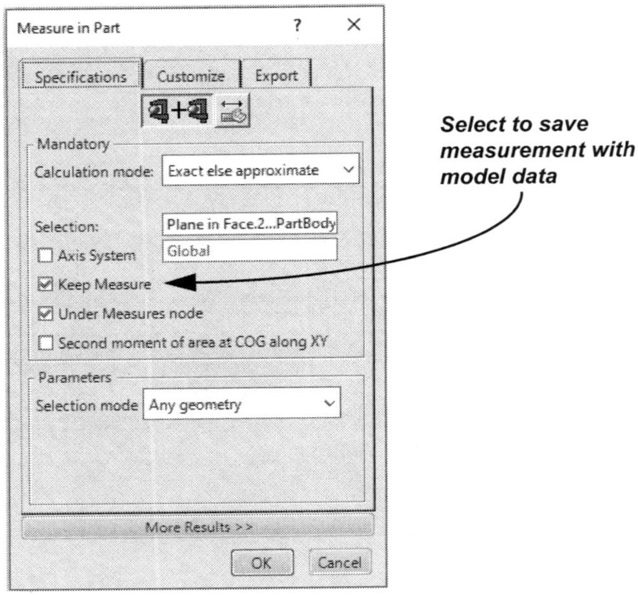

Figure 17–4

The measurement is then added to the specification tree, as shown in Figure 17–5.

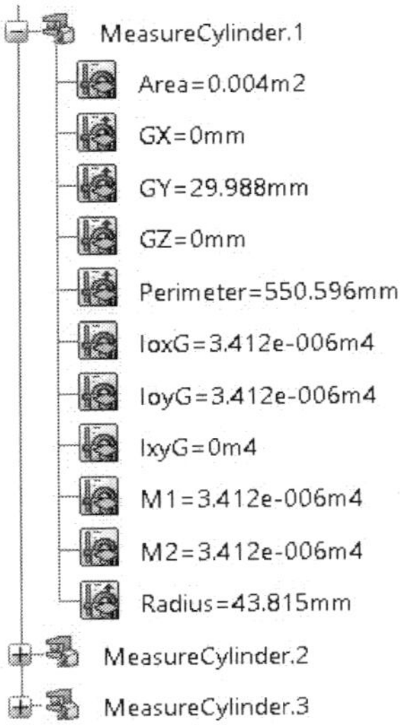

Figure 17–5

17.2 Updating Measurements

If modifications are made in the model that result in a change to a measured value (e.g., geometry change),  displays next to the measurement in the specification tree, indicating that the measured value is not updated.

To update the value, right-click on the measurement name and select **Local update**, as shown in Figure 17–6.

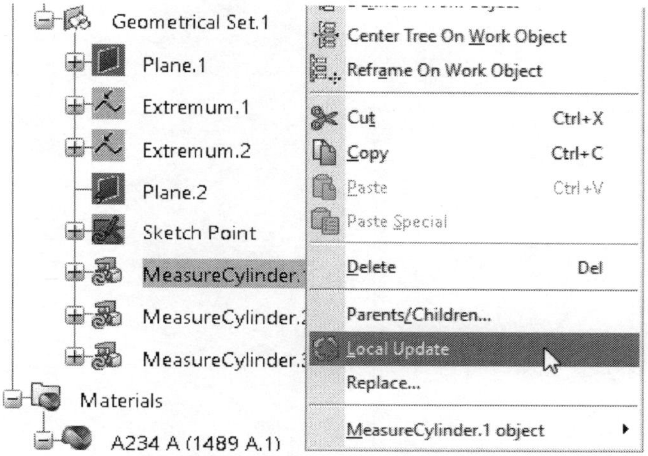

Figure 17–6

To automate the update of these measurements, enable the automatic update options by clicking **Me** > **Preferences** > **Common Preferences** > **Parameters**, **Measures, and Units** > **Measures** > **Measure Tools** > **Associativity** section, as shown in Figure 17–7.

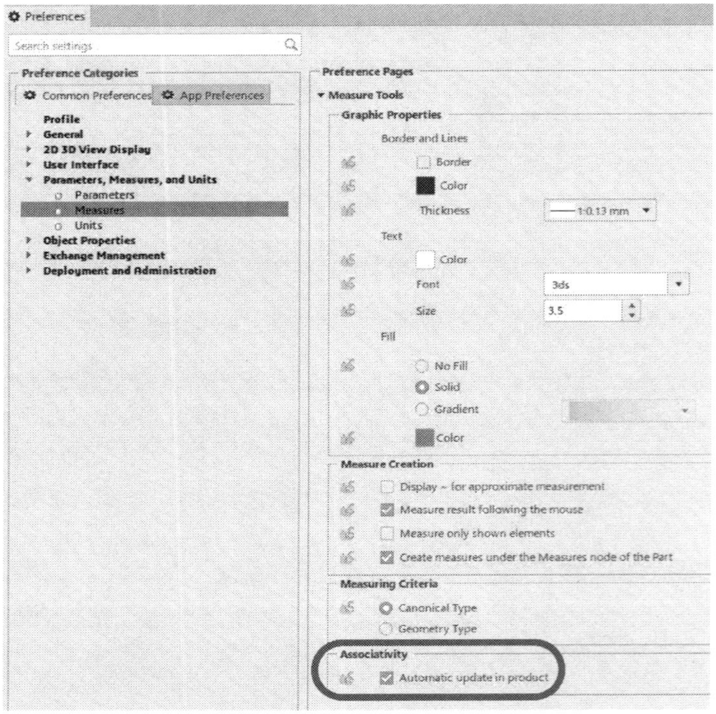

Figure 17–7

17.3 Measuring Between Items

Click  (Measure Between) in the *Tools* section of the Action Bar to open the Measure Between In Part dialog box, as shown in Figure 17–8.

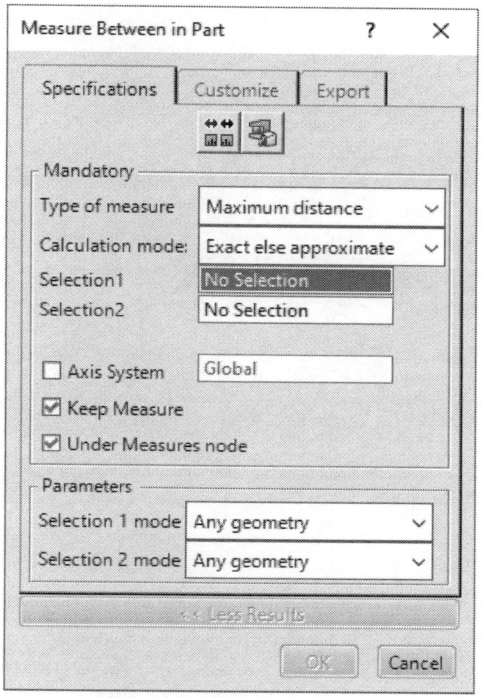

Figure 17–8

Measure Between in Part Geometry Selection

The **Measure Between in Part** tool is a two-click measurement tool that enables you to measure between two selected items of the same or mixed types. You can select from the specification tree or on the screen. The different selectable item types for the **Measure Between in Part** tool are shown in Figure 17–9.

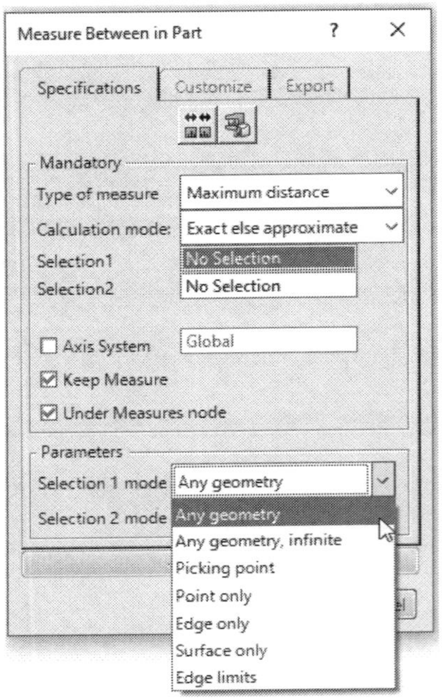

Figure 17–9

Using the **Any geometry** option, the software enables you to measure between geometry of any type. If this causes difficulty in selecting a specific type of element, select a more applicable element in the **Selection 1 mode** and/or **Selection 2 mode** drop-down menus.

The **Any geometry, infinite** option extends the selected plane, curve, or line infinitely to obtain an accurate minimum distance.

The two-click **Measure Between in Part** tool can be used to take measurements, such as the distance between items or angle between items.

An example of a measurement between two selected hole centers is shown in Figure 17–10. The results can be saved and customized using the same method as the **Measure Item** tool.

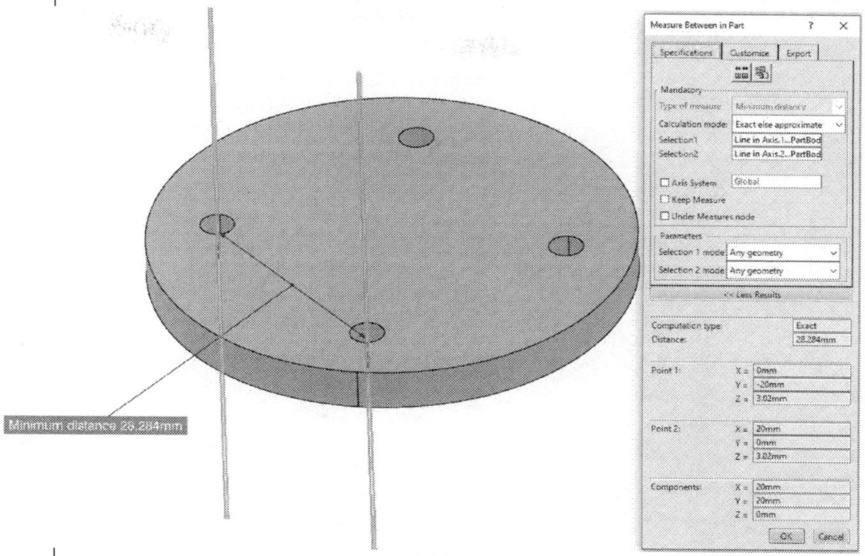

Figure 17–10

When selecting hole and arc centers, you can display an axis by moving the cursor over the approximate center of the hole and arc, as shown in Figure 17–11.

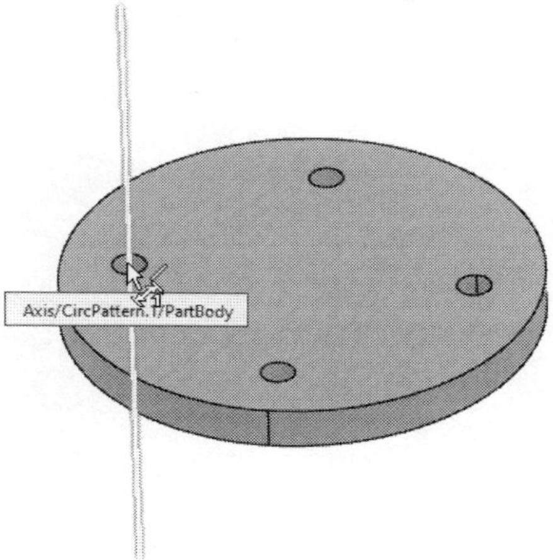

Figure 17–11

Measuring with Reference Elements

In situations where the part geometry is complex, such as models created using surfacing techniques, it is difficult to find planar references to measure between. In this case, reference elements can be constructed to generate an exact measurement reference.

For example, consider the simplified example shown in Figure 17–12. In this case, a Measure Between operation referencing the top and bottom faces can report the minimum and maximum distances. The software can select the location on the curved surface from which the measurement is made.

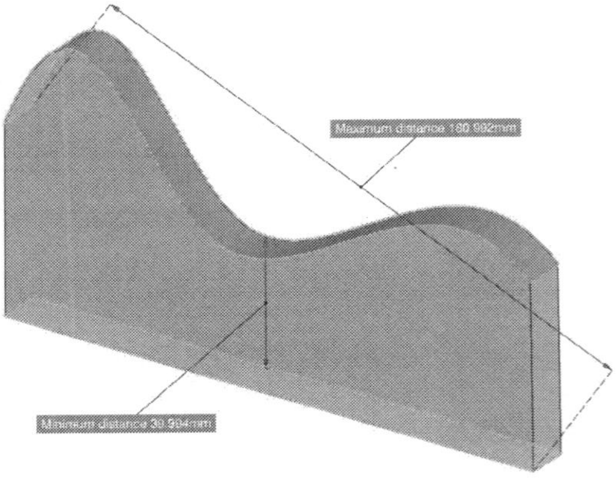

Figure 17–12

To measure the distance between an exact location on the top surface, a reference point can be created to define the location, as shown in Figure 17–13.

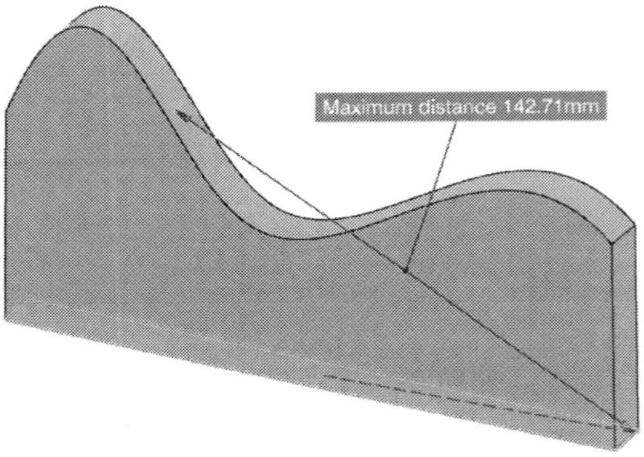

Figure 17–13

To further define the type of measurement, a reference plane can be created. This restricts the measurement direction to be normal to the plane, as shown in Figure 17–14. Another option is to use the **Components** option, accessed by selecting the **Customize** tab. This reports the X, Y, and Z components of a measurement, enabling you to extract the required direction.

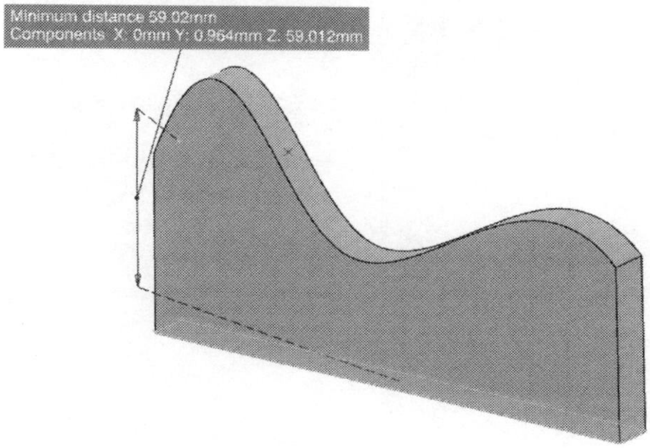

Figure 17–14

17.4 Measuring Inertia

Before measuring the inertia of the model, it is recommended that you first define the model's material properties.

Apply a Material

When you apply a material to a model, the properties of the model (such as density and Young's modulus) are defined. This ensures that accurate inertia values are computed for the model.

Use the following steps to apply a material:

1. Activate the model at the 3D Shape level as shown in Figure 17–15.

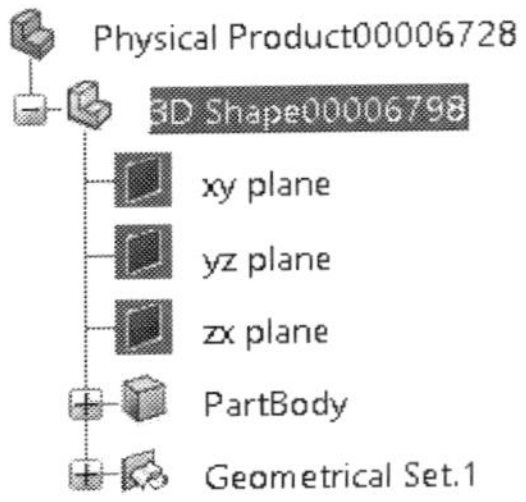

Figure 17–15

2. In the *Tools* section of the Action Bar, click  (Material Browser) to set the material for the model. The Materials dialog box opens as shown in Figure 17–16.

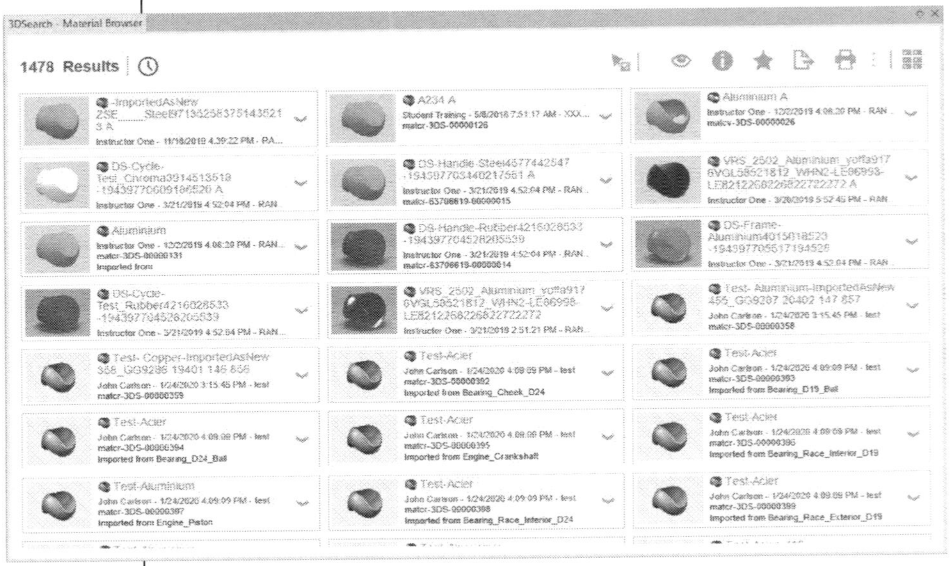

Figure 17–16

3. The view can be changed between Thumbnail, Tile, and Datagrid using the icon in the upper right of the Material browser, as shown in Figure 17–17.

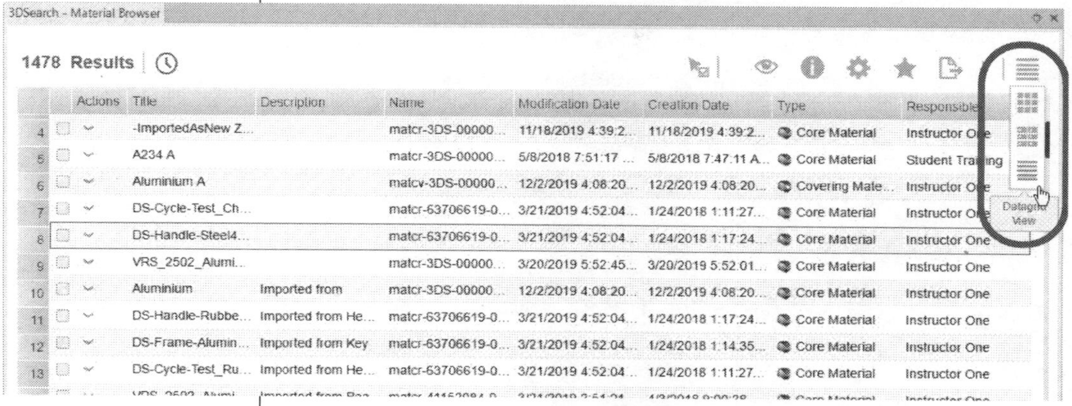

Figure 17–17

4. Select a material in the Materials results dialog box, right-click and select **Apply Material**, then click on the part body.

5. Click  (Exit Context Menu). The material is listed in the specification tree, as shown in Figure 17–18. All properties for the selected material are defined for the model to which the material is applied. The properties are also used in the inertia calculations.

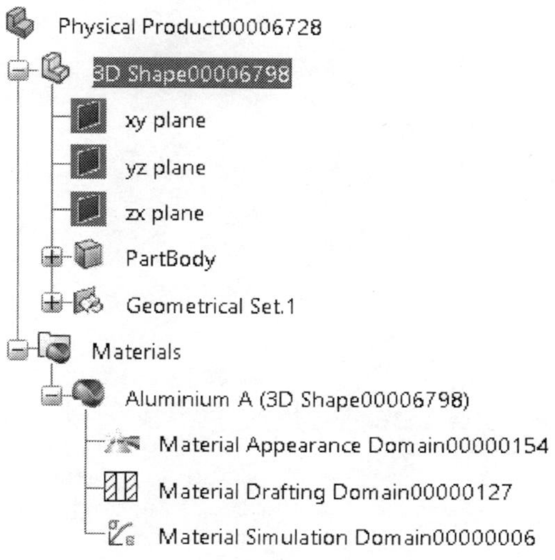

Figure 17–18

Viewing the Material

The model can also be viewed in a custom View mode with the material rendering applied.

In the *View* section of the Action Bar, click (View Mode), and then select (Shading With Material) to apply the material rendering to a model.

Changing Material Appearance

After a material is applied, you can change its properties. Double-click the material Rendering domain and the Material Definition: Appearance Domain dialog box opens as shown in Figure 17–19. Here you can edit the appearance by changing the **Transparency, and Sheen**, and so on.

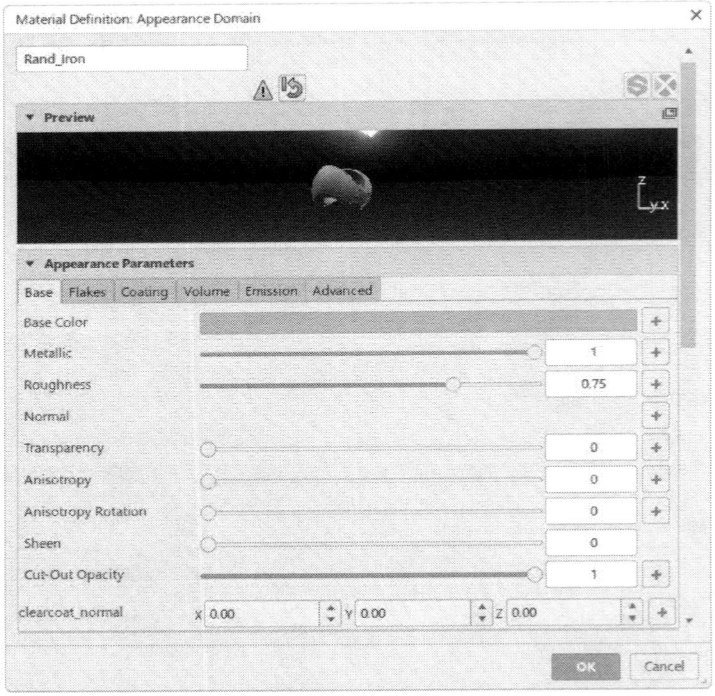

Figure 17–19

Measure Inertia 3D

The inertia of an object is defined as the property by which it retains its present velocity (speed and direction) so long as it is not acted on by an external force. An equivalent definition of inertia is the resistance of an object to a change in its motion.

To compute the model inertia using the model's current material properties, in the *Tools* section of the Action Bar, click

 (Create Inertia Data). You can select 3D entities (such as features or bodies) in the specification tree and measure their inertia. Select the **Volume** option, and the results display in the Measure Inertia dialog box, as shown in Figure 17–20.

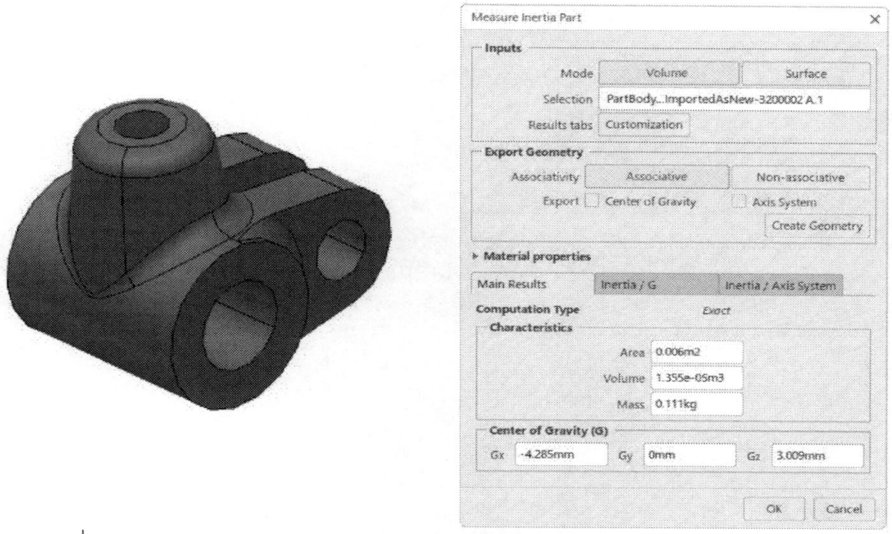

Figure 17–20

The dialog box reports the following information:

- Characteristics, such as volume, area, mass, and density.
- The center of gravity relative to the origin of the part.
- Inertia data of the part. (Inertia tabs)

The inertia data of the part can be measured with respect to a variety of elements by selecting one of the tabs described in the table below.

Tab	Meaning
Inertia / G	Measure inertia with respect to the center of gravity of the model.
Inertia / O	Measure inertia with respect to the origin of the model.
Inertia / P	Measure inertia with respect to a selected point.
Inertia / Axis	Measure inertia with respect to a selected axis.
Inertia / Axis System	Measure inertia with respect to a selected axis system.

The *Inertia / G* tab is activated by default. To activate the other four tabs, click **Customization** to open the Customization dialog box shown in Figure 17–21.

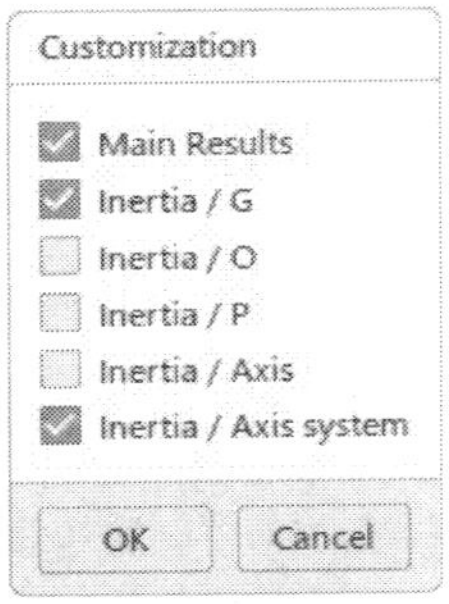

Figure 17–21

Each tab displays a variety of inertia data that is relevant to the measurement reference. For example, the parameters described in the table below are reported for an Inertia / G calculation.

Parameter	Meaning
Iox	Area moment of inertia about the X-axis.
Ioy	Area moment of inertia about the Y-axis.
Ioz	Area moment of inertia about the Z-axis.
Ixy	Mass moment of inertia on the XY plane.
Ixz	Mass moment of inertia on the XZ plane.
Iyz	Mass moment of inertia on the YZ plane.

The **Measure Inertia** tool also enables you to create a point and/or an axis system at the center of gravity in the part. To create geometry, click **Create Geometry** in the Measure Inertia dialog box as shown in Figure 17–22.

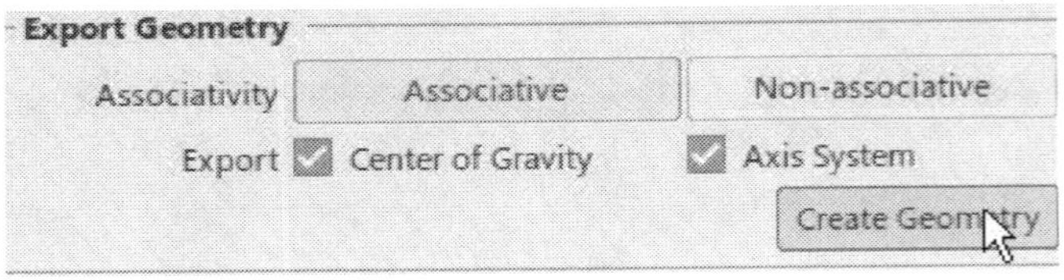

Figure 17–22

An axis system and a point at the center of gravity have been created in Figure 17–23 using the **Create geometry** tool.

Figure 17–23

Measuring the inertia of a section or surface is useful for rapidly determining the structural properties of complex shapes. With **Surface** selected, you can select solid faces from the model and measure their two-dimensional inertia properties. This tool is identical to its 3D counterpart, except that certain calculations that do not apply to two-dimensional surfaces (mass, density, volume, etc.) are not present. Also, only the *Inertia / G* tab is evaluated when measuring 2D entities.

17.5 Dynamic Sectioning

The Dynamic Sectioning enables you to position a section plane to visualize a 3D section view of a part, as shown in Figure 17–24. The section plan can be dynamically adjusted.

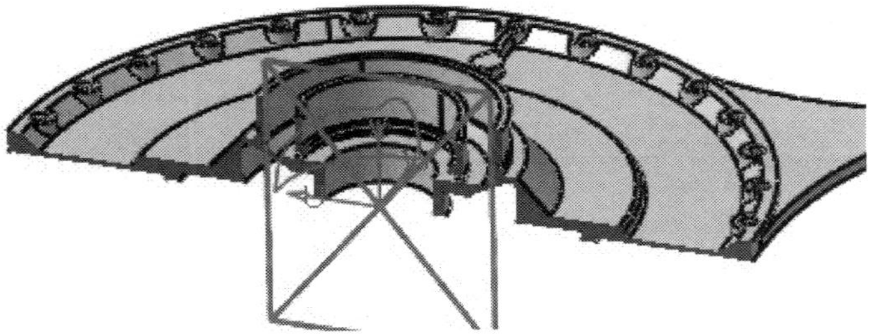

Figure 17–24

To use the Dynamic Sectioning tool, click (Dynamic Sectioning) from the *Review* section of the Action Bar. A red section plane is automatically displayed on the model.

The location of the section plane can dynamically be modified. To adjust the position, select an edge, surface, plane, or curve in the model. If you are selecting a reference in the model, a purple section plane locater icon displays, as shown in Figure 17–25.

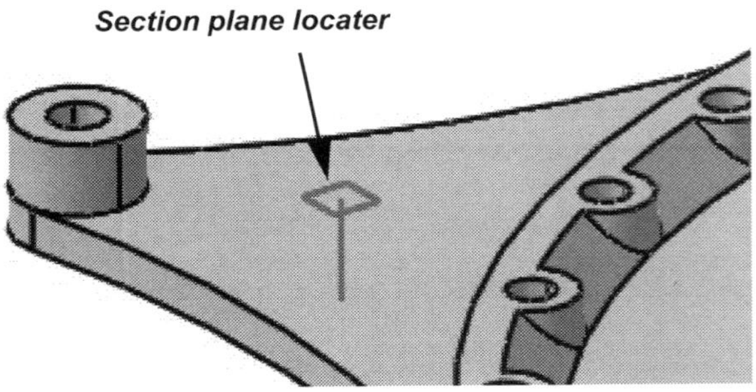

Figure 17–25

To translate the section plane along about the selected reference, hover the cursor over the red section plane, as shown in Figure 17–26. When the green arrow displays, click and drag the plane to the required location. The model is dynamically cut about the section plane as you click and drag.

To rotate the section plane, hover the cursor over one of the red arcs on the section plane compass. Click the arc, and drag the section plane to the required location, as shown in Figure 17–27.

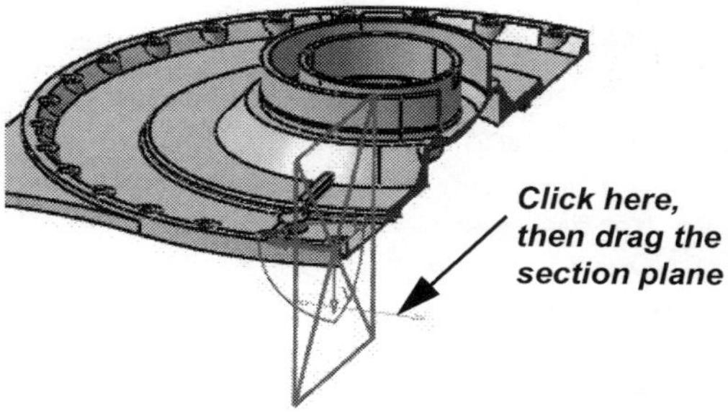

Figure 17–26

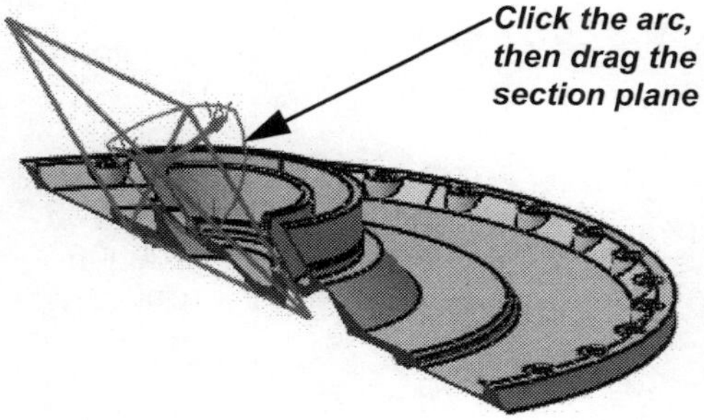

Figure 17–27

The section plane can be adjusted repeatedly. When done using the Dynamic Sectioning tool, deactivate by clicking

 (Dynamic Sectioning).

17.6 Feature Investigation

3DEXPERIENCE provides several tools to investigate a model. The investigation tools can be used to determine how a model is constructed. These tools are useful for the following situations:

- If a model is created by someone else.
- If it has been a long time since you worked on the part.
- If the model is complex and you need to modify the feature structure.

Scanning the Model

Scanning the model enables you to review the construction history of a model, one feature at a time. This is very useful when working with models that are created by other users. The **Scan** tool can give you an idea of the model creator's design intent and modeling techniques, by replaying and reviewing the design.

To use the **Scan** tool, in the *Review* section of the Action Bar, click  (Scan or Define In Work Object). The Scan tool opens in the lower left of the 3DEXPERIENCE window. You can leave the tool pinned, or can drag it out to be a stand alone toolbar, as shown in Figure 17–28. Use the control icons to play, step forward, rewind, or stop the model at the current feature creation location.

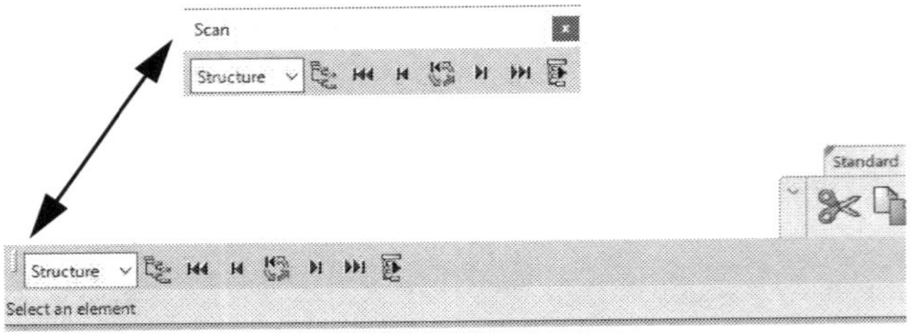

Figure 17–28

By default, the **Structure** option is selected in the Scan tool. With this setting, the software replays the features of the active body based on the feature order displayed in the specification tree. Features in other bodies or geometrical sets are not replayed.

If the **Update** option is selected, the software replays the features in the model in the order in which they are updated, as shown in Figure 17–29.

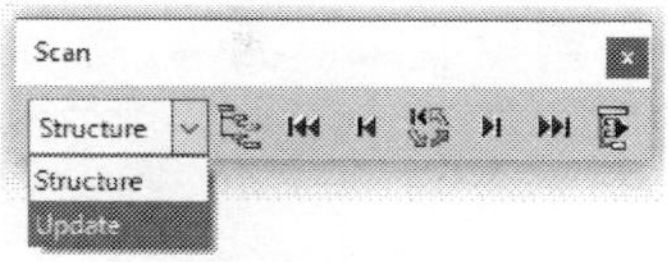

Figure 17–29

For example, consider the specification tree shown in Figure 17–30. The part was created by first adding a reference plane that was used as a support for Sketch.1. The scan order, based on the **Structure** or **Update** option, is shown in the table below.

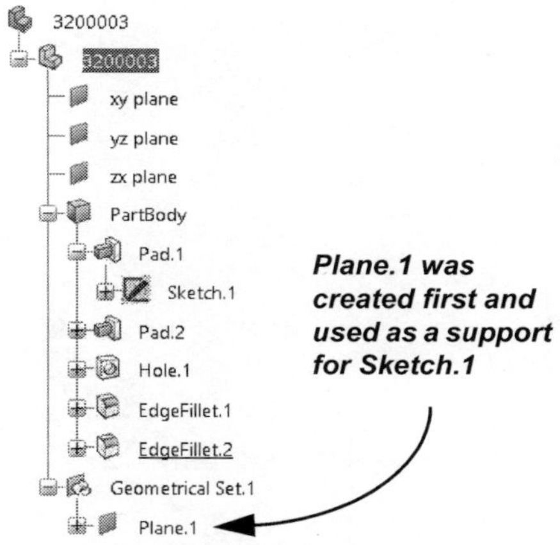

Figure 17–30

#	Structure	Update
1	Pad.1	Plane.1
2	Pad.2	Sketch.1
3	Hole.1	Pad.1
4	EdgeFillet.1	Hole.1
5	EdgeFillet.2	Pad.2
6	End	Hole.1
7		EdgeFillet.1
8		EdgeFillet.2
9		End

Practice 17a

Take Measurements

Practice Objective

- Review the feature creation history.
- Assign a material to the part.
- Determine the mass, volume, and surface area of the part.

In this practice, you will use the Scan tool to view the model's creation history. You will also assign a material to the part, take measurements of the part, and analyze some of its properties, such as mass and volume.

Task 1 - Import the part called Support_Info and review how it is modeled.

1. Import **Support_Info.3dxml**.
2. Right-click **Support** in the specification tree and select **Open**.
3. Set the view orientation to (* iso).
4. Set the display to (Shading With Edges) by using the (View Modes) command. The part displays as shown in Figure 17–31.

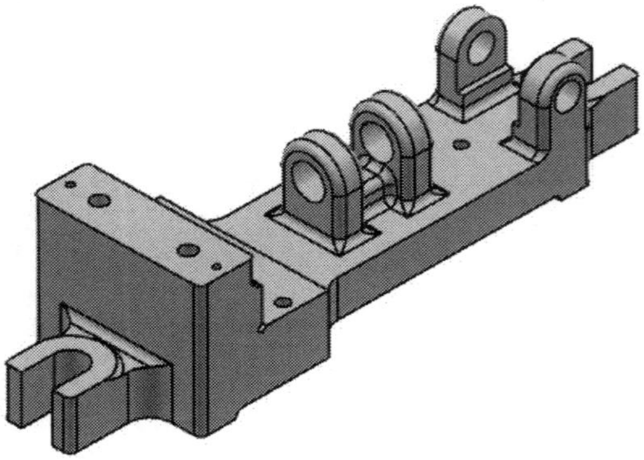

Figure 17–31

5. Note the feature order in the specification tree to review how the model is created.

Task 2 - Scan the model.

Design Considerations

Scanning the model is another way of reviewing its creation history. This is often a helpful tool if you did not create the model, but need to update it. The **Scan** tool enables you to review the creation process and grasp the original designer's design intent.

1. In the *Review* section of the Action Bar, click (Scan or Define In Work Object) to activate the **Scan** tool.
2. In the lower left of the 3DEXPERIENCE window, click (First) to reset the model to the first feature created. The model displays as shown in Figure 17–32. A Pad is the first feature created for the model.

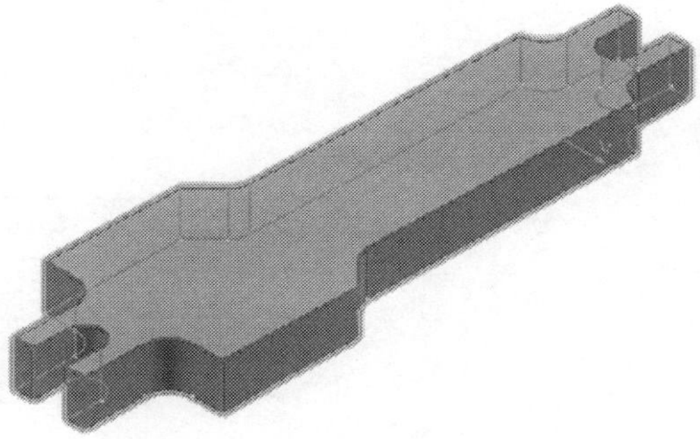

Figure 17–32

3. Click (Next) and note the addition of a second Pad feature.

4. Click (Play Update) and the software will automatically play the addition of the remaining features, as shown in Figure 17–33.

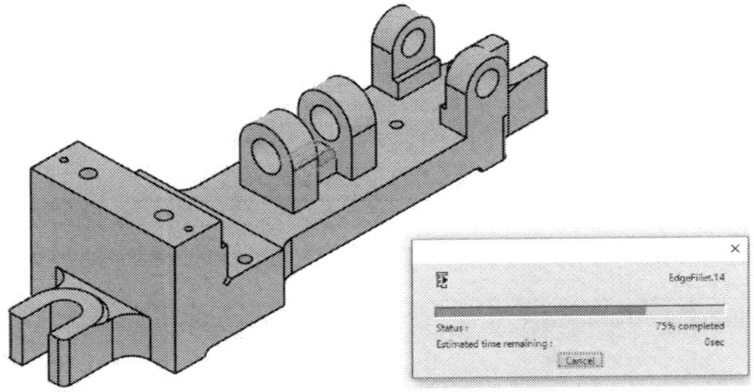

Figure 17–33

5. In the *Review* section of the Action Bar, click (Scan or Define In Work Object) to close the scan tool.

Task 3 - Review some of the parent/child relationships in the model.

1. Expand PartBody in the specification tree to display the features under PartBody.

2. A design change requires that the Shaft support of Pad.6 be modified. As a precaution before making modifications, it is a good idea to review the child features that rely on Pad.6 as a parent. Select the **Pad.6** feature in the specification tree, right-click and select **Parents/Children**. The Parents and Children dialog box opens as shown in Figure 17–34.

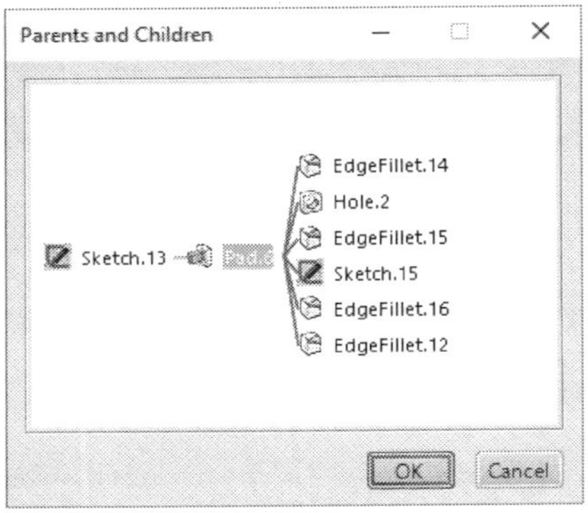

Figure 17–34

All of the items listed on the right side of Pad.6 are child features that reference Pad.6. Modifications to Pad.6 might result in modifications or failures with the child features. The parent feature (Sketch.13) is listed on the left side of Pad.6.

3. Double-click on various items in the dialog box to display further levels of the parent/child relations.
4. Click **OK** to close the Parents and Children dialog box.

Task 4 - Import a Material Library.

1. In the Top Bar, click (Add) **Import**.
2. In the Format drop-down list, select **3DXML with authoring (*.3dxml)**.
3. Change the path to **C:\Program Files\Dassault Systemes\B424_Cloud_Content\win_b64\resources\materials** as shown in Figure 17–35.
4. Select **DS Standard.3dxml** and change the Duplication String from to **RAND_** as shown in Figure 17–35.

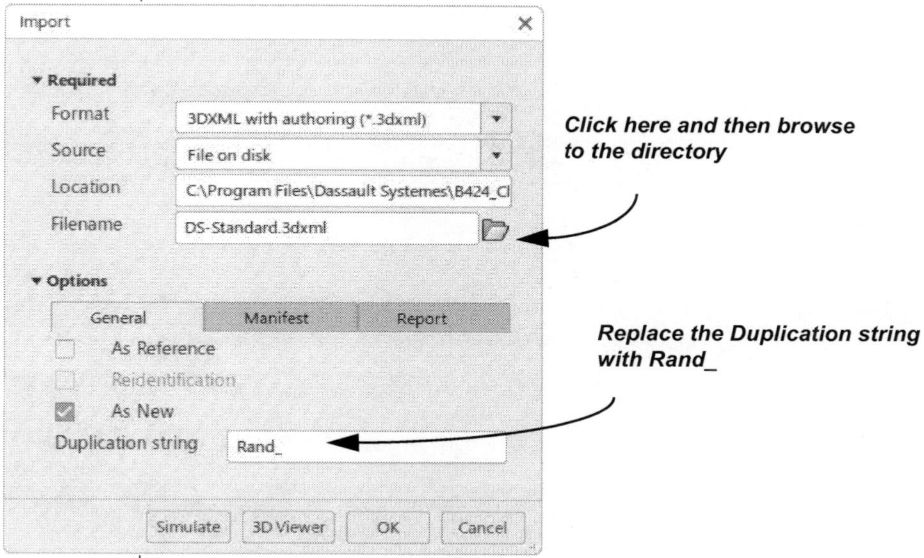

Figure 17–35

5. Click **OK**, and the Material Library will import and become available for use in the next task.
6. Click **OK** in the Operation Report dialog box.

Task 5 - Assign iron as the model material before you calculate inertia.

1. In the *Tools* section of the Action Bar, click (Material Browser) to open the material library.
2. Select **Rand_Iron** in the Material Browser window.
3. Right-click on the material and select **Apply**.
4. Close the Material Browser and select the **Support** 3D Part.
5. Click (Close Context Toolbar).
6. Note the Iron material listed in the specification tree, as shown in Figure 17–36.

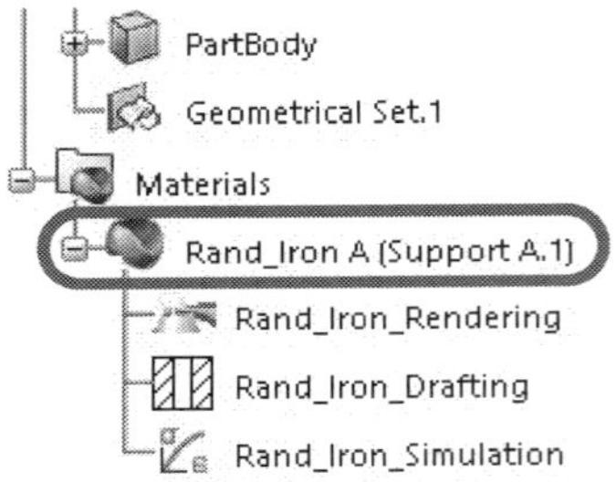

Figure 17–36

Task 6 - Display the model with iron material.

1. In the *View* section of the Action Bar, click (View Modes) then select (Shading With Material). The model is rendered with the material applied to it, as shown in Figure 17–37.

Figure 17–37

Task 7 - View inertia results using the iron material properties.

1. Select the part body in the specification tree, and in the Tools section of the Action Bar, click  (Measure Inertia Data) to measure the model inertia. The resulting data displays in the Measure Inertia dialog box as shown in Figure 17–38.

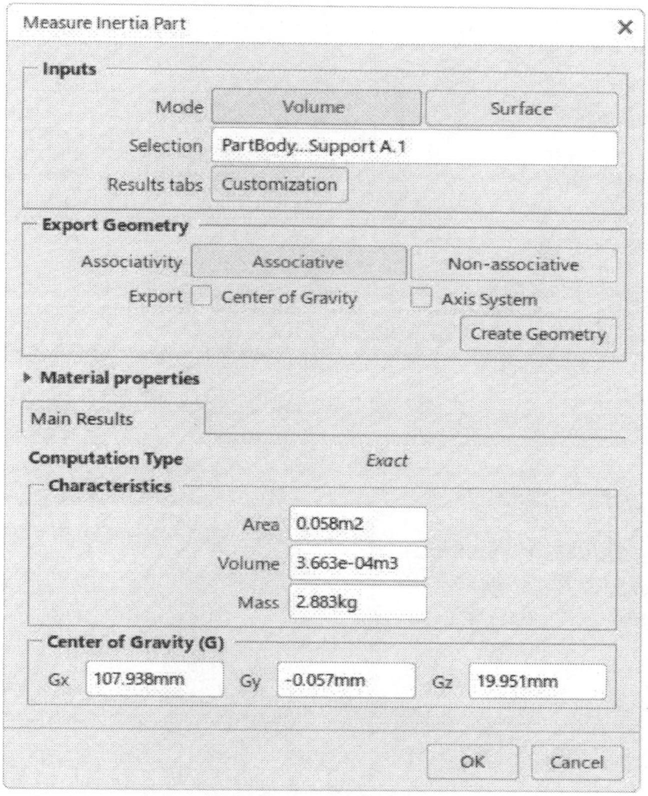

Figure 17–38

2. Note the surface Area value. This might be important if the part is powder-coated or plated.
3. Note the Volume value. This might be important in calculating the material cost of molded or cast parts.
4. Leave the Measure Inertia dialog box open.

Task 8 - Measure inertia with respect to an axis system.

1. If the *Inertia / Axis System* tab is not displayed in the Measure Inertia dialog box, click **Customization** and enable the **Inertia / G** and **Inertia / Axis system** options (if not selected) as shown in Figure 17–39.

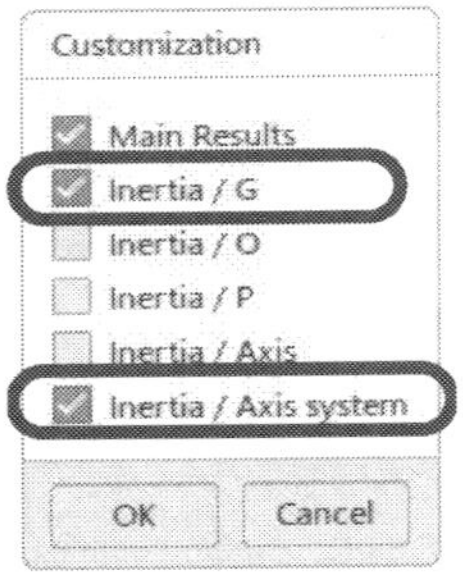

Figure 17–39

2. Click **OK**.
3. Select the *Inertia / Axis System* tab.
4. Select the **Select Axis System** option highlighted in Figure 17–40 and select **Axis System.1** as the axis system.

Note the Select Axis System option is immediately deselected when you click the axis system.

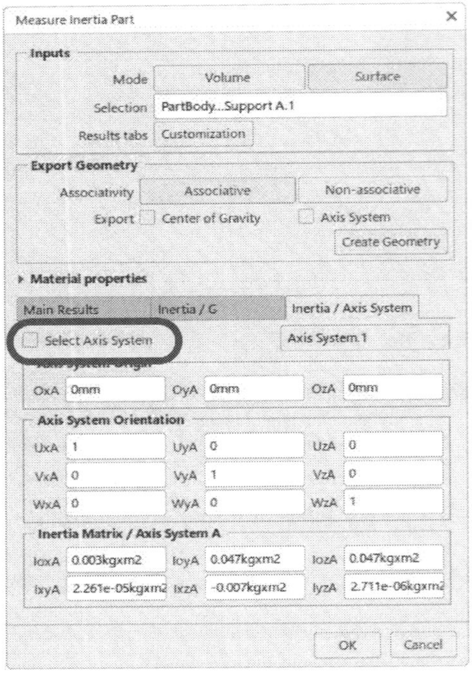

Figure 17–40

5. Note how the values of the Inertia Matrix are different than the values measured in the *Inertia / G* tab (select the PartBody to calculate).

6. Close the dialog box.

7. Change the View mode back to (Shading With Edges) using the (View Modes) command.

Task 9 - Take a series of one-click measurements.

1. In the *Tools* section of the Action Bar, click (Measure Item) to make some one-click measurements.

If the units for the area calculation are incorrect, select ***Preferences > General>Parameters and Measure****, select the Units tab and set the Area units to square meter.*

2. Select the cylindrical surface shown in Figure 17–41. Note that both the area and radius are displayed.

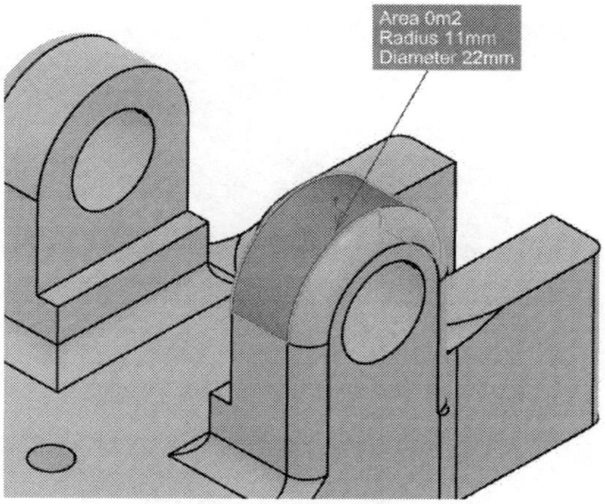

Figure 17–41

Design Considerations

Note that you obtain an area of $0m^2$. This is because the area of the cylindrical surface is relatively small. You can determine the correct area by changing the number of decimal places displayed for measurement.

3. Select **Me** > **Preferences** > **Common Preferences**> **Parameters, Measure, and Units**> *Units* section.

4. Select **Area** in the *Magnitudes* field.

Decimal places cannot be set globally. You must set the number of decimal places for each type of unit individually.

5. Change the value in the *Decimal places for read/write numbers* field to **7**, as shown in Figure 17–42.

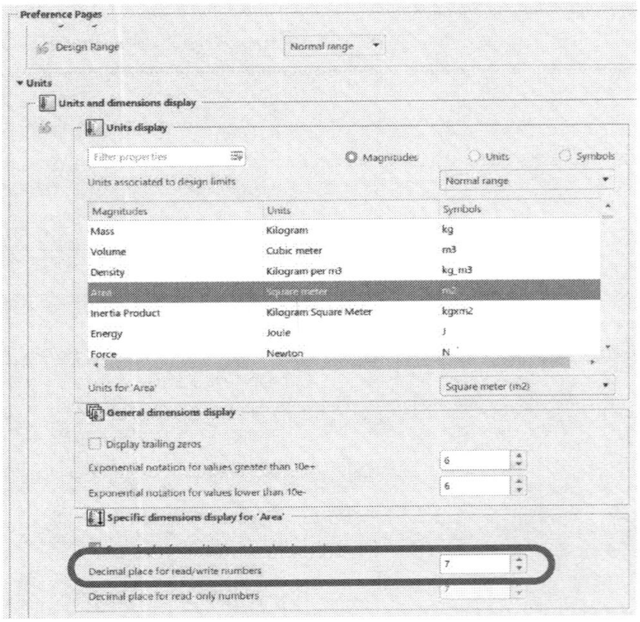

Figure 17–42

6. Click **OK** to close the Options dialog box.

7. Repeat the measurement of the cylindrical surface. The results display as shown in Figure 17–43.

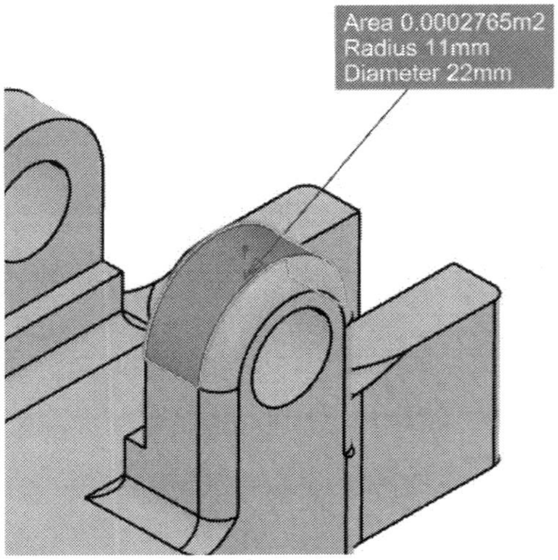

Figure 17–43

8. Take additional one-click measure item measurements for different items in the model, including flat surfaces, the part body, and a vertex.
9. Close the Measure Item dialog box.

Task 10 - Take a series of measure between measurements.

1. Click  (Measure Between) to take some Measure Between measurements.
2. In the Type of Measure drop-down list, select **Minimum distance**.
3. Select the flat face and hole axis to measure between, as shown in Figure 17–44.

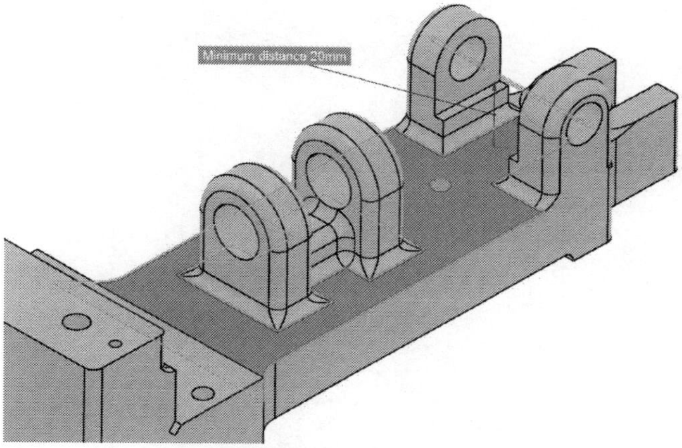

Figure 17–44

4. Note that the Angle dimension is calculated in the dialog box but not on the model. This dimension is not required.
5. Select the *Customize* tab to customize the results.
6. Clear the **Angle** option in the *Tab* column in the Measure Between Customization dialog box.
7. Click **OK**.
8. Repeat Step 3 for a different flat face and hole axis. Note that only the distance is measured and displayed in both the dialog box and on the model.

9. Practice making additional measurements using Measure Between.
10. Hide the parameters that you have just created.
11. Save the model and close the tab.

Practice 17b Measuring with Reference Geometry

Practice Objective

- Create reference geometry to perform measure operations.

In this practice, you will determine the maximum width, height, and length of the model. To do this, you will develop reference geometry, such as points and planes, to assist in your measurements.

Task 1 - Import GameController and take a measurement.

1. Import **GameController.3dxml**.
2. Right-click **GameController** and select **Open**.The model displays as shown in Figure 17–45.

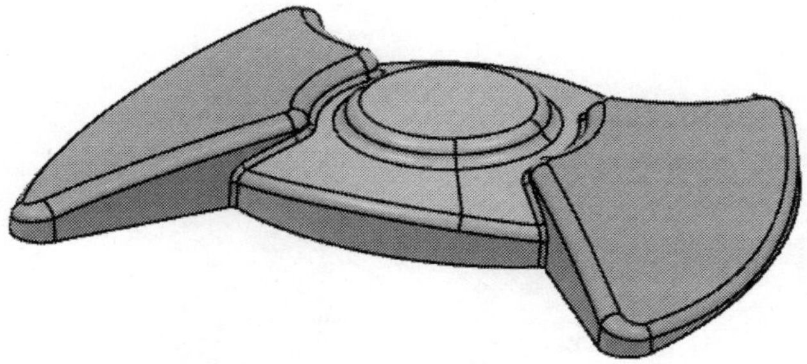

Figure 17–45

3. In the *Tools* section of the Action Bar, click  (Measure Between) and set the *Type of measure* to **Maximum distance** and ensure *Selection 1 and 2 mode* are set to **Any geometry**.

4. Measure between the two arc edges on the bottom of the model, as shown in Figure 17–46, to obtain the overall height of the model.

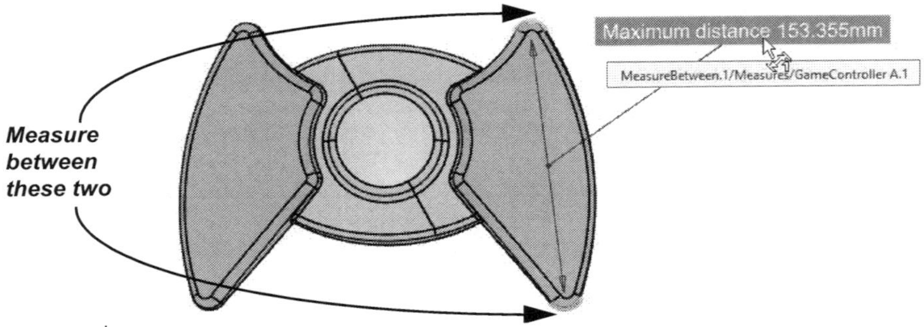

Figure 17–46

The software reports the distance between the centers of the two arcs, as shown in Figure 17–47. To obtain the overall height of the part, additional reference geometry must be developed.

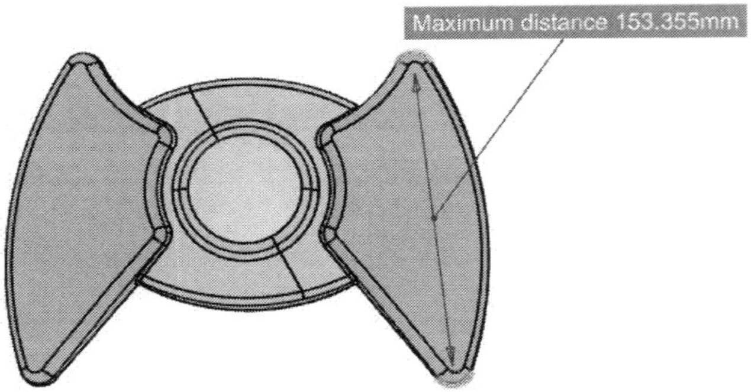

Figure 17–47

5. Cancel the measurement.

Task 2 - Create reference geometry.

In this task, you will build reference points that mark the extremities of the two arc edges that you previously measured. The **Tangent on curve** option is used in this case, as it forces the system to locate the outermost point of the selected curve when viewed from the selected plane.

1. Create a reference point using the following parameters:
    - Point Type: **Tangent on curve**
    - Curve: **Select the arc edge** as shown in Figure 17–48.
    - Direction: **ZX plane**

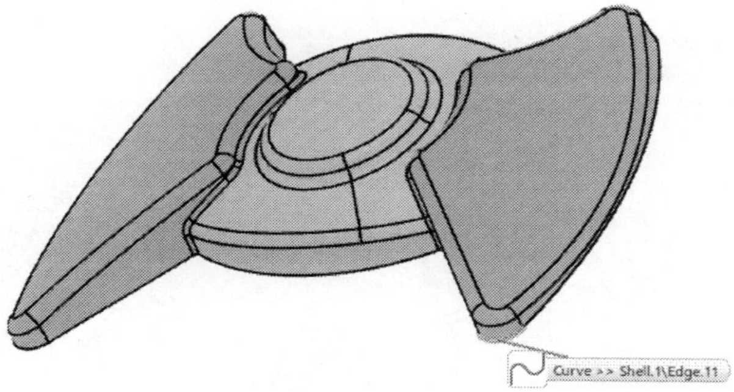

Figure 17–48

2. The resulting point displays as shown in Figure 17–49.

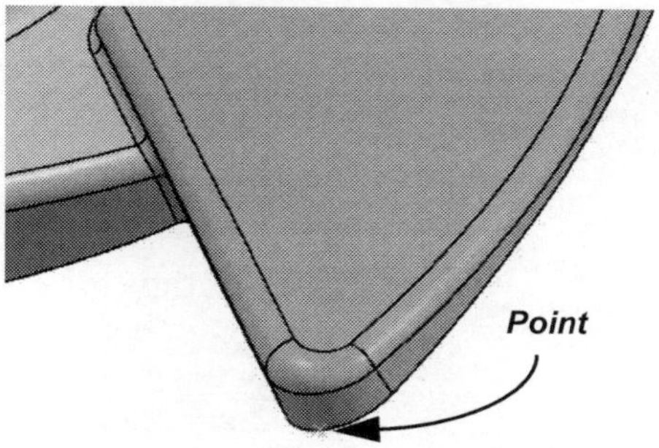

Figure 17–49

3. Repeat this process to create a point on the top arc edge. The point displays as shown in Figure 17–50.

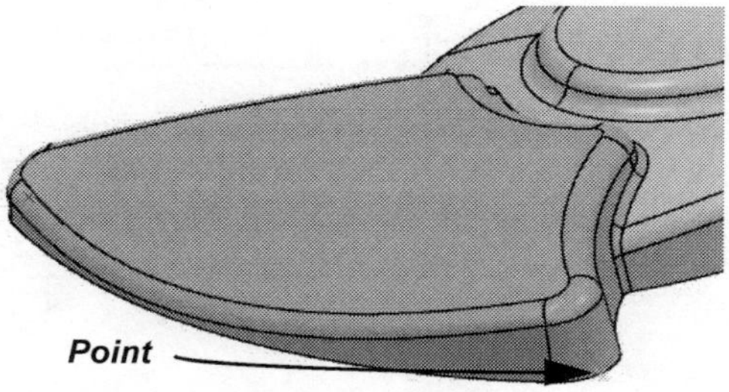

Figure 17–50

Task 3 - Take a measurement between points.

1. Repeat the **Measure Between** operation, selecting the two points that you created. The resulting measurement displays as shown in Figure 17–51.

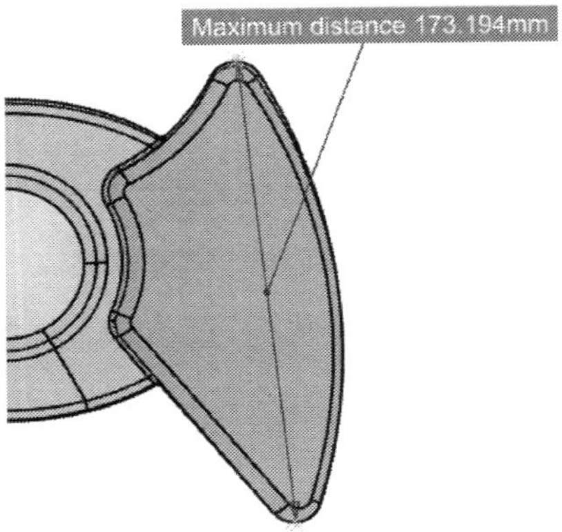

Figure 17–51

Design Considerations

The measurement still does not display the true height of the model. Since it cannot be guaranteed that the two points are vertically aligned, you can use the **Measure Between** tool to obtain the components of the measured distance.

2. Select the *Customize* tab and enable the **Components** option in both the *3D* and *Tab* columns. The dialog box updates to display the X, Y, and Z components of the measurement. The true height of the model is approximately 171.96mm.

3. Cancel the measurement.

Task 4 - Use reference planes to display distance in one direction.

In this task, you will build reference planes through the point elements. Measuring between two reference planes ensures that the measured distance is in the exact required direction. This also enables you to keep only the required component(s) of a measurement and display it on the model.

1. Create a reference plane using the following options:

- Plane type: **Parallel through point**
- Reference: **yz plane**
- Point: **Point.1**

The completed reference plane displays as shown in Figure 17–52.

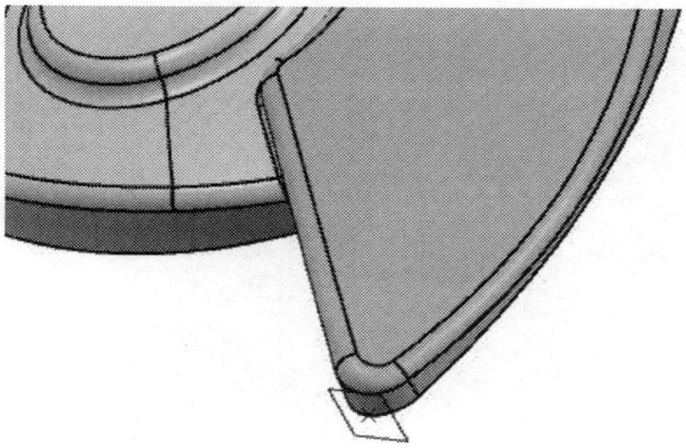

Figure 17–52

2. Create a second reference plane that is parallel to the yz plane and through Point.2. The model displays as shown in Figure 17–53.

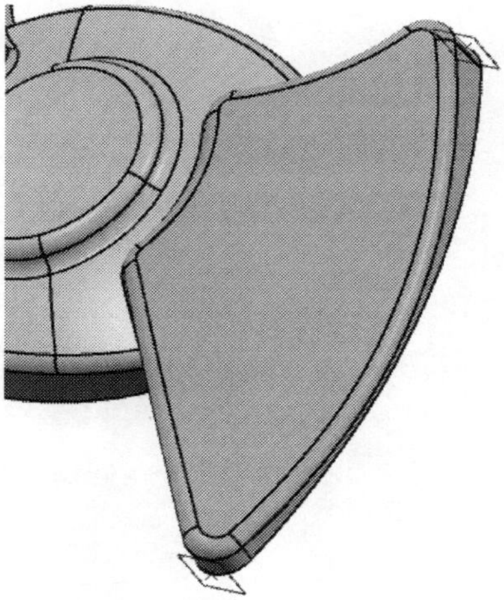

Figure 17–53

You can turn off the Component information in the Customize tab.

3. Measure between the two reference planes just created. The model displays as shown in Figure 17–54.

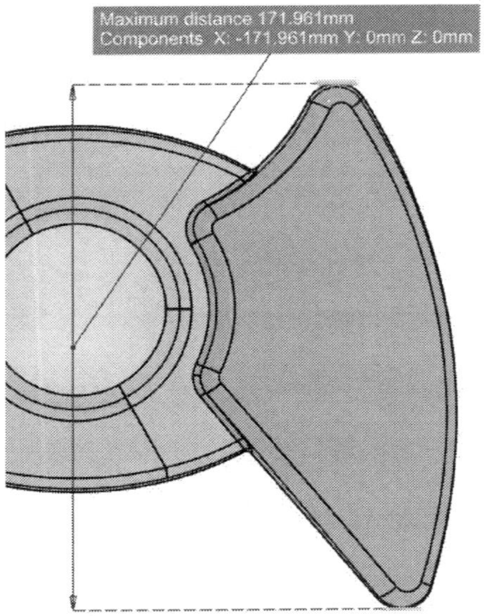

Figure 17–54

4. Click **OK** in the Measure Between in Part dialog box.

Task 5 - (Optional) Take additional measurements.

1. If time permits, use the techniques described in this exercise to determine the true width and depth of the model. The measured values should equal:
   - Width = **241.62mm**
   - Depth = **30.28mm**
2. Save the model and close the tab.

Chapter Review Questions

1. Which of the following items can be measured using the **Measure Item** tool? (Select all that apply).
   a. Point
   b. Edge
   c. Two planes
   d. Flat Surface

2. Measurements are always stored with the model data.
   a. True
   b. False

3. Measurement data is stored in the Results branch of the specification tree.
   a. True
   b. False

4. In Figure 17–55, the icon indicates that the measurement has not been updated.

   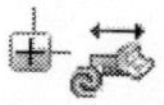

   Figure 17–55

   a. True
   b. False

5. When material is applied to a model, the properties (density, etc.) are defined which permits accurate inertial values.
   a. True
   b. False

6. The **Create Geometry** tool enables you to create an axis system and a point at the center of gravity.
   a. True
   b. False

Answers: 1abd, 4b, 3b,4a, 5a, 6a

Rib and Slot Features

Ribs and Slots are the swept solid features in CATIA that are used to create shapes where a single cross-section follows a reference path.

Learning Objectives in This Chapter

- Learn about Rib and Slot features.
- Understand the various options available for Rib and Slot features.

18.1 Ribs and Slots

The sketch plane of the profile must intersect the center curve.

A Rib feature adds material to your model by sweeping a sketched profile along a center curve. Figure 18–1 shows an example of a Rib. A slot is similar to a Rib feature, except that it removes material from your model by sweeping a profile along a center curve.

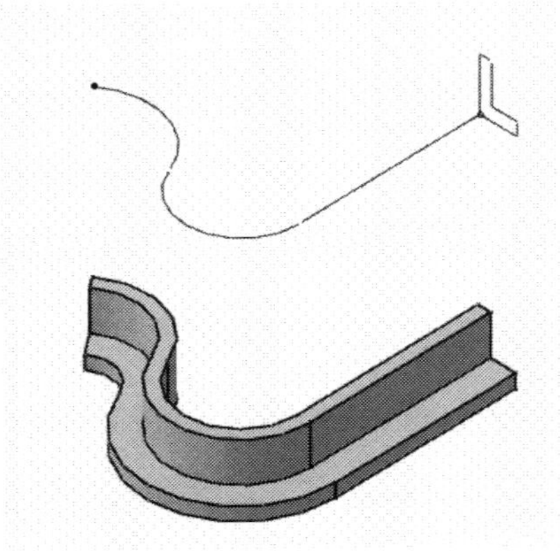

Figure 18–1

How To: Create a Rib Feature

1. In the *Essentials* or *Model* section of the Action Bar, click  (Rib) to open the Rib Definition dialog box, which prompts for a Profile selection and a Center curve sketch, as shown in Figure 18–2.

Figure 18–2

2. Specify the center curve. The center curve defines the path that the profile sketch follows. It must intersect the sketch plane of the profile.
3. Select a profile sketch to follow the center curve. As the profile follows the center curve, it can be controlled using the Profile control options. Three options are available from the drop-down list in the *Profile control* area.

   The Profile control options are described as follows:

Profile Control Option	Description
Keep angle	Maintains the existing angle between the profile sketch plane and center curve.
Pulling direction	Sweeps profile relative to a specified direction. A plane or edge can be selected.
Reference surface	Maintains angle value relative to the axis of the profile and a selected surface.

4. Click **OK** to complete the feature.

Slots

Slot features remove material from your model by sweeping a profile along a center curve. Slot features are created using a similar method to ribs. To create a slot, click  (Slot). Figure 18–3 shows an example of a slot.

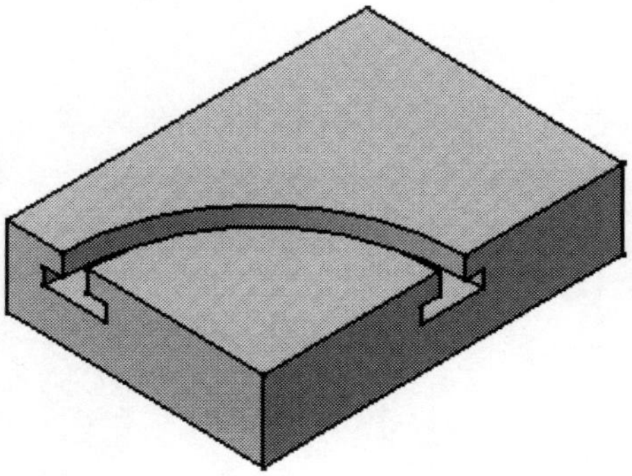

Figure 18–3

18.2 Rib and Slot Options

Merge Ends

The **Merge ends** option enables the profile to continue its trajectory and merge with a surface. Since the center curve is defined on the cup's surface, the profile does not extend into the cup body. However, if the **Merge ends** option is selected, the geometry merges with the cup body, as shown in Figure 18–4.

Figure 18–4

Center Curve

Only one edge can be selected for the center curve.

When specifying the center curve, an existing sketch can be used. If an existing sketch is not available, you can click  (Sketch) and create a new sketch on the selected plane. The center curve can also be specified by selecting an existing edge on a part surface, as shown in Figure 18–5.

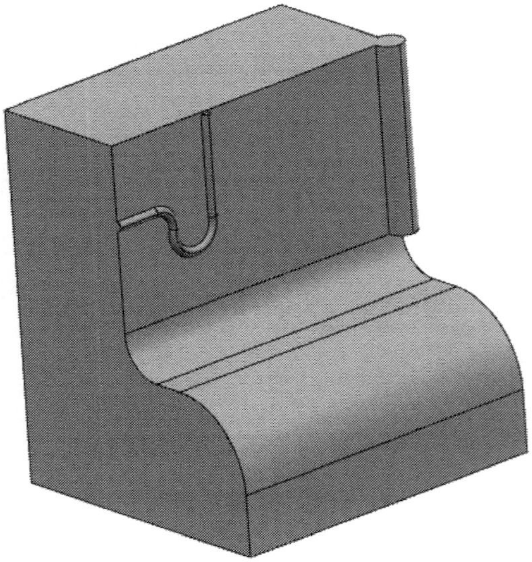

Figure 18–5

If entities in your center curve are non-tangent, sharp corners are produced. Note the difference in geometry from tangent entities compared to non-tangent entities, as shown in Figure 18–6.

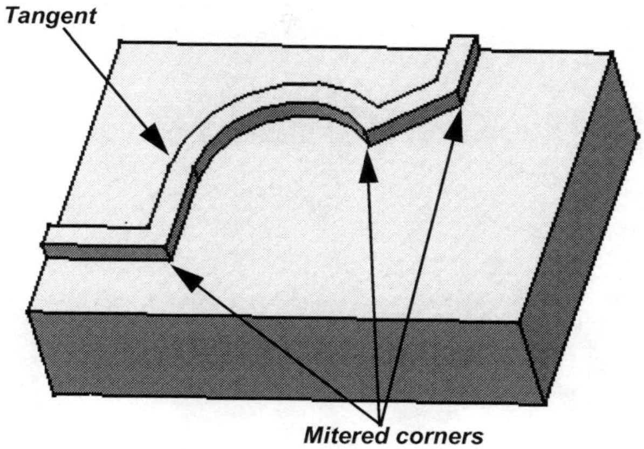

Figure 18–6

Overlapping Geometry

If the cross-section overlaps itself as it travels along the center curve, the feature aborts, as shown in Figure 18–7. If this occurs, modify the profile or the center curve.

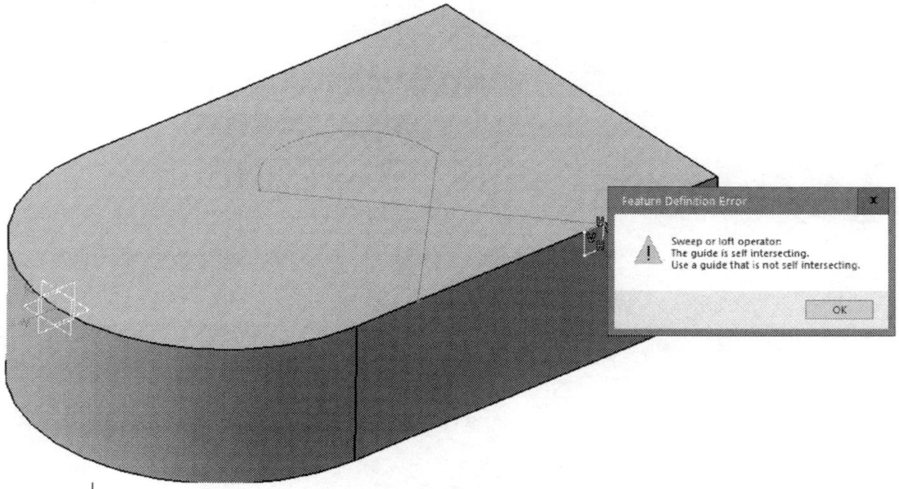

Figure 18–7

Practice 18a Slots and Ribs

Practice Objective

- Create and modify a Slot and a Rib.

In this practice, you will create the part shown in Figure 18–8. The part requires Slot and Rib features. You will also modify the slot and Rib features to merge their ends flush with the surface of the base feature.

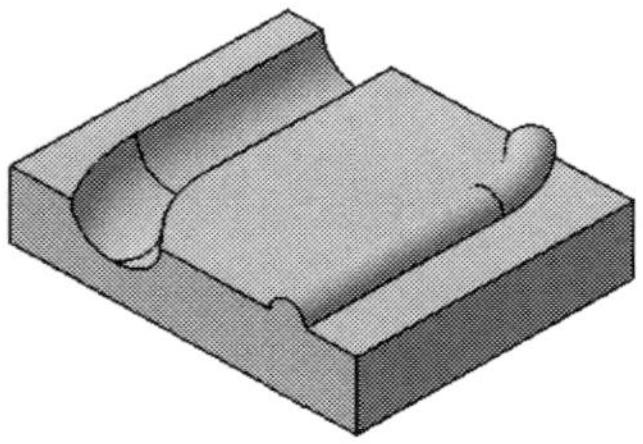

Figure 18–8

Task 1 - Create a Slot feature.

1. Create a new 3D Part titled ***Your_Initials*_Rib_Slot**. Title the 3D Shape the same.
2. Create a Pad 200 x 250 x 50 thick on the **xy plane**.
3. Create a positioned sketch using the top surface of the Pad feature as the sketch plane reference, as shown in Figure 18–9.

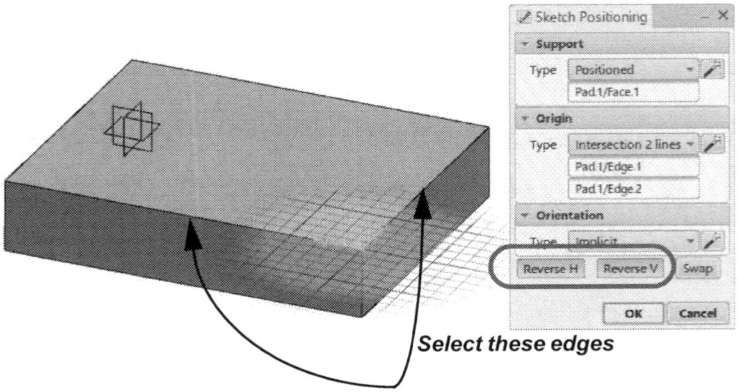

Figure 18–9

4. Hide the three default planes.

5. Dimension and constrain the sketch, as shown in Figure 18–10. It is used later for the center curve of a Slot feature.

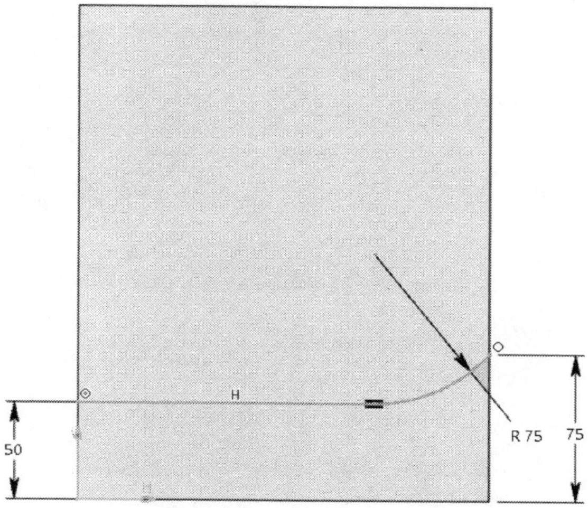

Figure 18–10

6. Create a positioned sketch with the sketch plane and origin defined, as shown in Figure 18–11.

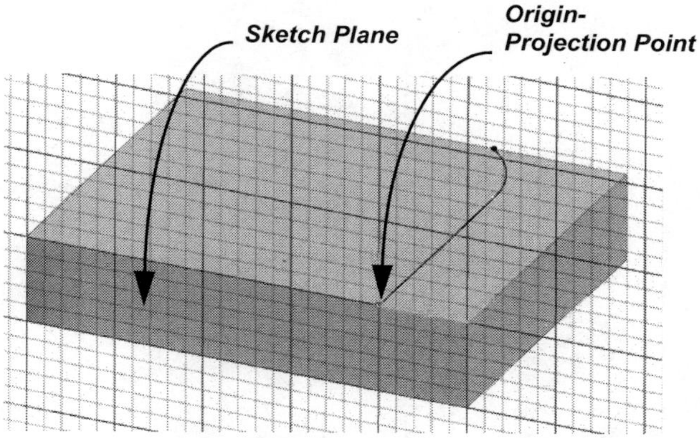

Figure 18–11

7. Sketch a circle with a *radius* of **25** and constrain it to the origin, as shown in Figure 18–12.

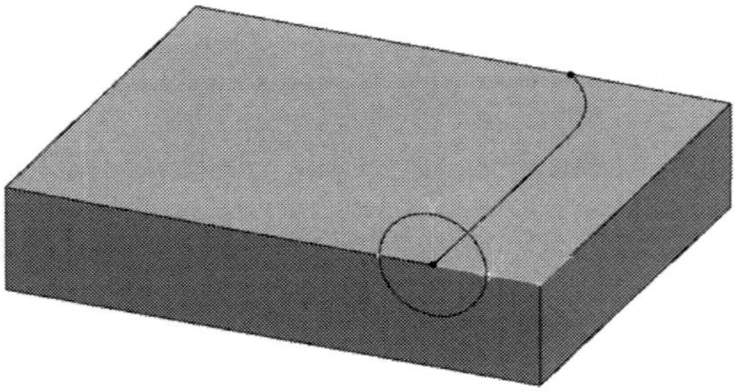

Figure 18–12

8. Create a Slot feature, by selecting the *Model* tab in the Action Bar and clicking  (Slot). The Slot Definition dialog box opens, as shown in Figure 18–13.

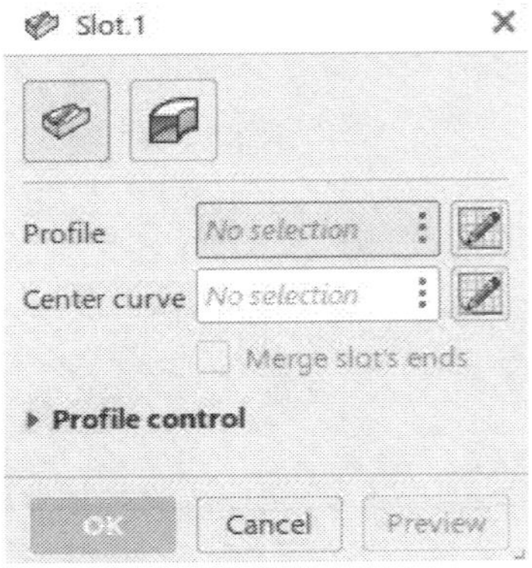

Figure 18–13

9. Select the following:
   - *Profile:* **Sketch.3** (if not already selected)
   - *Center curve:* **Sketch.2**

The name of the sketches could be different if created in a different order.

10. Click **OK**. The Slot feature displays as shown in Figure 18–14.

11. Double-click on the Slot feature to modify it.

12. Select the **Merge slot's ends** option and click **OK** in the Slot Definition dialog box. The slot displays as shown in Figure 18–15.

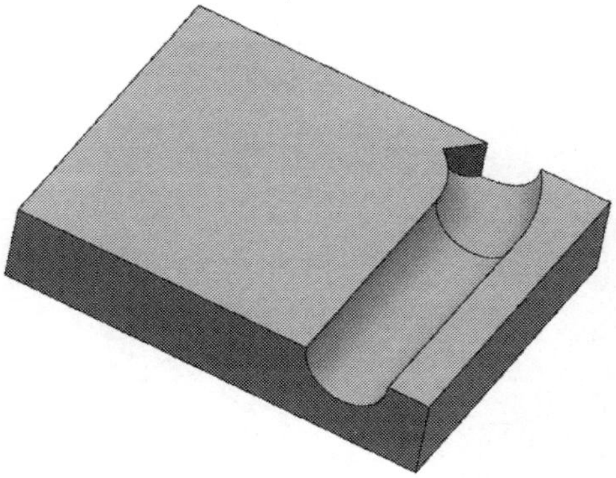

Figure 18–14

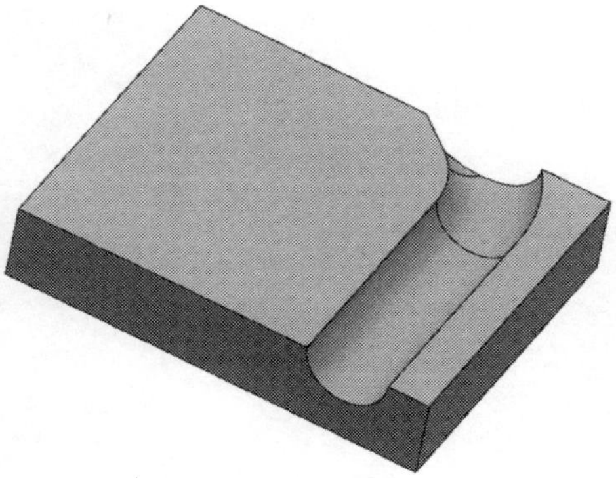

Figure 18–15

13. Double-click on the sketch of the slot center curve and modify the *arc radius* to **100.0**.

14. Exit the sketch and view the change in geometry.

Task 2 - Create a Rib feature.

1. Create a sketch, as shown in Figure 18–16.

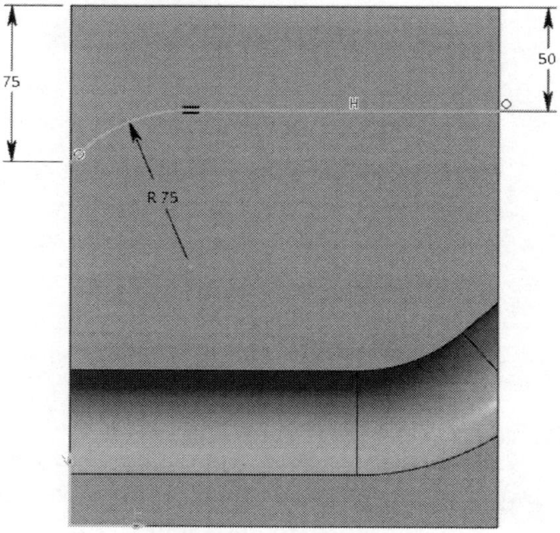

Figure 18–16

2. Create a Positioned Sketch on the back face as the planar support and select the end point of the previous sketch as the Origin, as shown in Figure 18–17.

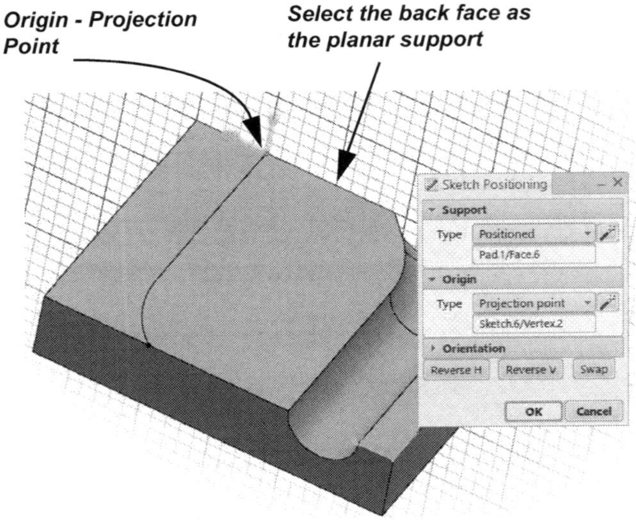

Figure 18–17

3. In the *View* section of the Action Bar, click (No 3D Background).

4. Create an arc profile as shown in Figure 18–18. Click (Usual) to return the solid geometry to display.

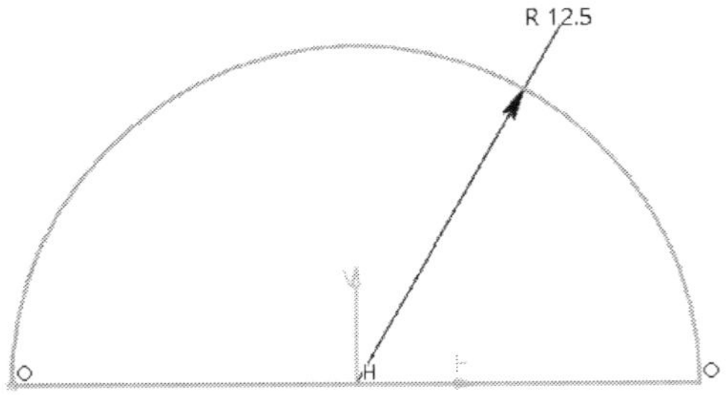

Figure 18–18

Design Considerations

It is recommended to close the profile section for Rib and Slot features. An open section can often cause unstable results during feature creation and downstream modifications. A closed profile provides a more robust model.

*Ensure that the **Merge rib's ends** option is cleared.*

5. Click (Rib) to create a Rib and select the appropriate profile and center curve sketches. The Rib feature displays as shown in Figure 18–19.

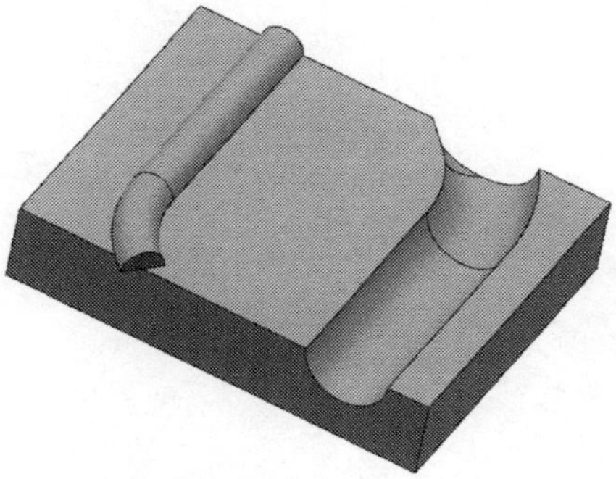

Figure 18–19

Design Considerations

You cannot merge ends with a surface that does not intersect the cross-section. Since the center curve does not cause the Rib to fully intersect the face, the **Merge rib's ends** option must be cleared.

Task 3 - Modify the profile control of the Rib feature.

1. Double-click on **Rib.1** in the specification tree. The Rib Definition dialog box opens.

2. In the Profile Control drop-down list, select **Pulling direction** as shown in Figure 18–20.

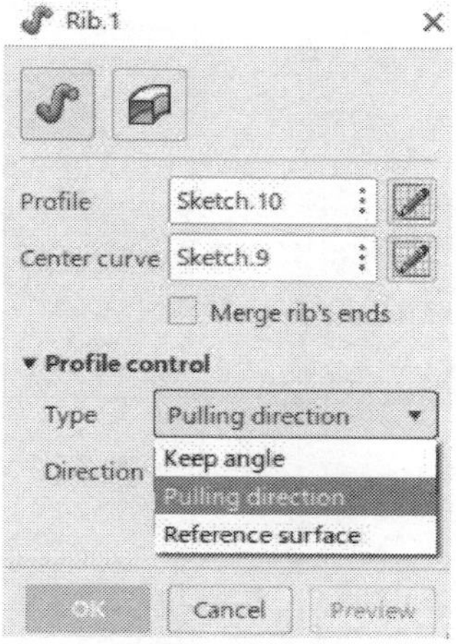

Figure 18–20

3. Select the edge shown in Figure 18–21 to define the pulling direction.

4. Click **OK** to complete the change. The part displays with the edge of the Rib feature now flush with the face of the part, as shown in Figure 18–22.

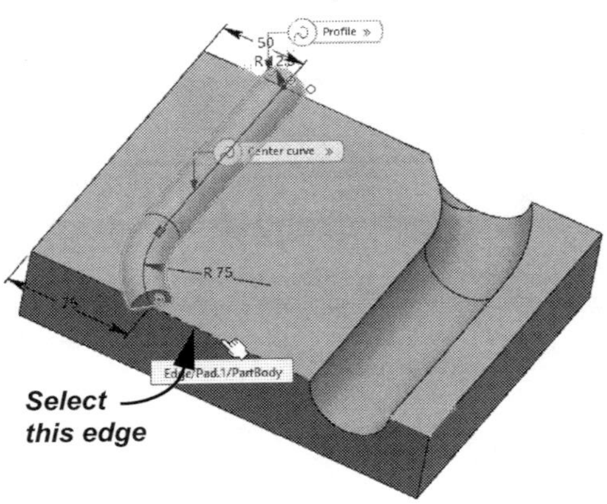

Figure 18–21

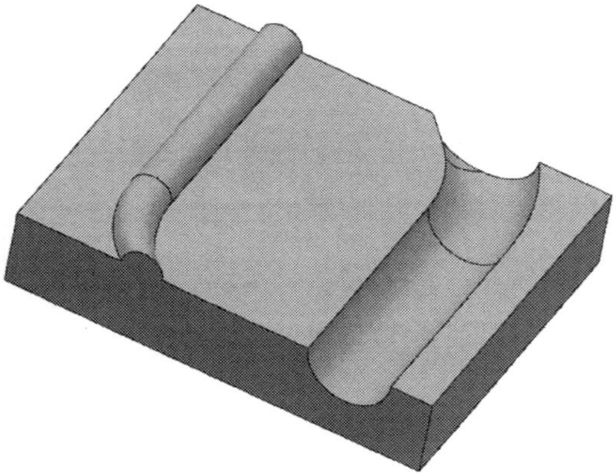

Figure 18–22

5. Save the model and close the tab.

Practice 18b Car Exhaust

Practice Objective

- Create a thick Rib feature.

In this practice, you will create two thick Rib features to define the geometry for the pipe and the tip of a car exhaust system. The completed model displays as shown in Figure 18–23.

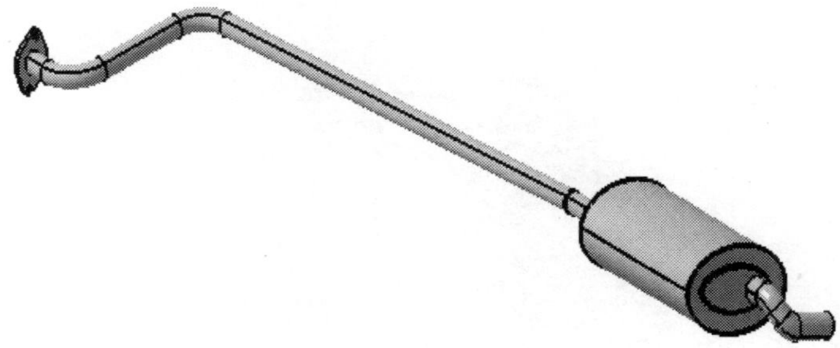

Figure 18–23

Task 1 - Open a part model.

1. Import **CarExhaust.3dxml**.
2. Right-click CarExhaust and select **Open**.
3. The model consists of two separate geometry items: the exhaust flange and the silencer. Each piece of geometry has been created in a separate body, which displays in the specification tree. In addition, two curves have been created that are used later as the center curves for the two Rib features.

Guide curves will be white instead of black in Catia by default.

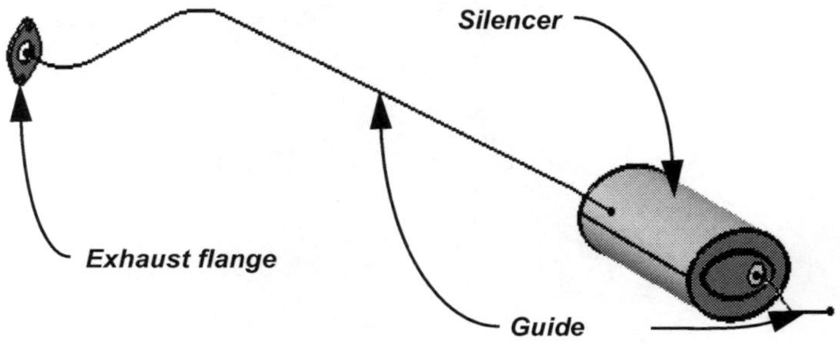

Figure 18–24

4. Verify that the PartBody is the active object.

Task 2 - Create the profile for the first Rib.

1. Create a sketch on the planar surface of the exhaust flange, as shown in Figure 18–25.

2. Prepare the sketch to insert the pipe into the hole of the flange. To create a parametric relationship between the pipe and the flange, use the edge of the flange geometry. Click  (Project 3D Elements) and select the circular edge of the flange, as shown in Figure 18–26.

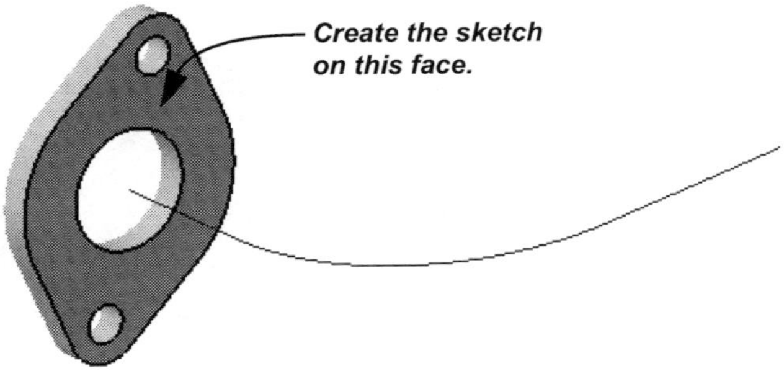

Figure 18–25

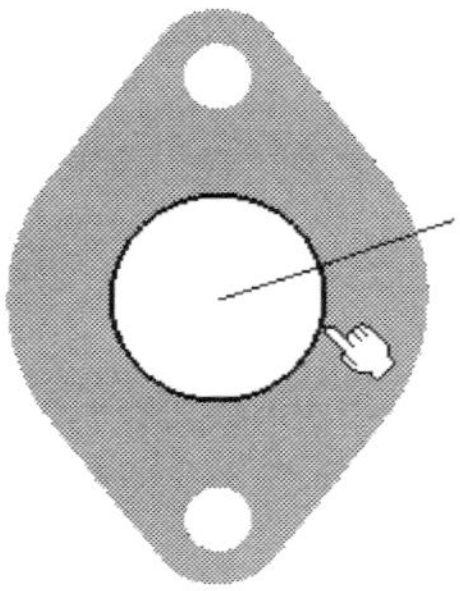

Figure 18–26

3. Exit the sketch.

Task 3 - Create the exhaust pipe.

In this task, you will use a Rib feature to define the shape of the exhaust pipe. The Rib will use the circular section for its profile and the polyline curve for the guide curve.

1. Create a Rib feature. Make the following selections:

   - *Profile:* Select the circular sketch just created
   - *Center curve:* **GuideCurve.1** from the PolylinePoints body
   -  (Thick Profile)*:* Select this option.
   - *Thickness1:* **0mm**
   - *Thickness2:* **2mm (0.079 in)**

   The completed Rib is shown in Figure 18–27.

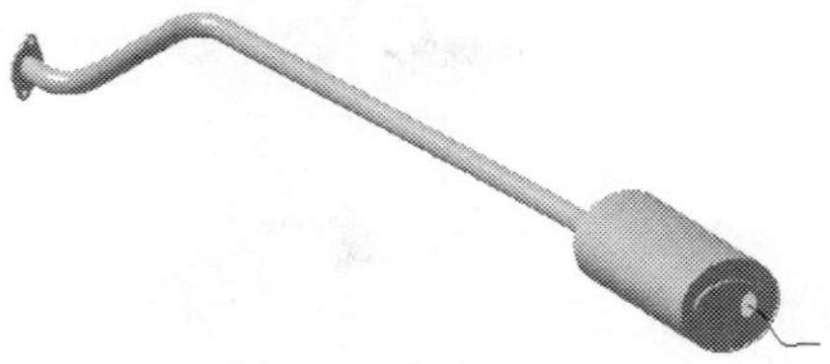

Figure 18–27

Task 4 - Create the exhaust tip.

In this task, you will create the exhaust tip geometry using a Rib feature. You will be given a minimum amount of instruction to complete this task. The completed Rib is shown in Figure 18–28.

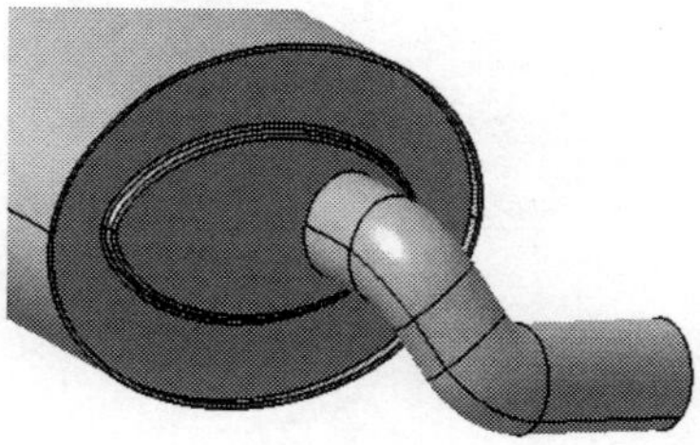

Figure 18–28

1. Create a sketch that has the circular section shown in Figure 18–29 projected onto the sketch plane.

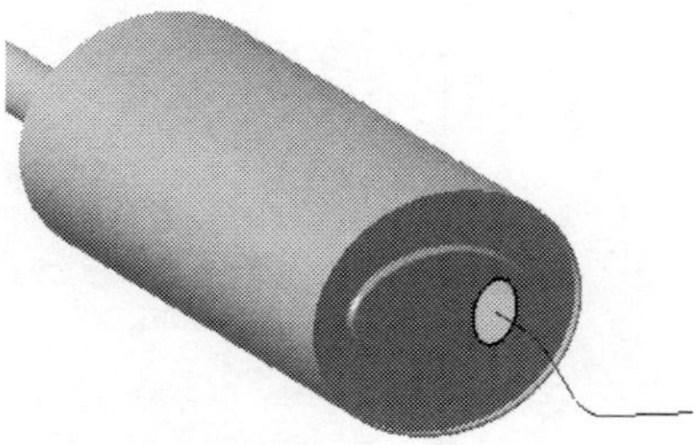

Figure 18–29

2. Create a Rib feature using this sketch and **GuideCurve.2**. Select the **Thick Profile** option and add a *thickness* of **2mm** to the outside of the circular profile.

Task 5 - Save the part and close the window.

1. Save the mode and close the tab.

NOTE: An additional rib/slot practice is found in Practice B16 at the end of this guide.

Chapter Review Questions

1. Which two elements must be defined to create a Rib feature?
   a. Profile
   b. Datum Plane
   c. Axis
   d. Center Curve
2. Which of the following statements regarding Rib features is true?
   a. A Rib creates a single feature whose geometry is blended between multiple profiles.
   b. A Rib creates a single feature whose geometry is swept along a defined path.
   c. A Rib can only be added to the model after the base feature has been created.
   d. A Rib path must intersect the sketch support of the profile.
3. The profile of a Rib must be closed.
   a. True
   b. False
4. Multiple edges can be selected as the center curve.
   a. True
   b. False
5. Non-tangent entities in the center curve of a Rib or Slot produce sharp corners while tangent entities produce smooth corners.
   a. True
   b. False

6. The Slot feature profile and center curve shown in Figure 18–30 fails because _____.

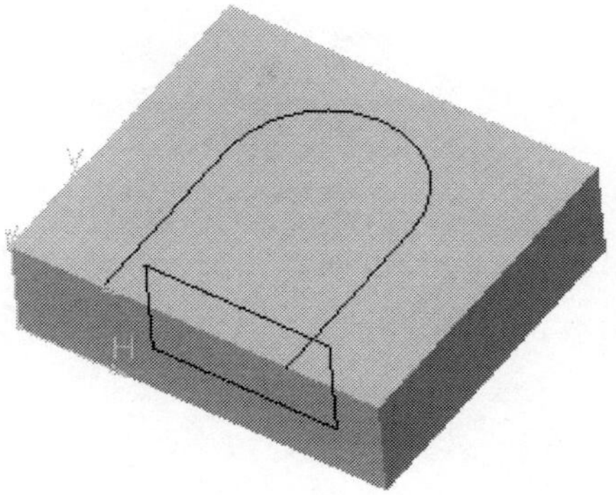

Figure 18–30

   a. The rectangular section is not fully in the solid.
   b. A rectangular shape cannot be used to follow a tangent curve.
   c. The resulting geometry overlaps itself.
   d. None of the above.

7. The _______ option can be used to blend the ends of a rib into existing geometry.
   a. Merge Ends
   b. Smooth Ends
   c. Blend Ends
   d. None of the above.

8. When creating a Rib or Slot, use the _______ option to maintain the angle value relative to the axis of the profile and the selected surface.
   a. Keep Angle
   b. Reference Surface
   c. Pulling Direction.
   d. None of the above.

Answers: 1ad, 2b, 3b, 4b, 5a, 6c, 7a, 8b

Chapter 19

Basic Multi-sections Solid Features

A Multi-sections Solid feature is an additional feature that can add or remove material from your model. Multiple offset sketches are selected and the software creates the transitional surfaces between the selected sketches to create the feature.

Learning Objectives in This Chapter

- Create multi-section solids to create complex geometry.
- Create multi-section solids to create transitions between existing geometry.

19.1 Multi-sections Solids

Multi-sections solids are used to create complex geometry or transitional surfaces between existing geometry. Multi-sections solids add material to your model. An example of this feature is shown in Figure 19–1. Removed multi-sections solids behave similar to multi-sections solids, except that they remove material from your model.

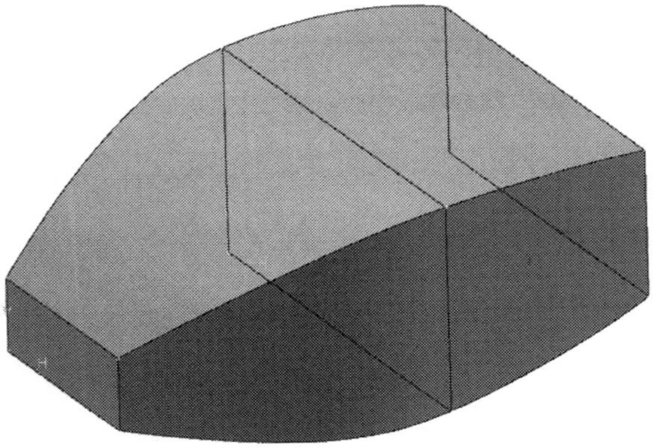

Figure 19–1

How To: Create a Multi-sections Solid

The order of section/sketch selection is important because the transitional surfaces are created in order between the sections.

1. Create all sketches that are required for the feature.
2. Click  (Multi-sections Solid) to open the Multi-sections Solid Definition dialog box, as shown in Figure 19–2.

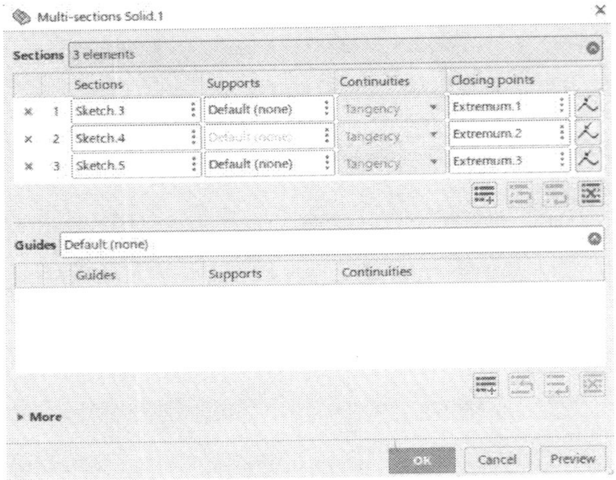

Figure 19–2

3. Select the sketches in the order of creation and click **OK** to complete the feature.

Closing Point

When the sketched sections are selected, the software selects a default closing point at one of the vertices in the sketch. The position of the closing point is used to calculate how the software connects the vertices. Figure 19–3 shows the closing points for the three sections.

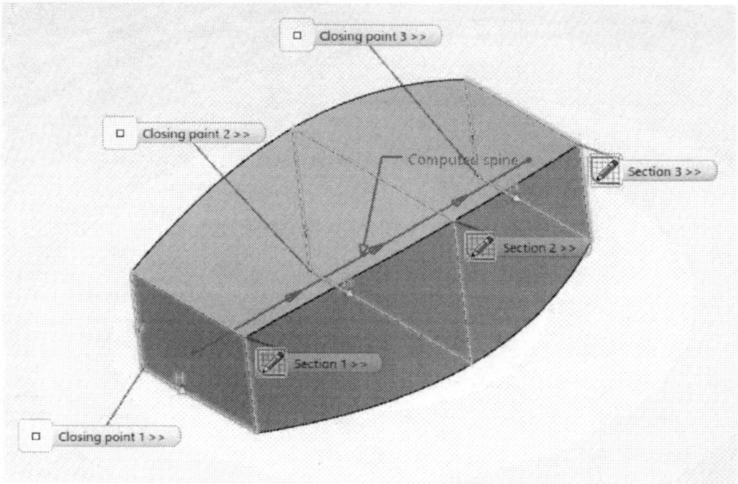

Figure 19–3

If the closing points are not aligned and/or are pointing in different directions, the transitional surfaces appear to twist as the software connects the vertices. The closing point of the last section is moved, as shown in Figure 19–4.

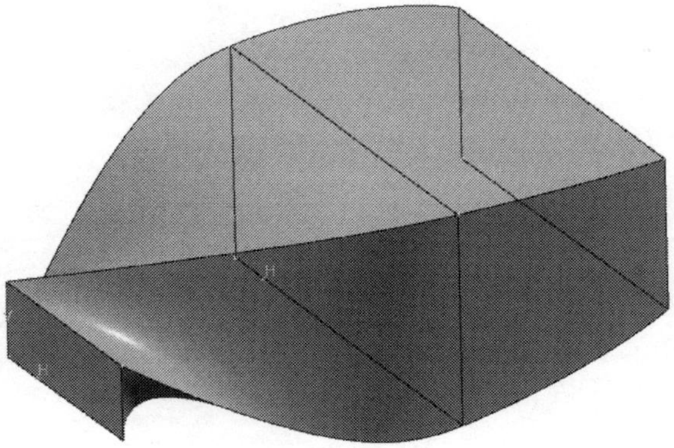

Figure 19–4

Changing Closing Points

*If a closing point is removed, it can be created again by right-clicking and selecting **Create Closing Point**.*

To change the closing point location, select the **Closing points** field in the section and select another vertex, as shown in Figure 19–5. Select another point to become the new closing point.

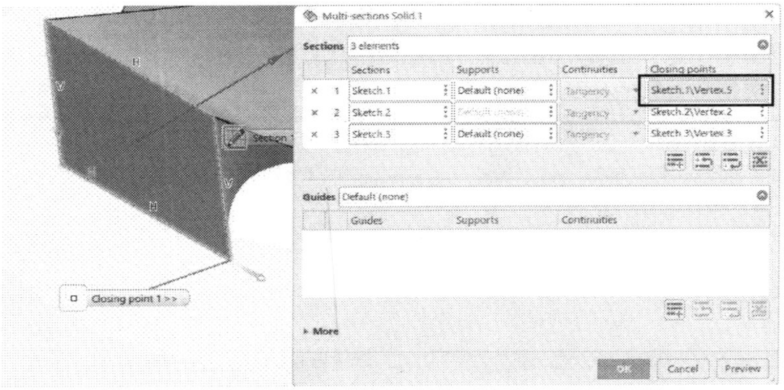

Figure 19–5

If a closing point is pointing in the wrong direction, zoom in on the arrow and select it to toggle the arrow direction.

Coupling

Click **More** to expand the Multi-sections Solid dialog box and open the advanced options. The *Sections coupling type* drop-down list is used to define the transitions between the sections, as shown in Figure 19–6.

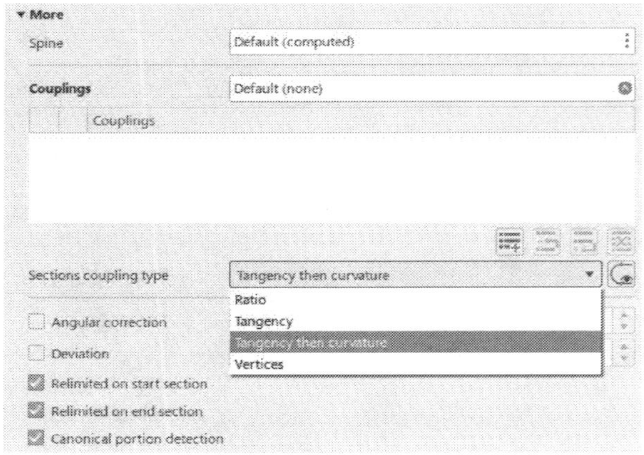

Figure 19–6

These options are described as follows:

Coupling Option	Description
Ratio	If the sections are connected at positions, the ratio is computed by the percentage of the section profile. This option is recommended when non-equal numbers of vertices are present in the sketch sections.
Tangency	If the sections have the same number of tangency discontinuity points, the points are coupled together between sections.
Tangency then curvature	If the sections have the same number of tangency and curvature discontinuity points, tangency discontinuity points are coupled together between sections, and then curvature discontinuity points are coupled together between sections.
Vertices	If the sections have the same number of vertices, these points are coupled together between sections.

- If a **Coupling** option is used and the criteria described are not met, an error message displays when attempting to generate the Multi-sections Solid feature.
- Setting the **Coupling** option to **Vertices** results in an error message when attempting to create transitions between a square and a circular section. This error occurs because the circular section does not have any vertices to couple with the square section.

Removed Multi-sections Solids

Removed Multi-sections Solids features behave similar to multi-sections solids, except that they remove material from your model. The software joins multiple sections by connecting vertices. Click  (Removed Multi-sections Solid) to create a removed multi-sections solid. Proceed using the same steps as the multi-sections solids.

Practice 19a Basic Multi-sections Solid Features

Practice Objectives

- Create a Multi-sections Solid feature.
- Create a Removed Multi-sections Solid feature.

In this practice, you will create a model using the Multi-sections Solid and Removed Multi-sections Solid features. During the creation of Multi-sections features, pay careful attention to closing points of the sections. If they are not correctly placed, the Multi-sections feature will contort. The final model should display as shown in Figure 19–7.

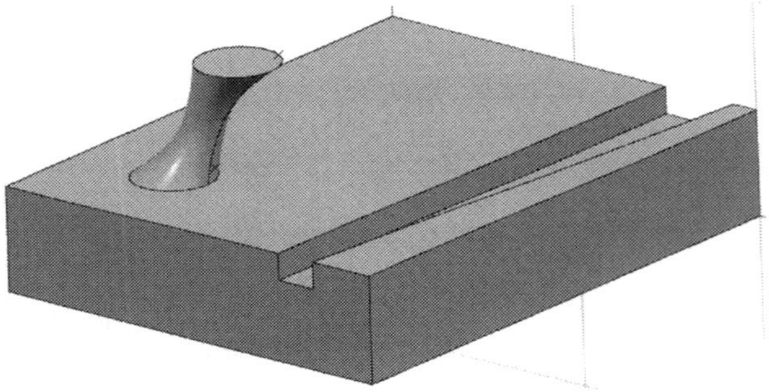

Figure 19–7

Task 1 - Open a model containing the base feature geometry.

1. Import **BasicMSS.3dxml**.
2. Right-click **BasicMSS** and select **Open**.

Task 2 - Create a Multi-sections Solid feature.

1. In the *Essentials* section of the Action Bar, click  (Plane) to create a reference plane.
2. Create a plane *offset* **25** from the top surface of the Pad. Select the **Repeat object after OK** option to create multiple copies.

3. Click **OK**. The Object Repetition dialog box opens. Do the following:
   - *Instance(s)* field: **1**
   - *Mode for Repetition:* leave **Absolute**
   - Disable the **Create in a new body** option.
4. Click **OK**. The updated model displays as shown in Figure 19–8.

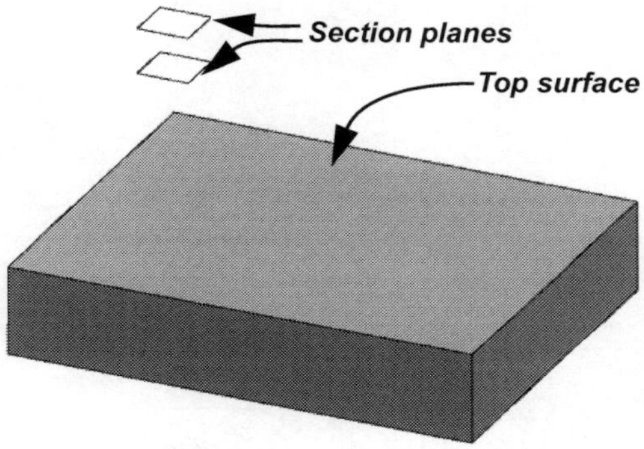

Figure 19–8

Design Considerations

The reference planes that you have just created will be used as sketching planes to create sections for the multi-sections solid.

5. Ensure that the PartBody is active. To set the active body, select PartBody in the specification tree and click (Define In Work Object), as shown in Figure 19–9.

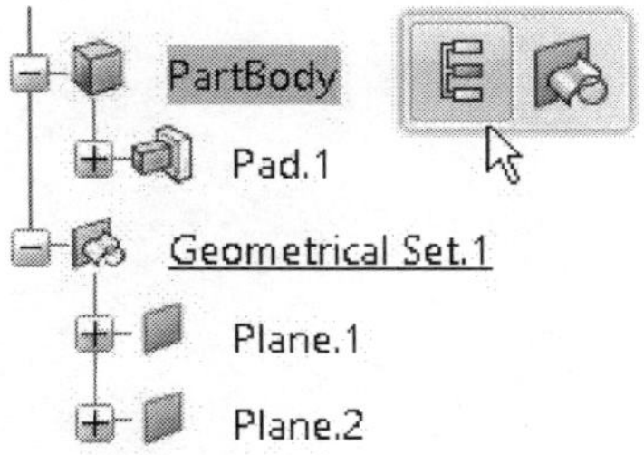

Figure 19–9

6. Select the top surface of the Pad and click (Sketch) to enter the Sketch app.

7. Sketch a **37.5** diameter circle with constraints, as shown in Figure 19–10.

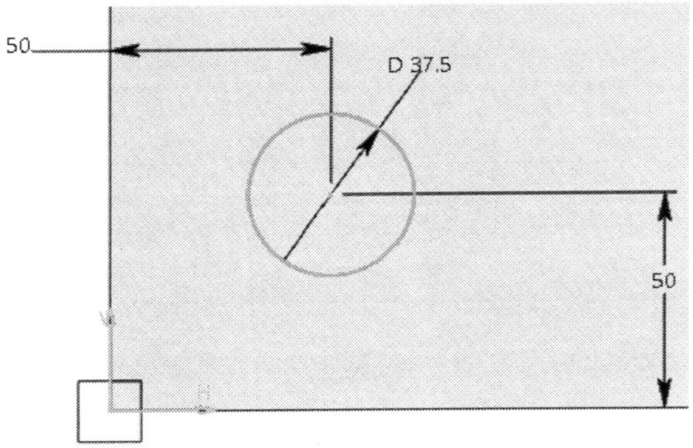

Figure 19–10

8. Click (Exit App) when the sketch profile is complete.

Task 3 - Create a sketch to be used for the Multi-sections Solid feature.

1. In the Essentials group, click (Positioned Sketch).
2. Select the plane shown in Figure 19–11.

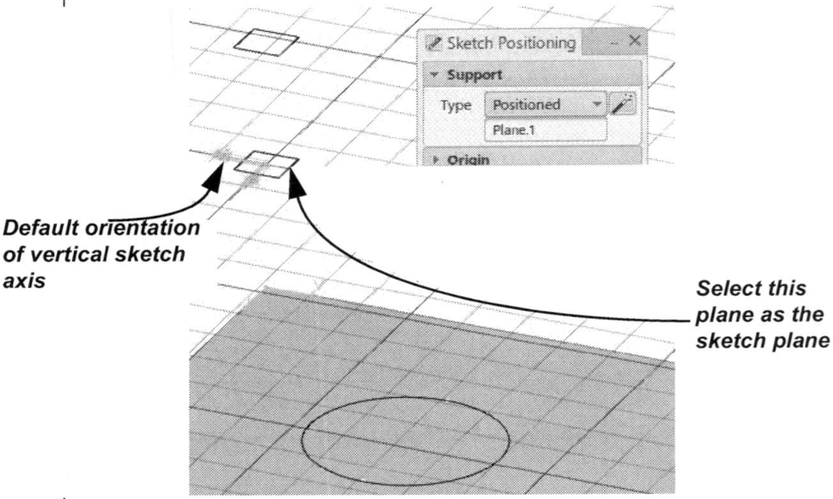

Figure 19–11

3. Leave the *Origin Type* as **Implicit.**

4. By default, the orientation (Horizontal and Vertical sketch axes) displays as shown in Figure 19–11. The Vertical sketch axis is flipped in the opposite direction from the way you viewed the sketch created in Task 3. To make the sketch orientation consistent with the previous sketch's orientation, select the **Reverse V** option, as shown in Figure 19–12.

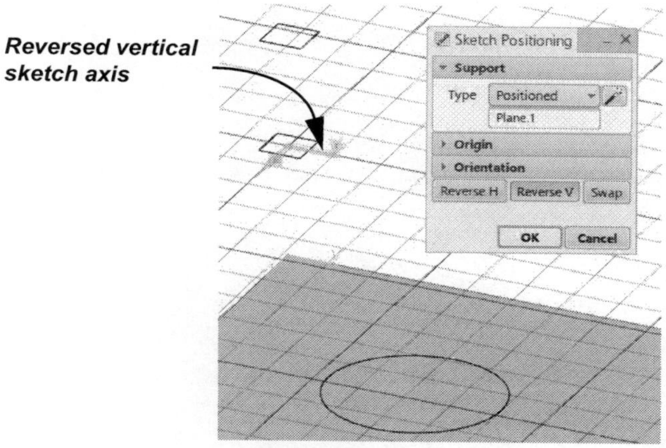

Figure 19–12

5. Sketch a **19** diameter circle on the selected plane and dimension the circle, as shown in Figure 19–13.

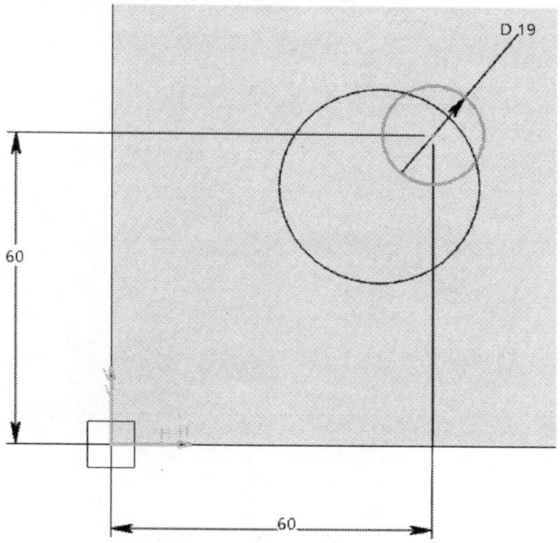

Figure 19–13

6. Create another positioned sketch using the second reference plane (the one furthest from the base Pad feature). Ensure that the sketch orientation is the same as the first two sketches.

7. Create a **37.5** diameter circle and dimension the sketch as shown in Figure 19–14.

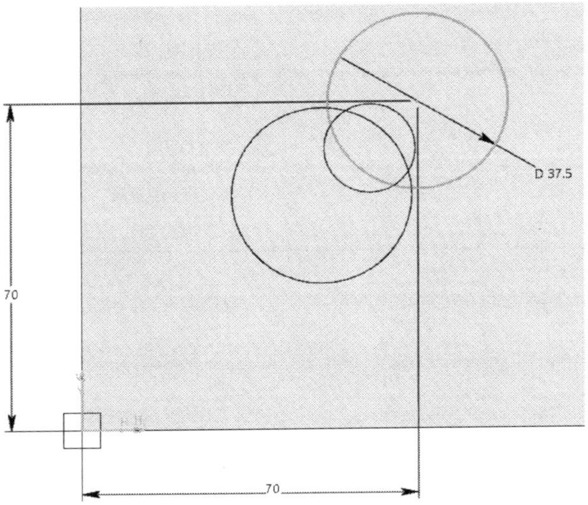

Figure 19–14

The model displays as shown in Figure 19–15. Note that in all three sketches the Horizontal and Vertical sketch axes face the same direction. If the sketches were not created as positioned sketches, the sketch axes for the three sketches would not all face in the same direction.

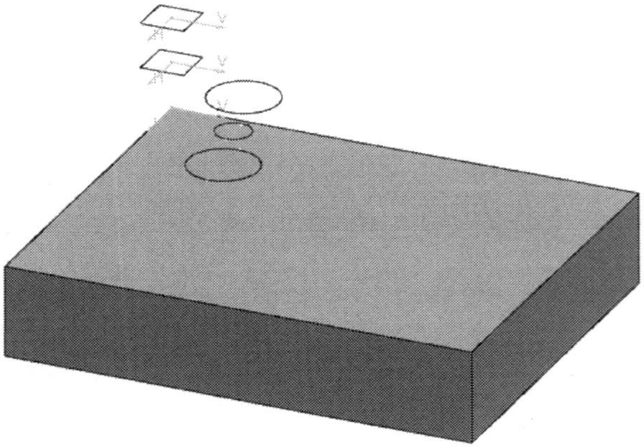

Figure 19–15

Task 4 - Create a Multi-sections Solid feature.

1. Select the *Model* section of the Action Bar and click  (Multi-sections Solid).

2. Select the three circular sections in the same sequence in which they were created to add them to the Multi-sections Solid Definition dialog box, as shown in Figure 19–16.

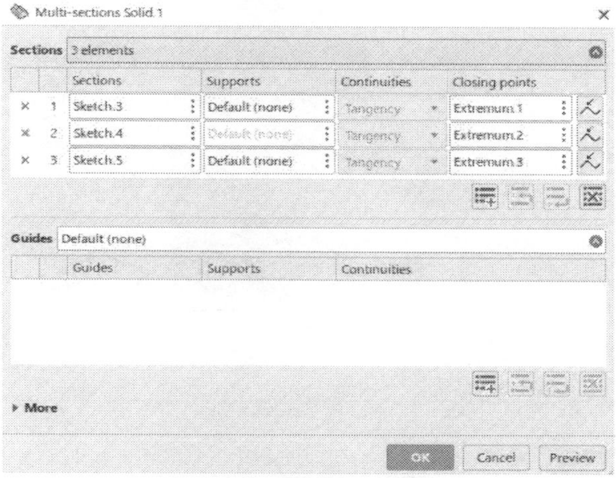

Figure 19–16

3. Ensure that the three closing point arrows point in the same direction, as shown in Figure 19–17. Select the arrows to toggle the direction, as required.

4. Click **OK** to create the Multi-sections Solid feature. It displays as shown in Figure 19–18.

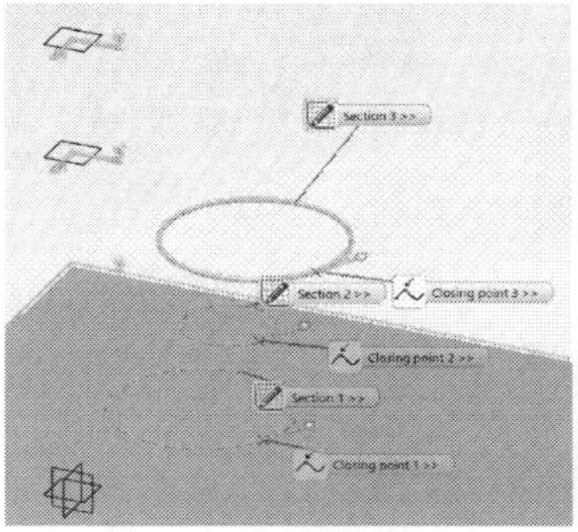

Figure 19–17

Figure 19–18

Task 5 - Create a Removed Multi-sections Solid feature.

Design Considerations

You will create two sketches, one on each of two opposing faces. These sketches will be used as the sections for the ends of the Removed Multi-sections Solid feature.

1. Hide the planes used to create the Multi-sections Solid.
2. Create a sketch using the surface shown in Figure 19–19 as the sketching plane.

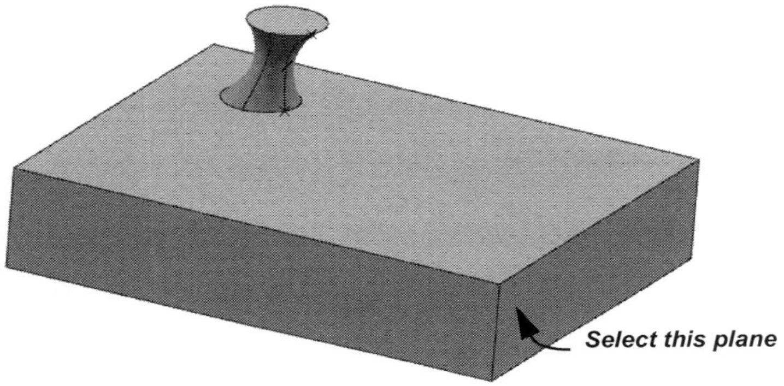

Figure 19–19

3. Sketch a **37.5 X 12.5** rectangle with constraints, as shown in Figure 19–20.

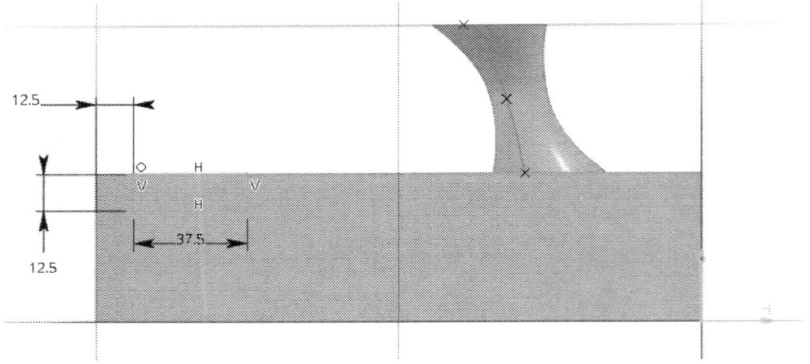

Figure 19–20

4. Click (Exit App) when the sketch profile is complete.

5. Create a sketch using the surface shown in Figure 19–21.

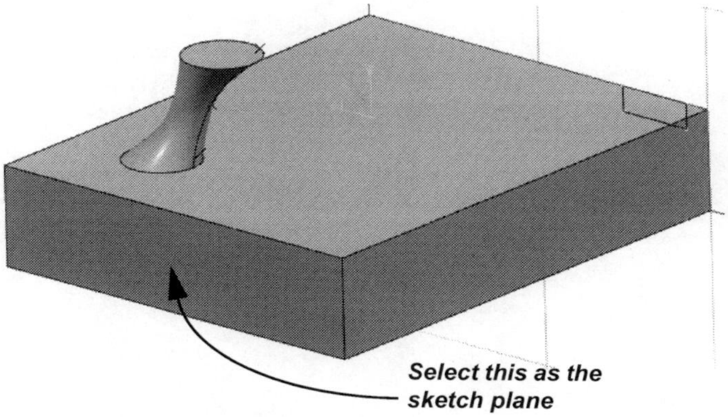

Figure 19–21

6. Sketch a **19** rectangle with constraints, as shown in Figure 19–22.

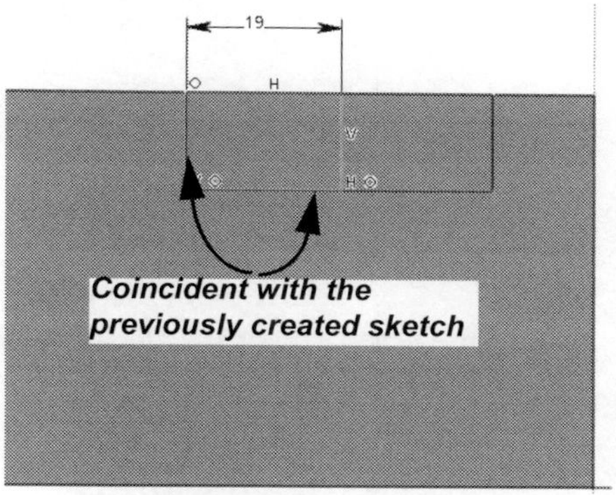

Figure 19–22

7. Click  (Exit App) when the sketch profile is complete.

8. Click  (Removed Multi-sections Solid) to create a Removed Multi-sections Solid feature.

9. Select the two rectangular sections to add them to the Multi-sections Solid Definition dialog box.

10. Verify that the closing points on each section are located on the corresponding vertex to be connected and are pointing in the same direction. For example, the two closing points, shown in Figure 19–23 are pointing in opposite directions and originate from non-corresponding vertices. You must move Closing Point2 to the upper right vertex in this view to correspond to Closing Point1.

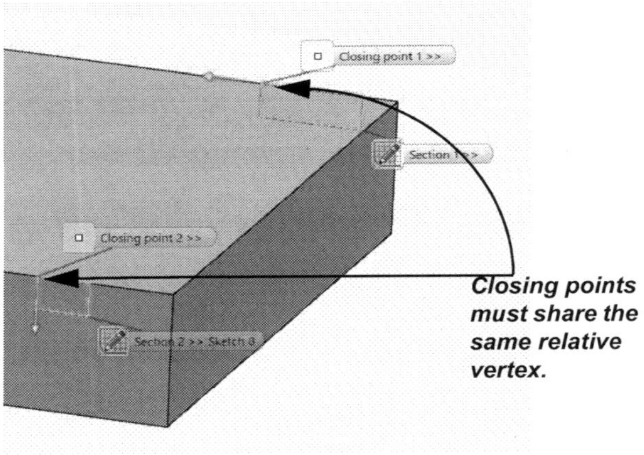

Figure 19–23

11. To move the closing point, select the *Closing point* field in the Section, and select another vertex.

12. Select the new point vertex location. This moves Closing Point2 to the new location.

13. Select the closing point direction arrow until the arrows point in the same direction, as shown in Figure 19–24.

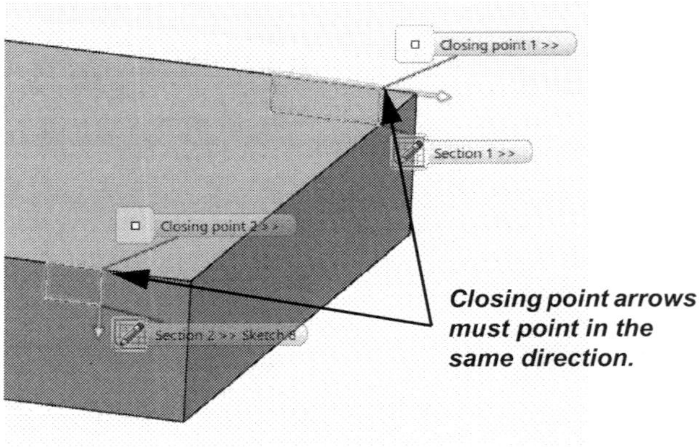

Figure 19–24

14. Click **OK** to create the Removed Multi-sections Solid feature. The model displays as shown in Figure 19–25.

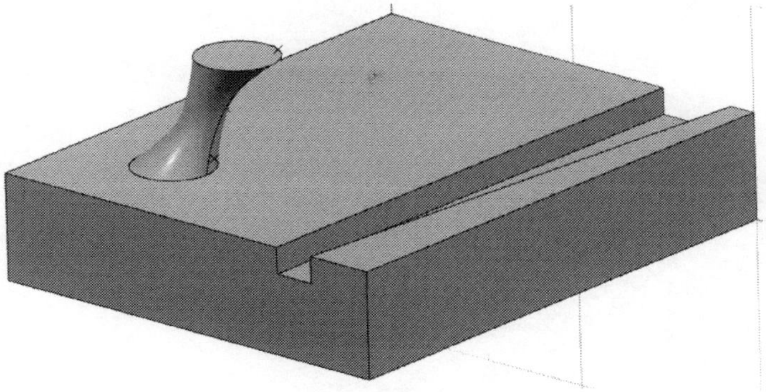

Figure 19–25

15. Save the model and close the tabs.

Practice 19b Transition Tube

Practice Objective

- Create a Multi-sections Solid feature.

In this practice, you will create the model shown in Figure 19–26. You will create one sketch and copy it into different planes. You will then modify the copied sketches to use them as the sections for the tube. After completing the Multi-sections Solid feature, you will shell it.

Figure 19–26

Task 1 - Create three reference planes.

Design Considerations

You will create three reference planes to use as sketching planes for profiles. These profiles will be used as some of the sections for a multi-sections solid.

1. Create a new 3D Part called ***Your_Initials*_TransitionTube**.
2. Create a reference plane offset **100** from the ZX plane. The reference plane displays as shown in Figure 19–27.

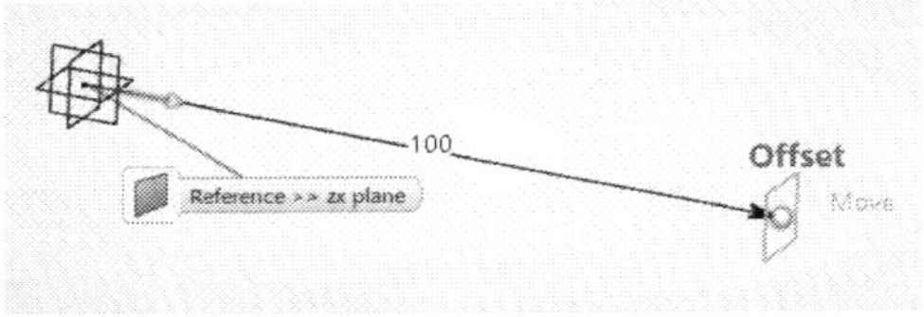

Figure 19–27

3. Create a second plane offset **175** from the ZX plane.

4. Create a third plane offset **250** from the ZX plane. The three reference planes are shown in Figure 19–28.

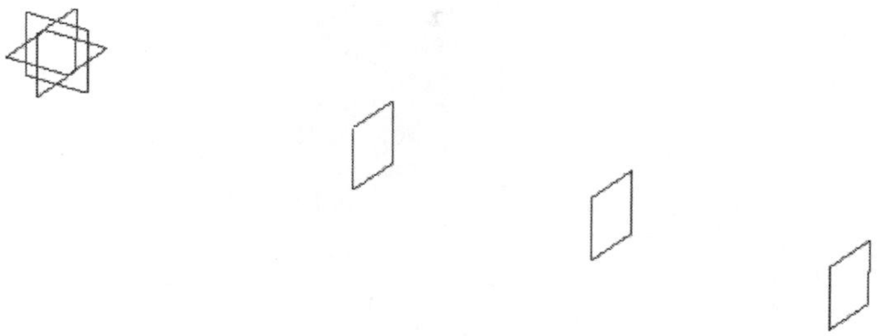

Figure 19–28

Task 2 - Create sketches to be used for a Multi-sections Solid feature.

1. If required, activate the PartBody.

2. Create a sketch on the ZX plane, as shown in Figure 19–29.

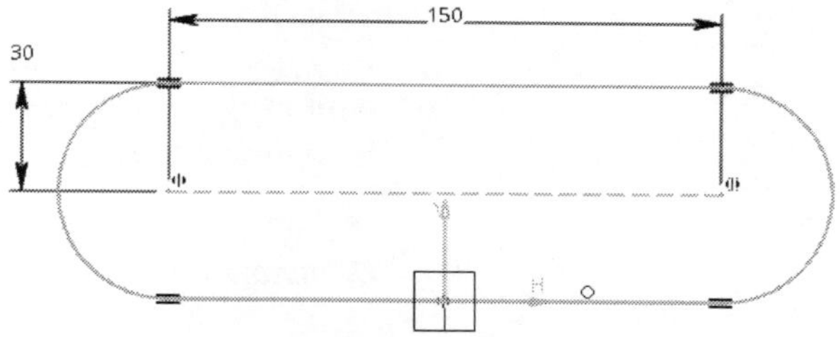

Figure 19–29

3. Click  (Exit App) when complete.

4. Copy **Sketch.1** from the specification tree and paste it onto **Plane.1** (your first reference plane).

5. Modify **Sketch.2** and change the **150** dimension to **120**.

6. Paste **Sketch.1** again on **Plane.2** (your second reference plane).

7. Modify **Sketch.3** and change the *150* length dimension to **5** and the *30* dimension to **50**.

8. Copy **Sketch.3** onto **Plane.3**. The model is shown in Figure 19–30.

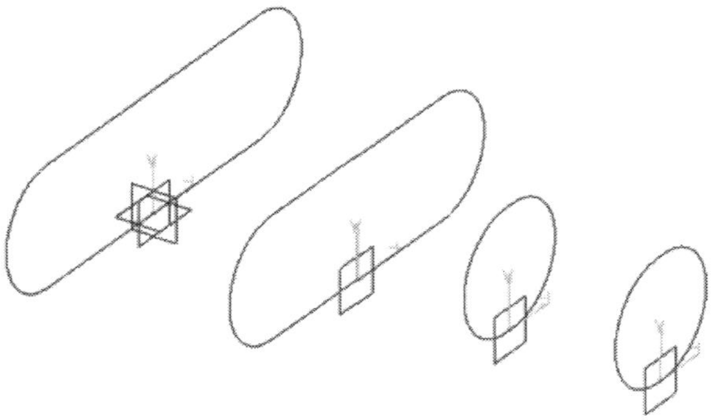

Figure 19–30

Task 3 - Reposition the sketches in the specification tree.

When pasting the sketches onto the three reference planes, the software places the sketch into the geometrical set. You must use the Change Geometrical Set operation to position them in the PartBody.

1. Select **Sketch.2**, **Sketch.3**, and **Sketch.4** using <Ctrl>, right-click, and select **Selected Objects>Change Geometrical Set**.

2. The Change geometrical set dialog box opens. Set *Destination* to **PartBody**, as shown in Figure 19–31.

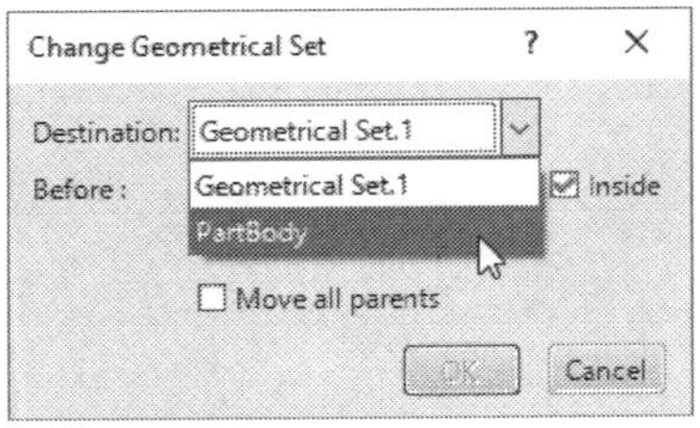

Figure 19–31

3. Click **OK** to complete the operation. The specification tree is shown in Figure 19–32.

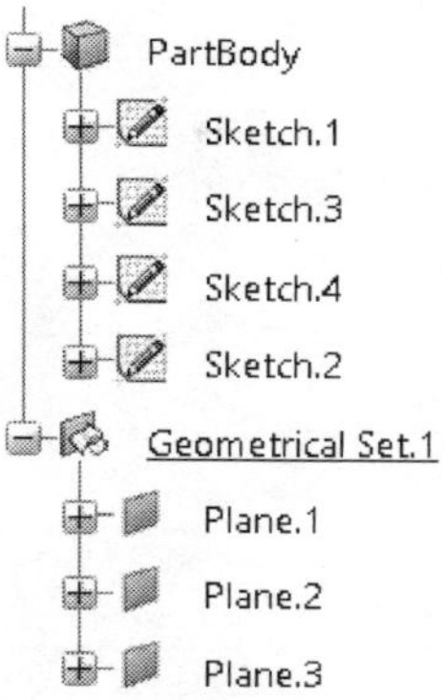

Figure 19–32

Task 4 - Create the Multi-sections Solid feature.

1. In the *Model* section of the Action Bar, click  (Multi-sections Solid) to create a Multi-sections Solid feature.

2. Select the four sketched sections in the order in which they were created to add them to the Multi-sections Solid Definition dialog box.

3. Verify that the four closing point arrows point in the same direction and are located at the same vertices in each section. Select the arrows to toggle the direction, as required. The model displays as shown in Figure 19–33.

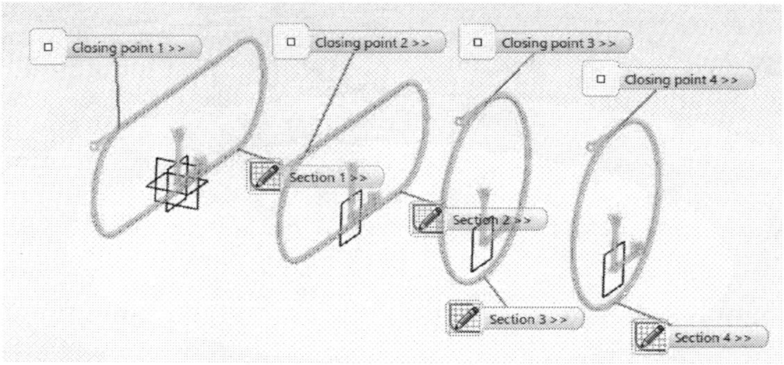

Figure 19–33

4. Click **OK** to create the Multi-sections Solid feature.

5. Hide all planes in the model. The model is shown in Figure 19–34.

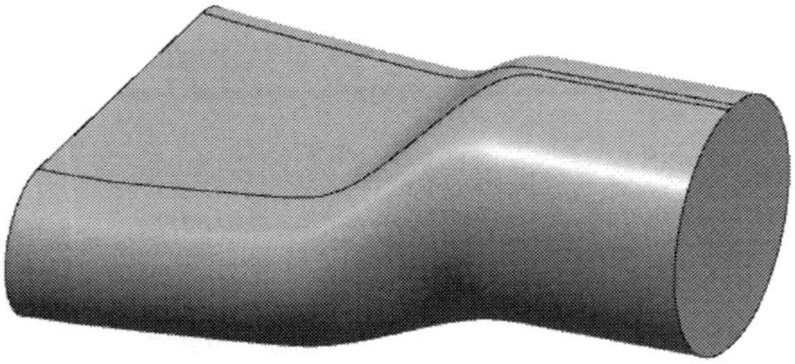

Figure 19–34

Task 5 - Shell the part.

1. Create a **4** inside thickness Shell feature and remove the two end faces of the model. The model displays as shown in Figure 19–35.

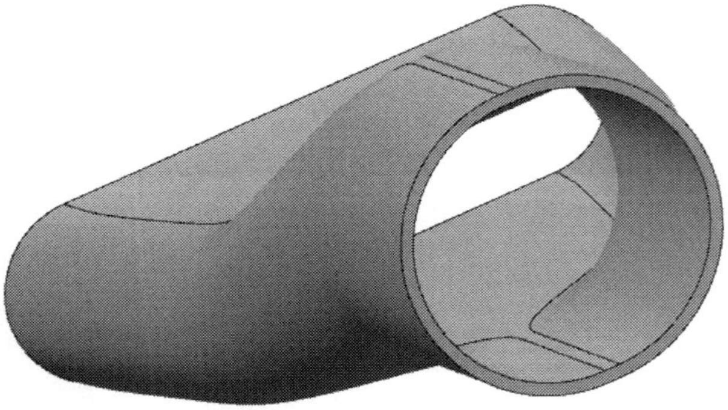

Figure 19–35

2. Save the model and close the tab.

NOTE: An additional multi-sections solid practice is found in Practice B17 at the end of this guide.

Chapter Review Questions

1. Which of the following statements regarding Multi-sections Solids is true?
   a. A Multi-sections Solid creates a single feature where the geometry is blended between multiple sections.
   b. A Multi-sections Solid can only be added to the model after the base feature has been created.
   c. The profiles for the Multi-sections Solid can only be sketched.
   d. The Multi-sections Solid creates a single feature whose geometry is swept along a defined path.
2. Sections must be selected in the required creation order.
   a. True
   b. False
3. What is the minimum number of sections that must exist in a Multi-sections Solid feature?
   a. 0
   b. 1
   c. 2
   d. 4
4. What is the maximum number of sections that can exist in a Multi-sections Solid feature?
   a. 2
   b. 4
   c. 36
   d. Unlimited
5. A Multi-sections Solid adds material and a Removed Multi-section Solid removes material.
   a. True
   b. False

6. You have accidentally created a Multi-sections Solid instead of a Removed Multi-sections Solid. To correct this, right-click on the feature, select Multi-sections Solid.object>Definition and select Removed Multi-sections Solid.
   a. True
   b. False
7. The twist shown in Figure 19–36 is not the design intent. The best way to correct the twist is to redefine the closing points and ensure they are all aligned and pointing in the same direction.

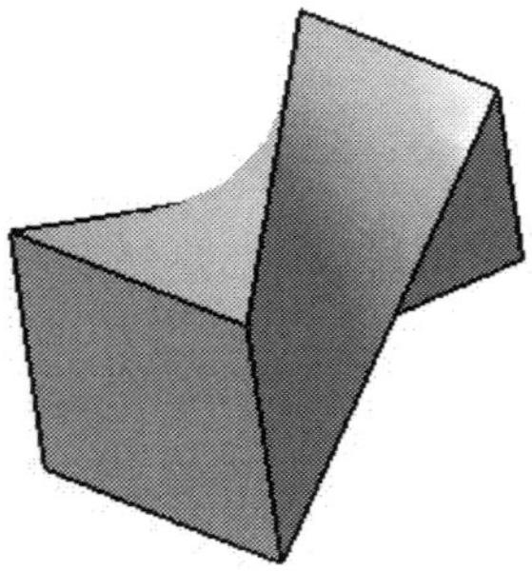

Figure 19–36

   a. True
   b. False

Answers: 1a, 2a, 3c, 4d, 5a, 6b, 7a

Made in the USA
Monee, IL
08 November 2026

68144951R00393